The Rise and Decline of the State

The state, which since the middle of the seventeenth century has been the most important and most characteristic of all modern institutions, is in decline. From Western Europe to Africa, many existing states are either combining into larger communities or falling apart. Many of their functions are being taken over by a variety of organizations which, whatever their precise nature, are not states. In this unique volume Martin van Creveld traces the story of the state from its beginnings to the present. Starting with the simplest political organizations that ever existed, he guides the reader through the origins of the state, its development, its apotheosis during the two world wars, and its spread from its original home in Western Europe to cover the globe. In doing so, he provides a fascinating history of government from its origins to the present day.

Martin van Creveld is a Professor in the Department of History at the Hebrew University, Jerusalem. His books include *Supplying War* (1978), *Fighting Power* (1982), *Command in War* (1985), *Technology and War* (1988), and *The Transformation of War* (1991).

The Rise and Decline of the State

Martin van Creveld

CAMBRIDGE UNIVERSITY PRESS

PUBLISHED BY THE PRESS SYNDICATE OF THE UNIVERSITY OF CAMBRIDGE
The Pitt Building, Trumpington Street, Cambridge, United Kingdom

CAMBRIDGE UNIVERSITY PRESS
The Edinburgh Building, Cambridge CB2 2RU, UK
40 West 20th Street, New York, NY 10011–4211, USA
10 Stamford Road, Oakleigh, VIC 3166, Australia
Ruiz de Alarcón 13, 28014 Madrid, Spain
Dock House, The Waterfront, Cape Town 8001, South Africa

http://www.cambridge.org

First published 1999
Reprinted 2000

Printed in the United Kingdom at the University Press, Cambridge

Typeset in Plantin 10/12 pt [VN]

A catalogue record for this book is available from the British Library

Library of Congress Cataloguing in Publication data
Van Creveld, Martin
    The rise and decline of the state / by Martin van Creveld.
        p.   cm.
    Includes bibliographical references and index.
        ISBN 0 521 65190 5 – ISBN 0 521 65629 X (pbk.)
    1. State, the. 2. World politics.   I. Title
JC11.V35   1999
320.1'90–dc21   98–30993   CIP

ISBN 0 521 65190 5 hardback
ISBN 0 521 65629 X paperback

Contents

Preface   *page* vii

1 Before the state: prehistory to AD 1300   1
   Tribes without rulers   2
   Tribes with rulers (chiefdoms)   10
   City-states   20
   Empires, strong and weak   35
   Limits of stateless societies   52

2 The rise of the state: 1300 to 1648   59
   The struggle against the church   62
   The struggle against the Empire   75
   The struggle against the nobility   87
   The struggle against the towns   104
   The monarchs' triumph   118

3 The state as an instrument: 1648 to 1789   126
   Building the bureaucracy   128
   Creating the infrastructure   143
   Monopolizing violence   155
   The growth of political theory   170
   Inside the Leviathan   184

4 The state as an ideal: 1789 to 1945   189
   The Great Transformation   191
   Disciplining the people   205
   Conquering money   224
   The road to total war   242
   The apotheosis of the state   258

5 The spread of the state: 1696 to 1975   263
   Toward Eastern Europe   264
   The Anglo-Saxon experience   281
   The Latin American experiment   298
   Frustration in Asia and Africa   315
   What everybody has . . .   332

6   The decline of the state: 1975–   336
      The waning of major war   337
      The retreat of welfare   354
      Technology goes international   377
      The threat to internal order   394
      The withdrawal of faith   408

Conclusions: beyond the state   415

Index   422

Preface

The state, which since the middle of the seventeenth century has been the most important and most characteristic of all modern institutions, is in decline. From Western Europe to Africa, either voluntarily or involuntarily, many existing states are either combining into larger communities or falling apart. Regardless of whether they fall apart or combine, already now many of their functions are being taken over by a variety of organizations which, whatever their precise nature, are not states.

Globally speaking, the international system is moving away from an assembly of distinct, territorial, sovereign, legally equal states toward different, more hierarchical, and in many ways more complicated structures. As far as individual states are concerned, there are good reasons to think that many of them will soon no longer be either willing or able to control and protect the political, military, economic, social, and cultural lives of their citizens to the extent that they used to. Needless to say, these developments affect each and every individual now living on this planet. In some places they will proceed peacefully, but in others they are likely to result in – indeed are already leading to – upheavals as profound, and possibly as bloody, as those that propelled humanity out of the Middle Ages and into the modern world. Whether the direction of change is desirable, as some hope, or undesirable, as others fear, remains to be seen.

In this volume I shall make an attempt to look into the future of the state by examining its past: that is, its prehistory, growth, maturation, and apotheosis, and the way in which it spread all over the world. Chapter 1 deals with the period – in fact, most of recorded and especially unrecorded history – when there were no states and, originally at any rate, not even government in the sense of the organized power that some men exercise over others. Chapter 2 covers the period from approximately 1300 (the *Res Publica Christiana* at its zenith) to 1648 (the Treaty of Westphalia); it shows how the state emerged out of the Middle Ages by fighting, and overcoming, ecclesiastical and imperial universalism on the one hand and feudal and urban particularism on the other. Chapter 3 continues the story from 1648 to the French Revolution. This period led to the separation of the state from "civil society" and the creation of many of its most characteristic institutions; including its bureaucracy, its statistical infrastructure, its armed forces, its police apparatus, and its prisons. The fourth chapter explains how states, having discovered the forces of nationalism as first proclaimed by the likes of Möser and Herder, trans–formed themselves from instruments for imposing law and order into secular gods; and how, having increased their strength out of all proportion by invading their citizens' minds and systematically picking their pockets, they used that strength to fight each other (1914–45) on such a scale, and with such murderous intensity, as almost to put an end to themselves. Chapter 5 describes the spread of the state from its original home in Western Europe to other parts of the globe, including Eastern Europe, the British colonies in North America and Australasia, the Spanish and Portuguese ones in Latin America, and finally the countries of Asia and Africa. Last but not least, chapter 6 deals with the forces which, even now, are undermining states all over the world, and which, in all probability, will cause many of them to collapse (as in Yugoslavia), give up part of their sovereignty and integrate with others (as in Europe), or decentralize and relax their hold over their citizens' lives (should the Republicans keep their 1994 "Contract with the American People") within the lifetime of the present generation.

As will readily be appreciated, compressing a subject such as the present one into a single volume represents a very large task. That it could be accomplished at all is due first of all to my comrade in life, Dvora Lewy. As usual, she has suffered from my repeated periods of blackest despair; had it not been for her constant encouragement and untiring devotion the work would never have been completed. I also wish to thank Professor Gabriel Herman and Professor Benjamin Kedar of the Hebrew University, Jerusalem, for reading part or all of my work, discussing it with me, making suggestions, and pointing out errors which otherwise might have escaped me. Above all, I want to express my gratitude to my stepchildren, Adi and Jonathan Lewy, for being with me through all these years. It is to them, with all my love, that this book is dedicated.

1 Before the state: prehistory to AD 1300

Definitions of the state have varied widely. The one adopted here makes no claim to being exclusive; it is merely the most convenient for our purpose. The state, then, is an *abstract* entity which can be neither seen, nor heard, nor touched. This entity is not identical with either the rulers or the ruled; neither President Clinton, nor citizen Smith, nor even an assembly of all the citizens acting in common can claim that they *are* the state. On the other hand, it includes them both and claims to stand over them both.

This is as much to say that the state, being separate from both its members and its rulers, is a corporation, just as universities, trade unions, and churches *inter alia* are. Much like any corporation, it too has directors, employees, and shareholders. Above all, it is a corporation in the sense that it possesses a legal *persona* of its own, which means that it has rights and duties and may engage in various activities *as if* it were a real, flesh-and-blood, living individual. The points where the state differs from other corporations are, first, the fact that it authorizes them all but is itself authorized (recognized) solely by others of its kind; secondly, that certain functions (known collectively as the attributes of sovereignty) are reserved for it alone; and, thirdly, that it exercises those functions over a certain territory inside which its jurisdiction is both exclusive and all-embracing.

Understood in this way, the state – like the corporation of which it is a subspecies – is a comparatively recent invention. During most of history, and especially prehistory, there existed government but not states; indeed the idea of the state as a corporation (as opposed to a mere group, assembly, or community of people coming together and living under a set of common laws) was itself unknown. Arising in different civilizations as far apart as Europe and the Middle East, Meso- and South America, Africa, and East Asia, these pre-state political communities were immensely varied – all the more so since they often developed out of each other, interacted with each other, conquered each other, and merged with each other to produce an endless variety of forms, most of them hybrid.

Nevertheless, speaking very roughly and skipping over many intermediate types, they may be classified into: (1) tribes without rulers; (2) tribes with rulers (chiefdoms);[1] (3) city-states; and (4) empires, strong and weak.

Tribes without rulers

Tribes without rulers, also called segmentary or acephalous societies, are represented by some of the simplest communities known to us. Before the colonization of their lands by the white man led to their destruction, they included so-called band societies in many parts of the world: such as the Australian aborigines, the Eskimo of Alaska, Canada, and Greenland, and the Kalahari Bushmen. Other communities discussed here were somewhat larger and their political organizations slightly more sophisticated. Among them are some East African Nilotic tribes such as the Anuak, Dinka, Masai, and Nuer made famous by the anthropological researches of Evans-Pritchard;[2] the inhabitants of the New Guinea highlands and Micronesia; and most – though not all – pre-Columbian Amerindian tribes in both North and South America.

What all these had in common was the fact that, among them, "government" both began and ended within the extended family, lineage, or clan. Thus there were no superiors except for men, elders, and parents, and no inferiors except for women, youngsters, and offspring including in-laws (who, depending on whether the bride went to live with the groom's family or the other way around, could be either male or female). In this way all authority, all rights, and all obligations – in short all social relations that were institutionalized and went beyond simple friendship – were defined exclusively in terms of kin. So important were kin in providing the structure of the community that, in cases where no real ties existed, fictive ones were often invented and pressed into service instead. Either people adopted each other as sons, or else they created the sort of quasi-blood tie known as guest-friendship in which people treated each other as if they were brothers. Among the Nuer, this system was taken to the point that women could, for some purposes, "count" as men.[3]

---

[1] In distinguishing between tribes without rulers and chiefdoms, I follow M. Fortes and E. E. Evans-Pritchard, eds., *African Political Systems* (Oxford: Oxford University Press, 1940). For some other classifications of tribal societies, see E. R. Service, *Origins of the State and Civilization* (New York: Norton, 1975), and T. C. Llewellen, *Political Anthropology: An Introduction* (South Hadley, MA: Bergin and Garvey, 1983).

[2] E. E. Evans-Pritchard, *The Nuer* (Oxford: Oxford University Press, 1940). This is probably the most complete and sympathetic description of a tribe without rulers ever produced.

[3] Evans-Pritchard, *Kinship and Marriage Among the Nuer* (Oxford: Clarendon Press, 1951), pp. 180–9.

Within the limits of the kin group the individual's position relative to everybody else was determined very precisely by his or her sex, age, and marital status. Conversely, those who for one reason or another were not surrounded by a network of kinspeople – such as foreigners originating in other tribes and, in many places, unwed mothers – tended to find themselves in a marginal position or with no position at all. An excellent case in point is provided by the biblical story of Ruth. Ruth, originally a Moabite, married an Israelite man who had settled in her native country. Left a widow by his death, she, together with her mother-in-law Naomi, moved from Moab to Israel. However, so long as she was not recognized and reintegrated into her late husband's family by marrying one of his relatives her situation in life remained extremely precarious. Not only was she reduced to beggary, but as a woman on her own she was exposed to any kind of abuse that people chose to inflict on her.

In the absence of any institutionalized authority except that which operated within the extended family, the societies in question were egalitarian and democratic. Every adult male was considered, and considered himself, the equal of all others; nobody had the *right* to issue orders to, exercise justice over, or demand payment from anybody else. "Public" tasks – that is, those tasks that were beyond the capacity of single family groups, such as worship, big-game hunting, high-seas fishing, clearing forest land, and, as we shall soon see, waging war – were carried out not by rulers and ruled but by leaders and their followers.[4] The operating units were so-called sodalities, or associations of men. In many societies, though not all, each sodality had its own totemic animal, emblem, and sacred paraphernalia, such as musical instruments, masks, festive clothes, and so on. The items in question, or at any rate the instructions for manufacturing them, were believed to have been handed down by the gods. They were kept under guard in specially designated places and were often considered dangerous for outsiders, particularly women and children, to touch or even look at.[5]

Membership in a sodality did not depend on a person's free choice but was passed along by heredity. Every few years a ceremony would be held; old men would be passed out, and their places taken by a group of youths, mostly related to one another through the network of kin, who joined the ranks of the sodality after passing through the appropriate rituals.[6] Within

[4] The early Germanic tribes expressed this relationship rather exactly by calling those who obeyed the leader his *Gefolgschaft* (literally "follow-ship"). See H. Mitteis, *The State in the Middle Ages* (Amsterdam: Elsevier, 1974), p. 11.
[5] See Y. Murphy and R. P. Murphy, *Women of the Forest* (New York: Columbia University Press, 1974), pp. 92–5, for an example of such arrangements.
[6] For the working of age-group systems, see B. Bernhardi, *Age–Class Systems: Social Institutions and Politics Based on Age* (London: Cambridge University Press, 1985).

each sodality leadership tended to pass from father to son. However, being well sired was of little use if the person in question did not also possess the necessary combination of personal qualities. Among them were a certain minimum age, eloquence, courage, experience, and, perhaps most important of all, proven skill in performing the various activities that made up the sodality's *raison d'être*. In many societies they also included a reputation for being able to command magic powers such as the ability, for example, to cause the game to appear at the appointed time and thus lead to a good hunting season.

Returning to the community as a whole, law, in the sense of a man-made, formally enacted (and therefore alterable), and binding set of regulations that prescribe the behavior of people and of groups, did not exist. In its place we find custom; in other words, an indeterminate number of unwritten rules which were partly religious and partly magic by origin. The rules covered every aspect of life from sexual mores to the division of an inheritance; thus our present-day distinction between the public sphere (which is covered by law) and the private one (where, as in ordering one's household or making one's will, for example, people are supposedly free to do as they please) did not apply. For example, custom dictated that a youngster *had* to pass through the appropriate initiation rites – and suffer the appropriate agonies – in order to be admitted to adult status, join the sodality to which the remaining members of his family belonged, and be allowed to marry. A newly married couple *had* to take up residence with the groom's family or with that of the bride. And brideswealth *had* to be shared with various male members of one's family, all of whom had a claim on it.

In the absence of the state as an entity against which offenses could be directed, another distinction which did not apply was the one between criminal and civil law; and indeed it has been said that the societies in question recognized tort but not crime.[7] Tort could, however, be directed not only against other people but – in cases such as incest or sacrilege – against the group's ancestral spirits and the deities in general. These were invisible, by and large malignant beings that dwelt in the air and took the form of wind, lightning, and cloud; alternatively they were represented by certain stones, trees, brooks, and other objects. Whatever their shape or chosen place of residence, they were intent on having their rights respected. If given offense, they might avenge themselves by inflicting drought,

---

[7] For an excellent discussion of these problems, see H. I. Hogbin, *Law and Order in Polynesia: A Study of Primitive Legal Institutions* (London: Christopher's, 1934), particularly ch. 4; and L. K. Popisil, *Kapauku Papuans and Their Law* (New Haven, CT: Yale University Press, 1958).

illness, or infertility not just on the perpetrator but on his relatives or, indeed, anybody else.

Once again a good illustration of the way things worked is provided by the Bible, this time in the book of Leviticus, which should be regarded as the codification of previous tribal usage. Much of the book is concerned with uncleanliness, especially but not exclusively of a sexual kind – menstruation, unintended ejaculation, and the like. Each rule is followed by the ways in which, if broken, it is to be atoned for, the understanding being that the Lord was particularly concerned with such problems and would not tolerate impurity in His people. Minor transgressions carried no particular penalty and could be obviated by the individual resorting to temporary seclusion, purification, prayer, and sacrifice. However, major ones such as incest were known as *tevel* (abomination). They carried the death sentence, usually by fire, or else the text simply says that the culprit should be "cut off" from the people (in other words, destroyed). Thus, and although there was no separate category of criminal law, there did exist certain kinds of behavior which were recognized as injurious not just to individuals but to God and, through His wrath, the community as a whole, and which, unless properly dealt with, would be followed by the gravest consequences.

As this example shows, tribal custom, far from being regarded as part of the nature of things and automatically obeyed, was occasionally violated.[8] In the simpler "band" societies it was the head of the household who arbitrated and decided in such cases, whereas among the more sophisticated East African pastoralists and North American Indians this was the role of the village council. The council consisted of elders, meaning not just old people but those who had undergone the appropriate rituals marking their status and, as a result, were considered close to the spirits and custodians of the group's collective wisdom. Even so, membership of the appropriate age group did not in itself qualify a person to speak in council; while every councilman had to be an elder, not every elder was a councilman or, if he was, could command attention. To become a "talking chief" one had to possess a reputation for piety and wisdom as well as a demonstrated record in maintaining the peace among the members of one's own family group. As the Berti of Sudan put it, he who is unable to strengthen his own cattle-pen should not seek to strengthen that of his neighbor.[9]

The initiative for summoning the council was taken by the parties

---

[8] See B. Malinovsky, *Crime and Punishment in Primitive Society* (London: Kegan Paul, 1926).

[9] L. Holy, *Neighbors and Kinsmen: A Study of the Berti People of Darfur* (London: Hurst, 1974), p. 121.

involved in a dispute or, more likely, by one of their relatives who had taken alarm and gone to summon help. Assembling at a designated place – often under the shade of a sacred tree – the council would hear out those directly involved as well as other witnesses drawn from among their kinspeople. In case of an invisible offense – i.e., where a misfortune was suspected to have its origin in witchcraft – a diviner would be called to discover the perpetrator; next, the accused or suspected would be made to undergo an ordeal, such as drinking poison or dipping an arm in boiling water, as a way to determine his or her guilt.[10] The way to settle interpersonal disputes up to and including murder was generally by means of retaliation – an eye for an eye, a tooth for a tooth – restitution, or compensation. The latter was itself based on the customary scale: so much for the death or injury of a man, so much for a woman, or for a youngster. All these, however, were due only in case the person offended against belonged to a different family or lineage; one did not pay for injuring one's own.

As they lacked anything like a centralized executive or police force, the sole sanction at the elders' disposal consisted of their ability to persuade the members of the group to follow their wishes and carry out the council's decision. What really mattered was one's personal standing and the number of relatives whom one might call to one's assistance; as in all other societies, the strong and influential could get away from situations in which the weak and the unconnected became entangled. A small, intimate, and tightly knit community might not find it too difficult to discipline, and if necessary punish, isolated individuals. However, taking similar measures against persons whose relatives were numerous and prepared to stand with them was not so easy, since it might readily result in the group dividing into hostile camps and even to feuding followed by disintegration. Once again there are examples of this in the Bible: for example, the book of Judges where an attempt to punish members of the tribe of Benjamin for an outrage committed on a woman led to full-scale civil war.

The absence of a centralized authority also determined the form and nature of another function normally associated with the state, namely warfare.[11] In some of the more isolated and less sophisticated societies it scarcely existed; instead there were ritualized clashes between individuals using blunt weapons or none at all. Such was the case among the Australian aborigines, where the rivals confronted each other staff in hand. It

---

[10] The classic treatment of divination and ritual is E. E. Evans-Pritchard, *Witchcraft, Oracles and Magic Among the Azande* (Oxford: Clarendon Press, 1976).

[11] The best work about the subject remains H. Turney-High, *Primitive War: Its Theory and Concepts* (Columbia: University of South Carolina Press, 1937).

also applied to the Eskimo, where the two parties would exchange derisive songs in front of the assembled community until one or the other gave way, at which point his rival was declared the victor. But most societies, notably those of East and Central Africa as well as New Guinea, Micronesia, and the Americas, did not content themselves with such friendly encounters among their own people. Using sodalities as their organizational base, they mounted raids – which were themselves scarcely distinguishable from feuds – against the members of other lineages, clans, or tribes.

The most important objectives of warfare were to exact vengeance for physical injury, damage to property (e.g., livestock or gardens), offenses to honor, and theft (including the abduction or seduction of women). Another was to obtain booty, and again this included not merely goods but marriageable women and young children who could be incorporated into one's own lineage and thus add to its strength. From Papua through Africa to North and South America, very great importance was attached to the symbolic trophies that war was capable of providing. These took the form of enemy ears, scalps, heads, and the like; having been dried, smoked, pickled, or shrunk, they could either be carried about on one's person or else used to decorate one's dwelling. As in more developed societies, a person who possessed such symbols could readily translate them into social status, sexual favors, family alliances, and goods. Hence the role that war played in men's lives was often very large: both the Latin *populus* and the Germanic folk could originally stand for either "people" or "army." Among the North American Plains Indians, men were known as "braves," while in the book of Exodus the term "members of the host" is synonymous with "adult men." In the absence of a centralized decision-making body, war itself might be defined less as a deliberate political act than as the characteristic activity of adult males, undertaken in the appropriate season unless they were otherwise engaged.[12]

On the other hand, it was precisely because every adult male was at the same time a warrior that military organization was limited to raiding parties. By no means should sodalities be understood as permanent, specialized, war-making armed forces or even popular militias. Instead they were merely associations of men which, lying dormant for much of the time, sprang into life when the occasion demanded and the leader succeeded in convincing his followers that a cause worth fighting for existed. Often raiding parties could maintain themselves for weeks on end and cover astonishing distances in order to make pursuit more difficult;

---

[12] For the way these things worked in one extremely warlike society, and the implications for humanity as a whole, see N. Chagnon, *Yanomano: The Fierce People* (New York: Holt, Rinehart and Winston, 1983 edn.).

they were also capable of disciplining their members, breaking their weapons (a grave insult), inflicting corporal punishment, and even putting them to death if necessary. However, once hostilities were over, sodalities invariably dissolved, leaving the leaders stripped of their authority. This was the case, for example, among the Cherokee with their so-called red chiefs; so also among the Pueblo, Jivaro, Dinka, and Masai.[13] None of these societies had a system of rent, tribute, or taxation that would have redistributed wealth and thus given rise to a class of individuals with the leisure needed in order to train for, and wage, war as their principal occupation.

In some of these societies, such as the Bushmen, institutionalized religion played hardly any role and every household chief was at the same time his own priest. However, the majority did recognize a religious head in the person of the shaman, prophet, or priest whose authority went beyond that of the individual lineage. Karl Marx to the contrary, the most fundamental difference separating humans from animals is not that the former engage in production for a living.[14] Rather, it is that they recognize the idea of incest, even if the rule against it is occasionally broken. In no known case anywhere around the world did the family-based, face-to-face groups in which people spent most of their lives habitually marry among themselves. Instead they sought their partners among the members of similar groups, normally those which were related to them, but not too closely.

In addition, and on pain of inflicting misfortune, the deities demanded to be worshipped. From Australia to Africa to the Americas, these twin social factors made it necessary to hold periodical gatherings, or festivals. Depending on its religious importance and the number of people whom it brought together, a festival could last for anything between three days and a fortnight. A truce was declared and peace, i.e., the absence of mutual raiding, prevailed; this enabled the members of the various clans to assemble in order to pray, sacrifice, eat their fill, socialize, and exchange women (either permanently, by arranging marriages, or else temporarily by relaxing social mores) and other gifts. Coming on top of its practical and religious functions, the festival also provided the people with an opportunity to reaffirm their own collective identity as a community; such is the case in other societies to the present day.

---

[13] For this kind of military organization, see P. Clastres, *Society Against the State* (Oxford: Blackwell, 1977), pp. 177–80; P. Brown, *Highland People of New Guinea* (London: Cambridge University Press, 1978); and J. G. Jorgensen, *Western Indians: Comparative Environments, Languages, and Culture of 172 Western American Indian Tribes* (San Francisco: Freeman, 1980).

[14] K. Marx and F. Engels, *The German Ideology* (New York: International Publishers, 1939 [1843]), p. 7.

The person who led the celebrations, though he might make use of female assistants to carry out his duty, was invariably male. His position is best described as a combination of sage, prophet, and high priest; by origin he had to belong to the lineage which, according to tradition, was considered closest to the tribe's principal divinity. Holding the position presupposed extensive knowledge of tribal lore, astronomy, magic rites, medicine, and so on, all of which could be acquired only by means of a prolonged apprenticeship. Priests were expected to train their own successors from among members of their family, either sons or nephews. Even so the succession was not automatic; instead it had to be confirmed by the elders of the priestly lineage who selected the candidate deemed most suitable by them. Among the East African Shilluk and Meru, for example, he carried the title of *reth* or *mugwe*, respectively.[15]

Once he had taken up his position, the priest was distinguished by certain symbolic tokens of office: such as body paint, headgear, dress, the staff that he carried, and the shape of his residence. He might also be subject to taboos such as being forbidden to have his hair cut, touch certain objects considered unclean, eat certain kinds of food, or marry certain categories of women. His influence rested on the idea that the fertility of land, cattle, and people depended on the accomplishment of rituals that he alone, owing to his descent and the learning that had been passed on to him by his predecessor, could perform; as a Bakwain (modern Mali) shaman once allegedly put it to the explorer David Livingstone, "through my wisdom the women become fat and shining."[16] In this way a close connection existed between the tribe's welfare and his own. Priests were responsible for the timely occurrence of climatic phenomena, such as rain, without which "cattle would have no pasture, the cows give no milk, our children become lean and die, our wives run away to other tribes who do make rain and have corn, and the whole tribe become dispersed and lost."[17] If they failed in their duty, they might be deposed and a substitute appointed in their stead.

Cases are known when capable priests manipulated their presumed magic powers to develop their influence into authority and make themselves into *de facto* tribal leaders. They acted as mediators, settled disputes, represented their people in front of foreigners, and instigated action in respect to other groups, including, in colonial times, the organization of rebellions against the imperial power. Although, by virtue of their sacred

---

[15] See L. Mair, *Primitive Government* (Harmondsworth, UK: Penguin Books, 1962), pp. 63ff.; and E. E. Evans-Pritchard, *The Divine Kingdom of the Shilluk of the Nilotic Sudan* (Cambridge: Cambridge University Press, 1948), pp. 13ff.

[16] Quoted in M. Gluckman, *The Allocation of Responsibility* (Manchester: Manchester University Press, 1972), p. xviiii.

[17] *Ibid.*

position, priests could not function as military commanders or participate in the fighting, they often conducted the opening and closing ceremonies that were considered necessary first in order to authorize bloodshed and then as a means of atoning for it. In return for their ministrations they could obtain presents in the form of food, since parts of the offerings made to the deities were set apart for them. Their reward might also include clothing, services such as help in erecting their dwellings, and, in some societies, women.

Still, priests, however important their position, did not make custom, but merely explained what it was and interpreted it to suit the case at hand. No more than anybody else did they possess the right to command obedience. They did not levy taxes, did not have an organized following that might enforce their wishes, and did not exercise command in war. Their weapons were persuasion and mediation, not coercion; insofar as the sole sanctions at their disposal were of a kind that we should call supernatural, their power fell far short of that of a chief or, indeed, any kind of ruler in the ordinary sense of that term. It is from Samuel's description of the arrangements which a king would institute once he had been duly anointed and installed that one can learn of the things that he himself, as a mere prophet, could not do:

This will be the manner of the king that shall reign over you. He will take your sons, and appoint them for himself, for his chariots, and to be his horsemen; and some shall run before his chariots.

And he will appoint him captains over thousands and captains over fifties; and will set them to clear his ground, and to reap his harvest, and to make his instruments of war, and instruments of his chariots.

And he will take your daughters to be confectionars, and to be cooks and to be bakers.

And he will take your fields, and your vineyards, and your oliveyards, even the best of them, and give them to his servants.

And he will take the tenth of your seed, and of your vineyards, and give them to his servants.

And he will take your menservants, and your maidservants, and your goodliest young men, and your asses, and put them to his work.

He will take the tenth of your sheep, and ye shall be his servants.

And ye shall cry out on that day because of your king which ye shall have chosen you; and the Lord will not hear you on that day.[18]

Tribes with rulers (chiefdoms)

Given that their social structure was almost identical with the extended family, lineage or clan, tribes without rulers were necessarily small and

---

[18] 1 Samuel, 8, 11–19.

rarely numbered more than a few thousand people. Though the Hob-
besian picture of these societies as living in a constant state of war of all
against all is probably overdrawn, by all accounts they were decentralized
and those of them that stood above the band level were wracked by
frequent feuds. Military operations were conducted on a small scale and
casualties were usually few in number. However, over time they could
represent an important factor in male mortality.

The way of life of these societies, regardless of whether it was based on
hunting–gathering, cattle herding, temporary gardening, or some combination of these, demanded a low density of population, wide open
spaces, and a nomadic or semi-nomadic lifestyle. Since well-developed
communications did not exist, the inbuilt tendency to split and disintegrate was strengthened. Disintegration must often have prevented feuds
from going to the murderous extremes observed in societies with a more
developed system of government. To this extent it constituted not only an
affliction but a blessing as well.

Whether in war or peace, these societies were incapable of taking
coordinated action on a scale larger than that of the sodality; the rare
exceptions, such as the short-lived Iroquois League created in the American Northeast, merely prove the rule. Small numbers, common ownership over the means of production such as land, forest, and water, and
relative economic equality also precluded specialization and a division of
labor other than that which, in all societies, is based on age and sex. Since
every household was almost entirely self-reliant in looking after its economic needs, standards of living and technological development remained
at the subsistence level. Whatever the pristine virtues that Westerners
from Rousseau and Diderot on have attributed to them, historically
speaking they have been and still are – those that survive – among the least
successful of all human societies. It was only in regions where they
encountered no more advanced forms of government, such as Australia,
parts of East Africa, and the North American Plains that tribes without
rulers could spread over large territories and maintain their way of life.
Everywhere else their fate was to be pushed into the jungles, as in South
America and Central Africa; deserts, as in South Africa; or the arctic
wastes of Greenland, Canada, and Alaska. And indeed it is only in such
undesirable environments that some of them managed to hold out until
recently.[19]

By contrast, tribes with rulers, also known as chiefdoms, may be found

[19] The idea that the simpler tribes without rulers are really the remnants of more complex
societies that disintegrated is advanced by E. E. Service, *Primitive Social Organization: An
Evolutionary Perspective* (New York: Random House, 1964). See also D. W. Lathrap, *The
Upper Amazon* (London: Thames and Hudson, 1970), and R. D. Alexander, *Darwinism
and Human Affairs* (Seattle: University of Washington Press, 1979).

in many parts of the world. They include many societies in Southeast, West, and South Africa, as well as others all over Southeast Asia, Polynesia, Hawaii, and New Zealand. By way of further examples, history tells us of the tribes that destroyed the Mycenean civilization and ruled Greece during the Dark Ages between about 1000 and 750 BC; the various Gothic, Frankish, and other Germanic tribes, as they were from the later centuries of the Roman empire (i.e., *not* those of Tacitus' day, who probably corresponded more closely to tribes without rulers) to the rise of the Carolingian empire in the eighth century AD; and the Scandinavian tribes during the tenth century AD, in other words just before they became Christianized and turned toward more centralized forms of government.

Chiefdoms were what their name implies: they had chiefs, i.e., individuals who were elevated over other people and possessed the *right* to command them. That right was invariably based on the chief's alleged divine descent, which in turn dictated that the normal method of succession should be from father to son. Still, a system whereby the eldest male descendant simply stepped into his predecessor's shoes seldom applied. The reason was that, as in present-day Saudi Arabia (which until the 1930s was merely a loose assembly of chiefdoms, all engaged in constant warfare against each other), most of these societies were polygamous *par excellence*. No doubt one motive for polygamy may be found in the pleasures of the bed; from King Solomon with his thousand wives to Chairmen Mao with his nurses, satisfying their sexual appetites has always been one of the privileges of rulers, so that the higher the status the more numerous the wives.[20] However, females by means of their labor also presented a source of wealth – note the numerous "women adept at spinning" who are passed from hand to hand in the pages of the Homeric poems. Those who were descended from noble lineages, or were particularly beautiful, could also act as status symbols for their owners.

The natural result of polygyny was a large number of sons who, when the time came, might present themselves as candidates for the succession. The potential resulting conflict could be made worse because the women belonged to various different classes: some were the chief's legally wedded wives, others concubines, others perhaps domestics, captives, or slaves who had been put to breeding uses in addition to their other duties. While a few women might have their children as a result of a purely temporary liaison, the great majority probably conceived as a result of being part of the master's household in one capacity or another. Given

[20] R. D. White, "Rethinking Polygyny: Co-Wives, Codes and Cultural Systems," *Current Anthropology*, 29, 1989, pp. 519–72.

these gradations, the distinction between legitimate and illegitimate off-spring was by no means always clear.

In practice, it made a great difference whether the individual in question was personally capable of providing leadership and, above all, who his mother was. Normally the chief's first, or principal, wife was descended from an eminent family. Having been formally given away by her kin, she was ceremonially wedded and later saw her offspring enjoy precedence over the rest. As the old ruler died and was replaced by one of his sons, the heir's mother would be a person of some importance since he owed his position to her; it is in this limited sense that the societies in question can be said to have been matrilineal. Once again, an example is provided by the Bible, this time by the book of Kings. As each new ruler of either Israel or Judea ascended the throne, the name of his mother was put on record, normally – unless she exceeded her proper role and tried to exercise power herself – for the first and last time. In the Germanic kingdoms of early medieval Europe, as well as in some African and Southeast Asian chiefdoms, it was customary for the chief to select one of his sons to be designated as his successor during his lifetime. To see that his wishes were carried out, a sort of regency council consisting of palace officials would be established.[21]

Next to the chief, society was generally divided in two different layers or classes. First came a privileged group, small in relation to the total population and consisting of the members of the chief's extended family, lineage, or clan. They enjoyed special rights such as access to the chief, much higher compensation to be paid in case of injury or death, and immunity from certain kinds of punishment which were considered degrading. Often they were distinguished by being allowed to wear special insignia and clothing or, in regions where the climate was favorable and clothes unimportant, tattoos. Considered as individuals, their position in society tended to be determined very exactly by their relationship with the chief, i.e., whether they were his sons, uncles, brothers, nephews, in-laws, and so on. Normally it was from among these people that the chief selected the provincial rulers. On the other hand, and precisely because they had some claim to the succession, they were rarely appointed to senior court positions such as *majordomo* or commander of the bodyguard.

Below the royal lineage, clan, or tribe was a much more numerous class of commoners: such as the ancient Greek laborers or *thetes* (also known

---

[21] For the way these things were done among the South African Bantu, e.g., see I. Schapera, *Government and Politics in Tribal Societies* (London: Watts, 1956), pp. 50ff. The Merovingians, too, had a similar system: I. Wood, *The Merovingian Kingdoms 450–751* (London: Longman, 1994), pp. 55ff.

under a variety of other derogatory names, such as *kakoi*, "bad ones"), the Natchez "Stinkers," and many others. They were subject to various kinds of discrimination, such as not being allowed to own cattle (the Hutu in Burundi and Rwanda), ride stallions (the bonders in pre-Christian Scandinavia), wear feather headgear (the Americas), or bear arms (many places around the world). If they were injured or killed by a member of the upper class, they or their families were likely to obtain little compensation or none at all; in the opposite case, their punishment would be particularly savage. The members of this class were not blood relations of the chief. On the contrary, for him and his close relatives to intermarry with them would, except under highly abnormal circumstances, be considered beneath their dignity, contaminating, and even dangerous. Particularly in Africa with its long history of tribal migration, settlement, and conquest, rulers and ruled often belonged to different ethnic groups. They did not necessarily share the same customs or even speak the same language.

The gap that separated them from the elite notwithstanding, the commoners were considered – and, so long as the community remained intact, considered themselves – subjects of the chief. They owed him their allegiance and, indeed, "belonged" to him in the sense that, directly or indirectly by way of the sub-chiefs of whom I shall speak in a moment, they were "his" people. In this way chiefdoms introduced a new and revolutionary principle of government. Blood ties continued to play an important role in determining who possessed what rights in respect to whom. This was true at the upper level, i.e., among the members of the chief's own clan, but it was also true at lower levels where, modified only by more or less strict supervision from above, the extended family group remained the basic entity in which most people spent their lives. The fact that chiefdoms were not based exclusively on such ties enabled the stronger among them to establish impersonal rule and achieve considerable numerical growth. With growth came at least some division of labor among various groups of the population: such as agriculturists, cattle-herders, fishermen, and even a few nonproducing specialists such as traders, artisans, and priests. More importantly for our purpose, much larger concentrations of political, economic, and military power could be created.

The chief's authority varied greatly. He might be little more than a head priest as described in the previous section: performing religious ceremonies, demanding presents, using those presents to maintain a few assistants, and lording it over his people by exercising his magic powers to reward or to punish. A critical turning point came when the members of the upper class, or some of them, became sufficiently elevated to cease working with their hands. This stage had not yet been reached in the Greek world around 1200 BC: legend has it that when King Agamemnon's messenger, sent to announce summons for the Trojan War, arrived he found Odysseus plowing his field. It *had* been reached among the Germanic tribes of Tacitus' time and also in Scandinavia before AD 1000.

Among the most powerful chiefdoms known to us were the nineteenth-century ones of Angkole, Bunyoro, and Buganda (East Africa), Dahomey (West Africa), and Zulu (South Africa), whose chiefs had developed into veritable monarchs. They owed part of their power to supernatural factors. They were considered sacred and tended to live in seclusion; the longer established the chiefdom, the more true this became. Often there were taboos which prohibited them from eating certain foods, taking certain postures such as kneeling, touching certain substances, or even walking on the ground. Similar taboos surrounded the regalia, such as umbilical cords, staffs, headgear, stools, and drums. All of these supposedly possessed magic powers, which were beneficent if properly used – for example, in bringing rain or curing disease – but otherwise dangerous to touch or even look at. Often they had to be guarded by a special college of priests and were taken care of by being offered sacrifices and the like.

The most powerful chiefs possessed life-and-death power over their subjects. The latter were bidden to approach them flat on their stomachs, if indeed they were allowed to do so at all; as a chief traveled or was carried from one place to another in his litter, speaking to him without permission or looking him in the face might constitute a capital offense. Insofar as chiefs were expected to follow religiously dictated custom, they cannot be said to have stood above the law, let alone to have created it in the manner of absolute monarchs. On the other hand it is true that their orders, decrees, and prohibitions represented the sole source of positive legislation inside the community. They also acted as head justice and chief executive, rolled into one.

Whenever the territory he commanded was at all extensive, the chief stood at the apex of a pyramid consisting of regional sub-chiefs. Except when he deposed them, which might happen if they had given offense or appeared to present a threat, the position of sub-chief was passed from father to son; at this point the resemblance to feudalism becomes evident. Far from being specialized, they were small-scale copies of the chief. They maintained their own courts, lorded it over their own peoples, and, subject to some supervision from above, performed duties similar to his. From time to time they would also be called to their superior's court to pay him homage and sit on his council.

A genealogical investigation of the sub-chiefs would probably show that most of them were related to the chief; where this was not the case, it was usually an indication that conquest and subjugation were of recent origin. Typically, indeed, chiefs engaged in a deliberate policy of reinforcing the structure of government by creating family ties. They sent out junior relatives to rule outlying provinces and presented their subordinates with women from the royal household to marry, thus building a ruling stratum whose members were linked to each other both by blood and interest. Representing another step in the same direction, the sub-chiefs' male offspring were often taken away when they reached an age of between six and nine and educated at court. In time, it was hoped, this practice would turn them into loyal supporters of the chief, useful either as provincial rulers or else as palace officials. Conversely, and, as was also the case in other societies such as early imperial Rome or feudal Japan, they served as hostages for their fathers' good behavior.

These types of personnel apart, both chief and sub-chiefs had retainers at their disposal. Though they were not close relatives, retainers were considered members of the household (the Anglo-Saxon term *huyscarls*, "house-braves," clearly indicates this status) and served the chief in various capacities. To make them easier to control they were often of foreign birth – in other words, either those who had been captured as children or else who were refugees from other tribes. In some cases they literally ate at his table, as did Scandinavian warriors before the introduction of more hierarchical forms of government under St. Olaf shortly after AD 1000 caused "kings" (best translated as "men of notable kin") to withdraw first to an elevated dais and them to their own quarters in quest of greater privacy.[22] Alternatively, as in many African, Asian, and Polynesian societies, they might be assigned some of the royal cattle to herd and/or a plot of land for the members of their families to cultivate.

As the Scandinavian chronicles and sagas in particular make clear, keeping the loyalty of subordinates – whether kinsmen, sub-chiefs, or retainers – depended in large part on the chief's ability to distribute wealth; this might take the form of food, clothing, cattle, land, and, in some societies, treasure as well as marriageable women. Some of this wealth originated as the spoils of war, while another part of it was owned directly by the chief. However, most of it derived from the idea that it was he who, by performing the proper rituals and making the proper sacrifices, was responsible for maintaining the land's fertility and ensuring that the harvest was good; it was also up to him to assign vacant land to people who had none. Hence anyone who cultivated land, grazed cattle

---

[22] For a step-by-step account of the withdrawal of Scandinavian kings into privacy, see Snorre Strualson, *Heimskringla, or the Lives of the Norse Kings*, E. Monsen, ed. (New York: Dover Publications, 1990), pp. 520–1.

on it, hunted on it, or exploited its resources in any other way owed part of the produce of his labor to the chief.

Thus chiefdoms became the first political entities to institute rent, tribute, or taxation (it is typical of most pre-state societies, classical city-states alone excepted, that the three could not be clearly told apart) – in other words compulsory, unilateral payments that would take goods out of the hands of the many ruled and concentrate them in those of the ruling few.[23] The precise nature of the wealth paid depended on the resources that the environment afforded and also on custom. Everywhere it consisted of a share of the staple crop, be it grain, rice, taro, or manioc. Then there would be prestige objects such as fine domestic animals and fish; choice parts of big game, such as the head, skin, or tail, which were often used to decorate a chief's person and mark his rank; cloth in its various forms; and, in some societies, women.[24] Some chiefdoms, ancient as well as modern, made use of a primitive form of currency consisting of items which were not meant for immediate consumption but were easy to store and preserve. Among them were whales' teeth (the Pacific), tigers' claws (Africa), wampum beads (North America), and cowry shells (many different regions). All of these could be used to make payments to the chief, whose stores were normally the largest, as well as for other commercial purposes. Finally, chiefdoms that came into contact with more complex, urban civilizations were often familiar with metal money. It might be obtained by trade, as were the *manila* bracelets which the Portuguese introduced to West Africa and which as late as the 1940s were being used to carry out minor transactions. However, there were also cases when they created their own currency, as did eleventh-century Scandinavian chiefs in imitation of Byzantium.[25]

Some of the tribute was paid into the chief's storehouses directly by his own tenants. The rest of the population made payments to the sub-chiefs who, having collected them, took their cut – generally as much as they thought they could get away with, so long as it did not bring the chief's wrath down on them – and passed the rest on. Both chiefs and sub-chiefs possessed additional sources of revenue originating in their right to exercise justice, such as fees, fines, the belongings of condemned persons, and often bribes as well. Very often there existed a sort of licensing system under which chiefs of all ranks might demand and receive payment for granting their subjects certain privileges. These included the right to hold

[23] See A. I. Pershits, "Tribute Relations," in S. L. Seaton and H. J. M. Claessen, eds., *Political Anthropology: The State of the Art* (The Hague: Mouton, 1979), pp. 149–56.

[24] For a good description of a tribute system while it was still in operations, see W. Mariner, *Natives of the Tonga Islands* (New York: AMS Press, 1979 [1818]), vol. II, pp. 230ff.

[25] See P. Einzig, *Primitive Money in Its Ethnological, Historical and Economic Aspects* (London: Eyre and Spottiswoode, 1949).

markets, engage in long-distance trade, go on raiding expeditions against other tribes (in which case the chief would most likely demand part of the booty), and so on. In short, scarcely any economic activity took place in which the chief was not involved and of which he did not take his share.

Part of the wealth that was gathered by such methods was consumed by the chief and the members of his household; from beautiful women to expensive riding animals, being able to engage in wasteful expenditure has always been one of the signs of government as well as one of its privileges. The rest would be saved and kept in storage in special structures that either formed part of the chief's own residence or else were scattered at strategic points throughout his domain. On certain festive occasions, as well as during an emergency such as famine or flooding or drought, the doors of the storehouses would be thrown open and the contents displayed – sometimes by way of potlatching – and used to feed the people. Such largesse could help reinforce the ties binding ruler and subjects. Alternatively one might regard it as a precaution because, under extreme circumstances, what was not readily distributed might be taken by force. There thus existed a sense in which the transfer of wealth was not unilateral but reciprocal. From Polynesia to Africa, its use for this purpose was one of the principal ways in which the entire system could be justified.

Above all, wealth could be used to engage and maintain followers; in this way it formed a basis for establishing, exercising, and increasing power of every kind. The entities that resulted tended to be much more centralized and more cohesive than tribes without rulers. They were also larger, starting in the hundreds but sometimes counting their populations in the tens and – though this was rare – hundreds of thousands; indeed it has been suggested that the pressure of population on resources was itself the most important factor that led to the establishment of chiefdoms and, with them, government proper.[26] Under such circumstances it might become necessary to divide the country into provinces and to build or clear at least some roads that would connect those provinces to the center. The latter assumed the form of a village larger than the rest. It contained, besides the chief's own residence, living quarters for his relatives and retainers as well as a temple for the deity from which he was descended.

Some chiefdoms, notably the prehistoric ones which probably erected the megaliths that dot the British countryside,[27] engaged in large-scale

[26] See above all E. Boserup, *The Conditions of Agricultural Growth: The Economics of Agrarian Change Under Population Pressure* (Chicago: Aldine, 1965). See also M. Harris, *Cannibals and Kings: The Origins of Culture* (New York: Vintage, 1977).
[27] See S. Shennan, "Wessex in the Third Millennium BC," paper given to Royal Anthropological Institute Symposium, 19 February 1983.

building enterprises, primarily for religious and military purposes. Messenger systems might be established and the chief's envoys provided with special insignia, such as palm leaves or staffs, that made their bearers inviolable and entitled them to receive food and other services from the local population. The core of the necessary labor force was probably provided by the chief's personal retainers. However, some of the more powerful African chiefdoms – such as the South African Zulu under their greatest "king," Shaka – also had available another and potentially much larger pool of manpower. This took the form of the members of certain age groups who, as a condition for being assigned land and allowed to marry, had to serve for a stipulated period – not that the chief was always scrupulous in releasing them after their obligation to him had been fulfilled.[28]

Whatever the source of the personnel, they could also be used for police work and war. Thus we find not only warriors but armed forces in the sense of a class of people who, by virtue of their status or age, were organized for engaging in violence, and at least some of whom were always at a chief's disposal. As far as we can follow them, e.g., in the case of the Zulu, the founders of chiefdoms were warlords who commanded their own forces. Trusting more to religion and less to force as a means of maintaining their power, their successors either appointed sub-chiefs to command or else selected other individuals from among their immediate collaborators. Sometimes there was a hierarchy of units, ranging from the royal guard through conscripted age groups all the way down to local forces. The latter, like the early medieval peasant-levy or *fyrd*, were made up of untrained or semi-trained personnel and mobilized only in an emergency.

Supported by force or the threat of force, chiefdoms were able to introduce hierarchy instead of equality; permanent authority instead of temporary leadership; tribute instead of more or less voluntary presents; and judgment, often reinforced by savage punishment, instead of the simple restitution and compensation that were the result of mediation by the village council. On top of engaging – or allowing their subordinates to engage – in the usual feuding, raiding, and booty-taking expeditions, they introduced conquest, subjugation, and domination of one group over another.[29] All these factors meant that boundaries between those who did and did not belong grew clearer, the more so because a settled way of life

---

[28] For Shaka and his cohorts, see most recently J. Taylor, *Shaka's Children: A History of the Zulu People* (London: HarperCollins, 1994), part I.

[29] The idea that government originated in conquest was particularly fashionable at the turn of the twentieth century. See L. Gumplowicz, *The Outlines of Sociology* (Philadelphia: American Academy of Political and Social Sciences, 1899), and F. Oppenheimer, *The State* (New York: Free Life, 1975 [1911]).

"caged" individuals and groups, by making it harder for them to move from the protection of one chief to that of another.

Stronger organization, larger numbers, and a greater capacity for coordinated action constituted the advantages which chiefdoms enjoyed over tribes without rulers. However, the fact that they were often able to expel or conquer the latter should not blind us to their limitations. The most important one was the tendency toward fission inherent in the system of government by hereditary sub-chiefs as well as the methods of succession. From biblical times through eleventh-century Scandinavia to nineteenth-century Africa, Asia, and Polynesia, the death of a chief often gave the signal for the start of a civil war. Rival candidates fought each other with every available means from assassination to full-scale battle; so did their mothers who, in case of defeat, might be put to death or, in some societies, suffer degradation by being assigned to the victor's harem. Sub-chiefs might use the opportunity to break away by ceasing to pay tribute, usurping their superior's rights, and establishing their independence. Neighboring chiefs might also intervene, seeking to increase their own power.

These factors explain why few chiefdoms, ancient or modern, lasted longer than a few generations. In those that did, most rulers came to power after winning a civil war and slaughtering the loser's relatives;[30] this "system," if resorted to often enough and taken far enough, was quite capable of causing development to be arrested and chiefdoms to be turned back into decentralized tribes without rulers.[31] To build stable, longer-lasting political organizations and avoid the repeated decimation of the social elite, new principles of government had to be introduced. It was necessary to regularize the succession to the chieftainship on the one hand, and prevent sub-chiefs from leaving their positions to their offspring on the other.

City-states

The societies described so far were overwhelmingly rural. Their members were nomadic or semi-nomadic, as many tribes without rulers were almost to the present day; alternatively they lived in villages that might be more or less permanent. Either way, their livelihood depended almost exclusively on hunting–gathering, cattle-raising, fishing, and agriculture

---

[30] The weaknesses of African nineteenth-century chiefdoms – the most sophisticated of all – are analyzed in M. Gluckman, *Politics, Law and Ritual in Tribal Society* (Oxford: Blackwell, 1965), pp. 147ff.

[31] The case for believing that chiefdoms frequently "devolved" into tribes without rulers is made by M. Mann, *The Sources of Social Power* (London: Cambridge University Press, 1986), vol. I, pp. 69–73.

practiced mostly at the subsistence level. Only in some of the more developed chiefdoms did the existence of a court and of an aristocratic ruling class create a demand for luxury goods and thus permit economic specialization and professions other than agriculture to emerge. Some chiefdoms, such as those of the ancient Goths and others in nineteenth-century West Africa, were familiar with writing, though normally it was imported from outside and used mainly for religious purposes by specialized personnel. Still, the number of the people engaged full-time in specialties other than producing food – they were often members of a separate, hereditary caste – was minuscule relative to the total population.

Cities, though, are a different matter. A city may be defined as a permanent settlement with houses constructed of a durable material such as stone or brick. It contains a temple, a market place such as the Greek *agora* and Roman forum, as well as a building or buildings devoted to government, and a considerable number of inhabitants who no longer depend on agriculture as their principal occupation.[32] Having mastered the art of writing or at any rate that of record-keeping, they engage in handicrafts, manufacturing, and trade, including, where conditions (usually access to waterways) permit, long-distance trade. Beginning already in late Neolithic times large numbers of such settlements emerged in many parts of the world, including China, India, and the Middle East. After a time lag of several millennia they also appeared in Central and South America.

Considered from a political point of view, cities may be divided into three classes. Probably the majority were ruled by petty chiefs. A chief was known as *lugal* in the ancient Middle East, *wanax* in the Mycenean world, and *kshatriya* in India;[33] in the biblical book of Joshua we find that each of several dozen cities occupied by the invading Israelites was ruled by a "king," though precisely what his powers were is nowhere specified. This type is distinguished from chiefdoms mainly by their more sophisticated administrative system and a more complex social structure. To aristocrats and commoners was added a group of appointed officials – who, since they had to be literate, were not simply sub-chiefs – as well as a separate class of unfree persons, or slaves. The latter might be owned by the ruler,

<hr/>

[32] See L. Mumford, *The City in History* (Harmondsworth, UK: Penguin Books, 1961), chs. 1 and 2.
[33] For what little is known about the way Middle Eastern city-states were governed, see T. Jacobsen, "Early Political Development in Mesopotamia," *Zeitschrift für Assyrologie und Vorderasiatische Archäologie*, 52, 1957, pp. 91–140; and N. Bailey, "Early Mesopotamian Constitutional Development," *American Historical Review*, 72, 4, 1967, pp. 1211–36. For Mycene, see L. R. Palmer, *Myceneans and Minoans* (London: Faber and Faber, 1965), pp. 97–107; for India, see B. Parsed, *Theory of Government in Ancient India* (Allahabad: India Press, 1926).

by private individuals, or, sometimes, by the temple.

A second class of cities did not represent independent communities at all. Instead they formed part of much larger political entities whom they served either as capitals or as provincial centers. Such, as far as it is possible to see, was the case in Mesopotamia after its unification at the hands of Sargon around 2350 BC; China from the time of the first imperial dynasties; India during the periods of centralized empire (320–185 BC, AD 320–500, and AD 1526–1707); and pre-Columbian Latin America as far back into history as we can see.[34]

Finally, the third type comprises self-governing cities. This type may have existed in pre-dynastic Mesopotamia, but in the main it was limited to the Mediterranean littoral. Only in such self-governing cities were Greeks, Romans, and possibly also Etruscans and Phoenicians (Carthage) able to come up with a new principle of government; only here was that form of government maintained during a period measured in centuries and constituting the "classical" world. Of the political system of the Etruscans, who have left few records behind, we know next to nothing. Of Carthage we know that it was a proper city-state and that Aristotle planned to include its constitution in his collection of 158 such documents, now lost; thanks to Rome, which did a thorough job in destroying not merely the city but the records that might have shed light on Carthage's history and government, that is more or less all we know. Hence it is on Greece and Rome, and on them alone, that the present section will focus.

The way classical city-states grew out of the communities which must have preceded them is largely unknown. Assuming, as recent research does,[35] that the communities in question originally consisted of "big-men" type societies in which government was largely confined to the household, at some time there must have taken place what subsequent Greek authors called a *synoikysmos* or "joining of the households." However it was brought about, from this point on government was neither confined to the extended family, as in tribes without rulers, nor concentrated in the hands of a single person as in chiefdoms; instead cities were regarded as collective enterprises and ruled by the many. To this purpose it does not matter whether any particular city was an oligarchy, as most initially were and many remained for a long period of time, or else went through a democratic transformation; nor, in the former case, does it

---

[34] For this kind of city and its government, see B. Sjoberg, *The Pre-Industrial City: Past and Present* (New York: Free Press, 1961), pp. 108–44, 182–255.

[35] For some modern attempts at explanation, see Y. Ferguson, "Chiefdom to City-States: The Greek Experience," in T. Earle, ed., *Chiefdoms: Power, Economy and Ideology* (London: Cambridge University Press, 1991), ch. 8; and M. Stahl, *Aristokraten und Tyrannen im archaischen Athen* (Stuttgart: Steiner, 1987), particularly pp. 140–4, 150–75.

make a difference whether the elite from among whom the rulers were drawn represented true aristocrats (which was how they liked to describe themselves), or merely oligarchs who owed their position to their wealth (which is how they tended to be seen by their opponents). Regardless of how many they were, or what the basis for their power was, the outstanding feature of classical city-states was that their citizens *appointed* certain persons among themselves to govern all of them. Those persons acted, or at any rate were supposed to act, on behalf of the community rather than merely for their own purposes. In other words, we are talking here not of rulers but of magistrates.

There is another way of looking at the matter. Under the political systems outlined so far – as well as the empires and feudal societies which I shall describe in the next section – the distinction between "government" and "ownership" was unknown or, at any rate, fuzzy.[36] Weak or strong, a ruler governed – that is led, commanded, issued decrees, judged, taxed, and if necessary punished – those who were "his," regardless of whether they were such as members of his lineage or as sub-chiefs, followers, domestics, retainers, tenants, or slaves (who, in the form of prisoners-of-war, did exist in some of the more developed chiefdoms). This is to say that "political" rule in the modern sense of that term did not exist; and neither, of course, did the term. In all these societies there were some persons who exercised authority over others, whether as simple lineage heads, as big men, or as full-fledged chiefs. However, without exception, they did so not as "public" officials but as individuals who, owing to their sex, age, divine descent, or some combination of these, were considered elevated over the rest and hence *deserved* to rule.

The situation in the classical city-state was entirely different. To be sure, both the Greek *polis* (as far as our information goes) and the Roman Republic for a long time retained traces of an earlier system. In both the citizens did not constitute a single body but were divided into "demes," "phratries," "curies," "centuries," and "tribes" which, in Rome at any rate, cast their votes *en bloc*. Still, neither was organized around blood ties; provided they were not closely related, citizens could freely marry each others' daughters. Nor, much less, were they based on any other form of "ownership" of one person by another. On the contrary, in both Greece and Rome "government" (*arche, imperium*) was defined as a form of authority exercised by some persons over others who, unlike family members and slaves, were their equals (*homoioi*) in front of the law and did *not* "belong" to them in any of the capacities just listed. They thus

---

[36] The situation just described has led to endless debate among scholars as to whether, in these societies, "private property" did or did not exist. See, e.g., A. M. Bailey and J. R. Llobera, eds., *The Asiatic Mode of Production* (London: Routledge, 1981).

drew a very sharp line between the private (*idios*, *res privata*) and the public (*demosios*, *res publica*) spheres. Within the house (*oikos*, *domus*), social relationships were based on ownership as exercised by the *pater-familias* over his related and unrelated dependents (the latter being slaves), who, of course, did not possess a legal persona of their own. Outside the house's walls there was political authority, or government.

As far as we can determine, these distinctions, like the *polis* itself, were still absent from the Mycenean civilization that spread over southern Greece and the Aegean during the second millennium BC. Nor are they found in Homer's *Iliad* which was populated exclusively by chiefs (*basileis*), the members of their lineages, and their – for the most part anonymous – followers.[37] Their existence is indicated for the first time in that other and presumably younger epic, the *Odyssey*. Written not long before 700 BC and thought to describe social circumstances as they were perhaps a century or two earlier,[38] it contains a passage where Telemachus, the hero's son, informs his host Menelaus that he came "on his own business, not of the people." As if to drive home the fact that a brave new world has appeared, there are two other places where the poet resorts to similar terminology. In the second of those the same Telemachus tells his mother's suitors, who were spoiling his inheritance, that "this is the house of [my father] Odysseus, not a public one."[39]

Additional evidence on the emergence of the *polis* as a new type of political entity comes from an inscription found in Crete and dated to the second half of the seventh century BC. In it, the citizens of Dreros solemnly lay down and decree that the magistrate known as *kosmos* should not hold the same office for the second time before ten years have passed; should he do so nevertheless, then he would be disenfranchised and "anything he should do *as kosmos* [emphasis added] will be null and void." Note the distinction between the office, which is temporary, and the person who occupies it and who will continue with his private life after he has laid it down. At present this is the earliest direct reference to a magistrate that we possess.[40]

As perhaps the most critical political invention of all time, the mature theory of the distinction between government and ownership – in what-

---

[37] See R. Drews, *Basileus: The Evidence for Kingship in Geometric Greece* (New Haven, CT: Yale University Press, 1983).

[38] The best modern analysis of the society that Homer described is M. I. Finley, *The World of Odysseus* (London: Penguin, 1979).

[39] The passages in the *Odyssey* (London: Heinemann, Loeb Classical Library, 1966), are IV.314, III.82, and XX.264–5.

[40] Inscription published in R. Meiggs and D. Lewis, eds., *A Selection of Greek Historical Inscriptions to the End of the Fifth Century BC* (Oxford: Clarendon, 1975), no. 2. I am grateful to my colleague, Dr. G. Herman, for bringing it to my attention.

ever form – probably took centuries to develop. Nor was the earlier point of view which confused the two easily laid to rest. In Athens, for example, it was only during the reforms of Solon in 594/3 BC that debt-bondage was abolished and an absolute line was drawn between free (citizen) and unfree (servile) status; in Rome the same reform had to wait longer still. The last important political theorist who, looking backward into history, wanted to govern the city *as if* it were an extended household was Plato in the *Republic*. For this he was criticized by Aristotle who pointed out, with perfect justice, that family and city were entirely different institutions and that the social principles that underlay the one were inapplicable to the other.[41] Using Plato as his punching ball, Aristotle, writing near the middle of the fourth century BC, devoted most of the first part of his *Politics* to working out the distinction in detail.[42] Nor was he wrong in placing it at the beginning of his book. Compared with it, all other constitutional arrangements which he discusses – or which existed in the daily life of various city-states – were of secondary, almost trivial, significance.

The city-state's organs of government did not correspond to our customary separation between executive, legislative, and judiciary.[43] Perhaps the most important single institution was the popular assembly. Rome seems to have been unique in that it did not have a single assembly but four different ones, each comprising a different section of the population, voting according to a different system, and attaining constitutional importance *vis-à-vis* the other three during a different historical period. Elsewhere there was a single assembly comprising all citizens, in other words all adult males who were neither part of the household of others (slaves) nor foreigners. It met at the request of the presiding magistrates, either at regular intervals or as the occasion demanded; in Athens, the only city about which we have such information, there seem to have been some forty meetings a year. The assembly's main function was to pass laws, known as *nomoi* in Greece and *leges* in Rome; but it also elected the magistrates and pronounced the final word on questions of war and peace. Finally, in Athens and possibly in other Greek cities as well, the assembly possessed the right to use ostracism in order to force citizens whom it considered a public danger into exile.

---

[41] On the relationship between *polis* and *oikos*, see J. Ober, "The *Polis* as a Society: Aristotle, John Rawls and the Athenian Social Contract," in M. G. Hansen, ed., *The Ancient Greek City-State* (Copenhagen: Royal Danish Academy, 1993), pp. 130–5.

[42] See W. J. Booth, "Politics and the Household: A Commentary on Aristotle's *Politics* Book I," *History of Political Thought*, 2, 2, Summer 1981, pp. 203–26.

[43] The best short account of the institutions of the ancient city-state remains V. Ehrenberg, *The Greek State* (New York: Norton, 1960 edn.).

Next in importance to the assembly were the various magistrates. Whereas many might be selected by lot, the most important ones were invariably elected. With few exceptions, the term of office was one year. Only in Sparta did the so-called kings rule for life; but even here they were little more than hereditary officials whose power was strictly limited and subject to supervision by a special group of five *ephors*.[44] Besides summoning the assembly, as has just been mentioned, the magistrates were responsible for running the city's day-to-day affairs. These included commanding in war (the Greek *strategoi* and *polemarchs*, the Roman consuls and dictator; the latter was a temporary commander elected for six months), looking after the finances (the Roman *quaestores*), erecting public buildings and supervising markets (the Roman *aediles*), and exercising justice, as well as keeping internal order (the Roman consuls and praetors together). In Greece – though rarely in Rome where aristocratic traditions were more powerful and lasted longer – the objective was usually to enable as many citizens as possible to rule and be ruled in turn. Hence the number of magistrates, especially those occupying minor posts such as supervising markets and keeping the streets clean, was often quite large.

Though the details are obscure, the military origins of government are betrayed by the fact that all cities probably demanded that citizens enlisted for service and participated in a prescribed number of military campaigns before standing for election to a magistracy. Many must also have maintained a minimum age which a person had to reach before he could be elected, though that rule – like the one which, in Rome, prohibited magistrates from serving twice in the same office – was sometimes waived in an emergency. Contrary to the practice of modern government organizations, in most cases there seems to have been no mandatory progression of offices through which an individual had to pass before he could reach the top; since, in the interest of avoiding tyranny, no magistrate possessed authority over the rest, government was diffused. Again the only known exception to the rule was Rome. Here there existed a highly structured *cursus honorum*, or honors career, which took the aspiring politician from the humblest positions to the most senior ones. Roman magistrates also possessed *coercitio* (the power to coerce), a power whose name speaks for itself and which was not shared by their Greek colleagues. Still, even in Rome the two consuls were co-equal. No policy could be carried out except by the consent of both; this led to the absurd arrangement whereby, until some time during the Second Punic War, they commanded the army on alternate days. Furthermore, and precisely

---

[44] See H. Mitchell, *Sparta* (Cambridge: Cambridge University Press, 1964), pp. 101ff.

because Roman government was so strong, it was found necessary to appoint special magistrates – the tribunes – to protect the plebes against any excesses that their rulers might commit, and also to give them at least some share in the government.

A further peculiarity of the system was that priests, too, were subject to annual rotation. Although in Athens and elsewhere some priestly positions were monopolized by certain families, as a rule the priesthood was not hereditary nor did it consist of specialists; instead priests were simply magistrates whose job happened to be that of serving the city's deities and keeping them happy. Each temple, god, and function had a college of priests which was responsible for it; Rome was unique because it had a *pontifex maximus*, or high priest, who exercised authority over official religion as a whole. Insofar as they were in charge of the various curses, auguries, and omens that permitted or prohibited certain actions, priests, whether individually or in their colleges, could and did influence the policies of the remaining organs of government; for example, they might decide whether this or that day was suitable for founding a temple, concluding an alliance, or fighting a battle. Still, the system meant that their influence could not become institutionalized or persist over time. A conflict between polity and church, such as very often arose in other societies, was thereby rendered impossible.[45]

The third organ composing the government of the city-state was the *boule* or council. The one in Sparta was known as *gerousia* and thus clearly originated in a tribal council of elders, and the same was true in other cities. Though the precise steps can no longer be traced, in historical times the councils of most cities lost their aristocratic character in favor of a system whereby members were appointed by lot and served for the usual period of one year. Only in Rome were the senators appointed *ex officio* from among ex-magistrates who had served their term. Unless disqualified by the *censores* (two magistrates who were elected every five years and whose responsibility it was to hold an inquiry into the property and conduct of each citizen), senators retained their position for life.

The council's principal functions were to prepare bills for presentation in the assembly and also to supervise the magistrates' work by checking their accounts and receiving complaints. In Greece it was normally the least important part of the government, but in Rome it acted as a sink where the political expertise of the republic accumulated. The Senate's influence over political affairs, both domestic and foreign, was immense. As well as exercising the above-mentioned functions, it replaced the

---

[45] A good account of the relationship between religion and polity in Rome in particular is D. Potter, *Prophets and Emperors: Human and Divine Authority from Augustus to Theodosius* (Cambridge, MA: Harvard University Press, 1994), pp. 147–58.

assembly in receiving the envoys of foreign rulers; it was authorized to suspend civil rights by declaring a state of emergency or *tumultus*; and, on at least one occasion, it used a technicality in order to invalidate consular elections and force new ones to be held.[46] Still, even in Rome at its second-century BC zenith, the authority (*auctoritas*) of the Senate was never formalized. Unlike a modern parliament it did not pass laws; the most it could do was deliberate and pass *consulta* (strictly speaking, advice) to the magistrates. However, it could not issue orders to them or hold them accountable, let alone override the citizen-assembly which always retained sovereignty – if the term is appropriate at all – in its own hands.

Finally, and as befits a community that had emancipated itself from the rule of an individual, the city did not have a unified juridical system. There existed neither appellate courts – decisions, once made, were final – nor a minister of justice, nor chief justices. Instead there was a variety of unrelated courts, each one meeting daily and often known, after the different premises in which they met, by such names as the New Court, the Triangular Court, the Small Court, and so on. The decision as to which case would be tried in which court was made by officials who specialized in that business, such as the Athenian *archontes* and *themosthetai* and the Roman praetors. Membership of the courts consisted of ordinary citizens. Like modern jurors, they served on a case-by-case basis without having received any special training for the purpose. In Athens from at least the time of Pericles they were given modest pay for their services – barely enough to keep them financially solvent, it would seem.

The jury system meant that a considerable part of the population was involved in the exercise of justice. Thus, in Athens, the assembly elected a pool of 6,000 potential jurors each year; to forestall bribery, the decision as to who would serve on each court each day was made by lot with the aid of a specially constructed machine.[47] The system meant that, instead of executive and juridical powers resting in the hands of the same persons, as was customary in all previous and most subsequent societies until well into modern times, they were separated. In this way the classical city-state became the first, and for a very long time only, political community to take juridical powers out of the hands of the ruler(s). No magistrate, not even the Roman consuls whose power was greater than that of all the rest, in an ancient city-state possessed the right to inflict capital punishment on a citizen in peacetime unless he had first been permitted to present his

---

[46] This happened in 163 BC: see M. T. Cicero, *De Natura Deorum* (London: Heinemann, Loeb Classical Library, 1967), II, 10–11.

[47] For the jury-selection system, see D. M. MacDowell, *The Law in Classical Athens* (Ithaca, NY: Cornell University Press, 1978), p. 34.

case before a citizens' court; which in some cases might be represented either by the council or by the assembly. In Rome this right, justly described by Cicero as a cornerstone of liberty, was known as *provocatio*.

In the absence of the state as a legal *persona* against which offenses could be committed, our modern distinction between civil and criminal jurisdiction did not apply.[48] It made no difference whether the matter brought before a court involved a dispute over an inheritance or murder; instead a line was drawn between cases which involved only individuals and those which, like peculation, treason, impiety, and – in Rome – insulting the greatness or *majestas* of the Roman people, concerned the community as a whole. In the former cases, the only ones who could bring suit were the injured person or, if he was no longer alive, his relatives; the second type could be prosecuted by any citizen who wished to do so. As a result it was sometimes used for getting rid of undesirables of whom the most famous one happened to be Socrates. In addition, persons who were involved in politics could persuade somebody else to press charges of this kind against an opponent, a method known as sycophancy.[49] In point of procedure a difference existed insofar as the number of jurors assigned to "political" offenses was much larger – either 501 or, in special cases, as many as 1,001. Still, even in such cases there was no state-appointed prosecutor in our sense of that term.

As they were governed not by the few but by the many, classical city-states failed to develop either specialized personnel, large administrative machines, or regular armed forces. It was a matter of principle that, with a few exceptions (such as those which, in some cities, restricted certain priesthoods to the members of certain families), any citizen could become a magistrate; after a prolonged struggle which pitted patricians against plebeians this became true even in Rome. Nor was there any attempt to prepare or train professional personnel in such fields as police work, accounting, diplomacy, etc. There seems to have been remarkably little administration. Initially, at any rate, even the laws themselves were regarded as god-given and available only in the form of oral traditions. Long after this had ceased to be the case and the laws were published – in Rome, this event took place in 451 BC when twelve bronze tables were inscribed and set up in the forum – the paperwork that did exist seems to have been carried out by the magistrates in person. They received no salaries but, at most, small sums of money intended as expenses. Having no staff except, in Athens, a secretary or two, they often employed their

---

[48] See R. Sealey, *The Justice of the Greeks* (Ann Arbor: University of Michigan Press, 1994), ch. 5.

[49] See R. A. Bauman, *Political Trials in Ancient Greece* (London: Routledge, 1990); and R. Garner, *Law and Society in Classical Athens* (London: Croom Helm, 1987), pp. 51ff.

own domestics, slaves, and politically ambitious relatives on administrative tasks.

Together with the secular character of government, the virtual absence of a bureaucracy in our sense of the term meant that Greek and Roman magistrates, unlike many other types of rulers before and since, were public figures first and foremost. The very fact that they had to stand for election made them such; having entered into office, they could be seen on a daily basis as they walked to and from the public assembly places in the center of the city. At most they might have a modest guard such as the *lictores* who attended Roman consuls and praetors. However, nothing could prevent people from accosting them in the streets in order to submit petitions and launch complaints; Pericles on one occasion provided a citizen who had insulted him with a light and had him escorted back home by a slave. It was in the open spaces of the *agora* and the forum, as well as the public structures surrounding them, that the magistrates carried out most of their duties. The remainder they probably performed from the privacy of their own homes.[50]

What was true of the administration also applied to the armed forces. In both Greece and Rome, whenever a war ended the troops – commanders and officers not excepted – simply dispersed and went home. Whenever a new one broke out, the responsible magistrates would proceed to the designated place – such as, in Rome, the Campus Martius or Field of Mars – refer to a list of citizens and hold a levy. They would take volunteers first, and only then turn to other citizens who had not yet served the number of campaigns stipulated by the law. In Rome and possibly elsewhere, each time a levy was held the men had to be sworn in afresh – not to the Republic, it should be noted, but to the person of the commanding consul. Should the latter die on campaign, then the ceremony had to be repeated in his successor's name. The citizen-soldiers, who of course did not wear uniform, were supposed to present themselves with their own arms, for which purpose they were divided into property classes.[51] Since war was seen as an affair of the people they did not receive pay for their services; at most, subsistence-money might be distributed.

Thus the city-state's armed force, known as *stratos* or *exercitus*, is best described as a host. Like the levies of tribes without rulers, but unlike regular armies, it was not clearly distinguishable from the citizen-body at large. It did not lead a separate existence as an organization, nor con-

---

[50] On the weaknesses of Greek and Roman public administration, see M. Finley, *Politics in the Ancient World* (Cambridge: Cambridge University Press, 1983), pp. 18ff.

[51] For the way these things were done in Athens, see Aristotle, *The Athenian Constitution* (London: Heinemann, Loeb Classical Library, 1942), 49.

sequently was it able to develop a militarist *esprit de corps*. Mercenaries could be and were employed, especially in Greece from the time of the Peloponnesian War on when they provided specialist troops such as archers, slingers, and javelin-throwers. But mercenaries, though often highly professional, by definition were not citizens. Instead of forming part of their employer's polity, they were paid off and dismissed as soon as possible and as far away as possible. Only in Sparta did the existence of helots – a class of hereditary serfs who performed most productive work – give the citizens leisure and enable war to be turned into a national industry, with the result that they were, in Plutarch's words, "professors of war."[52] Elsewhere it was carried on mainly by semi-trained amateurs, a shortcoming which Plato in the *Republic* identified and inveighed against.[53]

Remarkably, in view of the skills that some Romans in particular developed, the system also extended to commanders. Their position depended on their ability to get themselves elected by the people; hence they were almost always politicians first and military men second. If Nicias, who commanded in several campaigns and was finally chosen by the Athenians to lead the largest military expedition in their history, possessed any special training for the job, we are wholly ignorant of it. But even such a soldiers' soldier as the Roman consul Gaius Titus Flamininus, who in 197–196 BC defeated Macedonia and conquered Greece, had no specialized training as an officer. Instead he "learnt how to command others by being commanded himself."[54] For most city-states, and during most of their history, the system of unpaid amateur soldiers put strict limits on their ability to engage in military operations at a distance from home and also to conquer and dominate other cities.[55]

Possessing neither an extensive bureaucracy nor regular armed forces, city-states were for the most part able to do without directly taxing their citizens. A military emergency might call for the imposition of a special levy, especially on property or else in the form of a poll tax. In case the conflict was protracted this could become very burdensome; in 215 BC, for example, the Roman Senate both doubled the contributions due from each citizen and advanced the date at which they were collected. However, even on such occasions the fundamentally democratic and egalitarian nature of the community meant that there was always a tendency to shift the burden to the weaker, for which read non-voting,

---

[52] Plutarch, *Pelopidas*, in *Lives* (London: Heinemann, Loeb Classical Library, 1921), XXIII, 3.
[53] Plato, *Republic* (London: Heinemann, Loeb Classical Library, 1949), book II, 374.
[54] Plutarch, *Lives*, *Flamininus*, I, 3.
[55] See Y. Garlan, *Etudes dans la poliocrétiqve grèque* (Athens: Ecole française, 1974), esp. ch. 1.

classes. An excellent case in point is provided by the Roman Senate's attempt to tax rich widows during the Second Punic War. This caused the women to protest that, since they did not form part of the citizen-body and had no quarrel with Hannibal, they should not be made to bear its expenses.[56]

The normal method for meeting the expenditure of government in peacetime was to rely on market duties and the fruits of the justice system in the form of fines and confiscated property. For religious purposes there were the leftover parts of sacrificial animals, which were sold, as well as the financial operations of the temples which acted as depositories and lent out money at interest. Cities that were so fortunate as to have mines on their territory could grant individuals a lease on their operation and utilize the proceeds, either by devoting them to some public purpose (such as the Athenian navy, built on Themistocles' advice) or else simply by distributing them among the citizens. Some of the more cosmopolitan cities, such as Corinth, could count on customs, harbor-dues, and the payments made by foreigners in return for the right to reside and trade. Finally, a few of them were able to rule other cities. In exchange for the "protection" they offered, they received tribute. This was the case with Athens, which, having established its dominion over the remaining members of the Attic–Delic League, used the money it collected from them to pay its rowers and maintain its naval supremacy in the Aegean.

However, by far the most important source of revenue enjoyed by ancient city-states – Greek ones as well as Roman – consisted of the so-called liturgies. These are best described as contributions made by the richer citizens for specific purposes. It might be a question of staging a play; providing supplies to the gymnasium or exercise hall; erecting a public building; or constructing and even manning a warship.[57] Liturgies were assigned to individuals by the responsible magistrates on the basis of property lists which, of course, took into account contributions already made in the past; unlike modern charities, they were not voluntary but represented a civic duty that one could escape only by pointing to some-body else who possessed more but had given less. In a sense they were payments made by the rich in order to protect their property against being expropriated by the poor,[58] but in fairness it should be said that making those payments was considered honorable. Many donations were com-

---

[56] See Livy, *The Histories* (London: Heinemann, Loeb Classical Library, 1929), XXIV, xviii, 13–14.

[57] For Greece, see e.g. Pausanias, *A Description of Greece* (London: Heinemann, Loeb Classical Library, 1967), 10, 9, 2; also G. Gilula, "A Career in the Navy," *Classical Quarterly*, 1989, pp. 259–61. For Rome, see Livy, *The Histories*, XXIV, xi, 7–9.

[58] A. Fuks, "The Sharing of Property by the Rich with the Poor in Greek Theory and Practice," *Scripta Classica Israelica*, 5, 1979–80, pp. 46–63.

memorated in inscriptions set up either by the grateful recipients or by the donors themselves. Often citizens paid more than they had to as a means for obtaining popularity, influence, and, in the not unlikely eventuality of being taken to court, a measure of sympathy among the jurors; and indeed our knowledge of the subject owes much to cases of this sort.

The great variety represented by these sources of income meant that few if any cities maintained a single public treasury to which all money went and which, in turn, was responsible for making all public payments. Rome, which did not have liturgies in the same form and which at some unknown date developed the treasury or *aerarium*, was the exception to the rule. However, even here the magistrates often bore the burden of public expenditure, including what we today would regard as military expenditure, out of their own pockets. For example, during the Hannibalic War, the dictator Quintus Maximus Fabius Cunctator used his personal resources to pay for the release of some Roman prisoners. When the son of Scipio Africanus (who at that time was acting as *de facto* commander-in-chief) was captured during the war against Antiochus in 190 BC, it was he and not the Republic who had to come up with a ransom.[59]

As Rome grew wealthier and the gap between rich and poor widened, greater use was made of private money and private armed forces consisting of relatives and clients to accomplish public objectives. The system peaked in the careers of such figures as Crassus and Pompey who, in 73–71 BC, used their own resources to suppress the Spartacus Revolt, thus earning the gratitude of the Senate and the people. During the following two decades their example was followed by Julius Caesar, originally a minor nobleman who made his fortune first by vanquishing pirates in the Mediterranean and then by conquering Gaul which had been assigned to him as a province by the Senate. The three of them together attained so much power and popularity as to undermine and finally destroy the Republic.

Here and elsewhere the financial system, as best we can follow it, operated largely *ad hoc*. Specific sums were voted by the assembly, distributed among the classes according to their ability to pay, and collected for specific purposes. Most of the time this was done not at regular intervals but simply as the occasion demanded. Once the money had been collected it was deposited in a fund dedicated to some god; a case in point was the *aerarium* itself which was located in the temple of Saturn on the Capitol. In 431 BC, embarking on the risky enterprise known as the Peloponnesian War, the Athenians passed a resolution to

[59] Livy, *The Histories*, XXII, xxiii, 8; Polybius, *The Histories* (London: Heinemann, Loeb Classical Library, 1922–), xxi, 15.

the effect that, except in an emergency, anyone who proposed violating the 5,000-talent reserve kept in the temple of Athena would be put to death. Whatever the physical place where the money was kept, it was administered by the responsible magistrate or magistrates. There seems to have been no attempt to create a centralized accounting system to link the various funds, let alone an overall budget.

So long as they did not come under the dominion of an outside power or fall victim to a tyrant (in which case the *polis*, properly speaking, would cease to exist) each classical city-state enjoyed freedom (*eleutheria, libertas*) both in respect to its external affairs and internally. Externally "freedom" meant something very close to the modern sovereignty. The citizens worshipped their own gods and lived according to their own laws, i.e., they enjoyed *autonomia*; they were judged in their own courts, presided over by elected magistrates and manned by fellow citizens; they were not subject to, and did not pay, a compulsory tribute (*phoros, tributum*) to any other city or ruler; and, by way of guaranteeing all the above, they did not have to suffer a foreign garrison in their midst.[60] Internally it meant that citizens possessed the right to participate in political life and were considered equal before the law; nor, so long as normalcy prevailed, did they have to pay too many direct taxes. Short of a coup mounted by a tyrant, usually with the aid of mercenaries brought in from outside, the rise of arbitrary government was prevented by the elaborate system of checks and balances just described.

Above all, it was by separating the person of a ruling magistrate from the office that he held and making the latter both temporary and elective that classical city-states made a monumental contribution to political life. They thereby discovered a method which permitted the talents of every citizen to be freely mobilized on behalf of the polity as a whole; and which, in principle and very often in practice as well, could lead to a change of government without resort to conspiracy, civil war, or, indeed, violence of any kind. Since then their example has often been obscured and during certain ages it was even considered dangerous; in Russia Tsar Nicholas I (1825–55) went so far as to have all references to "republic" and "republicanism" removed from textbooks dealing with the classical world. Consider this description of the ancient city-state at its best:

Our constitution is called a democracy because power is in the hands not of a minority but of the whole people. When it is a question of settling private disputes, everyone is equal before the law; when it is a question of putting one person before another in positions of public responsibility, what counts is not membership of a

---

[60] For the Roman meaning of freedom in particular, see C. Wirszubski, *Libertas as a Political Idea at Rome During the Late Republic and the Early Principate* (Cambridge: Cambridge University Press, 1960).

particular class, but the actual ability which the man possesses. No one, so long as he has it in him to be of service to the *polis*, is kept in political obscurity because of poverty . . .

We are free and tolerant in our private lives . . . we give our obedience to those whom we put in positions of authority, and we obey the laws themselves, especially those which are for the protection of the oppressed, and those unwritten laws which it is an acknowledged shame to break.[61]

Empires, strong and weak

The communities discussed so far were relatively small. In the case of tribes without rulers this was due to a combination of factors, including an economy based on hunting, gathering, fishing, cattle-herding, and slash-and-burn agriculture; the nomadic or semi-nomadic lifestyle that these activities made necessary; the wide open spaces that they entailed; and the weakness of government itself. All this meant that whenever a group or tribe exceeded a certain critical size there was a tendency for it to split up. The heads of junior lineages would go their own way and start an independent life, though probably still acknowledging the various cultural, religious, and family ties that bound them to the parent group.

Though chiefdoms tended to grow larger than tribes without rulers, in their case the number of people who could be controlled from a single center was limited by the absence of an administration making use of the written word. As already noted, the resulting instability was reinforced by the prevalent system of polygyny which very often caused the rulers to beget numerous offspring. Unless great care was taken and proper arrangements made in advance, each time a chief died the result would be a succession crisis which threw the people into a turmoil and provided sub-chiefs with an opportunity to break away.

As for city-states, they were small by definition. The citizens of each one regarded themselves as a separate people descended from a single race and worshipping the same gods;[62] though Greek cities did acknowledge their common cultural identity, until the advent of the Hellenistic age (which, by subordinating most of them to larger political entities, reduced the differences among them), they were extremely reluctant to admit foreigners. Furthermore, and however small or large the number of those who possessed political rights, the essence of the city-state was a

---

[61] Thucydides, *The Peloponnesian War* (London: Heinemann, Loeb Classical Library, 1921), II, 36.

[62] For the Greek *polis* as a community of ancestor-worshippers, see above all N. D. Fustel de Coulanges, *The Ancient City* (Garden City, NY: Doubleday, 1956 edn.). For archeological evidence on how the community of the few was probably transformed into that of the many, see I. Morris, *Burial and Ancient Society: The Rise of the Greek City-State* (London: Cambridge University Press, 1987).

direct system of government in which all participated to one extent or another. Such a system required that nobody live too far away from the civic center where the assembly held its meetings and where the city's public buildings – such as temples, courts, theaters, etc. – also tended to cluster: say, the distance that could be conveniently covered by a man traveling on foot within a single day. Thus Athens, next to Syracuse the largest by far of all Greek city-states, probably had at its zenith a population of 250,000. Among them perhaps 30,000–40,000 were citizens; the balance was made up by their related and unrelated family members (the latter being slaves). All in all they lived in an area of no more than 600 square miles. Other city-states were much smaller. Often they counted their citizens in the low thousands and often only in the hundreds, as is illustrated by the fact that the Island of Crete alone was divided between no fewer than fifty different cities.

By contrast, empires – even the earliest ones – were often mighty organizations. Some were able to last for centuries and even millennia; this was particularly true of those which, like the ancient Egyptian and Chinese ones, were ethnically homogeneous and developed a political system that was all but identical with the culture in question. Homogeneous or not, empires often covered hundreds of thousands, if not millions, of square miles and counted their subject peoples – to the extent that they could be counted at all – in the millions and tens of millions. For example, the Inca empire measured over 2,000 miles from north to south and may have had 6 to 8 million inhabitants. The Roman empire at its zenith incorporated modern Italy, Yugoslavia, Romania, Bulgaria, Greece, Turkey, Armenia, Syria, Mesopotamia (for a short period under Trajan), Palestine, Egypt, the northern provinces of Libya, Tunisia, Algeria and Morocco, Spain, France, Britain, southern Germany, and Switzerland, as well as parts of Austria and Hungary; the number of people who lived under imperial rule is variously estimated at 50 million to 80 million. In the case of China the organization known as the empire even proved capable of ruling a population that eventually grew into the hundreds of millions over a period measured in millennia – albeit that control was not always complete and tended to be punctuated by recurring periods of decentralization, disorder, and rebellion.

The origins of some of the oldest empires, e.g., the Chinese and Egyptian ones, is unknown. Most of the remainder originated when one chiefdom conquered its neighbors – some of the most primitive of them, indeed, are perhaps best understood as chiefdoms grown large. This was the case with the Aztec and Inca empires, both of which owed their genesis to a series of exceptionally able warrior-chiefs: taking over from previous rulers, they went on to extend their rule in all directions, using

the members of their own tribes to create a new ruling class. The Assyrian, Babylonian, Persian, Arab, Mongol, Ottoman, and Mogul empires
also originated in the conquest by one chief and one tribe of many
others.

By contrast, Rome grew directly out of a city-state and indeed as late as
the beginning of the fourth century BC it was still possible for Constantine to claim that he had "avenged the *res publica* on the tyrant" (the
pretender Maxentius).[63] By the last decades of the second century BC,
Rome, though still maintaining its old republican system of government,
had expanded until it counted its citizens in the hundreds of thousands.[64]
With the advent of those two would-be social reformers, the brothers
Gracchus, the system began to break down; once the so-called social war
of 90–89 BC emancipated Rome's Italian allies and turned them into
citizens it became entirely impractical. While the citizens could be counted in the low millions and spread all over the entire peninsula, effective
power passed into the hands of the Roman mob. The latter continued to
be organized in its various assemblies and to be presided over by demagogues who, using bread and circuses, were able to sway it whichever way
they wanted. As mentioned above, for half a century these demagogues
fought each other, until the one who mobilized the largest and most
efficient army finally made himself emperor.

At the head of each empire there stood – unsurprisingly – a single
emperor. Early in the fourth century Diocletian attempted to divide
Rome between two emperors, known as *augusti*, each with a designated
successor to take his place when the time came; however, the attempt
broke down as soon as he himself resigned the reins of government and
does not seem to have found imitators since. In both Rome and China
some emperors tried to regulate the succession by appointing their own
sons – whether real or adopted – as co-regents during their own lifetime.
In the Ottoman empire, to prevent them from becoming the center of
intrigue, the emperors' often very numerous sons were brought up in a
part of the palace known as "the cage";[65] once a new sultan gained power
his first step was usually to order all his brothers strangled. Provided they
were sufficiently prominent, female members of the imperial family could
also play a role in the succession. Either they did so by engaging in
intrigue in favor of their sons, or else by outliving one imperial husband
and marrying his successor by way of an additional confirmation of his

---

[63] H. Dessau, ed., *Inscriptiones Latinae Selectae* (Zurich: Weidmann, 1967), vol. I, p. 156,
no. 694.
[64] P. Brunt, *Italian Manpower* (Oxford: Clarendon, 1971), pp. 44–90.
[65] Lord Kinross, *The Ottoman Centuries: The Rise and Fall of the Turkish Empire* (New York:
Morrow Quill, 1977), p. 333.

status; one tenth-century Byzantine princess even married three emperors in succession.

Like the chiefs that many of them originally were, most emperors claimed to owe their position to some kind of divine connection. This was true even in Rome, possibly the most secular-minded empire of all; already Caesar took the position of *pontifex maximus*, whereas his successor Augustus allowed temples to be built for him in the provinces, if not in Rome itself. Augustus' own immediate successors continued the practice, each of them – provided he had behaved himself during his lifetime – being formally proclaimed divine by the Senate as soon as he had died. Hadrian had his succession announced by Apollo whereas Marcus Aurelius was reputed to be capable of inspiring rain.[66] The process was completed in AD 218 when Varius Avitius Bassianus, ascending the throne, identified himself with the Syrian god Elgabalus. From this time until the empire became Christianized under Constantine, each successive emperor was *ex officio* a god and demanded to be worshipped as such both in the provinces and in Rome itself.

If Roman emperors took time before they developed into gods, elsewhere the connection was obvious from the beginning. Some were themselves god incarnate: so with the ancient Egyptians and the Inca, both of whom worshipped the sun, which proved to be a popular choice for imperial ancestor; so also in China, where the emperor was the son of *Tien* or heaven. Elsewhere the various arrangements that existed invariably implied a strong measure of supernatural support. Thus Mesopotamian emperors, though apparently not claiming to be divine themselves, were often represented in art as confronting the deity face to face and receiving its commands. Arab *khaliffs* claimed to be descended from Mohammed. As "heads of the faithful," they used their positions to exercise not just secular but religious government as well; and the same was true of the Ottoman sultans. Even when the emperor was neither a god nor a descendant of the prophet, as in Byzantium, he acted as head of the church and, indeed, it would be hard to say which one of his functions, the secular or the religious, was the more important. In fact perhaps the only emperor who did not unite secular and religious power in his own person was the Western Christian one; but even here the first among them, i.e., Charlemagne, regarded himself as head of the church as well. Accordingly he appointed bishops, summoned ecclesiastical councils, and in general imposed his will over such questions as feast-days and prayers without so much as referring to the pope in Rome.[67]

[66] Potter, *Prophets and Emperors*, pp. 122, 128–9.
[67] L. Halperin, *Charlemagne and the Carolingian Empire* (Amsterdam: North Holland, 1977), pp. 148–9.

Whatever their precise relationship with the gods, all emperors were absolute rulers who combined legislative, executive, and juridical functions in their own persons. There could be no question here of constitutional restraints of a separation of powers; as the Latin saying had it, *salus principis lex est* (law is what is good for the emperor) and *princeps legibus solutus est* (the emperor stands above the law). Similarly, Hellenistic rulers were *nomos empsychos*, law incarnate, ruling over both the bodies of men and their religious beliefs. To show what absolute power really meant Antiochus III on one occasion gave his own wife to his son, Antiochus IV, to marry. To the army, which had been assembled to witness the occasion, he explained that "this is not done according to the laws of god or man but because it is my will; and since they are both young, they will surely have children."[68]

Ideologically speaking, most empires developed doctrines whose purpose was to confirm the subject population in its obedience to the powers that be. Thus China had Confucianism in its two forms, "paternal" and "legal."[69] The former presented the empire as a vast family in which the young and the subordinate owed piety to their elders and betters, whereas the latter emphasized the role of discipline and prescribed drastic punishment for those who disturbed the heaven-mandated social structure. In the Arab, Ottoman, and Persian (from the middle of the seventh century on) empires, a similar role was played by Islam (the word itself means "submission") which in at least some of its versions emphasized fatalism, resignation, and obedience. Finally, the ancient philosophies such as cynicism, epicureanism, and stoicism all grew out of the ruin of the independent city-state and are best understood as reactions to despotism, whether Hellenistic or Roman. Thus the cynics taught that, to compensate for the loss of freedom, man should give up his possessions and withdraw from the world. Epicureanism suggested that men, likewise withdrawing into private life, should focus on enjoying themselves, whereas stoicism on the contrary put the emphasis on endurance, service to one's fellow men, and – if things became too hard to bear – suicide as a way of escaping to a world in which even the emperor's long arm could not reach.[70] In time all these ideologies were overtaken by early Christianity, which, in the words of its founder, gave Caesar what was

---

[68] Appian, *The Histories* (London: Heinemann, Loeb Classical Library, 1964), preface, 7.

[69] See W. T. de Bary, "Chinese Despotism and the Confucian Ideal: A Seventeenth-Century View," in J. K. Fairbank, ed., *Chinese Thought and Institutions* (Chicago: University of Chicago Press, 1984), pp. 163–200.

[70] On Hellenistic and Roman political thought, see M. Hammond, *City-State and World State in Greek and Roman Political Theory Until Augustus* (Cambridge, MA: Harvard University Press, 1951); and M. L. Clarke, *The Roman Mind: Studies in the History of Thought from Cicero to Marcus Aurelius* (London: Cohen and West, 1956).

Caesar's due while enabling the believer to focus on saving his own soul.[71]

So long as emperors behaved themselves, their rule might be beneficent. However, there always existed the danger that, motivated by need or greed or sheer madness, they would cease to do so, in which case the results would be unfortunate for the members of their immediate entourage in particular. Already in ancient Egypt we come across the story of an official who breathed a sigh of relief for not being punished after accidentally touching Pharaoh,[72] and the biblical Esther, having approached Xerxes without first asking permission, was fortunate to escape with her life. In China officials often wore heavy padding to cope with the floggings to which they were likely to be subjected and which could incapacitate a person for weeks on end; from the Middle East and pre-Columbian Latin America we have accounts of the spectacular punishments often inflicted by emperors on subordinates who displeased them. In Rome, according to the historian Seutonius, fear of the emperor sometimes drove people to commit suicide in self-defense *and* to leave everything they had to him.[73] In brief, an emperor could do anything to any of his subjects, whereas conversely any cruelties that he did not choose to visit on them counted as pure *indulgentia* on his part.[74]

As they appeared to their subjects as awesome, indeed almost divine creatures, another consequence of the emperors' position was their claim to be universal rulers. The modern state regards itself as one sovereign entity among others, but empires by definition could not accept equals. Looking beyond their borders they saw not other political communities with a right to an independent existence, but barbarians who at worst caused trouble and at best were not worth conquering. Already in Mesopotamia the earliest Accadian emperors claimed to reign over the "four quarters of heaven," a tradition later followed by their Assyrian and Babylonian successors right down to the Persian "kings of kings." The emperor of China carried the title of ruler of "all under heaven," whereas Rome identified itself with the *oikoumene*, Greek for "the inhabited world," which was said to stretch from the British ocean to the Tigris.[75] This notion was later taken up by Charlemagne who, like his successors, carried the orb to symbolize his position. All of them claimed to be the

---

[71] A good account of early Christian political attitudes is A. Cunningham, *The Early Church and the State* (Philadelphia: Fortress Press, 1982).

[72] K. Sethe, *Urkunden des ägyptischen Altertums* (Leipzig: Heinrichs, 1921), vol. IV, pp. 608–10.

[73] Suetonius, *Lives of the Emperors* (London: Heinemann, Loeb Classical Library, 1965), *Tiberius*, 49, 1; *Caligula*, 38. See also P. Plass, *The Game of Death in Ancient Rome: Arena Sport and Political Suicide* (Madison: University of Wisconsin Press, 1995), pp. 89ff.

[74] Pliny, Jr., *Letters and Panegyric* (London: Heinemann, Loeb Classical Library, 1975); H. Cotton, "The Concept of *Indulgentia* Under Trajan," *Chiron*, 14, 1984, pp. 245–66.

[75] E.g. Dessau, *Inscriptiones*, vol. I, p. 168, no. 754.

rightful rulers of the universe as a whole,[76] as did the emperors of pre-Columbian Mexico and Peru.[77]

To the extent that these and similar claims did not correspond to reality they could sometimes lead to comic results. Thus Suleiman the Magnificent once condescendingly wrote to Francis I of France that "your pleas for aid [against Charles V] have been heard at the steps of our throne"; refusing to accept Queen Elizabeth of England as his equal, Ivan IV the Terrible of Russia spoke of her as "a mere maiden." As late as the first decades of the eighteenth century, diplomats from European states seeking an audience with the Porte had to keep up the pretense of addressing a superior by donning Turkish dress over their own clothes. In the Far East, whenever a Japanese delegation visited the Chinese capital of the day they would demonstrate their independence by using language not appropriate for subjects, which offense the Chinese, provided of course they wanted to maintain correct relations, would magnanimously "forgive" by ascribing it to their guests' supposed ignorance of the correct forms.

Religion apart, the two pillars supporting imperial rule were the army on the one hand and the bureaucracy on the other. Few empires seem to have gone as far as Rome where the title "Imperator," or victorious commander, invariably headed the list of imperial offices, but the connection between political domination and military might was always clear. Compared to the polities previously discussed, the armed forces raised by empires were enormous. Nor did these forces consist simply of bands of warriors or personal retainers or popular militias. Instead, they were regular troops who made soldiering into their chosen career, served for long periods, were commanded by professional officers, and were centrally paid from the imperial treasury. Their numbers could grow into the hundreds of thousands – but here it is important to note that the extremely low degree of social and economic development of most empires (only a few ever carried their existence into the period of the industrial revolution, and those that did, such as the Ottoman and Chinese, expired within decades of encountering more advanced civilizations) prevented them from putting more than 1 or 2 percent of their populations under arms. Thus Rome, by no means the least developed among them, at its zenith counted only some 300,000 troops – and when that figure was doubled under the late empire its economy broke down under the strain. Elsewhere the figures were probably even lower.

[76] R. Foltz, *Le souvenir et la legende de Charlemagne dans l'empire germanique médiéval* (Paris: Société d'édition les belles lettres, 1950), pp. 81ff.
[77] R. F. Townsend, *State and Cosmos in the Art of Tenochtitlan* (Dumbarton Oaks Studies in Pre-Columbian Art and Archaeology, No. 20; Washington, DC: Dumbarton Oaks, 1979).

Furthermore, the cost of standing armies was such that most empires kept only a comparatively small number of regular troops; even in Rome, which probably went further in this regard, the first thing Vespasian, for example, did when setting out to subdue Judea in 66 BC was to gather auxiliaries.[78] Elsewhere the Persian Immortals, the Chinese Imperial Guard, and in the Ottoman empire the Janissaries hardly exceeded the (usually) lower tens of thousands. These units would serve the triple function of standing army, garrison for the capital, and police force responsible for dealing with internal uprisings. Meanwhile the bulk of the army did not consist of regulars but acted under some kind of feudal arrangement. In return for being granted land and exempted from taxation they would make themselves available on a temporary basis, as was the case of the Ottoman Sipahis. Alternatively they consisted of short-term conscripts who were normally available only for the defense of their home provinces, as was the practice in certain periods of Chinese history and among the Inca. As to navies, they were a much more expensive proposition still. Few empires in history were able to construct fleets of warships and maintain them for very long. The normal method was to rely on maritime cities which in time of war provided both the ships, suitably modified, and the crews.

Sharply differentiated from the army, the civilian bureaucracy consisted of *literati*. Originally they were probably priests who had mastered the sacred art of writing – such was the case in Egypt, where the script that they used is still known as hieratic (priestly), Mesopotamia (the Accadian and Babylonian empires), and among the Aztecs and the Inca. Later they came to be selected from the upper social classes. Once they had a foot on the ladder, promotion often proceeded on a more or less regular system, tempered, needless to say, by family connections and also imperial *ira et studio*; only in China since the days of the T'ang dynasty did there exist a system of examinations which was rigidly enforced as a vehicle of selection.[79] In theory everybody (except certain classes of convicted criminals) could present himself. In practice the time and expense needed to prepare for the examinations were such that only the sons of officials or of rich merchants could apply. Still, the system did prevent the creation of a hereditary aristocracy, as indeed it was designed to do.

Insofar as a collusion between bureaucrats and military commanders might prove fatal to the regime, it was the first concern of every emperor to keep the two apart. This achieved, the number of imperially appointed administrators was often surprisingly small. Both in Rome and in Ming China the bureaucratic positions directly under the emperor's control

---

[78] Josephus Flavius, *The Jewish War* (London: Heinemann, Loeb Classical Library, 1965), III, I, 3.

[79] See I. Miyazaki, *China's Examination Hell* (New York: Weatherhill, 1976), for the details.

probably numbered fewer than 10,000 – and in the latter case they ruled over a population estimated at 150 million.[80] It is true that each Roman official and each mandarin had his assistants in the form of ambitious family members, retainers, and slaves (or often freedmen) who were fed from their tables, served on their staffs, and could be made to carry out routine duties, go on errands, and the like. Even so, however, their overall numbers remained limited and certainly bore no relationship to modern administrative systems.

Just as the emperor himself combined various functions in his own person, imperial officials were administrators and judges rolled into one; though Roman senators during the early empire still had the right to be judged by members of their own class, the idea that the two ought to be separate was essentially a modern European development that does not date further back than the seventeenth or even eighteenth century.

These tasks apart, the most important responsibility of any official was to gather taxes on the emperor's behalf. Everywhere the two most important taxes were the land tax, consisting of a share of the crop, and a poll tax. In some of the more primitive empires, e.g., the Aztec,[81] Inca,[82] and early Chinese ones,[83] these had to be paid in kind; elsewhere they were usually commuted into money at rates that were set, needless to say, by the authorities themselves. To these sources of revenue would be added the imperial monopolies. From pre-Columbian America through Rome to China, the latter often consisted of the most valuable products including salt (a certain quantity of which had to be purchased by each family each year), metalware, precious stones, certain kinds of skins, furs, and feathers, and, in the case of Rome, the famous balsam that was grown on the shores of the Dead Sea. In most places mines, forests, rivers, and lakes were considered imperial property; in some empires the same applied to certain species of animals considered uniquely precious either because of the price that their products commanded or simply because they were large and hunting them was correspondingly prestigious. All these different kinds of resources would be exploited either directly by the emperor's own appointees such as office-holders, retainers, and slaves, or, which was perhaps more likely, leased to the highest bidder and exploited in return for a share in the profits.

A tribute-list drawn up by the Assyrian king Tiglat Pileser III (reigned

[80] For details, see R. Huang, *Taxation and Government Finance in Sixteenth-Century Ming China* (London: Cambridge University Press, 1974), ch. 2.
[81] See R. Hassig, *Trade, Tribute and Transportation: The Sixteenth-Century Political Economy of the Valley of Mexico* (Norman: University of Oklahoma Press, 1985), pp. 225–8.
[82] J. V. Murray, *The Economic Organization of the Inca State* (Greenwich, CT: JAI Press, 1980).
[83] T'ung-tsu Ch'u, *Han Social Structure* (Seattle: University of Washington Press, 1972), p. 92.

745–727 BC) included "gold, silver, tin, iron, elephant hides, ivory, multicolored garments, linen garments, blue-purple and red-purple wood, maplewood, boxwood, all kinds of precious things . . . flying birds of the sky whose wings are dyed blue-purple, horses, mules, cattle and sheep, camels, and she-camels together with their young."[84] With these and other sources of revenue at their disposal, many emperors were able to build spectacular fortunes; Augustus, for example, declared the whole of Egypt an imperial estate and closed it to members of the governing, that is, senatorial class. The forbidden city in Beijing, like Nero's *domus aurea*, contained untold treasures; those accumulated by the Aztec and Inca rulers have become legendary. When Alexander the Great entered the Persian capital in 330 BC he found Darius' treasury filled with 50,000 gold talents (whose late twentieth-century value would be $1,800,000,000–3,000,000,000) – this, on top of uncounted quantities of silver and other precious objects that had been hoarded over a period of perhaps two and a half centuries.

In the absence of the abstract state, it should be noted about all these riches that they belonged to, or at any rate were at the disposal of, the emperor in person. As in all pre-state polities except the city-state, he *had* to be the richest person by far in his domain; any competitors in this respect were *ipso facto* dangerous and had to be eliminated. In Byzantium, China, and elsewhere, attempts were sometimes made to keep separate receiving chambers for the two kinds of revenue, that originating in taxation and that deriving from the emperor's "private" property; likewise, two chambers were maintained to separate the expense of the palaces from those of the army and the administration. In practice, though, these distinctions could seldom be maintained. Thus Roman and Chinese emperors regularly forgave the payment of taxes by regions that had been struck by natural disasters; the praise for generosity that they earned as a result would have been wholly out of place if the sums in question had not been perceived as earmarked for their private pockets. Conversely, when in need of money for war or other purposes emperors very often resorted to their "private" resources. They sold plate, pawned palaces and estates, and even married their offspring to the highest bidder; when Charles V stood in need of money to fight the Protestants in Germany, he used the dowry brought in by his son Philip as a result of the latter's marriage to a Portuguese princess.[85] The prevailing system was curtly summed up by the Roman historian Tacitus when, on one occasion during the reign of Tiberius, the Senate voted to transfer money

---

[84] H. Tadmor, *The Inscriptions of Tiglat Pileser III, King of Assyria* (Jerusalem: Israel Academy, 1994), pp. 69–70.

[85] K. Brandi, *The Emperor Charles V* (London: Cape, 1967 edn.), p. 495.

from the old Republican *aerarium* to the imperial *fiscus* – "as if it mattered."[86]

What was true of the imperial possessions – one is at a loss to find a more accurate term – also applied to the army and bureaucracy. Both consisted of the emperor's men and served him rather than the state; some did so in his private capacity, others in his public one. In practice the distinction between the two was likely to break down. To add a certain luster to the court, some of the empire's highest dignitaries were often used to look after the emperor's personal needs such as bearing his cup, running his wardrobe, looking after the stables, and the like. Conversely palace servants, whether free or servile in the sense that they could be bought and sold, were often used on "public" tasks including command of the imperial bodyguard and filling vitally important administrative posts such as that of secretary to the emperor. Sometimes the personnel in question originated in the imperial harem (which itself meant not just the place where the emperor's women were kept but also included such institutions as the mint and the armory) and consisted of eunuchs. This was the case in the Persian, Byzantine, Arab, Ottoman, and Chinese empires, among others.

As the campaigns of the Byzantine general Narses and the Chinese admiral Zheng He – both of them eunuchs – demonstrate, government by household was not necessarily less competent or more corrupt than that which was exercised by the regular administration. It did, however, tend to circumvent the elite of high-born *literati* who saw their positions usurped, and their access to the emperor controlled, by persons whom they held in a mixture of fear and contempt. Reduced to political impotence, they would vent their spleen in writing. This probably explains the bad name that government by household has frequently acquired both at the time and in the eyes of many subsequent historians.[87]

Whether their personnel was free or not, both the members of the administration and those of the army owed their allegiance to the emperor as a matter of course. The oaths that they swore were addressed to him personally and had to be renewed each time a successor ascended to the throne; in return, they could normally expect to receive some kind of largesse. To ensure the continuing loyalty of senior administrators and officers, many emperors engaged in the practice of distributing presents to them at regular intervals, the value of each gift being carefully graded

---

[86] Tacitus, *Annales* (London: Heinemann, Loeb Classical Library, 1937), vi, 2. The same was true in Byzantium: W. Ennslin, "The Emperor and the Imperial Administration," in N. H. Baines and H. L. St. Moss, eds., *Byzantium: An Introduction to East Roman Civilization* (Oxford: Clarendon Press, 1948), p. 283.

[87] For an example of a mandarin inveighing against government by eunuchs, see de Bary, "Chinese Despotism and the Confucian Ideal," pp. 176–7.

according to the recipient's rank so as not to offend the others. The confusion between the private and the public was further accentuated by the fact that many members of the propertied classes, merchants in particular, were also in charge of collecting taxes – especially those on commodities – and were held personally liable for delivering them to the imperial treasury. If the latter faced a deficit, both merchants and officials could be called upon to make forced loans. Thus imperial service and private enterprise became fused. The abstract state being absent, the entire structure amounted to little more than a gigantic racket, one in which the emperor combined with his servitors, whatever their precise status, to fleece the remainder of the population.

The emperor's absolute power on the one hand and the absence of any clear distinction between the private and the public on the other meant that the one institution more or less safe from arbitrary interference was the established religion or church. Often it had a system of taxation running parallel to that of the emperor himself, as among the Inca; in other places it owned extensive estates second only to his, as in early medieval Europe. Even where the emperor also acted as the head of religion, as was the case in most empires, these factors gave it a certain autonomy. To be sure, the resources made possible by this autonomy often roused the cupidity of emperors who tried to appropriate them by various means. On the other hand, the fact that they owed their position to religion usually dictated a certain circumspection in dealing with it. To clash with the church openly might be to court disaster; many emperors who did so came to a bad end as did the Egyptian Tutankamun (Achenaton) after trying to substitute new gods for the old. The Secleucid Antiochus III was killed in 187 BC after robbing a temple of Ba'al; apparently one reason behind the easy Spanish success in Peru was the fact that, just before Pizarro and his men arrived, the Inca Atahualpa had quarreled with the priesthood in his attempts to reduce the expense of the imperial mummy-worship of which they were the principal benefactors.[88] Conversely, the relative security offered by the temple often turned it into a place where ordinary people flocked to deposit their belongings. This enabled it to engage in banking operations and turn itself into a center of commerce; the money-changers whom Jesus drove from the temple in Jerusalem would have been a common sight.[89]

Another factor capable of putting limits on the emperor's power was associated with time and distance. Given the extreme centralization of

---

[88] G. W. Conrad and A. E. Demarest, *Religion and Empire: The Dynamics of Aztec and Inca Expansionism* (Cambridge: Cambridge University Press, 1984), pp. 136ff.

[89] On the position of the temple as an alternate focus for hoarding wealth and exercising power, see M. V. Fox, ed., *The Temple in Society* (Winona Lake, MN: Eisenbach, 1988).

their political systems, once the armed forces of empires had been defeated in battle, conquering vast spaces was sometimes relatively easy and could be accomplished in a fairly short time; as both Alexander's conquests and those of the Mongols show, however, administering them was quite another matter and, indeed, the less homogeneous, ethnically speaking, any empire, the greater the difficulty. To overcome these handicaps the more long-lived empires left their physical mark upon the landscape in the form of massive "public," for which read imperially instigated (and sometimes paid for) works. The Chinese and Romans are famous for the fortifications with which they surrounded their borders. The Persians, Romans, and Inca all excelled as builders of roads, aqueducts, and bridges. Neither pre-Columbian Mexico, nor the Egyptian empire, nor the various Mesopotamian ones would have been conceivable but for the systems of canals that they built and which served for irrigation and transportation; as Tiglat Pileser boasted, "I dug out the Patti Canal . . . and made it bubble with abundant water."[90] Less durable, but equally important for holding the empire together, were the messenger systems that connected the provinces with the capital and which, in the case of Rome, were capable of distributing the imperial edicts to the remotest provinces in a matter of one to four months,[91] as well as carrying out the censuses held from time to time.

In Hellenistic Egypt, according to one surviving document, so tight was the system of imperial control made possible by these means that even a prostitute wishing to ply her trade for a single day in a given city had to apply for a license and, presumably, pay for it.[92] Byzantine emperors made repeated attempts to regulate the economy by prescribing everything from the opening hours of shops to the prices that could be charged for various commodities.[93] The Inca even developed a special system of recording – consisting of colored knots or *quippu* – for tax purposes. According to Garcilaso de la Vega, himself the son of a Spanish *conquistador* and an Inca princess and thus familiar with the culture, so thorough was the imperial information system that it proved capable of recording every last pound of maize and every last pair of sandals produced throughout the empire.[94]

On the other hand, there exist indications that the imperial records were often full of holes and that the results of the attempts to gain

---

[90] Tadmor, *The Inscriptions of Tiglat Pileser III*, p. 43.
[91] For the speed of the Roman imperial mail system, see R. Duncan-Jones, *Structure and Scale in the Roman Economy* (Cambridge: Cambridge University Press, 1990), pp. 15, 26–7.
[92] The document is printed in *Archiv*, 6, 1920, p. 220, n. 1.
[93] R. Runciman, *Byzantine Civilization* (New York: World Publishing, 1961), pp. 81–3.
[94] G. de la Vega, *Commentarios reales* (Buenos Aires: Plus Ultra, 1973 [1609]), pp. 281–4.

information were mediocre at best. For example, when Xerxes set out to conquer Greece in 490 BC he was entirely unaware of the existence of the second wealthiest person in the realm – so wealthy, in fact, that he could support the imperial army (according to one source, a million and a half strong) from his own private resources as they passed through his estates.[95] Though Hellenistic Egypt as the heir to millennia of imperial rule was probably among the most tightly governed of all empires, Ptolemy IV Philopater on one occasion found himself unable to determine whether in fact he had granted the city of Soli certain privileges (immunity from having troops quartered on them) as its citizens claimed.[96] Concerning both Rome and Ming China it has even been argued that the absence of good maps, good "data bases," and good communications reduced their emperors to passivity so that they dealt only with those cases that were brought in front of them or else were confined largely to ritual functions.[97] To be sure, it is hard to imagine how a person as enterprising as Septimus Severus, who had started his career as a junior officer, could have given up his active lifestyle after ascending the imperial throne in AD 193. On the other hand it is clear that no emperor could know everything and that these limitations often represented an important constraint on their ability to rule.

In fact, given the problems of time and distance as well as the limits of the information at their disposal, many emperors preferred to deal with entire communities – tribes, chiefdoms, villages, cities, even client-kings – rather than with individuals. In both Tenochtitlan and Quizco the Aztecs and the Inca used as their basic social building block not families, but wards known as *calpullin* and *alyu* respectively;[98] outside the capitals, too, their rule was indirect, being exercised by means of subordinate tribal chiefs whom they had conquered. China originally had the so-called eight-well system which counted peasant families by "wells,"[99] whereas Rome for a long time left administration to hundreds upon hundreds of autonomous city-states as well as numerous client-kings. Instead of counting their entire populations, empires preferred to calculate censuses by households or hearths. Both of these institutions were likely to contain unrelated as well as related "family" members, with the result that

[95] Herodotus, *The Histories* (London: Heinemann, Loeb Classical Library, 1943), 7, 27–9.
[96] C. B. Welles, *Royal Correspondence of the Hellenistic Period: A Study of Greek Epigraphy* (New Haven, CT: Yale University Press, 1934), no. 30, p. 136.
[97] F. Millar, *The Emperor in the Roman World, 31 BC–AD 337* (Ithaca, NY: Cornell University Press, 1977); Millar, "Emperors, Frontiers and Foreign Relations, 31 BC to AD 378," *Britannia*, 13, 1982, pp. 1–23; R. Huang, *1587, a Year of No Significance* (New Haven, CT: Yale University Press, 1981).
[98] Conrad and Demarest, *Religion and Empire*, pp. 52, 97.
[99] Ch'ien Mu, *Traditional Government in Imperial China: A Critical Analysis*, Chun-tu Hsueh and G. T. Totten, trs. (Hong Kong: Chinese University Press, 1982), pp. 23–6.

determining the correct multiplier must have proved as difficult for contemporary administrators as it has for subsequent historians.

The deficiencies in their administrative systems may also explain why many empires were reluctant to impose a single system of law upon all their inhabitants. Originating in conquest, many of them were heterogeneous by definition; hence, so long as subjects followed orders and paid their taxes, most emperors were content to leave them alone. Apart from the fact that many, possibly most, of those involved in running the empire never appeared on the imperial payrolls, the system meant that, when officials came to perform their duties, they very often saw themselves confronted not by individuals but by organized communities of the most diverse kinds. This probably reduced their power and in many cases must have reduced government to a bargaining process.

Another factor which tended to work in the same direction and impose practical limits on the emperor's power was of a financial nature. No empire in history ever seems to have reached the point where it developed a single treasury (whether "public" or "private") into which all revenues went and which in turn was responsible for making all payments, the most important reason being that, given the expense of transporting bullion and the attendant risk, a large part of the sums collected by taxation always remained in the provinces and was used to meet local expenses. The same was even more true of deliveries in kind, most of which were likely to stay in provincial storehouses; to say nothing of the *corvées* or forced labor that the subject population was often made to perform in working the imperial estates, erecting and maintaining imperial works, and providing transport and other services to imperial officials. Each of these factors meant that only a small fraction of the sums raised, or the labor expended, ever reached the capital and was put at the free disposal of the emperor. The rest remained at or near the place of origin and could profit him, if at all, only indirectly and to the extent that he controlled the local officials.

To prevent local officials from going their own way and appropriating imperial resources for themselves, emperors employed a variety of devices. Officials could be hindered from forming local ties by being rotated between one post and province and another. In Hellenistic Egypt there seems to have existed a dual administration, i.e., one set of bureaucrats charged with collecting taxes and another with supervising them;[100] elsewhere there were often roving inspectors such as the Roman *quaestores* (later replaced by the *agentes rerum*) and the Chinese visiting secretaries who appeared under a variety of titles but whose function was always the

---

[100] M. Rostovstzeff, *The Social and Economic History of the Hellenistic World* (Oxford: Clarendon Press, 1941), vol. I, p. 251.

same.[101] The kings of Assyria at its zenith formed the habit of appointing eunuchs – "the son of nobody" – to govern newly conquered towns,[102] a method which presumably had the additional benefit of humiliating the conquered.

Though each of these methods provided a practical answer to the problem, none was capable of solving it once and for all. Inspectors, whether traveling or permanent, could be misled or bought by the men on the spot. Transferring officials from one post to another merely meant that they did not have time to familiarize themselves with their districts and thus tended to increase the power of the heads of local communities at the expense of the center. The use of eunuchs obviously made it impossible for families to consolidate their hold on power but, for that very reason, probably endangered stability in other ways. In brief, an emperor might make himself absolute within his own capital. However, by and large the further away any particular province the harder it was to impose the imperial will.

Under such circumstances the danger always existed that subordinate authorities, whether religious or secular, would use any difficulty experienced by the center – often a war or a succession crisis – in order to cease obeying the emperor and to break away. In particular, provincial governors might use the economic resources at their disposal to build up armed forces, whereas military commanders might use their troops to appropriate an economic foundation. The task of both was often made easier by the self-governing communities that most empires contained. Unless they were physically removed from their original abodes and sent into exile, which was a regular practice among both the Assyrians and the Inca,[103] subject tribes often provided feudalism with ready-made building blocks. The ultimate outcome would be the disintegration of the empire and its replacement by a much more decentralized, if still strongly hierarchical, system of government;[104] and indeed feudalism itself could be regarded simply as the political structure that emerged when empires fell on evil days. This was the case in Western Europe during the Middle Ages and in Egypt and China during their various interdynastic periods,

---

[101] On the duties of second-century AD provincial inspectors, see the account of a contemporary Ts'ai Chin, printed in Wang Yu-ch'uan, "An Outline of the Central Government of the Former Han Dynasty," *Harvard Journal of Asiatic Studies*, 12, 1949, pp. 159–60.

[102] Tadmor, *The Inscriptions of Tiglat Pileser III*.

[103] For the Assyrians, see the biblical book of Kings; for the Inca, see M. A. Malpass, *Daily Life in the Inca Empire* (Westport, CT: Greenwood Press, 1996), p. 72.

[104] M. Weber, *Economy and Society: An Outline of Interpretative Sociology*, G. Roth and C. Wittich, eds. (New York: Bedminster, 1968), vol. III, ch. 12; and O. Hintze, *Staat und Verfassung: gesammelte Abahandlungen zur allgemeinen Verfassungsgeschichte* (Göttingen: Vanderhoek, 1961), vol. I, pp. 84–119.

as well as in a large number of other societies including Persia, Byzantium, India, and Japan at various points in their histories.[105]

Once the class of warrior-governors so characteristic of feudalism had come into being, it would invest heavily in military retinues as well as physical defenses that would enable them to defy the emperor. As each lord strove to make his domains as independent as possible the centralized information-gathering, transportation, and defense system would be allowed to decay and disintegrate. Bureaucracies – and, to a large extent, the necessary literacy among the non-religious classes – postal services, censuses, even the most elementary means of transport, disappeared; at no time were European roads as bad, and communications as difficult, as during the Middle Ages with its multitude of interlocking principalities. The regular armed forces too would melt away, perhaps to the point where they were reduced to a mere handful of retainers who were fed from the emperor's kitchen as he moved from one residence to another. Rights that had previously belonged to the emperor, such as the usufruct of economic resources (mines, forests, etc.), taxation, and coinage would become dispersed and pass into the hands of numerous lords and barons.

Reflecting the emergence of feudalism, the imperial ideology collapsed. Its place was taken by a system that put much greater emphasis on the collective rights of the aristocracy on the one hand and the religious establishment on the other. According to Thomas Aquinas, probably the greatest and certainly the most systematic among medieval "political scientists," government, far from being created by and for men, was an integral part of the divine order. As such it presented a seamless web in which each person and each class had his appointed place, which was not subject to arbitrary interference from above.[106] The stronger any emperor the more any privileges that any person, body, or class possessed were regarded as within his gift and revocable at his will; but in feudal societies privileges became attached to their owners who in this way acquired certain "constitutional" guarantees that were almost entirely absent from empires.[107]

Once the warrior-governors ceased to be appointed by the emperor and succeeded in making their positions hereditary, the process would have reached its logical conclusion and the empire come to a *de facto* end, however alive it might still be in name. The resulting structure was based

[105] For the history of feudalism in these countries, see R. Coulborn, ed., *Feudalism in History* (Hamden, CT: Archon Books, 1965).

[106] See D. Bigongiari, ed., *The Political Ideas of St. Thomas Aquinas* (New York: Hafner, 1981 edn.), particularly the introduction.

[107] The best modern accounts are M. Bloch, *Feudal Society* (London: Routledge, 1961), and F. L. Ganshof, *Feudalism* (New York: Harper, 1961).

neither on family ties (though such ties were important in helping people form alliances) nor on bureaucratic fiat. Instead it rested on a network of fealty that bound each member of the aristocracy both to his superiors and to his inferiors. By taking an oath, vassals would commend themselves to their lords and agree to serve them by offering counsel, bearing arms, and extending financial aid when necessary. In return they received protection, land for maintaining themselves and as many of their own vassals as were suitable to their station, and the rights that went with such land in the form of rent and various forms of labor services formerly due to the emperor and his representatives. Further down the social ladder, those who actually lived on the land and worked it tended to become *glebi adscripti*, tied to the soil. They were ruled over by the lord of the manor with hardly any interference on the emperor's part.

As the numerous transitions from centralized empire to decentralized feudal regime and back indicate, the two systems were not as far apart as would seem to be the case at first sight. Unlike tribes without rulers and city-states, empires whether strong or weak possessed a pronounced hierarchical character and a well-defined head even if, following feudalization, he was merely titular. Unlike the situation in chiefdoms these hierarchies were not simply based on ethnic identity and family ties but made use of relatively well-developed bureaucracies and standing armies on the one hand and of fealty on the other. Whereas emperors concentrated all power in their own hands to the extent that practical considerations permitted, feudalism ensued when some sort of crisis caused the imperial prerogatives to pass into those of his soldiers and administrators, who became fused into a single hereditary class. The relationship between the public and the private was the same, however, and differed notably both from the situation in city-states and from the one which obtains in the modern state. In the next section, the nature of that relationship will be explored more closely.

Limits of stateless societies

The above short survey does not cover all the different types of political communities that existed before the advent of the state. To do so it would have to mention several other, mostly intermediate types such as so-called big-men or rank societies;[108] and, standing somewhere midway between chiefdoms and bureaucratic empires, kingdoms of every period, size, and shape. Empires, having conquered tribes without rulers, often turned

---

[108] See M. D. Sahlins, *Tribesmen* (Englewood Cliffs, NJ: Prentice Hall, 1968), chs. 4 and 5; and M. H. Fried, *The Evolution of Political Society: An Essay in Political Anthropology* (New York: Random House, 1967), ch. 4.

them into chiefdoms by insisting that a single leader be appointed and take responsibility for such matters as internal administration and taxation; on the other hand, in subjecting chiefdoms they often de-capitated them and, in an attempt to forestall rebellion, turned them back into kin-based organizations. City-states, too, were likely to find their constitutions eroded by conquering or being conquered until, sooner or later, they themselves ceased to exist as independent self-governing communities. None of these communities represented new principles of government but merely recombinations, on one scale or another, of those already examined. What remains is to point out some political, social, and economic implications that followed from the struc-ture of pre-state societies.

In the absence of the state as a separate legal *persona*, most historical societies were unable to develop a clear distinction between government and ownership in their various forms. The resulting confusion between the public and the private spheres led to all sorts of paradoxes, such as Aristotle's claim that barbarians, who did not live in self-governing *poleis* but were subject to the will of their ruling chiefs or kings, were "by nature" slaves.[109] In Rome during the first centuries AD, we are confron-ted with the curious fact that the *cursus publicus*, or mail system, was anything but public, but could be used exclusively by the emperor or those acting on his behalf. The European Middle Ages went to the opposite extreme. With the collapse of Rome the public sphere, meaning simply that which belonged to the emperor, all but disappeared. In medieval Latin the term *dominium* – from *domus*, house or residence – could stand either for a prince's private property or for the country that he ruled,[110] and indeed lawyers often argued as to which was the correct usage. Meanwhile the word "privy" meant the one place where even the king went alone.

To be sure, these problems did not affect either Greek city-states or the Roman Republic in the same form – and indeed the latter in particular probably came closer to being a "state" than any other premodern political entity. Both were perfectly able to distinguish the functions of government from the private property of the individuals who, for a time, occupied the offices and acted as magistrates. Getting oneself elected was usually (though not invariably) expensive; however, there was no need for rulers to be the richest citizens of all. Many cities also maintained special

---

[109] See the discussion in Aristotle, *Politics* (London: Heinemann, Loeb Classical Library, 1977), I, ii, 19–21. This view is echoed in 1 Samuel, 51, 8, where the Philistine Goliath calls the Israelites Saul's "slaves."

[110] See J. F. Niermeyer, *Medicea Latinitatis Lexicon Minus* (Leiden: Brill, 1976), vol. I, p. 353; and J. H. Bruns, "Fortescue and the Political Theory of Dominium," *Historical Journal*, 28, 4, 1985, pp. 777–97.

boards, such as the Athenian *logistai* and the Roman *censores*, whose function was to ensure that peculation did not lead to the boundaries between the two being crossed.[111] Two of the greatest Greek and Roman statesmen, Pericles and Scipio Africanus, had their problems in this respect. To avoid suspicion of collusion with his Spartan kinsmen during the Peloponnesian War, the former felt compelled to turn over his property to the *polis*. The latter's political career never recovered from the accusation that he and his brother had helped themselves to King Antiochus' money during the Syrian War of 191–189 BC.[112]

As the orderly succession of magistrates shows, the system made it possible for a ruler to step down without at the same time losing everything else as well; or, which amounts to the same thing, for the ruled to change their rulers without resorting to a coup, revolt, rebellion, or violence of any kind. In particular, the largest city-states – Rome, Athens, and, during the first few centuries of its recorded history, Sparta – were able to preserve civil peace. By avoiding the repeated loss of life and property that political change often entailed elsewhere, they launched themselves on the road to success.

Government other than that of the *polis* was often powerless as in tribes without rulers and under feudalism in its looser, more decentralized forms. Alternatively it was arbitrary as in the more strongly governed chiefdoms and empires. In them the legislative, judiciary, and executive functions were all concentrated in the hands of a single ruler; with the result that, technical obstacles and the ever present possibility of rebellion apart, the only "legal" constraint on his power consisted of religion whose head, whether as the god's descendant or as his representative on earth, he was. As John Locke, writing in the 1680s, was perhaps the first to point out,[113] both kinds of political community had more in common than met the eye. Opposed as they were, neither was able, or indeed attempted, to guarantee the security of either the life or the property of individuals.

Under feudalism, anyone who owned anything was *ipso facto* forced to be a warrior as well, thus violating the principle of the division of labor and putting limits on economic effectiveness. Under an imperial regime whatever large-scale economic success could be attained almost always

---

[111] See R. A. Knox, "'So Mischievous a Beaste?': The Athenian Demos and Its Treatment of Its Politicians," *Greece and Rome*, 32, 1985, pp. 132–61.

[112] G. Herman, *Ritualised Friendship and the Greek City* (Cambridge: Cambridge University Press, 1987), p. 71; H. H. Scullard, *Scipio Africanus, Soldier and Politician* (London: Thames and Hudson, 1970), pp. 217ff.

[113] J. Locke, "Second Treatise," in *John Locke: Two Treatises on Government*, P. Laslett, ed. (Cambridge: Cambridge University Press, 1967), pp. 344ff. Here I take it for granted that, as Hobbes himself says, tribes without rulers roughly correspond to the late seventeenth-century "state of nature."

took the form not of market-oriented enterprises but of government-related activities – as in tax-farming (an occupation which in both Rome and China often gave rise to the largest fortunes), contracting to erect "public" works such as fortifications or aqueducts on the emperor's behalf, leasing imperial possessions such as forests or mines, and supplying the army. Ultimately such success was possible only to the extent that, and as long as, the entrepreneur found favor in the eyes of the ruler. Either way individuals had to resort to noneconomic means in order to amass and defend their belongings. This could be done by investing in fortresses, armaments, and military retinues as both European and Japanese lords did on a very large scale; by entering the imperial service, as during thousands of years of Chinese history from the Han Dynasty on; or by taking refuge in religion and entrusting one's belongings to the protection of the temple. In theory, although not always in practice, the first and second of these alternatives were mutually exclusive. Not so the third which could be, and often was, combined with either of the previous ones.

As Adam Smith said, the one thing more important than opulence is defense.[114] Insecurity, whether due to the weakness of government or to its excessive strength (in empires with their heterogeneous ethnic composition and far-flung territories, both factors sometimes applied) prevented the accumulation of a surplus among the people and the emergence of sustained per capita economic growth. Sporadic attempts to the contrary, not one of these societies was able to develop a paper currency or advance very far toward building something like a central bank. Simply put, the confidence in the government's ability and willingness to honor its obligations was non-existent; it is not for nothing that, in Hebrew, "sending one's money down the drain" is derived from a term whose original meaning was "public treasury" (Greek *timaion*).[115] This in turn meant that, in spite of the often remarkable ingenuity displayed by individuals, technological progress was obstructed, retarded, or prevented. Not much needs to be said of the backwardness in these respects of tribes without rulers and chiefdoms; it has led directly to their downfall which, under the name of modernization, is still proceeding in many places. More significant and less well known is the fact that, up to the first half of the nineteenth century, so primitive was Asia Minor under Ottoman rule that there were neither metaled roads nor wheeled vehicles of any kind. In the absence of maps, distances had to be measured by the number of hours traveled and thus varied in accordance with the quality

[114] A. Smith, *The Wealth of Nations*, E. Cannan, ed. (Chicago: University of Chicago Press, 1976 [1776]), vol. I, p. 487.
[115] I am grateful to my student, Ms. Talma Luft, for bringing this fact to my attention.

of the roads;[116] even the first printing press was established there only in 1783.[117]

Much the same applied even to the most advanced of these societies, such as early imperial Rome, Ming China, and Mogul India. All were the seats of sophisticated civilizations capable of conceiving and erecting immense "public" works. All also developed literary and artistic products that have never been surpassed for quality or splendor. And yet, with the partial exception of a class of merchants who were themselves dependent on the ruler, most of those products were earmarked for the court, its servants, and its favorites. Often they were manufactured in the imperial workshops or composed by imperial hangers-on; the name of one courtier, Augustus' friend Maecenas, has even become a byword for artistic patronage. Once the limits of court, capital, and provincial administrative centers had been left behind, civilization and its amenities all but disappeared. Not one empire ever succeeded in moving beyond the point where at least 90 percent of the entire population lived on the land, and where, often sharing their homes with their "domestic" animals, they eked out an existence at something very close to the subsistence level.[118]

As for city-states, they were small by definition and, equally problematic for their prospects of anything but modest economic success, they were jealous of their independence and autarchic by preference.[119] In theory the ideal city-state was the one which, being self-sufficient, did not need to engage in trade and was able to preserve the constitution handed down by the citizens' ancestors without change. In practice, the most prosperous among them were those which, like Athens, Corinth, Syracuse, and Carthage, used their geographical position to develop extensive networks of trade. As the case of Athens in particular shows, such cities were often open to change, vibrant with fresh ideas, and capable of providing many of their citizens with what they themselves regarded as a comfortable standard of living; yet ultimately their prosperity had its limits, owing to the primitive communications and transport technology at their disposal. The one exception to the rule was

[116] J. Brewer, *A Residence at Constantinople in the Year 1827, with Notes to the Present Time* (New Haven, CT: Drurie and Peck, 1830), p. 126.

[117] An earlier experiment in using print was made in 1727 but was soon abandoned: see Kinross, *The Ottoman Centuries*, pp. 381–2, for the details.

[118] For the role of property rights in promoting economic growth, see D. C. North and R. P. Thomas, *The Rise of the Western World: A New Economic History* (Cambridge: Cambridge University Press, 1973), ch. 1; for the economic limits of pre-state societies in general, see J. G. A. Pocock, "The Political Limits to Pre-Modern Economies," in J. Dunn, ed., *The Economic Limits to Modern Politics* (Cambridge: Cambridge University Press, 1990), pp. 121–41.

[119] For the economic limits of classical city-states, see M. Finley, *The Ancient Economy* (London: Cambridge University Press, 1975).

Rome where, thanks to its military prowess, immense fortunes were accumulated by means of booty and tribute.[120]

Partly because they refused to incorporate foreigners into the citizen-body, and partly because incorporating too many would inevitably have led to the loss of the democratic principle on which they were based, city-states could extend their dominion only so far. Going beyond that point, the larger political entities that they tried to build collapsed, the fate that overtook both Athens and Sparta; in the long run they found it impossible to maintain their rule over reluctant subjects. Alternatively they were taken over by an empire, as Greek ones were by Macedonia (and as may have happened in pre-dynastic Mesopotamia), or else themselves took the road of the Roman Republic toward empire and despotism. Here it is worth noting that, in spite of its unique origins, the impact of Roman despotism on the economy was similar to its effect anywhere else. Already during the second century AD, the towns' autonomy was being lost as imperial procurators were appointed to supervise their finances and ensure that their taxes would be paid. Gradually power was taken out of the magistrates' hands so that their only remaining function was to pay for the liturgies. Another hundred years passed and the demands of the government began to weigh so heavily on society that they threatened not just prosperity but urban life in general. Particularly in the West, where cities were more recent and less well established, the result was to force the inhabitants to flee to the countryside.[121]

Finally, the language used by our ancient historians makes it very clear that neither Greeks nor Romans ever conceived of the state as an abstract entity separate from its citizens. Where we could say "the state," they would write "the public" or "the people"; after all, it was the historian Thucydides who wrote that "the city *is* its men" and the lawyer Cicero who defined the *res publica* as "an assembly of men living according to law."[122] Thus premodern thought, regardless of civilization and degree of development, failed to come up with the corporation as an abstract legal entity separate from that of its officials and members. This helps explain the role which religion played in these societies; given the absence in both public and private life of the corporation, many of its functions, such as exercising ownership and providing legitimacy, were assigned to

[120] For the role of these factors in Rome's expansion, see J. W. Harris, *War and Imperialism in Republican Rome, 327–70 BC* (Oxford: Oxford University Press, 1979), pp. 58ff.

[121] For the collapse of urban life in third-century Rome, see R. MacMullen, *Soldier and Civilian in the Later Roman Empire* (Cambridge, MA: Harvard University Press, 1963), pp. 38ff., 136ff.

[122] Thucydides, *The Peloponnesian War*, 7, 77, 7; M. T. Cicero, *De Republica* (London: Heinemann, Loeb Classical Library, 1928), I, 39.

the equally invisible deities. So long as the state did not exist, the only way in which political units larger than chiefdoms and city-states would be created led through empire with all its imperfections. Thus understood, the state represents the second most important invention in history after the Greek separation between ownership and government. Its exact nature and functions will occupy us later; for now, we must focus on the process that led to its emergence out of feudalism and the Middle Ages.

2   The rise of the state: 1300 to 1648

The West European feudal system that followed the collapse of the Carolingian empire – itself a short-lived attempt to impose order on the disorder resulting from the barbarian invasion that had destroyed Rome – was decentralized even by the standards of similar regimes elsewhere. Under feudalism, government was neither "public" nor concentrated in the hands of a single monarch or emperor; instead it was divided among a large number of unequal rulers who were related to each other by ties of fealty and who treated it as their private possession. However, in Western Europe the situation was made even more complicated by the exceptional position of the church.

Whereas, in most empires, the emperor's position was strengthened by the fact that he was descended either from god or from his prophet, in Christendom he was neither one nor the other. This was also true in Byzantium; but here at least there was the saving grace that there were no politically independent Greek Orthodox communities outside the empire's borders. However, in the West from about AD 1000 there were always important countries and regions such as Ireland, England, northern Spain, Scandinavia, and Poland which, though Christian and therefore subject to the authority of the pope, did not pay homage to the emperor.

To make things worse, the secular and religious capitals did not coincide. Byzantium and the Ottomans had Constantinople, the Inca Cuzco with its palaces and temples; but European emperors kept moving from one place to another. Most of the time they were found either in greater Germany, which at that time included what are today the Low Countries, Lorraine, Alsace, Switzerland, and Bohemia, or else in northern or southern Italy. This meant that, during most of the Middle Ages, the pope in Rome was beyond the reach not only of the emperor but of any other secular ruler. Unlike his opposite numbers in other empires he had his own territorial domain, albeit one which was never secure and where his power had to be shared with the great noble families such as the Colonnas and the Orsinis. In the form of the military orders whose supreme overlord he was, he also had his own armed force, albeit one that was small and scattered in small groups over much of Christendom, the Mediterranean, and the Middle East.[1]

Finally, the Carolingian empire was unique in that the established religion was older than it and, technically speaking, well ahead of it. The church inherited the language of the Western Roman Empire as well as many of its legal and political traditions. For some centuries it exercised a virtual monopoly on literacy, with the result that its services were indispensable to any secular ruler whose domains were at all extensive and who hoped to make them into something more than a mere chiefdom or feudal fief. Charlemagne's attempt to solve the problem by providing for schools and education was short-lived. At the time of the Magyar and Norman invasions in the ninth and tenth centuries AD the church, and the monasteries in particular, remained almost the sole centers where something resembling an orderly civilization was able to survive at all. The church's assets were not concentrated in any one place but consisted of buildings and estates scattered all over Europe; hence it had to develop a sophisticated financial, judiciary, and administrative apparatus capable of overcoming distance and time. As late as 1300 that apparatus stood far in advance of anything of the sort available to secular rulers.

These factors explain why, after Charlemagne's death, his position as head of religion was lost. As his successors quarreled with one another they often called on the church to mediate. In return, either they gave it, or it was able to obtain, privileges much greater than in any other civilization. From about AD 1100 on it possessed, apart from the power to lay down and interpret divine law, the right to nominate and promote its own officials; immunity from secular justice, also known as benefit of clergy; the right to judge and punish both its own personnel and, in cases involving the care of souls, laymen; the right to offer asylum to fugitives from secular justice; the right to absolve subjects from their oaths to their rulers; and, to support the lot, immense landed estates, a separate system of taxation, and, here and there, the right to strike money as well. Not only were higher prelates almost always noblemen but, like other lords, the church could both give benefices and receive them from others. Throughout much of Europe, ecclesiastical domains and even principalities existed side by side with their secular counterparts; the main difference was that the ecclesiastical succession, instead of proceeding from father to (necessarily illegitimate) son, often went from uncle to nephew.

---

[1] See W. Ullmann, *Law and Politics in the Middle Ages: An Introduction to the Sources of Medieval Political Ideas* (Ithaca, NY: Cornell University Press, 1975), ch. 4.

Thus the church became integrated with the feudal system, being supported by the latter and, in turn, supporting it.

The church's power peaked between the time of Gregory VII (1073–85) and Clement IV (1265–8). The former clashed with Emperor Henry IV over the right to appoint bishops, excommunicated him, absolved his vassals from their oath, fomented rebellion against him, and finally forced him to go to Canossa where, on his knees, he publicly repented of his sins.[2] The latter mobilized much of Europe, engaged in a whole series of wars, and did not rest until he saw the last one of Henry's descendants – the sixteen-year-old Emperor Conrad – executed. Legally, too, ecclesiastical claims to supremacy grew bolder and bolder. Already Innocent III (1198–1216), building on earlier foundations, declared that the pope could judge everybody but be judged by none. Taking another tack, James of Viterbo (d. 1308) argued that secular government was tainted with original sin and could become perfect only provided it was supervised by the church, while Giles of Rome (1246–1316) told princes that "your domains belong to the church more than to you." The climax was reached in 1302 when Pope Boniface VIII issued his famous *Unam Sanctam Ecclesiam*. Quoting Jeremiah – "I have set thee over the nations and over the kingdoms" – the Bull proclaimed that secular power should be exercised *ad nutum et patientiam sacerdotis*, "at the command and sufferance of the priest."[3]

As noted above, the centrifugal tendencies that were present in most empires caused some of them to collapse: this was particularly true when external pressures joined internal ones and made the whole ungovernable, as in late imperial Rome. Other empires, notably the ancient Egyptian, Chinese, and Japanese, were able to overcome feudal particularism – sometimes repeatedly so – and reestablish central power after a shorter or longer period. Only in Europe was the position of the church so strong that, instead of finding itself resubjected to the imperial power, it fought the latter to a standstill. Thus feudalism, instead of coming to a comparatively rapid end, lasted for the best part of a millennium and was able to give its name to an entire historical age. More important from our point of view, the empire never recovered. In the chinks between the two great universal organizations there grew the great monarchies, which, much later, were destined to turn into states.

[2] U. K. Blumenthal, *The Investiture Controversy: Church and Monarchy from the Ninth to the Twelfth Century* (Philadelphia: University of Pennsylvania Press, 1982), ch. 4.
[3] For papist claims in regard to secular government, see E. Lewis, *Medieval Political Ideas* (London: Routledge, 1954), vol. II; and A. J. Carlyle, *A History of Medieval Political Theory* (Edinburgh: Blackwood, 1928), vol. IV. The text of *Unam Sanctam* may be found in H. Bettenson, ed., *Documents of the Christian Church* (Oxford: Oxford University Press, 1967), pp. 115–16.

The struggle against the church

When, in AD 1170, men sent by King Henry II of England murdered the primate of England – Archbishop Thomas Becket – in his own cathedral, the upshot was a sharp reverse for the royal cause. No sooner was the prelate dead than his grave became an object of pilgrimage and miracles began to take place on it; within two years, indeed, he was formally proclaimed a saint. Not only was the king forced to repent in public, but the extent of his surrender is indicated by the fact that England was subjected to a flood of papal decrees dealing with every aspect of government including, in particular, the clergy's right to be judged solely by men of their own kind.[4] Henry's son and second in the line of succession went further still. King John (1199–1216) spent much of his reign fighting Philip Augustus of France over Anjou and Maine. Requiring all the support he could get, he appropriated the revenue of the church only to find himself helpless when Pope Innocent III, acting in retaliation, quashed the election of his nominee to the most important ecclesiastical position in the country. The dispute, which climaxed in 1213, was finally resolved when John agreed to install the pope's man rather than his own. The king even went so far as to make England a papal fief, receiving it back on condition of paying 1,000 silver marks a year.

Ninety years after this surrender a somewhat similar incident took place in France, only to end very differently. The papacy's protracted, though ultimately victorious, struggle against the Empire had increased its dependence on the House of Capet; at the turn of the fourteenth century King Philip IV the Fair was the mightiest lord in Christendom. He and Boniface VIII quarreled, as rulers often do, over money. At issue were, first, the right of the French clergy to transfer funds out of the kingdom, and secondly the king's own right to tax them. Scarcely had the pope given way over this question – which, hoping for support in other matters, he did in 1297–8 – than another dispute, this time over the king's right to dismiss offending bishops and put them on trial, broke out. In the person of John of Paris (d. 1306), Philip found an ecclesiastic who was every bit as tenacious in defending the perfection of secular rule as the pope was in denying it.[5] As matters came to a head the king and his advisers held a secret meeting at the Louvre. There they fabricated all

---

[4] For the impact of Becket's murder on the relations between the church and the English monarchy, see Z. N. Brooke, *The English Church and the Papacy from the Conquest to the Reign of John* (Cambridge: Cambridge University Press, 1952), pp. 211ff.; and C. Duggan, "From the Conquest to the Death of John," in C. H. Lawrence, ed., *The English Church and the Papacy in the Middle Ages* (New York: Fordham University Press, 1965), pp. 87–93.

[5] See John of Paris, *De potestate regia et papali*, J. Leclercq, ed. (Paris: Vrin, 1942).

kinds of charges against Boniface, ranging from unlawful occupation of the Holy See to heresy.[6] One of them, Guillaume de Nogaret, was sent to Rome to see whether he could stir up an anti-papal rebellion among the noble families that held the town in their grip. In the summer of 1303 he and a party of armed men broke into the pope's residence, took him prisoner, and actually slapped him.

Though Boniface died shortly after this incident, the dispute was by no means at an end. His immediate successor, Benedict XI, reigned only for a few months; but when Clement V assumed the tiara, Philip, now unquestionably in control, forced him to annul *Unam Sanctam* insofar as it applied to France. In the summer of 1307 Clement, expecting to preside over an ecclesiastical council that was to be held in Tours, traveled to France. There he had to stand by as the king mounted a spectacular series of show trials in which the Knights Templar were accused of everything from heresy to homosexuality. What military force the church possessed within the realm of France was destroyed; its commanders were executed, its fortresses and revenues taken away and joined to the royal domain. Not wishing to turn his back while these proceedings were under way, Clement remained in France. In 1309 he selected Avignon, which though a papal fief was surrounded by French territory, as his residence, thus turning himself into the king's prisoner. During the next seventy years all popes were Frenchmen and, without exception, appointees of the French crown. The papacy's international character suffered, given that any measure suggested or taken by a pope was likely to receive automatic support from the French, Spanish, and Scottish clergies and, equally automatically, to be rejected by the English, Hungarian, Italian, and, above all, Imperial ones.[7]

In 1356, these quarrels led to the loss of the pope's right to participate in the Imperial election process. The papacy's return to Rome, which took place in 1378, was soon followed by the Great Schism. It was occasioned by the Roman population's insistence that the successor of Gregory XI (died 1378) should be not another Frenchman but an Italian like themselves;[8] lasting for thirty years, the Schism repeatedly led to the spectacle of two and even three popes all quarreling furiously with each other as to which of them was Christ's true vicar and which, on the contrary, the Antichrist. The condition of the papacy in these years can scarcely be imagined. One pope – Urban VI – so feared conspiracy that he

[6] For the details see J. Favier, *Philippe le Bel* (Paris: Fayard, 1978), pp. 373–6.

[7] See M. Keen, *The Pelican History of Medieval Europe* (Harmondsworth, UK: Penguin Books, 1969), pp. 198–9; and C. W. Previte-Orton, *The Shorter Cambridge Medieval History* (Cambridge: Cambridge University Press, 1952), vol. II, p. 961.

[8] For a modern account of these events, see W. Ullmann, *The Origins of the Great Schism* (London: Burns, Oates and Washbourne, 1948).

tortured and executed his own cardinals when, driven out of Rome, he roamed the south Italian countryside. Another – John XXIII – was accused of murder, rape, sodomy, and incest (the more serious accusations were suppressed) before, disguised as a crossbowman, he was forced to flee from the Council of Constance; afterwards his very name was erased from the official list of pontiffs. As popes excommunicated and deposed one another they called on the lay rulers to intervene on their behalf, waging war and laying siege to each other's seats of power in Rome and Avignon. By so doing they enabled those rulers to gain concessions of every kind.

Long after the schism had been brought to an end by the election of Martin V (1417), its residue continued to affect the relationship between ecclesiastical and secular government. The spectacle of popes being elected and then deposed had reopened the ancient question as to whose authority, that of the pope or that of the Council of the church, was supreme;[9] worse, contemporaries had become used to the possibility that an individual might both wear the tiara *and* be a heretic. In 1438 the Conciliarists showed what they could do by deposing Eugenius IV and electing Felix V in his stead. Ten years passed before the renewed split could be healed; no wonder subsequent popes held ecclesiastical councils in holy terror. For the next century – in fact, until the onset of the Counter-Reformation – the division of the church played into the hands of secular rulers. Whenever a conflict with the church appeared likely, e.g., over taxation, French and Spanish rulers in particular could turn to the pope for assistance; conversely, in dealing with the Roman curia they would threaten to summon an assembly of the prelates of the realm or else, in England, of Parliament. Calling on the clergymen's patriotism and contrasting it with the claims of "foreign" (or, in France, "ultramontane") Rome often presented a good way for obtaining their support, especially over benefices. And the later the date, the more true this became.

Throughout the first half of the fifteenth century the papacy continued to suffer additional blows. As the Albiginsian, Waldensian, Cathar, and Lollard movements in particular show, heresy – even large-scale, organized heresy supported by entire social groups – had by no means been rare during the Middle Ages.[10] However, the Hussite Revolt of 1419–36 was something else; it was the first to unite the greater part of a long-established Christian nation against the established religion. Hus himself made the mistake of trusting a safe conduct that had been granted to him

[9] See M. Wilks, *The Problem of Sovereignty in the Later Middle Ages* (Cambridge: Cambridge University Press, 1963), pp. 479–523.
[10] See H. A. Obermann, *Forerunners of the Reformation* (New York: Holt, 1961).

and ended up by being burnt at the stake. His supporters suffered savage repression at the hands of the Emperor and the German territorial rulers. Still, his principles were not forgotten. Protected by part of the Czech nobility, a Hussite (Utraquist) Church continued to operate in Bohemia.[11] Its practices, particularly in regard to the language in which services were held (Czech rather than Latin) and the wine of the Eucharist (which was taken by both priest and laymen) differed significantly from those of Rome; yet they had to be tolerated by the latter for close to two centuries to come. Much ecclesiastical property had also been confiscated by the same nobility and was not restored. Finally, the ease with which the movement was able to spread from its source through Saxony and Mecklenburg all the way to the Baltic coast acted as a forewarning of the Reformation to come.

Meanwhile the foundations of the church's secular authority were being attacked by the new humanist scholarship emerging in Italy. Its key concept was the admiration of everything classical, which itself implied that an orderly – even flourishing and intellectually superior – civilization was possible without the benefit of the Christian faith. One of the first indications of what humanism and its supporters, once they put their minds to the matter, could do to reduce the position of the church came in 1440. The exact origin and meaning of the so-called Donation of Constantine – one of the key documents used by the papacy to justify its claim to monarchical power over Rome, Italy, and the West – had been disputed at least since the tenth century;[12] now Lorenzo Valla, exercising his knowledge of classical Latin, ended the debate by exposing the Donation as an eighth-century forgery and not a very skillful one at that. Valla, who like many of his fellow Italians regarded the established church as a source of corruption, political division, and war, became famous overnight. He ended his declamation by expressing the hope that, since the church's claims had been exposed, its lands would be swiftly secularized and its functions reduced to the spiritual sphere which alone belonged to it.

By this time the most important monarchies had long since become established facts. Kings either pushed resolutions through their parliaments – as with the English Statutes of Praemunire (1351) and the French Pragmatic Sanction (1439) – or else they negotiated with the pope of the day and signed a concordat. Whatever the procedure used, invariably it led to the church's financial independence being lost and its

---

[11] See H. Kaminsky, *A History of the Hussite Revolution* (Berkeley: University of California Press, 1967), pp. 97–161.

[12] The debate around the Donation is summarized in D. Maffei, *La Donazione di Constantino nei giuristi medievali* (Milan: Giuffre, 1964).

property made subject to royal taxation. To mention only a few land-marks, already Edward II (1307–27) managed to squeeze more money out of the church than he did from his lay vassals.[13] In 1366 John of Gaunt, acting in the name of Richard II, formally renounced England's status as a papal fief; when the same king, having attained his majority, appealed to Rome in his dispute with the nobility, that very act was used as additional grounds for deposing him. In France the appointment of foreigners to vacant ecclesiastical positions was prohibited in 1439, though the prohibition became definitive only in 1516. Louis XI (1461–83) had the 600 most important ecclesiastical benefices listed and dec-lared subject to his own control, thus further reinforcing his grip over personnel and enabling him to exercise patronage; by bestowing them upon lay supporters, he turned them into one more instrument of royal government and a notoriously corrupt one at that.[14] Finally, in Spain King Ferdinand – who with his wife styled himself "the Catholic" – appointed himself master of the various military orders as the offices became vacant between 1477 and 1498. In 1531 Pope Adrian VI accep-ted the move as a *fait accompli* and confirmed it. It brought the crown lands as well as revenue; however, it was only ten years after this that Charles V followed the example of his French colleague and definitely prohibited foreigners from taking up ecclesiastical benefices in the coun-try.

The clergy's other rights, such as appealing to the pope against the royal justice system, were likewise being reduced. In France after the end of the Hundred Years War, Louis XI prohibited the Inquisition from persecuting heretics except at his own express command. He insisted that every sentence passed by an ecclesiastical court was subject to review by the *parlement* of Paris; to prevent priests from conspiring against him he prohibited them from traveling abroad without obtaining permission first. Francis I (1515–47) made them take the same oath to himself as was sworn by the rest of his subjects, thus moving one step closer toward ending their special status. Meanwhile, in England during the early years of Henry VIII, a comprehensive census was held – the first in 200 years – to determine just what properties were and were not owned by the church (and also which churches possessed the right to offer asylum). Some matters, such as the making and execution of wills, were removed from the church's jurisdiction. One – defamation – was struck off the books

[13] J. H. Denton, *Robert Winchelsey and the Crown 1294–1313* (Cambridge: Cambridge University Press, 1980), pp. 78–9, 297–301.
[14] See P. Ourliac, "The Concordat of 1472: An Essay on the Relations Between Louis XI and Sixtus IV," in P. S. Lewis, ed., *The Recovery of France in the Fifteenth Century* (New York: Harper, 1965), particularly pp. 146ff.

except insofar as it was directed against the king. Here as elsewhere the ecclesiastical authorities were now entirely dependent on the cooperation of the king's officers for carrying out the sentences that they imposed over whatever cases remained within their jurisdiction. This even applied to conservative Portugal and Spain; and indeed it has been said that no institution was so completely under royal control as the Spanish Inquisition. One way or another, the good old days when every senior prelate and every first-class abbot possessed their own jails were coming to an end.[15]

An even more important turning point in the triumph of the monarchs over the church came in the form of the Reformation. From the beginning one reason why Luther in particular gained so much more support than previous reformers was precisely because of his insistence that the movement he led had no revolutionary overtones; he believed that religion should not be allowed to invade the realm of the secular power.[16] This position led him to write vicious tracts in opposition to the Peasants' Revolt of 1525; in 1530 it was formalized when his collaborator, Melanchthon, drew up the Confession of Augsburg and quoted Christ's words to the effect that His Kingdom was not of his world. Other leading reformers, notably Zwingli, Calvin, Bucer, and Beza, dedicated some or all of their works to the secular rulers of the day in the hope of gaining assistance in spreading their views.[17]

Once the princes' fears concerning its political effects had been assuaged, Protestantism spread rapidly. Its victory was perhaps most complete in Scotland, the Scandinavian countries, and, though it took longer and ended in a different way, England; but it also took over large parts of Germany, Bohemia, Poland, Hungary, Switzerland, France, and the Low Countries. Whether in its Lutheran, Zwinglian, Calvinist, Anglican, or Presbyterian (Scottish) form, wherever it reached, its adherents renounced their obedience to the pope. They also dissolved the monasteries as the church's spiritual centers and, embarking on the large-scale confiscation of ecclesiastical property, reduced its economic power in general.

The process whereby the church's property was seized assumed various forms. In Germany entire principalities were secularized; the most spec-

---

[15] For developments in France during this period, see F. Laurent, *L'église et l'état* (Paris: Libraire internationale, 1866); for English ones, see R. N. Swanson, *Church and Society in Late Medieval England* (Oxford: Blackwell, 1989), as well as L. C. Gabel, *Benefits of Clergy in England in the Later Middle Ages* (Northampton, MA: Smith College Studies in History, No. 14, 1928).

[16] See above all his *Secular Authority: To What Extent Should It Be Obeyed?* (1523), in M. Luther, *Werke: kritische Gesamtausgabe* (Weimar: Weimarer Ausgabe, 1883–), vol. XI, pp. 245–80.

[17] For a list, see E. Cameron, *The European Reformation* (Oxford: Clarendon Press, 1991), p. 462, n. 32.

tacular instance took place in 1525. Employing Luther as his consultant, Albert of Brandenburg-Ansbach used his position as master of the Teutonic Order to appropriate it lock, stock, and barrel. He thus created a new political entity which, at its greatest extent, measured 120 by 200 miles and which is known to history as the Duchy of Prussia.[18] Elsewhere it was mainly a question of stripping churches of their plate, as during the "smashing of the idols" movement that swept over the Netherlands in 1566; in Sweden King Gustavus Vasa decreed that every church in the land should sacrifice a bell in favor of the exchequer. Most important of all, the Reformation enabled rulers to lay their hands on the ecclesiastical estates which, in some countries, amounted to 25–30 percent of all land. The tenants who worked the land often cooperated, being glad to rid themselves of monks and priests who were notorious for their strict enforcement of rent and other prerogatives. Once they had been confiscated, estates were sold for ready cash or, though perhaps less frequently, leased out to subcontractors. Either way, the result was to increase royal revenues – in some cases several times over, as in England where Henry VIII became the first monarch who was richer than all his magnates combined – and also to create institutional support for the reforms which, once they had reached into men's pockets, became much more difficult to undo.

Moreover, and though tens of thousands of monks and nuns were simply turned out and left without a living, the rest of the clergy had to be provided for. Traditionally priests had been members of a separate universal organization that looked after them by assigning them benefices. Now, either they were turned into royal servants whose duty happened to be looking after peoples' souls, as in Lutheran countries; or else, though retaining some autonomy in respect to internal organization and the election of priests, they were excluded from interfering in matters of government, as was the case in Calvinist countries. In the latter, rulers, though they did not formally appoint themselves heads of the church, made it their responsibility to keep an eye on its activities, including education (both of laymen and of priests), rituals, and preaching. In the former, they often went further and, consulting with their court theologians, themselves published new articles of faith. In England Henry VIII, being neither a Lutheran nor a Calvinist but simply a bigamist with absolutist tendencies, both eliminated the independence of the church *and* issued a whole series of binding beliefs for his subjects to study and profess. Any doubt concerning his intentions were removed in 1539 when

---

[18] For the details, see M. Biskop, "The Secularization of the State of the Teutonic Order in Prussia in 1525: Its Genesis and Significance," *Polish–Western Affairs*, 22, 1–2, 1981, pp. 2–23.

the clergy were obliged to exchange their old translation of the Bible for a new one that bore the royal seal. The title page showed an assembly of figures, all of whom were busily saying *vivat rex*.[19]

Continuing to acknowledge the pope's authority, Catholic rulers did not go quite as far in these respects. Still, though the clergy's immunities and juridical powers remained much more extensive than under Protestant rule, many of them tightened control over religion; in the Empire, their right to do so was sanctioned by the Peace of Augsburg (1555).[20] Turning necessity into virtue, they used the need to fight on behalf of the "true" religion as a convenient excuse for taking over ecclesiastical principalities, confiscating church property, and imposing taxes, as Charles V did in 1520 when he turned the *tercio reale* and the *Cruzada* from voluntary contributions into permanent levies. Francis I on his part ordered all ecclesiastical benefices worth over 100,000 *livres* to be sold and the proceeds put into the royal coffers. His successors developed extortion into a fine art. Church property was regularly confiscated and, equally regularly, sold back to its original owners; as Michel de L'Hôpital, chancellor from 1560 to 1568, put it, "everything they [the clergy] possess belongs to the king," who could sell it whenever he wished "without even informing them."[21] Toward the end of the century that paragon of piety, Philip II of Spain, was reducing the Castilian church to penury by siphoning away as much as half of its revenue. His income from it equaled that which, as the master of the largest and richest overseas empire in history until then, he derived from the New World.[22]

With the duke of Bavaria in the lead, one after another Catholic rulers set up councils – invariably with a majority of laymen among their members – to supervise the affairs of the church, including the distribution of officers and of benefices. Nor was the faith itself left alone. Charles V, though personally firm in the old belief, led the way; between 1520 and 1543 his theologians engaged on an unceasing quest for a doctrine that, giving equal satisfaction to Catholics and Protestants alike, could be declared binding on all of them. In France with its independent traditions – already in the fourteenth century the Sorbonne had presumed

[19] On the use of the Bible for reinforcing royal authority during this reign and the next, see G. Brennan, "Patriotism, Language and Power: English Translations of the Bible, 1520–1580," *History Workshop*, 27, 1989, pp. 18–36.

[20] See H. Tuechle, "The Peace of Augsburg: A New Order or Lull in the Fighting?," in H. J. Cohn, ed., *Government in Reformation Europe 1520–1560* (London: Macmillan, 1971), pp. 145–69; and J. Leclercq, "Les origines et le sens de la formule: cuius regio, eius religio," *Recherches de Science Réligieuse*, 37, 1950, pp. 119–31.

[21] Quoted in I. Clouas, "Gregoire XIII et l'aliénation des biens du clergé de France en 1574–1575," *Mélanges d'Archéologie et d'Histoire: Ecole Française de Rome*, 71 (1959), pp. 381–404; quote, p. 397.

[22] J. H. Elliott, *Imperial Spain, 1469–1716* (London: Edward Arnold, 1963), pp. 192–3.

to rule in matters of doctrine – the attempt of the Council of Trent to redefine the Catholic religion was itself greeted with alarm. French literature on the respective rights of king and church grew and grew. In 1594 Pierre Pithou in *Libertés de l'église gallicane* proclaimed that, within the frontiers of the realm, the pope's temporal power was nil and his spiritual authority limited to whatever had received the king's consent; when Blanche of Savoy, the bride of Henry IV (1598–1610), asked him to adopt the Tridentine articles as her wedding present she was told never to concern herself with matters of state. Returning to Philip II, though he did not lay down the principles of the faith, he *did* assert his power to the point that no papal bull could be published in many of his dominions without being approved by him first.

As secular rulers tightened their grip on the church, change also overtook the personnel of government. Encouraged by the spread of secular humanism, beginning in the fifteenth century laymen were increasingly able to get as good an education as ecclesiastics did. In time, this fact put an end to the situation in which rulers were dependent on "clerks" to staff their administration. For example, Thomas Wolsey – who was dismissed in 1525 – was the last cardinal to fill the post of lord chancellor in England. His successor Thomas More wore a hairshirt under his clothes; nevertheless he was primarily a lawyer whose way to the top led though Parliament, the Inns of Court, and a succession of business deals that made him rich. Subsequent English monarchs were usually at some pains to avoid appointing churchmen to state offices – something denied even to William Laud who, as archbishop of Canterbury, played a major role in the persecution of Puritans and other dissidents under Charles I. Here, as in other Protestant countries, the lay nobility was giving up its independent lifestyle and turning to royal service as a means of advancing themselves. As of the second half of the sixteenth century they flocked to the universities in unprecedented numbers in order to study, among other things, the newly established "political" science whose founders were Bodin and Justus Lipsius.[23]

Though slower off the mark, Catholic rulers followed. In Spain Cardinal Granvelle, who served his master for over twenty years before dying in harness in 1586, proved to be the last of his kind. Philip III's chief minister was the duke of Lerma. Philip IV appointed the count of Olivares and, after him, Don Luis Mendez de Haro. Only France, which in the days of Catherine de Medici (1559–89) and Henry IV (1589–1610) had been moving in the same direction, proved an exception to the general

---

[23] L. H. Stone, "The Educational Revolution in England, 1560–1640," *Past and Present*, 28, 1964, pp. 41–80; P. M. Hahn, *Struktur und Funktion des brandenburgischen Adels im 16. Jahrhundert* (Berlin: Colloquium-Verlag, 1979), pp. 206ff.

rule. For thirty-seven years – 1624 to 1661 – it was run by two red-hatted cardinals, Richelieu and Mazarin, who acted in the names of Louis XIII and the young Louis XIV respectively. It should be noted, though, that nobody could be more zealous in defending the "state" against the church in Rome (and also in accumulating offices for himself) than Richelieu himself – to the point that he has often been regarded as its true founder. Here, too, in any case, the experiment was not repeated. One of the first things Louis XIV did upon reaching his majority was to bring government by ecclesiastics to an end. Acting as his own first minister, he looked for his advisers among laymen such as Colbert and Louvois.

Meanwhile the very idea that orderly government depended on the sanction of religion was coming under attack. Once again, it was humanism that opened the doors. Commenting on his much admired Roman Republic, Machiavelli suggested that one of the secrets of political stability consisted of the upper classes using religion in order to keep the masses in their place.[24] The truth or untruth of these beliefs did not matter; for him, it was not the mandate of heaven but *virtù*, best defined as a mixture of patriotism and courage, that both created government and justified it. Nor was Machiavelli's the only voice to raise itself: three years after he had written *The Prince*, Thomas More published *Utopia* (1516). There he described an imaginary polity which exercised religious toleration without falling into disorder or, indeed, suffering adverse consequences of any kind. The only exception were atheists who would deny men an eternal soul; but even they remained unmolested so long as they did not publicly express their views. But for the fact that he was famous for his love of satire, we might well accept More as the first true modern. As it is, one is hard-pressed to say whether the proposal was seriously meant. He himself was an intensely religious person who during his term as lord chancellor persecuted heretics as zealously as he could. He ended by sacrificing himself in defending Catholicism against Henry VIII.

In any case the idea was destined to take hold in countries such as France and the Netherlands. As the former slid into civil war from 1561 on, religious tolerance was seen by Huguenot spokesmen as a way of protecting themselves against the Catholic majority; additional support came from the school of thought known as *politiques* (originally the opposite of *fanatiques*) who hoped to use it for overcoming religious divisions.[25] Both Charles IX (1560–74) and Henry III (1574–89) toyed with it from time to time, as did their mother who was the real power

[24] N. Machiavelli, *Discourses* (New York: Random House, 1950), ch. 13.
[25] M. G. Smith, "Early French Advocates of Religious Freedom," *Sixteenth-Century Journal*, 25, 1, 1994, pp. 29–51.

behind the throne.[26] Though personally a pious Catholic, Henry III ended up by appointing the Protestant Henry of Navarre as his successor, alienating many of his subjects but clearly putting the imperatives of government above those of religion. The king of Navarre himself was probably a skeptic at heart; however, and as his famous quip about Paris being worth a mass indicates, he was one who was prepared to follow external forms provided they served his ends. He converted to Catholicism and assumed the throne as Henry IV. His next step was to put an end to his predecessors' attempts at persecution and grant religious toleration in the form of the Edict of Nantes, which for ninety years turned France into a virtual patchwork of Catholic and Protestant communities. Throughout his reign his factotum and chief adviser was a Huguenot, the duc de Sully, a figure whom we shall meet again.

In the Netherlands religious differences were as acute as anywhere else but, in the north at any rate, they tended to be submerged by the desperate struggle for independence against Spain. William the Silent in his capacity as the first leader of the revolt did everything in his power to maintain unity, which explains why, during the late 1560s and early 1570s, he was found advocating formal equality between the Catholic and Calvinist churches. However, their mutual suspicions – particularly those of the extreme Calvinists, known as *Predikanten* – limited his success. In 1573 the Catholic inhabitants of the northern provinces lost their right to worship, though no attempt was made to deprive them of their liberty of conscience. Here, as in most other countries, centuries were to pass before all forms of religiously motivated discrimination were abolished, offenses against religion struck off the statute book, and a separation of church and state achieved – to say nothing of ending the church's dominant position in such fields as welfare and education.

Even as Catholic and Protestant rulers waged war in the name of their respective creeds, they were forced by the demands of politics and of commerce to deal with each other on an equal footing. The practice of establishing permanent representatives had originated in Italy after the Peace of Lodi (1454) where rulers dealt with each other on a daily basis and where there were no cultural differences standing in the way. From there it spread to countries such as Spain, France, and England whose kings often relied on experienced Italian personnel.[27] As the Reformation divided Europe into warring camps, development toward a modern diplomatic service was interrupted; however, from about 1600 on political

---

[26] L. I. Taber, "Religious Dissent Within the Parliament of Paris in the Mid-Sixteenth Century," *French Historical Studies*, 16, 3, 1990, pp. 684–99.
[27] J. G. Russell, *Peacemaking in the Renaissance* (Philadelphia: University of Pennsylvania Press, 1986), p. 68.

realities again prevailed and this evolution began to reestablish itself. Whenever ambassadors arrived at some foreign court one of the first questions that had to be settled was their right – and that of their staffs – to worship in their own manner. In most cases the demand ended up by being granted, first in private and then, increasingly, in public as well.[28]

By this time both Catholic and, *a fortiori*, Protestant rulers were beginning to treat their churches as if they were mere departments of state. In the former many of the ecclesiastics' privileges and immunities remained in place right up to the time of the French Revolution; but in the latter, particularly Prussia, Sweden, and England (where Henry VIII had called the clergy "only half our subjects"),[29] the differences between them and laymen were rapidly being eliminated. While most educated people probably continued to believe both in the divine right of kings and in the latter's right and duty to look after their subjects' spiritual welfare,[30] here too change was in the air. Perhaps the most radical position was found in England where Thomas Hobbes published *Leviathan* in 1651. Influenced by Galileo, Hobbes' goal was to base his political system on the physics of his day, eliminating all influence other than those that could be seen, sensed, and measured. He was the first to proclaim that the belief in God (if He existed) was irrelevant to politics; as to outer forms, he followed Machiavelli in recommending that subjects be made to practice the religion prescribed by the sovereign as best adapted to the maintenance of public order. During the English Civil War, Hobbes was attacked as a crypto-heretic and forced to flee abroad. However, it was symptomatic of the changing outlook that, even though the Protectorate was committed to Puritanism, under Cromwell he was permitted to return. From then until his death – which took place well after the Restoration and thus after another major change in religious policy – he was allowed to live in peace as the king's pensioner though, the plague of 1666 being blamed in part on his blasphemous views, from then on he was forbidden to publish.

The papacy, too, changed its character. The rise of the great monarchies had not gone unnoticed south of the Alps. It made the popes realize that their own future lay with a territorial principality in which they themselves would exercise absolute government independently of any-

[28] See G. Mattingly, *Renaissance Diplomacy* (London: Jonathan Cape, 1955), pp. 266ff.
[29] A. Fox and J. Guy, *Reassessing the Henrician Age: Humanism, Politics and Reform 1500–1550* (Oxford: Blackwell, 1986), p. 15.
[30] See, for England, S. Doran and C. Durton, *Princes, Pastors and People: The Church and Religion in England, 1529–1689* (London: Routledge, 1991), p. 100; for France, see W. J. Stankiewicz, *Politics and Religion in Seventeenth-Century France* (Berkeley and Los Angeles: University of California Press, 1960), pp. 164, 199; and, for Spain, J. J. Elliott, "Power and Propaganda in Spain of Philip IV," in S. Wilentz, ed., *Rites of Power: Symbolism, Ritual and Politics Since the Middle Ages* (Philadelphia: University of Pennsylvania Press, 1985), pp. 149ff.

body else. The work of building it was begun by the "terrible" (Jacob Burkhardt) Sixtus IV (1471–84). By surrendering to Louis XI what he could not protect – i.e., the right to tax ecclesiastical income and control over benefices – he bought French assistance, or at any rate neutrality, in his disputes with the remaining Italian rulers. The respite gained he used to capture the strongholds of the Colonna family and kill their leader, thus breaking their power and establishing papal rule over the city of Rome once and for all. However, Sixtus' attempts to continue his record of intrigue and assassination in order to extend his control over Florence as well was cut short by his death. His immediate successor, Innocent VIII, was ineffective and made no further headway. Innocent's successor, Alexander VI (the Spaniard Rodrigo Borgia) became involved in the series of Franco-Spanish wars that broke out when the French invaded Italy in 1494 and which were to last until 1559. By deftly switching alliances at several critical moments he provided himself with further opportunities for aggrandizement. However, his aim was not so much to strengthen the Papal State *per se* as to provide his relations – chief among whom was his son Cesare – with principalities which he distributed right and left.

Then it was the turn of Sixtus' nephew, the warrior-pope Julius II (1503–13). Concluding an alliance with Spain as the greatest power of the time, he donned armor and, commanding in person, campaigned all over central Italy. Cesare Borgia was captured, sold to Naples, and sent to Spain where he died in a skirmish; the lands lost by Rome under Alexander VI were recovered and additional parts of the Romagna annexed. When Julius was succeeded first by Leo X (1513–23), and then by Clement VII (1523–35), both members of the Medici family, it looked as if even Florence and indeed the whole of Tuscany were destined to come under papal government. It was not to be, and the sack of Rome by the troops of Charles V (1527) showed that the dangers to the Papal State were by no means over. However, from this time until the Napoleonic Wars Rome succeeded in maintaining itself as an independent political entity with the pope as its undisputed ruler. Its frontiers lasted even longer, remaining established for three and a half centuries to come and were done away with only in 1859 when Italian unification was achieved.

Yet in a different way the construction of such a state proved to be a double-edged weapon. Driven by the need to engage and maintain mercenary troops, the popes of the age engaged in venality to an extent not known before or, probably, since. Accordingly they sold indulgences (promising to get sinners out of purgatory) and quadrupled the number of offices that were open to purchase; particularly in Germany which did not have a single monarch to protect it, they also siphoned money away from the local ecclesiastical organization to Rome.[31] All of this raised the ire of believers – during his visit to Rome, which took place in 1510, Luther witnessed papal corruption at first hand – and, when the time came, helped him and his fellow reformers find their followers. Meanwhile the discussions by Guicciardini and Machiavelli show that contemporaries were becoming used to thinking of the church in terms of pure power politics. The former accused the Papal State of having abandoned even the semblance of Christianity in pursuing its secular ends. The latter saw it as a state among states, remarkable for nothing but its outstanding hypocrisy.

Given the circumstances of the time the use of intrigue, sword, and fire to establish a viable Papal State was inevitable. The Universal Church, its head saved from secular domination, was preserved. However, successive popes found it difficult to reconcile their role as the vicar of Christ with that of temporal ruler;[32] as time went on, their influence over international affairs came to be in proportion to the size of the territory that they ruled and the armed forces that they commanded. From the middle of the seventeenth century this meant that, outside Italy, it amounted to very little indeed: as Stalin was one day to ask, how many divisions did the pope have? As for the church's local organizations, regardless of whether or not they were reformed, they tended to come under the authority of the state. Stripped of their independent power, they found themselves surviving under the authority of the state with which they often forged a close alliance. Even when ecclesiastics and their institutions still opposed the state, as sometimes happened, inevitably they did so either within the state or by fleeing to such other states as would offer them asylum; the days when they possessed their own political communities were largely over.

The struggle against the Empire

As the kings were winning the struggle against the church, the Holy Roman Empire too retreated in front of their onslaught. Its position had been weakened by the dispute over the investiture; from the end of the eleventh century to the beginning of the fourteenth there was hardly an Emperor who did not suffer excommunication at some point during his reign. Meanwhile the balance of military power changed. At the Battle of

[31] On papal finances during this period, see J. A. F. Thomson, *Popes and Princes, 1487–1517* (London: Allen and Unwin, 1980), pp. 86ff.; for the opposition that the sale of indulgences encountered, see R. Kiermayer, "How Much Money Was Really in the Indulgence Chest?," *Sixteenth-Century Journal*, 17, 3, 1986, pp. 303–18.

[32] For this development, see N. S. Davidson, "Temporal Power and the Vicar of Christ: The Papal State from 1450 to 1650," *Renaissance and Modern Studies*, 36, 1993, pp. 1–14.

Bouvines (1214), Philip II Augustus of France defeated the last serious attempt made by an Emperor – Otto IV – to put back the clock to the days of Charlemagne. Next, the death of Emperor Conrad IV in 1254 was followed by a long interregnum during which the throne was vacant. By the time Rudolf I of Habsburg ascended the throne in 1273, it had led to the collapse of whatever reality Imperial power still possessed outside greater Germany. It was during this period that, exploiting the situation where rival claimants were fighting each other, the kings of Aragon, Hungary, and Bohemia assumed the Imperial orb and the so-called closed crown as symbols of their authority.

Even what "help" the Holy Roman Empire sometimes received from the papacy in its struggle against the monarchs could backfire. Thus, as a part of his lifelong campaign against Philip IV, Boniface VIII tried to interest Albert I of Habsburg in the French throne. Though the offer was gracefully declined, the pope continued to insist that the king of France was subordinate to the Emperor.[33] A lawyer among Philip's advisers responded by bringing into use the phrase *rex in regno suo imperator est* (the king is emperor in his own realm). In time it was to gain wide currency, not only in France but in other countries as well.[34]

On the other hand, that phrase itself reflected the Empire's superior status in all affairs that, transcending individual kingdoms, affected Christianity as a whole. However shadowy its real power the Empire, as heir to Rome, remained very much alive in men's minds; this was true not only in Central Europe but also in Italy where people were desperately looking for ways to counter the power of the church. A mere ten years after Boniface issued his *Unam Sanctam*, Dante Alighieri (1265–1321) published *De monarchia*. Intended by its author to be his prose *magnum opus*, the work was written against the background of the endless wars which afflicted the peninsula. Dante starts by explaining that temporal government has been instituted by God in order to keep human beings, a species of willful animals, in check. Next he argues that, since existing kingdoms cannot but engage in conflict with each other, a supreme secular authority is needed to exercise justice over them; that it is to the Roman people, and no other, that universal monarchy properly belongs; and that the monarch in question should be co-equal with, but in no way dependent on, the pope.

Less interested in things Roman, but even more determined in defense of the Empire were two close contemporaries of Dante's, Marsilius of

---

[33] Speech of 30 April 1303: J. P. Pfeffinger, ed., *Corpus Iuris Publicis* (Frankfurt am Main: Varrentrapp, 1734), vol. I, p. 377.

[34] See R. Feenstra, "Jean de Blanot et la formule 'Rex Franciae in regno suo princeps est,'" in *Etudes d'histoire canonique dediées à Gabriel le Bras* (Paris: Sirey, 1965), pp. 883–95.

Padua (1280–1343) and William of Ockham (1285–1349). The former was a Franciscan monk who spent a good part of his life in Paris. These were the years when the papacy was violently denouncing the Franciscans for insisting on the poverty of Christ and demanding that the church follow in his footsteps; perhaps in defense of his order, Marsilius put himself at the service of Lewis the Bavarian during the latter's attempt to gain the Imperial throne. Marsilius' masterpiece was the *Defensor Pacis* in which he argued that the Emperor and not the pope was primarily responsible to God for keeping the peace among men. The pope's position derived merely from his being the bishop of the Empire's capital; his mission was purely spiritual, which meant that the church should neither hold property nor enjoy any special immunities and privileges.

The treatise, originally written in Latin but later translated into French, was read by Pope Clement V, who found in it no fewer than 224 heresies and who denounced its author as "a beast from hell." This did not prevent Ockham, Marsilius' fellow Franciscan and political consultant to Lewis, from writing in his *Dialogus* that the Emperor was "over all persons and causes supreme." "However many liberties the Emperor may grant the French and other kings, still the realm of France and others may not be totally separated from the Empire, for to do so would be to destroy the Empire."[35] Later in the same work Ockham, displaying the kind of casuistry which earned him the nickname of "Invincible Teacher," declared that all kings were subject to the Emperor even though the latter in his wisdom had not so ordained by his express command.

Throughout this period the Emperor retained his titular position as the head of the feudal hierarchy. Holding his dominion directly from God, his rights were immutable and his writ, in theory, valid all over Christendom. As a "Roman" he stood over all nations and was fit to act as their judge; everywhere his name continued to be mentioned in the masses people said. Whenever an Emperor and another ruler met it was the former who enjoyed precedence, a situation which often led to diplomatic incidents. A king, such as Charles VI of France, who was visited by an Emperor had to guard against the danger that the guest might seat himself on the royal chair without asking for permission first.[36] Conversely an Emperor visiting a king was likely to find himself greeted by the declaration that he was *not* superior. To prove the point he might have a sword brandished in his face, as happened to Emperor Sigismund (1433–7) when he came to England; or else he might be assigned a black horse instead of the white

[35] Marsilius of Padua, *Defensor Pacis*, A. Gewirth, tr. (New York: Harper, 1956); William of Ockham, *Dialogus* (London: Oxford University Press, 1925), part III, tr. ii, lib. II, e. 7.
[36] Such an incident, which took place in 1416, is described in Juvenal des Ursin, *Histoire de Charles VI* (Paris: Panth. Litt. edn., 1898), p. 530.

one that was the symbol of suzerainty. Nor did such squabbles end when the Middle Ages did. As late as 1677 at Nijmegen, the French and English envoys gave proof of their masters' traditional inferiority complex by insisting the Emperor's delegates should not enjoy precedence over themselves.[37]

Nor was the Emperor's position without its practical significance. He was, after all, the only one who could create kings; as Emperor Maximilian (1493–1519) once remarked in jest, he was indeed "the king of kings" since all those theoretically under his authority aspired to be kings (and, as happened to Duke Charles the Bold of Burgundy in 1472, were sorely disappointed when their request was denied). Furthermore, at various times and places there were other actions that he alone could take. Thus Lewis the Bavarian appropriated to himself the right to permit marriages within the prohibited degree of consanguinity, with all that this implied for the distribution of inheritances, etc.;[38] in Scotland until the reign of James III (1460–1844) the Emperor alone was entitled to create public notaries. Finally, until 1356 – which was when the kings of Bohemia, Poland, and Hungary took it for themselves – the crime of *lèse majesté* could be committed only against him. Thus, strictly speaking, the Emperor alone among mortals stood for a type of law different from, and superior to, the one that governed disputes between individuals.

As had been the case ever since the ascent of Otto I in 962, the center of the Holy Roman Empire's power continued to be Germany where various Emperors owned their own hereditary lands – principally in Austria, Bohemia, the Tyrol, and Alsace. Unlike other princes, whose position had become hereditary by about 1300, Emperors continued to be elected. The procedure for doing so was regularized by the Golden Bull of 1356, which, among other things, took away the pope's right to participate and left him only the coronation ceremony to perform. On the other hand, the bull itself represented a significant step in the weakening of the Empire. It gave, or rather confirmed, the seven princes designated as electors in their possession of important rights such as mining (i.e., any resources discovered in their territories now belonged exclusively to them), levying customs, taxing Jews, and in some cases coining money. Most importantly, it ended their subjects' right to appeal against them to the Imperial court.

Still, the ability of the princes to strengthen themselves at the expense of the Emperor had its limits. Not only did he remain the sole individual

---

[37] See H. Durchardt, "Imperium und Regna im Zeitalter Ludwigs XIV," *Historische Zeitschrift*, 23, 3, 1981, pp. 555–81; and B. Guennée, *States and Rulers in Later Medieval Europe* (Oxford: Blackwell, 1985), pp. 8–9, for numerous other instances of this kind.
[38] See Wilks, *Problem of Sovereignty*, pp. 324–5.

with the authority to call out the Imperial forces, but control over common facilities such as fortresses, roads, and rivers remained in his hands. Created by and for the electors, the bull did not change the position of perhaps 300 secular and ecclesiastical lords of various ranks; nor that of some 2,000 knights who held land directly from the Emperor, nor that of eighty-five "free" or Imperial cities which were scattered from the Baltic Sea to Switzerland and whose role as centers of wealth and industry was growing all the time. All of them continued to be subject to the Emperor's jurisdiction as exercised first through the Hofgericht (Household Court) and then through the Kammergericht and Reichsgericht, which took its place during the fifteenth century. It is true that Emperor Maximilian met with little success in his efforts to set up an Imperial system of taxation as well as a unified Imperial army. On the other hand the repeated attempts of the princes to set up a new constitution that would enable them to further emancipate themselves were equally unsuccessful. Meanwhile the very fact that attempts at reform were being made lent new life to the idea of a common fate and a common authority positioned above that of individual princes.[39]

In Italy, too, though it had to affirm its position by means of countless wars, the Empire's suzerainty continued to be acknowledged. If only because the papacy fought tooth and nail to prevent Italian unification, the peninsula did not see the rise of a strong monarchy capable of subduing the squabbling city-states or, having failed to do so, at any rate regularize the positions of their rulers. This did not matter much so long as the latter were elected by their communities; but incipient capitalism and the growing polarization between rich and poor meant that the era of more or less democratic government was coming to an end. Beginning around 1300 most cities were swept by a wave of civic unrest as the middle classes, sometimes supported by the guilds and at other times opposed by them, rebelled against patrician rule.[40] As the common people and the peasantry joined in these often extremely complicated struggles they opened the way to the triumph of *condottieri*, such as those belonging to the Gonzaga, Visconti, and Sforza families, or else of successful bankers such as the Medicis. Whoever they were, they seized power to which they had no legitimate title, which meant that they needed the Emperor's consent to confirm their status.

Besides the explicit recognition of Imperial overlordship that it con-

[39] See H. S. Offler, "Aspects of Government in the Late Middle Ages," in J. R. Hale, et al., eds., *Europe in the Late Middle Ages* (Evanston, IL: Northwestern University Press, 1965), pp. 241ff.; and F. Hartung, "Imperial Reform, 1485–1495: Its Course and Character," in G. Strauss, ed., *Pre-Reformation Germany* (London: Macmillan, 1972), pp. 73–135.

[40] See M. Mollat and P. Wolff, *The Popular Revolutions of the Late Middle Ages* (London: Allen and Unwin, 1973), pp. 76–83, 98–107, 142–61.

tained, usually such consent could be had only for hard cash. For example, the Florentines in 1355 humbly begged to become an Imperial vicariate and even paid out 100,000 florins for the privilege. In 1359 Galeazzo Visconti likewise paid 100,000 florins in order to be recognized as duke of Milan. Amadeus VIII was made duke of Savoy in 1416, Giovan Franceso Gonzaga count of Mantua in 1432. In 1437, seeking to legitimize its control over the newly conquered *terra ferma*, even Venice – which had never in any case been part of the Empire – requested to be admitted as an Imperial vicariate and promised to pay 1,000 ducats a year. In 1452 Emperor Frederick III visited Italy and found the various cities vying with each other as to which one would accord him the greatest honors. He sold titles as if they were herrings; by way of disposing of the biggest herring of all he appointed Luigi III of Mantua a duke. As late as 1494 Lodovico Il Moro paid Emperor Maximilian 100,000 florins – which seems to have been the going rate – to be confirmed as duke of Milan. To be sure, these and similar deals should be understood not as an empty quest for titles but as part of a ruthless game of *Realpolitik* played by Italian rulers among themselves as well as by several foreign potentates. On the other hand, none of this would have been possible if there had not been very real advantages to obtaining the Emperor's recognition, which in turn serves as an index of the power, both legal and practical, that he still retained.

As poems, folktales, and prophecies show, during the last quarter of the fifteenth century the idea of empire as a universal organization was alive and well in the popular consciousness.[41] In Germany and Italy it seemed that the spirit of the age itself was turning its hopes on the Emperor; in countless minor works he was addressed as the one ruler who could, if he only would, deliver Christendom from the manifold evils that were besetting it. Always first on the order of priorities there appeared the defeat of the Turks who were causing trouble all over the Mediterranean and threatening Christendom's eastern frontiers in the Balkans and Hungary. Next came putting an end to the corruption of the church and compelling the princes to make peace among themselves so that murder and robbery would cease and the roads be rendered safe for travel. To crown it all the medieval idea of a crusade aimed at recapturing the Holy Sepulcher in Jerusalem remained very much alive. Once again, the person who was expected to lead it was obviously the Emperor.

How widespread such expectations were is shown by the fact that they found an echo in the one quarter where it could least be expected, namely

---

[41] See F. Kampers, *Die deutsche Kaiseridee in Prophetie und Sage* (Munich: Aalen, 1969 edn.), pp. 129ff.

France. To be sure, here it was on a French king rather than a German or Roman one that various authors centered their hopes. However, the contents of those hopes and the qualities attributed to the would-be Emperor himself bore a surprising resemblance to those which were being voiced in the Empire during the same period; here as elsewhere it was a question of a prince who, exercising *sacrum imperium* over the *populus praeelectus Christi*, would impose justice, unite Christendom, and lead a crusade.[42] Returning to Germany and Italy, the works of such figures as Cardinal Nicholas of Cusa and the humanist Aeneas Picolomini – both acting as advisers to Frederick III, and the latter destined to be elected pope in 1503 – prove that these popular aspirations were shared by at least some of the elite, as does Ariosto's famous poem, *Orlando Furioso*. These and other contemporary works[43] may help explain why, for all the Empire's weakness, most people were reluctant to take active steps that would lead to its disintegration. Surprisingly enough this even applied to the independent-minded Swiss. Forming part of the Empire but resisting incorporation into the hereditary lands, they had been fighting the Habsburgs since at least 1291. Early in the fifteenth century a federal council was created, uniting the various cantons into a loose confederation and launching them toward eventual statehood. Yet it was only in the Peace of Basel (1499) that they formally emancipated themselves from obedience to Imperial law.

The installation as Emperor of Charles V in 1519 represented a landmark. On the one hand he had to swear a coronation oath which, for the first time, allowed the princes a voice in Imperial affairs; this was extended by the establishment at the Diet of Worms in 1521 of a Reichsregiment, or Imperial Council, with twenty-two members that was to govern in his absence and preserve the peace. Side by side with these internal reforms he had his chancellor and mentor, Mercurio Gattinara, prepare two memoranda which spelt out his rights and duties as a "universal" Emperor.[44] Charles was a master of propaganda and the spectacle of the Emperor in his council did not fail to make an impression on contemporaries; at any rate the advisers of the French king, such as Jean

---

[42] Wilks, *Problem of Sovereignty*, p. 430; also W. J. Bouwsma, *Concordia Mundi: The Career and Thought of Guillaume Postel (1510–1581)* (Cambridge, MA: Harvard University Press, 1957), pp. 216ff.

[43] See F. A. Yates, *Astraea: The Imperial Theme in the Sixteenth Century* (London: Routledge, 1975), pp. 20ff.; and D. Perry, "*Catholicum Opus Imperiale Regiminis Mundi*: An Early Sixteenth-Century Restatement of Empire," *History of Political Thought*, 2, 2, Summer 1981, pp. 227–52.

[44] For Gattinara's designs, see H. J. Koenig, *Monarchia Mundi und Res Publica Christiana* (Hamburg: Lüdke, 1969), pp. 58–85.

Feu and Charles de Grassaille, persisted in their attempts to prove that their master was as good as the Emperor and in no way his subject. The same applies to Henry VIII of England who, on the occasion of the visit that Charles paid him in 1522, organized a *tableau vivant* that displayed Charlemagne in the act of handing out crowns to the both of them. For as long as he reigned, "the last medieval Emperor," as he is often called, retained his pretensions to act as supreme arbitrator among Christian princes of all ranks. He regarded himself as carrying an equal responsibility with the pope for maintaining the faith and defending it against heresy, and, of course, as God's own appointed leader in Christendom's struggle against the infidels who, as it happened, reached the peak of their power during those very years.

What gave these claims a new credibility was the fact that, in spite of the Empire's loss of real political power during the preceding two centuries, Charles was in a unique position. By birth he was simply the duke of Burgundy, a territory much of which had been lost by his grandfather to the French crown in 1477 and which neither he nor any of his successors was ever able to recover. However, a fortunate and entirely unforeseen series of dynastic accidents put him in possession of Spain (complete with its dependencies in northern and southern Italy), as well as Germany and his own native Netherlands. From Spain, where the last remaining Muslim principality had just been destroyed, came the world's best troops, "doctors of the military discipline" as the saying went.[45] Also from Spain, as well as the Netherlands and, increasingly, the New World, came the financial muscle with which to maintain those troops.[46]

A conscientious though somewhat ponderous ruler, Charles himself was concerned above all with maintaining his God-given patrimony. He regarded the many wars that he waged as purely defensive; to others, caught between his various territories and aware of the superior dignity attached to the Imperial title, they looked suspiciously like an attempt to reestablish universal rule, *monarchia mundi*, in all its former glory. Straddling the globe from Europe through the Americas to the Philippines, Charles' power peaked in 1525 when, following the Battle of Pavia, he took his main enemy Francis I prisoner and imposed his own terms on him. In 1527 his forces sacked Rome and took Pope Clement VII

---

[45] See T. S. Foreman, "Doctors of Military Discipline: Technical Expertise and the Paradigm of the Spanish Soldier in the Early Modern Period," *Sixteenth-Century Journal*, 27, 1, Spring 1996, pp. 325–54.

[46] E. J. Hamilton, *American Treasure and the Price Revolution in Spain, 1501–1650* (Cambridge, MA: Harvard University Press, 1934), p. 34, gives a table of bullion imported into Spain from America; Elliott, *Imperial Spain*, p. 200, emphasizes the role of the Netherlands in financing the campaigns of Charles V.

prisoner, thus showing the whole world who was master. Three years later he received the Imperial crown from the same pope in Bologna; as it happened, this was the last time that the ceremony was performed.

The really decisive watershed was probably reached when Charles, tired out and realizing his own inability to control such a huge realm, abdicated in 1555–6. He had toyed with the idea of leaving all of it to his only legitimate son, Philip; in the end, though, the latter received Spain (together with its overseas colonies), Sicily, South and North Italy, and the Low Countries. The Empire proper, plus the Imperial title, went to Charles' brother Ferdinand who, holding the title of king of the Romans, had acted as his deputy for three decades past and also ruled the Habsburgs' own hereditary lands. The two branches of the Habsburg house had much in common, being united by their hatred of France, the Protestants, and of course the Turks. Constantly intermarrying among themselves, they were to remain on close terms for a century and a half until the War of the Spanish Succession (1702–13) finally put a French Bourbon prince on the throne in Madrid. Still, once the Empire had been deprived of the Spanish financial and military resources, whatever dreams Vienna may have had concerning the reestablishment of universal monarchy were stone-dead.

Though the procedure whereby the Emperor was elected by seven of Germany's principal princes remained unchanged, Ferdinand's succession also marked another kind of turning point. It is true that the name of Habsburg had been associated with the Imperial throne for centuries and indeed that none but Habsburgs had occupied it from 1438 on. Still, as late as 1519 two princes who were neither Habsburgs nor Germans – Henry VIII and Francis I – had been able to launch serious bids for it; the last named even had to be fended off by means of close to a million thalers in bribes that the Fugger banking house of Augsburg paid to the electors on Charles' behalf. Now, the very ease with which Charles was able to pass on the reins of government to a designated member of his own family put an end to the situation whereby, in theory, any Christian regardless of nationality could become Emperor. Ferdinand on his part was a capable ruler who saw the writing on the wall. Unable to make the Empire pay for his wars against the Turks, he turned to the hereditary lands, laying the groundwork for an administration that included the first unified privy council, the first unified court of appeal, and a similarly unified chancellery and chamber of accounts. His election, and that of his successor, can be seen as setting in motion the process whereby the Empire, its title to the contrary, gradually turned from Germany to the Danube and crystallized into a dynastic state much like all others, until, at length, it came to be known under the name of Austria.[47]

By the time these events took place the Reformation was in full swing. Wherever it reached, Protestant rulers, seeking to assert their independence, hastened to deny the Emperor whatever special rights he still possessed concerning religion. In 1533, as part of his attempt to bring his own church under control, one prince – Henry VIII – broke all precedents by formally declaring "this realm of England an Empire [that] so hath been accepted in the world." To this claim the Arthurian legends clearly did not provide a sufficient foundation; the thing to do was to bring in consultants in the form of Italian humanists. Their leader was Polydore Vergil, formerly a papal employee in charge of collecting Peter's Pence who had risen to become archdeacon of Wales. They used their expertise to produce a whole series of complicated historical fabrications which showed Henry to be an "Imperator" whose title was derived from that of a more ancient fellow Briton, the Roman Emperor Constantine;[48] later part of their work, known as *English History*, was to become required reading in schools. Together with the imperial dignity Henry also took the title of "Majesty." In this he was soon followed by Francis I and, a generation later, Philip II whose own Spanish ancestors had been addressed simply as "Highnesses." All three also assumed the "closed" Imperial crown.

To top it all, Europe's overseas expansion was beginning to change people's views. As Cortés proudly wrote to Charles V in 1520, so immense were Spain's conquests and so numerous its new subjects as to deserve the appellation of a new empire in addition to the old; the possibility that he might style himself "Emperador de Indias" was, in fact, explored by Charles' advisers, only to be rejected.[49] Thus it was the Habsburgs' dominions in Central Europe which, up to the first quarter of the eighteenth century, continued to be known simply as "The Empire" and its officials as "Imperialists." Nevertheless, the notion of a supreme religico-political construct uniting the Christian world but excluding the infidel began to crack; the more so because a non-Christian ruler – the Ottoman Suleiman the Magnificent – was being drawn into European politics through the alliance that he made with Francis I. Out of the

[47] The process whereby the Empire lost its international character culminated in 1713 when Charles VI, adopting the Pragmatic Sanction, abolished the election process. See J. Bryce, *The Holy Roman Empire* (New York: Schocken, 1961 edn.), p. 267; and F. Heer, *The Holy Roman Empire* (New York: Praeger, 1968), p. 168.

[48] For this episode, see R. Koebner, "The Imperial Crown of This Realm: Henry VIII, Constantine the Great and Polydore Vergil," *Bulletin of the Institute of Historical Research*, 26, 1953, pp. 29–52.

[49] H. Cortés, *Letters from Mexico*, A. R. Pagden, ed. (New Haven, CT: Yale University Press, 1968), p. 48; Heer, *The Holy Roman Empire*, p. 168.

Empire's ruins can be seen to emerge, from about 1550 on, at least two other entities – the Spanish and the British – which, though neither universal nor in any sense Roman, by virtue of their far-flung territories demanded, and were considered by some to deserve, the same title.[50]

In 1598 the duc de Sully, claiming to act in the name of his master Henry IV, for the first time proposed a plan which, had it been accepted, would have led to the Holy Roman Empire's demise. The existing international regime whereby most rulers, in consequence of ancient feudal ties, were in one way or another dependent on others for at least part of their countries was to be abolished. The various countries were to be consolidated along geographical lines and Europe divided between fifteen equal states each possessing the full attributes of sovereignty. They in turn were to be united in a sort of prototype League of Nations. Unlike its twentieth-century successor it was to be itinerant; meeting for a year each time in one city selected out of a list of fifteen, it would combine the roles formerly played by both Empire and church by fighting the Turk, laying down international law, settling disputes, preserving the peace, and punishing transgressors. Sully specified that the League's armed forces would consist of precisely 117 warships, 220,000 infantry, 53,800 cavalry, and 217 cannon – a formidable force by seventeenth-century standards and one more than sufficient to overawe any of its members. Nothing came of the scheme, which in some ways was intended simply to end Habsburg rule in Germany and make Henry IV the arbiter of Europe. And indeed there is some doubt whether it was seriously meant.[51]

Exactly two decades later the Habsburgs, provoked beyond endurance by the Protestant challenge to their throne, launched the Thirty Years War in a last-ditch effort to restore the Imperial power in Germany if not throughout Europe. They started with Bohemia where the Protestant aristocracy was in revolt and where, following the Battle of White Mountain in November 1620, their victory was swift and complete. Eight years later, with his forces approaching the Baltic, Ferdinand II (1610–37) believed he had made sufficient progress to publish the Edict of Restitution. In it he commanded that property taken from the church since the Peace of Augsburg be restored to its former owners. While Lutherans

---

[50] For an example of the Spanish use of the word "empire," see Philip III's letter to his viceroy in the Indies, 28 November 1606, quoted in H. Grotius, *The Freedom of the Seas*, R. van Deman Magoffin, ed. (New York: Carnegie Endowment, 1916), p. 77. An example of English usage may be found in F. Bacon, "An Essay upon the Origin and Nature of Government," in Bacon, *Works* (London: Miller, 1720), vol. I, p. 103.

[51] For Sully's project, see C. Pfister, "Les 'oeconomies royales' de Sully et le grand dessein de Henry IV," *Revue Historique*, 56, 1894, pp. 307–30; A. Puharre, *Les projets d'organisation européene d'après le grand dessein d'Henry IV et de Sully* (Paris: Union federaliste inter-universitaire, 1954), pp. 51ff.; and D. Heater, *The Idea of European Unity* (Leicester: Leicester University Press, 1992), pp. 30–8.

would be tolerated, Calvinists were to be expelled; at a stroke of the pen, the Emperor thus attempted to restore his right to govern religion not only in his own hereditary lands but in the Empire as a whole. However, and even though perhaps a third of Germany's population perished, in the end the task proved too much for the Habsburgs. Their very victories, particularly in central Germany and culminating in the sack of Magdeburg in 1631, terrified Catholic and Protestant princes alike. The former withdrew their support to the point where they temporarily forced the Emperor to reduce his army, dismiss his commander-in-chief, and seek peace. The latter were driven to look for help outside the Empire's frontiers. First Gustavus Adolphus of Sweden, then Louis XIII of France intervened. Dutch money did the rest, and the tide of Imperial conquest was brought to a halt.

The Peace of Westphalia which, in 1648, concluded the war marked the monarch's triumph over both the Empire and the church.[52] Imperial territory was partitioned. The kingdom of Sweden came away with much of the Baltic coast, which gain was not to prove permanent and was later lost to Prussia; the king of France received a considerable part of Alsace, which was destined to remain in his hands. The Swiss, who as will be recalled had distanced themselves from Imperial law in 1499, finally broke away and thus achieved the complete independence which they still retain. More important from our point of view, knowingly or unknowingly the first half of Sully's program was implemented. As a sharp line was drawn between the territories that belonged to the Empire and those that did not, the Emperor lost whatever pretensions over other rulers that he still retained. Western and Central Europe were divided between secular, sovereign potentates – though their number, swelled by the German princes who were granted "territorial lordship" or *Landshoheit*, turned out to be considerably larger than fifteen. Those who were within the Empire were given practically all the privileges of sovereignty, including the right to maintain their own armed forces and, which in theory at any rate had been denied to them until then, the right to make alliances both among themselves and with foreign powers "so long as they were not directed against the Emperor." The entire complicated arrangement was guaranteed by two non-Imperial princes, the kings of France and Sweden. Thus the point had been reached where the Empire, instead of protecting the peace of others, needed protection itself.

The Treaties were also the first which, violating all previous usage, did not even mention God. The Edict of Restitution was canceled. The

[52] For the text of the treaty, see K. Muller, ed., *Instrumenta Pacis Westphalicae* (Bern: Lang, 1966).

terminus post quam for restoring confiscated church property was moved forward from 1555 to 1624, which meant that whatever changes had taken place between those two dates would not be undone and that entire bishoprics would remain in the hands of their secular rulers. The rights awarded to Lutheran rulers by the Peace of Augsburg were extended to Calvinist ones as well, so that there were now three official religions instead of two. Whatever the church to which they belonged, rulers were authorized to regulate the public exercise of religion in their territories; as to subjects' private beliefs, no binding articles were included, though the Treaties strongly recommended a policy of toleration which, in fact, tended to emerge in many states over the next few decades. As if to emphasize the triumph of politics over religion, the government of one disputed principality – the north German bishopric of Osnabrück – was made alternately Catholic and Protestant. No wonder Pope Innocent X, who had not been consulted, thundered against the Treaties, denouncing them as "null, void, invalid, iniquitous, unjust, damnable, reprobate, inane, empty of meaning and effect for all time."[53]

However, the times had changed since Charles V had raised the standard of the Counter-Reformation and declared war on Protestants. Though the Treaties were not able to prevent more wars from taking place, in a world that was growing tired of religiously motivated conflict and where the Empire was manifestly no longer capable of holding its own even inside Germany the world-view that they expressed held up remarkably well. The dawning age of the Enlightenment meant that awareness of the cultural unity of Europe was stronger than ever before; on the other hand, the old universal *Res Publica Christiana* with its twin hierarchical governments was finally dead. Out of the chaos of war a new order, based on a rough balance of power between the great states, emerged ready to take its place.

The struggle against the nobility

As the fight against the universality of church and Empire was being won, the monarchs were also making headway against feudal particularism. The two processes were, in fact, interrelated. Though the church was a universal organization, much of its power base was local in the form of bishoprics, churches, and abbeys, each with its own properties (including that source of all wealth, servile manpower), privileges, and immunities. Conversely, though the roots of the feudal nobility were usually local – each lord having his own estates and his own castle or castles – much of its

---

[53] The Bull *Zelo Domus Dei*, dated 20 November 1648, quoted in G. R. Cragg, *The Church in the Age of Reason 1648–1789* (Harmondsworth, UK: Penguin Books, 1960), p. 9.

position derived from its network of fealty and family connections that extended beyond individual realms. To make things worse, medieval monarchs themselves formed part of that network. There was scarcely a king whose entire holdings were located inside his own realm (whatever that may have meant); scarcely a king, too, whose realm was not riddled by independent and semi-independent principalities of every sort. In theory kings were supposed to be mightier than any of their subjects, possessing greater income, more land, and more vassals who could be made to do service in peace and war. In practice they were often the vassals of other men for at least part of their lands. As late as 1576 Jean Bodin in his *Six livres de la république* was able to argue that there was only one king, i.e., that of France, who was sovereign in all of his territories and did not owe homage to others for any of them; and, strictly speaking, he was right.

The speed with which, starting from this unfavorable situation, the position of kings was built up was not uniform but varied from one country to another. Occasionally it was subject to setbacks lasting for decades or more, which meant that a country that had advanced further on the way sank back into particularism and, as often as not, anarchy and war. A good example of the way in which an early movement toward centralization could backfire is provided by England. Thanks to the events of 1066, which meant that all English lands were in principle forfeit and could be distributed at will, William the Conqueror was able to rule England with an exceptionally strong hand. He built royal castles, held a comprehensive census (the famous Domesday Book), and sent out itinerant justices to enforce his will. His son William Rufus, who reigned from 1087 to 1100, maintained the Conqueror's achievement; but after the death of his second son, Henry I, the king's position started to deteriorate. First there took place the war of succession between Henry's daughter Matilda and her cousin Stephen (1135–42). This was resolved by the accession of Matilda's son Henry II, but not before he had granted his barons a charter and reaffirmed their rights in 1154. Though anything but a weak ruler, Henry II spent only fourteen of thirty-seven years in England. His last years were marred by the rebellion of his sons against whom, indeed, he died fighting.

Nor were things improved by the fact that Richard I the Lionheart (1189–99) chose to reign *in absentia*. He opened his reign by going on crusade in the Holy Land; on his return to Europe he was imprisoned and had to be ransomed. No sooner had he come home then he left England for the second time in order to fight for his possessions in France where he too met his death. Richard's brother John (1199–1216) tried to make good the damage done by his lion-hearted predecessor and originally it looked as if he might succeed. However, in 1204 the loss of his Duchy of

Normandy to the French king made him dependent on his English revenues alone. Attempting to squeeze the barons (and the church, with results that have already been pointed out), he quarreled with them and was forced to issue Magna Carta, in which he made extensive concessions to the nobility as well as the church and the towns. When Henry III (1216–72) succeeded John, the position of the monarchy touched nadir. Some of his own barons sided with the French dauphin Louis in his attempt to secure the English crown. Though that attempt was repulsed, Henry's reign ended, as it had begun, in civil war and, indeed, if England ever came close to disintegration it was during the seventh decade of the thirteenth century.

Thanks to the practice of marrying sons and daughters to the offspring of foreign princes, all of the above mentioned kings also possessed lands, or at any rate dynastic interests, in places as far apart as France, the Holy Roman Empire, Italy, and Spain. In the Middle Ages, war, far from being waged on behalf of the "public," was something that rival noblemen of all ranks engaged in to defend or extend their various possessions.[54] This required them to fight in person; and the need to fight in person explains why not only English monarchs but all others tended to lead itinerant lives that took them far away from the centers of their power. Thus German Emperors, to the extent that they were not away on crusade, spent much of their time campaigning in Italy. Some French monarchs also went on crusade but, even if they did not, were forever rushing around their domains in an attempt to prevent them from being partitioned by the Emperor, the kings of Aragon, Castile, Navarre, and England, the count of Flanders, and – particularly after 1356 – the dukes of Burgundy as well. There was, as yet, no foreshadowing of the idea that the territories of any single ruler ought to be unified by the nationality of his subjects, nor that they should have natural frontiers, nor even that they should be concentrated in one place rather than dispersed. Under such circumstances whatever progress toward centralization could be made was likely to be slow and, what is more, temporary. As often as not it backfired; sooner or later one's own native nobility was likely to rebel, join forces with a foreign invader, or both.

Beginning in the last decades of the thirteenth century, nevertheless, change was in the air. In England Edward I proved an exceptionally capable monarch. Putting an end to the rebellions that had plagued his father's reign, he pressured his magnates into rendering military service in Wales, Scotland, and France; he also built up the chancellery, the exchequer, and the royal justice system, all of which were now run on a

[54] See P. Contamine, *The Art of War in the Middle Ages* (Oxford: Blackwell, 1984), pp. 260–70.

professional basis and staffed by highly expert personnel.[55] His son, Edward II, became the first king to ascend the throne without being elected by the barons. Though this particular Edward was destined to be deposed and subsequently murdered by his wife, Isabella, and her lover, Mortimer,[56] an even stronger monarchy emerged under *his* son Edward III. By this time the characteristic English formula that a king ought to reign *in* Parliament had emerged and was in operation. Using it, Edward was able to obtain sufficient funds to start the Hundred Years War in order to make good his claim to the French throne; this was, it should be noted, an essentially personal cause (though of course he promised to share the loot with his vassals) rather than in any sense a "public" or "national" one. Though his conduct of the war was indecisive, at any rate there were no more baronial rebellions during Edward III's long reign (1327–77).

Much more than the heroism of the English longbowmen, the centralizing efforts of the Plantagenet monarchs explain why, though the kingdom that they headed was small and weak, they were able to contend with the much larger realm of France.[57] However, when Edward III died his son, Richard II, was only ten years old. For years he was helpless as various noble factions sought to manipulate the crown for their own purposes; the low point was reached when Parliament, led by a group known as the Lords Appellant, impeached his chancellor (1386) and set up a committee of eleven men to exercise the royal prerogative on his behalf.[58] Fighting back, Richard mounted a sort of *coup d'état*. Having declared his own majority in 1389, he was determined to emancipate himself from baronial rule by making himself the sole source of law, not bound by custom. To achieve this goal he tampered with the Rolls of Parliament; nullified statutes that had been agreed upon by both of the latter's houses; imposed a new oath on his provincial officers, the sheriffs; and sent his principal opponents into exile, and confiscated their lands right and left.

As events were to show, Richard, like his grandfather Edward III, was trying to do too much too fast. Once again rebellion was the result, and in 1399 he shared the fate of Edward II by being deposed and mur-

---

[55] See S. Carpenter, *The Rise of the Feudal Monarchies* (Ithaca, NY: Cornell University Press, 1951), pp. 75ff.

[56] See N. Fryde, *The Tyranny and Fall of Edward II 1321–1326* (New York: Cambridge University Press, 1979).

[57] See E. Perroy, *The Hundred Years War* (New York: Capricorn, 1965 edn.), pp. 34–60, for a comparison of the two adversaries.

[58] For these events, see J. S. Roskell, *The Impeachment of Michael de la Pole Earle of Suffolk, in 1386* (Manchester: Manchester University Press, 1984); and R. H. Jones, *The Royal Policy of Richard II: Absolutism in the Later Middle Ages* (Oxford: Blackwell, 1968), ch. 5.

dered. Under Henry IV and Henry V it looked as if the monarch had finally established itself; but this proved to be an illusion. Henry VI was just a year old when his father died in 1422. His minority was never officially ended, but from 1437 he was considered old enough to rule for himself. His main interests, however, were education and religion. Around him his noblemen fought for control – the more so since at least one of them, Richard, duke of York, by way of strict primogeniture had a better claim to the throne than the king himself. A period during which Henry was temporarily insane (1453–4) set the stage for the beginning of an armed struggle between the two branches of the English royal family, the House of York and the House of Lancaster. Henry, himself a Lancastrian, was captured in battle by the Yorkists (1461). The duke of York having died, Henry was deposed in favor of the latter's son who ascended the throne as Edward IV. He was released for the second time, fled to Scotland as a refugee, returned as the figurehead of an uprising against Edward, and was captured for a third time (1465). After being imprisoned in the Tower for five years, he was released, restored to the throne by the grace of a powerful nobleman, the earl of Warwick ("The Kingmaker"), defeated by the forces of Edward IV, and finally executed in 1471.

Nor did the so-called Wars of the Roses end at this point. Though he had briefly lost his throne to his predecessor in 1470, Edward IV, once restored in the next year, was able to reign in peace, and died in his bed (1483). Not so his two young sons Edward and Richard; within a matter of months they disappeared, apparently murdered by their uncle, Richard, Duke of Gloucester, who thereupon took the throne as Richard III. He had only just survived a noble rebellion led by the duke of Buckingham when yet another pretender to the throne, the Lancastrian Henry Tudor, left his exile in France and landed in Wales. Deserted by most of his supporters, Richard was defeated and killed in the Battle of Bosworth Field (August 1485), and Henry Tudor succeeded to the throne as Henry VII. Only then did the English crown cease to be the happy hunting ground of aristocratic faction.

Henry VII and, even more, his descendants Henry VIII and Elizabeth I, were finally able to establish their own ascendancy to the point that revolt on any scale no longer appeared practicable. Their principal instruments for doing so were the Court of Requests, the Prerogative Courts, and the dreaded Star Chamber, all of which shared the quality that they did not apply the common law. Instead of mobilizing armies of supporters as their fathers and grandfathers had done, nobles who fell foul of the crown were liable to be accused of treason and executed. By using confiscated church land to distribute favors on a grand scale, the monarchy was able to draw the upper levels of the aristocracy to itself.[59] In 1625 the accession of Charles I marked the first time in England's history when a new king felt sufficiently secure to refrain from executing some of his predecessors' noblemen and putting others in their place – a clear turning point. When civil war did break out once again in the 1640s, the nobility's status had been completely transformed. This time they did not mobilize their supporters and lead them against the king. Instead most of them were found fighting on his behalf and, later, sharing in his defeat as their estates were confiscated and they themselves driven into exile along with their master, the future Charles II.

Unlike their English colleagues, French barons never got to the point where they deposed their kings and executed them; still, in a different way, progress toward making the monarch not just *primus inter pares* but a real ruler was even slower. Both the population and the territory of France were much larger than those of England, making them more difficult to control. Even under ideal circumstances a letter sent from Paris to an outlying city such as Toulouse or Bordeaux might take between ten and fourteen days to arrive and as long again before an answer was received; but then circumstances were seldom ideal. Nor was there any question of a one-time conquest and consequent redistribution of all lands. Starting from the Ile de France, the realm was joined together piecemeal over a period of several centuries. It always contained independent enclaves as well as provinces whose laws, traditions, and even languages differed widely from each other.

Under such circumstances there could be no question of building a unified administration on the English model. Kings such as Philip II (1179–1223), Louis IX (1226–70), and Philip III (1270–85) had to proceed very carefully. They balanced the privileges of church, nobility, and urban communities against each other, all the while keeping a wary eye on their neighbors who stood ready to exploit any divisions that might arise to help themselves to outlying towns and provinces. To make things worse, the French system of inheritance differed from the English one. Time and time again vast royal appanages, i.e., nonhereditary estates, were created to support the reigning king's younger brothers on the scale that was considered their due; time after time they proved a source of trouble and had to be reabsorbed into the realm, sometimes by the use of force. Still, progress as measured by the increase of the number of royal servants such as seneschals, *prévôts*, and bailiffs was perceptible. Paid by the king – although, in practice, they tended to accumulate landed estates and turn into noblemen if they could – these royal servants supervised

[59] L. Stone, *The Crisis of the Aristocracy 1558–1641* (Oxford: Clarendon Press, 1965), ch. 8.

provincial affairs, levied taxes, and carried out the royal will in general.

These trends were particularly pronounced under Philip IV and his immediate successors, Louis X (1314–16), Philip V (1316–22), Charles IV (1322–8), and Philip VI (1328–50) in his early years. They began to take away seigneurial privileges, such as the right to strike money; introduced Roman law with its inherent centralizing tendencies;[60] appointed their own advisers to preside over courts in newly annexed provinces; and built up their positions as the "fount of justice," i.e., heads of the courts of appeals to which vassals could turn in cases brought against their lords and to which, indeed, the latter themselves were supposed to have resort. These measures were beginning to bear fruit when the Hundred Years War broke out in 1337. Unable to prevent invasion, the royal armies were defeated at Crecy (1346) and Poitiers (1356). This gave the signal for bands of English troops – some under royal control, others not – to pillage the helpless kingdom. They ranged far and wide not only in the northwest but in the south and southwest as well; the most famous of their raids covered no fewer than 600 miles and most of Languedoc before, laden with booty, it ended in Bordeaux. Meanwhile the French king, unable to come to his subjects' aid, saw his authority disintegrate.

The ground lost to the monarchy had only begun to be recovered during the last decades of the century when England, in the person of Henry V, found a formidable warrior. In 1415 he crossed the Channel and inflicted on the French the defeat of Agincourt. All of western France was now in Henry's hands or had made its peace with him; a real danger even existed of the kingdom being partitioned between the English and their Burgundian allies. Paris itself was lost in 1419, and in 1422 the Treaty of Troyes made Henry heir to the French throne. France's subsequent recovery had more to do with its people, as represented by Joan of Arc, the Maid of Orleans, than with the rule of the intermittently mad Charles VI (1380–1422). The turning point was reached in 1435 when Charles VII (1422–61) concluded the Treaty of Arras and split the Anglo-Burgundian alliance. In the next year he was able to reoccupy Paris; the English were finally driven out, their various French allies such as the duke of Brittany brought to heel, and royal control over the entire realm reestablished.

The Hundred Years War over, the task of rebuilding the authority of the French crown fell to Louis XI, whom we last met as he was establishing the rights of the monarchy over those of the church. The early years of his reign were hardly auspicious. The members of the higher nobility (including his brother, Charles of France) resumed the tradition

[60] P. Vinogradoff, *Roman Law in Medieval Europe* (Oxford: Clarendon Press, 1929), pp. 29ff.

of rebelling against him in the name of their ancient liberties. Intriguing with the king of England as well as with the duke of Burgundy, they formed the so-called League of the Public Weal with the aim of dividing up the government of France, plus the newly formed royal army, among themselves; the king's fortunes touched nadir in 1468 when, during a meeting with the duke of Burgundy, he actually found himself under house arrest. Having ended the war under humiliating conditions – huge pensions had to be paid to the rebellious lords – he was able to start rebuilding his authority. He freed the high nobility from their obligation to do homage to him as their liege lord, thus dispensing with the idea of mutuality; in its place he put a formula under which all alike were his subjects.[61] The number of tax-collectors was increased and royal taxation extended to additional territories that had previously been free from it. Provincial *parlements* were put under royal supervision, and a beginning was made on the construction of a comprehensive royal code of law in the hope of achieving greater centralization of justice.[62]

Still, Louis' greatest achievement was not of his own making. The occasion for it took place in 1477 when Charles the Bold, fighting the Swiss, was killed near the walls of Nancy. He left an only daughter, Marie, who was eighteen years old and who promptly found herself threatened by a rebellion of her own nobility in the Low Countries where she was staying at the time. The "damsel in distress" was rescued by the young Emperor Maximilian who literally arrived on a white horse and married her; however, by the time he did so, much of her inheritance both in France Comté and in Flanders had been occupied by Louis and nothing that Maximilian or his successors could do was ever able to change that fact.

Though the annexation of Burgundy did not bring the policy of creating royal appanages to an end, at any rate from now on it was no longer to resort to military force in order to reabsorb them into the realm. Louis' sons and successors Charles VIII (1483–98) and Louis XII (1498–1515) devoted themselves less to internal affairs than to a whole series of Italian campaigns, their goal being to carve out additional kingdoms for themselves. That they were able to do so was largely their father's achievement; when the constable of Bourbon, not having heard that the period of feudal anarchy had ended, rose in 1523 and conspired with Charles V he found only a few followers and was easily dealt with. More remarkable still, even the capture of Francis I at the Battle of Pavia in 1525 and his

---

[61] B. A. Poquet de Haut-Jusse, "Une idée politique de Louis XI: la subjection éclipse la vassalise," *Revue Historique*, 214, 1961, pp. 383–98.

[62] P. S. Lewis, "France in the Fifteenth Century: Society and Government," in Hale, et al., *Europe in the Late Middle Ages*, pp. 276–300.

subsequent imprisonment in Spain did not lead to any serious civil disturbances.

Toward the end of Francis' reign, though, the situation changed once again. Driven by the need for money for his anti-Habsburg campaigns, he initiated the policy whereby governorships of provinces were established and sold, either individually or in blocks comprising several at once, to the highest bidder. In general the purchasers proved to be members of the highest nobility such as the Guises, the Montmorencys, and the Rohans. Just at a time when their old feudal authority was ceasing to have any meaning, they were able to add the resources of office, such as emoluments and the proceeds of tax-farming, to their private ones; as in England a century earlier, this gave them a new lease on life and the capacity to stir up trouble.[63]

In 1559, when Henry II died unexpectedly as a result of a wound received during a joust, the results of this policy became evident. He left behind him a widow with an unsavory reputation, Catherine de Medici, as well as four sons, none of whom, as it turned out, were capable either of governing or of begetting an heir. By this time France, like other countries, was in the grip of the Reformation. As Catholics and Huguenots battled each other, they looked for leadership to their nobilities under the Houses of Guise and Condé respectively. No sooner was the war with Spain brought to an end by the Treaty of Cateau-Cambresis than civil war broke out. It was to last for some forty years and brought about as much destruction as any other episode in French history.

Anarchy peaked in 1589 when the last of Catherine's sons, Henry III, was assassinated. The heir apparent was now a distant relative, the future Henry IV, who was himself a Protestant and thus unacceptable to the majority. Engaged in a life-or-death struggle, both parties called on foreign rulers to assist them. The Huguenots repeatedly received Dutch money and English troops who were sent to defend – in reality, occupy – cities along the Atlantic coast. The Catholics on their part made use of papal mercenaries as well as inviting invasions by Prince Casimir of the Palatinate and Philip II of Spain, the latter their country's greatest enemy. Nine more years were to pass and several major battles had to be fought before Henry IV, who in the meantime had changed his religion, was able to establish his authority over the entire country.

Once established, Henry's reign proved to be relatively quiet. Not that it was safe: an amazing number of plots was hatched against him by various noblemen, most of them strict Catholics who refused to forget his Protestant origins or forgive his policy of tolerating the Huguenots. The

[63] G. Zeller, "Gouverneurs des provinces au seizième siècle," *Revue Historique*, 185, 1939, pp. 225–56.

last of these plots resulted in the king's assassination; the nature of the links that may have connected the actual murderer to the nobility and to Spain has never been cleared up.[64] That Henry's achievement was more of a personal nature than an institutional one is proved by the stormy history of the reigns of his successors, Louis XIII (1610–43) and Louis XIV (1643–1715). Both Richelieu and Mazarin saw the high nobility as the main enemies of the crown and did everything they could to reduce it to order. They razed such of its castles as were not located within the frontiers; they tried, though without much success, to forbid dueling; and they occasionally executed ringleaders *pour encourager les autres*.

Though Richelieu in particular is sometimes regarded as the real founder of the French state, actually the results were mediocre. The two cardinals succeeded in making themselves hated like few administrators before or since; throughout their terms of office, discontent, fueled partly by the heavy demand for taxes occasioned by France's intervention in the Thirty Years War and partly by religious strife, was widespread. Times beyond number, towns and peasantry rose in revolt and found persons among the higher – even highest – nobility to lead them. Many of the nobles themselves still acted as provincial governors; but now they found an additional cause for anger in the royal policy of adding another layer of officials in the form of the *intendants* who were appointed over their heads. One way or another, in forty years there were no fewer than eleven waves of revolts. Though not all were equally significant, all without exception were instigated, led, or at least joined by important noblemen. The last wave was known as the Fronde and was led by Prince Louis Condé whose surname of Bourbon is sufficient evidence of his status. It lasted from 1652 to 1658 and for a time even succeeded in holding Paris against the royal armies.

It was only when Louis XIV came of age in 1661 that a fundamental turning point was reached and the French nobility finally tamed in much the same way as the English one had been a century and a half before. The policy of depriving them of their provincial governorships and appointing *intendants* in their place was pushed through systematically. The very basis of their status was altered; completing a job begun by Henry IV, Colbert by means of his great *recherché de la noblesse* refused recognition to any titles except those demonstrably originating in a royal grant. Thousands of noblemen, particularly minor ones who did not have the financial means to fight their case in the provincial courts, lost their titles in this way. The remainder were stripped of their armed followings; the most important ones were given pensions and concentrated at court where the

[64] D. Bruisseret, *Henry IV* (London: Allen and Unwin, 1984), pp. 125ff.

king could keep an eye on them. Condé himself forgot about rebelling and, returning to obedience, put his formidable military talents at Louis' disposal. He ended his days rowing ladies around the lake at Versailles; his fellow noblemen were soon found wearing perukes and competing as to who would hold the king's chamber pot.

Whereas in both England and France there was at any rate a single king with no titular competitors, the same was not true in Spain. The country, with its complicated terrain, had been conquered province by province during centuries of military operations against the Muslims; as late as 1479 it consisted not of a single kingdom but of two separate ones, Castile and Aragon, whose laws and traditions were entirely different. In the former some measure of stability was first achieved by Henry II of the House of Trastamara (1369–79). His nicknames, Henry the Bastard and Henry the Fratricide, provide a sufficient explanation of the origins of his power and the way in which it was gained. His son John I (1379–90) was unremarkable; it was Henry III (1390–1406) who, playing the same role as Edward III in England, did most to reinforce the power of the crown *vis-à-vis* the nobility by building up royal institutions such as the council and the exchequer. Nevertheless the situation remained precarious. John (1406–54) succeeded his father as an infant. His entire reign was taken up by the quarrels of the nobility with his favorite, Alvaro de Luna, which finally made it necessary to confront and defeat the nobles in the Battle of Olmedo (1445).

The victory of Olmedo only settled the issue for the moment. When Henry IV took over in 1454, he inherited Luna, and again the result was several years of open civil war that lasted until the favorite was overthrown and executed. Though a capable commander – in 1464 he recaptured Gibraltar from the Muslims – Henry proved unable to dominate his nobles to the point that, in the very next year, they revolted and deposed him in effigy. The pretext for the quarrel was the succession which Henry wanted to give to his infant daughter. Spreading the rumor that he was impotent and therefore not her father, the magnates insisted that the throne should go to his half-sister Isabella, the real cause of the quarrel being, as usual, noble fears of royal centralization that would lead to the erosion of their privileges. At eighteen, Isabella herself confounded both her supporters and her opponents by eloping from the palace and secretly marrying Ferdinand II of Aragon. Thus the most important single event in the whole of Spanish history – the creation of a personal union of the two kingdoms – came about as the result of court intrigue and without the consent, or indeed the knowledge, of the king who supposedly was the most powerful in the peninsula.

In Aragon, as elsewhere, royal institutions made some progress during the fifteenth century[65] but this did not prevent its history from being as stormy as that of Castile. Ferdinand I (1412–16) was himself a Castilian prince. He owed his throne not to any hereditary succession but to his election by the Aragonese nobility which, of course, extracted its pound of flesh in the form of a famous coronation oath that made its obedience conditional on the monarch's good behavior. Alfonso V (1416–58) was a capable ruler who, however, spent most of his reign fighting to establish a claim over Sicily and southern Italy which he had inherited from his ancestors. In 1442, under the influence of his mistress Lucrezia de Alagno, he moved his court permanently to Naples. His wife and brother, who were left behind, were unable to control the nobility which did as it pleased and drove both the cities and the peasantry into revolt by its fiscal demands.

Then it was the turn of John II. Within three years of his accession he had to deal with a revolt in Catalonia, the most difficult province of all, where the magnates offered the crown to Peter of Portugal; when the latter died, still not satisfied, they appealed to Louis XI of France for aid against their master. The war lasted for nine years and very nearly cost John his crown before it could be brought to an end by the capture of Barcelona in 1471; even then the outcome was not the nobility's suppression but, on the contrary, a reaffirmation of its privileges accompanied by a general pardon for every ringleader but one, who was executed. John's son Ferdinand II, who later married Isabella, gained his own early military experience in these wars. Nor were the Castilian nobility at first inclined to accept him as their king. Instead they too called in the king of Portugal who himself had a dynastic claim. Discounting the years of the Aragonese revolt, it took the young couple ten years of near continuous war and, on Ferdinand's part, many heroic deeds before they were able to get themselves recognized in both countries. This did not prevent another major noble revolt in 1486, this time occasioned by the Catholic kings' attempt to recover land that had been alienated during the civil wars.[66]

Throughout this period Spain was undergoing what can only be called a process of aristocratization.[67] Not only did the members of all classes model their lifestyle upon that of the nobility, but the latter increased its economic power as its numbers declined to the point that, by the 1470s, there were only fifteen families of magnates left in Castile and two in

---

[65] J. M. Font y Ruis, "The Institutions of the Crown of Aragon in the First Half of the Fifteenth Century," in R. Highfield, ed., *Spain in the Fifteenth Century, 1369–1516* (New York: Harper, 1972), pp. 171–92.

[66] For these events, see T. N. Bisson, *The Medieval Crown of Aragon* (Oxford: Clarendon Press, 1986), pp. 133–61.

[67] Elliott, *Imperial Spain*, pp. 110ff.; L. Fernandez Suarez, "The Kingdom of Castile in the Fifteenth Century," in Highfield, *Spain in the Fifteenth Century*, pp. 95ff.

Aragon.[68] Against this background, progress in turning Castile and Aragon into a single country met with resistance on the part of both their assemblies and was abysmally slow. In 1507, following the expected death of Isabella and the unexpected one of her son, the duke of Medina Sidonia and the count of Urena revolted and threatened to dismantle Spain into its constituent parts. Using 4,000 troops, once again Ferdinand was able to gain the upper hand; however, by the time he died in 1516, the only tangible achievement toward the construction of common institutions was the introduction of a unified currency.

Under Charles V (Carlos I as he was known in Spain) and his son Philip II the grandees' landed holdings took on monstrous dimensions. In Salamanca, for example, some two-thirds of both the population and the territory found themselves under noble jurisdiction. One magnate alone, the Marquis Diego Lopez Pacheco, possessed no fewer than 25,000 square kilometers of land and 15,000 vassals who brought him 100,000 ducats a year; another, the Duke of Infantado, was lord of 800 villages and 90,000 vassals.[69]

Still, times were changing. Though the *reconquista* had been completed, the first two Habsburg kings needed the Castilian nobility's support against the towns and the middle classes who gave vent to their dissatisfaction by the revolt of the *communeros* in 1520–1. In return, they allowed them to exercise nearly absolute control over their estates, including seigneurial justice and the right to maintain private armies capable of holding their tenants in check. Thus reinforced in their positions the magnates finally made their peace with the royal government. Some of them entered its service as commanders and governors of overseas provinces – far from the center of power, it should be noted.

Not so in Aragon which, again thanks in large part to its nobility, was well on its way to becoming the most backward country in Western Europe. Nowhere else were feudal privileges as archaic or as extensive; during most of the sixteenth century the income which the province provided the crown was nil. Pursuing an old tradition, the grandees intrigued with their northern neighbor. This was carried to the point where there was some doubt whether, from the king's point of view, the province was an asset or merely a security risk.[70] In 1591 there was another revolt which took Philip II 14,000 troops to suppress.[71]

[68] See J. R. L. Highfield, "The Catholic Kings and the Titled Nobility of Castile," in Hale, et al., *Europe in the Later Middle Ages*, pp. 358–87.
[69] H. Kamen, *Spain 1469–1714: A Society of Conflict* (London: Longman, 1983), pp. 20, 155. Even higher figures are given by J. V. Vives, "The Economy of Spain During Ferdinand and Isabella's Reign," in Highfield, *Spain in the Fifteenth Century*, pp. 253–4.
[70] J. Lynch, *Spain Under the Habsburgs* (New York: New York University Press, 1981), vol. I, pp. 210–17.   [71] Elliott, *Imperial Spain*, pp. 279ff.

It was only then that the time for reckoning came. Though none of the province's institutions was abolished, they were reformed to reflect the royal will. For the first time the king gained the right to appoint non-Aragonese as governors. The monopoly of the nobility over the *justitia*, a kind of prototype constitutional court left over from the Middle Ages and intended to protect subjects against arbitrary government, was broken; its head was replaced by a royal official and the remaining members were made subject to recall at the king's pleasure. Finally, Philip reinforced the Inquisition – an instrument whose usefulness against political opponents as well as heretics had been demonstrated in Castile – by giving it a new fortified residence as well as a contingent of troops for its protection.[72] Thus it was only a few years before Philip's death that the task of bringing Aragon into line with the rest of the country was tackled and the independent power of the nobility finally broken, though this did not prevent further revolts during the seventeenth century.

In England, France, and Spain, the fight between crown and nobility at any rate proceeded more or less in the same direction and, sooner or later, yielded broadly similar results as the former was elevated far above the latter. This was not so in Germany where the situation was entirely different. However much the Holy Roman Empire was alive as an institution and as an idea – in spirit, one might say – its real power had been declining since the second half of the thirteenth century, a state of affairs that the Golden Bull of 1356 merely confirmed. Responsibility for the Emperors' weakness must be attributed to various factors including, not least, the sheer size of the countries they pretended to govern. On top of this came their struggle with the church on the one hand and their numerous commitments outside Germany on the other; rather than losing their independence, the most powerful members of the nobility were themselves able to build up their territories and launch them on the way to eventual statehood.

The factor that really opened their way was, once again, the Reformation. Until then the future of Germany had been in doubt; a modern historian has argued that an alliance between Emperor Maximilian with the south German cities in particular might have produced a united state.[73] The cities were, in the early years of the sixteenth century, at the peak of their power; as a contemporary rhyme put it, the splendor of Augsburg, the wit of Nuremberg, the artillery of Strasbourg, and the

---

[72] For these constitutional arrangements, see R. B. Merriman, *The Rise of the Spanish Empire* (New York: Cooper, 1962), vol. IV, pp. 595–9.

[73] T. A. Brady, *Turning Swiss: Cities and Empire, 1450–1550* (Cambridge: Cambridge University Press, 1985).

money of Ulm ruled the world.[74] By the 1520s all four, and a great many others as well, were giving Luther an enthusiastic welcome and were turning Protestant. Now the patrician merchant-bankers who ruled the towns in their own economic interests wanted nothing as much as peace and quiet. It is not inconceivable that they would have cooperated with Charles V against the territorial nobility; as they repeatedly told the Emperor, though, they were powerless to ignore the feelings of the common man and carry through his policy of enforcing religious uniformity. Conversely, if Charles himself ever contemplated relenting on the religious question we are ignorant of the fact. Given the firmness of his personal faith, he almost certainly did not – to say nothing of the effect that tolerating the Protestants would have had on his position as a universal, God-mandated Emperor.

During the first two decades of Charles' reign he was diverted away to other commitments in Spain, Hungary, Italy and North Africa. Hence he only returned to Germany in 1543–4, determined to tackle the problem. He brought with him Spanish troops under the command of the duke of Alba; at the Battle of Mühlberg in 1547, they easily scattered the haphazard forces assembled by the Schmalkaldic League of Protestant rulers. However, he had come twenty years too late. He was able neither to reestablish his authority over the cities nor to force them back into the Catholic camp; their defeat merely opened the way to the princes who were being encouraged by Henry II of France. The storm broke in 1552 when one prince, Maurice of Saxony, turned upon Charles, taking him unawares and forcing him to flee from Innsbruck to Villach in Carinthia. Short of funds, faced with renewed threats from the Turks in the Mediterranean and from Henry II in Lorraine, Charles struggled on for three more years. However, the attempt to reestablish Imperial power was hopeless and, as we saw, he abdicated in 1555. Meanwhile the princes, whether Protestant or Catholic, swept through the country like raging boars. They secularized church property and annexed cities right and left.

The way in which the princes themselves gained control over their nobilities is best exemplified by Bavaria.[75] During the fifteenth century, as a result of countless fratricidal wars, divisions, and redivisions, the nobility as represented in the Estates had remained almost the sole institution that held the country together. Their power peaked during the minority of Duke William IV (1508–50), i.e., the second decade of the sixteenth century; thereafter, though, it declined. The chink in the

---

[74] Quoted in K. H. Roth von Schrekenstein, *Das Patriziat in den deutschen Städten* (Tübingen: Laupp, 1856), p. 552.
[75] See F. L. Carsten, *Princes and Parliaments in Germany* (Oxford: Clarendon Press, 1959), pp. 357ff.

Estates' armor proved to be the huge debts undertaken both by William himself and by his successor, Albrecht V (1550–79). Repeatedly these debts threatened to bring government to a halt; repeatedly the Estates were compelled to assume them. Meanwhile a combination of ducal bullying and chicanery ensured that they should neither be able to maintain their own collecting machinery nor gain a veto on the contracting of future obligations. Nor were the Estates able to stop the dukes from obtaining more money by taxing their own peasants and, on pain of secularization, the church. The fact that he had money, or at any rate could obtain it on his own or his Estates' credit, enabled Albrecht to insist on taking only Catholics into his service. By the time of his death the Bavarian Counter-Reformation, and with it the construction of a close alliance between church and throne, was well under way.

The example set by Bavaria was followed, though later rather than sooner, by many of the remaining principalities including Prussia, Saxony, Hesse, Württemberg, and Austria. However, a difference did exist between Prussia and other parts of Germany. In the former the power of the nobility over its peasantry tended to grow after 1550 as hereditary serfdom was introduced and many old feudal burdens reimposed.[76] Though serfdom also existed elsewhere in Germany, at any rate a class of free peasants was permitted to continue and some of them were even able to achieve modest prosperity. Furthermore, the nobility's powers of police and jurisdiction were less extensive than in Prussia.

The German princes' march toward greater control over their nobilities was interrupted by the Thirty Years War, when most of them were reduced to playthings in the hands of much greater rulers whose forces invaded Germany from all directions. In 1648, though, it was resumed; there was nothing that contemporaries wanted more than law and order. This time the example was set by Frederick William of Prussia (1640–88). Nicknamed the Great Elector, he levied taxes in order to raise troops and then used the troops to send the Estates packing. His successor Frederick I gathered the fruits of his policy and, having obtained the Emperor's permission, was able to have himself declared king in Boroussia. Germany's remaining princes had to content themselves with less exalted titles; by way of compensation they built miniature imitations of Versailles and competed among themselves as to who could design the most extravagant uniforms for their troops. The Estates had not been defeated everywhere; in Württemberg in particular they remained alive and well. Still, and as the Treaty of Westphalia had confirmed, by the third quarter of the seventeenth century those among Germany's count-

[76] Carsten, *A History of the Prussian Junkers* (Aldershot: Scholar Press, 1989), pp. 7–16.

less principalities large enough to be considered something more than their rulers' private property were themselves turning into states.[77]

The monarchs' victory over their nobilities was, in some ways, bought at the expense of the rest of society. Except in England, where the Revolution of 1688 brought all classes under the common law, many of their privileges survived intact. Though varying from one place to another, normally these privileges included special juridical status, i.e., the right to be tried by courts made up of members of their own class and exemption from the more degrading forms of punishment; freedom from certain forms of taxation, both direct and indirect; and a near-monopoly over top positions in the administration, in the army, and at court. In addition to this, there were such symbolic *marques* as the right to meet the sovereign face to face, wear a sword, hunt (a right no longer economically significant to the members of the upper classes, but much resented by those of the lower ones to whom it was denied), and to maintain a family coat of arms.[78] No wonder that from this time until the cataclysm of 1789 – until, indeed, the upheavals of 1848 – whenever the monarchs were threatened the nobility rallied to their side. It stood by them, fought with them, and, as in France during the Terror, sometimes died with them as well. The deal that it cut with the throne was highly successful. Sometimes, as in Prussia and Spain, it was able to arrest the development of the towns while at the same time retaining and even extending its feudal rights over its own tenants.

However, the price of privilege was a loss of independence. From being he crown's competitors, the nobility was turned into its associates. From wearing armor, rallying to the royal cause, and carrying their own banners while fighting for it they were, shortly after 1648, made to don uniforms and thus literally turned into "the king's men." After that date not even the greatest nobleman in any country could hope to play the role of a Warwick, a Guise, a Condé, a Tilly, or a Wallenstein – to say nothing of the fact that, as the Holy Roman Empire declined and several kings assumed "Imperial" rights, the confirmation of old titles and the creation of new ones had itself turned into a royal monopoly. As the eighteenth century went on, the nobility's gradual loss of an independent role made its privileges more and more difficult to justify in the eyes of society at large. Before they could be abolished, though, the instruments which would enable royal power to assert itself had to be built.

---

[77] See V. G. Kiernan, *State and Society in Europe, 1550–1650* (New York: St. Martin's, 1980), ch. 9, for a short survey of developments in Germany.

[78] For a discussion of French *marques* to *noblesse* in particular, see E. Schalk, *From Valor to Pedigree: Ideas of Nobility in France in the Sixteenth and Seventeenth Centuries* (Princeton: Princeton University Press, 1986), ch. 7.

The struggle against the towns

Church, empire, and nobility aside, the fourth type of political organization that had to be overcome before the modern state could be created
were the urban communities. Particularly in Southern Europe, many of
these communities were leftovers from Roman times; if the people and
institutions did not display continuity from classical times, at any rate the
physical sites and sometimes the streets and fortifications did. Others
grew up spontaneously as distribution centers at places which were
convenient for trade – i.e., near mines, where roads crossed, or where
rivers entered lakes or became navigable – whereas others still, particularly in Germany, were artificial creations set up by secular and ecclesiastical princes of every rank who, seeking to attract trade, either granted
privileges to existing communities or else established completely new
ones. By 1340, just before the towns were decimated by the Black Death,
it is believed that approximately one-tenth of the entire population of
Western Europe – estimated as 60 million – lived in hundreds upon
hundreds of towns, albeit, for our calculations to reach such a figure, any
settlement with more than 5,000 inhabitants has to be included in the
list.[79]

From the beginning towns were corporate bodies. Whatever the extent
of their privileges and the way in which they were gained, these were
granted not to individuals but to all citizens who, being sharply differentiated from the rural population, possessed "free" – that is, nonservile –
status. In this way towns contradicted the very principles of feudal government which were based on the interlocking rights of superiors over
inferiors; nevertheless, from the point of view of the would-be centralizing
monarchs, the problem that the towns presented was much the same as
that posed by the nobility. Just as each nobleman was, to some extent, his
own lord and exercised power inferior to, but not essentially different
from that of the king, so towns had their own organs of government. This
included one or more elected chief magistrates known under a variety of
titles: *echevins* (France and the Netherlands), *consules* (Italy), *Schöffen*
(Germany), and *regidores* (Spain). In addition, towns had a variety of
other officials and a municipal council, both of them also elected; a
separate system of municipal dues; the right to make their own assess-
ments for the purpose of collecting royal taxes; and sometimes, by way of
an institution that was both profitable and symbolic, a mint as well.

Finally, towns differed from villages in that, on top of these privileges,
they possessed their own fortifications, guards responsible for the main-

---

[79] F. R. Bairoch, et al., eds., *La population des villes européennes* (Geneva: Droz, 1988), pp.
253–4.

tenance of public order, and, in the form of militias (particularly in Italy), mercenaries, their own armed forces.[80] To one extent or another this organization and these forces – backed by wealth derived from trade and manufacturing – enabled them to assert their independence both against their original founders and against the higher authority represented by the king; this capability often extended to the point of declaring and waging open war.

Also like noblemen, the influence of the towns was not purely local but supplemented by the connections that they maintained with each other across territorial borders. Trading relations represented one foundation on which such connections could be built; another was the commonality of institutions, given that newly established towns were often given, or else took for themselves, the laws and political organization of existing ones and were sensitive to any attempt to take them away. Whatever the basis for their feelings of solidarity, they often formed alliances or leagues aimed at securing the roads, maintaining the peace, and defending their interests in regard to freedom from tolls and the like. The most famous associations were those of northern Italy on the one hand and of Germany on the other. The former were created as early as the twelfth century. They successfully fought the German Emperors at Legnano in 1176, and were soon to witness the cultural flowering known as the Renaissance. The latter included the Rhineland League, the Swabian League, the Alliance of Heidelberg, and of course the Hansa. The last-named peaked during the fourteenth and fifteenth centuries when it held regular congresses and, thanks to its economic and naval power, was able to interact on equal terms with kings and Emperors. At that time it united some 100 trading towns scattered from the northern Netherlands all the way to the eastern Baltic.

Above all, medieval towns were often able to take advantage of the conflicts between the various monarchs, princes, and noblemen to press for their own interests and even conduct their own foreign policy. As fortified places they could refuse entry to one side or another, thus making it necessary to engage in a long and costly siege; as centers of wealth and manufacture they could demand political concessions in return for men, money, and arms. This was all the more so because, as the latter became more sophisticated following the introduction of gunpowder, they could no longer be provided by any rural blacksmith but had to be sought exclusively within or around the towns. As might be expected, the demands most frequently raised were for self-government on the one hand and immunity to various forms of taxation on the other. Seen from

[80] For a recent account of medieval urban institutions, see S. Reynolds, *Kingdoms and Communities in Western Europe, 900–1300* (Oxford: Clarendon Press, 1984), ch. 6.

this point of view, the rise of the great monarchies is largely the story of their rulers' attempts to reduce or eliminate those twin privileges.

As in the case of the nobility, the manner and speed with which the process was carried out differed markedly from one country to another. As in the case of the nobility, too, the results were broadly similar insofar as they led to the establishment of a strong central authority that towered above everybody else. It was most easily accomplished in England. Thanks partly to its insular position, partly to the Conquest, it became a unified country at an exceptionally early time; consequently the towns were unable to play off the king against foreign rulers as they did in so many other places. From the beginning, the towns' most important enemy consisted of the nobility, whose turbulence threatened to disrupt peaceful trade. Their natural ally was the crown; they soon became integrated with the royal administration, bearing those burdens and performing those tasks which for one reason or another it did not choose to undertake itself.[81] Although during the civil wars that marked the last years of Henry III there were some signs of dissatisfaction in the towns also,[82] these never reached the point where they rose in rebellion. On the contrary, already at the beginning of the fourteenth century the position was reached where, by simply issuing a chancery writ, the king and his officials were able to call on the services of any borough throughout England.

The relatively subordinate position of the towns meant that they could retain their old charters, or be granted new ones, without the central government feeling itself threatened.[83] It also permitted the uninterrupted development of their institutions which, in essence, continued in existence until the great reforms of the nineteenth century took power out of the hands of the urban oligarchies. Backed by royal power, their officials were able to avoid the ferocious struggles between guilds and patriarchate that marked their counterparts in every other country; moreover, the position of the towns explains why, though medieval England was as subject to noble revolts as any other country, from the time of Edward I on those revolts already bore a somewhat superficial character. The normal way in which aristocratic factions sought to gain control of the crown was by engaging in intrigue at court. At intervals they would also chase each other across the countryside, particularly in the north

[81] C. R. Young, *The English Borough and Royal Administration, 1130–1307* (Durham, NC: Duke University Press, 1961), pp. 16, 155–61.

[82] S. Reynolds, *An Introduction to the History of English Medieval Towns* (Oxford: Clarendon Press, 1977), pp. 109–10.

[83] From 1500 to 1700, no fewer than 160 new English towns were incorporated: P. Clark and P. Slack, *English Towns in Transition 1500–1700* (New York: Oxford University Press, 1976), p. 128.

where one side or both could often call on the Scots to join the fray. Given the noninvolvement of the towns and the early collapse of feudalism in England, the only people they could rely on for their quarrels were their personal retainers and such volunteers as chose to join the cause. Consequently their numbers were always small. However hard they might try, they seldom succeeded in disrupting the life of the country at large. Even at Bosworth Field, the battle that put an end to the Wars of the Roses and brought the House of Tudor to the throne, the effectives on both sides counted fewer than 10,000.

It was only during the Civil War that the situation underwent a temporary change. Most historians agree that the revolt against Charles I was initiated by the gentry, landed property-owners who made up no less than three-quarters of the House of Commons.[84] Still, it was the towns, with London at their head, that provided the financial muscle as well as the appropriate ideology in the form of Puritanism. The towns' readiness to involve themselves in the war meant that it was fought on a far larger scale, and wrought much more destruction, than any of its predecessors; this was all the more so because England had become, owing to the decline of the nobility as a military case, essentially an open country with few modern fortifications capable of withstanding serious attack. What saved the situation was the fact that, following a century and a half of powerful Tudor monarchs, the central government's control over the entire realm had long ceased to be questioned. The Protectorate that emerged from the war was, if anything, stronger and more centralized than the monarchy whose place it took. And indeed it was Cromwell who launched England, hitherto much smaller and weaker than either France or Spain, on its way to the status of a great power that it was to occupy in the eighteenth century.

Whereas English towns put few obstacles in front of the central authority, the same was not true of other countries including, above all, Italy and Germany. In Italy with its Roman traditions, towns arrived early and may, indeed, never have disappeared altogether. Though some of them were ruled by bishops, with hardly any exceptions they were neither founded by members of the feudal nobility nor governed by them.[85] From the beginning they stood out sharply from the countryside; far from having to be emancipated from it by the grant of privileges, the strongest of them started to conquer it in order to create an agricultural

[84] L. Stone, *The Causes of the English Revolution, 1529–1642* (London: Routledge, 1972), pp. 91ff.
[85] For the characteristics of Italian cities during this period, see G. Chittolini, "Cities, 'City-States,' and Regional States in North-Central Italy," in C. Tilly and W. P. Blockmans, eds., *Cities and the Rise of States in Europe, AD 1000 to 1800* (Boulder: Westview Press, 1989), pp. 28–44.

and commercial hinterland for themselves. Endless wars, most of them originating in commercial rivalry, also divided the towns from each other. As these wars caused the smaller ones to fall by the wayside, five large towns – Genoa, Venice, Milan, Florence, and Rome – emerged and succeeded in turning themselves into what were, for most intents and purposes, fully independent political communities. The power of the cities, both inside Italy and outside it by way of the networks of trade and banking that they created, peaked during the second half of the fifteenth century.

However, domination over others usually has its price and the Italian towns were no exception. As the most eminent of Florence's historians, Francesco Guicciardini, was well aware, ancient city-states such as Sparta, Athens, and Rome traced their origins to the voluntary symbiosis of villages. Engaging in its career of conquest, Rome in particular had been able to turn its Italian subjects into willing allies with whom, until the "social war" of 90–89 BC, it shared fortunes good and bad. Not so medieval Italian towns. As they made their power felt outside their walls, they did not incorporate the inhabitants of the countryside (including such smaller towns as it contained) into their citizen-bodies; instead they merely sought to exploit them by means of tolls, taxes, and various other forms of economic discrimination designed to prevent the development of industry.[86] Not only were they unable to count on their subjects to fight for them, but they even required armed force to hold them down. Consequently they were never able to create national armies but were forced to rely on mercenaries instead. The latter, besides occasionally turning against their employers and taking over, were expensive and seldom inclined to fight too hard.

The results of this policy became apparent in the years after 1494. In terms of economic and cultural accomplishment Italy led the world; however, neither quantitatively nor qualitatively could Italian armies match the much stronger foreign ones that invaded the peninsula and fought each other on its territory. Often, indeed, those foreigners were welcomed by at least part of the population which sought (as in Pisa) to reestablish its independence or (as in Florence) to replace oligarchic by democratic rule or *vice versa*. For over half a century northern Italy in particular was turned into a battlefield. Here Spaniards, French, and Imperialists – each in their turn supported by ferocious Swiss mercenaries – fought each other; as they were conquered and reconquered, one after another the cities lost their independence to central governments,

---

[86] F. Bocchi, "Città e campagna nell'Italia centro-settentrionale (secc. XII–XIV)," *Storia della Città*, 10, 1986, pp. 101–4; M. Berengo, "Città e contado in Italia dal XV al XVII secolo," *Storia della Città*, 10, 1986, pp. 107–11.

albeit such as were introduced from other countries. Notwithstanding Machiavelli's hopes as expressed in the last chapter of *The Prince*, out of the five candidates only two, Venice and Rome, succeeded in surviving as independent states. Venice, its days of economic greatness gone after 1550, was too small to play a significant political role and soon came to lead the dreamlike existence so well portrayed in the paintings of Canaletto, whereas Rome, by virtue of its unique ecclesiastical character, was and remained opposed to everything that an Italian state might have stood for.

In Germany towns were more numerous, and their origins more diverse, than anywhere else. Some, particularly in the south, had very ancient roots, having been established as Roman colonies; others, particularly in the north, were created completely *ex novo* during the great period of eastward migration between the eleventh and early fourteenth centuries.[87] For the northern towns in general, and for those united in the Hansa (originally meaning *An-See*, "on the sea") in particular, the turning point in their fortunes came during the second half of the fifteenth century. It was connected to a shift in the habitat of their chief product, herring, as well as growing Dutch commercial competition that led to their economic decline.[88] Whereas in England (and, as we shall see, France) there was usually the king to protect the towns against the worst that the nobility could do, in Germany the Emperor was too weak and remote to play that role – the more so because the center of his power was already beginning to shift to Bohemia and the Danube.

Thus, already in 1442–8 the elector of Brandenburg took advantage of the disputes between the patriarchate and the guilds of Berlin to deprive the town of its right of self-rule. From about 1480 on we begin to hear of cases in which townspeople were refused the right to harbor runaway peasants, were subjected to various tolls, and were even forced to render labor services such as hauling the lord's goods. By 1500 there were no free towns left in Brandenburg; in time the system was extended throughout Prussia. The legal differences between town and countryside were largely eliminated, all alike coming under the dukes' despotic rule. By the eighteenth century, instead of breathing the spirit of liberty and participating in the commercial revolution that was making English and French cities rich, any Prussian town that was selected to house a royal garrison considered itself lucky.

Some of the Hansa's members awoke to the dangers that faced them shortly after 1500. A number of congresses were held and various

---

[87] See H. Stoob, *Forschungen zum Städtwesen in Europa* (Cologne: Boehlau, 1979), vol. I.
[88] On the fate of the north German towns, see F. L. Carsten, *The Origins of Prussia* (Oxford: Clarendon, 1954), pp. 109ff.

schemes set afoot to reform the association and give it a more centralized character – including what it lacked most, a system of taxation and a common army. It was, however, a question of too little too late. German towns, though numerous, tended to be smaller than their Italian counterparts.[89] Surrounded by a very large number of petty noble domains, most of them had never been able to develop an independent power base by expanding into the surrounding countryside. Over the next hundred years some of them were simply annexed by the rulers of Denmark, Sweden, and Prussia with whom they had formerly been able to deal on equal terms. Others, though they retained their independence as free cities, sank into political – although, as the example of Frankfurt and Hamburg shows, not always economic – insignificance. The Thirty Years War hit some towns much harder than it did others; nevertheless, by demonstrating the Hansa's military impotence, it set the tombstone on the latter's grave. As a matter of fact some attempts were made to revive the association after 1648, but with little success.[90] Only in the eastern Baltic, where the kings of Poland proved too weak to play a role analogous to that of the German princes, did a few towns such as Danzig retain their privileges into the eighteenth century.

Dominating the great trading routes between Southern and Northern Europe as they did, and often containing valuable minerals on their territory, south German towns were generally more successful in maintaining their prosperity than north German ones. For a time around 1500 it looked as if they had the option of turning Swiss, that, is, of creating a genuine alliance between town and countryside that would enable them to resist the encroachment of the territorial princes. As in Italy, though, these plans were defeated by the oligarchic outlook of the commercial elites which cared only for their own interests, narrowly defined. The Peasants' Revolt of 1525 frightened the south German towns. Abandoned by an Emperor whose worldwide commitments made him manifestly unable to protect them, thereafter they were generally inclined to cooperate with the princes.

As had happened in the north, some towns were annexed outright and were henceforward subject to direct government by the princes' appointees. Others, retaining free or Imperial status, found themselves bypassed by history and deserted by trading routes which were shifting to the Atlantic; they sank into a torpor that lasted until the French Revolution

---

[89] In 1500 the largest German town, Augsburg, numbered 50,000 against over 100,000 for Venice or Milan. For some figures, see E. Ennen, *The Medieval Town* (Amsterdam: North Holland Publishing, 1979), pp. 187–9.

[90] See P. Dollinger, *The German Hansa* (London: Macmillan, 1964), part III, for the attempts to resuscitate the Hansa and its final decline.

and beyond. Perhaps the most fortunate ones were those selected as a *Residenz* or capital for the newly consolidating territorial states such as Munich, Mannheim, and Coblenz;[91] Vienna, from where Ferdinand I ruled the newly consolidated hereditary lands, was even able to achieve politico-economic leadership over the entire Danube basin. Here and elsewhere, however, there was a price to be paid. In 1521–2, following an abortive revolt, Vienna's privileges – including the right to maintain a mint – were revoked. Municipal elections came to an end, and the Burgomaster, one Siebenburger, was executed.

Somewhere in between those extremes fell France and Spain. In the former, relations between crown and towns closely paralleled those between crown and nobility. Some progress toward asserting royal control over both was made from the days of Philip IV on; as in the case of the nobility, though, the French kings lost their towns during the Hundred Years War when many of them, caught between the adversaries, were forced to negotiate on their own behalf and strike the best bargain they could. Particularly during the critical period of the war from 1415 to 1435, many towns behaved almost as if they were independent political entities. Abandoned by the king, they conducted their own foreign policy and often used their own armed forces in order to defend themselves against the depredations of all and sundry. Nor did this kind of thing come to an end after 1435. Many towns found themselves inside the newly consolidated realm and thus at the king's mercy. However, others – particularly those located near the frontiers of Burgundy – were able to continue playing the old games.

From 1439 to 1559 French kings, though not fundamentally opposed to the autonomy of their *bonnes villes*, did everything in their power to make them amenable to their demands, particularly in regard to finance.[92] Charles VII himself showed the way, renewing royal taxes such as the *taille* and the *gabelle* on communities which were liberated from English rule and occasionally using force to suppress those which, like Lyons, refused to pay.[93] Likewise, Louis XI aimed at making sure that they would obey the royal justice, supply royal armies as they passed through, and pay taxes. Given that his position was much stronger than that of his father, he sometimes went so far as to nominate their magistrates directly; normally, though, his method was to have the council

[91] H. Patze and G. Streich, "Die landesherrlichen Residenzen im spätmittelalterlichen Deutschen Reich," *Blätter für Deutsche Landesgeschichte*, 118, 1982, pp. 202–20.
[92] See B. Chevalier, *Les bonnes villes de France du XVe au XVIe siècle* (Paris: Aubier Montaigne, 1982), for a general account.
[93] R. Fedou, "A Popular Revolt in Lyons in the Fifteenth Century: The *Rebeyne* of 1436," in P. S. Lewis, ed., *The Recovery of France in the Fifteenth Century* (New York: Harper, 1971), pp. 242–64.

submit a list of three names to the bailiff to choose from. By the end of his reign many of the towns' fortifications were falling into ruin and their militias were no longer active.[94]

As in the case of the nobility, French towns were given a new lease on political life during the religious wars. Spreading from Geneva, the French Reformation differed from the German one in that it never really took hold among the masses in the countryside. Instead it was most influential among noblemen (including, in particular, noblewomen) on the one hand and townspeople on the other. Time after time the Catholic majority, composing 90–5 percent of the population, turned against their Huguenot neighbors in massacres great and small. Forced to defend themselves, from 1560 on they turned the country into a veritable archipelago of semi-independent communities, each with its well developed organs of government and armed forces. As the term "League" itself shows, both Catholic and Huguenot cities formed alliances among themselves as well as with noblemen of their respective creeds (sometimes, when pecuniary interests predominated, those of other creeds). All fought each other in a desultory way, at times allying themselves with the crown and at other times opposing it even to the extent of taking the king prisoner. Though open warfare ceased under Henry IV the underlying reality remained much the same. Communal independence was, indeed, reinforced by the Edict of Nantes which, besides granting the Huguenots freedom of worship, permitted them to maintain their own fortifications and their own armed forces. These privileges go a long way toward explaining why, throughout the time of disturbances from 1610 to 1661, the towns were able to play a role similar to that of the nobility and to cause the monarchy as much trouble as the latter.

Where the towns' internal government was concerned Henry IV chose not to introduce any revolutionary changes. The fifteenth-century system whereby the lists of candidates for the mayoralty were submitted to the king remained in force; though Henry sometimes overrode his subjects' proposals, this was not always the result of deliberate policy, since in some cases it merely reflected the towns' own inability to come up with an agreed-upon list. His ambiguous attitude was reflected in contemporary opinion concerning Paris, the most important city of all. Some thought Henry never interfered in the city's affairs, others that he was systematically trying to eliminate its independence. The truth seems to have been somewhere in between. In Paris and elsewhere the king made his power felt when the danger of tumults, or fiscal needs, rendered intervention necessary. From time to time he also saw a need to keep a well-

[94] B. Chevalier, "The Policy of Louis XI Toward the *Bonnes Villes*: The Case of Tours," in Lewis, *Recovery of France*, pp. 265–93.

known opponent from taking office or else used the offices themselves as a way of bestowing favor at no cost to himself. Otherwise, though, he was inclined to leave them alone.[95]

In the long run, much more dangerous to municipal independence were the attempts of Sully, as secretary to the treasury, to bring their finances under his supervision. As a condition for authorizing taxation, he demanded that they submit their accounts every three years; in time, this would have given him effective control. In the event both Sully and his master passed from the scene before that control was complete, leaving the task to Mazarin during his later years. To recall a few landmarks only, in 1655 an anti-fiscal revolt at Angers led to a three-month occupation of the town by royal troops under the *intendants*; the age-old system of municipal elections was definitely suppressed and *maire* and *echevins* were replaced by royal appointees. Aix, having revolted in 1658, suffered a similar fate. When Marseilles revolted in the same year, it was treated by Mazarin almost as an occupied city; troops were quartered on it, parts of the wall were razed, the urban militia disbanded, the inhabitants disarmed, a new citadel built, and the very title of *consul* traditionally carried by the elected magistrates abolished. In 1692 Louis XIV completed the process by putting an end to the election of magistrates in all French towns. From then on, it was the *intendants* who ruled.[96]

In Spain, thanks largely to the wars against the Muslims which forced successive kings to look to them for support, the tradition of self-governing towns was as strong as anywhere else.[97] However, during the last decades of the fifteenth century those wars were coming to an end. The Catholic kings were anxious to whittle away the towns' independence; the latter on their part were weary of anarchy and ready for a lead. Already since the fourteenth century occasional *corregidores* had been sent to some Castilian towns to oversee their affairs – then as now, the phrase "I am from the government; I am here to help you" was one of the greatest lies in any language. In 1480 it was decided to introduce them into all towns which did not yet have them and to make their office permanent. Originally judicial officers, subsequently the *corregidores* also acquired administrative authority. They acted as *de facto* royal governors, controlling all aspects of municipal administration including, in particular, finance. So long as Ferdinand and Isabella remained alive the system

---

[95] Bruisseret, *Henry IV*, pp. 164–6.
[96] For the story of how one French town lost its independence, see R. A. Schneider, "Crown and Capitoulat: Municipal Government in Toulouse, 1500–1789," in P. Benedict, ed., *Cities and Social Change in Early Modern France* (London: Unwin Hyman, 1989), ch. 6.
[97] See P. Fernandez Albaladejo, "Cities and the State in Spain," in Tilly and Blockmans, *Cities and the Rise of States in Europe*, pp. 170–3, for the relations between crown and cities during this period.

worked to the satisfaction of both sides. After their deaths, though, Charles V during his first brief sojourn in Spain in 1516–19 misused it to reward his favorites most of whom were both foreigners and ill qualified for the job; it was no wonder that the towns' ire was aroused.

When Charles, seeking the Imperial crown, turned his back on Spain in 1519, the towns thought that their time had come. Among the middle classes and artisans, resistance to aristocratic encroachment had been simmering for decades; now an additional grievance was found in the form of newly imposed royal taxes.[98] The sign for the rebellion was given in May 1520 when Toledo expelled its *corregidor*. In the next month the revolt spread to most of the cities of Old Castile. One by one they expelled royal officials and tax collectors – a few were unlucky enough to get killed in the process – and proclaimed a *communidad*. In July the representatives of four cities met at Avila. They set up a revolutionary *junta* which drove the regent, Adrian of Utrecht, out of Valladolid and established a rival government. The movement peaked in September when, now representing fourteen of eighteen towns and backed by an army of its own, the *junta* proclaimed that the kingdom stood above the king and that they themselves represented the kingdom. After initial hesitation, the regent reacted by coopting the representatives of the high nobility into the government. Mobilizing their forces as well as his own, he defeated the rebels at the Battle of Villalar in April 1521. The various towns were besieged in turn, until finally Toledo itself was forced to capitulate in October 1521.

Simultaneously with the *communeros*, the *germanias*, or popular associations, of Aragon wrested control of the cities out of the hands of the authorities, though the two movements never cooperated. As in Castile, the rebellion was carried principally by the middle classes and aimed as much against the growing power of the aristocracy as against the crown. As in Castile, too, it was the latter that emerged the victor when the movement was suppressed. However, the Spanish crown was less successful than the French one in balancing the nobility against the towns. In Aragon they were all but abandoned to the tender mercies of the grandees who for several centuries to come did everything they could to turn the country into a Mediterranean Poland. In Castile, defeat left them powerless, enabling Charles V and Philip II to suck them dry by means of royal monopolies, export duties, forced loans, and the repeated seizure of imported bullion.[99] Committed years in advance to support Spain's

---

[98] For the history of the *communeros* movement, see S. Haliczer, *The Communeros of Castile: The Forming of a Revolution, 1475–1521* (Madison: University of Wisconsin Press, 1981); and A. W. Lovett, *Early Habsburg Spain, 1517–1598* (Oxford: Oxford University Press, 1986), pp. 30ff.

[99] See data in R. Trevor Davies, *The Golden Century of Spain* (London: Macmillan, 1961), pp. 180ff.

military campaigns in the Mediterranean and, later on, the Netherlands, not even the growing flow of silver arriving from the New World could save the Castilian economy. The first signs of urban decay, occasioned very largely by the impossible demands of royal taxation which they were unable to resist, became evident in the 1560s.[100] Their piteous appeals for relief were to no avail. Between 1600 and 1700 Castile's urban population (except that of Madrid) fell by more than half,[101] thus launching Spain on the road to the economic and social backwardness from which it was to start emerging only after the Napoleonic conquest and, indeed, in the late twentieth century.

Finally, in two countries – Switzerland and the Netherlands – the towns, far from surrendering to royal government, were themselves able to take over. The greatest achievement of the Swiss towns consisted in that, unlike their Italian counterparts, they never lost the loyalty of the countryside – the cantons – over which they ruled.[102] As Machiavelli in *L'arte della guerra* noted, after Fornovo in 1494 Italian armies became notorious for their ineffectiveness, melting away before the first shock. Not so Swiss ones, which for several centuries past had built up a well-deserved reputation for courage and even ferocity. Consequently they were able to resist the Habsburg attempts to dominate them; later they were equally successful in fighting off the rulers of Burgundy, France, and Savoy. Having done so, they switched to the offensive and consolidated from a patchwork of scattered districts, connected only by mountain passes, to a fairly coherent country. Though formal secession from the Empire came only in 1648, long before that Zurich, Bern, and the rest had built a loose confederation that was practically independent. Already it was adopting the policy of armed neutrality that was to characterize it in future centuries. Interrupted only by the wars of the French Revolution, it lasted until the outbreak of a brief civil war led to the creation of a modern Swiss state in 1847.

From 1384 on the Netherlands, hitherto a motley assembly of provinces ruled by a variety of dukes and counts, had fallen under the domination of the House of Burgundy, which acquired them one by one. They underwent the same centralizing tendencies that prevailed in other countries; and indeed throughout the fifteenth century Burgundy had, if anything, been ahead of other monarchies in this respect.[103] The direction in which things were moving was dramatically illustrated in 1540.

[100] J. H. Elton, "The Decline of Spain," *Past and Present*, 20, 1961, pp. 61ff.; A. D. Ortiz, *The Golden Century of Spain* (London: Weidenfeld and Nicolson, 1971), pp. 184ff.
[101] Figures from Fernandez Albaladejo, "Cities and the State in Spain," p. 177, table 8.1.
[102] On the achievement of the Swiss, see M. V. Clarke, *The Medieval City-State* (Cambridge: Speculum, 1966 edn.), ch. 7.
[103] H. Pirenne, "The Formation and Constitution of the Burgundian State," *American Historical Review*, 14, 1909, pp. 477–502.

Charles V's own grandmother Marie had seen her rule threatened, and her advisers executed, by the magistrates of Ghent; now, using an antifiscal revolt as his excuse, the Emperor in turn executed some of the town's leading citizens and deprived it of its ancient privileges, particularly as regards to the right to collect its own taxes. In this way the power of a community which for centuries had given endless trouble first to the French kings and then to Charles' own ancestors was broken, never to be restored, as commercial greatness deserted it and passed to Antwerp.

However, in the next generation Charles' son Philip overplayed his hand by trying to suppress the Reformation and introduce new taxes – the famous *alcabala* or tenth pence – at the same time. Just as Charles had alienated the Spanish towns by introducing Flemish advisers, so Philip achieved the same effect in reverse when he sent a Spaniard (Nicholas Perenot) to succeed his own half-sister Margaret as governor of the Netherlands in 1565. By so doing he managed to do what few other rulers in any other early modern country had done: namely cause an alliance to be forged between the towns and at least part of the nobility. The outcome of the alliance, which directed its efforts against him, was the Dutch War of Independence. It lasted from 1568 to 1648 and was paid for almost entirely by the now highly prosperous, and prospering, cities of Holland and Zealand.

The United Provinces that came into being following the Treaty of Utrecht in 1579 did have a titular leader in the person of William the Silent. After his assassination in 1584 the position of *Stadthouder* or lieutenant-general was destined to remain in the hands of his family; far from being hereditary kings, however, each of his successors had to gain the approval of the Estates General before taking up the office. These princes lacked great private resources – having spent his fortune (quite modest, to begin with) to raise armies during the early stages of the revolt, William the Silent himself left nothing but debts. On the other hand, they did not have the right to levy taxes on their own. Hence, the House of Orange never even got close to establishing absolute rule toward which contemporary monarchs were working; indeed there were periods, as between 1650 and 1672, when the Provinces made do without any *Stadthouder* at all. Meanwhile the cities that were represented in the Estates, numbering no fewer than fifty-eight, kept their respective delegates on extremely tight leashes. To this extent they *were* the state.[104]

---

[104] On the political system of the Netherlands, see C. Wilson, *The Dutch Republic* (London: Weidenfeld and Nicolson, 1968), ch. 3; M. 'T Hart, "Intercity Rivalries and the Making of the Dutch State," in Tilly and Blockmans, *Cities and the Rise of States in Europe*, pp. 199–203; also, at greater length, 'T Hart, *The Making of a Bourgeois State: War, Politics and Finance During the Dutch Revolution* (Manchester: Manchester University Press, 1993).

The dominant position of the Dutch patriarchate meant that, as in Switzerland, evolution toward modern, unitary, centralized statehood was arrested or at least delayed. And yet, remarkably, neither country fell victim to their much more powerful neighbors. This was due, in the one case, to unique geographical circumstances as well as the demonstrated military prowess which from 1500 on turned the Swiss into the first choice as mercenaries for those who could afford them. And, in the other, the cause was exceptional wealth – which made for the maintenance of efficient armed forces – combined, from 1688 on, with a more or less permanent alliance with the strongest Protestant power of the time.

With these two notable exceptions, the task of bringing the towns under royal control had been very largely achieved by 1660 or so. As the example of England shows, municipal institutions were not suppressed everywhere; many towns continued to enjoy a measure of autonomy in their internal government or "police." It is also true that minor riots, most of them occasioned by poverty and unemployment, continued to be a frequent phenomenon in France in particular. However, neither riots nor urban self-government were capable any more of seriously threatening the growing power of the state. Except for providing the personnel for minor posts such as night-watchmen, supervisors of markets, and prison officials, the urban militias which in their heyday had been able to defy kings and princes were allowed to decay. In Prussia the term "militia" itself was outlawed after 1670, and in other places the term became an object of derision.

The consolidation of territorial states also meant that the fortifications of towns located inside the country were neglected – if, indeed, they were not deliberately destroyed – and soon fell into ruin. The rest passed out of municipal control and into the hands of the commanders of royal garrisons. In another century or so these factors were to revolutionize the role that cities played in war, changing them from centers of resistance to be besieged into mere fat, soft concentrations of wealth that an invader, following some battle, would occupy almost as an afterthought.[105] The population was disarmed and the "bourgeois" and the "warlike" went their separate ways. Except in times of civil war, as in France after 1789, no longer could there be any question of towns refusing to admit their rulers or conducting an independent policy in league with foreign princes across the border, let alone of their engaging in military operations on their own behalf.

---

[105] See M. van Creveld, *Technology and War* (New York: Free Press, 1989), pp. 27–8, 106.

The monarchs' triumph

With the benefit of hindsight – always the historian's best friend – the triumph of the monarchs during the period under consideration appears inevitable. Perhaps the most important single factor was represented by the prolonged, and as it were predestined, conflict between pope and Emperor which enabled the monarchs to play one off against the other; had the Emperor also been the head of the established religion, as was the case in virtually any other part of the world where similar political systems existed, then almost certainly his power would have proved suffocating and the modern state would never have been born. As it was, religious reform and the fragmentation of Imperial political power marched hand in hand, culminating in the Reformation. Almost regardless of whether they supported the reforms or opposed them, it was the monarchs who benefited.

As the list of their titles usually implies – almost without exception they were not only kings but marquises of this and counts of that – originally the monarchs themselves were merely great nobles who collected estates piecemeal until, one day and almost without noticing, they found themselves at the head of a state. To this extent the question as to why they succeeded in overcoming the rest is meaningless: it reminds one of the story of the philologist who, having spent twenty years in an effort to determine who composed the *Iliad* and the *Odyssey*, finally concluded that they had been written not by Homer but by another poet whose name was also Homer. This is but another way of saying that, of 500 or so contenders who presented themselves at the starting line and took part in the struggle,[106] some were more successful than their fellows in setting up institutions, mobilizing economic resources, and translating those resources into civil and military power. Hence they ended up by lording it over those fellows who submitted, and defeating (and if necessary killing) those who did not.

As with pope and Emperor, so *vis-à-vis* the cities, the monarchs were often able to play a game of divide-and-rule. On the one hand, and particularly in Spain and in Eastern Europe, it proved possible to harness the nobility in order to combat the cities and, if not to eliminate the latter altogether, at any rate to arrest their development and reduce them to political impotence. Elsewhere it was more a question of using the cities' own internal divisions – as between rich and poor, merchants and craftsmen, those who lived within the walls and those who inhabited the subject countryside – in order to gain the upper hand over them.

---

[106] See J. Anderson and S. Hall, "Absolutism and Other Ancestors," in J. Anderson, ed., *The Rise of the Modern State* (Brighton: Wheatsheaf, 1986), p. 31.

Frequently it was done by resorting to outright force, as in southern Germany in particular. In other cases it was an almost imperceptible process as royal appointees gradually curtailed urban democracy, took over the magistrates' functions, levied taxes in their master's name, and suppressed occasional revolts when and where they took place. Whether rulers such as France's Henry IV *intended* to put an end to their cities' independence has been endlessly debated.[107] The point is that, in the long run he, as well as his predecessors and his successors, did precisely that.

Regarded from yet another point of view, though, neither nobility nor the cities were defeated as decisively as this account might imply. As explained above, the former tended to retain both their privileges – such as exemption from taxes – and a near-monopoly on the upper ranks of government. The inhabitants of the latter lost their political independence and, as members of the Third Estate, saw themselves excluded from the ranks of government; but by way of compensation, the economic system of which they were both the main supporters and main beneficiaries was able to flourish as never before. Particularly in Western Europe, capitalism and monarchy marched together. Whether by means of taxation or loans, capitalism provided monarchy with financial muscle. Monarchy repaid its debt by providing capitalist enterprise with military protection both within the country and later, outside its borders; it also endowed the city-dwellers with privileges that set them apart from, and well above, the inhabitants of the countryside. Russia alone excepted, from at least the second half of the seventeenth century, the strongest states were also those with the largest and most powerful capitalist entrepreneurs. Later, and as Marx was to write in the *Communist Manifesto*, it was often a pertinent question as to who owned whom.

Having defeated their rivals by one method or another, the monarchs soon began to change the way they did business and presented themselves to the world. One of the earliest, and most important, changes took place in the military field. Owing partly to the personal nature of politics, partly to the knightly ethos, medieval rulers had normally commanded their armies in person and often fought hand to hand in the front ranks. Consequently casualties among them were by no means rare: some died; others were taken prisoner and had to be ransomed. For example, both the king of France and his heir were captured at the Battle of Poitiers in 1356. James IV of Scotland was killed at Flodden in 1513; as already noted, the Battle of Pavia in 1525 ended with the capture of King Francis I of France. Not to be outdone, Francis' rival Charles V fought hand to

---

[107] E.g. D. Parker, *The Making of French Absolutism* (London: Edward Arnold, 1983), pp. 66–7.

hand in front of the walls of Tunis in 1535 and had several horses killed under him. Titian's portrait of the Emperor at the Battle of Mühlberg shows him as the perfect Christian knight, glued to his mount – he was, in fact, an excellent horseman – with his jaw firm and his gaze set, albeit, on this occasion, there is no indication that he fought in person.

By contrast, Charles' prudent son Philip II preferred to direct his far-flung campaigns by bureaucratic methods, relying on field commanders whom he selected from the highest nobility and surrounded with closely worded letters of instruction. By the time of the Thirty Years War his approach had come to be shared by most of the principal monarchs involved, including his son and grandson, Philips III and IV, as well as Emperor Ferdinand II and James I of England. The one important exception was Sweden's Gustavus Adolphus. A *bona fide* military genius, he insisted on operating in the old fashion and commanding from the front. Not surprisingly he ended up by getting himself killed when, escorted by only two or three companions, he rode to the assistance of his endangered right flank at the Battle of Lützen in 1632.

During the eighteenth century, the decline in the number of royal field commanders continued. The only important exceptions were Gustavus Adolphus' descendant, Charles XII, and Prussia's Frederick II, but even they no longer fought hand to hand but commanded from a safe position in the rear.[108] To compensate themselves for the lost joys of battle, some eighteenth-century monarchs, especially Louis XIV, would present themselves at the end of a siege, assume formal command, and put on heroic airs. Others, including notably Russia's Peter III, played with tin soldiers whom he would even take to bed with him. Of the three emperors who were present at Austerlitz in 1805, only one – Napoleon Bonaparte – was a military man and exercised effective command. The other two, Russia's Alexander and Austria's Francis I, acted as hangers-on and did little but put obstacles in front of their own subordinates – but this is to anticipate our story.

Linked to the change in the military field was a shift from itinerant to sedentary government. In this connection there is no need to go back as far as John Lackland of England who spent most of his reign touring his realm attended by a few family members and servants, a treasure chest, and 200 hounds; Louis XI of France, as well as his contemporaries the Emperors Frederick III and Maximilian I, were almost as mobile as him. Both secular and ecclesiastical rulers traveled to wherever there was a problem to be settled, and, according to their preferences, spent the rest of the time hunting animals or women. Maximilian in particular seldom

---

[108] See M. van Creveld, *Command in War* (Cambridge, MA: Harvard University Press, 1985), pp. 52–5.

spent more than a night in the same bed; during his last days he was reduced to such penury that he could not find an innkeeper who would take him in. As the example of Charles VIII and Louis XII shows, some rulers continued to spend many years away not only from their capitals but from their countries. Even the medieval idea of monarchs going on a crusade and abandoning government for the good of their souls had not been entirely forgotten, albeit from the late thirteenth century it tended to result in mere empty posturing. Thus it occasioned Erasmus' advice in *The Education of a Christian Prince* that they had better stay at home and mind their subjects' welfare.[109]

As government became more centralized after 1550 or so, that advice began to be heeded. The first really sedentary monarch was, as already noted, Philip II. He struggled to govern from behind his desk, bending under the workload and often falling asleep over his papers. In England Elizabeth spent much of her reign traveling from one country house to the next; to her it was a question of saving money by living at the barons' expense. This was not the style chosen by her two successors, James I and Charles I. Together they exercised the closest thing that England ever came to absolute government – the years 1629–40 were known as the period of personal rule – and with short interruptions both of them chose to remain in or near London as they did so. Across the Channel, Catherine de Medici and her sons had been as itinerant as their predecessors, often spending months on the road. Once he had brought the civil war to an end, Henry IV normally resided in Paris; however, Louis XIII reversed the trend and often left his capital for months on end to inspect provinces, make "joyous entries," attend the weddings of his relatives, and oversee battles (he was incapable of exercising command). Then it was the turn of Louis XIV. A follower of Copernicus, he was the first French monarch who had his subjects revolve around him instead of the other way around. Not for nothing did he take the title, *le roi soleil*, and have the words, as well as the symbol itself, embossed on walls and furniture throughout the palace.

Reflecting their new position high above ordinary mortals, the choice of partners that royalty could take in marriage narrowed. Medieval and Renaissance kings used family alliances to cement feudal ties and join new territories to their domains; hence they had often wedded members of the high nobility, either foreign or their own, such as duchesses and counts. For example, England's Richard II contemplated an alliance with the lord of Milan's daughter before settling for Anne of Bohemia, herself of less than royal stock. France's Louis XI married Charlotte of Savoy

[109] Erasmus, *The Education of a Christian Prince*, L. K. Born, ed. (New York: Norton, 1964), p. 208.

(1451), Charles VIII Anne of Brittany (1497), and sixteenth-century French kings the daughters of the Medici ducal house. Now that provinces were ceasing to be regarded as private property and, except in Germany with its infinite number of petty principalities, most nonroyal families ceased to reign, monarchs sought to preserve their status by marrying exclusively into each other's families. The result almost amounted to a kind of racism; as Lady Fleming, who in 1550 was briefly privileged to act as mistress to Henry II of France, put it, "the king's blood is a smoother and sweeter liquid than any other."[110] By the later eighteenth century even the Russian tsars, though long regarded as latecomers by the rest of Europe, were following the trend in a way calculated to put them far above even the greatest of their subjects. Elsewhere, systematic inbreeding practiced over generations sometimes led to noticeable instances of degeneration.

The shift from itinerant to sedentary government was itself part cause, part outcome of the growth in the size and splendor of courts. Gone were the days when a king such as Louis IX could be found sitting under a tree dispensing justice amidst his assembled nobles; the later the period, the more pronounced the trend toward majesty and the greater also the expense involved. The leaders in the field were the dukes of Burgundy whose etiquette has been made the subject of a famous description by Johan Huizinga;[111] first in Dijon and later in Ghent even to arrange the cutlery in other than the prescribed order was treated as an affront to the ducal dignity. But then it was precisely this quality which commended it to others, including Charles V – who spent his own youth surrounded by its splendors – Francis I, and Henry VIII.

Between 1500 and 1700 the number of royal attendants often rose into the thousands and even the tens of thousands. From the princesses of the blood – who could sometimes be found running across the palace so as not to miss some ceremony in which their presence was expected – to the most humble lackey they were subjected to something like a military discipline which determined who would do what, how, when, and to whom; and which, in turn, could not be maintained unless the all-powerful monarch himself subscribed to it like the spring in a vast clockwork. As the duke of Saint-Simon said of Louis XIV, "with an almanac and a watch one could tell, three hundred miles away, what he was doing."[112] To house these retinues it was necessary to construct entirely new pal-

---

[110] Quoted in E. Le Roy Ladurie, *The Royal French State 1460–1610* (Oxford: Blackwell, 1994), p. 156.
[111] J. Huizinga, *The Waning of the Middle Ages* (Harmondsworth, UK: Penguin Books, 1965 edn.), pp. 39–44.
[112] Quoted in E. Lavisse, *Louis XIV* (Paris: Tallandier, 1978 [1905]), vol. VII, part I, p. 157.

aces. The first was the Spanish Escorial whose location at the exact center of the Iberian Peninsula made it well suited to the purpose for which it had been designed. Then came the French Palais Royal and Versailles (originally a hunting lodge that expanded into a community of 150,000 people); the Bavarian Nymphenburg, the Austrian Schönbrunn, and the Prussian Charlottenburg, to mention only some of the best known. Each one was partly residential, partly administrative, and partly ceremonial in character.[113] Each was surrounded by a formal garden where even the trees were made to obey their royal master by taking on geometrical forms; each came, or was soon provided, with a list of those whose status made them worthy of entering it. Rulers seldom left these residences, and then only on occasions of state and in the company of the entire court – when Louis XV on one occasion moved from Versailles to another place he insisted on his daughter-in-law, though she was desperately ill, coming along. The days when any subject could, in theory at any rate, hope to meet his or her king face to face and submit a complaint were coming to an end.

In a Christian civilization, to compare a monarch to God was tantamount to sacrilege. The Counter-Reformation had put an end to the situation whereby a king such as Olaf of Norway or Louis IX of France could be both great warriors *and* saints; however, humanist scholarship rose to the challenge. Now that rulers were no longer beatified, it made available an entire series of deities for them to identify with. The favorite choice for males was Hercules – as the title was passed from one monarch to another, Henry IV of France on one occasion was actually called "the Hercules who now reigns." Normally his female counterpart was the hunting goddess Diana; presumably Venus with her record of adultery would have proved too embarrassing. Name-calling apart, royal weddings, christenings, joyous entries, and similar ceremonies were frequently attended by deities including Jupiter, Juno, Apollo, Neptune, Minerva, and Bacchus, not to mention numerous nymphs who were often impersonated by young women in the nude.[114] Those who created the relevant paintings, sculptures, and *tableaux vivants* based themselves on handbooks especially written for the purpose, which provided illustrations and in which the gods' various qualities were spelt out. In this way European monarchs were able to

---

[113] For an analysis of the way these *palais* were laid out, see N. Elias, *The Court Society* (Oxford: Basil Blackwell, 1983), ch. 5.

[114] See A. Huon, "Le thème du prince dans les entrées parisiennes au XVe siècle," in J. Jacquot, ed., *Les fêtes de la Renaissance* (Paris: Centre national de la recherche, 1956), vol. I, pp. 21–30; and R. Strong, *Art and Power: Renaissance Festivals 1450–1650* (Woodbridge, Suffolk: Boydel, 1973), which presents a detailed analysis of the way absolutist themes rose to dominance.

cavort with divinities, albeit such as were pagan and taken only moderately seriously.

The monarchs' triumph over their various competitors also found its expression in the way they themselves were painted and sculpted. Medieval kings up to the second half of the fifteenth century were often shown mixing freely with their nobles while engaged in such activities as hunting or banqueting. Others, more religiously inclined, may be seen at prayer humbly kneeling in the company of their patron saints. An immense distance separates these works from their successors from the time of the Counter-Reformation on. Already Vasari toward the end of his life (he died in 1574) painted the "Apotheosis" of Duke Cosimo de Medici. Within the next fifty years Rubens, Velazquez, and van Dyck – all three of them immensely successful court painters – could be found producing vast canvases which show royalty, either alone or in exclusive family groups, dramatically portrayed against a background calculated to enhance their splendor such as a garden, hunting trophies, or a siege. Hung in the palace, the largest paintings were intended as *coups de théâtre*, confronting visitors with a different angle of their master's august person each time they entered a new building or room. Others, produced on a smaller scale, were meant to decorate the king's private quarters or else for presentation.[115]

Medieval rulers often had vertical statues of themselves placed inside niches on the walls of churches, whereas graves were decorated with horizontal effigies that represented them and their wives. During the second half of the fifteenth century the place of both styles began to be taken by larger than life, free-standing, equestrian statues made of bronze. Instead of being enclosed by buildings, their purpose was to decorate public squares, a fashion that started in Italy where people had the one of Marcus Aurelius on the Capitoline Hill to serve as an example. Around 1475 the Sforza rulers of Milan became the first to commission statues of themselves on horseback, though they were never completed. Much later their example was followed in other countries such as France (Louis XIII) and Prussia (the Great Elector). Often the less martial a ruler the more heroic his statue. A case in point is the one of Charles I made by Hubert le Sueur in 1630. While the king is shown wearing jousting armor, it was precisely during his reign that the sport, which in any case had long lost any resemblance to real-life war, was abandoned.[116]

Whichever way one looks at it, the dawning age of absolutism found rulers raised to splendid heights rarely attained, if indeed contemplated, by their relatively humble medieval predecessors – including also the

[115] See C. Brown, *Van Dyck* (Oxford: Phaedon, 1982), particularly ch. 4.
[116] J. Pope-Hennessey, *Italian Renaissance Sculpture* (London: Phaedon, 1971), pp. 52–9.

newly found, and eagerly sought after, ability to cure various diseases by a touch of the hand.[117] Having destroyed their competitors or harnessed them to their own service, kings had power that in theory was unprecedented. In practice, though, the isolated sites of the palaces that they built for themselves, the number of attendants by whom they were surrounded, and the amount of ceremonial on which they insisted all pointed in the opposite direction. As we shall see in the next chapter, other things being equal, the more absolute any monarch the greater his dependence on impersonal bureaucratic, military, and legal mechanisms to transmit his will and impose it on society at large. In the end, those mechanisms showed themselves capable of functioning without him and were even destined to take power away from him.

[117] See M. Bloch, *The Royal Touch: Sacred Monarchy and Scrofula in England and France* (London: Routledge, 1973).

3 The state as an instrument: 1648 to 1789

Growing out of feudalism and harking back to Roman imperial times, the system of government that appeared in Europe during the years 1337–1648 was still, in most respects, entirely personal. The state as an abstract organization with its own persona separate from that of the ruler did not yet exist. Thus, in Italy around 1500 the term stood for "the machinery of government," as when Guicciardini wrote of "the state of the Medicis" and "those in Florence who seek to change the state."[1] Thus to say, as many historians have done, that it was the state which overcame church, empire, nobility, and towns is incorrect. In fact it was the achievement of autocratically minded kings; or, as in Germany, rulers whose titles were less exalted but whose positions *vis-à-vis* their own societies as well as their colleagues bore an essentially monarchic character. To their contemporaries, the territories of Lodovico Sforza, Francis I, Charles V, and the rest were known as marquisates, counties, duchies, kingdoms, and of course the Empire. Each such territorial unit might contain "states" (French *états*): such as the aristocratic one, the ecclesiastical one, and the common one. Conversely, the "state," meaning situation and resources (particularly financial resources) of each unit might be such and such. They themselves, though, came to be called states only during the first half of the seventeenth century.[2]

Those same contemporaries also continued the medieval tradition, manifest both in ecclesiastical chronicles and in the *chansons de geste*, of writing the histories of political communities of every kind and size almost entirely in terms of the personalities who governed them. Not for them institutions evolving, impersonal forces driving, and various factors clustering to produce this outcome or that; at most there was the medieval idea of the wheel of fortune, itself geared to the rise and fall of individuals and now often impersonated, as in Machiavelli, by the classical goddess

[1] F. Guicciardini, *Ricordi* (Milan: Rizzoli, 1951 edn.), series 2, 64.
[2] See N. Rubinstein, "Notes on the Word *Stato* in Florence Before Machiavelli," in R. G. Rose and W. K. Ferguson, eds., *Florilegium Historiale: Essays Presented to Wallace K. Ferguson* (Toronto: University of Toronto Press, 1971), pp. 313–26.

fortuna.[3] Normally the actors were rulers, the members of their families, their opponents, their advisers, and of course their mistresses. Either they allied themselves with each other or else they fought and intrigued against each other.

As late as 1589, according to Justus Lipsius in his hugely successful *Politicorum sive civilis doctrinae libri sex,* personal government meant that revolts might ensue because rulers had no children or because they suffered from a facial disfigurement or an incurable disease. Those of them who depleted the treasury by cultivating some hobby or allowed a love affair to determine the fate of a kingdom might be criticized for frivolity; still, in the end the gains to be made, and the losses to be suffered, were their own and nobody else's. It is true that rulers had long been told that, to save their souls (and prevent rebellion), they had better look after their subjects' welfare. However, the frequent comparison between the latter and a flock of sheep – owned as the latter are by their shepherd and raised for his benefit – speaks for itself. It was only after ascending the throne in 1660 that Louis XIV arrived at the point where he could distinguish between his own glory and the good of the *état* that he headed. Or so, at any rate, he claimed in his memoirs.[4]

To put it in a different way, centralization on its own does not the state make. As we saw in chapter 1, from the time of ancient Egypt on many of the political constructs known as empires had been as centralized as possible, at least in theory and as far as the available technological means permitted. Not surprisingly, seventeenth-century monarchs deliberately tried to emulate the Roman empire in particular, which resemblance often extended into details as they Latinized their names (e.g., Louis became Ludovicus), adopted the symbols of the Caesars, and propagated the ideology of resignation and service that is known as neostoicism.[5] Conversely, the real story of the absolute state is not so much about despotism *per se* as about the way in which, between 1648 and 1789, the person of the ruler and his "state" were separated from each other until the first became almost entirely unimportant in comparison with the second.

That story, which represents an almost purely West European development and which was exported to other continents only at a much later date, will be told in four parts. First, I shall trace the rise of the bureaucratic structure and the way in which it emancipated itself both from royal control and from civil society. Secondly, I shall show how that structure

---

[3] N. Machiavelli, *The Prince* (Harmondsworth, UK: Penguin Books, 1963), ch. 25.
[4] *Mémoires de Louis XIV*, J. de Lognon, ed. (Paris: Tallandier, 1927), pp. 280–1.
[5] G. Oestreich, *Neostoicism and the Origins of the Modern State* (Cambridge: Cambridge University Press, 1982).

strengthened its hold over society by defining its borders, collecting all sorts of information about it, and taxing it. Thirdly, we must examine the way in which bureaucracy and taxes together made it possible for the state to create armed forces for external and internal use and thus establish a monopoly over the use of violence. Fourthly, it is necessary to trace the way in which political theory both accompanied all these developments and justified them.

Building the bureaucracy

However weak or strong, no ruler in charge of a political unit larger than a family can operate without subordinates who look up to him and, in one way or another, are dependent on him. In tribes without rulers the position of the priest was largely explained by the fact that he did not have any permanent followers except for the members of his own family and, perhaps, an assistant or two; conversely, in chiefdoms and empires the position of the ruler was very much a reflection of the number of people who, whether as clients, retainers, servants, or slaves, manned the administration and carried out the orders given them. Thus the history of political communities – including the one known as the state – almost amounts to the story of the growth in the number of executives, the way they were organized, and the way they received their living or were compensated for their efforts; incidentally it also explains the tendency of most rulers, be they Chinese emperors or modern presidents, to present themselves in public with as many attendants as possible.

During the period under consideration, the outstanding change was the one which led from indirect rule by feudal lords to direct government exercised by salaried officials on the king's behalf. Attempts to move in this direction had been made since the time of France's Philip Augustus (1179–1223); however, the obstacles produced by time, distance, and the king's own irregular income proved decisive and it was only around the middle of the fifteenth century that real progress began to be made under King Louis XI. By 1610, the year in which Henry IV died, the process had gone far enough for the difference between the two kinds of personnel to be defined very precisely by a French lawyer, Charles Loyseau. The former derived their power from the possession of land and the rights which they exercised over their own vassals; the latter were appointed by the king whom they served with or without pay. Consequently they could be transferred, promoted, and dismissed at the monarch's will.

As their titles indicate, originally the royal servants attended the king's person. They were in charge of the various departments of the household, such as the wardrobe, the kitchen, and the stable; others kept the seal or looked after the women's quarters.[6] As monarchs expanded their power at the expense of church, aristocratic landowners, and towns, these officials were turned from appointees who looked after the royal domains into government administrators. For example, it was common for the master of the castle (*castelan*) to assume responsibility for various public works and also for public morality, sumptuary laws, and the like. The master of the wardrobe found himself looking after financial affairs; the chancellor, originally a clerk, concerned himself with the day-to-day working of the justice system; and the marshal – whose original responsibility was to maintain order among the royal bodyguards – began acting as commander-in-chief in war, now that monarchs were decreasingly inclined to do so themselves.

In principle the household, consisting simply of servants great and small, was independent of the feudal hierarchy. In practice the two were always intertwined; the reason being that, both in order to enhance the authority of his servants and by way of giving a certain luster to the court itself, its officials were often selected from among the nobility. To guarantee a steady supply, the sons of feudal lords were often brought to court where they served as pages and acquired an education considered appropriate to their status. Conversely, men of humble birth might distinguish themselves in the king's service and, by way of their reward, marry into the feudal aristocracy and thus obtain estates as well as tenants and rights over them.[7] Except in England, where most forms of aristocratic privilege were abolished after 1688, the two hierarchies retained their incestuous links as long as the *ancien régime* lasted. They became separated only after the French Revolution, but even then it remained customary for the rulers of countries such as Prussia and Austria to reward their close collaborators by promoting them into the nobility.

Sooner or later, the expansion of the household into additional fields led to its transformation. Its development into a public administration was arrested; instead, overwhelmed by its own size and the extent of its responsibilities, the situation was inverted. A royal official whose job was, say, looking after the country's financial system could not at the same time attend to the expenditure of the palace; nor could an army commander-in-chief take responsibility for the royal bodyguard, particularly now that kings no longer took the field: so the two became geographically separate. Such tasks, which were minor by comparison, were delegated to

---

[6] A very good overview of one household establishment is P. G. Thiler, *Die Verwaltung des Ordenstaates Preussen, vornehmlich im 15. Jahrhundert* (Cologne: Boehlau, 1965), pp. 31–120.

[7] For the career of one knight who did just that, see G. Duby, *Guillaume le Maréchal* (Paris: Fayard, 1984).

others. The household was swallowed by its own offspring, so to speak: it became simply one of a great many administrative departments whose responsibility happened to be looking after the monarch's person, his residences, his property, and the like.

Possibly because it was always highly centralized, the first important country to witness the transformation was England. Throughout the fifteenth century, and especially after the Wars of the Roses had come to an end, the size of the household grew and grew; after 1507 this process coincided with the personal characteristics of Henry VIII who, unlike his father, preferred activities such as hunting, composing music, and womanizing to attending the affairs of government. This combination of circumstances enabled the chancellor, Thomas Cromwell (served 1532–40), to bring about a "revolution in government."[8] By way of an indication of what was happening the great seal became the official sign of the realm, while the signet and private seal declined into insignificance, continuing in use simply as the king's personal signs in letters that he sent to his relatives and similar missives. Spain followed England during the reign of Philip II from 1556 on; France under Richelieu during the first decades of the seventeenth century. The reversal of roles marked a decisive step toward the establishment of a modern bureaucracy and, with it, of the modern impersonal state.

Now that they were no longer simply the king's attendants, top administrative officials changed their titles from mere secretaries – as was still the case under Emperor Charles V – to the more grand-sounding secretaries of state. The peace conference held at Cateau-Cambresis in 1559 was probably the first in which the representatives of both France and Spain carried that title; shortly afterwards we find Florimond Robertet, known to history as *le père des secrétaires d'état* and the third official in a line bearing that name, countersigning decrees issued by the sovereign.[9] The developing impersonal character of the office is obvious from the fact that he, like his opposite number in England, William Page, performed his duties under several monarchs in a line; when finally dismissed by Henry III in 1588, he found it necessary to compose an Instruction for his successor. The first full-sized manual intended for the use of secretaries of state was written in 1631 by another Frenchman, Jean de Silhon. Clearly the position was being institutionalized.

The rise of bureaucratic organization also meant that the traditional household ordinances were no longer adequate to their task. The first

[8] For a short summary of the change, see G. R. Elton, *The Tudor Revolution in Government* (Cambridge: Cambridge University Press, 1953), pp. 415ff.

[9] For his career, see N. M. Sutherland, *The French Secretaries of State in the Age of Catherine de Medici* (London: Athlone Press, 1962).

such ordinance on record was produced for France's Louis IX in 1261; widely imitated by other courts, its function was to define the duties of various cooks, servants, and other assorted personnel responsible for their master's welfare. Between 1600 and 1660 they were replaced, or rather supplemented, by the various systems of government published in countries such as Sweden, England, and Prussia. The background to the preparation of these documents varied. In Sweden the *Regeringsform* of 1634 owed its existence to Chancellor Oxenstierna and the need to do without a reigning monarch during the minority of Gustavus Adolphus' daughter, Christina. In England it resulted from the Civil War and the establishment of a new form of government, the Protectorate. In Prussia under the Great Elector, Frederick William (1640–88), it was made necessary by territorial consolidation. As additional provinces, some of them far away, were joined to Brandenburg the elector sought to create a common framework that would cover them all, a process that was imitated on a greater scale by Austria's Maria Theresa after her army's defeat at the hands of the same Prussians in 1740–8.

Unlike the personnel that had served previous rulers, early modern European bureaucrats were neither priests, nor slaves, nor necessarily aristocrats. Over time their sources of income also changed; regarded as a method for remunerating governors and administrators, feudal rent – i.e., the assignment of lands and tenants in the form of a fief – had become unimportant by the second half of the fifteenth century. Starting with France and the Papal State, in most countries it was replaced by a system whereby offices were sold to the highest bidder. While many offices did carry salaries, those were almost always niggardly in relation to the standard of living expected and the expenses involved, the more so since holders were supposed to pay the latter (including the maintenance of their subordinates, of "families") out of their own pockets. This was a fact which many rulers understood but, owing to financial constraints, could not change. Consequently they were forced to agree to a system of compensation by way of rights that were attached to the office, fees that were due to it, and monopolies that its holder could exercise.

The system of venal offices continued to develop throughout the sixteenth and seventeenth centuries. In France it reached its apogee during the reigns of Henry IV, Louis XIII, and Louis XIV, all of whom, pressed to raise money for their wars, created new offices and sold them by the hundreds. In 1604 the Paulette, named after Secretary of State Paulet, put the final touch on the structure. Offices were turned into private property. In return for paying an annual sum, theoretically one-sixtieth *ad valorem* but tending to be fixed in practice, their owners were granted security of tenure. They were also allowed to buy, sell, and otherwise transfer their offices to other persons as they wished. Except at the highest levels, where the selection of the *intendants* depended entirely on the king's will, the way to advance in the hierarchy was by turning each office to profit and then using the latter in order to purchase one's way from one to another until one reached the highest offices of all.

Nor was there anything to prevent a person from holding multiple offices. Richelieu, for example, was a master at this practice; he bought and sold offices until, in addition to his principal one of first secretary of state (with its salary of 40,000 *livres* per year), he held several governorships as well as tax-farming rights in numerous provinces (raising his real income into the millions).[10] Accumulating offices was one way of making oneself powerful, additionally so as the king was often dependent on his officials for loans; on the other hand it explains why historians are so often frustrated in their efforts to determine who was responsible for what. Offices could be willed to one's heirs (as happened to Montesquieu who inherited the one that had belonged to his uncle), and even be assigned as dowries. In this way they almost came to resemble family heirlooms.

In two countries, England and Prussia, venal offices failed to develop to the same extent. In England, where the landowning class was rich, the justices of the peace had made their appearance as a result of the Peace Act in 1361. In theory it was the king who appointed them from among local notables; in practice, by the second half of the fifteenth century, doing so had become the responsibility of the lord chancellor and the lord keeper of the seal, who in this way exercised considerable powers of patronage. The justices worked without pay, carrying out administrative duties and supervising public order in each county; the day-to-day cost was borne by means of "funds" into which went the proceeds of fees, licenses, confiscations, and the like. The system's greatest advantage, which commended it both to sovereign and Parliament and explains its extraordinary longevity, was that it was cheap to run. This was all the more so because the justices' subordinates, i.e., the sheriffs and the constables, were maintained at the expense of the counties and parishes rather than out of the royal exchequer. The result was that much of the King's Justice, though carried out in his name, had little to do with him.

In Prussia, by contrast, the nobility was poor and tended to get poorer after the devastation suffered during the Thirty Years War and the Great Northern War. This fact enabled the electors – later, the kings – to draw it into their own service by offering salaries; the role played by other forms of income was, by comparison, minor. In 1723 Frederick William I took

---

[10] R. Knecht, *Richelieu* (London: Longman, 1991), pp. 27–9.

the final step by prohibiting the sale of offices altogether and ordering that all the revenues generated by the administration be passed directly into his own treasury instead of remaining in locally administered funds, as previously.[11] Thus one country bypassed, and the other cut short, the period in which offices could be bought and sold and their owners compensated themselves out of the proceeds. Toward the end of the eighteenth century, the typical Prussian system whereby the administration was staffed by university-educated bureaucrats at the top and by ex-NCO types at the bottom was in operation. Pummeled into shape by Frederick the Great, it became the most advanced in Europe. At the other extreme England was both run by amateurs and underadministered by continental standards; an impersonal, salaried bureaucracy failed to develop.

The move from feudal lords through state entrepreneurs to appointed, salaried officials also led to a shift from a geographical to a functional division of labor. The first secretaries of state who, rather than being jacks of all trades, specialized in any particular function appeared in France during the reign of Henry IV. Around the middle of the century both France and Prussia introduced the so-called *generalités*: in other words, administrative divisions whose responsibilities were not limited to certain provinces but covered the entire realm and involved specialization in some particular field. As might be expected, the earliest *generalités* looked after justice, finance, and military administration where they took care of recruitment, supplies, and pay. Somewhat later they were joined by a secretary of the navy.

Perhaps the most important characteristic of the modern state is its territoriality. Therefore it is somewhat surprising to find that the distinction between internal and external affairs, and the establishment of separate administrative structures for each, appeared only comparatively late in the day. Owing to the ties that linked them to each other as well as the often scattered nature of their domains, medieval rulers up to the sixteenth century did not have centralized foreign ministries; instead each provincial governor was also responsible for looking into the affairs of his neighbors across the border. Diplomatic affairs were conducted by means of *ad hoc* envoys on the one hand and intermediaries (who were often ecclesiastics) on the other.[12] Far from being strictly salaried employees working for each party, the persons who made up both categories expec-

---

[11] See H. Rosenberg, *Bureaucracy, Aristocracy and Autocracy: The Prussian Experience, 1660–1815* (Cambridge, MA: Harvard University Press, 1953), pp. 27–9.

[12] See D. E. Queller, *The Office of Ambassador During the Middle Ages* (Princeton: Princeton University Press, 1967).

ted to be maintained and rewarded by the rulers with whom they negotiated.

As we saw, the practice of establishing permanent diplomatic representatives with foreign princes originated in Italy after 1450. Interrupted by the Reformation and, above all, the Counter-Reformation, the use of such representatives was resumed after 1600 or so, by which time the term "ambassador" had replaced the earlier agent, legate, factor, procurator, or orator and was confined exclusively to personnel sent by the ruler of one state to represent him in the court of another. After 1648 their numbers grew. France, for example, had twenty-two in 1660 and thirty-two in 1715; whereas William III of England appointed 80 diplomatic representatives during his reign, his successor Anne commissioned 136. By this time even a minor German principality, such as Hanover, found it necessary to maintain no fewer than sixteen officially accredited ambassadors.

Numerical growth soon made it necessary to have a central directory that would look after the ambassadors, send them instructions, and read their reports, all in addition to running the apparatus which transmitted messages from and to foreign capitals and which, for reasons of secrecy, was usually kept separate from the public mail systems developing inside each country. From the 1620s on France had an unbroken line of secretaries of state whose task was to look after foreign affairs. Under Louis XIV the post was held by a succession of able diplomats such as Lionne, Pompone, Colbert de Croissy, and Torcy.

Though sovereigns not seldom circumvented their own assistants and engaged in personal diplomacy, around 1720, Spain, Prussia, Sweden, and Austria all had more or less well organized foreign ministries headed by a single secretary of state. Britain proved an exception; reflecting the way in which the country had been put together, it had a secretary for the south, who in addition to England and Ireland looked after Catholic countries, and a secretary of the north who looked after Scottish affairs and also after relations with Protestant ones (as well as Poland and Russia). It is true that there was often a tendency for one secretary to dominate the other, so that in practice there was a foreign minister; such was the situation under Bolingbroke in 1711–14, Stanhope in 1714–21, and the elder Pitt in 1756–61. Still, it was only in 1782 that George III – the most efficiency-minded English ruler in three centuries – succeeded in having separate home and foreign secretaries instituted.[13]

Compared to the empires which had preceded them, these early modern states were remarkable for the number of their administrators. Rome,

[13] D. B. Horn, *The British Diplomatic Service* (Oxford: Oxford University Press, 1961), p. 2.

about which our information is relatively abundant, at its zenith may have had 50–80 million inhabitants; yet the Empire was governed by no more than a few thousand centrally appointed bureaucrats, all the remainder being local magistrates selected by the cities (later they were appointed by the *procuratores* or else their positions became hereditary) and client rulers. By contrast, France, with a population fluctuating between 18 and 20 million, had 12,000 officials in 1505, 25,000 in 1610, and perhaps 50,000 during the early years of Louis XIV.[14] The number of top-ranking *intendants* also increased, from an average of two per year appointed between 1560 and 1630 to no fewer than eight or nine assigned to their posts each year from 1630 to 1648. By the time Richelieu died in 1642 every single royally governed province, or *pays d'élection*, had its own *intendant*. As already mentioned, the growing power of the *intendants* presented an irritant to the nobility and was one factor behind the series of noble uprisings collectively known as the Fronde. This did not prevent the French example from being imitated elsewhere, particularly in Spain, Prussia (where the corresponding officials were known as *Generalkommis-saren*), and Sweden.[15]

Even more spectacular than the growth in the number of officials was the rise in the quantity of paperwork that the invention of print permitted. From about AD 1000 on, medieval rulers were no longer illiterate; for all that he preferred the sword to the pen Richard the Lionheart could write as well as anyone. Still it is said that, on one occasion when Emperor Charles called for pen and paper, none could be found within the walls of the palace. Whether or not the story is true, certainly he began his reign by traveling from the Netherlands to Spain with the most important government papers packed in chests which were carried on the back of mules and, from time to time, abandoned in some castle as they became too heavy to carry about. By the end of his own reign such a solution was no longer practicable, and under his son Philip II the situation was entirely transformed. In the 1580s a single inquiry into the affairs of a royal governor lasted for thirteen years and consumed 49,545 sheets of paper. The age of modern bureaucracy had truly arrived.

Besides producing overwhelming amounts of paperwork, the invention of print had other results. Previously, administrative papers of every sort, produced in a very small number of copies, could easily be lost or destroyed. Hence the best way to preserve them (and also to protect them

---

[14] Figures from R. Mousnier, *Le conseil du roi de Louis XII à la révolution* (Paris: Presses universitaires de France, 1971), ch. 1.

[15] For the development of these officials, see O. Hintze, "The Commissary and His Significance in General Administrative History: A Comparative Study," in *The Historical Essays of Otto Hintze*, F. Gilbert, ed. (New York: Oxford University Press, 1975), pp. 267–302.

against counterfeiting) was to have their contents inscribed on some durable material and displayed at a prominent public place. Such was the case of the laws of classical antiquity – not, as the Roman Twelve Tables show, that this method was always foolproof. The use of print solved the problem, making royal decrees and ordinances available to anybody who wished to consult them and all but eliminating the possibility of falsification; already the Tudors were familiar with the saying *ars typographia artium omnium conservatrix* (the art of print conserves all other arts).[16] Before long scarcity was replaced by its opposite, surfeit. Mountains of material were produced, filling chambers and lining corridors; unless properly looked after, they would soon become so disorderly as to be impossible to use. It became necessary to find entirely new systems for storing and retrieving documents. It is no wonder that, from about 1550 to 1650, one ruler after another is found establishing a central state archive.

In the long run, this kind of bureaucratic expansion itself made it necessary for officials to operate according to fixed rules. The latter governed entry into the service, working hours, division of labor, career management, and the *modus operandi* in general. Partly in order to break the control of the local nobility over appointments, partly under the influence of the *chinoiserie* that was fashionable at the time, Frederick II in 1770 instituted a system of entrance examinations. His example was soon followed by Bavaria, which during the third quarter of the eighteenth century developed one of the world's most advanced administrations. In 1771 it was to became the first modern country to take a nationwide census, albeit the work was done in a rather desultory way and took ten years to complete. Thus officials begot paperwork, and paperwork officials.

The purpose of the various measures was to ensure uniformity, regularity, and a reasonable standard of competence, and in this they were generally successful. On the other hand, every step taken toward professionalism also brought with it a reinforced *esprit de corps*. Already the introduction of entrance examinations meant that monarchs were no longer free to decide whom to take into their service; it was found that the more centralized any government the more indispensable the officials who ran it on the monarch's behalf. This in turn translated into an ability to insist on their rights and enforce them even against his will, if neces-

---

[16] For the motto and its significance, see E. Eisenstein, "The Advent of Printing and the Problem of the Renaissance," *Past and Present*, 44, 1969, pp. 29ff.; for printing in the service of government, see A. J. Slavin, "The Tudor Revolution and the Devil's Art: Bishop Bonner's Printed Forms," in D. J. Gutch and J. W. McKenna, eds., *Tudor Rule and Revolution* (Cambridge: Cambridge University Press, 1982), pp. 3–24.

sary. Among the most important such rights were freedom from arbitrary dismissal, acceptable pay, a regular promotion ladder based, for the most part, on seniority, old-age pensions, and a certain dignity which they shared with the king.

The term "bureaucracy" itself was coined in 1765 by Vincent de Gourmay, a French *philosophe* who specialized in economic and administrative matters. The context in which he did so was pejorative; to him it was a new form of government added to the three that had been laid down by Aristotle, i.e., monarchy, aristocracy, and democracy. Significantly for the future he saw a need to reduce the number of pen-pushers in favor of *laissez faire*, a term he also invented.[17]

By this time officials, who for centuries past had been the king's men, were beginning to think of themselves as servants of an impersonal state. The process whereby *Staatsdiener* were separated from *königliche bediente* spread from the bottom up. The latter lost status until they degenerated into mere flunkies, whereas the most important among the former were soon coming to be known as ministers. It climaxed in 1756 when no less an authority than Frederick II described himself as "the first servant of the state." As if to emphasize the growing separation between the court that looked after his personal affairs and the administration that was now running the Prussian state, he also ended the system whereby the latter's employees were fed from the royal kitchens.

The fact that the growing size and power of the administration was not without its dangers was understood at an early time. Already one of Philip II's ambassadors, when rebuked by his master for insisting on ceremonial, found it in him to reply that *Vuessa Majesta misma no es sino una ceremonia* – "Your Majesty himself is nothing but a ceremony."[18] By the 1640s the Spanish bureaucracy, which unlike the French one was not torn to pieces by civil war, had become the most advanced in Europe. No wonder that commentators such as Saavedra Fajardo and Quevedo y Villegas took alarm. They expressed the fear that it might undermine personal government and, indeed, end up by rendering the king himself superfluous.[19]

As the next century established "legitimate" government – meaning that the king's identity, provided only he had been born to the right woman and in the right bed, no longer mattered much – that fear began to be turned into reality. The monarchs' own reactions to this development varied. Some were content to allow the process to run its course while

[17] *Baron Grimm and Diderot, correspondance littéraire, philosophique et critique, 1753–1769* (Paris: Caillot, 1813), vol. IV, p. 186.
[18] Quoted in J. H. Elliott, *Spain and Its World 1500–1700* (New Haven, CT: Yale University Press, 1969), pp. 15, 142.
[19] See J. A. Maravell, *La philosophie politique espagnole au XVIIIe siècle dans les rapports avec l'esprit de la contre-réforme* (Paris: Vrin, 1955), p. 241.

simultaneously denying that it existed. Such was the case of France's Louis XV: while spending almost half of his time hunting and the rest with Madame de Pompadour, in 1766 he issued a ringing declaration to the effect that "it is in my person alone that sovereign power resides . . . the whole system of public order emanates from me."[20] Others, such as Prussia's Frederick II, vainly tried to swim against the tide by working unceasingly. He also sneered at his French colleague, claiming that it was not Louis XV who governed but a group of four, namely the secretaries of war, of the marine, of foreign affairs, and the controller-general.

Frederick's Prussia was, in fact, the perfect example of the dilemma that bureaucracy created. On the one hand he vehemently demanded "system" as indispensable for running the country and making the best of its limited resources. On the other he inveighed against those who, even as they manned the system and provided the information on which it rested, "wanted to govern despotically while their master is expected to be satisfied with the empty prerogative of signing the orders issued in his name." Well aware of his subordinates' tendency to procrastinate and obstruct when it suited their purpose, he tried to contain the problem by loosing salvo after salvo of edicts and rebukes. In the 1770s he even resorted to divide-and-rule by importing French officials to occupy top positions in the postal system and the treasury, which caused his own native bureaucrats to complain about "despotic and arbitrary methods . . . in the fashion of the Spanish Inquisition."[21] Given that no country was as dependent on its bureaucracy as Prussia – an entirely artificial creation lacking both tradition and geographical unity – it is no wonder that, in the long run, his efforts availed him little. The older he became and the greater Prussia's population – during his reign it increased from 2.5 to 5 million – the more his rule restricted itself to inspection tours and occasional acts of capricious interference.

At the end of the eighteenth century the Prussian bureaucracy was, relative to the population, the largest in the world,[22] thus making certain that the trend set under Frederick the Great would continue under his less capable successors. Frederick William II (1786–97) was primarily a *bon vivant*. His chief interest in life was his mistresses; once provided with those, he took little further interest in affairs. Frederick William III (1797–1840), though conscientious (a "perfectly honest man" is how he was once described by Napoleon)[23] did not have it in him to oppose his

[20] Quoted in M. Antoine, *Le conseil du roi sous le règne du Louis XV* (Paris: Droz, 1970), p. 9.

[21] Quotations from Rosenberg, *Bureaucracy, Aristocracy and Autocracy*, p. 197.

[22] See the tables in M. Mann, *The Sources of Social Power* (Cambridge: Cambridge University Press, 1993), vol. II, appendix A.

[23] Napoleon I, *Correspondance* (Paris: Plon, 1858–), vol. XIII, p. 368, no. 11026, Bulletin No. 9 of the Grande armée, 17 October 1806.

ministers or, for that matter, his formidable wife Queen Louise. Both were "absolute" kings who soon discovered that their real role was limited to putting their seal on the recommendations made to them by their ministers. By that time the judiciary, too, had become independent and the sovereign had lost the prerogative of meddling with the juridical decisions that his subordinates made. As Frederick II recognized toward the end of his reign, doing so was to diminish their authority, throw a spanner into the system's works, and render the laws upon which it rested ineffective.

Far from suffering a setback, the story that began during the later Middle Ages culminated after Napoleon's defeat of Prussia in 1806. Into the gap created by the failure of the royal cabinet, the army, and the top levels of civilian government, there stepped a tiny but determined clique of *gebildete* – meaning university-educated – officials of bourgeois origin such as von Stein and von Hardenberg, both of whom had recently been ennobled. Centering around the Council of State or *Staatsrat*, the system they built was essentially one of enlightened bureaucratic despotism tempered by the will of the upper classes; as Stein himself was to write, Prussia was ruled by "buralists" who, "come rain or sunshine . . . write, write, write . . . in silence, in offices behind closed doors, unknown, unnoticed, unpraised, and determined to raise their children as equally usable writing machines."[24] Technically they were responsible to a king who, carrying the title of *Allerhöchste* or "all highest," remained the legitimate sovereign and an active power not subject to human judgment. In practice he operated through the ministers – whose countersignatures to all royal ordinances were required – and his personal intervention in the operation of the administrative machine was all but eliminated.

Fifteen years before the Prussian collapse, the entire vast French system of venal administration had been brought down at a single blow together with the *société d'ordres* in which it was anchored. As in Prussia, the bureaucracy was pulled up by the roots and taken out of civil society, so to speak; as the divorce between the two, which had been in the making since the second half of the seventeenth century, became final as the former developed a separate identity and was set up over the latter. Addressing the National Convention, Mirabeau put it as follows: henceforward France would recognize only two kinds of persons, i.e., citizens on the one hand and government officials on the other. These brave words were soon followed by deeds. Napoleon cleared away the debris left by the Revolution. The old mishmash of *intendants* and provincial governors, *pays d'état* and *pays d'élection* (the latter subject to direct royal

[24] H. F. C. von Gagern, ed., *Die Briefe des Freiherrn von Stein an den Freiherrn von Gagern, 1813–1831* (Stuttgart: Cotta, 1833), pp. 90–2.

rule, the former not), was abolished. Its place was taken by an ultra-modern, highly centralized, salaried government apparatus whose top echelons consisted of the cabinet and the *conseil d'état* and whose tentacles spread uniformly into every *département* and *arrondissement*. Later it became the model for every country occupied by the French including Italy,[25] the Netherlands,[26] much of Germany,[27] and Spain.[28]

Since the Revolution had eliminated the *société d'états* as well as the provincial parliaments, flattening and atomizing society, the power of the French bureaucracy soon reached unprecedented heights. During the next century the forms of government were designed to undergo many changes from empire to absolute monarchy to constitutional monarchy to republic and (after another empire) to republic again. Each time a revolution took place the administrative structure was shaken. However, after a few individuals had been executed or dismissed, it emerged stronger than before; much as the waves of the ocean do not affect the underlying currents, so the foundations laid in 1800–3 have, in many ways, survived to the present day. In theory it was a fine-tuned machine completely under the government's control and responsive to its commands. In practice not even a Napoleon – as a contemporary saying went, "il sait tout, il peut tout, il fait tout" – was able to run a country of 30 million by decree, the more so because he was often absent on campaign.

By this time Britain with its centuries-old system of unpaid administration sustained by corruption had fallen far behind. From the 1790s on, the demand for reform began in earnest. One voice which called for an end to the prevailing confusion between the private and the public was that of Jeremy Bentham; despairing of being heard in his own country and influenced by the French example, he even wrote many of his works in French.[29] Whereas Bentham was a philosopher and a liberal, Burke was a parliamentarian and a conservative who in many ways led British public opinion in opposing everything that the Revolution stood for. Hence it is surprising to find him calling for the creation of a class of men "wholly set apart and dedicated for public purposes, without any other than public duties and public principles; men without the possibility of converting the

[25] M. Broers, "Italy and the Modern State: The Experience of Napoleonic Rule," in F. Furet and M. Ozouf, eds., *The French Revolution and the Creation of Modern Culture* (Oxford: Pergamon, 1989), vol. III, pp. 489–503.

[26] J. P. A. Coopman, "Van Beleid van Politie naar Uitvoering en Bestuur, 1700–1840," *Bijdrage en Mededelingen betreffende de Geschiedenis der Nederlanden*, 104, 1989, pp. 579–91.

[27] I. Mieck, "Napoléon et les réformes en Allemagne," *Francia*, 15, 1987, pp. 473–91.

[28] C. Muñoz de Bustilo, "Remarks on the Origins of Provincial Administration in Spain," *Parliaments, Estate and Representation*, 14, 1, 1994, pp. 47–55.

[29] See in particular his *Introduction to the Principles of Morals and Legislation* (New York: Methuen, 1970 [1789]).

estate of the community into a private fortune; men denied to self-interest, whose avarice is for some community; men to whom personal poverty is honor, and implicit obedience stands in the place of freedom."[30]

In the event, the British government took several measures to modernize the country's administration. The Regulating Act which Lord North, as prime minister, passed through Parliament in 1773 prohibited tax collectors and persons engaged in the administration of justice from taking part in trade or accepting presents. The percentage of senior officials who received salaries rather than fees increased; the fact that ministers spent more time in Parliament, thus leaving day-to-day administration in the hands of their permanent undersecretaries, also represented a step toward bureaucratization. These steps had gone into effect only when the Revolutionary and Napoleonic Wars broke out and gave government more important things to worry about than Bentham's "felicific calculus," the formula by which he hoped to figure out the measures best adapted to maximize the happiness of each person in the realm. The old creaky machinery was retained. On the whole it functioned admirably, financing the country's own military effort, subsidizing that of its allies, and ending the war on terms that made Britain the greatest power on earth. Progress resumed only in the 1830s, by which time industrialization had transformed the country, creating a strong urban middle class which insisted on ending the old aristocratic corruption.

After the Reform Bill of 1831 had abolished the rotten boroughs and extended the electorate by 60 percent the last sinecures were done away with. New legislation was passed, barring members of Parliament from holding offices; next, in the 1840s, the reforms of Sir Charles Trevelyan led to the institution of the modern civil service with regular entrance examinations, a promotion ladder, retirement pensions, and a fixed if sometimes whimsical way of doing business. Remarkably enough, it was modeled upon the system first organized by the East India Company – the private organization to which the government had delegated control over the subcontinent – where Trevelyan had spent fourteen years of his career.[31]

Though the details varied, in all countries the century and a half after 1648 was characterized above all by the growth in the power of state

[30] E. Burke, *Reflections on the Revolution in France* (London: Oxford University Press, 1920 [1791]), p. 174.
[31] For these reforms, see E. W. Cohen, *The Growth of the British Civil Service, 1780–1939* (London: Allen and Unwin, 1941), ch. 5; and E. T. Stokes, "Bureaucracy and Ideology: Britain and India in the Nineteenth Century," *Transactions of the Royal Historical Society*, 30, 1950, pp. 131–56.

bureaucracy, both that part whose function was internal administration and the division responsible for external affairs. However, the more powerful and the more centralized the bureaucracy rulers needed in order to control their states, the more it tended to take that control out of the rulers' hands and into its own. Among the first to sense which way the wind was blowing were those excellent weathervanes, the great aristocratic families of France and England. Even before 1789 they were beginning to desert their respective courts, the latter in favor of London (where real power tended to become concentrated at Whitehall) and the former in favor of their country seats.[32] By 1798 things had progressed far enough for the Dictionary of the French Academy to define bureaucracy as "power, influence of the heads and staff of governmental bureaus." Fifteen years later a German dictionary of foreign expressions explained it as "the authority of power which various government departments and their branches abrogate to themselves over their fellow citizens."[33] As for royalty itself, from 1848 on many of them resumed their travels by making use of the railways. With real power for the most part taken out of their hands, the place where they found themselves at any one time did not matter too much anyway. This applied even to Germany's Wilhelm II, who, though still closer to absolutism than any other monarch except for the Russian tsar, absented himself from Berlin for months on end and acquired the nickname of *Reisekaiser* (traveling-emperor).

Though its pace varied, the growth in the number and power of the bureaucracy that has been documented in this section took place regardless of the state's lineage, i.e., whether it was absolute, constitutional, or parliamentarian; had been set up by armed coercion, as was mostly the case in France, Austria, and Prussia, or with the aid of capital as in the Netherlands and, in a different way, England; and ultimately even whether it was national or multinational, centralized or federal, monarchical or republican. If lazy rulers such as England's Henry VIII and France's Louis XV found themselves trapped and sidetracked by their own bureaucracies so, though for the opposite reasons, did industrious ones such as Spain's Philip II and Prussia's Frederick the Great. If hereditary rulers enjoying lifetime power failed to master the machinery they themselves had created, so, though again for the opposite reasons, did elected ones with their much shorter terms of office. As Hegel recognized, by the beginning of the nineteenth century the point had been

---

[32] M. von Boehm, *Frankreich im 18. Jahrhundert* (Berlin: Weidemann, n.d.), p. 67, notes how the Rohan, Noailles, and Montmorency clans withdrew from the court of Louis XVI.

[33] Académie française, *Dictionnaire de la langue française* (Paris: Bassagne and Maison, 1798 supplement); J. H. Campe, *Wörterbuch* (Braunschweig: Bouvier, 1813), p. 161.

reached where the bureaucracy itself *became* the state, elevating itself high above civil society and turning itself into the latter's master.

Creating the infrastructure

Bureaucracy both presupposes the existence of information – the indispensable grist to the administrators' mill – and enables more of it to be generated. One of the earliest and most important steps in this direction was to arrive at an exact definition as to which territories belonged to which ruler. During the Middle Ages this had mostly been done on an *ad hoc* basis; an estate reached from this hill to that river, a province from town A to mountain B. In an illiterate society facts of this kind had to be retrieved with the aid of reliable old men, as the formula went, and recorded with the aid of local witnesses. To make sure the witnesses kept things well in mind, they were sometimes dunked into the river or else given a resounding slap – which incidentally also accounts for the custom of dubbing knights by striking them with the flat of the sword.

Until the middle of the seventeenth century, when the Dutchman Willebord Snell (Snellius) started using trigonometry for the purpose, maps capable of accurately representing entire countries or even provinces did not exist. Corresponding with Italy's exceptional degree of development, the first attempts to draw such maps were made there during the second half of the fifteenth century.[34] In France, a map showing the entire realm was produced in 1472; however, it was merely a sketch intended to give a general idea, without any particular scale and suitable neither for diplomatic purposes nor for administrative ones. In the absence of maps the modern system of representing the shape of a country, let alone measuring its territory, could not be applied. As late as the 1690s the great military engineer Vauban, working for Louis XIV, submitted estimates as to France's area which differed from each other by as much as a third; elsewhere the situation was even worse. The absence of good maps also meant that, whenever war or agreement led to a transfer of land from one ruler to another, the territory in question could rarely be described in cartographic terms. Instead it had to be handled in terms of counties, districts, or communities, in short of small subdivisions whose frontiers were more or less known to both rulers and inhabitants. And indeed countries tended to be seen as consisting of such subdivisions.

The first border to be marked on the ground by means of stones was the

---

[34] See J. Marino, "Administrative Mapping in the Italian States," in D. Buisseret, ed., *Monarchs, Ministers and Maps: The Emergence of Cartography as a Tool of Government in Early Modern Europe* (Chicago: University of Chicago Press, 1992), ch. 1.

one established between Sweden and Brandenburg at the end of the Thirty Years War.[35] At the conference of Nijmegen in 1678–9, rivers were used to delimit borders between two states, in this case France and the southern Netherlands. In 1718 a treaty between Emperor Charles VI and the Dutch set another precedent: the written text was accompanied by a map with lines drawn across it marking the new borders.[36] Credit for the idea that the territories ruled by each monarch or republic should be painted in the same color goes to the Hamburg geographer Johan Hebner (1680–1713). Later during the century the use of different markings to distinguish between international borders and those separating provinces also became standard; still, as late as 1762 the British ambassador to Copenhagen trying to mediate a diplomatic dispute discovered that a map showing the border between Holstein (which was part of the Empire) and Denmark (which was not) did not exist. The one he eventually procured contained information that was over 160 years old.[37]

By this time the British, French, and Austrian governments were all employing professional surveyors in order to produce, for the first time, maps of entire countries that would be based on triangulation rather than on guesswork. Relying on the primitive equipment of the day, the projects took decades to complete. In the cases of England and France, they bore fruit just before the French Revolution; in Austria, it took until 1806.[38] Conversely, regions where states had not yet penetrated were characterized by inaccurate maps or none at all – which, among other things, explains why Napoleon during his retreat from Moscow found himself operating in *terra* that was largely *incognita*. In other parts of the world the situation was even worse. Though the fashion of "drawing elephants for want of towns" (as Alexander Pope put it) was slowly dying out, blank patches were still large and numerous. For example, during much of the eighteenth century nobody could say for certain where Virginia ended and Louisiana began. Much of the border between the United States and Canada remained unmarked until well into the nineteenth century, to say nothing of the situation in much of Africa and Asia, where, of course, there were no states and, consequently, no sharply defined borders but only intermediate zones subject to rulers on both sides or to none at all. As time passed the ability of a political organization to be represented by a colored patch on a map of the globe grew into one of the most important

[35] G. Parker, *The Thirty Years War* (London: Cambridge University Press, 1984), p. 217.

[36] G. Clark, *The Seventeenth Century* (London: Clarendon, 1966 edn.), p. 144.

[37] J. Black, *The Rise of the European Powers, 1679–1793* (London: Edward Arnold, 1990), pp. 194–6.

[38] For the history of that map, see J. Vann, "Mapping Under the Austrian Habsburgs," in Buisseret, *Monarchs, Ministers and Maps*, pp. 163ff.

symbols of statehood. And indeed the more solid the patch, the more powerful, other things being equal, the state.

Once the problem of determining states' borders and measuring their areas had been more or less solved, the next question was to find out what resources, human and material, were available to rulers *within* each state. From the time of the Domesday Book on, occasional censuses had been held in many European countries; however, it lay in the nature of the decentralized political system (as well as the primitive technical means available for the purpose) that they very seldom kept up with demographic and economic change. In 1516 Thomas More suggested that the problem be evaded by giving all communities, all towns, and all provinces exactly the same size – an idea that would have been useful, even if it was utopian. Almost as utopian was the proposal of the English merchant Gerrard Winstanley in *The Law of Freedom* (1652) that each parish elect two "postmasters." They would report to eight "receivers," two for each part of the kingdom, east, west, south, and north. The parish postmasters would "every month bring up or send by tidings, from their respective parish to the chief city, of what accidents or passages fall out, which is either to be the honor or dishonor, hurt or profit of the Commonwealth." Once collated the information would be printed: "the benefit lies here, that if any part of the land be visited with plague, famine, invasion, or insurrection, or any casualties, the other parts of the land may have speedy knowledge and send relief."[39]

On the Continent, where political entities tended to be either larger or more fragmented (sometimes both), the problem of gaining information as the basis for administration was, if anything, even more difficult. During the 1580s, both Jean Bodin and Justus Lipsius had suggested that national censuses be taken in their respective countries so as to make taxation more equitable. Preparing for the Estates General of 1583, Henry III's accountants did in fact take some measures in that direction; but so long as the civil wars continued, and disorder remained endemic, there was no chance of the proposal being carried out. Then it was the turn of Louis XIV whose advisers, such as Louvois and Colbert, were well aware of the problem and repeatedly suggested measures to correct it.[40] According to Voltaire, the Sun King tried to obtain a systematic picture of his realm by way of the *intendants*; however, he was defeated by the difficulty of designing a standard form that would provide for the very different conditions found throughout the kingdom. "What would have

[39] G. Winstanley, *The Law of Freedom* (Cambridge: Cambridge University Press, 1983 [1652]), pp. 354ff.
[40] See R. Blomfeld, *Sebastien le Prestre de Vauban, 1633–1707* (London: Methuen, 1938), ch. 10.

been most desirable was for each *intendant* to give, in columns, an account of the number of inhabitants in each district – nobles, citizens, farm workers, artisans, and workmen – together with livestock of all kinds, land of various degrees of fertility, the whole of the regular and secular clergy, their revenues, those of the towns and those of the communities."[41]

The first modern countries to hold population censuses were Iceland (1703) and Sweden (1739), both of which were motivated by fear of depopulation.[42] The French in 1736 set another precedent: all parish priests were ordered to record births, marriages, and deaths in duplicate, keeping one copy and sending the other to the government in Paris. Both the advantages and the limitations of the system are illustrated by the efforts of Jacques Necker, in his capacity as minister of finance to Louis XVI in 1767–72, to find out the number of France's inhabitants. Relying on the available data, he averaged the number of births in each of the years in question. The outcome he multiplied by 25.5, or 24.75, or whatever other guesstimate was available on their proportion in the general population.

Following the example set by Sweden as early as 1748, the French National Assembly in 1791 established a proper statistical office, independent of the government ministers and charged with the compilation of regular statistical reports. Its first head was a great scientist, Antoine Lavoisier, whose other achievements as a public servant included the new metric system of weights and measures. From this point on, not only did the state count everybody and everything but, as if to emphasize the extent of its power, it also determined the units in which this was done. As for Lavoisier himself, among other fields in which he had been active was tax-farming. Accordingly, his reward was to be taken to the guillotine and executed.[43]

Returning to Britain, the first systematic attempt to gain statistical information – known as "political arithmetic" – on the number, wealth, and income of the inhabitants of the island was made in the 1690s by Gregory King. By profession he was a surveyor, mapmaker, and architect who laid out many of the squares of London and Westminster. In his spare time he wrote *Natural and Political Observations and Conclusions upon the State and Conditions of England* (1696) which gave the best

[41] Voltaire, *The Age of Louis XIV* (New York: Twayne, 1963 [1751]), p. 143.

[42] For Iceland, see T. Thorsteinsson, "The First Census Taken in Iceland in 1703," in *25th Session of the International Statistical Institute* (Washington, DC: International Statistical Institute, 1947), vol. III, pp. 614–23; for Sweden, see E. Arosneius, "The History and Organization of the Swedish Official Statistics," in J. Koren, ed., *The History of Statistics* (New York: Macmillan, 1918), pp. 537ff.

[43] On Lavoisier's work in these fields, see D. McKie, *Antoine Lavoisier: Scientist, Economist, Social Reformer* (London: Collier, 1980).

available picture of any country's population and wealth in history until then. However, the volume remained in manuscript, being of no interest to the general public. No systematic attempt was made to improve the information in the hands of the government. In 1753 a proposal for taking a national census was rejected by Parliament as inimical to liberty; six years later the same fate overtook an attempt to follow the French example by having parish priests provide the state with information on all vital events.[44] One result of this policy was that, in Britain as in other countries, witnesses to the early years of the industrial revolution – 1760–1800 – observing that enclosure was beginning to empty the countryside, expressed the fear that the population was decreasing, whereas in fact it was growing as never before.[45] Only in 1801 did both Britain and France follow the example of the United States (1790) and hold their first nationwide censuses; but even then it took another half-century before the British government, for one, bothered to register the names of every man, woman, and child in the country. As to Gregory King, he was vindicated in 1801 when his work was rediscovered and published.

The most important use to which statistics were put – and which explains why, from the time of King David on, attempts to gather them often gave rise to a storm of protest – was taxation. During the Middle Ages, taxes in our sense of the term did not exist; the king, like any other feudal lord, was supposed to "live off his own," i.e., the rent, fees, and other feudal payments due to him from his tenants and, in theory at any rate, not subject to change without their consent. To supplement his "private" income, he might ask the Estates for "aid" – especially in times of war or for covering some other kind of extraordinary expenditure, and usually in return for correcting "grievances." So important was this system of voluntary taxation that when Charles V created the first French treasury in 1373 he called it the *cour des aides*.

To focus on a few landmarks only, possibly the earliest "national" tax imposed in any country were the export duties on wool and hides that were voted by Parliament to Edward I in 1275 and which became permanent from 1347 on. Other rulers tried to follow his example; however, since their domains did not constitute islands, collection was more difficult and they were often frustrated either by the extent of their territories (if they were large) or by the ability of trade to avoid levies by going elsewhere (if they were small). In 1383 Charles V instituted the *gabelle*, or

---

[44] See K. Johanisson, "Society in Numbers: The Debate over Quantification in 18th-Century Political Economy," in T. Frangsmyr, et al., eds., *The Quantifying Spirit in the Eighteenth Century* (Berkeley: University of California Press, 1990), p. 349.

[45] See D. V. Glass, *Numbering the People: The Great Demographic Controversy* (Farnborough: Saxon House, 1978), esp. pp. 11ff.

salt tax, which obliged each household to buy a set amount at prices set by the king; described by Louis XII as "the easiest, simplest and most straightforward subsidy that could ever be levied," it soon found imitators in Castile, Provence, Florence, Genoa, and the Papal Territories. Next came the *taille*, or land tax, which Charles VII instituted in 1452 in order to pay for his standing army of *compagnies d'ordonance*. By forbidding the nobility to impose similar levies of their own he simultaneously created the first distinction between rent, which was due to a variety of feudal lords, and taxation, which was the sole prerogative of the king.

Reflecting the way in which France had been put together, both the *gabelle* and the *taille* were paid at very different rates by different provinces. Some, such as Brittany, escaped altogether and continued to do so right down to the Revolution of 1789; in others, the tax-farmers' demands drove the agricultural population to the verge of destitution. Nevertheless, by 1500 these and other taxes were transforming the financial situation of rulers, particularly those whose countries were the largest and in which the differentiation of the "public" sector from the "private" household was, accordingly, the most vigorous. The greater the growth of government, the less important the role played by the monarchs' private resources in financing it; conversely, the share of taxes went up and up. This led to different results in different countries. In France, a decisive step was taken in 1523 when Francis I published the edicts of St. Blois and St. Germain-en-Laye. A single treasury, the *trésoir d'épargne*, was established. The distinction between ordinary and extraordinary revenue – corresponding to that between money arbitrarily collected by the king and that which had been voted to him by the Etats généreaux – was abolished; and the basis for royal absolutism was laid for almost three centuries to come. This was not so in England, where Henry VIII, having sold off confiscated church land in order to finance his wars, found himself in a worse situation than his father had been in and became the first king who was entirely dependent on Parliament. The long-term outcome was an equally solid system of parliamentary government, albeit one from which his daughter Elizabeth, as well as the first two among her Stuart successors, did their best to escape.

Regardless of whether the taxes were levied by the king on his own or voted to him by some assembly, the income available to rulers increased relative to that of all other individuals and also in comparison to that of society as a whole. Under Henry VIII it tripled; in France between 1523 and 1600 it quadrupled.[46] The increase was greatest during the years

[46] More detailed figures are in M. S. Kimmel, *Absolutism and Its Discontents: State and Society in Seventeenth-Century France and England* (New Brunswick, NJ: Transaction Books, 1988), pp. 58–9.

before 1550, after which it tended to be swallowed up by the so-called price revolution caused by the influx of precious metal from the Americas as well as the increase in demand resulting from rapid population growth. Nevertheless, the reality of the trend is attested to by its persistence into the first half of the seventeenth century, a period of bad weather (the "little ice age"), agricultural disasters, stagnant economies, and low inflation or even deflation.[47] For example, England's Charles I was able to more than double the income received by his father James I, raising it from £400,000 annually at the beginning of the reign to £900,000 on the eve of the Civil War. By that time even the rulers of small countries such as Bavaria, Prussia, and Denmark were relying much more on taxation and less on their private resources.[48] This was a trend which their subjects resented but which by and large they were powerless to resist.

In both England and France the reluctance of the population to pay taxes contributed to the unrest, civil war, and revolutions that swept over them between around 1620 and 1660;[49] however, by the latter date both had largely overcome their difficulties in this respect. England in 1664 became the first country all of whose citizens were equal under the law. The privileges which still existed – specifically the right of clergymen to vote taxes in convocation – where abolished, so that everybody regardless of status paid whatever sums the government sought to levy and Parliament to grant. In France, the rising prestige of the king's *trésoriers* received symbolic expression in 1643 when, at the funeral of Louis XIII, their wives and daughters were allowed the same clothing as other magistrates. It is true that the distinction between *pays d'élection* and *pays d'état* remained in force; however, Mazarin and his successors were able to circumvent it to some extent by introducing a whole series of new "extracurricular" taxes not covered by the ancient privileges and, therefore, applicable to the realm as a whole. As early as 1670 – i.e., before Louis XIV engaged on the long and costly wars that marked the second half of his realm – Colbert in his *Mémoire au Roi sur les finances* argued that the king was, if anything, collecting too much. According to him, royal revenue stood at 70 million *livres tournois* annually. The ratio between this

---

[47] See E. Hobsbawm, "The General Crisis of the European Economy in the Seventeenth Century," *Past and Present*, 5, 1954, pp. 33–59, and 6, 1955, pp. 45–65.

[48] For Denmark, see G. Rystad, ed., *Europe and Scandinavia: Aspects of Integration in the Seventeenth Century* (Lund: Esselte Studium, 1983), p. 15; for Prussia, see K. Breysig, "Der brandemburgische Staatshaushalt in der zweiten Hälfte des 17. Jahrhunderts," *Jahrbuch für Gesetzgebung, Verwaltung, und Volkswirtschaft in Deutschen Reich*, 16, 1892, pp. 1ff., 449ff.

[49] On these revolts, their causes, and their outcomes, see Kimmel, *Absolutism and Its Discontents*.

sum and the amount of silver in circulation, estimated at 120 million, was 7:12, whereas the ideal ratio was thought to be 1:3.

In the second half of the seventeenth century, taxation was probably lightest in England which, though already engaged on the construction of a regular navy, had neither a standing army nor a paid bureaucracy to look after. It was heaviest in Prussia where the sums collected by the Great Elector, Frederick William, often with considerable brutality, were used to create a standing army of 30,000 men and thus change his domains from a motley assembly of provinces into a medium-ranking European power. Though comprehensive statistics are hard to come by, other countries must have stood somewhere in between. In many of them, as long as the *ancien régime* lasted, the real problem facing governments in their attempt to increase revenue was not so much the depressing effect this had on the economy as the tendency of the sums collected to get lost on their way to the central treasury. For example, out of 8,277,166 *livres* raised in Languedoc in 1677, 34.5 percent remained in the hands of various provincial notables. Of the remaining 65.5 percent, half – in fact, 50.3 percent – was tied to royal expenditure in the province itself. Thus only 33 percent, or just under one-third, ever reached Paris and could be used by the king to cover the expenditure of the state, which at that time consisted mainly of the army on the one hand and the court on the other.[50]

In spite of these limitations, between 1689 and 1714, France spent no less than 5 billion *livres* – or £300 million. This almost equaled the sums spent by its three principal enemies, England, the Holy Roman Empire, and the Netherlands combined, thus justifying Louis XIV's proud boast of being *nec pluribus impar*.[51] The screws of taxation had been turned to the limit. Unable to tighten them still further without risking a revolt, the king and his advisers resorted to borrowing. Here the fact that the administration was a venal one could be turned to advantage, since the list of persons entitled to receive tax-money as a reward for the offices that they held read like a who's who of French society. In return for allowing its officials a share of revenue the state demanded that they advance it money. Having been extensively used during the wars of religion in particular, the system was anything but new, but under Louis XIV it grew to monstrous dimensions. In 1714, the year that the War of the Spanish Succession ended and the one before the king's death, the government's debt stood at thirty times its annual income and the resulting payments

---

[50] M. Beik, *Absolutism and Society in Seventeenth-Century France* (London: Cambridge University Press, 1985), pp. 260ff.
[51] For more details, see P. G. M. Dickson and J. Sterling, "War Finance, 1689–1714," in J. S. Bromley, ed., *The New Cambridge Modern History*, vol. IV (London: Cambridge University Press, 1970), pp. 284–315.

consumed nearly the entire state revenue. By comparison, in 1994 the US national debt – the one considered so intolerable that it led to the Republican victory in the elections of that year – amounted to only three times annual revenue.

Thus, so long as it remained "absolute" the power of the French state found its fiscal limits.[52] Its debts to its own officials continued to increase, the problem being not so much the country's inability to pay as the inequitable distribution of taxes, particularly the *taille* from which almost everybody except the peasantry (including, in particular, large landowners in the form of nobility and church) was exempt. Collection continued to be by tax-farming, tax-farmers being employed by the central treasury, the provincial estates, and the municipalities, all of whom deducted what was due to them before sending the remainder to the *receveur-général* in each of sixteen collection districts. Not only did tax-farmers make themselves thoroughly hated – during the Terror many of them were put to death – but the ultimate result was that the state slid slowly into bankruptcy. In 1750, in a desperate attempt to tap the hitherto exempt resources of the upper classes, a 5 percent tax was imposed on all landed incomes; however, it was a case of too little too late. Meanwhile trust in the government's ability to meet its obligations, and with it progress toward a modern financial system, suffered.

When the break finally came, it was radical indeed. As the National Assembly put it in the Declaration of Rights (1789), for the maintenance of the public forces and the expenses of administration a common contribution was indispensable; but henceforward this contribution was to be equally divided among all citizens in proportion to their means. The entire vast system of exemptions and privileges was abolished at a stroke. With it went the ancient customs duties that still separated one province from the next, thus for the first time turning France into a single market (and state) of 30 million people. From this time to the reemergence of so-called free trade zones during the years from 1975 on, customs duties were something that one paid upon passing from one state to another, not so long as one remained inside its borders. Under Napoleon the yield from property taxes alone increased from 80 million to 200 million *livres*; but he also added a whole series of new taxes to the existing ones. Among them were an excise – which in time came to be hated almost as much as conscription – a levy on salt, a state tobacco monopoly, and a system of external tariffs that was destined to remain in place for the rest of the nineteenth century. Even more important, taxation became truly national. Not only did all revenues – including those extracted from other

[52] See J. B. Collins, *Fiscal Limits of Absolutism: Direct Taxation in Early Seventeenth-Century France* (Berkeley: University of California, Press, 1988).

countries in the form of booty or reparations – accrue to a single treasury, but the system whereby part of the sums raised in each province could only be spent in that province came to an end, thus for the first time giving the government full control over all its funds.

Having already gone through *its* revolution a century or so earlier, the British state was governed with the consent of the upper classes and thus in a much better position to squeeze the pips without risking too much opposition. In particular, the series of anti-French wars of 1689–1714 represented an extraordinary achievement for a country of perhaps 5.5 million people which had long been located on the fringes of civilization and had only recently broken into the ranks of the great powers. The wars were financed by an entire series of new taxes, such as a property tax, a tax on beer, and a tax on windows which was imported from the Netherlands; a similar one was imposed on the American colonies and, as can be seen in Charleston, South Carolina, to this day, led to the construction of narrow, elongated buildings facing away from the streets. In 1692 Britain became the first country to abandon tax-farming in favor of paid collectors, leading to a sharp reduction in the percentage of revenue that got stuck on the way. The upshot was that Britain handled its finances much better than France. By 1714, although the government's debt had grown to three times annual income, interest rates were actually falling.

Around the middle of the century the British state was draining away perhaps 20 percent of the country's wealth. Its main instrument for doing so consisted of indirect taxes which brought in two-thirds to three-quarters of all sums collected; as Prime Minister Robert Walpole (1721–42) once explained, people who would otherwise have squealed like slaughtered pigs allowed themselves to be fleeced like sheep.[53] A series of efficiency measures, such as the establishment in 1787 of a single consolidated fund into which the entire yield of customs and excises was paid, continued the transition toward a modern state with a centralized national treasury. Since it did not have to share its revenue with its office holders, Britain with a much smaller population than France found the resources to wage a whole series of world wars (1740–8, 1756–63, 1776–83), subsidize any number of continental allies, *and* easily carry a growing debt, albeit one that did lead to moderate inflation. In 1799 the younger Pitt, faced with the need to finance the war against France, felt strong enough to introduce an income tax of 5 percent on incomes over £200 per year. Considering that a fully employed unskilled laborer could make

---

[53] P. Mathias and P. O'Brien, "Taxation in Britain and France, 1715–1810: Comparison of the Social and Economic Incidence of the Taxes Collected for the Central Government," *Journal of European Economic History*, 5, 1976, pp. 601–50.

about £25 a year, and a skilled one double that sum,[54] this was not too much to ask. However, the tax was the first of its kind imposed in any country and a clear harbinger of much worse things to come.

By way of a final illustration of what a well-administered modern state could do to rob its citizens and concentrate financial power in its own hands, consider the development of Prussia. The country, such as it was, was incomparably smaller and less fertile than either Britain or, *a fortiori*, France. Around 1700 its population, numbering perhaps 1 million souls all told, stood at only 6 percent of the French; and, to make things worse, was scattered in a number of discontinuous provinces some of which were only barely recovering from the Thirty Years War. Even as late as the accession of Frederick the Great in 1740 the yield of the royal domain, amounting to one-third of all Prussian land and farmed with ruthless efficiency by the soldier-king, his father, accounted for half of his revenue. By the end of the reign further rent-racking had increased the income from this source from 3 to 7 million thalers, but this did not prevent its share as a part of all state revenue from falling to one-third. During the same period total revenue rose more than threefold, a feat achieved mainly by increasing indirect taxes.[55]

In the 1750s Frederick's income – including all kinds of services and *corvées* which continued to burden the peasantry – probably swallowed around 34 percent of the Prussian national product, a figure much higher than that attained in any other country at the time and which was soon augmented by massive British subsidies.[56] As in France, the most important single tax was the *Kontribution*, a levy on landed income which fell mainly on peasants since the nobility was exempt. While the system was far from uniform and riddled with inconsistencies, compared to France the Prussian state under Frederick the Great enjoyed several advantages. From 1723 on tax collection was concentrated exclusively in the hands of paid personnel. This meant better control over corruption, less loss along the way and, most important, no need to pay interest on loans made to the state by its own officials. Thanks partly to the efficiency of the bureaucracy, and partly to the king's own efforts, much better information was available on economic conditions in the various provinces and the income that could be expected from them. Moreover, the longer the century went on the more Prussia tended to follow the French example by imposing state monopolies (on coffee as well as tobacco and salt) and the British

[54] P. Deane, *The First Industrial Revolution* (Cambridge: Cambridge University Press, 1965), p. 262.
[55] A. Zottmann, *Die Wirtschaftspolitik Friedrichs des Grossen* (Leipzig: Deuticke, 1929), pp. 21ff.
[56] D. Stutzer, "Das preussische Heer und seine Finanzierung 1740–1790," *Militärgeschichtliche Mitteilungen*, 2, 1979, p. 30.

one by relying on indirect taxes, including, besides the usual ones already enumerated in connection with other countries, a tax on all kinds of meat except pork.

At the time he died in 1786, Frederick the Great, though he had waged two major wars (1740–8, 1756–63) plus a minor one (1778–9), left a treasury of 50 million thalers, equal to about two and a quarter years of revenue. He also had an army of close to 200,000 men, which besides being Europe's fourth largest (after those of France, Austria, and Russia) was considered the best of the lot. Basking in his achievement and perhaps fearing the consequences if they persisted, his successors chose to relax the pressure a little. They canceled some of the royal monopolies, sent the French experts who administered them packing, and adopted a more generous policy in regard to the unfortunate tenants of crown lands. Within four years the surplus had disappeared; but the Prussian state remained solvent and, a remarkable feat, maintained its ability to pay even during the extremely difficult years that followed its defeat at the hands of Napoleon. Still, its modernity should not be exaggerated. For example, the establishment of a single treasury responsible for all payments and receipts had to wait for the reforms of von Stein and von Hardenberg, while internal customs frontiers between the various provinces persisted and were abolished only in 1818.

To summarize, the period here under consideration was characterized above all by the creation of the instruments that would enable the state to do away with various intermediaries and squeeze its citizens as never before. As part of the process, borders had to be marked, maps drawn, and statistical information of every sort gathered; including in particular such as pertained to population, property, production, and incomes. As government expanded both in terms of the number of bureaucrats that it employed and the tasks that it undertook, the importance of the ruler's private resources *vis-à-vis* the country's overall budget naturally declined; until, sooner or later, it sank into insignificance. The change was reflected in the way that financial obligations were handled. Erasmus, assuming that the expenses of the court were responsible for a sizable fraction of the fiscal burden borne by subjects, had urged his Christian Prince to live modestly. Louis XIV on occasion was still reduced to selling plate (including a cherished set of 5,000 silver toy soldiers) to pay for his wars. But in 1689 William III of England, having just arrived from the Netherlands, could not be expected to step into his predecessor's shoes; accordingly he became the first monarch in history who could not be held personally liable for his government's debts. In 1770, the final step was taken and the total separation between king and country achieved.

Under the new system, the Post Office – established by Cromwell in

1652 and operated as a royal monopoly from the time of the Restoration on – as well as the remaining crown lands were taken over by the state. In return, King George III began to receive an annual stipend of £800,000 which was voted to him by Parliament and which was used to defray the expenses of running the court. This reform was subsequently imitated by other countries, including France (after the Revolution) and Prussia (where it took place in 1820).[57] Here it is worth adding that, although the link between the ruler's private property and that of the state was severed, the former usually remained substantial and, in most cases, enjoyed privileged status. For example, it was not until 1993 that the queen of the United Kingdom, the richest person in the realm, began paying income tax like anybody else.

The history of taxation itself was marked by a gradual switch from indirect taxes to the harder to collect, but much more remunerative, direct ones. To this should be added the growing profits derived from state monopolies, including, in many countries from the 1830s on, the railways. In one country after another the system was extended, exemptions abolished, and additional provinces brought into the network. Meanwhile internal customs borders were abandoned, central receiving funds established, and privileges of every sort canceled – albeit in some cases it took either a bloody revolution or defeat in war to accomplish that feat. Between 1760 and 1820 alone, the nominal value of taxes collected by the treasury increased fourfold in Austria, fourfold in France, and more than sixfold in Britain.[58] Needless to say, none of this would have been possible had the administration not been reformed, venal offices replaced by salaried ones, and professionalism – more and more based on university education – substituted for class, property, and connections as a means for advancement. To make good on its pretensions the state had to increase the instruments of violence at its disposal until there was nobody left capable of talking back – a subject to which we shall turn in the next section.

Monopolizing violence

During the Middle Ages, war, rather than being waged on behalf of nonexistent states, had been embedded in society, so to speak. Armies – let alone navies, which are extremely capital-intensive – *qua* separate organizations did not exist; war was the vocation of the upper classes whose members, representing little but their own interests and sense of

[57] See D. E. Brady, *Frederick William IV and the Prussian Monarch 1840–1861* (Oxford: Clarendon Press, 1995), p. 19.
[58] Mann, *Sources of Social Power*, vol. II, appendix, tables A6, A7, A8.

justice, donned armor and fought each other as the occasion demanded. As had also been the case in tribes without rulers, chiefdoms, and city-states, the modern "trinity" consisting of a government whose job is to direct policy, armed forces that fight and die, and a civilian population that supposedly enjoys immunity provided it does not interfere with the proceedings did not exist in the same form. Given the knightly ethos, rulers of every rank felt themselves obliged to fight in the front ranks and, as we saw, were frequently killed or captured; so long as they did so, they could scarcely be said to govern. The people on their part were hardly considered part of society at all. Looking at war as one would regard a natural disaster, a plague, or a famine – hence the four horses of the apocalypse – they watched as their betters battled each other and, of course, often paid the price.

The story of the transition from feudal hosts to mercenary forces and thence to the regular, state-owned armies and navies that made their appearance after 1648 has been told many times.[59] A good starting point is provided by the introduction of gunpowder, which was invented in China and must have been brought to Europe either by the Mongols or by the Arabs via North Africa and Spain; in any case there are scattered references to it in sources dating to the second half of the thirteenth century.[60] The use of cannon, or some other noise-making device probably based on gunpowder, is mentioned for the first time in connection with the Battle of Crecy which was fought between the English and the French in 1348. Shortly thereafter we find it employed in siege warfare also;[61] from the end of the fourteenth century on, references and pictures multiply, while the earliest extant specimens, such as "Mons Meg" at Edinburgh Castle, date to the middle of the fifteenth century. Though edged weapons and mechanical missile-throwing machines did not disappear at once, throughout this period the role played by gunpowder continued to grow. Toward the end of the Hundred Years War the French king in particular made systematic use of artillery in order to reconquer Normandy. As the fall of Constantinople in 1453 showed, by that time no walls in the world were strong enough to withstand its impact.

In the long run, nevertheless, gunpowder did less to change the balance between offense and defense than is often supposed.[62] Instead it forced

---

[59] The best short account is probably M. Howard, *War in European History* (Oxford: Oxford University Press, 1976), chs. 2–5.

[60] See J. R. Partington, *A History of Greek Fire and Gunpowder* (Cambridge: Heffer, 1960), ch. 3; and J. F. C. Fuller, *Armaments and History* (New York: Scribner's, 1945), pp. 78–81.

[61] Jean Froissart, *Chronicles* (Harmondsworth, UK: Penguin Books, 1968), pp. 88 (n. 2), 121.

[62] G. Quester, *Offense and Defense in the International System* (New York: Wiley, 1977), pp. 45–55.

the latter to look around for different methods by which to erect fortresses, a problem which during the second half of the fifteenth century gave employment to the very best minds from Leonardo, Michelangelo, and Albrecht Dürer down. By 1520 or so, after many false starts, an Italian engineer by the name of Michele San Michele had hit upon the solution. Essentially it consisted of replacing the tall, thin, medieval curtain-walls by extremely thick, squat walls that were sunken *into* the ground; at the same time, the place of towers was taken by the angular structures known as bastions which projected from the walls and provided cover both to the latter and to each other.[63] The resulting fortifications were much larger than their medieval predecessors and, as time went on and the range of cannon grew, tended to become larger still. Spreading from Italy to other countries, by the seventeenth century entire belts of them were girding the borders of France, the Netherlands, and the Empire. Anticipating the possibility of a Spanish invasion, even England built a few, though they were destined to remain unused as the Armada was defeated.

Not only was the new type of fortress much larger than the previous one, but it was also much more expensive. Though the cost of construction should not be underestimated, a medieval castle was within the reach of a comparatively large number of people. In France alone the remains of perhaps 10,000 are known, albeit the majority consist only of a simple bailey, or tower, and moat. Lords of every rank built castles for themselves, the difference between the most powerful monarch and the lowliest baron or count consisting not so much in the nature of the fortifications they erected as in the number of the castles that they owned, often in widely scattered places. The invention, and subsequent spread, of the so-called *trace italienne* brought this situation to an end. Only the richest and most powerful rulers could afford the new structures, while their sheer size meant that, instead of being located on the spurs of hills as previously, they tended to be built in the plains and even, as in the Netherlands, in country that was completely flat.[64]

As the nobility's castles became defenseless in front of cannon, its military position was also weakened in other ways. Contrasting sharply with those of antiquity, medieval armies had been based mainly on cavalry. So long as the terrain was suitable the mounted man-at-arms enjoyed a tremendous advantage, even to the point where the chronicles often fail to mention the foot-soldiers who were also present and whose

---

[63] J. R. Hale, "The Development of the Bastion, 1440–1453," in Hale, et al., *Europe in the Late Middle Ages*, pp. 446–94. See also S. Pepper and N. Adams, *Firearms and Fortifications* (Chicago: University of Chicago Press, 1986).

[64] For the evolution of fortifications from 1500 to their peak around 1700, see I. V. Hogg, *Fortress: A History of Military Defence* (London: Macdonald, 1975), chs. 3–4.

role on the battlefield consisted of being massacred by the heavier, taller, and faster knights. During the fourteenth century, though, the role of cavalry began to be undermined by the reintroduction of two ancient weapons, the pike and the longbow. Both originated with comparatively rude peoples – the Welsh, the Scots, and the Swiss – who inhabited mountainous countries that did not offer much scope for the operations of cavalry; and both instead demanded the creation of disciplined formations which, whatever their precise appearance, would stand together facing assault. From the time of the Battle of Morgarten (1315) on, and with increasing frequency, such formations began to be created and to show that they could stand up to the knights' attacks. The knights in turn tried to meet the challenge by piling on more and more armor, a solution which tended to make their equipment much more expensive and ended up by undermining itself even when, and to the extent that, it succeeded. After 1550 or so they simply gave up. Starting at the feet and reaching upward, complete suits of armor were gradually discarded. Those still being produced were intended for use mainly in tournaments, which by this time had turned into fantastically elaborate affairs with little but entertainment value.

Besides the military-technological developments that initiated it, the shift away from medieval warfare also had its financial aspects. As early as the thirteenth century the revival of an urban-based, commercial economy began to put money into people's hands. As a result, rulers sometimes released their vassals from the obligation of fighting for them, demanding shield-money or *scutagium* instead. The sums that were raised in this way could be used to engage mercenaries;[65] and by the second half of the fifteenth century mercenaries had, except perhaps at the highest levels of command, largely taken over from their feudal predecessors. The way to form an army now consisted of commissioning – the term is still in use – an entrepreneur to raise troops, clothe them, equip them, and train them. Having done so, he was also expected to lead them in war, all in return for good money which the entrepreneur received from his employers and which he shared with those under his command while trying to shave off as much as possible.[66]

During the sixteenth century, inspired first by the Swiss and then by the Spaniards, armies came to consist mainly of massive blocks (known as *Haufen* or *tercios*) of infantrymen armed with a mixture of pikes and arquebuses and organized for mutual protection. Field artillery was

---

[65] See, for the case of England, M. Prestwich, *War, Politics and Finance Under Edward I* (Totowa, NJ: Rowman and Littlefield, 1972).

[66] On the way these things were done, see F. Redlich, *The German Military Entrepreneur and His Work Force* (Wiesbaden: Steiner, 1964).

slower to develop, the early guns being heavy and their rate of fire RD
low; however, after 1494 these limitations were gradually overcome.
Cannon, which contrary to previous usage began to be mounted on
mobile carriages, appeared on the battlefield in growing numbers. Cavalry, too, remained in existence, though its effectiveness as a shock arm
declined as did its numerical proportion to the rest of the forces. As the
three arms assumed something like their modern form, more and more
the outcome of battles depended on the ability to coordinate them,
employing each one in such a way as to put the enemy on the horns of a
dilemma: for example, by the demonstrative use of cavalry to compel him
to form squares before opening up with one's cannon to blast those
squares to pieces. This was the way in which such master-tacticians as
Gonsalvo de Cordoba, Maurice of Nassau, and Gustavus Adolphus
operated. All three were well aware of the need for combined arms, and
the latter two constantly experimented with smaller formations and
lighter guns to bring it about.

Given that states in our sense of the term still did not exist, the
objectives for which war was waged had not changed much from medieval
times. Rulers such as Charles V, Francis I, and their contemporaries
fought each other to determine who would rule this province or that. The
personal nature of their quarrels is indicated by the fact that the Emperor
repeatedly offered to fight his rival in a duel; in addition, the peace treaties
signed after each war often included some clause that provided for a
marriage between the protagonists, their sons, sisters, daughters, and
other family members in such a way as to produce an heir who, as the
offspring of both sides, would – it was hoped – solve the problem that had
given rise to the war. At a lower level, the fact that armies were made up of
independent or semi-independent entrepreneurs helps explain the wave
of civil wars that swept over countries such as England, France, and
Germany. An army of mercenaries, often including its commander, remained loyal to the ruler whom it served only so long as pay lasted. Once
that changed, the troops would mutiny, switch sides, strike out on their
own, or simply disperse and go home.[67]

The climax of these developments was reached during the Thirty
Years War, which marks both the end of the old system and the beginning of the new. It started, as we saw, as an attempt by the Habsburg
Emperor to reassert his authority over Germany and, possibly, the Empire in the wider sense of that term. However, it soon degenerated into a
free-for-all in which Emperor, kings, territorial rulers of various ranks,

[67] The military revolts mounted by mercenary forces are well described in G. Parker, *The
Army of Flanders and the Spanish Road* (London: Cambridge University Press, 1972),
ch. 8.

religious leagues, free cities, and commissioned and noncommissioned military entrepreneurs (many of them scarcely distinguishable from robbers and, unless willing to change sides, often treated as such) fought each other with every means at their disposal. All, needless to say, did so at the expense of the peasantry whose fields, orchards, and domestic animals enabled armies to march on their stomachs, to say nothing of meeting the remaining natural requirements of heroes such as looting, burning, and raping. Where the peasants did not allow themselves to be victimized but tried to put up a defense, they merely added to the confusion, so that for three decades much of Central Europe was literally engulfed in war.

In the long run, nevertheless, the outcome of chaos was order. Once the Treaties of Westphalia were signed, many of the mercenary forces that had fought the war – those who were not were absorbed into the standing armies or *militia perpetua*, as they were known – were sent home. Officers did not at once cease to be businessmen; in France it was only around the middle of the century that units ceased to be known after their commanders and the purchase of military rank was abolished, whereas in Britain the latter reform had to wait until the Cardwell Reforms of 1874. Still, throughout the period their role as independent entrepreneurs was gradually narrowed down. Such tasks as recruiting the troops, enrolling them, paying them, clothing them, equipping them, and promoting them were centralized in the hands of the newly emerging war ministries. The replacement of entrepreneurs by officers – who, increasingly, had to attend a military academy before being commissioned – turned the latter into loyal servants of the state, while the switch from temporary mercenaries to long-serving regular troops made it possible to improve the discipline of the rank and file. The crowds of unruly scarecrows that had infested Europe during much of the century before 1648 largely disappeared. The name of General Martinet of France, who acquired fame by the bastinadoes that he inflicted for every missing button and every ill-fitting garter, has even entered the language.

By this time the entire structure of war, which hitherto had been waged for personal reasons, was beginning to change in the direction of the impersonal state. In England Queen Elizabeth I had often entered into commercial contracts with her subjects, the most prominent of whom were Francis Drake and Walter Raleigh, with the objective of despoiling the Spanish overseas possessions.[68] A hundred years after her death such a system had become unthinkable; and indeed already during the first half of the eighteenth century there grew the conviction that, to the extent that

[68] K. R. Andrews, *Trade, Plunder and Settlement: Maritime Enterprise and the Genesis of the British Empire, 1480–1630* (Cambridge: Cambridge University Press, 1984), pp. 14–15.

rulers still went to war for their personal profit, they were little better than criminals.[69] The state's growing monopoly over war also made itself felt overseas. Throughout the seventeenth century there had been many occasions when two countries fought each other in Europe but not in the colonies, or the other way around, as, for example, during the twelve-year truce between Spain and the Netherlands, which lasted from 1609 to 1621 and which was limited to Europe. After 1714 this situation came to an end. More and more the various West and East India Companies came to be regarded simply as an extension of their governments' power, and more and more this was actually the case.

Another field in which the shift from personal war waged by the ruler to impersonal warfare conducted on behalf of the state made itself felt was the different treatment meted out to prisoners of war. Previously they had been regarded as their captors' private property and had to ransom themselves; until they did so, they could be swapped, sold, and otherwise put to profit by private individuals who, accordingly, often quarreled among themselves as to who had made which catch. However, the establishment of standing armies and the centralization of military power in the hands of rulers brought this system to an end. After the War of the Spanish Succession, prisoners were taken out of their captors' hands. Ransom, instead of being settled by the individuals in question, was now a question for the belligerent state which negotiated with its opposite numbers on the basis of a fixed scale of payment – so much for a private, captain, or, at the very top, a *maréchal de France*.[70] Next, following the Seven Years War, the requirement for ransom was dropped altogether. From commodities to be traded, prisoners became guests of the opposing governments, though unless they were officers and able to look after their own accommodation (captive enemy commanders were routinely put on parole) they seldom found their quarters too comfortable.

The switch from personal to impersonal warfare also led to the invention of a new legal category, the wounded. Although war had always resulted in injuries, previously those who suffered them did not enjoy any special rights; instead they merely made their way off the battlefield as best they could. As late as Hugo Grotius during the first decades of the seventeenth century, whether or not quarter would be offered depended solely on the goodwill of the victor. However, the move toward regular forces during the last years of the seventeenth century gave rise to the idea

[69] L. E. Traide, ed., *Horace Walpole's Miscellany* (New Haven, CT: Yale University Press, 1978), p. 77; C. de Montesquieu, *Persian Letters* (Harmondsworth, UK: Penguin Books, 1973), p. 177.
[70] J. G. von Hoyers, *Geschichte der Kriegskunst* (Göttingen: Rosenbusch, 1797), vol. II, pp. 614–19, gives a detailed table of the ransom due for a prisoner of each rank.

that the troops on both sides were not criminals fighting for some nefarious ends but simply men doing their duty to their respective sovereigns, or states. Once such men had become incapacitated, there was no sense in punishing them further, and indeed eighteenth-century international lawyers considered the idea preposterous. Consequently it became comparatively easy to make agreements – first bilateral, then multinational – which promised the wounded, provided only they did not continue fighting, immunity from further military action as well as medical treatment and even special places of asylum which were not to be attacked: in short, protection as good as circumstances permitted.[71]

From 1660 or so the tendency to look at combatants as servants of the state also began to have a clear effect on the way wars were commemorated and monuments to them built.[72] From the time of the ancient Egyptian pharaohs all the way to the time of the Counter-Reformation, gloating had been one of the rewards of victory – e.g., Tiglat Pileser III, whom we have already met, boasted of having "impaled" his enemies "alive" and "cut off their hands."[73] Likewise, the plastic arts often showed enemy dead in profusion and prisoners being maltreated, as, for example, in the reliefs commissioned by the same king, his ancestors, and his successors, depicting their capture of cities all over the Middle East and used by them to decorate their palaces at Nineveh and elsewhere. Nor were such practices confined to the "barbaric" East. Looking up the column erected by Trajan, supposedly one of the more civilized Roman emperors, in the forum that bears his name, those with keen eyesight can see Dacian prisoners being decapitated.

However, during the second half of the seventeenth century, such presentations of joy on one's own side and suffering on the other ceased to be regarded as *bon ton*. Though monuments continued to be built for victories and commanders – witness Berlin's Brandenburg Gate or London's Trafalgar Square, overlooked by a statue of Nelson – from now on it was only very seldom that they showed the enemy in the act of being defeated, let alone tortured, mutilated, or executed. Not that such things ceased to take place either in European or, especially, colonial warfare; during World War II, American troops in the Pacific sometimes took Japanese ears as trophies.[74] Even in Nazi Germany, care was taken to hide the atrocities from the gaze of the public; or, failing that, blame them

---

[71] For the rise of *ius in bellum* during the eighteenth century, see G. Best, *Humanity in Warfare* (New York: Columbia University Press, 1980), pp. 53–60.

[72] See, for this entire subject, A. Borg, *War Memorials from Antiquity to the Present* (London: Cooper, 1991).

[73] Tadmor, *The Inscriptions of Tiglat Pileser III*, pp. 49, 79.

[74] J. W. Dower, *War Without Mercy: Race and Power in the Pacific War* (New York: Pantheon, 1986), p. 64.

either on military necessity or on the enemy who had been the first to violate the rules.

Since rulers for the most part had already ceased to command in person, the modern distinction between a government that wages or "conducts" a war at the highest politico-military level and the armed forces that fight and die came into being. By the middle of the eighteenth century, rulers' personal property could be clearly distinguished from that of their states. Consequently it became sacrosanct; when, during the Seven Years War, Frederick II went into a pique and tried to demolish a castle belonging to one of his Austrian opponents, he encountered opposition on the part of his own generals.[75] By way of another indication that war was ceasing to be regarded as a personal affair, even as they fought one another rulers now addressed each other as *monsieur mon frère* and exchanged elaborate compliments. This was a far cry from the days when, for example, as Francis I and Henry VIII prepared to meet at the Field of the Cloth of Gold, each side presented himself with an agreed-upon number of armed retainers for fear of being kidnapped or assassinated.

While government and armed forces were being separated in this way, the third leg of the "trinity," population, was also being created – or rather, shut out of the conduct of war – by the introduction of uniforms. Originating in the liveries which had long been worn by the servants of monarchs and lesser aristocrats, the purpose of the first uniforms was not to distinguish the two sides from each other; instead, following the demise of armor and the concentration of war in the hands of the state, it was to distinguish those who were licensed to fight on its behalf from those who were not. From 1660 on, uniforms, contrasting sharply with the extravagant dress of the higher classes but also with the more sober garments worn by the townspeople, became the norm. Their purpose had never been strictly utilitarian; over time, though, they became more and more elaborate as rulers competed with each other to see who could dress his troops in the most impressive manner. The peak of military sartorial splendor was reached between about 1790 and 1830. Thereafter, owing to the rise of quick-firing weapons, it declined, but without giving up the essential distinction between the military and civilians which, as one of the cornerstones of the modern state, had to be maintained at all cost.

Dress, though, was but one of the marks which set the military apart. Previously, armed forces – apart from those responsible for the rulers' person who, logically enough, had been housed in or around his castle or palace – had existed only during wartime; now that they had become permanent, it was necessary to find housing for them, which in one

---

[75] C. Duffy, *The Army of Frederick the Great* (London: Purnell, 1971), p. 9.

country after another led to the construction of barracks. Once they were cooped up inside their barracks, the troops and their commanders, often serving for periods that could be measured in decades, developed a culture of their own. Gone were the days when they themselves constituted society, as during the Middle Ages. Gone, too, were the times when they were considered social outcasts, as during much of the sixteenth and early seventeenth centuries. Instead, eighteenth-century professional armies – and, to a considerable extent, their successors up to the present day – formed autonomous groupings which in many ways stood outside "civilian" society and, needless to say, regarded themselves as superior to the latter.[76] This was the period when a separate code of military justice, separate customs as the salute and (for officers) the duel, and even separate ways of bearing oneself develop; with the result that, in our own day, American officers as representatives of the state are prohibited from such effeminate forms of behavior as carrying an umbrella or pushing a pram. Soon the feeling of solidarity, which first arose within countries, spread across them, so that soldiering (from the German *soldat*, somebody who received *Sold*, or pay) became a profession with numerous international links.

Throughout the eighteenth (and nineteenth) centuries, the growing separation between armed forces and society manifested itself by two opposing trends. On the one hand, armies increasingly took upon themselves tasks which had previously been contracted out to civilians; such as engineering, supply, administration, medical, and even spiritual services, all of which were increasingly provided by men who themselves wore uniforms and were subject to military discipline. On the other, the developing body of international law – the law of nations, as it was called – tended to prohibit people who did not wear uniforms from taking part in their rulers' quarrels. The original idea was to prevent the troops on each side from robbing civilians, or, strictly speaking, to do so on their own without any benefits accruing to the armies of which they were members; to this end bilateral treaties were concluded between the rulers of such countries as France, the Holy Roman Empire, and Prussia. By midcentury this had been turned into a system, even a philosophy, whereby civilians, as long as they behaved themselves and paid up, were supposed to be immune from the horrors of war. As the greatest eighteenth-century lawyer, Emmeric Vattel, put it, war ought to be waged exclusively by sovereign rulers on behalf of their respective states. For anyone else to intervene in it was itself an offense, and as such they deserved to be both condemned and punished.[77]

[76] See A. Vagts, *A History of Militarism* (New York: Free Press, 1959), pp. 52ff.
[77] E. Vattel, *The Law of Nations* (Philadelphia: Johnson, 1857 edn. [1758]), pp. 317–18.

By that time the point had long been reached where the uniformed, disciplined, state-owned armed forces with their heavy horsemen, cannon, and well-dressed volleys of musket-fire could be withstood only by other organizations similar to themselves. After 1700 the growing capacity of government to impose order as well as slowly improving economic conditions meant that it was seldom necessary any more to employ first-line troops for internal purposes. Doing so became the characteristic task of light cavalry – hence the term "to dragoon." In 1795 it took a mere "whiff of grapeshot" to disperse the crowds that menaced the National Assembly in Paris. There was, however, a price to be paid. Units that were earmarked for fighting against others of their kind tended to be stationed on the frontiers rather than in the towns where riots were mostly likely to occur, and they did not possess the special skills necessary for internal disorder. Finally, the closer to the end of the century we come, the better able governments were to control the movement of their citizens and prevent them from going abroad if necessary. Hence there was a tendency to draw on citizens rather than foreigners as recruits; this in turn limited their usefulness against fellow citizens, since the danger always existed that they would use bayonets against the authorities rather than on the latter's behalf.[78]

These developments both reflected and made necessary the separation between the armed forces and the police, the other uniformed arm of the modern state, and by no means the least important of the two. The first West European to use the term seems to have been Melchior von Osse who, around 1450, served as chancellor to the elector of Saxony. To him, as to Nicholas de la Mare who published his *Traité de la police* in 1750, it simply meant "public order"; as late as the 1770s it was in this sense, and in this sense only, that it was used by Hector Crevecoeur in his *Letters of an American Farmer*. As an organization it reflected the growth of the towns. Since the Middle Ages, the latter had at their disposal an array of minor officials such as lantern-lighters, nightwatchmen, supervisors of markets and of slaughter-houses, companies of guards, and prison wardens – in short personnel whose work covered every aspect of municipal government at the lower levels.[79] Sharing the general preference for venal office, most of them were not municipal employees and did not receive a salary. Like today's companies that are licensed to tow away illegally parked cars, the normal practice was to have them contract with the town.

---

[78] On these problems, see A. Corvisier, *Armies and Societies in Europe, 1494–1789* (Bloomington: Indiana University Press, 1979), pp. 100–2.

[79] For the way these things were done, see L. Martines, *Violence and Civil Disorder in Italian Cities, 1200–1500* (Berkeley: University of California Press, 1972), pp. 203ff., 315ff.

This meant that they reimbursed themselves out of the proceeds of their work or, in the case of wardens, at the expense of the prisoners and their families. Others, such as the English thiefcatchers, set up private guilds and made their living by claiming a share out of stolen goods recovered, not seldom from themselves. A famous case was that of the London racketeer Jonathan Wild around 1725. Not only did he operate a network that specialized in stealing goods and selling them back to their owners, but he also caught "unauthorized" thieves (in other words, such as operated without his permission and did not share their proceeds with him) and handed them in to the authorities.

These urban officials apart, various forces existed to look after the security of the countryside. England had long had the sheriffs and the constables; the former were unpaid county officials, whereas the latter were elected personnel maintained out of the taxes paid by the parishes. In other countries provincial governors had their guards whose character was partly public, partly private. Commanded by a special official known in France as the *prévôt*, they could be used to quell disorder, maintain public safety, look into criminal matters, and the like. All of these forces were semi-professional and tied to the districts in which they were raised. It was only in the 1760s that the first national police, the French *maréchaussée*, was established; as its name indicates, originally it was a highway patrol whose mission was to prevent robberies. Compared with the forces that the king maintained for combating his external enemies, it was very small. In a country whose population probably stood at about 26 million, the former could reach 400,000 men and seldom fell below 200,000 even in peacetime; but the *maréchaussée* counted only some 3,000 men, divided into thirty companies of a hundred each. To make up for their numerical weakness, their uniforms were particularly splendid, a tactic later adopted by many of their foreign counterparts such as the Italian *carabinieri*.

By this time Paris already possessed a *lieutenant général de police* with twenty district commissioners and a total of 700 men – a third of them mounted – under his command. Originating in the second half of the seventeenth century, the system was soon imitated in other places; a medium-sized city such as Lyons or Bordeaux would probably have a guard consisting of several dozen men and even a small provincial town of some 50,000 inhabitants was likely to have four or five policemen to maintain law and order within its precincts and an additional area of, say, 250 square kilometers. The appointment of these *chefs de police* was in the hands of the mayors, who as we saw had themselves ceased to be elected but were appointed by the *intendant* on the king's behalf. All these forces were responsible for a very large variety of duties, from public sanitation through looking after markets to controlling vagabonds, in addition to police work in the narrow sense of that term.

One of the first rulers who tried to establish a Directory of Police or Polizeidirektion was that centralizing monarch, Emperor Joseph II of Austria, after he took over from his mother in 1780.[80] At first it had only two employees in addition to its head, one Franz von Beer; before long it expanded both in terms of personnel and the fields of activity that it covered until it had branch offices throughout the Empire. However, Beer's attempt to set up a single countrywide organization that would look after all types of police affairs was resisted by the Austrian Estates, which saw it as a threat to their liberties, and had to be abandoned. Foiled in this, he and his men found themselves limited to state security, including a *cabinet noir* that specialized in opening the letters of political suspects as well as foreign ambassadors. Routine police matters that were not considered to endanger the regime continued to be handled by a very great variety of provincial and municipal authorities, backed up by the armed forces when strictly necessary, a situation which began to change only after the failed Revolution of 1848.

In this way the distinction of setting up the first nationwide police force responsible for all forms of internal security belongs to Napoleon. Beginning in 1799, he systematically merged the various forces already existing with each other and put them under a single minister, Joseph Fouché. A sinister genius – he was certainly not above plotting against the emperor to whom he reported daily – Fouché developed his command into a vast organization; the number of provincial *commissaires de police* alone rose from thirty at the beginning of the empire to four times that number ten years later. Even so, the uniformed police which now made its presence felt in every district and town only represented the tip of the proverbial iceberg. Not visible to the public eye was the *Sûreté*, established in 1810 and at first headed by a reformed criminal and daredevil jailbreaker, François Vidocq, to say nothing of a very large number of professional, semi-professional, and amateur informers known as *mouchards*. Often recruited from among the lowest classes – concierges, footmen, barbers, prostitutes, and the like – they infested every street corner, coffee house, and saloon. Here they collected vast amounts of information, most of it too trivial to use.[81]

Hard on the heels of the police came another characteristic device of

---

[80] On the origins of the Austrian police, see H. Hoegel, *Freiheitsstrafe und Gefängnisswesen in Österreich von der Theresiana bis zur Gegenwart* (Graz: Moser, 1916), pp. 38–9.

[81] J. Ellul, *Histoire des institutions* (Paris: Presses universitaires de France, 1955), vol. II, pp. 708–10, gives a good description of the system built by Fouché. On the rise of the police in general, see G. L. Mosse, ed., *Police Forces in History* (London: Fertig, 1975).

the modern state, prisons. If only because incarceration is expensive and requires a long-term commitment, pre-state political communities had seldom used it as a method of punishment. Either it was limited to important personages whom, for one reason or another, one did not want to execute, as in Roman times when Augustus confined his daughter and granddaughter.[82] Alternatively it served to detain those who were awaiting trial. Like other offices, jails were often run on a contractual basis by operators who sought to make a profit out of their unfortunate charges. In the absence of a well-developed bureaucratic machine capable of enforcing long prison sentences, the penalties meted out by justice had to be swift and cheap. The ones most frequently used included fines, confiscation of property, humiliation (either pillorying or forcing the culprit to wear some kind of shameful garment), exile, floggings, mutilation, and of course executions. The latter in particular were regarded as an edifying spectacle that was put up by the authorities for the benefit of their subjects. By the middle of the eighteenth century they were being carried out by a variety of exciting methods. Witness the case of a would-be French regicide who first had his flesh torn from his body; then had several different boiling liquids poured into the wounds; then was drawn and quartered by horses (to help them do the job, he had to be cut into pieces first); and finally had his remains burnt and his ashes scattered so that nothing, but nothing, should remain of him.[83]

Within fifty years, though, the state had grown so powerful that displays of ferocity, instead of emphasizing its might, merely tended to arouse sympathy for the victim. Sustained by the Enlightenment belief in the essential goodness of men, and prodded by reformers such as Jeremy Bentham and his Italian fellow *philosophe* Cesare Beccaria,[84] the state did not merely want to punish transgressors. Instead it tended to regard them as a blemish on its own record; hence it undertook the much more difficult task of reforming them at the hands of its own officials in the hands of special institutions designed for the purpose. Among the methods employed were isolation, enforced silence (both of which were supposedly good for the soul), the imposition of a strict daily routine, and, above all, work.[85] Historians have traced the origin of the modern prison

[82] Suetonius, *Lives, Augustus*, 65.
[83] The proceedings are described in A. L. Zevaes, *Damien le régicide* (Paris: Rivière, 1937), pp. 201–14.
[84] Bentham's most important work on the subject was *Théorie des peines et récompenses* (1811; English translation, *The Rationale of Punishment*, London: R. Heward, 1830). Beccaria wrote *Dei delitti e delle penne* (1764; English translation, *Essay on Crime and Punishment*, London: Bone, 1801).
[85] See J. Bentham, *Panopticon: or the Inspection House* (London: Payne, 1974); and, much more succinctly, J. Mill, "Prisons and Prison Discipline," in Mill, *Political Writings*, T. Ball, ed. (Cambridge: Cambridge University Press, 1992), pp. 195–224.

system to certain seventeenth-century antecedents such as the orphanages and workhouses into which the magistrates of Protestant cities sometimes put foundlings and various types of minor offenders.[86] Yet another model for incarceration was provided by armies and especially navies; every time a war broke out the result was likely to be a set of criminals released and put into uniform. Fleets of galleys, such as the one maintained by Louis XIV, had their rank and file formed almost entirely of convicts.[87] Both armed forces and workhouses were seen as a way of ridding society of offenders – including, often, serious ones condemned to death but pardoned – while at the same time continuing to make use of their labor.

By the time Joseph II died in 1790 he had all but abolished the death penalty, replacing it with imprisonment and forced labor in the form of hauling barges along the marshy Hungarian plains. Twenty years later the criminal part of the Code Napoleon came into force; it made loss of freedom into the principal form of punishment between fines and death. From about 1800 on prisons, housed in buildings either specially constructed or (as was frequently the case in France and Austria) confiscated from the church and adapted to their new purpose, began to dot the European countryside. As if to parody the structure of government, an elaborate hierarchy was created. Fouché himself set the example, establishing *maisons de police* (the lowest degree of all), *maisons d'arrêt*, and *maisons de correction*. The top level was formed by a handful of particularly prestigious *maisons centrales*; in them hardened criminals and those who were considered dangerous to the state found a more or less permanent home. Once prisons had opened their gates, their appetite turned out to be insatiable. During the forty years between the fall of the *ancien régime* and the rise of the July Monarchy, the number of people kept under lock and key at any one time is said to have increased tenfold,[88] a development paralleled in French-administered countries from 1794 to 1814.[89]

With the establishment of the regular armed forces, the police (both in and out of uniform), and prisons, the proud structure of the modern state was virtually complete. A century and a half after the Thirty Years War, its domination over external conflict had grown to the point where war itself was coming to be defined as a continuation of policy by other

[86] J. A. Sharpe, *Crime in Early Modern England 1550–1750* (London: Longmans, 1984), pp. 178–80.
[87] P. W. Bamford, *Fighting Ships and Prisons* (Minneapolis: University of Minnesota Press, 1973), is the best modern account of this system.
[88] M. Foucault, *Discipline and Punish: The Birth of the Prison* (London: Penguin Books, 1979), p. 116.
[89] N. Finash, "Zur 'Oekonomie des Straffens': Gefängniswesen und Gefängnisreform in Rör-Department nach 1794," *Rheinische Vierteljahresberichte*, 4, 1989, pp. 188–210.

means,[90] whereas the attempts of lesser groups or people to use violence for *their* ends acquired a stigma by being called civil war (if it was waged on a sufficiently large scale), rebellion, uprisings, guerrilla warfare, banditry, crime, and, most recently, terrorism. Meanwhile, in the states that pleased to look on themselves as the most civilized, the violence that they directed against their own citizens did not so much diminish as disappear from public view. More and more it took place behind walls, whether of prisons or fortresses or, much later, concentration camps where – in an ironic twist that would have made Bentham shudder – "Arbeit macht frei." Like so much else it took on a bureaucratic character with an elaborate hierarchy of administrators, offices, filing cabinets, and finally computers; governed by elaborate rules, it was known by such euphemisms as "correction," "discipline," or "reeducation." In theory at any rate all these praiseworthy activities were carried out not by, or for, some private person or persons but on behalf of the impersonal state whose understanding of how to treat criminals and other social misfits exceeded that of anybody else. And so it is to the development of that state, as reflected in political theory, that we must next turn our attention.

The growth of political theory

With the exception of the classical city-states and their magistrates, none of the political communities which existed until 1648 distinguished between the person of the ruler and his rule. An African chieftain, a Hellenistic king, an Inca emperor, and their colleagues regardless of their titles and the size of the countries that they ruled *were* the government, which also explains why those who worked for or under them (the two were equally indistinct) were, initially at least and so long as the administration did not grow too large, their own relatives, clients, companions, and "friends."[91] In the absence of the political as a separate sphere of activity, government tended to be presented in terms of the dominance of a father over his family, a master over his slaves, or even – from Augustine on – a shepherd over his sheep. The first approach is exemplified by Chinese Confucianism which for over two millennia presented the empire as if it consisted of a single large family whose members owed filial piety to their superiors. The second is illustrated by the Bible which very often speaks

[90] C. von Clausewitz, *On War* (Princeton: Princeton University Press, 1976), book 1, chs. 1 and 2; M. van Creveld, *The Transformation of War* (New York: Free Press, 1991), ch. 2.
[91] The Hellenistic king's top officials were known as their *haeterioi* (companions), or *philoi* (friends); on them and the courts that they formed, see G. Herman, "The Courts Society of the Hellenistic Age" (unpublished paper, History Department, Hebrew University, Jerusalem).

of high-ranking officials as the "slaves" of this or that king.[92] Nor was this merely a figure of speech. As late as the first half of the nineteenth century, the subjects of the Ottoman Porte were, legally speaking, his slaves for him to do with whatever he pleased; private property that could not be confiscated at any moment and for any (or no) reason simply did not exist. The idea was summed up succinctly by a league of Alsatian cities which wrote in 1388: "[we pledge our support to] our Lord the Emperor Lewis, who is the Empire" ("unsern Herren Keiser Ludwigen, der das Reich is").[93]

Another outcome of the age-old identification between ruler and rule was that the idea of a conflict of interest stopped short at the steps of the throne. Officials of every rank might – and often did – receive bribes; these might come either from people subject to their authority or else from foreign rulers who hoped to influence policy or even to foment a revolt. Such cases might be detected and, if they seriously affected the ruler's interests, punished. The annals of all monarchical governments are full of such cases, often falling under the rubric of *lèse majesté* or of treason. However, the same did not apply at the very top. Not only were king or emperor beyond human judgment in practical terms, but in their case the distinction between their person and the government did not exist and, of course, neither did corruption. Throughout history monarchs large and small were accustomed to receiving presents both from their own subjects and from foreign rulers in search of alliances or favors. By definition, they could not accept bribes.

Reflecting the fact that most rulers attributed their positions to the gods that be, political theory, to the extent that it existed at all, tended to be a subdivision of theology. This was the case, for example, in ancient Egypt, where it is hard to say whether certain hymns were written in praise of Ra or Pharaoh (who, after all, was himself a god);[94] so also during the Middle Ages at the hands of Thomas Aquinas, Jean Gerson, and others, all of whom followed Augustine in that they saw government not as an artificial entity established by him and for his own benefit, but as part of the order that had been created by the Lord. Depending on how centralized, powerful, and intrusive government was – in other words, whether it was an empire or a feudal system that we are talking about – doctrines of this kind might well elaborate on the structure of the community; the nature

---

[92] For example, 1 Samuel, 18, 19 (the "slaves" of King David); Samuel II, 7, 6 (the "slaves" of the Aramean King Hadadezer); 1 Kings, 5, 15 (the "slaves" of King Hiram of Tyre); and numerous other places.

[93] Historische Kommission bei der Bayerischen Akademie der Wissenschaften, ed., *Deutsche Reichstagsakten* (Munich: Rieger, 1867–), os, vol. IV, no. 268.

[94] A. Gardiner, *Egypt of the Pharaohs: An Introduction* (London: Oxford University Press, 1961), pp. 51ff.

of the bonds that held it together; the rights and duties of both rulers and ruled; and even on what either side was entitled to do in case the other violated its god-mandated obligations. Unlike Aristotle's *Politics*, though, they did not have their roots in human action and thus did not amount to political theory in the modern sense of that term.

Another traditional approach to what we today would call the science of politics consisted of handbooks for rulers. Some were mere literary exercises and were written without any particular person in mind; others were produced in the service of, and often dedicated to, individuals from whom the author hoped to receive some kind of favor in return. One of the earliest known works of this kind is the *Cyropaedia*, composed by the Athenian Xenophon around 364 BC. It is an idealized account of the education and career of a Persian pretender to the throne, Cyrus the Younger, with whom Xenophon took service as a mercenary commander and whom he presents as a paragon of virtue. In antiquity, and throughout the Middle Ages, Xenophon's example was followed by a very large number of works by secular and ecclesiastical writers.[95] All alike tended to emphasize the importance of good breeding and a sound education in instilling such qualities as piety, wisdom, temperance, and clemency (the foursome which Emperor Augustus claimed to possess). More to the point, the ruler is invariably treated as if he were a mere private individual. Though his station may be more exalted and his responsibilities more onerous than those of others, the code he is urged to follow is no different from that recommended to anybody else in the society in question. And indeed one reason why such treatises were written in the first place was not merely to educate princes – whose numbers, after all, were limited – but to enable ordinary people to model themselves upon their betters' supposed virtues and live accordingly.

One of the last, and best, works of this genre is the *Institutes Principis Christianis* (best translated as *The Ways of a Christian Prince*) written by Erasmus while in the service of the future Charles V and published in 1517. A humanist and a Christian, Erasmus saw the prince as appointed by God and responsible to Him; he never tires of warning his student that, in the end, earthly rulers will be taken to account by the one who sits in heaven. Accordingly, the first thing that any ruler must do is to select a proper tutor for his son so as to give his designated successor a sound moral education; compared to the ability to distinguish between right and wrong everything else that the prince may study (including, specifically, the state of the realm) is secondary. Once he has come to the throne the prince is to treat his subjects as his wards, looking after their welfare in

---

[95] For a long list of such works, see Erasmus, *The Education of a Christian Prince*, pp. 44–132.

much the same way as a *paterfamilias* would look after his dependents or a master (*dominus*) after his servants. The worst vice is tyranny, i.e., disregarding divine law by putting power to selfish uses. Thus Erasmus' prince is not to fill "his" treasury in order to indulge in unnecessary luxuries; nor to try to increase "his" glory by waging war at the expense of his subjects; nor to marry a foreign woman (let alone engage in debauchery); nor spend more time away from "his" realm than is made strictly necessary by the need to look after "his" affairs: briefly, as a ruler he should not be tempted to do that which, as a private citizen, he would avoid. His conduct is to be like that of any other decent person whom fortune has charged with the welfare of others. He should try to gain and maintain his subjects' "love" – all in order to leave his realm in a better state than the one in which he himself received it from his predecessor.

While it cannot be shown that Charles V was directly influenced by Erasmus – he probably never read the work, which was dedicated to him – the two were entirely at one in regarding government as a personal affair. A glimpse into the emperor's world is offered by the two great testaments that he wrote for his son Philip, then sixteen years old, in 1543. Paradoxically the one that deals with the prince's person, the way he ought to behave (also in regard to his relations with women), and the qualities he ought to adopt is semi-public in character; it consists of pious advice concerning the need to trust in God, exercise sexual restraint, take one's responsibilities seriously, etc. Conversely, the one that is devoted to what we today would call political affairs is strictly "eyes only." It contains a number of shrewd pen-portraits of the emperor's closest collaborators, some of whom he trusted more than others. Charles' inability to distinguish between the private and the public is further accentuated by his constant references to "my" (or, where he means the Habsburg family as a whole, "our") treasury, "my" resources, "my" servants, "my" commanders, "my" army, "my" countries, and even "my" peoples; the possibility that the two spheres might be anything but identical never entered his mind.

In the eyes of Charles and his contemporaries, provinces, money, armies, ministers, and princesses were simply assets. They belonged to rulers, and were freely passed from one to another by means of diplomacy or war. All alike were pawns in the vast game of chess whose ultimate aim was to maintain "our" inheritance undiminished, if possible while keeping the subjects happy but if necessary even at the cost of taxing them heavily and putting other burdens on them. In this world-view there was no government in our sense of the term, only people who served the emperor in this capacity or that; no civil society, but only subjects great and small who had to be treated differently according to their different stations in life; and no foreign states to deal with, only rulers belonging to other dynasties who either allied themselves with Charles or stood in his way.

An even more interesting example of the inability to distinguish between government on the one hand and the ruler's private affairs on the other is that of Machiavelli. As a student and admirer of ancient Rome – he probably never mastered Greek – he must have been aware that the great men to whom, in his own words, he looked for political wisdom[96] were magistrates and not kings who ran the city as their private property; yet when he produced his masterpiece, *The Prince*, he wrote as if that distinction did not exist. Like Erasmus' *Institutes*, *The Prince* with its dedication to Lorenzo Medici the Younger does not constitute political science as we understand that term, but belongs to the type of handbook known as Mirrors for Princes. Unlike Erasmus, whose reader is supposedly a prince who is either destined for the throne or elected (on the political processes that may lead to the election Erasmus has absolutely nothing to say), Machiavelli wrote, as he says, for the "New Prince" ("il nuovo principe").[97] Since Machiavelli's prince owes his position to his own efforts, the difficulties that he faces in reaching and maintaining his position are that much greater. All the more he deserves to be given advice based not on the world as people would like it to be, but as it is.[98]

Seen in this light, Machiavelli, far from being a revolutionary, was entirely a man of his times. Neither in the type of book that he wrote nor in his confusion between the private and the public spheres did he differ from his contemporaries. Like Erasmus he was incapable of distinguishing between the prince's personal life and his political role, to the point that he included a paragraph on the need to leave the citizens' daughters alone.[99] In an Italy whose cities were for the most part ruled by ferocious, often self-made tyrants, what set him apart was merely the secular tone of his work. Considered as an individual, Machiavelli's prince might well go to hell after his death. Considered as a ruler, he is neither appointed by God nor, in any practical sense, responsible to Him. Though he would be well advised to maintain an outward show of piety, there could be no question of a ruler maintaining his government by kindliness of the sort advocated by Erasmus and many of his predecessors; instead it was necessary to play the game of politics, which for the first time since antiquity was given a separate identity by a set of rules to be known,

---

[96] Machiavelli to Francesco Vettori, 10 December 1513, in *Lettere* (Milan: Feltrinelli, 1962), vol. V, p. 305.

[97] For the expression *il nuovo principe* and its special significance, see S. de Grazia, *Machiavelli in Hell* (New York: Harvest Wheatsheaf, 1989), pp. 232ff.

[98] Machiavelli, *The Prince*, p. 90.

[99] *Ibid.*, p. 102.

shortly after Machiavelli, as *raison d'état*.[100] Since men are at heart base, cowardly, and treacherous, those rules cannot be the same as those which apply inside the house or family (although little is known about his personal life, Machiavelli seems to have been a good husband by the standards of the times). The qualities most required are not piety and clemency but force and guile.

By putting God to one side, Machiavelli also knocked away those twin pillars of government that were closely dependent on Him, i.e., justice and right. The success of political action as reflected in the greatness and prosperity of the country became its own reward. Rulers owed their positions not to any kind of heavenly mandate but to their prowess or *virtù*, which in this way was turned into the cardinal pillar on which everything else rested. Yet Machiavelli was also aware that outstanding *virtù* is seldom attained by persons whose only goal in life is to advance themselves; as Napoleon, who knew about such matters, once put it, the pleasure an emperor derives from a duchess in her boudoir is no greater than that which a farmboy gets out of a shepherdess in a barn. *Virtù* can reach its own heights only provided it is inspired by an ideal which, in Machiavelli's case, was represented by his much beloved *patria* (whether he meant his native city of Florence or Italy as a whole is moot): hence the famous last chapter of *The Prince* where he calls upon the reigning Medici prince to take the lead in expelling the barbarians from Italy. Modern scholars have often argued that this text represents either a careless afterthought or gross flattery to the ruler. In reality it constitutes the justification both for Machiavelli's own work and, even more importantly, for the prince's existence and the nature of the methods that he employs.

Given that he set out to strip political life of hypocrisy, it is no wonder that Machiavelli met with a frosty reception, to the point that his most famous work remained unpublished while he lived. A mere four years after *The Prince* was written (1513), Luther nailed his ninety-five theses to the church door at Wittenberg; this act marked the beginning of a period which lasted for over a century and which was largely dominated by religious strife as to who was the *true* God on whom society, and with it the system of government that keeps order within it, could be based. The course of the struggle varied from one country to the next. In some, such as Italy, Spain, England, and Sweden, the established authorities prevailed quite easily. Either they confirmed the established religion or they changed it in the direction they considered desirable – with the result that the number of victims, in the form of heretics who were condemned and executed, came only to hundreds or, at worst, thousands. In other, less

---

[100] See F. Meinecke, *Machiavellism: The Doctrine of Raison d'Etat and Its Place in Modern History* (London: Routledge, 1957), particularly pp. 25–48.

fortunate countries, the outcome of the Reformation was nothing less than the disintegration of government. This left the way open to decades of civil war, as happened in France, Germany, and what is now the Czech Republic.

It was against such a background that the next great political author, Jean Bodin, did his work in France. Bodin, whose personal life is some- thing of a mystery (even the religion he professed is uncertain), was probably around thirty years old when civil war broke out in 1561; no wonder much of his career consisted of an attempt to find a solution. Neither the old theological approach nor the Mirrors for Princes had much to offer, given that the former was anchored in a God whose identity had become a matter for dispute and that the latter had manifest- ly failed to help French monarchs carry out their task of imposing order and justice. Accordingly, Bodin turned his back on both traditions. Starting at the beginning, he focused neither on the way God had con- structed the universe nor on the education of princes but on the nature of the *république* as such – a problem which both Machiavelli and Erasmus (let alone Charles V who, though he was an astute and conscientious ruler, was anything but a theorist) had entirely ignored. Naturally Bodin's model was Aristotle's *Politics*, which he followed very closely even as he criticized some of the detailed arrangements which it proposed. Seeking a new, nonreligious basis for government, Bodin in *Les six livres de la république* became the first writer in modern history to discuss the dif- ference between government *within* the household, as exercised by the husband over his dependants and by the master over his slaves, and political power which prevailed between people who were, if not yet equal, at any rate born free and possessed of a legal persona of their own.[101]

Trained as a lawyer – at one point in his career he was active as an *avocat* to Henry III – Bodin rejected Machiavelli's argument that force and guile, rather than law, rule political affairs. Instead he adopted Cicero's definition of a *res publica* as a community of people governed by law; from this he derived the proposition that the most important duty of any ruler was precisely to lay down the law. However, if order was to prevail then law alone was not enough. He who is responsible for legis- lating should also decide on war and peace, appoint the most important officials, mete out the principal rewards and punishments, act as the supreme appellate justice, and determine the currency of the land (Bodin was very interested in political economy, on which he wrote a separate treatise). In principle there was nothing to prevent these functions from

[101] J. Bodin, *Six Books of the Commonwealth*, M. J. Tooley, ed. (Oxford: Blackwell, 1967), pp. 40–9.

being exercised either by a single person or by an assembly of people; the point was that, to prevent conflicts and disorder, they should be united in the same hands. As Bodin points out, sovereignty – a term which he did not invent, but which owes much of its popularity to him – should be one, indivisible, and perpetual. When there are two sovereigns neither is truly so; where sovereignty is not perpetual anything that has been done by a sovereign can be undone by his successor.

In a world where God is no longer capable of providing a consensual basis for political life, Bodin wanted to endow the sovereign with His qualities and put him in His place, at any rate on earth and as pertained to a certain well-defined territory. Aristotle had inquired into the justification of government, finding it in the free consent of family-heads; to Bodin the question did not matter and nowhere in his massive work did he pay much attention to it. What *did* matter was the sovereign's ability to create order out of chaos by instituting good laws and governing through them. Bodin, however, was unable to disassociate himself from the medieval idea of law as something that existed independently of the human will. Accordingly, good laws meant not simply those that served the community best but those that were based on, or at any rate did not conflict with, divine law on the one hand and the law of nature on the other. The former had been laid down in the Bible and, in Bodin's view, also dictated that the form of succession should be by primogeniture. The latter were really little more than the rules of equity which dictated, for example, that a person should not be deprived of his property without cause (Bodin has often been portrayed as an early defender of capitalism). What means were to be used in order to make sure that the sovereign, whose power came closer to absolutism than that of any of his predecessors, should indeed abide by the principles of natural and divine law Bodin failed to say, nor, given the extreme weakness of the French monarchy in his day, did it matter.

Another problem which was implicit in Bodin's work, but to which he did not really provide an answer, was how the sovereign's position was to be maintained over time. Speaking of sovereignty as perpetual was all very well; but humans, including kings, did die and at no time were people more aware of the fact than during the sixteenth century when paintings were constantly showing how death swept away emperors and commoners alike. For dealing with the problem, the late Middle Ages had invented the doctrine of the "king's two bodies."[102] The king's physical body was manifestly as mortal and as perishable as that of anyone else. However, he also possessed a "mystical body" (*corpus mysticum*), an idea

[102] See E. H. Kantorowicz, *The King's Two Bodies: A Study of Medieval Political Theory* (Princeton: Princeton University Press, 1957), pp. 128ff., 336ff., 401ff., 446–7, 501ff.

whose origins are disputed but which may have grown out of Christianity where God, after all, is believed to possess no fewer than three different bodies. It was to this mystical body, rather than to the physical one, that the king's dominion, prerogatives, and duties were attached. As a result, far from having to be renewed each time a monarch died and was replaced by another (which was standard practice in all premodern empires), they were passed on automatically. To close the hiatus between the death of one king and the coronation of another the formula *le roi est mort, vive le roi* was devised and sounded for the first time at the funeral of Louis XII in 1512. Another way of expressing the same idea was to prepare an effigy that would continue the reign until a new king could be crowned. This ceremony was in use from the death of Charles VI in 1422 and was carried out for the last time following the death of Henry IV in 1610.[103]

By the last quarter of the fifteenth century the notion that there existed (in Germany, Italy, and sometimes France) a "state" or (in England and also in France, a "crown") was slowly emerging out of the no-man's-land between the ruler's private property and his public responsibilities. Attempting to make a subordinate carry out an unpalatable order, France's Louis XI was capable of writing that "you are a servant of the Crown as well as I."[104] Nevertheless, usage remained unsettled and the modern meaning of the term did not yet exist. When Bodin wrote the *Six livres*, he was at a loss to find a word for the kind of entity he had in mind, with the strange result that, though his preferred form of government was monarchical, he was compelled to use the old Latin expression *res publica*. As late as 1589, Giovanni Botero defined the *stato* as "a stable rule over a people" and *ragione di stato* as "the knowledge by which such a dominion may be founded."[105]

From this point things developed quickly. By the third decade of the seventeenth century, Cardin le Bret, a collaborator of Richelieu's, found it possible to distinguish between treason directed against the king's person and that which, affecting the state, deserved to be punished much more harshly.[106] Hard on le Bret's heels came Thomas Hobbes and *Leviathan*; to him belongs the credit of being the first to define the state as an "artificial man" separate from the person of the ruler. Like Bodin, Hobbes lived at a time when his country was swept by civil war (his last book, *Behemoth*, was written in order to explain its causes). Like him,

---

[103] See C. Geertz, "Centers, Kings, and Charisma: Reflections on the Symbolics of Power," in S. Wilentz, ed., *Rites of Power: Symbolism, Ritual and Politics Since the Middle Ages* (Philadelphia: University of Pennsylvania Press, 1985), p. 56.
[104] Quoted in P. Kendall, *Louis XI* (London: Allen and Unwin, 1971), p. 320.
[105] G. Botero, *The Reason of State* (London: Routledge, 1956), p. 3.
[106] See R. E. Giesey, et al., "Cardin le Bret and Lèse Majesté," *Law and History Review*, 41, 1986, pp. 23–54.

Hobbes' goal was to restore order by putting in place an extremely powerful sovereign whose attributes he took over almost unchanged from his predecessors' great work.[107] But Hobbes differed from Bodin in that his model was not Aristotle, but Galileo whom he had met during his travels on the Continent and whom he much admired. Hobbes' aim, discussed in the first nine chapters of *Leviathan* and, at much greater length, in his *De corpore*, was to endow politics with the kind of precision hitherto attained only by physics – in other words, to do away with all factors except those which, like bodies and motions, could be sensed and measured in an objective manner. This "scientific" approach led him to define man as a machine, mere matter acted upon by the motion of various bodies which triggered off this reaction or that. Bodies were divided into two kinds, i.e., "natural" (such as man himself), and "feigned" or "artificial" ones. Artificial bodies also fell into two kinds, private and public. The former were formed by individuals on their own initiative, whereas the latter were created by the state. In this system the state was simply the most important public body of all. It authorized the rest (in the sense of determining whether or nor they were lawful) but was authorized by none.[108]

In this way Hobbes deserves the credit for inventing the "state" (or, to use his own synonym, "commonwealth") as an abstract entity separate both from the sovereign (who is said to "carry" it) and the ruled who, by means of a contract among themselves, transferred their rights to him. As with Bodin, Hobbes' chief "magistrate" could be either an assembly or a single person; if the latter was preferred, this was merely a matter of convenience designed to ensure unity of government and prevent conflict. However, Hobbes' wish to dispense with "immaterial bodies" and "transubstantiate" influences other than those that could be objectively perceived also made him do away with those twin pillars of Bodin's theory, divine and natural law. Carrying positivism to extremes rarely attained before or since, Hobbes saw law as something that exists solely *within* the commonwealth and is enacted by it; in the state of nature, where no organized community existed, "covenants without swords are but words." Bound by no law except that which he himself laid down (and which, of course, he could change at any moment), Hobbes' sovereign was much more powerful not only than the one proposed by Bodin but, *a fortiori*, any Western ruler since late antiquity. In Rome and

---

[107] On the nature of sovereignty as understood by Bodin and Hobbes, see P. King, *The Ideology of Order: A Comparative Analysis of Jean Bodin and Thomas Hobbes* (London: Allen and Unwin, 1974), pp. 140–57, 237–43.

[108] T. Hobbes, *Leviathan or the Matter, Forme and Power of a Commonwealth* (Oxford: Blackwell, 1946 edn.), p. 146.

elsewhere, emperors were to some extent bound by religion, even if it was one of which they themselves were the heads, and even if they themselves were regarded as living gods. Not so Hobbes' sovereign. Following a train of thought already developed by Machiavelli in the *Discourses*, this sovereign dictated his subjects' beliefs in the way best calculated to maintain public order and thus became the most absolute ruler in all history.

Against the background of the seventeenth-century struggle between king – later, lord protector – and Parliament, the draught prepared by Hobbes proved too strong for most of his countrymen to swallow. Like Machiavelli he saw man as basically evil; unlike Machiavelli he did not even endow him with *virtù* or love of country. Man's greatest quality, his reason, also enabled him to peer into the future; motivated by fear of the latter, he spent his entire life seeking power after power *vis-à-vis* his fellow men, the struggle ceasing only in death. It was in his attempt to restrain this creature that Hobbes had set up the sovereign. However, before long it became clear that the sovereign in question was so powerful as to present as great, or greater, a threat to his subjects than they did to each other.

This problem preoccupied the English philosopher John Locke (1632–1704). Though he seldom mentions his illustrious predecessor by name, much of Locke's work in the field of politics can only be understood as a direct reply to Hobbes. At the bottom of Hobbes' system had been the assumption that even the worst government was preferable to its absence, i.e., the state of nature; accordingly Locke's first step was to take another look at that state in order to find out whether it was really as bad as its reputation.

As an early representative of the Enlightenment, Locke in the *Second Treatise on Government* (probably written just before the Glorious Revolution but published only when it was over) discarded the assumption, which had guided Western thought since Augustine, that man was basically an evil creature who needed to be restrained by government. For him as for Hobbes, man's essential quality was his rationality; but, whereas Hobbes saw that quality leading to the war of all against all, Locke thought it would translate into enlightened self-interest which, most of the time, would enable people to live in peace with each other, even in the state of nature where there was no common ruler. The latter's most important task was not so much to constrain men as, on the contrary, to safeguard the rights with which they had been endowed by nature – i.e., the trio of life, liberty, and property. The thing to be avoided at all costs was *absolute* (the emphasis occurs repeatedly in the original) government. Government was to be based on consent: not such as had been given once and for all and was irrevocable, as with Hobbes, but such as was repeatedly confirmed by means of elections. Just who was to possess the vote Locke did not explain but, good bourgeois that he was, if pressed he would probably have proposed some kind of property qualification such as actually existed in most European countries until the early years of the twentieth century. Another way of preventing the rise of absolutism was to divide the sovereign's power between a legislative, an executive, and a "federative" authority charged with the conduct of war and foreign policy, an idea which was in the air at the time and whose form was much influenced by the English political system as it then existed.[109]

Having devoted the entire *First Treatise on Government* to showing that paternal and political power were *not* the same, Locke wasted little time on working out the distinction between the ruler and the state which, following Hobbes, he took very much for granted. Equally beyond question was the distinction between civil society and state; not only did Locke proclaim that the former preceded the latter, but it had actually created the state in a deliberate attempt to defend itself both internally against disturbances of the peace and externally against all comers. As Bodin had been the first to point out, and as Locke again explained at length, subjects were emphatically *not* members of their ruler's household. Therefore the principles applying to their government were *not* the same as those used to rule married women, children, or sheep.[110]

Insofar as he abhorred absolute rule, Locke's goals were opposed to those of Hobbes; still, together they ended up at the point where the only remaining constraint on the power of the state (as distinct from that of each of the three authorities separately) were certain rights which a benevolent nature had bestowed on man – a flimsy barrier, as Hobbes had already pointed out, but one which Montesquieu now set out to demolish in *The Spirit of the Laws*. Paradoxically, the background to Montesquieu's work was formed by the reaction to absolutism that grew up among the French nobility, to which he belonged, after the death of Louis XIV.[111] Like Locke, whom he much admired – he also spent a couple of years in England studying that country's political system – Montesquieu's chief goal was to discover ways to protect civil society against the arbitrary power of the sovereign, without which protection despotism would ensue and any kind of civilized life would become difficult if not impossible.[112]

---

[109] See H. C. Mansfield, *Taming the Prince: The Ambivalence of Modern Executive Power* (New York: Free Press, 1989), pp. 161–4.

[110] See *Second Treatise on Government*, in Locke, *Two Treatises on Government*, pp. 301–48.

[111] See N. Hulliung, *Montesquieu and the Old Regime* (Berkeley: University of California Press, 1976), pp. 15–33.

[112] C. de Montesquieu, *The Spirit of the Laws* (New York: Harper, 1949), ch. 17.

While Montesquieu was mulling over his great work during the twenty years before its publication in 1748, the philosophical foundations of the belief in the law of nature were being knocked away by David Hume (1711–76). Unlike Locke, who was active as a largely self-trained physician, Hume was unfit for any occupation except that of philosopher and, as such, in a constant anguished quest for first principles. Locke blithely assumed that such a thing as objective reason (by which, of course, he meant the reason of an enlightened Englishman of his age) existed; furthermore, that it was identical with the laws laid down by a benevolent nature. To Hume, on the contrary, reason was subjective and, in the last resort, merely a servant of the passions which dictated the ends toward which it should be directed. Not only was it manifestly untrue that such a thing as "objective" reason capable of being shared by all people existed, but even if it had existed any connection between it and the intentions of nature would have been completely undemonstrable.[113]

Montesquieu, accordingly, definitely relegated the law of nature – which Hume had deprived of its support, "reason" – to the back seat. To avoid tyranny, it was still necessary that government should be based on law – not such law as had been laid down once and for all by some external force or authority, however, but such as man (Montesquieu was fond of speaking of "the legislator") himself made for himself and wrote down in accordance with the kind of community he had in mind. In this way Montesquieu completed the process, which had been going on since the late Middle Ages, in which the force of laws other than those made first by the ruler and then by the state was whittled away and finally abolished. As had already been the case with Hobbes, from now on law, good or bad, was simply that which the state enacted and put on the books in due form.

Montesquieu, to be sure, was careful to qualify his words. The kind of law he had in mind was not to be enacted arbitrarily. On the contrary, it should be made to fit the varying climatic and geographical circumstances in which each community found itself, the need to do so being Montesquieu's special hobbyhorse and the part of his work that earned him the greatest fame among his contemporaries. Even more important, the standard whereby various political communities were to be judged was liberty.[114] To guarantee the latter, the absolute power of the state over the members of civil society was to be vitiated by dividing sovereignty among three authorities. Besides Locke's legislative, there was an executive branch and a judiciary one; this was the first time in history when

[113] D. Hume, *Treatise on Human Nature* (London: Longmans, 1874 [1739]), esp. pp. 484, 520, 526, 567.
[114] See N. Hampson, *Will and Circumstance: Montesquieu, Rousseau and the French Revolution* (London: Duckworth, 1983), pp. 19ff.

such a separation was established, so that no magistrate who possessed authority over a person or group was also in a position to act as their judge. Thus the absolute power of the state to pass such laws as it saw fit was compensated for by the way in which its various organs balanced each other. Though applauded, so long as Montesquieu himself lived and the *ancien régime* persisted, the idea remained without influence in his native France. As destiny had it, the first country in which it was realized was the USA.

Between Hobbes and Locke, the theoretical structure of the modern state was substantially complete. Basing themselves on the separation between public rule and private authority – a distinction that had escaped both Erasmus and Machiavelli, and whose real founder in modern Europe had been Bodin – they set it up as an abstract entity separate from both ruler (the sovereign) and the ruled (civil society) but including them both. Louis XIV might boast that *l'état* (not, significantly, the *res publica* or *civitas* or *communitas* or some similar expression) *c'est moi*; however, the very fact that he, unlike any of his royal predecessors at any other time and place, could make that claim itself shows that the two were no longer the same. Surprising though it may seem to those who remember him principally as a liberal, that state was made all-powerful by Montesquieu who, completing the demolition job already begun by Hobbes and continued by Hume, tore up its roots in any kind of law except its own. Divorced from both God and nature, and no longer bound to observe custom except insofar as it had been ratified by itself, the state as envisaged by Montesquieu and his successors was capable of doing *anything*. The only remaining condition was that the three authorities among which sovereignty was divided should coordinate their actions with each other; and that they should follow the laws which, of course, they themselves enacted and interpreted and carried out.

Following four and a half centuries of development that had started around 1300, the state found itself perhaps the most powerful political construct ever. Relying on its regular armed forces – first the military, then the police and the prison apparatus as well – it imposed order on society to the point that the only organizations still capable of challenging it were others of the same kind. Those armed forces themselves rested on unprecedented economic muscle; steadily improving statistical – the word itself comes from "state" – information about every kind of resource available within the state's borders; and a bureaucratic machine capable of extracting those resources, husbanding them, and wielding them without any need for intermediary bodies. No longer identical with the person of the ruler, and liberated from the religious, legal, and quasi-legal constraints that had hampered most previous forms of government, the state stood poised at the beginning of a spectacular career. Before we can trace that career, though, it is necessary to examine some other aspects of life within the Leviathan.

Inside the Leviathan

Once the state had been brought into being, the very terms in which people thought about government changed. Already during the last quarter of the sixteenth century that time-honored form of literature, Mirrors for Princes, began to go out of fashion. The more rulers lost power *vis-à-vis* their own bureaucracies, the less important their personal qualities, foibles, loves, and hates became, and the greater the tendency to replace the Mirrors with textbooks by the likes of Bodin and Lipsius which were edited, where necessary, *ad usum delphinium*.

As for religion, the words *fidei defensor* continued to appear on British coins and *Gott mit uns* on the belts of German soldiers. Though rulers continued to be instructed in it as a matter of course, more and more it was relegated to private life. Luther, Calvin, and their fellow reformer Beza still had much to say about the institutions of government and the rights of magistrates; but John Wesley, who founded Methodism during the 1740s, was content with the existing regime so long as it afforded him and his followers freedom of religion.[115] From the time of the Enlightenment on, "monk-ridden," said of a ruler, became a term of abuse, one which was applied, for example, to Spain's Philip II and to France's Louis XIV during his declining years. Considered as a basis for government, theology lost most of its influence. This of course did not mean that its replacement, i.e., political science, could not be equally incomprehensible and even more long-winded.

Like that of classical Greece, but in contrast to most of its predecessors in other times and places (and also in contrast to some present-day doctrines), modern political science was couched almost entirely in secular terms. For two centuries after 1650 the idea that rulers deserved obedience because they had received their mandate from heaven continued to figure in children's catechisms. However, probably the last significant writer to argue in this way was an Englishman, Robert Filmer. His book, *Patriarcha*, was written around the middle of the seventeenth century and against the frequently fertile background of civil war. In it he tried to trace the origins of government to God's original gift to Adam. The latter had passed it on to his eldest son and so on to the author's own time – even though much of the process was carried out by usurpation

[115] See J. C. English, "John Wesley and the Rights of Conscience," *Journal of Church and State*, 37, 7, 1995, pp. 349–65.

which itself, Filmer argued, could succeed only because God approved of it.[116] At the hands of Locke, within less than three decades of his death, Filmer had been turned into a butt of ridicule, which in the eyes of many he has remained to the present day.

During the fifty years leading up to the French Revolution the belief spread that the units in which humanity lived ought to be states – and, increasingly, that people who did not live in states, as was the case outside Europe, belonged to inferior "tribal" civilizations and were scarcely human.[117] In France, England, Germany, and the United States *inter alia* the debate as to the constitutional arrangements that ought to exist *within* each state was to continue into the nineteenth century and beyond. Where agreement could not be reached, the result was revolution, a seventeenth-century concept which was borrowed from astronomy and which, since previous political entities only knew palace coups, revolts, rebellions, and mutinies of every sort, itself represents a product of the state.[118] Those, and there were always some, who disputed that man should be subject to the state at all came to be known as anarchists.[119] To the extent that they took action to realize their views – and, often, even if they did not – they were persecuted with all the power of the police.

In day-to-day life, the question whether one was a citizen of this state or that became one of the most important aspects of any individual's existence besides the biological facts of race, age, and sex. As late as the end of the *ancien régime*, Lawrence Sterne, author of *A Sentimental Journey*, was able to travel from Britain to France even though they were at war with each other; and, having arrived there, to be received with every sign of honor in the social circles to which he belonged. However, the nineteenth century put an end to such civilities. In the words of the US citizenship oath, those belonging to one state had to abjure all loyalty to foreign rulers, princes, or potentates. All states during wartime, and some during peacetime too, imposed restrictions on whom their citizens were and were not allowed to marry; while hostilities lasted, enemy nationals were likely to be interned and have their property confiscated. The time was even to come when not to be accepted as a citizen by one state or another turned into one of the worst of all possible fates. Such people were literally deprived of the right to live; always subject to deportation, sometimes

---

[116] R. Filmer, *Patriarcha* (London: Chiswell, 1685). This work was originally written just after the publication of *Leviathan*.

[117] *Leviathan*, p. 80. In our own politically correct days, the term "tribal" is sometimes regarded as an insult and is therefore taboo.

[118] On the origins of the political use of the word "revolution," see I. B. Cohen, *Revolution in Science* (Cambridge, MA: Belknap Press, 1985), pp. 51ff.

[119] For the origin of the term, see R. Williams, *Keywords: A Vocabulary of Culture and Society* (London: Fontana, 1976).

shuttled from one country to another (as notoriously happened to the Jewish refugees abroad the *St. Louis* in 1939), or concentrated in refugee camps, or left to starve in no man's land. Even if they were graciously admitted and allowed to reside within the stomach of this or that particular Leviathan, usually they were not permitted to take on legal employment and were left to lead a furtive existence.

Having grown out of the instruments that had helped monarchs turn themselves into absolute rulers, the state acquired a life of its own. Like some latter-day monster, it loomed over society; and, in turn, subjected that society to a flattening process unequaled in history until then. Aristotle, Bodin, and Montesquieu[120] had all noted the tendency of tyrants to eliminate social differences and privileges of every sort in order to reduce all their subjects to trembling equality in front of themselves. However, from the Persian Darius, through Alexander – who, as legend has it, was taught to cut off the heads of taller stalks of corn in a field – Nero, and the Sublime Porte, to Louis XIV, the power of the despots whom they had in mind was as nothing compared to that of their impersonal, invisible, and indivisible successor – one who, made up of armies of bureaucrats in and out of uniform, could not be swayed by human feeling while at the same time enjoying an immortality not granted even to the most powerful of emperors. As already noted, the construction of a specialized government apparatus implied the switch from indirect to direct rule and made the *société des ordres* in which social status equaled political power superfluous. The result was that *société*'s final demise, whether suddenly and at a stroke as happened in France, or gradually during the nineteenth century as in Germany and Austria.

To look at it in another way, by transforming rulers from owners and masters into magistrates who acted on *its* behalf, the state did away with the need to endow them with any special qualities or privileges. The first to suggest that all men were equal in respect to their physical and mental attributes – indeed that they did not possess any other attributes, such as strength, special wisdom, or divine favor, which made them fit to rule – was that great iconoclast, Thomas Hobbes. To Hobbes also belongs the credit of being the first political thinker since antiquity to base his system on that belief. In the state that he constructed all men were to be equal; from the sovereign down, whatever power some people exercised over others, and whatever special rights they enjoyed, derived not from their own qualities but solely from their position as government officials.

Later, the idea that men were born equal was taken up by Locke and spread by *philosophes* such as Voltaire, Thomas Paine, and others. From

---

[120] *Politics*, V, ix, 2–5; *Six Books of the Commonwealth*, p. 63; *The Spirit of the Laws*, pp. 58ff.

at least the middle of the eighteenth century on, the pressure for legal and political equality among all citizens could be seen to build up. At first, and as had already been the case in the ancient city-states, it was only applied to men; by 1918 or so, universal suffrage for the latter had become the rule in all the most advanced countries. However, an even better indication of its long-term strength is presented by the fact that, after an interval of about a century and a quarter (1789–1914), it began to be extended even to that supposedly inferior form of life, women. In one country after another, those who resisted the trend in the name of property, education, or sex were defeated. The equality of all citizens was built into the structure of the modern state, so to speak. Give up your special rights, all ye who enter here.

While the flattening process meant that the power exercised by the state within its borders grew and grew, most of the bonds that had linked earlier political communities to each other were either deliberately cut or allowed to lapse. Already Bodin had noted that the concept of sovereignty was incompatible with the existence of feudal ties between rulers on different sides of the border. Either one was sovereign and thus not the vassal of anybody else, or one was not; and indeed his work, representing a French point of view and thus very much concerned with the relationship between *le roi très chrétien* and the Emperor, can be read as a call for such ties as still remained to be abolished. Twenty years after the *Six livres* were published, Sully, as Henry IV's loyal servant, floated his scheme for breaking the Habsburg's overlordship over the German princes, and by the middle of the seventeenth century this feat had in fact been accomplished. The shift away from feudal ties among rulers was to prove both rapid and permanent. As early as 1667–8, Louis XIV, trying to revive them as a pretext for extending his borders, found himself opposed by most of Europe in the so-called War of Devolution. Later, as the European state began reaching outside its original home, the ability to impose direct rule while dispensing with intermediaries was turned into something of an index for modernization.[121]

It is true that rulers belonging to different dynasties continued to marry each other's daughters and sisters, and indeed their exalted status scarcely left them a choice. However, and in contrast to the situation as it has existed before 1648 and, even more so, 1550 or so, such family ties were now almost completely without political significance. Princesses continued to be provided with dowries; but the time when they had consisted of provinces which were transferred from one royal house to another was past. When Holland's William III became king of England, there was

[121] See e.g. B. Eccleston, "The State and Modernization in Japan," in Anderson, *The Rise of the Modern State*, pp. 192–210.

never any question of the two countries being united, and after his death they went their separate ways in foreign policy too. When Louis XIV put his grandson Philip on the Spanish throne by means of the War of the Spanish Succession, he declared that the Pyrenees had ceased to exist. This turned out to be a mere figure of speech, since the two countries continued to be entirely separate and no French king was ever to rule Spain as well. Later in the eighteenth century the fact that Louis XVI of France married Marie Antoinette, daughter of Maria Theresa and sister of Emperor Joseph II, did very little to influence relations between their respective countries. As to Napoleon, within three years of him marrying Marie-Louise he and his father-in-law, Emperor Francis, were engaged in all-out war.

Nor did the collapse of political entities superior to the sovereign state go unnoticed by contemporaries. To the proponents of both church and empire it was, of course, an unmitigated disaster. By contrast, in the hands of both Hobbes and Locke, it was turned into proof that "the state of nature" was not merely a fiction but existed in reality. The former regarded international relations as the arena in which fear, greed, and the lust for power ruled unchecked and where the war of *omnes contra omnium* was therefore able to unfold without beginning, pause, or end. The latter saw them in a more benevolent light as a field where states, though occasionally engaging in a quarrel and clobbering each other, on the whole allowed themselves to be governed by enlightened self-interest and behaved sufficiently well to allow civilized life to develop.[122] Whichever of the two views we adopt, the demise of any authority above that of the state meant that the unity of Europe which eighteenth-century *philosophes* from Voltaire and Gibbons onward were so fond of talking about was limited almost entirely to the republic of letters. In our own day many authors have argued that "international anarchy" as it exists among states is the root cause of war. What they forget is that war made its historical *début* long before the state; and, to all appearances, is destined to outlast it as well.

---

[122] On the views held by the *philosophes* on these questions, see E. Silberner, *La guerre dans la pensée économique du XVIe au XVIIe siècle* (Paris: Libraire de recueil Sirey, 1939), particularly part 2.

4   The state as an ideal: 1789 to 1945

The state as it emerged between about 1560 and 1648 was conceived not as an end but as a means only. During a period of intense religious and civil conflict, its overriding purpose was to guarantee life and property by imposing law and order; anything else – such as gaining the consent of the citizens and securing their rights – was considered secondary and had to wait until peace could be restored. This explains why, even in England with its relatively well-developed parliamentary tradition and even as late as Hobbes, the choice of the sovereign was irrevocable and liberty, as he put it, merely consisted of the cracks left between the laws which that sovereign enacted.[1] True, neither Locke nor Montesquieu nor most of their eighteenth-century successors accepted Hobbes' conclusions in this respect; however, in regarding the state as a mere instrument for making a civilized people, they were entirely at one with him. As late as the 1790s Jeremy Bentham in Britain still considered the state in purely utilitarian terms as a machine whose only mission was to secure "the greatest happiness for the greatest number." The prevailing attitude was succinctly explained by another Englishman, Alexander Pope: "for forms of government let fools contest/whatever is best administered is best."

In view of these attitudes one should scarcely be surprised to find that the demands that the early modern state made on its subjects were, compared with what was to come later on, fairly limited. From the upper classes it took administrators and officers; from the middle ones, taxes; and from the lower ones both taxes and cannon fodder. Enlistment in the armed forces was, however, voluntary in most cases; moreover, in terms of percentages, neither the number of soldiers enlisted nor the amount of taxes levied by the "absolute" state even approached the burdens imposed by its democratic, liberal, twentieth-century successors. During the two and a half centuries after 1700 the former figure approximately doubled: from 5 to a maximum of about 10 percent of the population

---

[1] Hobbes, *Leviathan*, p. 139.

were drafted in wartime,[2] while the share of national income drained away by Frederick II's Prussia, the most heavily taxed eighteenth-century state by far, was almost exactly equal to that levied by the United States as one of the most lightly taxed modern states, in 1989, i.e., *before* the increases instituted by the Bush and Clinton administrations.[3] It is of course true that the absolute state denied the great majority of its subjects any form of political participation while demanding obedience from all alike. However, so long as that was granted – or, at any rate, so long as the state encountered no overt resistance to its demands – it was usually content to leave those subjects to their own devices; it did not make a systematic attempt to tutor them or to influence their views.

Considered from another angle, the relationship between the early modern state and its citizens was based not on sentiment but on reason and interest. The idea of just war having been abandoned by Hugo Grotius twenty years before the Treaty of Westphalia was signed, Enlightenment rulers did not go to war against one another for reasons of personal hatred. The role of patriotism in providing motivation for both soldiers and civilians was limited;[4] as Austria's Francis I supposedly said of the Tyroleans, "today they are patriots for me, tomorrow against me."[5] The need to prevent the emergence of revolutionary demands did not allow rulers to burden their subjects too heavily, and also caused most of them systematically to recruit foreigners into their armed forces. Scotland, Wales, Ireland, Switzerland, Italy, and certain German states all exported soldiers; Frederick the Great even claimed to wage war in such a way that the local population should not notice it was going on.[6] When Napoleon defeated the Prussians at Jena in 1806 the governor had posters placed in which he announced that, the king having lost a battle, the subjects' first duty was to stay calm.

Even as the state was reaching maturity around the middle of the eighteenth century, however, forces were at work which were about to transform it from an instrument into an end and, later, a living god. At first the ideas in question, surfacing in the works of French, Swiss, and

---

[2] For figures on the size of the military from the eighteenth century to the present, see J. A. Lynn, "The Pattern of Army Growth, 1445–1945," in Lynn, ed., *Tools of War* (Urbana: University of Illinois Press, 1990), pp. 100–27.

[3] For Prussian taxation see chapter 3, n. 55, in this volume; for modern American taxes, see R. B. Reich, *The Work of Nations: Preparing Ourselves for 21st-Century Capitalism* (New York: Vintage Books, 1991), p. 260.

[4] See C. Duffy, *The Military Experience in the Age of Reason* (London: Routledge, 1987), pp. 7–10.

[5] Quoted in E. Hobsbawm, *States and Nationalism Since 1780* (London: Cambridge University Press, 1990), p. 75.

[6] Frederick II, quoted in J. Luvaas, ed., *Frederick the Great on the Art of War* (New York: Free Press, 1966), pp. 100–11.

German intellectuals, were harmless enough. But before long they spread to the masses, causing them to take on an aggressive, chauvinistic tone that boded ill for the welfare of humanity. Partly driven by these forces, partly in an attempt to keep them within limits, the state took them under its own aegis. This led to the bureaucracy extending its tentacles into fields which had previously been largely free of government interference – such as education, health, and ultimately such fields as sports and social welfare as well. As the twentieth century entered its first few decades, a number of states even reached the point where they themselves took over all those activities and services, prohibiting any that were not state-owned; the outcome was the emergence of the "totalitarian" regimes of both the left- and right-wing variety. Finally, once the state had become so powerful that it was able to determine what did and did not count as money, the financial restraints which had always limited the actions of previous rulers also dropped by the wayside. The ultimate outcome of all these developments was an increasingly violent series of explosions, beginning with the French Revolutionary and Napoleonic Wars, and culminating in the era of total war between 1914 and 1945.

The Great Transformation

The man who did more than anyone else to start the Great Transformation was, perhaps, Jean-Jacques Rousseau (1712–78).[7] Of *petit-bourgeois* origins – his father, though full of his own importance, was a watchmaker – he spent much of his life away from his native Geneva as a penniless exile; the more extensive his wanderings the more he harked back to it, painting it in splendid hues and glorifying its supposed virtues. Like most of his fellow *philosophes* from the time of Locke and Leibnitz on, Rousseau rejected the Christian idea of original sin and started from the notion that man was naturally good. However, to them the *patrie* was merely "a community of interests arising out of property rights,"[8] whereas to him it was the source from which all the individual's mental and moral faculties derived. Man being formed by the community in which he was born and in which he spent his youth, outside it no true humanity – no language, no property, no morality, no freedom, no happiness – was possible.[9] In the *Social Contract* of 1762, Rousseau went further still, suggesting that this community had a corporate persona – a

---

[7] Rousseau's contribution to the rise of the modern state is discussed in J. L. Talmon, *The Origins of Totalitarian Democracy* (London: Mercury Books, 1961), ch. 3.

[8] F. M. Voltaire, *Dictionnaire philosophique* (Paris: Cluny, 1920 [1776]), p. 259.

[9] J.-J. Rousseau, "Patrie," in J. d'Alembert and D. Diderot, eds., *Encyclopédie* (Paris: Briasson, 1755–65), vol. XII, pp. 178–81.

moi commun – represented by the general will. To go against one's creator, as against one's parents, was turned into the worst of all vices. Conversely, patriotism – the active submission to, and participation in, the general will – became the highest of all virtues and the source of all the remaining ones.

While the transformation of the *patrie* from the place where one had been born into the highest of all earthly ideals was thus accomplished almost at a single stroke, still Rousseau was no nationalist. As he made clear in the *Confessions*, to him the essence of the *patrie* consisted not of some lofty ideals but of the most humdrum aspects of its existence: such as the language its people spoke, the clothes they wore, the customs they observed, the festivals they celebrated, even the streets and houses they built in a style that was uniquely their own and in which they spent their lives. Precisely because of the extremely intimate link that he saw as existing between it and the individual, the community had to be small, possibly indeed no larger than Plato's ideal city-state to which his father had often compared Geneva and to which his thought owed so much. Decentralization, not its opposite, was Rousseau's goal. The world which he envisaged was anything but modern. It consisted of a loose confederation of autonomous city-states, each one living in relative isolation from its neighbors and populated, as far as possible, by warlike yet peaceful farmers who drew their own nourishment from the soil. Thus, and only thus, would each one also be able to represent the supreme ideal to its inhabitants who both drew their life from it and were supposed to lay down their lives on its behalf if necessary.

These were the days when, reacting to the universalistic ideas of the Enlightenment (man, essentially a rational creature, was the same everywhere), the first stirrings of nationalism made themselves felt in several countries.[10] The writers in question sought to rescue what was unique in each people's culture from the clutches of the *philosophes*: particularly as most of the latter spoke and wrote in French. Thus, in Switzerland, Franz Urs Baltheassar's *Patriotic Dreams of a Swiss* (1758) sang the praise of the simple, virtuous, and free lives supposedly led by the Swiss peasants in their mountain huts. Using as his vehicle the first modern Zurich newspaper, which was published by his friend Heinrich Füssli, Baltheassar sought to rescue anything that was native and authentic, even going so far as to suggest that Swiss girls choose their husbands for their patriotic virtues rather than for wealth. Less utopian was the founding of the Helvetic Society which represented the first organized manifestation of modern Swiss nationalism and whose most important

---

[10] See J. H. Shennan, "The Rise of Patriotism in Eighteenth-Century Europe," *History of European Ideas*, 13, 6, 1991, pp. 689–710.

member was the famous educator Pestalozzi. It sought to rescue native customs such as dress, folksongs, and the like by recording them and giving them the largest publicity possible.

In Germany during those very years a role similar to that of Baltheassar was being played by Justus Möser and his weekly paper, the *Patriotic Fantasies*. A jurist by trade – he had served as chief judge on the criminal court of his native Osnabrück – and a follower of Montesquieu, Möser before he turned into a social critic had witnessed petty tyranny at first hand. His *bête noire* was the arbitrary laws which such tyranny had imposed on the German states; his chief demand, that they be changed so as to suit the national spirit or *Nationalgeist*. However, Möser differed from his French master in that this spirit was not a neutral factor and did not stand merely for the characteristics of each nation as impressed on it by the facts of race, geography, climate, history, etc. What to Montesquieu had been merely an observable fact that had to be taken into account for the sake of good government was turned into something uniquely precious; like Rousseau, Möser saw in it both the source of the individual's life and, more pertinent for our purpose, that which held different nations together while separating them from each other.

The most important eighteenth-century representative of what one author has called "humanitarian" nationalism[11] was, however, another German publicist, Johann Gottfried von Herder (1744–1803). As an early Romantic, Herder was only incidentally interested in law, that system of dry-as-dust regulations by which each ruler surrounded himself. Instead his concern was with the *Wesen* or inner being of each nation which, to him, was no less a thing than a manifestation of the divine. He denounced the Enlightenment emphasis on the rational and the uniform in favor of the unique and the different: "no individual, no country, no people, no history of a people, no state is like any other. Therefore, the true, the beautiful and the good are not the same for all of them. Everything is suffocated if one's own way is not sought, and if another nation is blindly taken as a model." Each nation had its own culture, character even. Nurtured by soil and climate, they were passed on from one generation to the next and would stay intact for some generations even if, by some extreme mischance, a nation were transported from one geographical location to another. Culture manifested itself in dress, habits, and, above all, language; and indeed so strong were the connections between one's mother tongue and one's personal identity that no one was ever capable of learning a foreign one perfectly. On

---

[11] C. J. Hayes, *The Historical Evolution of Modern Nationalism* (New York: Russell and Russell, 1968 [1931]), ch. 2.

the contrary, "civilization itself consists primarily in the potentialities of a nation, and in the making use of them."[12]

Again it cannot be emphasized too strongly that, whatever the kind of community in which they lived or which they had in mind, these and other eighteenth-century intellectuals were no nationalists in the modern, political sense. Some, having replaced Christianity with deism, merely studied different cultures as a way of bringing out the beauty of the creation in all its manifold forms – like a garden of separate flower beds each worthy of being admired on its own. Others, slightly more practically minded, were motivated by the need to understand the spirit of each nation as the basis for doing away with antiquated laws and creating a just social order. Some, such as Rousseau, held democratic and even revolutionary views, whereas others were inclined to accept almost any political regime so long as it allowed culture to develop freely. Herder himself went on record as saying that nothing was so ridiculous as the pretensions of any one nation to superiority, let alone claims of political domination which, far from advancing culture, would create "a wild mixture of breeds and nations under one scepter." His attitude was typical for German intellectuals of his day. As late as 1796, Schiller, Germany's greatest dramatist and poet, was able to write that Germans should forget about becoming a nation, and educate themselves to be human beings instead.[13]

It was only in the years after 1789, when some of the intellectuals came to power and when their ruminations were married to the pretensions of the state, that the picture changed. Leaving the study, nationalism took on an aggressive, bellicose character; nowhere was this more true than in Germany, previously celebrated as the country of "poets and thinkers" in which close acquaintance with French bayonets, French rule, and French marauders led to a violent reaction from 1806 on. In particular, Napoleon's victory over Prussia transformed one philosopher – Johan Gottlieb Fichte, hitherto known mainly as a harmless follower of Kant – into a rabble-rousing orator of remarkable force. In his *Addresses to the German Nation* (1807–8), Fichte elevated anti-French sentiment almost to the rank of a religious principle; from that point on even to teach one's daughter French, the common language of the Enlightenment, was to deliver her into prostitution. His work marks the point where German national feeling, long cosmopolitan and inclined toward pacifism, ceased

---

[12] J. G. Herder, *Werke*, E. Kühnemann, ed. (Stuttgart: Union deutsche Verlagsgesellschaft, 1889), vol. I, p. 402.

[13] J. W. Goethe and F. Schiller, "Xenien," in *Schillers Werke*, J. Peterson and F. Beissner, eds. (Weimar: Nationalausgabe, 1943), p. 321.

to be so and assumed the militant and chauvinistic character that it was to retain during much of the period until 1945.[14]

During the very years that Fichte was thundering away from his University of Berlin chair, the marriage of nation and state was consummated at the theoretical level by another and greater professor, Georg Wilhelm Friedrich Hegel. A native of Stuttgart in southwestern Germany, Hegel had been brought up to follow his father as a Protestant pastor; however, during his period of study at the University of Tübingen he met with wine, women, and song, and lost his faith in a personal God. He spent time as a private tutor at Bern – where, like Möser half a century previously, he came to know and detest the petty tyranny that characterized city-states at their worst – and Frankfurt before settling down at Jena in 1801. Initially he welcomed the universalistic ideas of the French Revolution; to him they represented the final separation of state from society and thus an end to the corruption which the *ancien régime* necessarily entailed. However, his position changed after the cataclysmic events of 1806–7, during which Saxony was occupied and his own house burnt down.

Though he was in many ways a child of the Enlightenment and thus inclined to believe in rationality as the supreme good, Hegel's loss of faith left him with the question as to whose reason directed the affairs of society and of man. For an answer he turned from the personal God of Christianity to the impersonal Spirit of History or *Weltgeist*, thus setting up a secular religion whose high priest, needless to say, was Hegel himself. Where Hegel differed from others, however, was that he attributed reason – and thus the shaping of history – neither to humanity as a whole nor to the individuals of which it consisted but to the separate political communities or states in which they lived. Composing civil society, individuals merely reproduced themselves without change from one generation to the next. Their principal occupation in life consisted of haggling with each other for petty economic advantage; as they were self-serving and capricious, their doings were scarcely worth noting by the philosopher concerned with higher things. By contrast, states were mighty, hence important and "world-historical," organizations. Each one was not just a system of government but an idea incarnate which manifested itself in that system. Like Hobbes, Hegel saw the state's most important characteristic and the one in which it differed from other organizations as its sovereignty. Unlike Hobbes, he did not see this sovereignty merely as an instrument for imposing law and order but endowed it with high ethical content. Acknowledging no superior, alone

[14] On Fichte and the origins of German nationalism in this period, see above all H. Kohn, *The Mind of Germany* (New York: Scribner's, 1966), pp. 68–98.

of all institutions on earth the state possessed the freedom to develop in accordance with its own nature, a freedom which it bestowed on its citizens (so long as they cooperated with it) and which provided it with its justification. From a machine designed to serve this purpose or that, the state was elevated into nothing less than "the echo of God's footsteps on earth."[15] History itself was transformed, turning from a formless mass of facts into the record of states rising, growing, clashing with each other, reaching maturity, and decaying in an everlasting search for a more perfect political order that was at the same time a more perfect truth. Moreover, and standing in sharp contrast to Locke as well as the Fathers of the American Revolution, Hegel considered that true freedom for the individual was possible *only* within the state. Take the state away and man was reduced to nothing at all, a puny biological creature whose life was divorced from the world-spirit and, in this sense, devoid of ethical significance.

Like Fichte, Hegel spent his last years at the University of Berlin where his lectures were much admired but little understood (his greatest work, *The Philosophy of Right*, took twenty years to sell 500 copies). His death in 1831 marks the end of the Great Transformation that had been started by Rousseau; but whereas Rousseau, harking back to a primitive past, had still spoken of the organized community as his ideal, Hegel was unhesitant in pointing to the state as the community's highest, indeed sole, representative. Embodying freedom and acknowledging no judge above themselves, the one way for states to play out their historical destiny was to pit themselves against other states by means of war, which thus became the principal tool whereby the world-historical spirit unfolded itself; without it everything tended to sink into selfishness and mediocrity.[16] The result was that each state had to be made as strong as possible. For all that he saw the task of the state as protecting the national culture and creating a suitable environment for its development, Hegel would not have been Hegel had there not been present in his thought a strain that adored power politics as such.

Nationalists coming after Hegel frequently disputed the idea that the Prussia of 1820 or so was the best of all possible states, preferring to bestow that distinction on their own countries instead. Some, such as the Frenchmen François Guizot and the Italian Giuseppe Mazzini, were dyed-in-the-wool liberals; if not necessarily in favor of popular democracy, at any rate they did their best to combine national greatness with personal freedom for the individual. Others, particularly in Germany and Eastern Europe but with strong representation in France also, dis-

[15] *Hegel's Philosophy of Right*, T. M. Knox, tr. (Oxford: Clarendon, 1952), p. 279.
[16] See S. B. Smith, "Hegel's Views on War, the State and International Relations," *American Political Science Review*, 7, 1983, pp. 624–32.

agreed. Fully prepared to do away with personal freedom if it failed to serve national goals, they adopted either an authoritarian and reactionary standpoint or else a populist and even revolutionary one.[17] Whatever their views concerning the kind of regime that was most suitable for their respective national cultures, almost without exception they agreed with Hegel concerning the need for their own states to develop their independence and power. If possible this was to be done in harmony with others, as Mazzini in particular hoped; but if necessary it could be at the expense of their neighbors and by using as much armed force as it took to achieve national liberation (also of fellow nationals currently living in other states), natural frontiers, a place under the sun, or what other phrase could be made to justify territorial expansion. All this helped fuel the kind of interstate rivalry that was to be such a prominent feature of the period from 1848 to 1945 and which, exploding into flame, ultimately led to two world wars as well as a whole series of smaller ones.

Born in the dreamlike visions of a few intellectuals and subsequently dressing itself in a respectable academic mantle, nationalism could not have acquired the force that it did had it not been able to transform itself into a mass movement as well. The first state to deliberately mobilize the masses for its own purposes was Revolutionary France; the magnitude of the task can be judged from the fact that, in 1789, the country was still divided into eighty provinces, each of which had its separate laws, customs, and political traditions. What patriotic feelings existed among the people at large were almost entirely local; as the French Academy put it, "a Frenchman's country [was] merely that part of it in which he happened to be born."[18] To make things worse, it was judged that only between 1 and 13 percent of approximately 27 million Frenchmen who lived within the country's 1792 frontiers could speak French "correctly." Even in the region of the *langue d'oïl*, it was spoken only in the towns, and not always in the suburbs, whereas in the south it was not spoken at all. This was clearly an obstacle to state unity and, in particular, to its more centralized and militant version as envisaged by the Jacobeans. As Henri Gregoire, a clergyman who was at the same time a radical member of the national Convention, put it in his "Report on the need to eliminate *patois* and universalize the usage of the French language" (1794): only when all citizens speak the same tongue can they enjoy equal access to state citizenship.[19]

In the event, the rulers of France between 1789 and 1815 took few

---

[17] For the forms that nationalism took in different countries, see J. Breuilly, *Nationalism and the State* (New York: St. Martin's, 1982), particularly pp. 43–118.

[18] Quoted in J. M. Thompson, *The French Revolution* (Oxford: Blackwell, 1944), p. 121.

[19] Quoted in M. de Certaue, et al., *La Revolution française et les patois: l'enquête de Gregoire* (Paris: Galimard, 1975), p. 295.

positive steps to correct the alleged linguistic deficiencies of their countrymen (in this they showed better sense than some of their successors
who, trying to go further, merely covered themselves with ridicule). What
they did do, though, went far enough. Sweeping away the old administrative divisions, they set up a centralized bureaucracy with a uniform
structure and branches throughout the country. They also established
general military service for all males aged nineteen to twenty-six; a comprehensive legal code with authority over all Frenchmen regardless of
status, creed, or province of residence; and a new state-directed secondary and tertiary education system that in many ways was without precedent in history. No less important, the turbulence caused by the Revolution and the series of wars in which the Republic engaged within three
years of its foundation meant that Frenchmen originating in the four
corners of the country were brought together for a single purpose and
mingled with each other as never before. For the first, but certainly not
the last, time war became the crucible of the nation as well as of the state
in which it organized itself.

To put muscle behind its claims, the Republic initiated a series of huge
popular festivals in which it sought to celebrate itself and which it hoped
to substitute for the old religious ones. The first one took place in
November 1789 when some 12,000 people from various towns and
villages in Languedoc and Dauphine gathered more or less spontaneously
at Etoile on the Rhone and swore an oath "to offer our arms and our
wealth to the common fatherland . . . flying to the aid of our brothers of
Paris or of any other town of France which may be in danger." From
January to May of the next year similar gatherings were held at Pontivy
and Lyons, culminating in a massive gathering on 14 July 1790, Bastille
Day, which was thereby established as the anniversary of the Revolution.
At the Champ de Mars, the newly designated parade-ground outside
Paris, 300,000 "patriots" from all over France were assembled for the
Fête de la Fédération. It was presided over by Talleyrand, an aristocratic
member of the National Assembly who had been bishop of Autun under
the old regime but had turned his coat (not for the last time) and become
one of the most vocal revolutionaries. To the incongruous sound of
masses being chanted and cannon being fired, the assembly swore to
forego regional differences. From now on there were to be no more sons
of the Dauphine, Artois, Vendée, and so on: only Frenchmen who joined
together in taking an oath to the constitution. During the next nine years
the ceremony was to be repeated annually, often assuming bizarre forms
as when Robespierre enthroned the Goddess of Reason, planted the tree
of liberty, and the like. It also served as the model for countless smaller
ones held in provincial cities.

Not content with occasional ceremonies, the founders of the Republic marked the event by the adoption of a new national flag – the tricolor – as well as a new national calendar starting in the year one. Designed by the poet Fabre d'Eglantine, it deliberately divided the year into weeks of ten days rather than seven; no better way of giving citizens the clearest possible indication of the state's power to change their working habit and run their lives for them could have been invented. Taking yet another leaf out of the book of the discredited church, France in 1795 became the first country to be blessed with an official anthem for use on public occasions. The *Marsellaise*, a uniquely stirring marching song, had been written in 1792 by captain of the artillery Claude Joseph Rouget de Lisle who, as it happened, was stationed in Strasbourg at the time. It received its name from a contingent of troops whose native city was Marseilles and who sang it as they marched toward Paris. It was banned by Napoleon who feared lest the central message, i.e., the need to fight against "the bloody banner of tyranny," might be interpreted as referring to his own regime; restored by the Orleanists in 1830, it was banned for the second time by Napoleon III and officially reinstated in 1871. Increasingly surrounded by its opposite numbers in other countries, it has remained in favor ever since, to be sung on public occasions amidst gestures previously reserved for religious hymns.

During the Revolution and the First Empire, poetry, literature, and the plastic arts were all systematically mobilized to glorify *la patrie* and the emperor who took it over and stood at its head. A special architectural style, known as the *architecture parlante*, was even developed; from the Arc de Triomphe onward its results can still be seen across the length and breadth of France. Painters such as David celebrated Napoleon's deeds – even to the point of showing him unshaven to emphasize that he spent nights as well as days in the service of France. Like many other things that the emperor did, the art he promoted tended to be heavy-handed. From beginning to end, there was no place for subtlety in delivering the message, and even less room for doubt concerning the supremacy of the state.

Whereas France became the first country where the nationalist cause was married to that of the state, elsewhere development often followed a different pattern. Where nation and state did not coincide, as was the case in much of Europe between 1815 and 1860, rulers had cause to fear popular nationalism rather than to encourage it. Consequently it arose without them and, in many cases, against them, incidentally putting an end to whatever still remained of the old idea that rulers and state were one and the same. The outstanding case in point was Germany, stirred to red-hot patriotism during the Wars of Liberation but thereafter once again divided into thirty-eight states – excluding, Austria which, though a member of the Federation or *Bund*, was in large part non-German.

The early representatives of post-Napoleonic German nationalism were figures such as Friedrich Ludwig Jahn and Ernst Moritz Arndt. Like Hegel, both of them came from a pietist background; like him, they were led by the events of 1806–15 to shake off their earlier political apathy and turn from rather dreamy, religiously minded patriots into burning advocates of the German fatherland. Besides giving nationalist speeches, they started planning and organizing festivals whose purpose was to advocate national unity and celebrate the deeds of the German people ever since the time when their ancestors had triumphed over the Roman legions. The movement was surprisingly quick to take hold; by 1817, when the famous Wartburg Festival was held, crowds attended and an entire liturgy had been created out of thin air. It was modeled on that of the Protestant church, complete with the singing of hymns such as *Deutschland über Alles*, marching about, and preaching; but differed from it in significant points such as the tendency to hold services in the open air rather than indoors, the display of national flags, and the replacement of bells by trumpets. The one held at Hambach in 1832 was attended by 30,000 students, and this was even before the advent of modern transportation and modern means of communication allowed such meetings to be held on a truly national scale.[20]

Initially these popular gatherings, in which much beer was drunk and some windows (and heads) might be broken, were regarded with suspicion by the authorities. They considered them hotbeds of Jacobinism, sent plainclothesmen to spy on participants, arrested leaders, and incarcerated them. However, from the middle of the century on, the direction of the wind changed. The gatherings were taken over by the increasingly nationalized state, which transformed them and made them serve *its* ends. Naturally not all attempts at doing so were crowned with success. Planning a festival, and then making it appear spontaneous, is never easy, particularly if the purpose is to show deference to the authorities rather than to express opposition or simply release steam. For example *Sedantag*, instituted by law to commemorate the battle of 1870 and scheduled to take place on the first day of each September, proved too heavy-handed and did not really attract popular enthusiasm. People, even Germans, preferred occasions which granted a greater measure of popular participation. To fill the void, the state found it necessary to resort to parades and other military displays.

By this time the industrial revolution, having started a century earlier in Britain, had long reached the Continent and was in full swing. Dedicated

[20] For the history and significance of these festivals, see G. Mosse, *The Nationalization of the Masses* (New York: Fertig, 1975), pp. 73–160.

to perpetual economic growth, industrial society meant change and a constant game of musical chairs as people gained or lost new employment and as fortunes were made or lost. But it also led to a vast increase in the individual's ability to move from one place to another; with the spread of the railroads from the 1830s on, the ties that had hitherto bound the common man to the community of his birth were broken for the first time. Thus industrial society weakened or destroyed the older institutions in which people used to live together on a face-to-face basis: such as the extended family, clans, tribes, villages, and guilds, even the relatively small urban communities which, surrounded by their walls, had existed for centuries but which now took on monstrous dimensions owing to the influx of newcomers from the countryside.[21] Their demise left people feeling rootless and naked, exposed as never before to the vast "market forces" that seemed to rule their lives and over which they could not exert the slightest control. Against this background, already around the middle of the century "alienation" was being recognized as a cardinal social problem to which all sorts of remedies were offered by revolutionaries and conservatives alike.[22]

Rising to the challenge, the state, embracing nationalism, deliberately sought to turn the situation to its own advantage and began to sing its own praises by every means at its disposal. Gone were the days when such things as national food, national costume, and national habits could be left to the care of mere patriotic societies; by means of its education system, to be discussed in greater detail in the next section, the state sought to harness not only them but also "culture" in the form of history, painting, sculpture, literature, drama, and music. All these ceased to be either a matter for lone individuals or part of the common human enterprise. Instead they became compartmentalized into English, French, German, or Russian as the case might be; often coming under the auspices of some ministry of culture (which might or might not be the same as the ministry of education), they were subsidized and studied primarily as a means of glorifying the national heritage.

As one of the greatest expressions of human freedom and spontaneity, sport too became nationalized. Previously it had been organized on a purely local scale as fights, races, and athletic demonstrations were used to enliven popular fairs and as neighboring schools sometimes sent their students to compete against each other; now, however, it was taken over

---

[21] An excellent early analysis for the alienating effects of modern industrial society is K. Marx and F. Engels, *The German Ideology* (New York: International Publishers, 1932 [1844]), pp. 23ff.

[22] For the links between nationalism and the Industrial Revolution, see E. Gellner, *Nations and Nationalism* (Oxford: Blackwell, 1983), particularly ch. 3.

by the state which turned it to *its* ends, including above all preparations for war.[23] Furthermore, the spread of the railways made it possible to organize competitions first on a national and then on an international basis with teams representing their various states. The signal was given in 1896 when the first rejuvenated Olympic Games were held in Athens. From then on, the greater the prestige of any single sporting event, the more likely it was to start with a raising of national flags and to end with the playing of national anthems, to say nothing of the displays of national rowdiness that often took place in between.

From Argentina to Spain,[24] the second half of the nineteenth century also saw the invention of a whole series of new festivals: such as Independence Day, National Day, Armed Forces Day, Jubilee Day, Flag Day, Heroes' Day, Memorial Day, Victory Day, Great Trek Day (for the Boers of South Africa), or whatever they may have been called. Some of these were grafted upon existing religious and royal feasts. Others, generally less successful in the long run, were literally conjured out of nothing. The central festival was invariably held at the capital with the head of state in attendance, listening to and delivering speeches. But every city, town, and village felt obliged to set up a modest copy of the original; the more important the state dignitaries who condescended to come their way, the greater the reflected glory and the more successful the event. Depending on the occasion there would be a holiday celebrated by parades, preferably by the armed forces[25] but, since the latter could not be present everywhere, if necessary by some less august body such as the local sharpshooters' association or gymnastic club. Then there would be tattoos, choruses, speaking choruses, flags, banners, some kind of sacred flame to be ceremoniously lit and carried about and extinguished, and of course the inevitable fireworks. To conclude the proceedings the masses were provided with open-air parties and opportunities for drinking, dan-

[23] A. Krieger, "Sieg Heil to the Most Glorious Era of German Sport: Continuity and Change in the Modern German Sports Movement," *International Journal of the History of Sport*, 4, 1, 1987, pp. 5–20; J. Tollener, "Formation pour la vie et formation pour l'armée: la Fédération nationale des sociétés catholiques de gymnastique et d'armes de Belgique, 1892–1914," *Stadion*, 17, 1, 1991, pp. 101–20; L. W. Burgener, "Sport et politique dans un état neutre: l'instruction préliminaire en Suisse, 1918–1947," *Information Historique*, 48, 1, 1986, pp. 23–9; M. Spivak, "Un concept mythologique de la Troisième République: le renforcement du capital humain de la France," *Information Historique*, 4, 2, 1987, pp. 155–76.

[24] L. A. Bertoni, "Construir la nacionalidad: héroes, estatuas y fiestas patrias 1887–1891," *Boletin del Instituto de Historia Argentina y Americana*, 5, 1992, pp. 77–111; M. A. Civera, "Origen y desarrollo de la fiesta de la Hispanidad," *Historia y Vida*, 25, 295, 1992, pp. 92–101.

[25] See J. P. Bois, "L'armée et la fête nationale, 1789–1919," *Histoire, Economie et Société*, 10, 4, 1991, pp. 505–27, on the way the armed forces came to dominate Bastille Day in particular.

cing, and carousing, while those able and willing to pay could enjoy dramatic and orchestral performances with stirring patriotic content.

During the last few decades before 1914, the existence of any state without such celebrations had become almost unthinkable. Dreaming about a future Jewish homeland, Theodore Herzl as the founder of Zionism became fascinated with the problem; his diary is peppered with descriptions of imaginary spectacles, the more grandiose the better.[26] Though all states participated to one extent or another, the real masters of this kind of thing turned out to be the postwar Communist, Fascist, and, above all, Nazi regimes. In their hands the festivals turned into gigantic occasions such as October Revolution Day, May Day, March on Rome Day, Memorial Day to Fallen Heroes, the Nuremberg Party Day, German Workers' Day, Summer Solstice Day, and the like. Even more than their counterparts in other countries, these occasions quickly lost whatever spontaneity they may have possessed at the outset. Becoming ritualized, they were destined to be repeated with dreadful monotony year after year.[27] The number of participants, not those who presented themselves voluntarily but who were shepherded to the spot by the authorities, rose until it reached tens and even hundreds of thousands, all marching and singing and saluting in unison, to say nothing of the additional millions who received the message by means of those new technical media, the state-controlled radio and film. Sometimes, as in the case of Moscow's Red Square and Rome's Piazza Venezia, the festivities made use of existing structures or adapted them to the new purpose. Elsewhere entirely new ones were built, such as the Zeppelinfeld near Nuremberg and numerous "giantic" (*sic*; a favorite expression in 1930s vintage English-language German guidebooks) open-air theaters which the Nazis constructed all over the country.

As these occasions were designed to demonstrate, by this time state-worship had reached the point where the original distinction between it and civil society was itself being abandoned. For all that he held up the state as the idea, Hegel had never regarded it as the *sole* ideal; on the contrary, he had always insisted on the need for strong private institutions to maintain themselves, balancing both each other and the state so as to make liberty possible.[28] This part of his message was destined to be ignored, not to say falsified, by his totalitarian successors on both the right

---

[26] Theodore Herzl, *The Complete Diaries of Theodore Herzl*, R. Patai, ed. (New York: Herzl Press, 1960), vol. I, pp. 27, 33, 39, 43, 67.

[27] For Hitler's own ruminations on this subject, see A. Speer, *Erinnerungen* (Berlin: Propylaen Verlag, 1969), pp. 67ff.

[28] For Hegel's views on civil society, see S. Avineri, *Hegel* (London: Cambridge University Press, 1972), pp. 141–7, 161–75; and H. Ottman, "Hegel's Philosophy of Right: Changing Paradigms for Its Interpretation," *Clio*, 13, 4, 1984, pp. 315–30.

and left wings of the twentieth-century political spectrum. Each in their own way, Communists and Fascists sought to abolish civil society; of its institutions, only those that had been put under state control and acted in step (or, to use the Nazi expression, were *gleichgeschaltet*) with its ends were permitted to survive.[29] In theory, and sometimes not merely in theory, every stamp-collecting association carried out its activities in pursuit of some political goal and every *Hausvater* became a miniaturized Führer barking out orders at his unfortunate family. Citizens were supposed to address each other in the state-approved way and sign their letters in state-approved words; those who still tried to express any kind of opinion except for the officially approved ones were likely to land in a state-run concentration camp. As Mussolini was to put it in his article on "Fascismo" in the 1935 edition of the *Encyclopaedia italiana* (itself, of course, an étatist design) – "everything inside the state, everything for the state, nothing against the state." In Nazi Germany, according to Minister of Propaganda Joseph Goebbels, the only time the individual was free of state control was in his dreams.

It must be conceded that liberal countries such as France and, in particular, Britain never went nearly as far as their totalitarian opposite numbers. Following the tradition first established by Locke and Montesquieu, they defined liberty in a different way; nor, in spite of numerous excesses that took part during some of France's revolutionary periods in particular, did they ever completely forget the need to protect individuals and institutions *against* the arbitrary will of the state. But when everything is said and done the difference was merely one of degree. Not only did twentieth-century France have an influential fascist movement in the form of the Action française, but the "strong" version of Hegelianism had its followers even in Britain where "the name of the little territory which encloses Weimar and Jena" was said to "stir the imagination of thousands of our youths of both sexes even as the name of Jerusalem moved the hearts of men in centuries behind us."[30] Whereas Voltaire had still spoken of patriotism as the scoundrel's last refuge, after 1789 it was only the socialists who doubted that it represented the highest virtue or that loyalty to the state in its capacity as the organized expression of society was the first duty of the patriot. The meaning of the word itself changed, from somebody who "makes the welfare of mankind his care" (the definition provided by the *Encyclopédie*) to a person prepared to fight

[29] The best account of totalitarian regimes in terms of the relationship between state and civil society remains H. Arendt, *The Origins of Totalitarianism* (New York: Meridian Books, 1951), esp. ch. 12, "Totalitarianism in Power."

[30] R. B. Haldane, "Hegel," *Contemporary Review*, 67, February 1895, p. 232; see also B. Bosquanet, *Philosophical Theory of the State* (London: Macmillan, 1899).

(some would say, create havoc) on his state's behalf. As treason to the state took the place of *lèse majesté* as the supreme crime, other forms of treason declined or disappeared. Thus, in Germany, *Landesverrat* far eclipsed mere *Hochverrat*; whereas in England *petite trahison*, otherwise known as murdering one's husband and considered a more heinous offense than simply killing one's wife, ended by being struck off the statute book during the 1830s.[31]

Of much greater significance to the lives of most people was the fact that, acting in the name of all these lofty ideals, the state now appropriated for itself the *right* to claim the highest sacrifice from its members. The danger which Voltaire had feared, namely that an excess of "patriotism" would lead to war, had been abundantly realized during the French Revolutionary and Napoleonic period. During the last decades before 1914, intense efforts were made by anarchists, socialists, and pacifists in many countries to build international bridges of every sort and thus prevent the most important states from fighting each other. However, when the call for sacrifice came, the barriers that they sought to erect proved to be far flimsier than anticipated by the states themselves and were easily swept aside.[32] With very few exceptions, potential soldiers flocked to the mobilization centers, and parliaments, even those in which socialist representation was strong, voted for war credits. The ultimate result of the marriage between nationalism and the state was to be slaughter conducted with an intensity, and on a scale, which the members of previous political organizations could not even have imagined. Before we can turn to that story, though, it is necessary to trace some of the more concrete means by which the state came to dominate civil society.

Disciplining the people

The state's transformation from an instrument into an ideal could never have taken place if it had not also reinforced its grip on society far beyond anything attempted by its early modern predecessor. For books on folklore to be written, patriotic speeches to be given, and national festivals to be held, even in the presence of kings, presidents, and prime ministers, is all very well. In the long run, though, what counts is neither periodical celebrations, nor the ruminations of a handful of intellectuals, but the

[31] See M. E. Dogget, *Marriage, Wife Beating and the Law in Victorian England* (London: Weidenfeld and Nicolson, 1992), p. 49.
[32] See M. Ferro, *The Great War 1914–1918* (London: Routledge, 1969), ch. 1; and A. Offner, "The Working Classes, British Naval Plans and the Coming of the Great War," *Past and Present*, 107, May 1985, pp. 225–6.

daily grind as experienced by the great majority of the ruled. To make sure that the daily grind would in fact be under its own control and, as far as possible, subservient to it was the goal of every post-1789 state both in Europe and, increasingly, overseas, the most important means for the purpose being the police and prison apparatus, the education system, and the welfare services.

As has been shown in an earlier section, two of the most characteristic features of the modern state are its specialized police forces on the one hand and the prison system on the other. The former was made necessary by the French Revolution and the *lévee en masse* which it was the first to introduce. The latter itself was a typical state-owned bureaucratic instrument, presupposing as it did whole armies of forms, regulations, wardens, physicians, social workers, psychologists, and of course the fortified structures in which their unfortunate wards were incarcerated. While the connection between them and the state is thus strong and intimate, both of them also reflect the fact that, once the Napoleonic Wars were over, the nature of the internal security problem facing the state underwent a decisive change.

From the time of the earliest empires on – and as the establishment of tyrannies in such ancient and medieval city-states as Corinth, Syracuse, Rome, Milan, and Florence *inter alia* also showed – traditionally the persons most in need of supervision had been the great. In the words of one sixteenth-century expert, "the rich are reluctant to submit to rule because they are fortunate"; though the lone assassin might succeed in murdering a king or magistrate, political change could usually be achieved only by those already "distinguished by their noble birth and influential positions."[33] With the establishment of the modern state that proposition became decreasingly valid. As feudal ties weakened and the church lost its right to govern, the switch to "legitimate" government meant that rulers had nothing to fear even from the greatest of their subjects. On the other hand, private property took over as the cement on which all relationships outside the nuclear family (and, often enough, inside it as well) were based. From the time of Bodin and Hobbes the protection of private property was turned into one of the principal functions of the sovereign.[34] Conversely, the success of the early modern state was itself explained partly by its willingness and ability to protect the property of its supporters.

With Locke and Montesquieu, the need to defend property against all comers – be it non-property-owners or the ruler himself – was elevated to

---

[33] Botero, *The Reason of State*, p. 83.
[34] See C. B. McPherson, *The Political Theory of Possessive Individualism: Hobbes to Locke* (London: Oxford University Press, 1962), particularly pp. 264–5, 197–221, 247–8.

the rank of a cardinal principle of political theory. The former made the right to property into an inalienable law of nature, even to the point that he defined life itself as a "possession" of which no person should be deprived without cause. The latter devoted some of the most critical parts of his work to a detailed explanation of the ways in which that right was to be enforced in practice. In the event, the first state explicitly to adopt the principle as one of its foundations was England after the "Glorious Revolution" of 1688. The United States and France followed, the former as soon as it adopted its constitution and the latter in the Declaration of the Rights of Man (1789). In Prussia, the inviolability of private property emerged gradually during the eighteenth century and was enthroned by the reforms of 1807–13. No wonder that, as the nineteenth century unfolded, the great – which, all other social ties having been dissolved, translated into the rich in nine cases out of ten – were almost always found on the side of the state. Save for a few eccentric Russian princes with anarchistic leanings, such as Bakunin and Kropotkin, they could be counted on to resist any attempt to upset the existing order, to the point that Marx in 1848 was able to define the state itself as nothing but a committee set up by "the entire bourgeoisie" to manage affairs on its own behalf.[35]

The acquiescence, often even the enthusiastic support, of the possessing classes having been secured in this way the early nineteenth-century state set out to extend *its* law and *its* order into those parts of the population which, up until then, were usually considered to be beneath its notice. Previously in most countries, crime among the lower social classes had been understood as the "depravity" of individuals. However regrettable from a moral point of view, it did not endanger society, the more so because most of it took the form of petty neighborhood quarrels directed by the poor against each other. As the emergence of the modern state caused the members of the upper classes to be disarmed, and as industrialization caused vast numbers of have-nots to concentrate in the rapidly growing cities, this situation changed. The events of 1789–94 had demonstrated what the mob, provided it was properly aroused and led, could do even to the most powerful and best organized state in history until then. During the decades after 1815 the emerging "social question" came to be seen as threatening the foundations of the establishment; and, with it, the working discipline that modern capitalism and industry required.

Whatever their exact motivation, during the two decades after 1810 one country after another set out to imitate Napoleon, establish new

[35] K. Marx and F. Engels, *The Communist Manifesto*, A. J. P. Taylor, ed. (Harmondsworth, UK: Penguin Books, 1967 [1848]), p. 82.

police forces, and centralize existing ones. To mention some of the most important developments only, between 1815 and 1825 the old Prussian municipal "citizens' guards" (*Burgergarden*), which had hitherto been responsible for dealing with petty crime, were abolished. Their place was taken by the police and (in rural districts) gendarmes, both of whom were paid and maintained exclusively by the state. At mid-century a typical provincial Prussian town was blessed with approximately one policeman per 3,000 inhabitants; by the even of World War I this had risen to over one in a thousand.[36] In 1811 in Russia, Tsar Alexander I, wishing to stamp out disloyalty in anticipation of a probable French invasion, established a Police Ministry by taking a rib of the existing Ministry of the Interior.[37] Renamed "The Third Department" by Nicholas I, it was given a virtual *carte blanche* to gather "information concerning all events, without exception": by the 1840s it had run so far out of control that it put the emperor's own son under supervision without his knowledge.[38] Assuming various guises, it was destined to remain active as long as the tsarist regime itself lasted. Eventually it served as the model for its even more notorious Communist successors, the Cheka, OGPU, NKVD, and KGB.

Among the main European countries, the one with the strongest liberal traditions was Britain. Though individual members of Parliament repeatedly protested the effect on liberty, here too the growth and centralization of state-run, regular police forces proceeded apace; in 1829 the city of London received its "bobbies" (after Home Secretary Robert Peel). In 1835 Parliament ordered all incorporated municipalities to follow London's lead, and twenty-one years after that the County and Borough Police Act made police forces mandatory all over the country. Meanwhile roads, railroads, and telegraphs had all begun to put an end to the isolation of local police forces both in Britain and abroad. During the 1870s police pay, discipline, and criteria for enlistment were taken out of the hands of local authorities and put into those of the Home Office; another landmark occurred in 1890 when it became legal to swap policemen or even entire units between one local force and another. By 1906 no less than a third of the business of the Home Office was accounted for by its Criminal Department – which by this time looked after everything

---

[36] Figures from A. Luedtke, *Police and State in Prussia, 1815–1850* (Cambridge: Cambridge University Press, 1989), pp. 41–2, 86; and E. Glovka Spencer, *Police and the Social Order in German Cities* (DeKalb: Northern Illinois University Press, 1992), pp. 166–7.

[37] On the origins of the Russian police, see P. S. Squire, *The Third Department: The Establishment and Practices of the Political Police in the Russia of Nicholas I* (Cambridge: Cambridge University Press, 1968), pp. 29ff.

[38] W. Bruce Lincoln, *Nicholas I, Emperor and Autocrat of All the Russians* (DeKalb: Northern Illinois University Press, 1989), p. 89.

from controlling foreign-born waiters to petty crime. Even so, compared with what was going on elsewhere, Britain lagged behind. For example, it was only in 1929 that arrest procedures were standardized throughout the country.

By the time these developments were taking place, the state, originally a purely European invention, had started the march of conquest that was to make it master of the world. The process of expansion will be studied later in this volume; here we must merely note that the British system of professional police forces was exported to the most important colonies which naturally looked to the mother country for a solution to their problems. In the United States, as the most important extra-European state by far, New York became the first city to create a municipal police force in 1845. Originally it numbered 800 men – massive for its day, but soon rendered out of date by a population which, over the next two decades, expanded from 400,000 to 650,000.[39] The year 1865 saw the establishment of the Secret Service, the first nationwide police force, whose mission was to protect the president. In 1905 Pennsylvania became the first US state to set up a state police, a measure that was later imitated by New York (1917), Michigan, Colorado, and West Virginia (1919), and Massachusetts (1920). By 1920 the Bureau of Investigation – later renamed the Federal Bureau of Investigation or FBI – had been in existence for twelve years. It was created by the executive over the objections of Congress, some of whose members feared that their own affairs would be among those investigated. Originally its mission was to look into anti-trust cases, several kinds of fraud, and certain crimes committed on government property or else by government officials. Like all bureaucratic organizations, it proceeded to expand its organization until it covered a whole array of "federal" crimes.

Having put their forces in place, these and other US states proceeded to impose order both on the countryside and on those lower-class urban neighborhoods which had previously been almost entirely beyond their reach. Patrolling the streets, monitoring markets, beer-houses, and brothels (but careful to avoid those known to be frequented by the state's own high officials), the police soon made their presence felt, though this was more true in Europe than in the United States with its wide open spaces and frontier society. Again Britain with its relatively liberal traditions provides a good measuring-rod. The number of prosecutions grew sevenfold between 1805 and 1842; compared to the population the

---

[39] See J. F. Richardson, *The New York Police: Colonial Times to 1901* (New York: Oxford University Press, 1970), pp. 82–123. For some comparative figures on the strength of British municipal police forces at the time, see F. C. Mather, *Public Order in the Age of the Chartists* (Manchester: Manchester University Press, 1959), pp. 111–17.

increase was by a factor of four and a half. Given the new emphasis on public order – for example, the UK Vagrancy Act of 1824 made it possible to prosecute people merely for being on the streets – it is not surprising that the vast majority of those indicted belonged to the lower classes. The results deserve to be called dramatic. After 1848 it was seldom necessary any longer to bring in troops for quelling riots, etc.; in Britain between 1850 and 1914 (when the curve changed direction and became horizontal), the rate of burglary per 100,000 of population declined by 35 percent, that of homicide by 42 percent, and that of assault by 71 percent.[40] Using the need to discipline the people as its excuse, the state set out to conquer entire city quarters that previously had been out of bounds, and remake them in its own image.

Even as its police forces were imposing acceptable standards of behavior on the people, the nineteenth-century state felt that the time had come to invade their minds as well. During most of history, education had been left almost entirely to the family and to the established church. Sparta, of course, was a notable exception; reflecting the practices of earlier tribal societies, male children were taken away from their parents at the age of six and raised in special dormitories from which they only emerged in order to marry. Prominent men of other ancient city-states also sometimes founded schools, but they did so in order to display their generosity to their fellow citizens, as part of the liturgies to which they were subject, rather than in a comprehensive attempt to control the minds of the young.[41] The Carolingian, Inca, Ottoman, and Chinese empires all boasted imperially run schools; but their student intake consisted almost exclusively of the relatives of court officials and, perhaps, some of the aspiring members of the bureaucracy. Whatever the system, and again with the very partial exception of the ancient city-states, the vast majority of the people were left to cope as best they could. Throughout history, this meant that the rural population in particular received scarcely any formal education at all.

Proposals aimed at setting up a state-run education system may be found in the works of such seventeenth-century utopian writers as Valentin Andrea and Gerrard Winstanley, whom we already met as an advocate of a national information-gathering apparatus. Possibly influenced by the Spartan example and also by Plato, Andrea wanted children of both sexes to be taken away from their parents at the age of six and raised in dormitories. Winstanley suggested that the "Common-

---

[40] Figures from *Cambridge Social History of Britain* (London: Cambridge University Press, 1993), p. 290.
[41] See A. R. Hands, *Charities and Social Aid in Greece and Rome* (Ithaca, NY: Cornell University Press, 1959), pp. 111–17.

wealth" assume responsibility for ensuring that no future citizen should be without the requisite moral and professional education needed for making a living, though just how this was to be done he did not explain. As the eighteenth century progressed schemes of this kind multiplied. All wanted to see education taken out of the hands of the church; but while some were motivated by what we today would call patriotic and national considerations, others merely reflected the desire to provide the nascent bureaucracy with a steady stream of compliant penpushers. The first type was exemplified by Rousseau who, in his *Considerations concernant le gouvernement de Pologne* (1772), suggested that the goal of education should be to make students replace the words *ubi bene ibi patria* (home is where life is nice) by their opposite.[42] The second included several detailed schemes submitted by Prussian and Bavarian theologians – Konrad von Zeydlitz and Heinrich Braun – to their respective royal masters during the 1780s.

In the event, so long as the old regime lasted, little came of these and similar proposals. Focusing on the negative side, most monarchs were content to make sure that nothing should be taught in church schools that was likely to undermine their own position; beyond that, it was merely a question of providing money and sometimes buildings for instruction in whatever subjects which for one reason or another excited their interest. Thus Louis XIV, prompted by Colbert, gave his support to a short-lived Académie politique as well as a few technical colleges, the most important of which was to develop into the subsequent Ecole des ponts et chaussées.[43] Another field that attracted the attention of the powers that be was officer training. Previously officers had been persons who, either working with their own capital or with that provided to them by others, received "commissions" from rulers to recruit soldiers. With the advent of regular armed forces after 1648 or so, the system changed: cadet schools intended for the sons of the impoverished nobility became fairly common, each of the main states (except Britain, where the form used by regimental commanders to enlist officers did not include a blank for education) founding at least one. By the end of the eighteenth century, they had spread from Europe to the new state across the Atlantic. Here two of them – the one at West Point and the one at Annapolis – were preparing themselves for a great future.[44]

The first ruler to take a practical interest in the education of his subjects

[42] J.-J. Rousseau, *The Government of Poland* (Indianapolis: Bobbs Merrill, 1977), p. 14.
[43] G. Thuillier, 'L'Académie politique de Torcy, 1712–1719," *Revue d'Histoire Diplomatique*, 97, 1–2, 1983, pp. 54–74; F. B. Artz, *The Development of Technical Education in France* (Cleveland, OH: Society for the History of Technology, 1966), ch. 1.
[44] On the origins of officer schools, see M. van Creveld, *The Training of Officers: From Professionalism to Irrelevance* (New York: Free Press, 1989), ch. 1.

at large was Prussia's Frederick William I. In 1717 he claimed to have learnt that children were "grossly ignorant . . . of those things that are most necessary for their welfare and eternal salvation"; thereupon a royal decree was issued which ordered all parents to send their children to school, but since nothing was done to follow the matter up the results, if any, were minimal. Frederick the Great in his *Landschulregiment* (1763) decreed that all children between five and thirteen should attend school; nine years later he set aside 200,000 thalers to pay teachers and rescue his newly acquired Pomeranian subjects from what he called "their Polish slavishness."[45] Again little came of the matter, not least because parents were too poor, and local authorities unwilling, to bear the cost. For example, as late as 1792 only one out of six East Prussian villages had a school. In West Prussia the percentage was even lower; throughout the kingdom such schools as did exist tended to be concentrated in the royal domains, whereas Prussia's Junkers did little to educate their serfs. Frederick did, however, complete his father's work by bringing secondary and university education under the control of a state department. A school-leaving examination known as *Abitur* was instituted and became a condition for admission both to the universities and to the ranks of the Prussian administration. As the nineteenth century progressed, it also became a prerequisite for those who aspired to commissioned rank in the military.

While Prussia dawdled, Bavaria acted. The Peace of Luneville (1801) put an end to the old *sancta Bavaria* as it had existed from 1648 on. Not only was the country drawn into a tight alliance with Napoleonic France, but the annexation of territories formerly belonging to Austria brought with it a massive infusion of Protestants and Jews who could not be assimilated by the old system. Accordingly, in October 1802, the Council for Ecclesiastical Affairs was abolished and a Ministry of Education, the first of its kind in any country, founded. Besides making entry into the civil service conditional on the completion of high school, as in Prussia, the Bavarian authorities instituted compulsory schooling for all children, compliance to be secured by issuing a school-leaving certificate that would be required for permission to purchase real estate, practice a trade, or marry. Most of the cost was to be covered by fees paid by parents; the rest would come out of church property which was being secularized as fast as possible. A law of 1804 went further still, placing all existing schools under state supervision and making them nonconfessional. The curriculum was given a secular, utilitarian bent. Once instituted it was

---

[45] M. Baer, *Westpreussen unter Friedrich dem Grossen* (Osnabrück: Zeller, 1965 [1909]), vol. I, p. 550.

destined to remain in force until the next wave of reforms swept it away during the 1860s.[46]

Whereas in Bavaria commitment to education flagged after the Restoration, in Prussia things went the other way. Thanks to the efforts of Frederick William III, who took a personal interest in the question, a department of education was set up in 1808; nine years later its importance was formally acknowledged when it received cabinet rank. With higher and secondary education already under its own control, no sooner had the Wars of Liberation ended than it, provided with relatively ample means, began to found schools by the hundred. Finance came partly from the parents themselves, partly from contributions made by local government. The system covered girls as well as boys; not only Germans but Poles and even Jews were admitted, a real innovation for the time. The task of providing faculty fell on twenty-eight specially organized, state-funded boarding schools. In Königsberg, such was the shortage of qualified teachers that orphans in state institutions were summarily designated as future educators and, once their training had been completed, unleashed upon their fellow youngsters.

The results of the state "being turned into an educational institution writ large," as one official in charge of the curriculum put it,[47] did not take long to bear fruit. By 1837, 80 percent of Prussian children were attending school and, to allow them to do so, the first child labor laws were being passed. By mid-century 80 percent of the adult population were literate, compared to only 50–65 percent in Britain and France; among Prussian army recruits, only one in ten had failed to receive any schooling at all.[48] The final steps were taken by the constitution of 1849 which turned all teachers – including university professors, some of whom had to be dragged by the neck – into state employees. After 1871, and making use of the fact that the remaining states had long been in control over their own schools, the system was extended over the whole of Germany. As liberals turned their coats and gave their support to Bismarck, any doubts that the aim of schooling was to help make the Reich good and strong were overcome and the direction of German education

---

[46] See, for these reforms, K. A. Schleunes, *Schooling and Society: The Politics of Education in Prussia and Bavaria, 1750–1900* (Oxford: Berg, 1989), pp. 43–4; and G. Zuber, "L'école primaire de la Prusse à la veille de la fondation du Reich," *Revue d'Allemagne*, 20, 3, 1988, pp. 311–21.

[47] Johann Suevren, quoted in G. Giese, *Quellen zur deutschen Schulgeschichte seit 1800* (Göttingen: Musterschmidt, 1961), p. 92.

[48] P. Flora, "Die Bildungsentwicklung im Prozess der Staaten und Nationenbildung," in P. C. Ludz, ed., *Soziologie und Sozialgeschichte* (Opladen: Westdeutscher Verlag, 1972), p. 432.

was well and truly established on lines that were to be altered, if at all, only after 1945.

For reasons that cannot be examined here, other countries were slower off the mark. Bills which would have led to the establishment of parish schools were put before the British Parliament in 1796, 1797, 1807, and 1820; all were rejected, however, and it was only in 1833 that a paltry sum – £20,000 – was set aside "in aid for the education of the poorer classes."[49] By 1858, funding had increased to £700,000, not a negligible sum (among other things it provided for the training of 14,000 pupil-teachers), but this was still far short of the £24 million spent on defense in the same year. Meanwhile, motions for the establishment of universal and compulsory instruction controlled by a Ministry of Education continued to be defeated. In the face of opposition on the part of ratepayers, steps to extend schooling to larger segments of the population progressed only very slowly. In the main, they were limited to parliamentary committees of inquiry which looked into the way the sums which had been voted were spent.

By and large, and in spite of the existence of a much more centralized political system, the same was true in France. Napoleon's greatest contribution to the French educational system consisted of the two "great schools" – the Ecole polytechnique and the Ecole supérieure d'administration – that he founded. He also set up a series of *lycées*, intended for the sons of the middle classes and run on military lines; however, his interest in elementary education was limited and, far from ordering its expansion, he was content to have existing institutions placed under state supervision. In his capacity as secretary of education to Louis-Philippe, the historian François Guizot ordered the opening of an elementary school in each community. However, implementation was haphazard and those few institutes which were put into operation were run jointly by the state and the parish priest.

In the event, what galvanized both countries – and others as well – into action was the series of Prussian military victories that began in 1864. In 1866 von Roon, the minister of war, informed King William I that "the victor at Königgrätz was the Prussian *Volkschule* teacher."[50] Von Roon's original intention was probably to rob von Moltke's rapidly rising general staff of some of the glory; however, the phrase served other countries as their cue. The first step, taken in France, was to establish an *école normale primaire* in each *département*. Within a few years whole armies of teachers had been mass-produced and had embarked on their designated task of

---

[49] For the rise of state-directed education in Britain, see E. Midwinter, *Nineteenth-Century Education* (London: Longman, 1970), pp. 32ff.
[50] R. Rissman, *Deutsche Pädagogen des 19. Jahrhunderts* (Leipzig: Klinkhardt, 1910), p. 219.

turning every Frenchman into a burning patriot ready to give his (nobody yet thought of a woman being made, let alone asking, to give *her* life) for Alsace-Lorraine.[51] Several other measures followed, until the process was crowned by the establishment of universal free compulsory education in 1882.[52] The person most responsible for pushing the scheme through parliament was Prime Minister Jules Ferry. Not accidentally, he also played a major role in the expansion of France's colonial empire into Tunisia, Madagascar, Tonkin, and the French Congo.

Faced with "the challenge of Germany,"[53] other states felt they had little choice but to follow. Compulsory, universal education – which sooner or later was bound to be made free as well – reached Japan (where it was part of the process known as the Meiji Restoration) in 1872. Italy's turn came in 1877, that of Britain in 1890, and that of Spain in 1908. But whereas in Germany it was the states which made up the empire that laid down the curriculum, the political system of most other countries tended to be more centralized, with the result that, around the turn of the century, it was claimed that the French minister of education, for example, could tell you what was being taught in each one out of a hundred thousand classrooms by simply looking at his watch. By the time World War I ended the measure had even been adopted by many Latin American countries,[54] albeit from then to the present day it has often remained largely on the statute books.

This was not so in the most advanced countries, where the reform had largely accomplished its goals. In 1895, 82 percent of all eligible British children were in fact attending school and the system was even beginning to provide some medical care as well as subsidized meals. On the eve of World War I, the social reformer Beatrice Webb was waxing lyrical over the "utopian" picture in front of her eyes: "7,000,000 children emerge every morning, washed and brushed . . . traversing street and road and lonely woodland . . . to present themselves at a given hour at their 30,000 schools where each of the 7,000,000 finds his or her own individual place,

[51] On the nationalization of French schools, see J. F. Scott, *Patriots in the Making* (New York: Macmillan, 1916).

[52] S. T. Greshman, "Good Workers and Good Soldiers: Attitude Formation in the Primary Schools of the French Third Republic, 1880–1914," *Proceedings and Papers of the Georgia Association of Historians*, 6, 1985, pp. 32–42; M. Garnier, et al., "The Strong State, Social Class, and Controlled School Expansion in France, 1881–1975," *American Journal of Sociology*, 95, 2, 1989, pp. 279–306.

[53] A. M. Kazmias, *Politics, Society and Secondary Education in England* (Philadelphia: University of Pennsylvania Press, 1966), pp. 107ff.

[54] C. Newland, "La educación elemental en Hispanoamerica: desde la independencia hasta a la centralización de los sistemas educativos nacionales," *Hispanic American Historical Review*, 7, 2, 1991, pp. 335–64, provides an overview of these developments.

with books and blackboard and teachers provided."[55] Reality, to be sure, was less idyllic. As early as the 1880s escorting truant children to school – and sometimes jailing their parents for failing to force them into doing so – had become a routine police duty in the "best-ordered" countries such as Germany.

Possibly because it costs more on a per student basis, the situation in respect to secondary and tertiary education was more variable. State funding to pay the way of the talented sons (much later, daughters as well) of the poor who wished to attend high school began to be provided during the 1880s, and again Britain provides a good case in point. From 1902, when a centralized organization took the place of the earlier school boards, 56 places out of every 1,000 in rate-supported schools had to be provided free of charge. Twenty-seven years later that figure was doubled; in 1932 a means test was introduced to distinguish between parents who were able to pay for their children's education and those who were not. Though parallel measures were taken in many other countries, by and large secondary education remained limited to the offspring of the middle classes, and it was only after 1945 that it was made anything like universal and free. In most countries the school-leaving age, which had originally stood at eleven, was raised first to fourteen and then to sixteen, that being a limit which not even the modern state, for all its self-righteousness and the unprecedented apparatus of coercion at its disposal, dares cross.

Since tertiary education requires high expertise on the part of the faculty, by and large governments were less able to control it. Relatively few countries followed the German example in turning all universities into state-owned institutions and all tenured faculty into *Beamter* (officials). Elsewhere there was a tendency for government to subsidize universities; for example, in Britain between the world wars the government provided one-third to one-half of their income. Surprisingly, one of the first countries to establish "state" universities was the United States. The first one to open its doors was Rutgers, the New Jersey State University, in 1766. This was followed by the University of Georgia in 1785, the University of Vermont in 1791, the University of Tennessee in 1794, and the University of Cincinnati in 1819.[56] Many of these public universities were set up in places too remote and too recently settled to be reached by money-conscious private ones. Perhaps not surprisingly, their prestige (and, presumably, their educational standards) has tended to lag behind the latter from the time they were founded to the present day.

[55] Quoted in A. Trop, *The Schoolteachers* London: Heinemann, 1957), p. 195.
[56] *World Almanac and Book of Facts, 1998* (Mahwah, NJ: K-III Reference Corporation, 1998), pp. 234–8.

Whereas, except in totalitarian countries, universities were for the most part given license to determine their own curriculum, the same was not true of secondary and, *a fortiori*, elementary schools. Consequently the instruction that they offered often became subject to the political demands of the moment; depending on how much states feared their citizens or trusted them, now practical subjects were emphasized, now more theoretical ones. While schools in all countries tended to replace religion with (national) history, German and French schools in particular were caught in the struggle between church and state. In Germany, Bismarck waged the *Kulturkampf* from 1872 on; in France a Radical government came to power in 1900 and closed all religious schools until 1914, when they were allowed to reopen. In an age when more and more people were receiving the vote, the state's desire to dominate the curriculum was partly motivated by the need to "educate our masters" (as one British MP put it in 1867). However, democratization could not explain why, in virtually every country, children were increasingly forced to study the "national" language at the expense of their mother tongue – quite the contrary. Nor can it account for the constant parading, flag-saluting, anthem-singing, and hero-worshipping that went on in many places, to say nothing of the need to "foster loyalty to one Kaiser, one army, one navy" (Germany); assist the "race" in its "battle for life" (Britain); and prevent "the power of national defense from lagging behind that of other countries" (the United States).[57]

Last but not least, having established a firm grip on the minds of the young, the state moved to acquire the allegiance of those old enough to perceive that their real interests consisted not of circuses but of bread. By and large, the early nineteenth century had been the heyday of *laissez faire*. Many of the old institutions were dead; having finally succeeded in drawing a clear line between government and ownership, the state had no desire to place limits on what might be done in the name of the latter. However, already during the 1830s the direction of the wind began to change. In Britain as the most industrialized country by far, there were no fewer than thirty-nine royal commissions appointed to look into the conditions of the poor between 1831 and 1842 alone. What they brought to light was masses of people living in squalor; neglected children who, to keep them quiet as their parents were at work, were given opium instead of an education; fourteen-hour work-

---

[57] Quotations, dating to the years around 1900, from prominent officials in all three countries in Schleunes, *Schooling and Society*, pp. 172, 226 (Germany), 230 (Britain), and 236 (United States). On the nationalization of education as it applied to Britain in particular, see also L. Simpson, "Imperialism, National Efficiency, and History, 1900–1905," *Journal of Educational Administration and History*, 16, 1, 1984, pp. 28–36.

days for young and old; working conditions which, in many cases, could only be called appalling; wages which, even at the best of times, were barely sufficient to keep body and soul together; and no insurance against unemployment, accidents, illness, and old age.[58] Some reformers were motivated by a genuine concern for the welfare of the people; others, perhaps more numerous, by fear of the revolutionary consequences that might follow if nothing were done. Whatever the cause, states started laying their hands on social and economic life in ways, and to an extent, that would have been wholly beyond the imagination of previous political communities.

The first Factory Acts, prohibiting the employment of children under nine and limiting the working hours of persons under eighteen to twelve a day, were passed in Britain in 1834. As the name implies, originally they applied to factories only; they were extended to mines in 1842, merchant shipping in 1876, and railways in 1889. An 1844 law prohibited women from being employed for more than twelve hours a day – this being the first of a very long list of statues which the modern state, claiming that women were weak and needed special protection, enacted in their favor. As early as 1847 Parliament passed a ten-hour bill; however, it was not until 1874 that it was applied to all factories, whereas other workers, particularly those employed as shop assistants and in domestic service, began to have their working hours limited only early in the twentieth century. To enforce these laws, as well as the safety regulations gradually being enacted from the 1840s on, a system of inspection was established. During the early days it often met with resistance, not only on the part of employers who resented the intrusion but also on that of the workers themselves who did not want limits on the earning power of their youngest family members. Other countries followed Britain's lead, albeit reluctantly and often after a considerable interval. For example, Germany got the twelve-hour day only after unification in 1871; France, where conditions were in some ways worse than anywhere else, even later.

With working conditions increasingly falling under its own control, the state started expanding its power into other spheres of public welfare. In 1834 in Britain the old Speenhamland system of outdoor relief, dating to Elizabethan times, was abolished. Not only had the burden risen beyond the ability of individual parishes to bear; but its decentralized nature was incompatible with the demographic changes brought about by urbanization. Its place was taken by state-owned workhouses which admitted

---

[58] A classic account of the life of the masses is F. Engels, *The Conditions of the Working Class in England* (London: Allen Unwin, 1936 [1846]). For a succinct modern treatment, see H. Haerder, *Europe in the Nineteenth Century, 1830–1880* (London: Longman, 1966), ch. 6.

people on the basis of a means test. In an attempt to keep costs down, they were run on prison-like lines with conditions deliberately made as harsh as possible. Families were separated, and most forms of innocent amusement, such as smoking or playing games, prohibited, while the work provided was onerous and unpleasant. The reform's aim – namely, cutting cost – was achieved; until the 1860s, the sums spent on welfare actually fell. Precisely for that reason, it probably did little to help the poor. Still, this was the first time when authority was taken away from the Justices of the Peace and put into the hands of a central supervisory board. As such, it marked a major step toward the construction of the modern British civil service.

The first Public Health Bill was passed in Britain in 1848 and led to the appointment of local Boards of Health with power over water supplies as well as the paving, draining, and cleansing of streets. The act proved unpopular and in 1854 it was not renewed, the London *Times* claiming that John Bull had wearied of the "perpetual Saturday night" of cleanliness. Much to the chagrin of ratepayers, though, the setback turned out to be temporary. To note a few landmarks only, in 1853 vaccination against smallpox became compulsory (in 1898, the right of religiously minded parents not to have their children inoculated was recognized). In 1858 the General Medical Council was created to oversee education and licensing in the fields of medicine, surgery, and midwifery; in 1860 the Adulteration of Food Act was passed, and fifteen years later local authorities were given the power to appoint food analysts in order to enforce the law. A Lunacy Act, making compulsory hospitalization of the mentally ill conditional on the approval of a state-appointed physician, was passed in 1890; 1899 saw the establishment of the first ante-natal and maternity clinics, though the scheme became nationwide only in 1919. Finally the state began to build its own institutions for the physically and mentally ill, thus taking over from the church. As law followed law and inspector was piled on inspector, the call arose for a centralized organization; and a centralized organization inevitably sought to undertake additional tasks. The ultimate outcome was the establishment of a Ministry of Health, which took place in 1919.

Already by the 1840s these developments had gathered sufficient momentum to find their expression in socialist thought. Previous writers such as Saint-Simon, Fourier, and Owen – to say nothing of Rousseau – had put their faith for the salvation of mankind not in bureaucracy but in its opposite. To them the answer to contemporary social problems consisted of dismantling modern life and returning to the land; there groups of workers, having established autonomous communities with their own laws, would look after their own economic needs while living in freedom and equality among themselves.[59] However, the advent of modern industry caused such a solution to lose its appeal. For all that the black satanic mills were undoubtedly evil, their contribution to industrial production was such that to turn one's back on them merely meant condemning oneself to isolation, backwardness, and even hunger. Hence would-be reformers such as Etienne Cabet in France and Edward Bellamy in the United States turned their hopes to the state. As they saw it, states as they existed in their time merely represented the political framework of capitalist exploitation; the problem was to make them work for society as a whole. Taking over from private enterprise, future states would substitute cooperation for competition and planning for individual caprice, thus vastly increasing production while at the same time providing employment, welfare, and plenty for all.[60] This optimistic view of the benefits of centralized planning was even shared by those visionaries who, like Marx and Engels, predicted that the state would "wither away."

The first to declare the citizen's "right to work" were the French revolutionaries of 1848. Attempting to turn theory into practice, Louis Blanc established his social workshops or *atéliers nationaux* of 1848–9; whether through his own fault or through that of his opponents, they turned out to be a disastrous failure and were soon closed. Other, perhaps wiser, minds set their sights lower and called for insurance plans that would ease the workers' lot during periods of hardship. The first such schemes to be turned into reality were promoted by Chancellor Otto von Bismarck of Germany whose goal was to wean his country's proletarians away from the growing Social Democratic Party. In 1881–5 old-age, sickness, and unemployment insurance schemes were pushed through the Reichstag and became law. The state, the employers, and the employees were all made to contribute; initially applying to factory workers only, the plan was later extended to other groups until, during the Weimar Republic, virtually all trades received coverage.[61] Quickly taking up the German example, the Scandinavian countries established their own schemes and by 1914 several of them were in operation. In 1893 Switzerland, too, began to experiment with a state-run, voluntary unemployment insurance scheme. It proved unable to meet its commitments and went bankrupt within four years; however, this failure did not deter others. By 1920 Sweden, Denmark, New Zealand, France, the Nether-

[59] The most important nineteenth-century "utopian" writers are analyzed in M. Berneri, *Voyage Through Utopia* (New York: Schocken Books, 1950), pp. 207–92.

[60] E. Cabet, *Voyage en Icarie* (Paris: Bureau populaire, 1848); E. Bellamy, *Looking Backward* (Boston: Ticknor, 1888). For a nineteenth-century caricature of the complete welfare state, see E. Richer, *Pictures of the Socialist Future* (London: Jarrolds, 1933 [1892]).

[61] See L. Preller, *Sozialpolitik in der Weimarer Republik* (Dusseldorf: Atheneum, 1978 [1949]), pp. 233–4, 282–5.

lands, Finland, and Belgium all possessed voluntary, state-run and state-subsidized unemployment insurance systems.

Having been the first country to industrialize, Britain was remarkably slow to establish any kind of social security system; still, in 1908–11 ten years of argument were brought to a close by the Liberal Party in the person of its remarkable chancellor of the exchequer, David Lloyd George. As in Germany, the reforms included a compulsory health and unemployment insurance system with contributions by employers, employees, and the state; on top of this came a 30-shilling ($7.50) maternity benefit and a universal, non-contributory, scheme for paying flat pensions to persons over sixty-five years of age with no other sources of income. Described by its originators as "the greatest scheme of social reconstruction ever attempted," the reform immediately ran into trouble because almost twice as many people turned out to receive benefits than had been expected – money having a remarkable power to flush out individuals whose very existence had previously gone unnoticed. By 1914 the cost of the program had doubled from the planned £6 million to £12 million annually, while the cost of all "social" spending combined rose from a modest £22,6000,0000 in 1891 to a staggering £338,500,000 in 1925.[62] This, however, did not prevent other countries, notably Germany and Ireland, from going way beyond the British model in extending their own social services during the interwar years.[63]

By that time even the United States, traditionally the stronghold of rugged individualism and low taxes (to make the House of Lords vote money for his plans, Lloyd George had threatened to create the necessary number of new peers), was feeling the need to do something for its working population. A modest first step had been taken in 1912 when the Commonwealth of Massachusetts passed a law requiring the payment of minimum wages. However, it only lasted a few years; in 1923 a Supreme Court decision declared a State of Oregon minimum-wage law for women unconstitutional. Other measures to extend government control and limit private enterprise were equally unsuccessful. For example, the number of persons who benefited from a government vocational education scheme instituted in 1917 was so small that statistics about it simply ceased to be published. In 1920 a law calling for the abolition of child labor failed to make it through Congress. Five years later, a Kansas law for the compulsory arbitration of industrial disputes was similarly thrown out of the High Court. In 1929, the last year of prosperity, all

[62] E. Barker, *The Development of Public Services in Western Europe* (London: Oxford University Press, 1945), p. 77.
[63] P. H. Lindert, "The Rise of Social Spending, 1880–1930," *Explorations in Economic History*, 31, 1, 1994, pp. 1–37.

American federal welfare expenditure combined only amounted to $0.25 per head of population,[64] which constituted perhaps one percent of its British equivalent.

In the event it took the Great Depression and 12 million unemployed to shake the United States out of the world of *laissez faire* and into the one in which, whatever the names attached to the various schemes, welfare came to be financed out of taxation. The foundations were laid in 1933 when President Roosevelt, ignoring howls of Republican opposition, set up the Federal Emergency Relief Agency (FERA). Its first director was a social worker, Harry Hopkins; armed with a war chest of $500,000,000, it provided work for at least some of those who needed it.[65] Over the next six years this and numerous other programs led to the spending of some $13 billion over and the construction of 122,000 public buildings, 77,000 bridges, and 64,000 miles of roads *inter alia* – all, however, without making a real dent in the Depression which only ended in September 1939 when, following the outbreak of war in Europe, the stock exchange went through the roof.

Administratively speaking, the *annus mirabilis* of the New Deal proved to be 1935. That year saw the introduction of social security including old-age insurance and assistance, unemployment compensation, aid to dependent children, and aid to the blind. In 1939 survivors' and disability insurance, already a standard feature in the most advanced European countries, were added to the list. By that time every American citizen had been issued with his or her social security card and the Department of Health and Human Services had been created to oversee the system's operation. Even the Supreme Court was prepared to cooperate, though not before Roosevelt, having fought a battle royal with Congress, packed it with his own supporters. In 1937 a Washington State minimum wage law was declared constitutional. Another ruling did the same for social security itself; the age of big government had truly begun.

Finally, just as totalitarian states went further than anybody else in indoctrinating the people, so they took the lead in disciplining them. This was particularly true of the USSR which turned itself into the complete welfare state – one that, however harsh the discipline it exercised and however low the quality of the services it provided, did try to cover the individual's needs from the moment that he or she was born to the time he or she was put into the crematorium or grave. Though neither Fascist Italy nor Nazi Germany went nearly as far as this, both regarded themselves as rooted in the common people. Neither embraced capitalism whole-

---

[64] E. D. Berkowitz and J. McQuaid, *Creating the Welfare State* (Lawrence: University of Kansas Press, 1988), p. 76.
[65] See W. R. Brock, *Welfare, Democracy and the New Deal* (Cambridge: Cambridge University Press, 1988), ch. 5, for the details.

heartedly, looking instead for a "third way" that was neither reactionary nor socialist.[66] Each, according to its lights, designed its social security system with the explicit aim of ending class warfare, restoring the dignity of the working people, and harnessing them to the state's aims.[67] In many ways – e.g., providing for paid vacations – these programs differed little from those of other countries.[68] Italy and Germany did, however, put an unusual emphasis on benefits such as marriage allowances, housing loans, and child payments (sometimes made conditional on the wife not working outside the home), all of which were meant to spur population growth and prepare the country for war.

The "totalitarian" regimes also made a determined effort to control the minds of the young by way of formal and informal schooling, often against the will of their parents who distrusted the experiment – with good reason, as it turned out. Except in Fascist Italy, where Catholic education was never completely suppressed and where the Concordat of 1929 led to its revival,[69] schools other than the state's own were simply shut down. The rest had their faculty vetted for political reliability, their curricula dictated from above in accordance with ideological considerations, and their classes subjected to supervision so strict that one could hardly turn a corner without being gazed upon by the Sun of Nations, Il Duce, or Der Führer.

Finally, and by way of backing up their control over both welfare and education the Communist, Fascist, and Nazi states also established police organizations far more terrible than anything seen in history until then. Thanks to the fact that they operated without requiring juridical authorization, the NKVD, OVRA (Organizazione Vigilanza Repressione Antifascismo), and Gestapo (Geheime Staatspolizei) counted their victims in the millions; their names still send shudders down people's backs. To compare the security forces run by the likes of Lavrenty Beria, Arturo Boccini, and Heinrich Himmler with the police apparatus maintained by the democratic countries of the West is less than fair. Yet it should be kept in mind that, however great the differences that separated them, in the end they were all offshoots of the same tree whose roots had been so firmly planted by Napoleon. All sought to achieve the same end, namely to make sure that no person and no institution should be in a position to

[66] See above all E. Nolte, *Three Faces of Fascism* (New York: Holt, 1969).

[67] For Nazi welfare policies, see D. Schoenbaum, *Hitler's Social Revolution* (New York: Norton, 1966), pp. 73–113; and T. W. Mason, *Social Policy in the Third Reich* (Oxford: Berg, 1993), pp. 151–78. For their equivalents in Fascist Italy, see E. R. Tannenbaum, *Fascism in Italy* (London: Allan Lane, 1972), pp. 214–30.

[68] G. Cross, "Vacations for All: The Leisure Question in the Era of the Popular Front," *Journal of Contemporary History*, 24, 4, 1989, pp. 599–62.

[69] See D. A. Binchy, *Church and State in Fascist Italy* (Oxford: Oxford University Press, 1970), ch. 1.

resist any "lawful" demands made on it by the state. The torture chamber and the concentration camp merely completed the work that the class-room had begun:

> What did you learn at school today
> Dear little boy of mine?
> What did you learn at school today
> Dear little boy of mine?
> I learnt our country is good and strong!
> Always right and never wrong!
> I learnt our leaders are the best of men!
> That's why we elect them again and again.
> What did you learn at school today . . .

Conquering money

The extension of the states' control over society, which is the most prominent development of the years 1789–1945, could never have taken place had it not also acquired unprecedented financial means to back up its claims. Previously the people and institutions that ruled society, such as noblemen and the church, had often possessed their own independent sources of revenue in the form of land and the serfs who worked it; although this made them less subject to central control, on the other hand, the arrangement had the advantage that, if the central authority broke down, the local one could carry on for what were often very considerable periods of time. Not so modern state-run police forces, education systems, and social services: possessing no resources of their own – and given that whatever fees they require are supposed to be transferred directly to the treasury – all of them are absolutely dependent on their expenses being paid, and paid regularly, if they are to function. To make such payment possible the state not only had to raise more money than ever before but to redefine the very meaning of that com-modity. Once it had done so the financial constraints that had often held previous polities in check fell away, and the state's road toward war and conquest was opened.

As best we know, the first coins were minted in Lydia during the seventh century BC, though the use of gold bars of a set weight was known in ancient Egypt and is much older.[70] From Lydia the idea spread to the Aegean and the Greek cities all over the Mediterranean; the conquest of Asia Minor by Persia during the sixth century BC caused coined money to spread into Asia as well. Alexander's conquests opened up huge new sources of bullion and thus led to a very great increase in the

---

[70] See P. Grierson, *The Origins of Money* (London: Athlone Press, 1977), ch. 1.

use of money in the Hellenistic age as compared to the classical one. During the third century, it began to reach the Gauls on the western and northern shores of the Black Sea. From there it expanded westward to France, England, Ireland, and Scandinavia.

While the use of money spread, its nature remained unchanged. Unlike their successors, premodern rulers and communities did not themselves *create* value by fiat; instead, all they could do was to confirm, by adding their seal, that *existing* valuable commodities (mostly pieces of gold and silver, but sometimes also copper, bronze, and iron used for small change) did in fact conform to a certain standard of purity, weight, etc. In fact, the earliest coins seem to have been minted by private individuals, such as wealthy merchants, who used them for making payments among themselves. During the sixth century BC, control drifted into the hands of the temples which, in these as well as other societies, acted as banks; only during the fifth century did city-states assert their own control. However, it is characteristic of pre-state communities that, city-states apart, the concentration of all minting in a single hand was seldom achieved. For example, Augustus after he became *princeps* took the production of gold and silver coins into his own hands; but he left the minting of bronze coins to the Senate (for Italy) and to local authorities (in the provinces). In medieval Europe the – usually very profitable – operation of producing coins out of precious metal was dispersed among local lords, municipalities, and even abbeys.

Over time, the value of most coins tended to decline as rulers fiddled with their weight and the percentage of precious metal that they contained – especially but by no means exclusively as a method for financing wars. For example, between the time of Augustus and that of Diocletian three centuries later, the silver *denarius* lost 99 percent of its value, most of the loss being concentrated in the period from Nero on.[71] Another age-old factor that worked against stability was bimetalism. Rulers had no control over the relative availability of gold and silver. As new sources opened up, others ran dry: so long as both metals were in use as material for coins, the relative value of those coins tended to fluctuate. The ratio of gold to silver was set at 1:13.3 in the Persian empire, 1:10 by Alexander, and varied between 1:6 and 1:11 in sixteenth-century England. Often the official ratio did not correspond to reality or else there were different values set on the two metals in different countries. Either disparity could lead to the disappearance from circulation of either silver or gold coins, thus diminishing liquidity and hindering commerce.

Apparently the first rulers who tried to produce paper money, i.e., a

[71] For Roman inflation, see A. Cailleux, "L'allure hyperbolique des dévaluations monétaires," *Revue de Synthèse*, 101, 99–100, 1980, pp. 251ff.

medium of payment that would not be dependent on precious metal and thus entirely under their own control, were some Chinese emperors between about AD 800 and 1300. The last of these attempts was made by the Mongol emperor, Kublai Khan (reigned 1260–94). It became the subject of an enthusiastic description by Marco Polo who lived in China from 1275 to 1292;[72] like its predecessors, though, it was destined to end in monumental inflation as too large a supply caused the value of the currency to fall. Apparently influenced by the Chinese example, the shah of Iran tried to imitate it in 1294, issuing paper money known as "chao" and imposing the death penalty on those of his unfortunate subjects who refused to accept it. The experiment, which was limited to the city of Tabriz, was a complete disaster and had to be ended after just two months.

Given the decentralized nature of the political system and its instability, European rulers during the Middle Ages were generally in no position to imitate their oriental counterparts. Beginning already during the fourteenth century, though, banking and commerce revived; Italian banks in particular made great fortunes and were soon opening branch offices throughout the Continent. Bills of exchange were developed to facilitate financial transactions between those branches, and to the extent that they were made out to the bearer rather than to any individual they may be regarded as the first nonmetallic money in Europe. During the next two centuries the system spread to France, Spain, the Low Countries, and finally England. Note, however, that the money in question was produced not by the slowly emerging state but by private institutions. Before 1700 attempts to develop credit systems succeeded only in those places where private banking and commerce were so strong as to virtually exclude royal authority; in other words, where merchants *were* the government as in sixteenth-century Genoa and early seventeenth-century Amsterdam.[73] Common wisdom held that, whereas merchants could be trusted with money, kings could not. Concentrating both economic and coercive power in their own hands, all too often they used it either to debase the coinage or to seize their subjects' treasure.

While private institutions were thus beginning to develop paper money, rulers, on their part, were slowly imposing a monopoly on coinage. During the fourteenth century the thirty-two mints existing in France were successively closed down: e.g., Melgueil in 1316, Le Puy in 1318,

[72] Marco Polo, *Travels* (Harmondsworth, UK: Penguin Books, 1972), ch. 22. For a modern account of the Chinese experiments, see F. T. Lui, "Cagan's Hypothesis and the First Nationwide Inflation of Paper Money in World History," *Journal of Political Economy*, 91, 1983, pp. 1067–74.

[73] See V. Barbour, *Capitalism in Amsterdam in the Seventeenth Century* (Ann Arbor: University of Michigan Press, 1961), ch. 2.

and Rodez in 1378. Seigneurial coinage disappeared from circulation until, at the end of the fourteenth century, royal coins reigned supreme throughout the realm.[74] Shortly before 1500 Ferdinand and Isabella closed the last private mints still operating in Castile; as already mentioned, the last remaining ecclesiastical mint in England was suppressed by Henry VIII in 1543–4. France, which owing to the civil wars had lost its early lead, followed suit under Henry IV in 1600. By this time the idea that the right to mint was one of the prerogatives of sovereignty had gained wide recognition. Though private individuals continued to operate mints, more and more they did so only as licensees of the king or government. It was typical of the *ancien régime* that minting itself was turned into a form of capitalist enterprise. Only in 1696 did the English exchequer create the first mint that operated entirely as a public service – i.e., at the hands of state employees and without charging a fee.

The earliest modern attempts to create a paper currency, thus dissolving the link between money and bullion and theoretically putting unlimited sums at the disposal of the government, were made in Spain and Sweden. In Spain during the 1630s the duke of Olivares, desperately in need of money to pay for the country's involvement in the Thirty Years War, confiscated consignments of silver arriving from overseas and compensated the merchants by means of *juros* or interest-bearing letters of credit. As might have been expected, their value depreciated rapidly. The result was financial chaos as well as the collapse of Spanish trade with the New World; either the colonists preferred to buy from other suppliers – both the Dutch and the English stood ready to take the place of Spain in this respect – or else they suspended trade altogether. Olivares' failure did not prevent Sweden from imitating his example in 1661. Finding the treasury empty and the country exhausted by decades of war (1631–60), the government made a serious attempt to create a negotiable paper currency backed up not by gold and silver, which it did not have, but by copper. Again, however, overproduction resulted in inflation, causing the attempt to end in a failure that was as spectacular as it was rapid.

Meanwhile events in England followed a different course. Compared to the Continent the country had long enjoyed relatively stable money. Only during the reign of Henry VIII did a great devaluation take place; and then the damage that it did was partly repaired by his stingy successor, Elizabeth, whose chief adviser for the purpose was none other than Sir Thomas Gresham (after whom the law is named).[75] This stability made people willing to accept tallies, a form of wooden money on which

---

[74] See S. Piron, "Monnaie et majesté royale dans la France du XIVe siècle," *Annales, Histoire, Sciences Sociales*, 51, 2, March–April 1996, pp. 325–54.
[75] See C. Read, *Mr. Secretary Cecil and Queen Elizabeth* (New York: Knopf, 1955), ch. 9.

debts owing by the exchequer were recorded and which could be transferred to third parties.[76] Things came to a head in 1640 when King Charles I, having quarreled with Parliament, found himself in dire financial straits and suspended the payment of coins produced by the mint to his creditors, the goldsmiths and merchants of London. Like their opposite numbers in other countries, the latter had used the deposits of bullion in their safes as backing for letters of credit, which were negotiable; hence the king's action threatened to ruin not just them but all who had business with them. Against this background, pressure was applied on Charles, who eventually relented and paid his debt in full. However, the episode did show how important it was to have a public, or national, bank that would be immune to arbitrary interference by the throne.

Given that people were already accustomed to token money, proposals for establishing a public, note-issuing bank modeled on that of Amsterdam met with a favorable reception. The first successful attempt to turn it into reality was made in 1694, the year which marked the founding of the Bank of England. A privately owned joint-stock company, the Bank agreed to lend money to the government which was strapped by the expenses of the seemingly endless wars that had to be fought against France. In return, it received a lien over the revenues from certain custom duties as well as an assurance that all the money at the disposal of the government would henceforward be deposited exclusively with it. Using these revenues and deposits as its security, the Bank issued notes which it sold to the public and which were negotiable. All notes were printed on the same blank form, so that the sum in question had to be entered by hand.

The number of notes printed was too large at first, leading to a financial crisis in 1696. However, and contrary to similar experiments in other countries, the Bank survived. Though privately owned, it came to be accepted almost as a government institution. Though it did not enjoy a monopoly, following the Bubble Act of 1720 it was the only institution licensed to print notes redeemable in less than six months; hence it could beat its competitors and watch its notes circulate side by side with coin. Between 1685 and 1700 the establishment of the Bank contributed to a spectacular increase in government borrowing, from £800,000 to £13.8 million. By 1714 it had more than doubled again; yet the Bank remained solvent and had no trouble meeting its obligations. Since people were ready to take new paper in repayment of the old, the loan became permanent or revolving, meaning that the real cost to the Exchequer consisted of the interest paid which at first stood at 8 percent but later fell to 5 and even 4 percent. Lenders received what were, in effect, annuities.

---

[76] G. Davies, *A History of Money* (Cardiff: University of Wales Press, 1994), pp. 150–1.

The reforms of 1694–6 constituted the key to the financial power of Britain during the eighteenth and nineteenth centuries.[77] For the first time in history money in the form of notes was created and remained stable, thus leading to a vast increase in its supply without bringing about a notable increase in inflation. The difficulties resulting from the variable ratios between gold and silver also disappeared. Though silver coins remained in circulation, their importance diminished and, after 1750, the minting of new ones having all but ceased, Britain was effectively on a gold standard.[78] Once an expanding yet stable currency that was free from arbitrary interference existed, the road toward the industrial revolution, which from the 1760s on was to make Britain into the world's economic leader, opened. What really made success possible was the separation between the monarch's person and the state. After 1694 it was no longer the former but the latter, operating by means of the Bank and resting on an alliance between the government and the city, which guaranteed the notes.

Meanwhile, on the continent, financial developments proceeded at a slower pace. When Louis XIV died in 1715, the regent, the duc d'Orléans, found the treasury empty; attempting to fill it he turned to one John Law, a Scotsman who had fled to France after killing a man in a fight over a woman. Already famous for his skill with numbers, Law was author of *Money and Trade Considered, with a Proposal for Supplying the Nation with Money* (1705). His Banque de France assumed part of the government's debt, and in return was given permission to open a note-issuing bank in Paris; security consisted not of specie but of the fabulous wealth allegedly contained in the French territories in Louisiana to which Law and his partners in the Mississippi Company had purchased the rights. So successful was the scheme during its first three years that the shares of the Mississippi Company rose to thirty times their nominal value. Then, however, the wind changed and the public tried to cash in on its paper profits. On one day, so many people besieged the bank clamoring to have their money back that fifteen of them were crushed to death. While Law fled abroad, the failure of his company dragged others in its wake and ended by setting back the cause of paper money in France for the better part of a century. Absent a central bank free from royal interference, French *billets d'état* could not inspire public confidence and often had to be sold at 30 or even 40 percent below face value.[79]

Though all continental countries continued to use metal currency, one

---

[77] For the establishment of the Bank of England and its results, see E. Lipson, *The Economic History of England* (London: Black, 1931), vol. III, pp. 240ff.

[78] C. Oman, *The Coinage of England* (London: Pordes, 1967 [1931]), p. 352.

[79] J. P. du Verney, *Examiné du livre intitulé "Réflexions sur les finances et le commerce"* (Paris: n.p., 1754), vol. I, p. 225.

by one they also opened giro (i.e., note-issuing) public banks whose paper circulated side by side with coin and took the latter's place in carrying out large-scale transactions. By 1710 both Holland and the Austrian empire possessed such institutions; a Prussian giro bank was founded by Frederick the Great in 1765, and during the 1770s similar experiments were being made in Spain, Russia,[80] and (again, after an interval of seventy years) France where the *caisse d'escompte* was set up by Turgot in 1776. However, none of these banks was nearly as successful as the Bank of England either in handling the government debt or in increasing the amount of money in circulation. In particular, the *caisse d'escompte* ended in spectacular failure: caught between the need to repay the royal debt *and* to meet military expenditure at a time of rapidly falling revenue, the National Convention printed so many assignats that hyperinflation and the collapse of the currency ensued.[81] By 1797, when the Directory used the loot brought by Napoleon from Italy to put an end to the experiment, France had returned to a more primitive monetary system and was back on coin, if not barter. Meanwhile, in sharp contrast, Bank of England notes had become virtually the sole currency used in London, as the greatest commercial and banking center of the time. Only in the provinces were notes issued by other banks, all of them much smaller than the central one, still in circulation.

Even so, the real demonstration of the power of the Bank of England – and, with it, of the British state – to control money was yet to come. On 22 February 1797 a contingent of French troops, comprising ex-convicts, landed on Carregwastad near Fishguard in Wales; they were quickly rounded up and taken prisoner, allegedly because they had mistaken a distant gathering of women in Welsh costumes for Redcoats. Before it could be contained, however, rumors of the "invasion" caused a run on the Bank of England. The result was to bring about "so violent an outrage upon credit, property, and liberty as . . . has seldom been exhibited by the alliance of bankruptcy and tyranny" (Edmund Burke).[82] Under the Bank Restriction Act of 3 May 1797, the convertibility of paper into gold was suspended, first as an emergency measure for seven weeks and then for fully twenty-four years; turning Bank of England notes (together with those issued by the Bank of Scotland) into a "forced currency."[83] In 1812

[80] For the origins of Russian paper money, see W. M. Pinter, *Russia's Economic Policy Under Nicholas I* (Ithaca, NY: Cornell University Press, 1967), pp. 207–9.
[81] For the *caisse d'escompte* and its failure during the Revolution, see J. F. Bosher, *French Finances, 1770–1795* (Cambridge: Cambridge University Press, 1970), particularly pp. 231–75.
[82] Burke, *Reflections on the Revolution in France*, p. 134.
[83] Today we would speak of a currency that is inconvertible. Earlier, however, currencies were linked not to each other but to gold. A forced currency was one that was not linked to gold so that people had to be "forced" to accept it.

a *cause célèbre* brought before Parliament led to the creation of a new term, "legal tender," meaning that paper *had* to be accepted in settling all debts, even those originally contracted in gold. As might be expected, the move caused a decline in the value of the pound both against precious metal and against foreign currencies. From 1793 to 1810, the number of notes in circulation grew by 170 percent. Yet the result was only moderate inflation, and Britain's economy kept on growing rapidly throughout the period.

By this time France and the United States both had banks which, though privately owned (in France, Napoleon and his family were themselves among the largest shareholders), carried out some of the functions of central banks by receiving government deposits and using them to issue notes. However, in neither country were the US Bank and the Banque de France the sole note-issuing bodies; even the Bank of England had to wait until 1844 before it was able to obtain that monopoly. Meanwhile a bewildering variety of notes belonging to many institutions remained in circulation, constantly changing their value against each other and occasionally losing all value as a panic struck or a bank went under. The road toward the establishment of a state monopoly in the United States proved particularly tortuous. Though minting had been centralized in 1798–9, President Jackson in 1833 removed government deposits from the US Bank into the state banks – pet banks, as they were called – thus turning the former into a mere *primus inter pares*. The decision of the Supreme Court in 1837 to uphold the note-issuing rights of state and private banks led to a banking free-for-all that lasted until 1861. In 1859 *Hodges' Genuine Bank Notes of America* listed no fewer than 9,916 different notes issued by 1,365 different banks. Even then, another 200 genuine – and 5,400 counterfeit – notes failed to be included.

With the advent of the Civil War, nevertheless, the United States government gave an even more impressive demonstration of what a modern state could do with the financial power in its hands. At the beginning of the conflict, the US Army numbered just 28,000 men all told; by the time it ended the Federals alone numbered around 1 million (to say nothing of 450,000 Confederates at their peak). This, too, in many ways was the first modern war. Sustained by the railways and connected by telegraphs, armaments and logistics grew to monumental dimensions beyond anything seen in history until then.[84] Obviously there was no way in which such an effort could be financed by traditional means, i.e., by paying out bullion or even making promises of future payment in bullion. In December 1861, to conserve the nation's supply of precious metal for the war effort, Congress put an end to convertibility. Three months later

[84] The federal logistic effort is outlined in J. C. Huston, *The Sinews of War* (Washington, DC: OCMH, 1966), pp. 159–239.

the federal government received approval for the Legal Tender Act which authorized it to issue "greenbacks," not redeemable in gold or silver.

Once the legal obstacles were out of the way, the printing presses were set to work. By 1865 no fewer than $640 million had been produced out of thin paper – a staggering sum, given that average federal expenditure in 1856–60 amounted to only $69 million annually, but dwarfed by the national debt which rose from some $170 million before the war to $2,756 million at its end.[85] In the same year a 10 percent levy was placed on the conversion of other notes into federal currency, effectively taxing them out of existence. The process was crowned by an Act of Congress that finally did away with all notes except those of the US Treasury. The decision did not go unchallenged. In 1870 in *Hepburn v. Griswold*, the Supreme Court rejected the government's monopoly as contrary to the Fifth Amendment; however, President Grant promptly added two chief justices, causing the court to reverse itself in the following year. Federal paper, properly printed (and often, it seems, counterfeited), has remained the national currency ever since. In 1875 the Resumption Act permitted the government to resume payment in specie from 1879 on. However, by that time public trust was such that people did not ask for gold and silver but accepted greenbacks instead.

Not surprisingly, the Civil War also marked a turning point in taxation. The first income tax in US history was imposed on 5 August 1861. Next, the Internal Revenue Act of 1862 led to a whole series of new taxes including stamp taxes, excise taxes, luxury taxes, gross receipt taxes, an inheritance tax, and a value-added tax on manufactured goods. To collect these taxes the Bureau of Internal Revenue was created. It quickly spread its tentacles through a network of 185 collection districts, turning itself into the most coercive civilian organ of the federal government and bringing many citizens into direct contact with it for the first time. It is true that the income tax was abolished when the war ended; however, many other wartime taxes – the sin tax, excise taxes, inheritance taxes, etc. – proved permanent. By 1865 the share of internal taxes out of total federal revenue had more than tripled from 20 to 65 percent, nor was it ever again to fall below 32 percent. As if this added burden were not heavy enough, in the North taxes paid to the individual states also rose by a factor of three to six between 1860 and 1870.[86]

---

[85] Figures from R. F. Bensel, *Yankee Leviathan: The Origins of Central State Authority in America, 1859–1877* (Cambridge: Cambridge University Press, 1990), p. 169; and US Bureau of the Census, *Historical Statistics of the United States: Colonial Times to 1970* (Washington, DC: US Government Printing Office, 1975), part 2, p. 1106.

[86] E. Foner, *Reconstruction: America's Unfinished Revolution 1863–1877* (New York: Harper and Row, 1988), pp. 469–70.

From 1850 on, the discovery of new gold fields in California and Australia caused a temporary decline in its value as compared to silver.[87] One after another the most important countries seized the opportunity to demonetize the latter, leaving their currencies linked to the former only. When the United States, a latecomer to the field, followed suit in 1894, the switch was substantially complete. By that time Britain (since 1819), France, Italy (after a period of *corso forzato* in 1881–8), Belgium, Germany, Switzerland, Denmark, the Netherlands, Austria-Hungary, and Russia were all on a gold standard.[88] In theory any person in any of these countries was free to walk into the bank and exchange his notes for gold; except in London, though, those who had the nerve to try were likely to be sent away empty-handed whenever the sums in question were anything but trivial.[89] As time went on the banks of various countries vied with each other to see who could print the smallest notes (in Sweden, e.g., one-kroner notes, worth scarcely more than one British shilling or $0.25, were issued), thus causing even more bullion to disappear into their own vaults. Yet so much had the power of states grown that it scarcely mattered. Whereas French Revolutionary assignats were trading at 0.5 percent of nominal value within seven years of being issued,[90] the notes of pre-1914 states were literally as good as gold.

Even as states used all the above methods in order to impose their own control over money, they also increased the role of their central banks.[91] Regardless of whether they were privately or publicly owned, originally each such bank had only been one note-issuing institute among many, albeit one that, serving as the sole haven for the state's own deposits, led a charmed life and could hardly fail to grow at the expense of the rest. By 1870 or so, not only had they monopolized the issue of notes in most countries but they were also beginning to regulate other banks. Given that the central bank's reserves easily outstripped those of all the rest, it was inevitable that they should come to be treated as lenders of last resort. Acting as such, they not only set interest rates (the so-called discount rate) but were able to insist on the size of the reserves to be held by other

---

[87] Figures on the production and relative value of the two metals can be found in K. Helfferich, *Money* (New York: Kelley, 1969 [1927]), pp. 109–11.

[88] See M. de Cecco, *Money and Empire: The International Gold Standard, 1890–1914* (Totowa, NJ: Rowman and Littlefield, 1975), for the details.

[89] G. Cassell, *The Downfall of the Gold Standard* (Oxford: Oxford University Press, 1936), pp. 15–19.

[90] Data from H. See, "Histoire économique de la France," in F. H. Capie, ed., *Major Inflations in History* (Aldershot: Elgar, 1991), p. 11.

[91] See C. Goodhart, *The Evolution of Central Banks* (Cambridge, MA: MIT Press, 1988), pp. 1–12; and, in much greater detail, V. C. Smith, *The Rationale of Central Banking* (Indianapolis: Liberty Press, 1990 [1936]).

banks, thus putting a cap on their operations.[92] Sooner or later the informal supervisory power thus created was anchored in law; some countries went further still, charging the central bank with licensing other banks, auditing them, and even setting the fees which they were permitted to charge. The United States as usual was slow to adopt these changes; but even here the era of free banking ended with the creation of the Federal Reserve in 1913. From this point on, not only the currency but also the money supply as dictated by private lending came under state supervision.

In the event, the state's movement toward imposing its own control over money did not come a moment too soon. World War I broke out in August 1914. Within a matter of days all belligerents showed what they *really* thought of their own paper by taking it off gold, thus leaving their citizens essentially empty-handed. Draconian laws were pushed through, requiring those who happened to own gold coins or bullion to surrender them. Next the printing presses were put to work and started turning out their product in previously unimaginable quantities. Precisely because the United States was only marginally involved in the war – German submarines apart, the nearest enemy soldier was thousands of miles away – it can usefully illustrate these developments without fear of exaggeration. Thus, in October 1917, the possession of specie was made into a criminal offense punishable by a $10,000 fine or, in the case of "a natural person," up to ten years' imprisonment (the government that can put a corporation in jail has not yet been invented). By 1919 the amount of currency in circulation had grown from $3.3 billion to $5.1 billion, whereas the total money supply, which had stood at $22 billion in 1916, had passed the $33 billion mark. Meanwhile the cost-of-living index (with 1914 as base 100) went from 118 in 1916 to 218 in 1919, an increase of 83 percent.[93]

That prices did not rise even more was, of course, the result of the state draining away the public's income and savings by taxes on the one hand and loans on the other. US federal non-debt receipts rose from $782 million in 1916 to $4.6 billion three years later; of this increase the lion's share – almost $2.5 billion – was due to the dramatic growth in the income tax paid by individuals and corporations. To this were added five successive "Liberty" and "Victory" loans, each but the last (which was floated in April 1919, i.e., when the war was already over) larger than the

[92] For the way the Bank of England, for one, came to regulate the rest, see W. Bagehot, *Lombard Street* (London: Murray, 1927 [1873]), pp. 280–2.
[93] These and other figures are from C. Gilbert, *American Financing of World War I* (Westport, CT: Greenwood Press, 1977), tables 18 (federal spending), 20 (nondebt receipts), 41 (government loans), 62 (money supply), and 76 (cost of living index).

previous one and eventually raising $24 billion between them. Matching the rise in income, federal spending went up from $742 million in 1916 to almost $19 billion in 1919. The bulk of this increase (about $11 billion) was accounted for by the War Office and the Navy; but other federal agencies also looked after themselves. As it happened, the largest single increment was enjoyed by the so-called independent bureaus – in other words, the huge variety of agencies and boards newly created for the war and which stood outside the existing departmental structure. The sum they commanded rose from $7.2 million in 1916 to $1.1 *billion* in 1918 and $2.7 billion in 1919; if this was not the season for penpushers, what was?

Having entered the war earlier and stayed in longer, the governments of other countries had to do much more in proportion. In Britain, e.g., total government expenditure had stood at approximately 15 percent of GNP during the last years before the war, which itself represented an approximately 50 percent increase since the Liberal government had taken office in 1906. By 1916–17 it had reached fully 85 percent, a figure so high that it could barely be improved on even during the largest conflict in history, i.e., World War II.[94] As in the United States, the increase in expenditure was paid for partly by printing money, partly by taxation ("tax them till they squeak" was the response of Lord Rothschild when asked by Lloyd George how to raise money to pay for the war) and partly by issuing bonds at what were, by the inflationary standards that prevailed during much of the late twentieth century, remarkably low interest rates. Again the infusion of huge sums into the economy – between 1913 and 1920 government spending rose from £342 million to just under £1.7 billion annually[95] – led to inflation, though the bulk of it occurred *after* the war because, so long as it lasted, a combination of controls and scarcity meant that there was little to buy anyhow. Nor was Britain by any means the worst affected country. On the contrary, most of the remaining European belligerents made a much greater effort in terms of the number of troops raised per head of population, to say nothing of foreign occupation, physical destruction, and defeat suffered.

Except in the Soviet Union, on which more below, the "Great War Robbery" of 1914–18 was followed by a return to "normalcy" during the 1920s. Everywhere government budgets and taxes fell, though never again to pre-war levels which, in retrospect, appeared like the dream of a *laissez faire* enthusiast. For example, in Britain public spending fluctuated

[94] Figures from U. K. Hicks, *British Public Finances, Their Structure and Development, 1880–1952* (London: Oxford University Press, 1954), pp. 12–13.
[95] Figures from Hicks, *The Finance of British Government, 1920–1936* (Oxford: Clarendon Press, 1970 [1936]), p. 380, table 2.

between 25 and 30 percent of GNP (double the pre-war figure); to finance this outlay, standard income tax rates had risen by a factor of three and a half. Meanwhile, across the Atlantic, the effect of the war on ordinary Americans may be gauged from the fact that the number of individuals and corporations subject to income tax leaped from fewer than 500,000 in 1916 to almost 7 million in 1920.[96] Sitting on top of history's largest gold mountain – acquired in return for goods of every sort shipped to the Allies during the conflict – and little fearing that anyone would seriously try to buy it up, the United States resumed payments in gold almost as soon as the war was over. Britain followed in 1925, and by 1929 most other major countries – including even Italy, the poorest but, under Mussolini, by no means the humblest of the lot – had done the same.

As it happened, the return to the gold standard proved largely illusory. Not only were gold coins not returned to circulation, but the times were long gone since anybody in his or her sound mind dreamt of making large payments by physically transferring bullion from one place to another. In this way about the only effect of the move was to contribute to a severe deflation which in turn put obstacles in front of trade and thus helped trigger the Great Depression of 1929.[97] To cut a long story short, in September 1931 a threatened pay cut caused the sailors of the British navy to go on strike. The newspapers exaggerated the event into a mutiny; a panic resulted, and the consequent run on the banks caused sterling and other currencies to be taken off gold, this time for good. In the United States, President Roosevelt, claiming that "gold held in private hoards serves no useful purpose under present circumstances," imposed drastic penalties to make owners disgorge their wealth. In March 1933 a bank holiday was proclaimed; when those venerable institutions reopened their doors the dollar had been devalued by no less than 41 percent.[98] The refusal of the Treasury to allow private citizens to exchange their dollars for monetized gold even at this rate meant that, from now on, all means of payment other than paper were definitely concentrated in the hands of the state. Conversely, whatever was paid out by the state was, by definition, made of paper.

With every major currency depreciating fast against gold – the French franc, as the last to hold out, was devalued in 1936 and public confidence

[96] G. K. Fry, *The Growth of Government* (London: Cass, 1979), p. 193; US Bureau of the Census, *Statistics*, part 2, p. 1110.
[97] J. K. G. Galbraith, *Money: Whence It Came, Where It Went* (Boston: Houghton Mifflin, 1975), pp. 164–82, describes the return to the gold standard under the title "the self-inflicted wound."
[98] See E. Cassell, *The Downfall of the Gold Standard* (London: Cass, 1969 [1936]), pp. 112–35.

in it destroyed – many countries returned to forced currencies as did Germany, Italy, and, above all, the Soviet Union. In the former two this development was brought about by the world economic crisis; in the latter (in spite of its being the world's largest producer of gold) a forced currency had been in existence from the time of the 1917 Revolution and was backed solely by the word of Lenin, Stalin, and company. Whether called rubles or marks or lire, these currencies were inconvertible, which meant that in most cases they could be used only by citizens in transactions among themselves. The conduct of international business was monopolized by the state, which either created its own organs for the purpose or else operated through an elaborate licensing system. Often the shortage of "hard" currency was such that imports had to be paid for in gold (the Soviet Union) or by means of barter (all three countries, particularly in their dealings with each other and with the underdeveloped Balkans). Those who found themselves unable to trade and, indeed, threatened with death or a concentration camp if they ventured to do so were the unfortunate citizens.

So far from the totalitarian countries proving an exception, the road toward control over the currency that they took during the 1930s was followed, with only minor modifications, by the "free" ones during World War II itself. To repeat the story already told in connection with the events of 1914–18 would be tedious. There was little new except for even more stringent financial controls, even greater spending, an even tighter turning of the fiscal screws, and even greater loans. Even in the United States, as the richest and least affected country by far, expenditure exceeded revenue by a factor of one to two or three in each one of the war years 1942–5 – in spite of the fact that drastic tax increases caused that revenue itself to grow by a factor of six between 1939 and 1944.[99] As in World War I, the fact that spending and income no longer stood in any kind of reasonable relation to each other led to a sharp rise in prices. Again as in World War I, so long as hostilities lasted, attempts were made to keep the lid on inflation by various administrative mechanisms such as rationing. When those were lifted, the citizens of the victorious countries found that the value of their savings had been greatly reduced, while with the losers money had literally turned into so much paper and could be used, if at all, only for such purposes as patching up broken windows.[100]

Even more interesting than these developments was the change that

---

[99] Figures from *Economic Report to the President, 1974* (Washington, DC: Government Printing Office, 1974), p. 324. Parallel figures on other countries can be found in G. Findlay Shirras, *Federal Finance in Peace and War* (London: Macmillan, 1944), pp. 77 (Canada), 149–50 (Australia), 171–2 (South Africa), and 217ff. (India).

[100] Data on US prices may be found in *Economic Report to the President, 1975* (Washington, DC: Government Printing Office, 1975).

came over the nature of money itself. Savings apart – what happened to savers has just been explained – to individuals it had always represented a means of purchasing commodities; to governments, a method by which they controlled the economy and allocated resources. Now, however, both functions were largely lost. From the citizens' point of view, this was because anything worth buying could be had, if at all, only in exchange for coupons. These were distributed on the basis of noneconomic criteria such as age, sex, and the amount of calories demanded by the kind of work in which one was engaged (needless to say, those with their hands on the levers of power looked after themselves; as Ludendorff once wrote, had he been made to eat ordinary rations, he "could not have existed"). From the point of view of the state, the reason why money lost its function as a tool of government was precisely because its supply, depending solely on the printing machines, had become essentially unlimited. Consequently it could no longer be used to determine which products and services would be purchased and which ones would not. Thus total war marked the culmination of a 200-year process by which the state imposed its control over money. Having done so, the result was to leave that commodity without any real value – leading to some cases to a return to barter, as when urbanites traded their kitchen utensils for potatoes. By way of other not-so-subtle indications of what was taking place, the Bank of England was absorbed into the machinery of state[101] and the British secretary of the exchequer lost his traditional position as the first (after the prime minister) among equals; after 1940 he was no longer even a member of the war cabinet.[102]

Once money had been conquered – meaning that it could no longer place any limits on what government could buy – the extent of the war effort in each country came to be determined by the physical means of production. The most important ones were shipping, transport, raw materials, factory space, energy, and transportation, and of course the labor on which all the rest depended and for which they often competed among themselves. Already in World War I, all the most important belligerents had pushed through laws that effectively overrode their citizens' property rights and enabled governments to take those means into their own hands when necessary. These controls they used to decide who should produce what, how, where, at what prices, and with the aid of which workers possessing which professional qualifications and working at which wages during how many hours a day or week. To focus on the most important countries only, in Germany the task was entrusted to the

[101] See R. S. Sayers, *Financial Policy, 1939–1945* (London, Longmans, 1956).
[102] See A. Milward, *War, Economy and Society, 1939–1945* (Berkeley: University of California Press, 1977), pp. 99ff.

industrialist Walter Rathenau and his Raw Materials Department, an organization established against considerable opposition on the part of the military, who did not want civilians interfering with the conduct of the war. In Britain it was carried out rather more easily by the overbearing politician Lloyd George (later succeeded by Churchill) at the head of the newly established Ministry of Munitions; finally, in the United States it was done by the WIB or War Industries Board, whose chairman was the financier Bernard Baruch.[103]

But whereas in most Western states most of the controls were dismantled in 1918–19, in one country – the Soviet Union – they proved permanent. Large, ramshackle, and provided with comparatively few railways per square mile of territory, the tsarist empire had been less successful than most in mobilizing its resources for war.[104] Initially it was the armed forces which ran out of weapons and ammunition; by 1916–17 rampant inflation as well as shortages of virtually everything had made the country ready for revolution. Once the Bolsheviks took over power in 1917 they set out to change things with a vengeance. Not content with mere controls, they carried out their program of expropriating all means of production as well as services such as banking, insurance, communications, and transportation down to retail commerce and hairdressing. With control over labor equally complete – in a communist state any breach of working discipline was automatically turned into a criminal offense – the modern Behemoth swallowed up the economy lock, stock, and barrel.

The result of the revolution was the bureaucrat's dream come true. Claiming to serve the general welfare, but in fact working almost exclusively on its own behalf, the state owned everything, ran everything, produced everything, and bought and sold everything – all at prices, needless to say, which were determined by itself and which often had nothing to do either with the actual cost to producers or with the choices that consumers might have made if left to their own devices.[105] To carry out all these multitudinous functions and prevent them from running at odds with each other it also kept files and supervised everything by means

---

[103] German mobilization for World War I is covered in M. Feldman, *Army, Industry and Labor in Germany, 1914–1918* (Providence, RI: Berg, 1993). For Britain, see S. J. Hurwitz, *State Intervention in Great Britain: A Study of Economic and Social Response 1914–1919* (London: Columbia University Press, 1949); and, for the United States, R. D. Cuff, *The War Industries Board: Business–Government Relations During World War I* (Baltimore: Johns Hopkins University Press, 1973).

[104] See N. Stone, *The Eastern Front 1914–1917* (London: Hodder and Stoughton, 1975), pp. 144–64, 194–211.

[105] For an analysis of the communist state very similar to the one here adduced, see M. Djilas, *The New Ruling Class: Analysis of the Communist System* (New York: Praeger, 1957).

of an administrative apparatus unlike any in history. In 1980 it was estimated that the mature communist state was producing 100 *billion* documents per year, which avalanche of paperwork was backed up by the education system, the propaganda machine, the secret police, the concentration camp, and, all too frequently, the execution wall.

Though other states did not at once follow in the wake of the Soviet Union, the respite granted their economies proved temporary. Throughout the interwar period socialist parties everywhere kept demanding that the most important means of production be nationalized so that their profits, instead of going to individuals, could be put to use on behalf of the community at large. In one country after another, some of their demands were met; this applied in particular to new industries such as broadcasting, telecommunications, air transport, and electricity generation. Additional pressure in the same general direction sometimes came from the nationalist right. For example, Rathenau as the part-owner and chief executive officer of the Allgemeine Elektrizität-Gesellschaft, one of Germany's largest industrial combines, was certainly no socialist; yet before the war was over he summed up his experience in *The New Economy* (*Die Neue Wirtschaft*, 1918). Partly a blueprint for increasing national power, partly a preemptive response to the socialist demand for eventual nationalization, the book argued that the days of unrestricted capitalism were over. Instead he advocated a new partnership between state and industry – one which, needless to say, translated into greater control by the former over the latter.

Nor did the dictators who came to rule Germany and Italy need Rathenau to teach them this lesson. Both Mussolini and Hitler shed their original socialist leanings at a comparatively early age. Having discovered which side of the bread was buttered – when Mussolini turned interventionist in 1915, his fellow socialists greeted him by crying "chi paga" (who pays)[106] – they were quite prepared to sing the praises of private enterprise; and in return, happily accepted its financial contributions during their struggle for power. Having seized it, they quickly moved to meet their obligations to their supporters by forbidding strikes, prohibiting collective bargaining, dismantling the existing trade unions, and putting their leaders in prison. This, however, did not mean a return to early nineteenth-century *laissez faire*; instead they proceeded to conscript labor by means of the new, state-run corporations and Deutsche Arbeitsfront. The next step for both Nazis and Fascists was to establish direct controls over industry, the best-known instance being the 1936 Four-Year Plan which made Herman Goering into Ger-

---

[106] G. Seldes, *Sawdust Caesar: The Untold Story of Mussolini and Fascism* (London: Barker, 1936), p. 46.

many's economic tsar. Both also embarked on constructing a whole series of state-owned industries in fields considered vital to the war effort but which for one reason or another could not attract private investment.[107] Among them were steel, synthetic oil, and rubber (the latter manufactured with the aid of concentration-camp labor), and, of course, the famous Volkswagen car.

Once World War II had broken out, the mobilization plans of 1914–18 were taken out of the drawers and dusted, in some cases literally so as those responsible went to see their predecessors, several of whom were still alive, to ask for guidance. Regardless of whether their regimes were communist or fascist or liberal, all states hastened to assume control over the means of production or, if they already controlled them, tighten supervision even further by introducing the police into the factories and prescribing draconian penalties for any "slackers." It might even be argued that a "democratic" country like Britain was able to go faster and further than "totalitarian" ones such as Germany, Italy, and Japan. None of the three had an elected government; hence, and for all the police apparatus at their disposal, initially at any rate, they proved more fearful of imposing sacrifice on their populations.[108] Be this as it may, once again the bureaucratic machines grew and grew. In the United States the number of federal employees rose from 936,000 in 1933 to 3,800,000 in 1945, though half of those were discharged after the war; in Britain the newly created Ministry of Food alone expanded from 3,500 bureaucrats in 1940 to 39,000 in 1943, only to melt away once hostilities had ended. By the end of the year the point had long been reached where, in theory and to a considerable extent in practice, not an ounce of raw material could be worked nor a screw produced unless it had first received government blessing and had been declared vital to the war effort.

The states having finally succeeded in their drive to conquer money, the effect of absolute economic dominance on the states themselves was to allow them to fight each other on a scale and with a ferocity never equaled before or since. Practiced to a larger or smaller extent, central planning and central control enabled hundreds of thousands of tanks and aircraft to come off the assembly lines and go straight into battle. While

---

[107] For the German Four-Year Plan, see Militärgeschichtliches Forschungsamt, ed., *Germany and the Second World War* (Oxford: Clarendon Press, 1990), pp. 273–315; for Italy, see V. Castronovo, "La stratégie du conglomerat: l'état banquier et entrepreneur en Italie," *Entréprises et Histoire*, 1, 1992, pp. 13–25; and L. Ceva and A. Curio, "Industrie de guerre et l'état dans l'impérialisme fasciste des années 30," *Guerres Mondiales et Conflicts Contemporaines*, 41, 61, 1991, pp. 31–50.

[108] The measures taken to maintain German workers' morale in particular are discussed in S. Salter, "Structures of Consensus and Coercion: Workers' Morale and the Maintenance of Work Discipline, 1939–1945," in D. Welch, ed., *Nazi Propaganda* (London: Croom Helm, 1983), pp. 88–116.

business, fed by titanic state contracts, often made equally titanic profits, the effect on the lives of ordinary people in most countries was described in that grim caricature of World War II life, George Orwell's *1984*:

Always in your stomach and in your skin there was a sort of protest, a feeling that you had been cheated of something that you had a right to . . . there [was] never enough to eat, one never had socks or underclothes that were not full of holes, furniture was battered and rickety, rooms underheated, tube-trains crowded, houses falling to pieces, bread dark-colored, tea a rarity, coffee filthy-tasting, cigarettes insufficient – nothing cheap and plentiful except synthetic gin.[109]

The road to total war

The concentration of all economic power in the hands of the state would not have been necessary, nor could it have been justified, if its overriding purpose had not been to impose order on the one hand and fight its neighbors on the other. Already Hobbes, the man who really invented the state, was prepared to do away with every kind of freedom (including specifically freedom of thought) in order to achieve peace; in his view any government was better than no government at all. Having gone through two total wars in a single generation and seen what states and governments can *really* do in the way of war and destruction once they put their minds to it, perhaps we ought to know better.

As has been noted in a previous section, the establishment of the state was very soon followed by the development commonly known as the military revolution.[110] Until then no European ruler had had more than a few tens of thousands of men under his command: the Battle of Rocroi, e.g., which in 1643 led to the replacement of Spain by France as the greatest power of the time, was fought by 48,000 men all told. Three decades later, the forces raised by Louis XIV and his opponents already numbered in the low hundreds of thousands. This kind of growth could not go on for ever and during the eighteenth century the size of warfare on land tended to stagnate. With a total of about 200,000 French, Imperial, British, and Dutch combatants involved on both sides, the Battle of Malplaquet (1709) proved the largest in European history until Napoleon, whereas the armies with which Louis XV waged the Seven Years War were scarcely, if at all, larger than those of his great-grandfather Louis XIV.[111]

If the scale of warfare on land did not increase by much, the eighteenth

[109] George Orwell, *1984* (Harmondsworth, UK: Penguin, 1977 [1949]), p. 251.
[110] M. Roberts, *The Military Revolution* (Belfast: Belfast University Press, 1956); J. S. Levy, *War in the Modern Great Power System* (Lexington, MA: Lexington Books, 1983).
[111] For some figures on the size of European armies during the last years of the *ancien régime*, see Duffy, *The Military Experience in the Age of Reason*, p. 17.

century did see an explosion in military operations at sea. The principal seventeenth-century naval powers had been Spain (which, until 1660, had been united with Portugal) and the Netherlands; now, however, their fleets were completely overshadowed by those of Britain and France. Put on a sound organizational footing by the likes of Samuel Pepys and Colbert, depending on the period in question the British and French navies each possessed between 50 and 150 so-called ships of the line. Each such ship measured approximately 1,000 tons and carried between 80 and 120 bronze cannon weighing as much as 3 tons each, to say nothing of innumerable smaller vessels known under a variety of names and suitable for a variety of purposes from carrying dispatches to raiding trade.[112] Provided with navigational aids such as the sextant, which were far superior to anything previously seen in history, these wind-driven armadas for the first time provided their owners with an almost unlimited reach. Soon there was no continent and no sea left on which they did not fight each other, often on a very considerable scale as dozens of French, British, and Spanish ships clashed in Far Eastern or West Indian waters. In this way the War of the Spanish Succession opened the era of global warfare, one which may only now, thanks to the breakup of one so-called superpower and the growing reluctance of the other to sacrifice its young people, be coming to an end.

Meanwhile, both the scale of war on land and its intensity remained comparatively limited. In part this may have been due to humanitarian sentiment, arising out of a reaction to the excesses of the Thirty Years War: as Montesquieu, representing all that was best in Enlightenment thought, wrote in his *Spirit of the Laws*, in peace nations ought to do each other as much good as they could and in war as little injury as possible. In the main, though, the limitations that governed eighteenth-century war were the result of the political structure of each of the principal war-making states. Having been imposed on their peoples, often by main force, governments (except for the British one, and then within certain limits) knew themselves to be unrepresentative of the latter. Being so, they did not care to impose intolerable economic burdens, introduce universal conscription, or distribute arms: there was always the danger that the troops thus raised and armed would fight against their rulers rather than on their behalf.

Consisting of men who felt no commitment to the state that they served – "the filth of the nation," as France's minister of war, the Comte Saint-Germain, once put it[113] – eighteenth-century armies could be kept

---

[112] The best work on eighteenth-century naval warfare remains A. T. Mahan, *The Influence of Seapower upon History, 1660–1763* (Boston: Little, Brown, 1890).

[113] C. L. Saint-Germain, *Mémoires de M. le Comte de Saint-Germain* (Amsterdam: Libraires associés, 1799), p. 200; see also General James Wolfe, quoted in J. A. Houlding, *Fit for*

in existence only by means of a ferocious discipline under the open eye of their aristocratic officers. The requirement for discipline, plus some of the technical characteristics of the weapons in use, made it imperative that they move and fight in comparatively tight formations advancing shoulder to shoulder in serried, orderly ranks. The need for such formations in turn dictated that they could not easily be used as skirmishers, on the pursuit, in terrain that was hilly or wooded, or at night. In addition certain logistic constraints applied. The dependence of eighteenth-century armies on their "umbilical cords of supply" has often been exaggerated; however, it is true that most troops could not be trusted to forage on their own but had to be very carefully supervised by a cordon of NCOs that used to be thrown out around them. Even if they could be trusted, many regions did not have a sufficiently dense population to permit large-scale warfare to take place in them.[114]

Eighteenth-century battles could be as ferocious as any. There was, as a rule, no attempt at taking cover or adopting camouflage; dressed in long, straight lines, approaching each other to the sound of drums at exactly seventy-five paces in the minute, the troops would halt at a range where they could see the whites of each other's eyes and start blasting away. As a result, it was common for as many as a third of them to become casualties within a period, say, of between six and eight hours.[115] On the other hand, soldiers were expensive and battles risky. Accordingly, commanders such as Turenne and the maréchal de Saxe spent entire campaigning seasons maneuvering against their opponents with only the occasional minor clash to relieve the boredom of marching and countermarching; the latter even wrote that a good general might spend his entire career without being brought to battle. In addition, there was the notion that the safety of each state depended on a careful balance of power with all the rest. Consequently it was thought that no war should be pushed too far[116] or allowed to end in the complete destruction of a belligerent; and indeed the possibility that this might happen often led to the reversal of alliances

　　　Service: The Training of the British Army, 1715–1798 (Oxford: Clarendon, 1981), p. 268.
[114] On the logistics of eighteenth-century armies, see M. van Creveld, Supplying War: Logistics from Wallenstein to Patton (London: Cambridge University Press, 1978), ch. 1; and G. Perjes, "Army Provisioning, Logistics and Strategy During the Second Half of the Seventeenth Century," Acta Historica Academiae Scientiarum Hungaricae, 16 (Budapest: Academy of Sciences, 1965).
[115] For some figures, see D. Chandler, The Art of Warfare in the Age of Marlborough (London: Batsford, 1976), pp. 302–7; Duffy, The Military Experience in the Age of Reason, pp. 245ff.
[116] See the contemporary military writer Friedrich Wilhelm von Zanthier, quoted in M. Jahns, Geschichte der Kriegswissenschaften vornehmlich in Deutschland (Munich: Vorein, 1889–), vol. III, pp. 296–7; and M. S. Anderson, The Rise of Modern Diplomacy 1450–1919 (London: Longmans, 1993), pp. 163–80.

and the creation of new ones. War was a question of occupying a district here and a province there, whether in Europe or, even more frequently, overseas, where some of the most significant exchanges took place.

With the outbreak of the French Revolution, these and other limitations on eighteenth-century warfare disappeared. The trinitarian division of labor between the government that directed the war, the armed forces that fought and died, and the people who paid and suffered remained as it had been since 1648; in some ways it became even stricter than before, given that officers ceased to be independent businessmen but came to depend exclusively on the state for advancement and remuneration. What did change was the forging of very strong links between the first and the last elements of the trinity, which in turn made it possible to vastly expand the second. As Clausewitz later explained, the real achievement of the Revolution was to enable the state to wage war with the full power of the nation – something which, in Europe at any rate, only very few political regimes had been able to do since the days of the Roman Republic at its zenith. The Revolution's opponents put it less politely, describing the French troops as "monsters . . . savage beasts . . . foaming at the mouth with rage and yelling like cannibals – hurling themselves at top speed upon soldiers whose courage has been excited by no passion."[117]

The first to institute the *levée en masse* was the French National Convention in its famous decree of 25 August 1792.[118] Written by Bertrand Barère, it called for the "permanent requisitioning" of men, women (who were to "work at the soldiers' clothing, make tents, and become nurses"), old men (who were to "betake themselves to the public squares and preach the hatred of tyrants"), and even children, who were to make lint of old linen. So much did the delegates like the rhetoric that they asked for the decree to be read twice over; from this time every citizen was to be a soldier and every soldier a citizen. In practice the infrastructure necessary for implementing the decree was deficient and the results less than perfect – the only persons actually called up were men between eighteen and twenty-five years old, and then only if they were unmarried. Even so, martial enthusiasm did not last for long; staying in France as a prisoner in 1807, Clausewitz was surprised and not a little disgusted to see recruits led to the *préfecture* in chains.[119] The size of the French army doubled from 400,000 or so during the Seven Years War to perhaps 800,000 in

---

[117] Mallet du Pan, quoted in H. Nickerson, *The Armed Horde* (New York: Putnam, 1942), p. 91.

[118] An English translation of the text is in J. F. C. Fuller, *The Conduct of War 1789–1961* (London: Eyre and Spottiswode, 1962), p. 32.

[119] P. Paret, *Clausewitz and the State* (Princeton: Princeton University Press, 1976), p. 130.

1795–6, though not all of them could be trained, armed (the shortage of muskets at one time led to the production of pikes), or even properly clothed.

Having taken over from Carnot as "the organizer of victory," Napoleon used the full power of the police to break such opposition to conscription as still existed.[120] Not only was the imbalance between men and arms soon corrected, but the result was to provide the French state with forces larger than any since Herodotus had Xerxes lead a million and a half men into Greece in 480 BC; however, there was nothing mythical about the Grande armée. Instead of marching in a single block, as had been standard practice from the day of the Greek phalanx to that of Frederick the Great, willy-nilly the French troops had to be spread out over a much wider front in order to live and move. The construction of such fronts both demanded and was made possible by the organization of the forces into *corps d'armée*. First proposed by the National Convention in 1796, each corps or "body" possessed a permanent commander in the person of a maréchal de France, a title which Napoleon did not invent but to which he gave a new, more precise significance. Each had its own staff and its own proper combination of the three arms (infantry, cavalry, and artillery), as well as its own intelligence, engineering, and logistic services. Each one constituted a miniature army in its own right, one which, as common wisdom went, was capable of performing its mission independently of the rest and of holding out for two or three days even in the face of a superior force attacking it.

With the reorganization of the forces, the entire nature of strategy changed.[121] Previously armies had maneuvered against each other in fronts that were seldom more than four or five miles wide; but Napoleon's corps were capable of moving 25–50 miles from each other while at the same time operating in accordance with a coherent, centrally dictated plan. Whereas eighteenth-century armies had merely tried to conquer provinces, now they sought to subjugate entire countries in rapid succession. Whereas previously they had been forced to besiege each fortress on their way, now the great majority of fortified places could simply be bypassed (whereas Vauban at the beginning of the eighteenth century had reckoned that there were three sieges for each battle, the number of sieges that Napoleon conducted may be counted on the fingers of one hand). Living off the country and aiming straight for the jugular, French armies

---

[120] I. Wolloch, "Napoleonic Conscription: State Power and Civil Society," *Past and Present*, 1986, pp. 101–29.

[121] For these changes and the revolution in strategy that they wrought, see van Creveld, *Command in War*, ch. 2; and R. Epstein, *Napoleon's Last Victory and the Emergence of Modern War* (Lawrence: University of Kansas Press, 1994), ch. 2.

marched for the enemy's capital. If they found their way blocked, they used their superior command-and-control system to focus overwhelming numbers at the decisive point and defeat the enemy in one of those tremendous *batailles rangées* of which Napoleon boasted to have commanded no fewer than sixty. The results of this system were as rapid as they were spectacular. Starting in 1799, the time of Napoleon's second Italian campaign and the first one in which he was in command of all of the country's military resources, it took the French fewer than ten years to overrun the whole of Europe from the Pyrenees to the Vistula.

By 1813, when Napoleon himself conceded that "ces animaux ont apprenu quel'que chose" (these animals have learnt a thing or two), the armies of other states were imitating the French methods. The process is perhaps best studied at the hands of Prussia which, following its defeat in 1806, set out to reform its army during the years that followed.[122] Conscription, which hitherto had followed the old *Kantonen* system and brought in only the doltish inhabitants of the countryside, was extended and applied to the educated sons of the middle classes. They were given the choice between serving for two years, like everybody else, or for one year at their own expense, a privilege that most of them took since it enabled them to acquire the much-desired rank of Reserveleutenant. The officer corps, which hitherto had been governed by social status on the one hand and by seniority on the other, was reformed in such a way as to put greater emphasis on schooling (including that remarkable finishing school for officers, the Kriesgakademie) and competence. A corps organization modeled on the French one was put in place. To control it, a proper general staff with headquarters in Berlin and branches throughout the army was established; during the years of the Second Reich it was to become the most prestigious institution in the country.[123] In the persons of Gerhard von Scharnhorst, August von Gneisenau, Carl von Clausewitz, and their comrades, the Prussians were also fortunate to possess officers who, in addition to their practical ability to command in war, displayed an exceptionally deep grasp of its history and theory. This quality enabled them to institutionalize the reforms so that they were passed from one generation to the next.

With all states busily reforming and expanding their armies to resist the French battalions, the scale of warfare changed out of all recognition. In 1812 Napoleon invaded Russia with no fewer than 600,000 men –

[122] The literature on the rebuilding of the Prussian Army is vast. See W. Goerlitz, *The History of the German General Staff, 1657–1945* (New York: Praeger, 1971 edn.), esp. pp. 15–49; and D. Showalter, "Retaming Bellona: Prussia and the Institutionalization of the Napoleonic Legacy," *Military Affairs*, April 1980, pp. 57–62.
[123] Goerlitz, *History of the German General Staff*, pp. 60ff.

perhaps three times as many as had been concentrated in a single theater of war since history began. The largest contemporary battle was fought around Leipzig in October 1813; had it not been dubbed the Battle of Nations, it would have deserved the title Mother of All Battles. The total number of combatants present stood at 460,000 of whom 180,000 were French, the rest Prussian, Russian, and Austrian (assisted by a few Swedes). Indeed so large was the scale on which military operations were now conducted that it proved impossible to bring all the troops to bear on each other at the same time and place. Instead of lasting for one day, as had been the case of virtually all battles from prehistory until then, the one at Leipzig lasted for three. It really comprised three separate engagements fought simultaneously, with Napoleon himself rushing from one to another and controlling, if any, only one.[124]

During the years 1815–66 no other battles as large as this one took place between modern armies, though those which *did* take place were, relative to their size, quite as bloody.[125] This was the period of the Restoration and of the Reaction. Its outstanding characteristic was the fact that, from Moscow through Berlin and Vienna all the way to Paris, the crowned heads who occupied the various thrones feared their own populations more than they did each other. Accordingly there was a tendency to make armies less representative of the nation. France and most other countries did away with conscription, albeit not completely and in ways that usually made considerable reserves available to the standing peacetime forces.[126] The most important use to which armies were put was not to wage interstate war but to guard against revolution – *gegen demokraten hilfen nur Soldaten* (soldiers are the only cure for democracy), as the saying went. Thus French troops helped the Spanish government fight the series of civil conflicts known as the Carlist Wars. In 1830–1 a Prussian Army of Observation cooperated with the Russians as they put down the Polish insurrection in Warsaw. In 1848–9 French troops saved the pope by putting an end to Mazzini's Roman Republic, Austrian troops resorted to an artillery bombardment to reconquer their own capital, and Prussian ones were sent to drive the revolutionaries out of the southwestern German state of Baden. The climax came in May

[124] On the Battle of Leipzig and Napoleon's loss of control, see Vitzthum von Eckstädt, *Die Hauptquartiere im Herbstfeldzug 1813 auf dem deutschen Kriegsschauplätze* (Berlin: Mittler, 1910).

[125] Compare figures on the Battles of Leipzig (460,000 combatants, 90,000 casualties), Solferino (240,000 combatants, 40,000 casualties), and Gettysburg (160,000 combatants, 50,000 casualties), from *Harbottle's Dictionary of Battles* (New York: van Nostrand, 1981, 3rd edn.).

[126] For these developments, see G. Best, *War and Society in Revolutionary Europe, 1789–1870* (London: Fontana, 1982), pp. 191–309; and J. Gooch, *Armies in Europe* (London: Routledge, 1980), pp. 50–80.

1849 when Russian forces, acting on the invitation of the government in Vienna, invaded Hungary to extinguish the revolution there, an operation which they had to repeat in Warsaw fifteen years later.

While the scale of warfare was limited by its being put into a pressure cooker, so to speak, military technology flourished as never before. This is not the place to delve into the nature of the scientific revolution or the industrial revolution that followed it after a comparatively brief interval. Suffice it to say that, before the rise of the state around the middle of the seventeenth century, no weapon was capable of firing to a distance of more than perhaps half a mile or of moving faster than the pace of a galloping horse, while at sea the largest ships were still made of wood and possessed no more than 500–600 tons of deadweight. Given that military technological progress – including, above all, the invention of gunpowder – began to accelerate several centuries before the state appeared upon the scene, to blame the latter for the former would be less than fair, the more so since it is not at all clear whether military technology "pulled" technology (as Trotsky and others have suggested) or whether, on the contrary, weapons and weapons systems were merely one offshoot of technological progress as a whole.[127]

Even when all this is taken into account, however, the fact remains that modern means of death and destruction would never have been possible without the state, its ministry of defense (which, until 1945, was called simply the ministry of war), and its regular, uniformed, bureaucratically managed armed forces.[128] The forces of most previous political entities had been too disorganized and too temporary to offer scope for sustained military-technological progress. This was particularly true of feudal levies and mercenaries, both in Europe and in other parts of the world. The former were part-time warriors who, if not engaged in hunting and similar aristocratic pursuits, spent most of their time looking after their estates. The latter either led a nomadic life, moving from one employer to the next, or else simply went home each time a war was over. However, it was almost equally true of the standing armies built by some of the empires discussed in chapter 1 of this volume. Few of those really amounted to professional forces in the modern sense of the term, given that their officers were often selected less for their military ability than for their loyalty.

Once the modern state started introducing regular, standing armies

---

[127] See on this question J. M. Winter, *War and Economic Progress* (London: Cambridge University Press, 1976).
[128] The relationship between the state, its regular army, and the takeoff of military technology has never been investigated. For some remarks, see M. van Creveld, "The Rise and Fall of Military Technology," *Science in Context*, 7, 2, 1994, pp. 329ff.

and navies, the situation changed. To a greater extent than any of their predecessors, such forces provided a permanent market for weapons and weapons systems. Already toward the end of the seventeenth century the navy was the largest employer (as well as the largest buyer of goods and services) in the entire British economy;[129] such was the demand for uniforms created by the forces of Louis XIV that it led to the invention of the first primitive machines used for sewing buttons on cloth.[130] Almost for the first time in history, there now existed forces that received their entire income directly from the state and which, however much they might detest the ruler of the moment, were seldom engaged in conspiring against the institution itself. Increasingly excluded from participation in political life, gradually deprived of other functions such as police work, and deliberately isolated from civilian society, they possessed unprecedented freedom to devote their full attention to discovering new and better ways of killing and destroying others of the same kind.

When developing professionalism was joined to the industrial revolution spreading outwards from Britain, the results could not be anything but explosive. Armed with cannon manufactured according to the new Gribeauval system, Napoleon's forces would have made short shrift of Frederick's army a mere thirty or forty years earlier; but whatever progress took place during the years from 1760 to 1815 was dwarfed by the changes that started following each other from 1830 on. First came percussion caps, which finally did away with the need for flints to generate sparks and set off the powder. Next the muzzle-loading musket, which except for the replacement of wooden ramrods by iron ones had remained almost unchanged from Blenheim to Waterloo, was replaced by rifles capable of firing three to six times as often for a greater distance and, after some early experimentation, with greater accuracy – to say nothing of the fact that, being loaded from the breach rather than through the muzzle, for the first time in history they enabled men to fight while taking cover and without necessarily standing on their feet. Developments in artillery proceeded in parallel. Beginning in the 1850s, smoothbore bronze and iron muzzle-loaders were progressively replaced by rifled steel breech-loaders. By 1870 the best cannon were the Prussian ones. Manufactured by the firm of Krupp, they were capable of firing three times as far as their Napoleonic predecessors and possessed a rate of fire four or five times as large. For the first time since the sixteenth century, too, ammunition began to show some progress, with solid iron balls replaced by shrapnel

---

[129] J. H. Plumb, *The Origins of Political Stability: England 1675–1725* (Boston: Houghton Mifflin, 1967), p. 119.
[130] L. Mumford, *The Myth of the Machine* (New York: Harcourt, 1970), pp. 150–1.

and high explosive shells which were provided with clockwork fuses.[131]

Even more important to the development of war and conquest at the hand of the state was the improvement that took place in the infrastructure of war. Traditionally military transport had been limited to horse-drawn wagons and military communications to mounted messengers; but now telegraphs and railways began to cover entire countries (later continents) with networks in such a way as to revolutionize the state's control over its territory, population, and armed forces. The first telegraphs – optical, not electrical – were constructed in France during the early years of the Revolution and, as might be expected, were no sooner completed than they were used for the conduct of war.[132] During the next three decades, Spain (which claimed to have designed a more important system than France itself),[133] Britain, Prussia, and Russia all followed, building systems that reached from London to Dover and Portsmouth, from Berlin to Trier, and from Moscow to Warsaw. While each of the systems was slightly different from a technical point of view, from the beginning all of them had as their overriding purpose serving the military needs of the state. After 1830 or so the place of optical telegraphs was taken by the more efficient electric ones. Their construction was paralleled by that of the railways; given that the efficient operation of the latter depended on the correct use of the former, the two tended to run together like siamese twins.[134]

Already during the 1850s the French engaged on the construction of a railway net specifically designed for military purposes, one that served them very well in the war of 1859 against Austria. Had it not been for rails and wires the American Civil War would have been absolutely inconceivable. The conflict of 1861–5 does, indeed, deserve to be called the first railway war; given that both sides very often made their moves dependent on the availability of track – as Sherman's invasion of the South was – or else aimed at disrupting that of the enemy (Sherman again, this time in his operations against Atlanta in 1864). Railways alone made it possible for the Federals to call up no fewer than 2 million men during the conflict, an achievement which, against a population basis of only 27 million dispersed over a huge country, was unparalleled until

---

[131] A short account of the nineteenth-century military-technological revolution is B. Brodie and F. Brodie, *From Cross Bow to H Bomb* (Bloomington: Indiana University Press, 1959), pp. 124–71.

[132] A. S. Field, "French Optical Telegraphy, 1793–1855: Hardware, Software, Administration," *Technology and Culture*, 35, 2, 1994, pp. 315–47.

[133] A. Rumeu de Armas, "La línea telegráfica Madrid–Cadiz (1800), primera de España y segunda de Europa," *Hispania*, 42, 152, 1982, pp. 522–63.

[134] See for this entire story D. Showalter, *Railroads and Rifles: The Influence of Technological Developments on German Military Thought and Practice, 1815–1865* (Hamden, CT: Archon Books, 1975).

then. Almost equally unparalleled was the number of dead, which in a mere four years amounted to no fewer than 600,000 on both sides.

The real demonstration of what the marriage of the state and technology could do, however, was still to come. Unlike most European states, Prussia had not done away with conscription after 1815. More than most European states, its central position and flat, featureless terrain put it in a position to use the railways once the necessary capital and know-how became available – not a great step for a nation which, as we saw, already possessed the best education system in the world. Beginning in the 1850s, these factors led to the construction of an incomparably efficient railway network. Though the network was not governed exclusively by military considerations, Moltke as chief of the general staff was an *ex officio* member of the commission that governed it; that he was also a shareholder in the railways is interesting but, for our purposes, beside the point. Plans for mobilization were developed and rehearsed time and again with painstaking accuracy. In 1866, when the first great trial came, the world held its breath as the world's smallest great power called up over 300,000 troops and concentrated them on the Austrian border, all with unprecedented order and at unprecedented speed. Indeed, such was the superiority of the Prussian use of their railways in 1866 and 1870 that both wars in question were decided almost before the first shot was fired. Having been thrown off balance, both Austrians and French found themselves on the defensive and never recovered.

Whereas the American Civil War was all but ignored in Europe – as Moltke himself put it, there was nothing there but two mobs chasing each other across an enormous, half-deserted countryside – the Prussian victories were studied very closely. Beginning in 1873, one country after another did away with its antiquated military system and introduced universal conscription of the male population. By 1914 this even applied to Japan, which had only recently adopted what was known as "the standard of civilization"; the only remaining exceptions were Britain and the United States, both of which, however, followed the example of the rest during World War I. Conscription and an effective reserve system – itself made possible by the railways – in turn enabled monstrous armed forces to be created; when August 1914 came the most important powers counted their members not in the hundreds of thousands but in the millions.[135] Nor was this by any means the end of the story. Thus the German Army, which including its various reserves numbered almost 4.5 million men at the beginning of the war, grew to approximately 6.5 million in 1917 – most of the increase being concentrated in the technical

[135] For the strength of 1914 armies, see H. Kuhl, *Der deutsche Generalstab in Vorbereitung und Durchführung der Weltkrieg* (Berlin: Mittler, 1920), pp. 16, 63, 87, 103.

arms such as the artillery, the air service, and, above all, the signals corps. Between 1914 and 1918 the number of those who wore German uniform exceeded 13 million. Of these, approximately 2 million lost their lives. The total number of dead is estimated at about 10 million, not counting perhaps as many who died of war-related diseases.

By this time the railway and the telegraph had been joined by the motor car, the telephone, and the teleprinter. Making use of those instruments, the war also proved a turning point in terms of the ability of the state to mobilize its economy for military purposes. The result was a conflict fought on a scale inconceivably larger than anything before it. Thus, between 1914 and 1916 alone the average daily consumption of supplies per army division increased by a factor of three from 50 to 150 tons.[136] Whereas, at the beginning of the conflict, an army was considered very well prepared if it had in stock 1,000 rounds per artillery barrel, four years later there were batteries which fired that quantity of ammunition *per day*; meanwhile the German army's consumption of small arms ammunition had reached 300 *million* rounds a month. Other items, some of them traditional – throughout the war horse-fodder remained the single most bulky commodity shipped from Britain to France – and others newly invented were consumed or expended in proportion. Among the innovations were land and sea mines, produced and sown in the millions by all the belligerent states. Then there were hundreds of thousands of miles of barbed wire – to say nothing of that World War I specialty never before or since used on a similar scale, i.e., poison gas.

During the years 1919–39 much thought and goodwill were spent in attempts to find ways to prevent states from involving humanity in another catastrophe of the same kind.[137] As the failure of these attempts was to show, even greater efforts were devoted to discovering even more effective ways for states to fight each other. Some of these attempts were specifically designed to avoid a recurrence of the slaughter, as, for example, those of the British military pundit Basil Liddell Hart. Having been born in 1895, Liddell Hart was of exactly the right age to be gassed at the Somme in 1916 and thus knew the horrors of war at first hand. As he watched the names of most of his fellow students in pre-war Cambridge University appear on the memorial tables erected after 1919, he lost his previous faith in the wisdom of the British general staff.[138] The rest of his life he devoted to finding better (read faster and more economical) ways of

[136] Pre-war figures are from Oberste Heeresleitung, *Taschenbuch für Offiziere der Verkerhrstruppen* (Berlin: Oberste Heeresleitung, 1913), p. 84; 1916 ones are from A. Henniker, *Transportation on the Western Front, 1914–1918* (London: HMSO, 1937), p. 103.   [137] See below, ch. 6, "The waning of major war," pp. 337–54.
[138] The most recent work on Liddell Hart's intellectual development is A. Gat, "The Hidden Sources of Liddell Hart's Ideas," *War in History*, 3, 3, July 1996, pp. 293–308.

fighting. His first suggestion was the so-called indirect approach, consisting of sophisticated operations launched not against the enemy's front, as in 1914–18, but into the spot where they were least expected and would do the greatest harm. Later, influenced by his fellow British military reformer, Colonel (later Major-General) John Frederick Fuller, he sought to carry out the operations in question by means of the new armored forces then being established. By the mid-1930s Liddell Hart had gained an international reputation and could justly claim to have invented the kind of operation that was later to become known as the Blitzkrieg, although in truth there is little to show that his views had any great influence on the practical soldiers of the time.[139]

Whereas Liddell Hart's attempt to find cheaper – read more effective – ways of waging war at least had the merit of sparing the civilian leg of the trinity, the same cannot be said of his Italian fellow theorist, General Giulio Douhet. Originally an army officer, Douhet had had plenty of opportunity to observe the futility of infantry attacks against a fortified defense – between 1915 and 1917 there were no fewer than eleven offensives on the Isonzo, all of which failed with horrendous casualties. There simply *had* to be a better way, and by the time the war ended he believed he had discovered it in the form of the aircraft. First used for military purposes during the 1911 Italian–Turkish war and then, on a vastly greater scale, in 1914–18,[140] the aircraft's outstanding qualities were its speed and flexibility, qualities which enabled it to switch from one target to another regardless of the intervening terrain and regardless (almost) also of the distance between them. Since all points could not be protected at the same time, this made it into an offensive weapon *par excellence*. Instead of wasting one's airpower to attack the enemy's strongest sector, i.e., his armed forces, Douhet wanted to see it used first against the enemy's air bases in order to obtain command of the air (a term he took from naval warfare and defined as the ability to fly while denying that ability to the enemy) and then his civilian population centers.[141] Basing himself on the German attacks on London during World War I, which had led to a handful of casualties as well as considerable panic, Douhet confidently expected such "strategic" bombardment to bring any country to its knees within a matter of days, even to the point where ground combat would be both unnecessary and useless.

[139] See B. Bond, *Liddell Hart: A Study of His Military Thought* (London: Cassell, 1976), particularly pp. 215ff.
[140] See L. Kennett, *The First Air War 1914–1918* (New York: Free Press, 1991).
[141] G. Douhet, *Command of the Air* (London: Faber and Faber, 1943), esp. ch. 1. A good account of interwar debates on airpower is E. Warner, "Douhet, Mitchell, Seversky: Theories of Air Warfare," in E. M. Earle, ed., *Makers of Modern Strategy* (Princeton: Princeton University Press, 1943), pp. 485–503.

In the event these and other visions of future war were destined to be overshadowed by, or perhaps one should say incorporated in, the work of another and, if not greater, at any rate more experienced thinker, the German Erich Ludendorff. As wartime quartermaster-general of the German army and *de facto* ruler of Germany, Ludendorff had an unrivaled opportunity to observe war at the top. Having spent two years in charge of the mightiest military establishment ever seen, he did not share the belief that a modern great power could be brought down by a few operations, however indirect, or even by fleets of aircraft bombing whatever there was to bomb. Both, to be sure, were to be employed for all they were worth; not only was Ludendorff himself unmatched as an operational expert – a quality he had proved by the series of brilliant victories won over the Russians in 1914–16 – but he was anything but squeamish in his resolution to use whatever methods were necessary for achieving victory. Modern war, however, could be won only by the total mobilization of all the state's demographic, economic, and industrial resources under the rule of a military dictator. Since such "in-depth" mobilization took time, it had to be started in peacetime, which in turn meant that the dictatorship, presumably under none other than the Feldherr Ludendorff himself, was to be made permanent.[142]

When World War II broke out in 1939 it at first tended to confirm the visions of Liddell Hart and Fuller in particular. Whether or not the operations that finished off first Poland and then Norway, the Low Countries, France, Yugoslavia, Greece, the British imperial positions in the Middle East, and (almost) Russia were indirect is moot; what is not moot is that they were spearheaded by armored forces made up of tens, later hundreds, of thousands of machines ranging from light reconnaissance vehicles (jeeps) all the way to personnel carriers, motorized or self-propelled artillery, and tanks. Maneuvering this way and that, those forces were supported by fleets of aircraft, albeit they owed little to Douhet and, initially at any rate, concentrated on military targets rather than civilian ones.[143]

However, the early victories proved misleading. If small and medium powers could be wiped off the map by a handful of Panzer divisions and the air fleets that accompanied them and provided them with cover, continental ones such as the Soviet Union and Germany itself could not. First the Wehrmacht, then the Red Army, and finally the armies of the Western Allies learnt that their reach was limited. Such were the logistic requirements of modern mechanized offensives that, whenever

[142] E. Ludendorff, *The Nation at War* (London: Hutchinson, 1938), pp. 11–85.
[143] See M. van Creveld, *Airpower and Maneuver Warfare* (Maxwell AFB, AL: Air University Press, 1994), ch. 2.

they passed the 200-mile mark, they tended to collapse under their own weight, even when, as in Russia in the summer of 1941 or France in the autumn of 1944, enemy resistance was weak or absent.[144] As a result, though operational movements were much bolder and progressed much deeper than in World War I, World War II, like its predecessor, developed into a vast struggle of attrition.

As the belligerents proceeded to mobilize their entire economies for this struggle, they also turned to strategic bombing as a means to disrupt the other side's mobilization – thus demolishing the distinction between government, army, and people that had been built up so laboriously from 1648 on. The first who tried to bring entire countries to their knees by means of aerial bombardment were the Germans in Warsaw and Rotterdam (though the attack on the latter may have been the result of a communications failure). Next, they launched the so-called Blitz against Britain; but the German air force, having been built with a different style of war in mind, did not really have the aircraft or the staying power necessary for the purpose. In this way the honor of being the first – and, to this day, almost the only – ones to apply "strategic" bombing on a really large scale belongs to Britain and the United States. Whether or not their air commanders had read Douhet – and they probably had not – they were not backward in proposing that mighty fleets of aircraft, each propelled by four engines and each carrying perhaps three to five tons of explosive, could win the war against the Axis almost unaided. In the event their claims proved exaggerated; once they had been joined with radar, aircraft proved that they could fight quite as effectively on the defense as on the offense. Whether, given the technological realities of World War II, a better way of overcoming Germany and Japan than bombing their cities could have been found remains in dispute to the present day.[145] What is not in dispute is that some 2.5 million tons of bombs were dropped by the US Air Force and Royal Air Force together. When Allied troops entered German towns in 1945, they found them abandoned even by the birds.

Meanwhile, in an attempt to discover even more effective ways of demolishing each other, states had started mobilizing science for the purpose; instead of being left to private initiative, as had usually been the case before 1914, the process of scientific-technological invention itself was conscripted and put at the disposal of the state.[146] During World

---

[144] K. L. Privatsky, "Mobility Versus Sustainability," *Military Review*, 67, 1, 1987, pp. 48–61.

[145] The most recent contribution to the debate is R. Overy, "World War II: The Bombing of Germany," in A. Stephens, ed., *The War in the Air 1941–1945* (Fairbairn: Air Power Studies Centre, 1995), pp. 113–40.

[146] See W. H. McNeill, *The Pursuit of Power: Technology, Armed Force and Society Since AD 1000* (London: Weidenfeld and Nicolson, 1982), pp. 170–4.

War II the scale of the effort was expanded, to the point that tens of thousands of scientists were set to work full-time in order to develop better weapons and incidentally, find out what the enemy might have had up his sleeve. Military-technological progress, which until the middle of the nineteenth century could usually be measured in decades, was accelerated until it took only a few years or even months to design a new weapons system and bring it into operation. For example, the German Messerschmidt 109 and British Spitfire fighters both made their debut in 1938–9. By 1944–5 the former had gone through nine model changes, the latter through fourteen, at which point both were replaced by new, even more powerful types.[147] This experience was entirely typical. A 1940-vintage tank did not stand the slightest chance against one produced only two or three years later, while the aircraft carriers with which the US navy, for one, ended the war were about twice as large as the ones with which it entered it.

The state's greatest triumph was, however, yet to come. Between 1939 and 1945 somewhere between 40 and 60 million people were killed with the aid of conventional arms; still not content with this, states continued the search for more powerful weapons. In secret desert locations, protected by miles upon miles of barbed wire, the best minds were concentrated, provided with unlimited funds, and set to work. In 1938 Otto Hahn in Berlin became the first to split the atom. The significance of the discovery having been explained to him by his former assistant, Lise Meitner, within two years articles on nuclear physics had disappeared from the international scientific literature – a clear sign that the defense establishments of the most powerful states had taken over and that not even the most basic secrets of the universe were any more safe from their clutches.[148] Such was the magnitude of the task that it could be accomplished only by the state, and then by the largest and most powerful state of all. On the other hand, the speed with which it was accomplished is astonishing, thus providing yet another proof of what the state could really do once it had made up its mind. Less than three years passed from the appointment of General Leslie Groves, an excellent organizer hitherto known mainly for his mania about secrecy, to head the Manhattan Project to the detonation of the first bomb at Los Alamos.[149] On the sixth of August 1945, a fine summer day, a single heavy bomber appeared over Hiroshima and dropped a single bomb. Moments later the sky was torn

---

[147] Details in E. Angelucci, *The Rand McNally Encyclopaedia of Military Aircraft, 1914 to the Present* (New York: Gallery Books, 1990), pp. 185–6.

[148] F. Rhodes, *The Making of the Atomic Bomb* (New York: Simon and Schuster, 1988), is the best account of the Manhattan Project.

[149] See his firsthand account in *Now It Can Be Told* (New York: Harper and Row, 1962).

open. A thousand suns shone, 75,000 or so people lay dead or dying, and total war, which the states of this world had spent three centuries perfecting, abolished itself.

The apotheosis of the state

Born in sin, the bastard offspring of declining autocracy and bureaucracy run amok, the state is a giant wielded by pygmies.[150] Considered as individuals, bureaucrats, even the highest-positioned among them, may be mild, harmless, and somewhat self-effacing people; but collectively they have created a monster whose power far outstrips that of the mightiest empires of old. One reason for this is because, unlike all previous ruling groups, they do not have to pay the expenses of government out of their own pockets. On the contrary, they draw their nourishment from it; the rooms in which they meet, the desks at which they sit, and the computers with which they (nowadays) work are all government-provided. Another is that, again unlike most previous ruling groups, they operate according to fixed regulations and procedures without either anger or passion – although, to be sure, such as favor their own interests above all. But the most important reason is because they, unlike Caligula or Genghis Khan, e.g., possess a collective personality which makes them immortal. By merely waiting, the state can easily outlast any "natural persons" who dare cross its path. Hence ideally it should be able to rule its subjects by the buttocks rather than the fists – not that it has often been reluctant to use the latter, either.

At the time it first saw the light of day the state was comparatively small and weak, even to the point where megalomaniac rulers could sometimes look down on it and claim that it was identical with their own persons. From then on, however, it grew and grew. Stage by stage it separated itself from, and raised itself above, civil society. As it did so, it commissioned maps and used them to make political statements about itself; it built up an infrastructure of "statistical" information; it increased taxes, and, which is perhaps more important, concentrated them in its own hands. To complete its dominance, it set up police and security forces, prisons, armed forces, and specialized organs responsible for looking after education and welfare – all of which, as Max Weber noted, were themselves bureaucratic institutions *par excellence* and in some ways simply reflected the mechanism which they served.

Beginning in Britain during the last years of the eighteenth century, one

---

[150] The phrase is from H. de Balzac, *Bureaucracy* (Boston: Roberts, 1898; translation of *Les employées*, 1836), p. 84.

state after another also felt strong enough to spread its wings over the most important commodity of all, i.e., money. To be sure, the early attempts were hesitant and led to at least one spectacular bankruptcy; but after 1800 the switch from bullion toward state-issued paper imprinted with the picture of the sovereign proved unstoppable. During the nineteenth century most states still maintained the link between money and precious metal. Once World Wars I and II had caused that link to be severed and money had become simply so much paper, though, states used the need to fight other states as the excuse for dominating the economy directly by means of their own laws, regulations, and fiats. By and large, the process whereby the meaning of money was transformed took place not simply in this state or that but was very much part of the development of the state as such. From Washington DC, through London and Paris, and Rome and Berlin, all the way to Moscow and Tokyo, the principles were the same. The main difference between "free" and totalitarian states consisted in the fact that the former chose their rulers by democratic elections; although, as Hitler once pointed out, judging by his own popularity, the Nazi regime may have been the most democratic in history.[151] Hence they did not have to employ the instruments of coercion at their disposal quite as ruthlessly, or to the same extent, as the latter.

Initially the state was conceived as a mere instrument for imposing law and order: a body, made up of institutions and laws and people who served in them and carried them out, which would run like a machine in performing its task. However, almost exactly midway in its development between 1648 and 1945, it came across the forces of nationalism which, until then, had developed almost independently of it and sometimes against it. The seventeenth- and eighteenth-century state had demanded no special affection on the part of its subjects, provided only its decrees were obeyed and its demands for money and manpower met; but now it could draw on nationalism in order to fill its emptiness and provide itself with ethical content. As conceived by Rousseau, Herder, and the rest, nationalism – if that is the proper word – had been a harmless preference for one's native country, its language, its customs, its modes of dress, and its festivals; once it had been adopted by the state, it became aggressive and bellicose. Digesting the stolen spiritual goods, the state turned itself from a means into an end and from an end into a god. Whether it lived in peace with them or fought against them, that god was usually quite prepared to respect the rights of other gods like itself to a sovereign existence – witness the elaborate courtesies that rulers and diplomats,

---

[151] Speer, *Errinerungen*, p. 79.

often even soldiers, extended to each other even in wartime (when Napoleon III was captured at Sedan in 1870, not only did he come to no harm, but he was allowed to go free). But from its subjects it demanded absolute loyalty even unto death, inflicting savage punishment on them if they dared disobey or evade service, a double standard which shows what it *really* thought of them.

Protected and often abetted by the state, modern science and modern technology were able to flourish as never before. As noted above, had it not been for printed forms on the one hand and gunpowder on the other, the state could never have seen the light of day. Later both Hobbes, as the person who really invented the state, and his fellow English political scientist, James Harrington, took a keen interest in science and resorted to scientific models as underpinnings for the political constructs they had in mind.[152] Tackling the problem from the opposite direction, Francis Bacon in *New Atlantis* (1637) described an imaginary state which systematically harnessed science to increase its own power. While jealously keeping its own secrets, the state dispatched sleuths to ferret out new discoveries from all over the world; as a result, not the least of their achievements were cannon capable of firing balls further, and with greater force, than anything that existed until then. Bacon's ideas caught on rapidly, as is shown by the fact that forty years had not yet passed since his death before all the most important European monarchs had established Academies of Science, one of whose main functions was to investigate problems and come up with inventions useful for the state.[153] By the beginning of the eighteenth century, the notion that science could be used to increase the power of the state had even reached backward Russia in the person of Peter the Great.[154]

These, however, were just the beginnings. Not only did the state use science and technology to enhance its military capabilities for combating other states, but the same devices also reinforced its grip on every inch of territory and the life of every individual. Thus, from about 1850 on, the governments of France, Prussia (later Germany), Piedmont (later Italy), and Canada all systematically promoted the construction of railways with the objective of linking their various provinces with each other and bringing them under central control.[155] In the United States, it was

[152] For Harrington, see B. I. Cohen, "Harrington and Harvey: A Theory of the State Based on the New Physiology," *Journal of the History of Ideas*, 55, 2, 1994, pp. 187–210.

[153] See R. Briggs, "The Académie royale des sciences and the Pursuit of Utility," *Past and Present*, 131, 1991, pp. 38–88; and, in general, P. Carroll, "Science Power, Bodies: The Mobilization of Nature as State Formation," *Journal of Historical Sociology*, 9, 2, 1996, pp. 139–67.

[154] A. J. Rieber, "Politics and Technology in Eighteenth-Century Russia," *Science in Context*, 8, 2, 1995, pp. 341–68.

primarily political considerations which led to the construction of the north–south lines linking the midwest with the Gulf of Mexico as well as the east–west network, with the result, for example, that almost a generation had to pass before the transcontinental railway began to run more than one train a week and was able to show a profit. In Russia, as a comparative newcomer to the world of states,[156] so close was the link between the railways and the government which financed them that, to quote Lenin, "when the trains stop that will be the end."[157] Limiting ourselves to those countries which have been made the subject of detailed research, France, Russia, Japan, Argentina, and Australia all deliberately exploited the telegraph for the same purpose – even if, as happened in the first-named, the price to be paid for imposing a state monopoly over the field of telecommunications was technological backwardness.[158]

Finally, the transformation of the state into a god on earth both presupposed the existence of the popular press and helped the latter find a focus for its interests. This is not the place to trace the increase in readership that was brought about by the combination of improved technology with greater literacy. Suffice it to say that, in Britain alone, the annual number of newspapers sold increased from 7.5 million in 1753 to 25 million in 1826;[159] and this was before further advances which took place during the late nineteenth century brought circulation to millions *per day*. In Britain as in most other countries, what national papers existed were invariably based in the capital. Even where governments did not seek to keep them in their own hands, as was in the case of Russia in particular,[160] the outcome was to create an entire class of "public," meaning state-related, affairs which previously had concerned but a small minority and to impose them on the consciousness of the masses. The role of the press in fanning, for example, the Crimean War, the scramble for Africa, and the Anglo-German naval race has been amply documented. In addition, it was capable of manufacturing events out of nonevents as when the assassination of President Garfield made "all the English

[155] M. Merger, "Les chemins de fer italiens: leur construction et leurs effets," *Histoire, Economie et Société*, 11, 1, 1992, pp. 109–20; B. Mazlish, ed., *The Railroad and the Space Program: An Exploration in Historical Analogy* (Cambridge, MA: MIT Press, 1965), pp. 29–30.   [156] See below, ch. 5, "Toward Eastern Europe," pp. 264–81.

[157] On the history of Russia's railways, see V. Y. Larechev, "The Trend Towards State Monopoly in Pre-Revolutionary Russia's Railways," *Journal of Transport History*, 6, 2, 1985, pp. 37–47; the Lenin quote is from J. N. Westwood, *A History of Russian Railways* (London: Allen and Unwin, 1964), p. 7.

[158] P. Grisset, "L'état et les télécommunications internationales au début du XXe siècle en France: un monopole stérile," *Histoire, Economie et Société*, 6, 2, 1987, pp. 181–207.

[159] Figures are from G. A. Cranfield, *The Press and Society: From Caxton to Northcliffe* (London: Longman, 1978), p. 139.

[160] L. Reynolds, "Autocratic Journalism: The Case of the St. Petersburg Telegraphic Agency," *Slavic Review*, 49, 1, 1990, pp. 48–57.

race" mourn a person of whose very existence they may previously have been unaware.[161] By the time of World War I, another US president, Woodrow Wilson, was meeting the press twice a week – as good an indication as any of its ability to make public life revolve around the state.

In return for fostering technological development which made possible a much-augmented standard of living the state exacted protection money. Essentially it consisted of unlimited blood and treasure, a development which climaxed during the first half of the twentieth century. Reveling in total war, the state demanded and obtained sacrifice on a scale which, had they been able to imagine it, would have made even the old Aztec gods blanch. Nor were the differences between the "totalitarian" and "democratic" countries as great as people at the time liked to believe. Other things being equal, those states whose regimes were most efficient in squeezing the last ounce of marrow out of their citizens' bones went on to victory, whereas those which were smaller or less successful in performing this praiseworthy task went down to defeat. As usual the price was paid by the citizens, not by the state *per se*. In the defeated countries a few leaders lost their heads, whether with or without a trial; they were, in any case, dispensable, as is proved by the fact that, without exception, the states in question had risen out of the ashes and were back on their feet within less than five years after the largest war in history had ended. The stage was set for the state's Indian summer – one last shining rise in its power before its inevitable decline. Before we can turn to that story, however, it is necessary to explain how the state spread from Europe, where it originated, to the remaining areas of the globe.

[161] M. Sewell, "'All the English Race is in Mourning': The Assassination of President Garfield and Anglo-American Relations," *Historical Journal*, 34, 3, 1991, pp. 665–86.

5 The spread of the state: 1696 to 1975

The earliest political units deserving to be called states were France, Spain, Portugal, Britain, the countries composing the Holy Roman Empire and Scandinavia, and the Netherlands. During the first century or so of their existence all of these combined occupied only between 2 and 3 percent of the earth's surface: to be precise, 1,450,000 square miles out of a global land mass of 57,000,0000. All other parts of the world continued to be inhabited, as they had been since time immemorial, by tribes without rulers, more or less centralized chiefdoms, and empires of various sizes and descriptions. Here and there, as along the East African coast and also in parts of what are today Malaysia and Indonesia, history points to the existence of city-states too sophisticated to be called chiefdoms and not subject to larger empires. However, there were apparently none that were run on nonproprietary, democratic lines like those of ancient Greece and Rome.

This much granted, the spread of the state into other continents and its victory over other polities may be studied in one of three ways. The first would be to proceed chronologically without regard to location: in other words, to follow the march first of imperialism and then of decolonization as it took place. The second would be to proceed geographically: i.e., divide the world into various regions and trace the way each one separately came to be divided into, and ruled by, states. The third would be to look at the *methods* whereby states developed in regions outside Western Europe – whether by imitation, as in Japan from the middle of the nineteenth century on, or by conquest and subsequent liberation, as in most other places, or by some combination of the two. Insofar as those methods were largely dictated by the degree that civilization – including, not least, political civilization – had developed in each region before it was touched by the state, obviously these paths are interrelated. What follows here represents a compromise between all three.

Toward Eastern Europe

The first country other than the ones just listed to acquire a state, or something like it, was Russia. Its construction got under way when Peter I the Great assumed effective power; conversely, those regions which did not prove capable of developing states soon found themselves eclipsed and overtaken by their neighbors. The story to be told in this section is, accordingly, that of Russia on the one hand and of Poland on the other. With the aid of their contrasting fates, the importance of political modernization may be illustrated.

Russia during the sixteenth and seventeenth centuries is perhaps best characterized as a developing patrimonial empire ruled by a tsar whose position, thanks to the conquest of new land, was becoming increasingly absolute.[1] He was surrounded by a hereditary nobility which drew its political and economic power from the lands that it occupied, whether as allodial, hereditary estates, known as *votchiny*, or in the form of the feudal fiefs or *pomest'i* which began to be created under Ivan III from the 1470s on. As in other countries, the subject population was overwhelmingly rural. But whereas in most of Europe west of the Elbe this population was steadily moving toward ownership over the land and greater personal liberty, in Russia development proceeded in the opposite direction. During the first half of the seventeenth century whatever freedom of movement the serfs still possessed was gradually taken away; those who gave shelter to fugitives could be made to pay compensation to the owner. Soon a situation was created in which serfs could be bought, sold, and rented out as individuals or in groups with or without the lands on which they lived and worked.

The opening of a series of great wars against more developed countries to the west – first Poland and then Sweden – from 1632 on increased the tsar's dependence on his nobility and led to the *Sobornoe ulozhenie* of 1649.[2] Given the immensity of the trackless Russian wastes and the frequent absence of navigable rivers, the development of towns had always been slow. Now, in an attempt to keep the serfs from escaping, their segregation from the countryside was completed and the towns were subjected to tighter controls than ever before. Deprived of fresh manpower, towns languished, with the result that even as late as 1815 they accounted for only some 4 percent of the total population.[3] The serfs

---

[1] The best analysis of Russian patrimonialism is R. Pipes, *Russia Under the Old Regime* (Harmondsworth, UK: Penguin Books, 1974), esp. pp. 52–4, 69–70, 77–9.

[2] For the main provisions of the *ulozhenie*, see R. E. F. Smith, *The Enserfment of the Russian Peasantry* (Cambridge: Cambridge University Press, 1968), pp. 141–52.

[3] For this and other figures on Russia's population, see J. P. LeDonne, *Absolutism and Ruling Class: The Formation of the Russian Political Order 1700–1825* (New York: Oxford University Press, 1991), ch. 2.

themselves, left to be ruled by their owners with little or no supervision from above, fell into four groups. Perhaps 10 percent were owned by the church. Collectively the nobility owned around 40 percent, whereas the imperial family accounted for another 5 or 10 percent depending on the period in question. The one exception to private ownership, and one whose importance tended to grow as time went on, was formed by the *kazennye* – literally, "peasants of the treasury" – who composed perhaps one-third of the total. Concentrated mainly in the north and south, they lived mostly on recently conquered lands, with the result that, instead of being incorporated directly into the tsar's domains, they became subject to "public" ownership.

Thus the vast majority of the country's population (perhaps 90 percent) was reduced to a condition little better than that of chattel slaves. Except when they were sold or banished (in theory landowners were forbidden to kill their serfs; banishment therefore served as an equivalent to a death sentence), they could expect to live and die on their masters' estates. Whatever development of the state that could have taken place in Russia was thereby arrested for over two centuries. Government failed to acquire a persona of its own, which is the essence of what took place elsewhere; instead the country was run by a partnership between the tsar, who to the middle of the nineteenth century was able to speak of his "fatherly solicitude," and the nobility. The latter composed perhaps 0.5 of the total population and only they were considered eligible for any kind of position in the government, whether civilian, military, or ecclesiastical. Priests and well-to-do townsmen alone exempted, the remaining members of the population did not have any legal persona at all.

Having succeeded in making half of Russia's population into their personal property, the nobility by and large allowed itself to be controlled by the tsar – though not without the occasional revolt by boyars who refused to see that the world around them was changing. An important early step was taken in 1682 when Tsar Theodore II ceremoniously burnt the Books of Precedence in which the nobility's traditional titles had been recorded, thus establishing his own freedom to employ them as he saw fit. Between 1712 and 1714 the work of enserfment was completed by Peter the Great. The old distinction between *votchiny* and *pomest'i* was abolished. From now on, all land was to be held conditionally and in return for service, so that the very word for noble was replaced by *dvorianin* or imperial servitor.[4] A whole series of new titles such as count and baron were imported from the West. Depending on the number of serfs they possessed, nobles were divided into grades ranking from one (the highest) to fourteen. The six upper ones were hereditary, the remainder merely

---

[4] For a brief account of these reforms, see E. V. Anisimov, *The Reforms of Peter the Great: Progress Through Coercion in Russia* (Armonk, NY: Sharpe, 1993), pp. 186–93.

personal. A nobleman could serve the tsar by entering into one out of four distinct hierarchies, i.e., the army, navy (newly created by Peter), the civilian administration, and the court. Promotion from one rank to another was delegated at the lower levels but further up it was strictly controlled from the top. In practice it goes without saying that not even a genius of the caliber of Peter I could supervise every member of a machine which, toward the end of his reign, was made up of 5,000 officers, besides an unknown number of civilian bureaucrats. Hence the system amounted to a vast network of patronage shot through, from top to bottom, with corruption.

The creation of a system whereby all noble titles were socially and etymologically derived from the court also enabled Peter to do away with the old boyar's council, or duma, as the highest institution in the realm. Its place was taken by an appointed senate which concentrated judicial, administrative, and legal-consultative functions in its own hands. Nine colleges, or boards, each one under a president and bearing collective responsibility to the senate, carried the burden of government work at the highest level. Below them the country was divided into eight administrative gubernias or regions; each of which was later divided into provinces and districts. A peculiarity of the system was that the existing maze of *prikazy*, or agencies, run from Moscow and responsible for a variety of often conflicting functions, was not abolished; however, gradually they and their staffs were taken over by the new governors. The latter transmitted the tsar's power throughout an empire which, by West European standards, was already inconceivably large (6,500,000 square miles in 1700) if so sparsely populated that entire regions were little better than wilderness.

Aided by this administrative system, Peter was able to impose new taxes. The old land tax was replaced by capitation, or poll tax (first on households, then on individuals) and quitrent. In contrast to the West, a commercially underdeveloped economy offered few opportunities for indirect taxation; they were, however, imposed both on salt and on that other indispensable prerequisite of Russian life, vodka. Then there were *corvées* and, to complete the burden, payments in kind. Government officials as well as troops in transit had to be quartered and fed, and transportation in the form of horses and carts provided for them. As in other old regime countries, the nobility and the upper grades of the church were exempt from all but some indirect taxes. The rest of the population, including also the townspeople, paid and paid: as an imperial decree put it, not even the village idiot, the blind, the badly crippled, and the senile were to be considered exempt. The average burden per serf is said to have grown five times over between 1700 and 1708, even as the average size of their holdings fell. And this before we add the fees which the various *prikazy* continued to demand in return for services rendered and grievances looked into.

By 1725, government expenditure, which in 1700 had stood at 3.5 million rubles, had reached almost 10 million. Much of this was spent by Peter to build a new capital, and not a cheap one either; the site selected was marshy and before building could begin had to be drained by engineers especially imported for the purpose from Holland. However, the bulk of the money was used to fund a military machine which, during his reign, increased its size from the low tens of thousands to about 200,000 men and was thus on par with those of other major countries. These, moreover, were Western-style forces. Beginning already around 1640 the old *pomest'e* cavalry, designed for fighting the Tatars and other semi-nomadic peoples, had been giving way to other troops. First to appear on the scene were the *strel'tsy* or palace guards. Having risen in rebellion in 1698, they were forcibly suppressed and their leaders executed, some by Peter's own hands, and were replaced by a regular army consisting of disciplined infantry, cavalry, and artillery regiments.[5] They were commanded by members of the nobility – though individual noblemen could be found serving in the ranks as well – and manned by serfs who were called up on the basis of so many per hundred persons in each village and usually served until they died by combat or disease. The necessary arms and equipment were manufactured in government-owned factories that began to be established around the middle of the seventeenth century and were greatly expanded during Peter's reign. Managed by foreign experts with a labor force consisting of conscripted serfs, throughout the eighteenth century they provided the army with equipment roughly as good as that of its Western opposite numbers.

A few years before his death Peter also took the last step toward absolute government by bringing the church under his own control. Always on the lookout for additional revenue, the tsar had appointed no successor when Patriarch Adrian died in October 1700. An "Overseer" by the name of Yavorsky was, indeed, selected; but real power was in the hands of the newly established Monastery Bureau whose head, Ivan Mushin-Pushkin, was not a clergyman but a secular nobleman. While these measures enabled Peter to siphon off a considerable part of the church's wealth during what proved to be a twenty-year interim period, it still remained to put the reform on a regular footing. This was made the task of Feofan Prokopovich, previously archbishop of Pskov and an exceptionally well-educated person, who in 1718 replaced Mushin-

---

[5] For the rise of the Russian army, see R. Hellie, *Enserfment and Military Change in Muscovy* (Chicago: University of Chicago Press, 1971), pp. 151ff.

Pushkin as overseer and from now on worked hand in hand with Peter himself.

In 1721 Feofan published his *Spiritual Regulation*, a document which for the next two centuries was to form the bedrock of the Russian Orthodox Church.[6] The situation whereby "simple hearts" considered the patriarch co-equal with the tsar had become intolerable and had to be remedied. To correct it the patriarchate itself was abolished – if one anecdote is to be believed at the point of a steel dagger wielded by Peter, who was, at six and a half feet, a formidable threat. Its place was taken by a collective leadership in the form of the Most Holy All-Ruling Synod with a standing equal to that of the senate. Though the synod itself was made up of clergymen, real power was now in the hands of a layman carrying the title of *ober-prokuror* – in this case, as in others, importing foreign terms into Russia's developing bureaucracy had interesting results. To emphasize their standing as government officials the members of the synod were paid salaries, though this formed only a small part of their income, as was the case of other government officials of equivalent rank. The church's lower members lost their tax-exempt status. Numerous new prayers were introduced to celebrate Russian victories and the so-called table holidays invented to commemorate important events in the tsar's life; indeed, so close was the relationship between empire and official religion that, until the second half of the nineteenth century, leaving the state religion constituted a criminal offense.

At the time Peter died in 1725, a political entity that, for lack of a better name, can only be called an autocratic empire was in place. Unlike contemporary states, it did not possess a civil society. As the governor of St. Petersburg noted in 1718, Russia at the time did not even have a term corresponding to the French assembly. Explaining the meaning of "an unsupervised meeting" to the capital's inhabitants proved a matter of considerable difficulty; and indeed, it was expected that such meetings would take place only occasionally. So small was the number of books in circulation that Peter personally censored each one that was published, nor were there any printing presses in existence except for the three government-owned ones.[7] Not that it mattered, for well over 90 percent of the population consisted of downtrodden, illiterate serfs. So far were they from forming "society" that when one or another was killed his death was often treated as a civil question, to be settled not by putting the

---

[6] See A. V. Muller, ed., *The Spiritual Regulation of Peter the Great* (Seattle: University of Washington Press, 1972). The reforms as a whole are discussed in J. Cracraft, *The Church Reform of Peter the Great* (London: Macmillan, 1971).

[7] See G. Marker, *Publishing, Printing and the Origin of Intellectual Life in Russia 1700–1800* (Princeton: Princeton University Press, 1985), p. 77.

murderer on trial but by compensating the owner for the loss suffered. With the partial exception of a tiny class of merchants, themselves organized into guilds that carried administrative burdens as well as fiscal ones,[8] whoever was not a serf was *ipso facto* a secular or ecclesiastical government official. Peter III, at a later date, even tried to force officials to wear uniform, but this met with resistance and had to be abandoned.

As we saw, the emergence of the state in other countries owed much to the internal cohesion and discipline of their rising civil services. The first forms of government, written down by Peter personally and modeled upon the Swedish ones, were laid down in 1718–19. Toward the end of the eighteenth century the Russian administration, like that of other states, was starting to develop regular procedures which governed entrance, remuneration, promotion, and similar matters.[9] However, the Russian administration operated behind closed doors. Affairs which in other countries were discussed freely enough were treated as state secrets – a tradition which was maintained throughout the tsarist period, carried on into the Soviet Union that succeeded it, and is only now being dismantled. This as well as the arbitrary tradition emanating from the emperor down – as late as 1850, an old regulation which authorized officials to dismiss their subordinates without having to give a reason was reaffirmed – prevented the one most important element of the modern state, i.e., its bureaucratic *esprit de corps*, from emerging. Where it did emerge it was aimed not so much at serving a nonexistent state as at operating like a society of thieves and fleecing the people, if possible with the tsar's consent but if necessary behind his back. Beginning already with Peter the Great it sometimes pleased Russian tsars to present themselves as (God-appointed, to be sure) stewards of the people for whose welfare, both physical and spiritual, they carried the responsibility. However, the accession of each new one usually served as an occasion to reconfirm the "autocratic" nature of the regime – to remove all doubt, Alexander I in 1799 even enacted a special law which put the entire imperial family outside, and above, the normal framework of civil and public law. For these emperors to follow Frederick II and assume the role of a servant of an impersonal state would have been logically absurd even if this idea had occurred to anybody.

Russia's comparative backwardness during this period did not prevent it from becoming an increasingly prominent actor in the international system, albeit one that was regarded as barbaric by most of the rest. Possessed of a modern bureaucracy, a modern army, and modern arms, the tsar proved more than a match for his enemies to the south and east,

---

[8] For details on the merchant, or *posad*, estate, see J. Michael Hittle, *The Service City: State and Townsmen in Russia, 1600–1800* (Cambridge, MA: Harvard University Press, 1979), pp. 97–167.   [9] See Pipes, *Russia Under the Old Regime*, pp. 285–6.

i.e., the Turkish and Persian empires and the various Tatar khanates. The former two lost huge tracts of territory and were to continue to do so right up to the last years of the nineteenth century. The latter were reduced to the status of third-class opponents and protected, if at all, from Russian power mainly by distance, terrain, and the simple fact that they possessed nothing that the tsar and his nobles, now slowly adopting Western ways, considered worth having. In the West, too, Russian power made itself felt. The victory won by Peter himself over Sweden's Charles XII does not need recounting. The next decade saw Russian forces successfully engaging the Poles over Belarus; when the Seven Years War broke out in 1756, its forces found themselves fighting a Central European state, i.e., Prussia, for the first time. Throughout the 1770s and 1780s Russian strength in Europe continued to grow, mainly at the expense of Poland.

The climax of these developments was reached in the years after 1792. Having gained the lion's share in the third and final partition of Poland, Russia sent its forces to join the various coalitions which arrayed themselves against Revolutionary France; soon they found themselves operating in places as far from home as Switzerland and the Adriatic. Their role grew even larger from 1806 on when Napoleon's victories over Austria and Prussia left Tsar Alexander I as his only opponent besides Britain. Reflecting the French triumph at the Battle of Friedland in particular, the Treaty of Tilsit (1807) all but excluded Russia from Poland. However, it did not prove lasting: within five years of its signature Russia was being subjected to a massive French invasion. While the details of the campaign do not concern us here, its importance in breaking the power of the Grande armée is a matter of record – of a force of 600,000, less than a third ultimately returned. Another two years passed and the Russian army, having played a key role in winning the Battle of Leipzig, entered Paris. At the Congress of Vienna, Alexander played the role of a *primus inter pares*. Between one dance and the next, he and his fellow rulers proceeded to dictate the fate of Europe.

At this time the Petrine political – if that is indeed the correct term – system was still basically intact. To be sure, the eighteenth century had seen some changes. Already Empresses Anne (1730–40) and Elizabeth (1741–61) had raised the age at which nobles had to enter imperial service, originally fixed at fourteen, to twenty-five; in 1762 obligatory service was abolished by Peter III. In 1782–5 Catherine II ended conditional ownership over estates, turning them into private property, including also the right to will them to whomever the owner chose instead of to the oldest male, as previously. With many landowners choosing to lead an absentee life in Moscow and St. Petersburg, there began to appear a class of people who, however few they might be relative to the total population, were neither serfs nor officials nor officers nor ecclesiastics: in short, the nucleus of a civil society. Among this elite, liberal ideas from the West, their absorption made all the easier by the fact that Peter and his successors had compelled some of their subjects to study abroad, began percolating. After 1771 permission was even given for people to publish and read books other than government-produced ones, though none that had not been censored in advance. Both Catherine II and Alexander I at the beginning of their respective reigns played with liberalism,[10] but both soon found out that to do so was to put the regime at risk. The upshot of the "one step forward, two steps back" game played by the government was the Decembrist Revolt of 1825 mounted by aristocratic officers who had been exposed to French ideas. Failing to take hold, it was brutally suppressed by troops loyal to the tsar's brother, Prince Nicholas Pavlovich.[11] Soon afterwards he ascended the throne as Nicholas I, thus confirming the rule of the knout for another generation.

From then until the end of the reign Russia was put on hold, so to speak. While the West was undergoing the tremendous upheaval euphemistically known as industrialization, which in turn led to repeated outbreaks of revolutionary violence in 1830 and 1848–9, social and economic change in the gigantic empire to the east proceeded at a glacial pace. Its ruler, Nicholas I, was almost as tall as his illustrious ancestor; but there the resemblance ends. Though still undergoverned by Western standards, Russia's bureaucracy was expanding.[12] So were the regulations that governed its behavior: in the Code of Law of 1832 they occupied no fewer than 869 paragraphs, many of them concerned with the forms of deference to be shown by *dvoriane* of inferior rank to their superiors. For the first time a line was drawn between offenses directed against the tsar's person and those which concerned state employees – a mixed blessing, as Nicholas himself pointed out when he distinguished between the German nobility, which served "the state," and the Russian one, which served "us."[13] In 1837 a Ministry of State Domains was created so that court officials were no longer *ex officio* ministers and state revenue was no longer the same as the emperor's personal income. In this way Russia was brought to the point which, in England, for example, had been reached between 150 and 300 years earlier.

[10] On Catherine's attempts to do so in particular, see M. Raeff, *The Well-Ordered Police State: Social and Institutional Change Through Law in the Germanies and Russia, 1600–1800* (New Haven, CT: Yale University Press, 1983), pp. 235ff.

[11] See A. B. Ulam, *Russia's Failed Revolutions: From the Decembrists to the Dissidents* (London: Weidenfeld and Nicolson, 1981), pp. 3–65.

[12] In the 1830s Russia had 1.3 officials per 1,000 inhabitants, Britain 4.1, and France 4.8: S. Frederick Starr, *Decentralization and Self-Government in Russia, 1830–1870* (Princeton: Princeton University Press, 1972), p. 48.   [13] Quoted in Lincoln, *Nicholas I*, p. 52.

In time these reforms might have led to autonomy and the emergence of a state – known in Russian as *obshchestvo*, an eighteenth-century neologism – separate from the person of the ruler. Nicholas, however, recognized the threat. As individuals, the members of the aristocracy were powerless; as army officers and administrative officials they represented a danger. By setting up a new organ of personal government known, appropriately enough, as His Majesty's Own Chancery and not subject to any control except his own, he nipped this threat in the bud. Internal controls were tightened, also by the construction of a political police apparatus under one of his own *aides-de-camp* as related in a previous section. These measures enabled Nicholas to act as Europe's gendarme, sending troops to suppress democracy and nationalism – in this period, they usually marched hand in hand – wherever they appeared. The empire also continued to acquire new territories, mainly at the expense of the Turks who were being defeated once every generation on the average. The campaign of 1829 brought Russian troops all the way to the gates of Constantinople where only a combination of plague and protests on the part of the powers obliged them to withdraw. As the Battle of Sinope (1853) was to show, by mid-century the tsar's navy was capable of blasting the Ottoman fleet out of the water any time it chose to do so.

Behind the imposing facade of the so-called Nicholas system, the structure whose foundations had been so well laid by Peter the Great was starting to crack. In Britain, the first mechanized spinning machines began operating around 1760; from the 1830s on Western economic and technical growth – itself made possible by the framework which the state provided – far outstripped that which even the most powerful command structure in history could achieve. The production of power, iron, and coal soared. With them came better communications, better transport, and, perhaps most important of all, the kind of sustained technological progress that made running forward as fast as possible a condition for keeping up: in Britain, e.g., the number of new patents registered each year increased twenty times over between 1650 and 1850.[14] Largely deprived of these advantages, Russia wallowed in its own backwardness more than ever – between 1830 and 1860 its GNP, which at the earlier date had accounted for 24 percent of that of the leading five European powers combined, declined to less than 20 percent.[15] By 1850 Britain was producing 2 million tons of pig iron a year, France, 400,000 tons, and

[14] H. van der Wee, *De economische ontwikkeling van Europa 950–1950* (Louvain: Acco, 1950), p. 133.
[15] Calculation based on P. Kennedy, *The Rise and Fall of the Great Powers* (New York: Vintage Books, 1987), p. 171, table 9. For more figures on Russia's economic position *vis-à-vis* the remaining powers during this period, see *ibid.*, p. 149, tables 6 and 7.

Russia, with a population almost as large as that of both combined, a mere 227,000.[16] The results became painfully evident during the Crimean War (1854–6). "The war that refused to boil," as it has been called, saw British and French troops operating at the end of a long maritime line of communications; in the person of Lord Raglan it was also commanded by some of the worst blunderers in the whole of military history. Yet even so the allies were able to hold off, and ultimately defeat, the forces of Holy Russia on the latter's own soil, a feat which they crowned by storming Sevastopol. For the tsar's empire the writing was on the wall – not only were the Western troops better armed than the soldiers of Holy Russia but the latter's organization, transportation, and supply systems had all failed.[17] Russia had either to reform, or to turn into the next Turkey and be divided among the other powers.

With the accession of Alexander II – incidentally the first Russian ruler in 130 years to occupy the throne without having to stage a coup of some sort – the time for change arrived. Beginning with Catherine the Great, various Russian rulers had questioned whether the system whereby the great majority of the population were the personal property of a small minority was, in fact, compatible with the existence of a modern state and contemplated the abolition of serfdom.[18] Catherine herself had moved no fewer than 20,000 villages out of the church's domain and into that of the treasury; her successors made timid attempts to cut back the number of those in private ownership, whether by refusing to assign new lands to individuals or by passing legislation that facilitated emancipation.[19] Still, in the end she, her son, and her two grandsons all shrank back in the face of expected opposition on the part of the *dvoriane*, and it was only when the Crimean War was over that the die was finally cast. With the separation of the judiciary from the executive in 1861–4 arbitrary government was brought to an end in at least one crucial respect. A uniform code of law and a system of independent courts, staffed by lifelong judges whose decisions not even the tsar could overturn, were established – reforms that brought Russia to the point that Prussia, for example, had reached between about 1760 and the publication of the *Allgemeines Landesrecht* in 1795. Most important of all, over 40 million serfs were emancipated

---

[16] For more detailed figures, see J. Blackwell, *The Beginnings of Russian Industrialization* (Princeton: Princeton University Press, 1968).

[17] See J. S. Curtis, *Russia's Crimean War* (Durham, NC: Duke University Press, 1979), for the details.

[18] See J. G. Eisen and G. H. Markel, "The Question of Serfdom: Catherine II, the Russian Debate and the View from the Baltic Periphery," in R. Bartlett, ed., *Russia and the Enlightenment* (London: Macmillan, 1990), pp. 125–42.

[19] On the origins of the reforms that led to the liberation of the serfs, see R. A. Zaionchovsky, *The Abolition of Serfdom in Russia* (Gulf Breeze, FL: International Academic Press, 1978), pp. 4–81.

either from private ownership or from that of the crown. For the first time they were given an independent legal persona, including the right to own property.

To be sure, there were limits to how far even Alexander II was prepared to go. Though subject to judiciary review in ordinary matters, the Third Department – which changed its name to the Department of Political Affairs – retained the right to isolate and banish persons considered dangerous to the regime without having to state its reasons publicly and without appeal.[20] At the lowest level, the peasants continued to be governed by communal law. Theoretically they were free to live wherever they chose; in practice they remained bound to their communities by the need to repay the treasury for the value of the land which they had acquired, often at exorbitant rates. Still, from 1870 on sufficient social mobility was created to make possible some movement from the countryside into the towns. This and the firm foundation provided to private property in turn helped industry to take off – between 1848 and 1896 the number of industrial workers rose from 220,000 to 1,742,000.[21] Funded by the treasury, a gigantic railway-building program was launched, thus knitting together a vast continent and permitting its resources to be exploited. From the 1890s on it was followed by an equally spectacular expansion of heavy industry in particular, much of which was also state-financed and served the state's needs. While the overwhelming majority of the population continued to live on the land where its per capita income was abysmally low, by 1913 these reforms had made Russia into the world's fifth largest economy after the United States, Germany, Britain, and France. They had also restored its position as Europe's largest, if certainly not the most efficient, military power.

Under these circumstances a civil society, numerically small (as late as 1900, less than 1 percent of the population had attended high school) finally emerged; its liveliness is indicated by the fact that the number of political and literary periodicals increased from about twenty at the death of Nicholas I to seven times that figure thirty years later. However, in Russia, building industry and acquiring large-scale property were still very much a function of persuading the government to give assistance in the form of tariffs, subsidies, and loans.[22] Hence for the most part the *intelligentsia* – a term which first became popular during the 1860s – consisted of educated persons who were not property-owners, such as

---

[20] See R. Hinsely, *The Russian Secret Police* (New York: Hutchinson, 1970), for these and other aspects of arbitrary government in Russia during this period.

[21] Figures from E. H. Carr, *The Russian Revolution* (New York: Grosset and Dunlap, 1965), vol. I, p. 15.

[22] On the connection between the state and Russian industry in this period, see L. Kochan, *The Making of Modern Russia* (Harmondsworth, UK: Penguin, Books, 1965), pp. 155–7.

doctors, lawyers, teachers, low-level officials, and students: briefly people with everything to gain and nothing to lose.[23] Some of the members of the *intelligentsia* – including, notably, a handful of aristocratic men and women – leaned toward anarchism. Many more were liberals who admired the West and wished to emulate it, whereas others still were Slavophiles who rejected modernism and tended to look back nostalgically at a pristine, pre-Petrine Old Russia where people were devoted and government was a combination of Orthodoxy and paternalism.[24] Whatever their ideas, very early on they began to clash with the authorities, demanding reform, while claiming that their education and concern for social questions entitled them to a share in government. In fact the question of democratization, which by establishing a parliament and political parties would have enabled these people to vent their energies, was repeatedly considered by the last three tsars. Yet in the end none of them could bring themselves to grant a constitution – as Alexander II himself reportedly said, he would have done so "that very day" had he not been convinced that it would result in "Russia falling into pieces."[25]

Its political aspirations frustrated, the *intelligentsia* set up various opposition circles. Numerically they were too weak to achieve anything; hence they turned to an alliance with "the people" as did the various "Will of the People," "Way of the People," "Return to the People," and "Revenge of the People" – all movements that were made up of a handful of intellectuals. Regularly broken up by the police, which mistook their radical talk for active subversion, just as regularly they reemerged. Each successive group tended to be better organized and more resolute than the last. From revolutionary talk they passed to bombings and assassinations, the most important victims being Tsar Alexander II (1881) and Prime Minister Stolypin (1911). By the 1890s several Marxist-oriented factions had arisen, the most radical of whom were to become Lenin's Bolsheviks. Even before 1914 the propaganda of these groups was making some headway toward radicalizing the masses, particularly in the towns. Although trade unions were prohibited, a few were set up anyway.

In 1904–5, the weakness of the tsar's rule was signaled by Russia's defeat in the war against Japan as well as the abortive revolution that followed it.[26] Last-minute attempts to broaden the regime's support by way of democratization soon faltered; in the end it was World War I

---

[23] For the development of the *intelligentsia*, see D. Mueller, *Intelligentcija: Untersuchungen zur Geschichte eines politisches Schlagwortes* (Frankfurt am Main: Roediger, 1971).
[24] See A. Gleason, *European and Muscovite: Ivan Kireevskii and the Origins of Slavophilism* (Cambridge, MA: Harvard University Press, 1972), esp. ch. 9.
[25] Quoted in Ulam, *Russia's Failed Revolutions*, p. 123.
[26] For a short history of these years, see W. Bruce Lincoln, *In War's Dark Shadow: The Russians Before the Great War* (New York: Simon and Schuster, 1983).

which, by drastically reducing their already low living standards and turning them into cannon fodder, made the Russian masses ripe for revolution. The Communist polity established after 1917 did away with the last vestiges of patrimonialism – henceforward individuals no longer owned their houses, let alone entire countries. But at the same time it made *everybody* into a servant of the state, not out of necessity and in time of war as in Western, liberally minded countries but permanently and as a vital part of the official ideology. Instead of a clear line being drawn between the private and the public, which elsewhere was the very essence of political modernization, the former was swallowed up by the latter. In theory and to a considerable extent in practice as well, not an action could be taken nor a thought remain in anybody's head that was not state-mandated.

In Russia, the decisive factor that both made possible the construction of a successful centralized polity and prevented it from turning into a full-fledged state was the conscription of the nobility combined with the "privatization" of the rest of society, most of which consisted of serfs. Not so in Poland, which during the later Middle Ages reached the point where it was the nobility, the *szlachta*, which dominated the crown instead of the other way around.[27] Partly this success was made possible by sheer numbers: at 7 percent of the population, the *szlachta* was more numerous and more influential than anywhere else. The first critical step was taken in 1374 under the terms of the Pact of Kosice, also known as the Polish Magna Carta but destined to launch the country on a course very different from that of Britain. As the throne was being contested between King Louis' daughter and his wife, the nobility put its weight behind the former. In return they were able to insist that its members should be taxed at no more than two groschen a year – a sum so small that it was soon no longer worth collecting – and that no other taxes should be passed without their consent. On top of this, justice and coinage were to remain under their own control; and, most important of all, the hitherto hereditary monarchy was made elective so that future candidates could take up office only with the nobility's agreement and after having submitted to the conditions imposed on them.

These developments caused political authority in Poland to pass into the hands of the high nobility. Its main organ was the Privy Council; in 1493 the latter was transformed into a senate with 100 members. The senate in turn became the upper house of the parliament or Sejm whereas

---

[27] For the way this was achieved, see A. Wyczanski, "The System of Power in Poland, 1370–1648," in A. Maczak, et al., eds., *East-Central Europe in Transition: From the Fourteenth to the Seventeenth Century* (Cambridge: Cambridge University Press, 1985), pp. 140–52.

a lower house, numbering 150 and also known as Sejm, was occupied by the lower nobility. In 1505 enacting laws became the sole privilege of the Sejm; having already obtained the right of habeas corpus in 1434, the Polish nobility was now the most emancipated in Europe, possessed of what they pleased to call *aurea libertas* and what did, in fact, yield golden fruit for the largest of them. From then until the country's demise at the end of the eighteenth century some 200 meetings of the Sejm were held, all of them dominated by the Act of Nihil Novi (No Innovations) which was also adopted in 1505. As in Russia, the first use to which the nobility put its rule was to enserf the peasantry. In 1518 the latter were forbidden to appeal from seigneurial to royal courts; from now on, Polish landowners could not be called to account even for killing their serfs.

In 1572 the death of the last representative of the great Jagellonian dynasty led Poland into an interregnum that lasted three years. The opportunity was used to transfer the right to elect kings from the senate to the Sejm as a whole. In theory it was elected by the entire nobility. In practice it became the stamping ground of fewer than 300 wealthy families, who treated the lesser nobility as their retainers and extended their influence over entire districts – the top ninety landowners, for example, possessed an average of 1,000 hearths each. Once they had passed through the *sejm*'s doors all members were considered equal. Formally in 1652, but in practice much earlier, they adopted the *liberum veto*, an arrangement which gave each one the right to veto not only the bill under consideration but also all other acts adopted during the session.[28] To "safeguard those freedoms which our ancestors won through bloody combat," as one nobleman put it,[29] the members claimed the right to attend meetings armed, on horseback, and accompanied by their retainers – who were sometimes so numerous as to be grouped in "regiments." These procedures contributed little toward good order during the proceedings. Often they degenerated into brawls with delegates throwing books and drinking cups at each other and hiding under benches to avoid them. Still, at any rate, it turned the sessions into a spectacle well worth watching.

The second half of the sixteenth century was also the period when, to use a phrase coined by a famous historian, Europe was divided.[30]

---

[28] For details on the development of the *liberum veto*, see *The Cambridge Medieval History* (New York: Macmillan, 1971–), vol. VIII, pp. 566–7; and *The Cambridge History of Poland* (New York: Octagon, 1971–), vol. I, p. 193.

[29] Quote from C. S. Leach, ed., *Memoirs of the Polish Baroque: The Writings of Jan Cryszostom Pasek, a Squire of the Commonwealth of Poland and Lithuania* (Berkeley: University of California Press, 1976), p. 213, describing the Sejm convened for the 1609 royal elections.

[30] J. H. Elliott, *Europe Divided, 1559–1598* (London: Fontana, 1968), particularly pp. 43–50.

Whereas, in the West, populations expanded, towns flourished, and the first large-scale capitalist enterprises made their appearance, the wide open lands of Eastern Europe – Prussia and Poland above all – turned themselves into the granaries of this developed West. As had also been the case in Prussia, but to a far greater extent, this development worked in favor of the Polish nobility – especially, as always, the higher nobility – and against the towns. During the Middle Ages the latter had been quite as advanced as Western ones, developing flourishing handicrafts as well as an intellectual life second to none. Now they were transformed into nothing but *entrepôts* for the grain trade where foreign ships – first German and Dutch, later English – loaded their cargoes, thus laying the foundation for their subsequent decline.[31]

The events of 1572 having turned Poland into an aristocratic republic (Rzeczpospolita), from then on its throne came to be occupied by a succession of noblemen, some native and others foreign. Among the latter were an heir to the French throne, an elector of Brandenburg, several Swedish (Vasa) princes, and two electors of Saxony, to say nothing of a string of unsuccessful candidates including, at one point, Ivan the Terrible. Once elected, all remained entangled in the politics of their native countries. Closely bound by the coronation oaths imposed on them by their Polish subjects, none of them succeeded in establishing dynasties that lasted more than two generations. While other countries were busily transforming royal institutions into state-owned ones, in Poland there was no royal chancery; no royal bureaucracy; no attempt to centralize taxation (just two noble families, the Radziwils and the Potockis, between them were able to match the resources of the crown itself); and scarcely any royal judiciary except for a weak system of appellate courts which, of course, applied only to the nobility and to nobody else. Nor was the condition of the army any better. Like their aristocratic counterparts elsewhere, but with greater success, the Polish nobility resisted military modernization. Absent either a bureaucratically managed ministry of war or a large number of fortified cities, they could not follow the universal trend toward more infantry, artillery, and engineers operating in disciplined formations. Instead they stuck to cavalry – the Polish lancers' reputation for valor preceded them – each member of the gentry being, in fact, his own commander and bringing his undertrained, underequipped, disorderly, and often drunken retainers with him.[32]

---

[31] See M. Bogucka, "The Towns of East-Central Europe from the Fourteenth to the Seventeenth Century," in Maczak, et al., *East Central Europe in Transition*, pp. 97–108.

[32] See the description of the "Polacks," in H. F. Fleming, *Der vollkommene Deutsche Soldat* (Leipzig: the author, 1726), vol. I, p. 41; and E. Wimmer, "L'infanterie polonaise aux

During the second half of the seventeenth century, the Poles, though they lost control of the Baltic littoral to Prussia's Great Elector, Frederick William, were still able to score impressive victories over Russia (which was even more backward) and Turkey (albeit more Austrian than Polish troops took place in the relief of Vienna in 1683). However, the wars of the period caused the population to fall from 10 million to perhaps 7 million.[33] After the death of the legendary soldier Jan Sobieski in 1696, things began falling apart. The Great Northern War of 1700–21 ended by turning the country into a virtual Russian protectorate. Having beaten the Swedes, Peter the Great took Livonia for himself. Formal limits were imposed on the size of the Polish army, while the employment of Prussian officials who might have turned things around was explicitly prohibited. By the 1760s, though Poland still controlled a territory larger than that of France and a population comparable to Britain's, the national army could muster only 16,000 men. In addition, individual nobles had their own private armies, e.g., the Czartoryski family 3,000–4,000 men, the Potockis 2,000, and the Radziwils (father and son) perhaps 15,000. While Prussia as the smallest of the powers possessed 150,000 disciplined regulars, the Poles were barely able to muster one-third of that number *in toto*. As Frederick II put it in a characteristically barbed phrase, Poland had become "an artichoke, ready to be eaten leaf by leaf."[34] The first partition took place in 1772 and cost the country almost 100,000 square miles (almost 30 percent of its territory) as well as 4,500,000 people (35 percent of the population).

Spurred by the imminent threat to their existence, the Poles under King Stanislaw II Poniatowski (1764–95) finally started enacting reforms inspired by the ideas of Montesquieu, Rousseau, and Washington among others. After the United States, Poland in 1791 became the second country in history to adopt a written constitution. The *liberum veto* was abolished, albeit only for an experimental period of twenty-five years. This enabled Poniatowski to set up the first modern cabinet, which in turn soon led to a reform in the tax system and to the creation of the nucleus of a modern army including, in 1765 and 1774, the first officer school and artillery school respectively.[35] By 1790 the number of regular

---

XV–XVIIIe siècles," in W. Biegansky, et al., eds., *Histoire militaire de Pologne: problèmes choisis* (Warsaw: Edition du Ministre de la defense nationale, 1970).

[33] For some figures, see E. Fuegedi, "The Demographic Landscape of East-Central Europe," in Maczak, et al., *East-Central Europe in Transition*, p. 57.

[34] Figures and quote are from J. Lukowski, *Liberty's Folly: The Polish-Lithuanian Commonwealth in the Eighteenth Century 1697–1795* (London: Routledge, 1991), p. 34.

[35] On the officer school, see E. Malicz, "Die Rolle des gebildeten Offiziers im Europa des 18. Jahrhunderts: die Polnische Ritterakademie in den Jahren 1765–1794," *Zeitschrift für Ostforschung*, 38, 1, 1989, pp. 82–94.

troops had grown to 65,000; the beginnings of a diplomatic corps and a Ministry of Public Education (Komisja Edukacji Narodowei, the first in any country with responsibility for two universities and eighty high schools or gymnasiums) had also been established. It is true that legislation aimed at emancipating the serfs never got anywhere; one writer, Tomasz Dluski, even proposed that anyone who suggested such a measure should have his sanity examined in court. Still, even in this field sufficient progress was made on the initiative of private noblemen to make Poland attractive to half a million immigrants from neighboring countries.

Though the obstacles they met were enormous – in the 1780s, the Polish enlightened class numbered 2,000 persons at most – these reforms, had they been given the opportunity to develop, might conceivably have turned Poland into a modern state. In reality they raised the ire of neighboring rulers who feared that their own subjects would become infected – as the Prussian ambassador, Ewald von Hertzberg, put it, his country could not hope to defend itself against "a populous and well governed nation." In the eyes of Catherine the Great, the goings-on in Warsaw had "outdone all the follies of the Parisian National Assembly."[36] Thus the reforms, instead of achieving their purpose and saving Poland, helped bring about the second and third partitions which took place in 1793 and 1795 respectively. Significantly, what resistance the invaders encountered was not coordinated by the government, whose heads, led by the royal family itself, were the first to flee into exile; instead it took the form of popular rebellions led by the likes of Tadeusz Kosciuszko and Henryk Dabrowski, both of them members of the nobility and graduates of the Warsaw officer school. Wiped off the map, Poland was to undergo various transformations. First Napoleon established the so-called Grand Duchy of Warsaw. Then the Russians, returning after 1812, established "Congress Poland" as a sort of protectorate. However, after the abortive rebellion of 1863–4 the very name of Poland was erased; in its place there appeared the "Lands of the Vistula." An independent Polish state was resurrected only in 1918 when two of the occupying powers (Germany and Austria) had been defeated and the third (Russia) undergone a revolution which would be followed by the destructive civil war of 1918–19. As has been remarked, Poland was like a canary that had swallowed three cats.

The contrasting fates of Russia and Poland illustrate, each in its own way, both the expansion of the state and the consequences of failing to adopt its institutions. In Russia the construction of a state apparatus

---

[36] Both quotes are from Lukowsky, *Liberty's Folly*, p. 253.

proceeded mainly by imitation and often at the hands of Western experts, both civilian and military, specifically imported for the purpose. This state without a state – a better term is hard to find – enabled the country to hold its own internationally and to develop internally, albeit at the expense of conscripting the nobility and enserfing most of the population, and then only up to a point. When history, propelled by the steam engine, passed that point, the country saw itself left behind by its competitors. Though some changes were made, it was a question of too little too late. In the end the Revolution broke out and swept away the entire antiquated apparatus as well as killing hundreds of thousands of its members.

In Poland, to the contrary, the nobility refused to follow the example of either West or East and enter into a partnership with the monarchy – to the point that, to this day, the Polish term for state is *panstwo*, "a thing of nobles." Legally emancipated, and possessed of relatively enormous economic and military resources, it aspired to govern by assembly in its own name and on its own behalf. The result was that the monarchy was weakened, the bureaucratic organs of government remained embryonic, civil society remained confined to a very small number of educated urbanites, and a proper state failed to appear at all. This failure to achieve political modernization had to be paid for by the disappearance of the country for over a century – a fate which elsewhere overtook only non-European polities, and not even all of those. In the words of the Polish national anthem:

> And yet is Poland not lost.

The Anglo-Saxon experience

The expansion of the state into Eastern Europe took place against the background of populations which, though not exactly advanced for their age, at any rate were comparable to those of the West in terms of civilization, race, and religion. Not so the spread of the British colonists into North America, Australia, New Zealand, and (following the Dutch, who preceded them by over two centuries) South Africa. Here the local populations were extremely sparse. Only in South Africa had they so much as entered the iron age; in most other places – notably Australia and much of North America – they were still limited to tools made out of stone and had not yet crossed the border dividing tribes without rulers from chiefdoms. Again with the exception of South Africa, on which more below, the opposition that the white man encountered in conquering these countries was negligible. In North America around AD 1000, the natives were too backward to even resist the landing of a handful of

Vikings, who, accordingly, nicknamed them *Skraelinge* or weaklings.[37] From the beginning there was a tendency to treat them as foreign nations, whether friendly or hostile. For all these reasons there could be no question of their political institutions, such as they were, exercising influence upon the states that eventually emerged.

The earliest region to be settled by the Anglo-Saxons was the Atlantic seaboard of North America. The settlements were established at a time when "absolute" government in the mother country was at its zenith and government itself in many ways a form of capitalist enterprise by rulers; hence the colonies tended to assume a patrimonial character. In return for giving or advancing the crown – which in an era of conflicts with Parliament was chronically short of funds – sums of money, various individuals, groups, and companies were granted huge tracts of land that was largely unexplored, seldom mapped, and rarely provided with clear borders. With the territory came authority to import people into it, so as to turn what were supposedly rich agricultural lands to profit: so in Virginia, Maryland, Massachusetts, Pennsylvania, and New Jersey. The last-named colony was originally granted to Charles II's brother, James the Duke of York, who later transferred his rights to two other people: so also the Carolinas and Georgia.

The settlers' own motives varied.[38] Some, such as the Puritans who came to live in New England, were driven by religious dissent and the wish to set up a new, sin-free Jerusalem; accordingly, for years on end they discouraged others from following them. Others shared the perennial human need for additional cultivable land, while others still were probably adventurers hoping to strike it rich in various honest and not so honest ways. Whatever their motives, sooner or later they were bound to come into conflict either with each other over religious issues – as was the case in Massachusetts and elsewhere – or else with the concessionaires who, having been granted the land, attempted to bind their human charges to themselves and exploit them as much as possible for as long as possible. Some of the dissatisfied moved out of Massachusetts, as did the founders of Rhode Island, New Hampshire, and Connecticut. Others sought to redress their grievances by appealing to the crown. Either way the ultimate result was likely to be a transition to direct rule – in other words, the appointment of a royal governor who either took over from the concessionaires or else established a government *ex novo*.

Compared to earlier empires, the British one in America arose at a time when the difference between private proprietorship and political rule was

[37] *Vinland Saga* (Harmondsworth, UK: Penguin Books, 1965), p. 61 and n. 1.
[38] For a short account, see M. A. Jones, *American Migration* (Chicago: University of Chicago Press, 1960), ch. 1.

becoming firmly established. At no point could there be any question of royal governors owning the colonies in any way; on the contrary, their very establishment was meant to take those colonies out of private ownership and put them under a political regime presumably more able to resolve conflicts and secure the inhabitants' loyalty to the crown. In other places the distinction between the public and the private spheres took centuries or even millennia to develop – if, indeed, it developed at all. In North America it became firmly established almost from the beginning. Here rulers were neither fathers nor lords nor masters; and conversely the ruled were neither slaves nor serfs nor family members but, at worst, indentured servants who had rented out their labor for a number of years but who, once that period was over, reverted to full freedom.

Equally decisive for America's future political development was the fact that governors did not have extensive bureaucracies at their disposal. In part this continued the tradition of England as being undergoverned by continental standards; but mostly it reflected the desire to economize so as to make the colonies turn a profit to the homeland as well as the sheer size of North America itself. Deprived of a proper administrative machine, willy-nilly the governors sought to avail themselves of their subjects' aid by means of councils recruited from preeminent Americans, mainly prominent landowners and merchants. The first councils were appointed from above; later they tended to become elected. Increasingly they concentrated the functions of government, including legislation, taxation, and the payment of officials, in their own hands. They also offered the population scope for political activity that was unusual for the time. For example, in the colonies of the Chesapeake area, 80 to 90 percent of the free adult male population was permitted to vote.

By 1752, the year in which Georgia got rid of its proprietors (the Oglethorpe family) and received its first royal governor, all of the then existing colonies had emancipated themselves from private ownership. At Westminster, responsibility for looking after them fell to the Board of Trade whose main concern was to use them as a vehicle for increasing Britain's own wealth. To this end it imposed various restrictions, including, at one time or another, a prohibition on the colonies to engage in maritime trade with each other, an obligation on them to sell their products solely in the London market, and an obligation on all vessels bound for the colonies to stop at London and pay duties. Enforced by the Admiralty Courts – this at a time when Britain itself was already governed by the common law – the so-called Navigation Acts did not fail to raise the ire of the colonists whose numbers and wealth were growing. From just over 50,000 in 1650 the population had risen to little short of 2 million during the 1760s. More and more of them were not English but of

Scottish, French, German, Dutch, and Swedish origins. Each of these groups arrived with their own religious ideas and, in the case of the Irish, a strong resentment against everything English.

So long as the French and Spanish maintained a threatening presence in Canada and Florida respectively, the alliance between Britain and its North American colonies held in spite of occasional tensions. No sooner had the threat been removed by the French and Indian War, however, than tensions erupted: the more so since the colonial militias had played an important part in the conquest of Quebec in particular and were consequently flushed with confidence in their own military prowess.[39] The various disputes over taxation, representation, Britain's right to maintain standing armies, etc. that finally led to the outbreak of the Revolution need not be recounted here. Suffice it to say that, perhaps for the first time in history (or at any rate since the tyrannicides of classical antiquity), this was a revolt conducted not by would-be rulers and their followers but by elected representatives on behalf of a nascent abstract state; or, to be precise, states, since relationships among the various colonies and the form that their common institutions would take had by no means been worked out even by the time the struggle ended and independence from Britain was achieved.

Reflecting its origin in diverse colonies spread over a vast territory – excluding Florida, which reverted to Spain, from north to south it was equal to the distance between Stockholm and Palermo – the United States under its first constitution was an extremely loose entity. Not only did Article II of the Articles of Confederation (1781) expressly reserve sovereignty to the states, but the document even envisaged the possibility that one state might go to war against a third party without necessarily calling on the others. Understood less as a form of government than as an alliance between sovereign entities, the Articles could be revised only with the agreement of nine out of the thirteen states, while any major changes required the consent of all. So weak was the central authority that the governments of individual states were soon issuing their own currencies (the one issued by the Continental Congress having lost over 99 percent of its value during the revolutionary struggle itself) and using their own resources to repay their citizens for debts owned by the Congress. By the mid-1780s they were even beginning to set up customs barriers against one another. Indeed there was talk of the confederation breaking up into three or four regional groups, which would possibly one day go to war against each other over new land being opened up in the west.

---

[39] For the pretensions of the American military, such as they were, see D. Higginbotham, "The Military Institutions of Colonial America: the Rhetoric and the Reality," in Lynn, *Tools of War*, pp. 131–54.

In the event, the decisive factor that finally caused the governing elites of the various states to put their differences aside was probably the fear of a revolution by the underprivileged classes – a fear which Shay's Rebellion of 1787 did nothing to allay. Originally the purpose of the Philadelphia Congress, which met in May of 1788, was merely to amend the Articles of Confederation; but this was overtaken by the so-called Virginia Plan which envisaged the creation of a much more centralized polity on which, to quote John Marshall, "the prosperity and happiness" of the people depended. The Constitution which was adopted in 1788 was based primarily on the ideas of Locke and Montesquieu. The former contributed the notion of a government that was based on consent and whose main function was to protect the individual, including specifically his liberty and his right to own property and enjoy it without being disturbed. The latter triumphed insofar as the United States became the second country in history (after Britain) to adopt the separation of powers, and that in a form remarkably similar to the one which the French *philosophe* had suggested in his book. But whereas neither Montesquieu nor Locke had necessarily envisaged a democracy – Locke in particular thought in terms of a franchise limited to property-owners – the United States proceeded to adopt the principle of one (male, white, tax-paying) person, one vote.

With all political power ultimately resulting from popular elections the new polity, though surely dwelling under God, owed less to Him than any of its predecessors. Originally different states had their differing views and policies concerning religion: for example, Massachusetts and Connecticut came close to persecuting both Quakers and Baptists. Once they had finally agreed to join together, there was a strong tendency among the colonies to overcome these differences by keeping religion and government apart. Perhaps most importantly of all, the American system of government, instead of being built on top of existing foundations, was deliberately created almost *ex nihilo*. This gave it an artificial quality of which people who visited the country at the time were quite conscious[40] and which from then to the present has been by no means its least important characteristic. If there is anything wrong with the United States, the citizens get organized by means of a "grass-roots" movement and set out to fix it. Should they fail to achieve perfection and build a heaven on earth, then perhaps to a greater extent than the citizens of any other country they have nobody to blame but themselves.

The adoption of the Constitution, as well as the first ten amendments introduced in 1791, did not end the debate between the advocates of state

[40] See, e.g., A. de Tocqueville, *Democracy in America* (New York: Vintage, 1945 [1835–40]), vol. II, ch. 8.

rights on the one hand and those of the federal government on the other. As usual, at the heart of the conflict there was money: in other words, whether there should be a single national debt (and, consequently, a central bank to manage it) or whether each state should be responsible for its own. Support for the former view came from the Federalists who were concentrated in the north, whereas the opposite one was held by the Republicans and the southern states. At the head of the Federalists was Alexander Hamilton, a New York politician who was acting as George Washington's secretary of the treasury and whose main concern was to "borrow cheap" in case of another foreign war. In return for agreeing to have the Republic's capital city moved from Philadelphia and established on Virginia's northern border, as the South demanded, Hamilton was able to push the Bank Act through Congress and establish the US Bank. Thus it was by his efforts that a single national debt was brought into being – though nowadays few people, watching the clock in New York race through its figures, would share his view that it represented "a national blessing."[41]

The election of Jefferson as president in 1800 effectively put an end to the Federalist Party and opened an era of Republican government, Nevertheless, by and large the drive toward greater centralization continued. Partly this was because of continued expansion to the West; as critics such as Aaron Burr did not fail to point out, the more territory came under federal rule (even temporarily, until new states could be established), the greater the power of the government in Washington, DC. Inspired by John Marshall, the Virginia lawyer who had been appointed Chief Justice in 1800 and served until 1835, several Supreme Court decisions also tended to strengthen the Union at the expense of state rights. Thus *McCullogh v. Maryland* (1819) instituted the doctrine of "implied powers," enabling Congress to act in matters which, though not specifically written into the Constitution, were a "proper and necessary" part of government – in this case setting up the second central bank after the first one had been closed. In 1824 *Gibbons v. Ogden* gave Congress power to regulate interstate commerce even if it overrode state law by doing so; finally, *Weston v. Charleston* (1829) prohibited the states from taxing federally issued bonds.[42]

These developments were preceded by the War of 1812 which, having ended in a devastating (if unnecessary) victory over the British at New Orleans, brought about a new sense of power and, for a time at any rate,

[41] See Hamilton's Report on Public Credit, 9 January 1790, reprinted in G. R. Taylor, ed., *Hamilton and the National Debt* (Boston: Heath, 1950), pp. 8–18.
[42] The decisions are printed in S. I. Kutler, ed., *John Marshall* (Englewood Cliffs, NJ: Prentice-Hall, 1972), pp. 54–61, 61–3, and 84–8.

unity. They were soon followed by the transportation revolution which, beginning in the 1820s, started knitting together a huge and rather disparate continent into a single integrated polity. More federal money was spent on transportation under Andrew Jackson (1829–37) than under all previous administrations put together; but even so the government only put up a fraction of the sums invested by private individuals, corporations, and the states. As had been the case in seventeenth- and eighteenth-century Europe, the first great projects involved waterways. Among many smaller works, the Erie Canal and the Chesapeake and Ohio Canal acquired well-deserved fame as triumphs of organization and engineering skill. From the 1830s on the advent of steam-propelled paddleboats revolutionized shipping on the Great Lakes. By turning the Mississippi River system into the backbone of the United States, they also enabled people and goods to be transported from north to south and *vice versa* with previously undreamed-of convenience and reliability. But whereas steamships proved profitable, canals, coming perhaps half a century too late, by and large did not. That they did not was due to that other all-important nineteenth-century invention, the railways.

As noted by Adam Smith in *The Wealth of Nations*, throughout history the cost of transport by water had been a mere fraction of its price by land, thus explaining why the earliest commercial and industrial civilizations always arose either near the sea or where navigable rivers existed. Railways were the first technical device to reverse that relationship; by so doing they enabled polities which did not rely primarily on waterways to grow as large, and as cohesive, as those which did. Given proper management, the effect of railways was to permit large states to mobilize their resources almost as efficiently as small ones – sometimes more so, indeed, since there exists a limit below which both rail transport and the construction of the lines themselves becomes uneconomic. Thus their development worked in favor of those who were in possession of land masses – the United States and, after an interval of some decades, Russia – at the expense of the rest.[43] Already Napoleon during his exile at Saint Helena was able to prophesy the development of those two states into what, during the Cold War, people were fond of calling "superpowers." *Pace* some modern historians,[44] such a development could never have been brought about without the timely appearance and spread of the railways.

Against the background of slowly increasing centralization and rapidly,

[43] H. Mackinder, *The Scope and Method of Geography and the Geographical Pivot of History* (London: Royal Geographical Society, 1951 [1904]), pp. 30ff.
[44] R. W. Fogel, *Railroads and America's Economic Growth: An Econometric Inquiry* (Baltimore: Johns Hopkins University Press, 1964).

even spectacularly, growing economic and industrial power the question of slavery continued to prove a bone of contention between North and South. As it tended to become more rather than less profitable,[45] its role in the question of federal versus state rights grew and grew, the more so because it became entangled with other questions such as that of high tariffs favored by the northern states against the low ones demanded by the southern ones. In the long run the contradiction between a modern, nonproprietary, politically governed state and a situation whereby a considerable part of the population was considered the private property of others proved intolerable. This is not the place to spell out the immensely complicated train of events that led to the Civil War, let alone describe the course of the conflict. Suffice it to say that the war was the most decisive single event in American history; not for nothing is Gettysburg, where a special structure still marks "the high tide of rebellion," by far the most visited of all American battlefields. There and at Vicksburg on the Mississippi, but perhaps most of all during Sherman's march through Georgia which made the price of rebellion plain for all to see, it was determined that the United States should not be a loose gathering of states, each with the right to secede when it pleased. Instead there was to be a Union, one and indivisible and jointly ruled by the three powers, however constituted. All had their seat within a mile or two from each other in Washington, DC – a remarkably small area from which to govern a country that was soon to reach "from California to the New York island" and occupy no fewer than 3,680,000 square miles.

Symbolized by the completion of the first transcontinental railway line in 1869 – by which time the United States possessed almost 40,000 miles of track, more than all the rest of the world combined – industrial expansion proceeded even more rapidly after the Civil War than before. Between 1880 and 1900 alone, the quantity of steel coming out of the factories each year increased from 1,400,000 to over 11,000,000 tons, while the value of all manufactured goods increased from $5.4 billion to $13 billion.[46] By 1929 manufacturing output was almost as large as that of the remaining powers together; though it failed to retain that position during the Depression, it remained the largest single economy by far.[47] Long before that, the United States, having developed into a giant, felt the urge to match itself against others, as giants will. The War of 1812 had already put an end to the ability of any other state to threaten American

---

[45] R. W. Fogel and S. L. Engerman, *Time on the Cross: The Economics of American Negro Slavery* (New York: Norton, 1974).

[46] Figures from *Encyclopaedia Britannica* (Chicago: University of Chicago Press, 1993), vol. XXIX, p. 242, "United States."

[47] See data in H. C. Hillman, "Comparative Strength of the Great Powers," in A. Toynbee, ed., *The World in March 1939* (London: Royal Institute of International Affairs, 1952), p. 439.

security, effectively turning Canada into a hostage for Britain's good behavior in the New World. First the detachment of Florida from Spain (1819), then the Monroe Declaration (1823), and then the conquest of Texas and the Southwest from Mexico (1845–8) made the western hemisphere into an American domain; once the Civil War was over, the execution of Emperor Maximilian in 1867 marked the last time any other power was able to seriously interfere on the continent. In 1851 the Hawaiian Islands, hitherto governed by tribal chiefs with hand-thrown spears as their principal weapon, were brought under American protection. This led to the establishment of a forward base several thousand miles off the California coast and, as Japan in particular was very soon to find out, turned the United States into a Pacific force to be reckoned with.

Aware of its growing power, during the late 1880s and 1890s the United States also began to develop a robust nationalism. Its most important organs were William Randolph Hearst's *American* and Joseph Pulitzer's *World*, its principal representatives, Captain Alfred T. Mahan, Theodore Roosevelt, Elihu Root, Herbert Crolie, and their coterie. Roosevelt in particular represented a generation too young to have taken part in the Civil War and forever marked by their elders' tales of heroism – the war, after all, claimed as many lives as all other conflicts fought by the United States combined. Another factor that may have been instrumental in creating the new mood was the closing of the frontier, announced by historian Frederick Turner Jackson in 1893[48] and perhaps serving to turn the nation's energies outward. Unlike many of their opposite numbers in other countries, the exponents of American imperialism were not reactionaries but self-styled "Progressives." Usually they paid at least lip service to the democratic principles on which, after all, their ability to attain and maintain power absolutely depended. Concerning foreign affairs, however, their doctrines differed little from those advanced by contemporary European nationalists such as Heinrich von Treitschke and Theodor von Bernhardi in Germany.[49] It was in tune with the spirit of the age that such people thought of "strong" and "weak" races; the states that these races set up for themselves were thought of as animal species engaging one another in a Darwinistic struggle for survival. Both the states and the ideologues who claimed to speak on their behalf were usually quite prepared to go to war even if they did not positively hanker for it to happen – as Theodore Roosevelt, with his constant talk of the "rougher and manlier virtues," clearly did.[50]

[48] For a good discussion of Turner's ideas, see above all R. A. Billington, *The Frontier Thesis* (Huntington, NY: Krieger, 1966).
[49] For nationalist attitudes to war before 1914, see M. Howard, *The Causes of War* (Cambridge, MA: Harvard University Press, 1984), pp. 23ff.
[50] A good account of the rise of American imperialism is R. Hofstaedter, *The American Political Tradition* (New York: Vintage Books, 1948), ch. 9.

To accuse the United States of being the aggressor in the Spanish–American War – let alone World War I, World War II, and subsequent conflicts such as Korea, Vietnam, and the Persian Gulf – would be going much too far. From the atrocities committed by the Spaniards in their attempt to put down the Cuban rebels, through the German sinking of the *Lusitania* and the Japanese aggression against China, to the occupation of Kuwait by the Iraqis, US wars were triggered by the actions of others. However, all also involved an exceptionally, some would say disproportionally, strong response on the part of the "chip-on-the-shoulder nation" – a term coined by the greatest American anthropologist, Margaret Mead. Colonial conflicts apart, most other twentieth-century states fought wars against enemies from whom they were separated by only a line on the map and who, accordingly, presented an immediate, sometimes overwhelming threat to their interests, territory, and even existence. Not so the United States which, fortunately for it, occupies the position of a global island. Any attempt to invade it across the Atlantic or Pacific Ocean was, and remains, sheer lunacy; even in 1939–45, the largest war in history, the closest any enemy came to threatening the continent involved a handful of fire-balloons which the Japanese sent in the general direction of the Californian coast. Except for the Mexican episode of 1916, itself more a punitive expedition than a war, from the occupation of the Philippines onward, the United States has invariably sent its troops to fight several thousand miles away. No wonder American parents often took a long time before they could be convinced of the need to commit their sons – of late, daughters too – on other continents, even other hemispheres, to causes for which they did not care and among people of whom they knew nothing.

The absence of a serious external threat fact also helps explain why the US armed forces and central government apparatus took such a long time to develop even at a time when, as was clearly the case after 1865, the economic muscle for building both had come into being. It is true that the navy began to expand during the 1890s; driven by Mahan's theories concerning the need to command the sea as well as the interests of big business,[51] after 1919 it attained parity with Britain's. However, except for the years 1917–18 the land army remained almost ridiculously small.[52] During the late nineteenth century it numbered in the low tens of thousands; as late as 1940 it still had fewer than 300,000 men (including

---

[51] See K. J. Hagan, *This People's Navy: A History of American Sea Power* (New York: Free Press, 1991), ch. 9.

[52] On the efforts to expand the US Army during these years, and their failure, see S. Skowronek, *Building a New American State: The Expansion of National Administrative Capacities, 1877–1920* (Cambridge: Cambridge University Press, 1982), pp. 85–120.

the army air force) and scarcely any battle-ready reserves. Following the tradition whereby its main function had been to fight Amerindians, its formations were scattered in small groups all over a huge continent. As a result, hardly any large-scale exercises could be held and readiness for waging modern war was lower even than what these figures suggest.

Nor did the United States go nearly as far as other countries in building the fourth organ of government, namely a centralized bureaucracy. Originally there were just three departments of the government, Foreign Affairs, Finance, and War; but even in 1800, after Customs, Lighthouses, US Attorneys, Marshals, the Post Office, Revenue Cutters, Indian Superintendents, Commissioners of Loans, Internal Revenue, Surveyor General, Land Tax, and Land Offices had all been added, the federal workforce totaled only 3,000 persons. Throughout the nineteenth century, the Post Office remained the largest federal agency by far; as late as 1913 the government had only 230,000 employees compared with 700,000 in Austria-Hungary, 700,000 in Italy, and 1.5 million in Germany – all with much smaller populations, let alone territories – during the last years before the war.[53] Though the New Deal did something to change the picture, its achievements were limited; in the event, it was World War II and the subsequent Cold War which really ushered in the age of Big Government. In chapter 6 of this book the rise and decline of that government will be studied more closely. Meanwhile suffice it to say that the United States, living in a world of states and often engaging in competition with them, behaved much as other states did. Internal and external power grew *pari passu*. During the Truman and Eisenhower administrations, unprecedented prosperity provided the muscle for an equally unprecedented military buildup both at home (where it was known as the military-industrial complex) and abroad (which saw the stationing of hundreds of thousands of American troops). The climax came in the form of the "imperial presidency" of the Johnson and Nixon years when the United States, having humiliated the USSR over Cuba, seemed to bestride the globe like a colossus – until, with startling suddenness, the tide turned and the retreat of both the military machine and the industrial complex that supported it got under way.

The achievement of American independence, which took place in 1783, served the British government both as an example and a warning: an example since it showed what a well-governed, democratic state established in what was practically virgin country (North America's

[53] The US figure is from B. Porter, *War and the Rise of the State: The Military Foundation of Modern Politics* (New York: Free Press, 1993), p. 271; the European ones are from P. Flora, *State, Economy and Society in Western Europe 1915–1975* (Frankfurt am Main: Campus, 1983), vol. I, ch. 5.

population at the time of the European discovery is estimated at 1.5 million) could achieve; a warning since it proved that continued possession depended absolutely on granting the colonists "the rights of Englishmen" and allowing them to run their own affairs as soon as they were willing and able to do so.[54] In the event the warning was heeded and the construction of the Dominions proved to be a smashing success. Sooner or later it enabled each one to attain the status of a fully independent state complete with its own government, laws, and courts whose judgments were not subject to review in the mother country; armed forces, as well as diplomatic services, followed. Symbolically maturity came in 1919–20 when the Dominions, which hitherto had their foreign affairs run for them by Whitehall, insisted on putting their own signatures on the peace treaties and gained seats in the League of Nations; in the same year Canada appointed its first independent diplomatic representatives (to Washington, DC) instead of working through the British Embassy as it had previously. Only in South Africa did the clash of British imperialism with the Dutch settlers lead to the use of force on any scale, but even there it soon led to a remarkably generous peace settlement and, shortly thereafter, complete self-government. In sum, the various constitutional arrangements – whose crown was formed by the Imperial Statute of 1931 – preserved the colonies' allegiance to the mother country during the years, from 1914 to 1945, when it needed them most. This was a triumph of diplomacy that is probably unequaled before or since.

It is true that, from one continent to another, the development of the Dominions displayed striking variations. The largest and most important one was Canada. Conquered from France at a time when its white population numbered only 7,000, it was the first to develop its own institutions; modeled on those of Britain, in many ways they were strikingly different from those of the neighboring, and, after 1816, by and large friendly United States. The first attempt at responsible government, taking the form of the Quebec Act of 1774 which excluded the French majority, proved unworkable. This led to the Constitutional Act of 1791 which gave Quebec a government with a governor, an executive council, a legislative council, and an assembly elected on a franchise wider than that of Britain itself, with the result that, when the first elections were held in the next year, the new assembly already had a majority of French members. As they have done ever since, the French, dissatisfied with British government but on the whole disinclined to use violence in resisting it, promptly began creating difficulties for the English-speaking population.

---

[54] For the lessons that Britain drew from the events of 1776–83, see A. L. Burt, *The British Empire and Commonwealth from the American Revolution* (Boston: Heath, 1956), pp. 56ff.

And, as they have done ever since, many new immigrants who were deterred by these difficulties chose to settle further west where they created their own institutions under British guidance.

In 1841 Canada West (Upper Canada) was united with Canada East (Lower Canada) under a single government. Between then and 1873 it was joined by British Columbia as well as the smaller, English-speaking maritime colonies; the one exception was Newfoundland, which remained a British colony until 1914. By this time Britain, having turned itself into the workshop of the world and switched to free trade, no longer felt inclined to use force in order to hold on to the "wretched colonies" – or so Disraeli, with much public opinion behind him, said in 1852. Yet paradoxically British indifference made the Canadians themselves seek closer union with Britain. It was feared that, if they did not form a united front, the western territories and possibly even some of the provinces themselves might be swallowed up by the powerful and extremely dynamic neighbor to the south; nor did the United States during the years immediately following the Civil War make any secret of its wish to expand if the opportunity presented itself. Both factors together prepared the way for the establishment of the Dominion of Canada. Effectively it took place in October 1864: the relevant questions having been informally discussed for years, a congress made up of representatives from all the provinces needed only two weeks in order to pass no fewer than seventy-two resolutions. The work was completed in 1867 when the British North America Act came into force.

Unlike the United States the new polity was provided with a parliamentary system of government, so that the prime minister, instead of being directly elected, was dependent on a majority in parliament. Like the United States, it had a written constitution and a supreme court responsible for interpreting it. Like the United States, too, Canada was a federation – although Canadians, anxiously watching the Civil War and determined to prevent anything similar from taking place in their country, gave the government in Ottawa much greater powers over justice and banking in particular. On the other hand, the huge empty spaces made the relationship between the Canadian government and its people resemble that which prevailed in the United States, more than the one which existed in densely populated, long-united Britain. Not even the onset of a terrible economic depression during the 1930s persuaded Quebec and Ontario to prop up the prairie provinces whose plight was the worst; thus it was only in 1940 that the first nationwide scheme of social insurance came into being. However, a late start proved to be a good start. Using the tremendous mobilization effort during World War II as its starting point, the Canadian government surged ahead after

1945, creating a welfare state similar to most European ones and far surpassing that of the United States.

Thus the evolution of the Canadian state was shaped – as, in some ways, it continues to be – by the different pulls exercised by the British and American models on the one hand and by friction between French- and English-speaking people on the other. The first factor also applied to Australia; but the second did not. Following a century and a half of exploration along the coast, the first white settlers arrived in 1788 in the form of 980 people, 730 of whom were convicts and the rest royal marines charged with overseeing them. As additional immigrants, some convicts and some free, came in, they settled in widely dispersed locations; having little in common, each one subsequently became the nucleus of a separate colony. Though the system of government in each colony was never proprietary – the governors were officers and wardens, not owners – initially it was strongly authoritarian and run on prison-like lines. The turning point came between 1810 and 1820 when the colonists, having discovered sheep-raising, got on their economic feet. The first executive and legislative councils, both of them nominated, were set up in 1824 and 1829 respectively. As in Canada, the need for revenue soon led to democratization. In 1842 the colony of New South Wales became the first to hold elections on the continent; fifty years later South Australia gained the distinction of becoming one of the first countries to enfranchise women. On the other hand, progress toward establishing a unitary state was slower than in Canada, given that settlement was extremely sparse and limited to the rims; the interior was, and remains, essentially a desert.

When it came, the impetus toward unity and eventual statehood was provided by the fear of German imperialism on the one hand and of Asian, particularly Chinese, immigration on the other. The former caused the government of Queensland to force the hand of a reluctant Gladstone and take possession of New Guinea. The latter soon resulted in a veritable Asiaphobia which in some ways has persisted to the present day. The first continental congress, whose purpose was to discuss common measures against both threats, met in October 1883, opening the way to the first constitutional conventions which were held between 1891 and 1898. By 1900 they had worked out a constitution for what, developing on Canadian lines, was soon to become a Dominion whose continuing relationship with Britain was based entirely on a voluntary association. As in Britain, there was a prime minister elected by parliament and dependent on maintaining a majority among its members. As in the United States, the lower house of that parliament was based on a popular franchise, while the upper one had an equal number of representatives from each state. As in the United States and Canada, too, there was a written constitution and a high court responsible for interpreting it.

With these arrangements in place, the real turning point toward the establishment of a unified Australian state proved to be World War I. At one time or another almost 10 percent of the population served in the military; as Australian units distinguished themselves at Gallipoli – the anniversary of the landing, which took place on 25 April 1915, became a national holiday equivalent to the Fourth of July – and other battles a new sense of unity was created. Riding a nationalist wave, the movement toward centralization continued and in 1927 Canberra was officially designated as the national capital. Next, the shift in global power resulting from World War II caused a shift from a British to an American orientation; in the 1960s Australia was one of the few nations, and the only white one (apart from New Zealand), to send troops to Vietnam. Unlike Canada, which in 1982 went independent and set itself up as a new state centering around the maple leaf, Australia, though completely sovereign, did not cut the constitutional link with Britain, though it may yet do so in the future. More prosperous than most, it was slow to expand government authority into social affairs. State-run old-age and invalid insurance schemes were provided in 1908, but there matters got stuck. Only in the late 1950s and the early 1960s did the welfare state arrive, and even then the rule of the Labor Party, which introduced the reforms, lasted for only a few years.

The Dominion model was equally successful in New Zealand, which to this day remains more English in character than any other. Coming under the British crown in 1839, it was given responsible government in 1852. Once the Maori Wars had ended, it developed peacefully from 1870 on, going further than Australia in constructing a welfare state which is now (from the early 1990s on) being dismantled. Peace, however, did not prevail in South Africa where the situation was much more complicated. The European settlement at the Cape originated as a trading station where ships bound for Asia stopped to refresh their provisions and crews. For a long time it remained the property of the Dutch East India Company; but already during the eighteenth century some Boers, or farmers, broke away. Using their ox-drawn wagons as mobile homes they moved inland. There they developed their own language – a combination of colloquial Dutch interlaced with French words introduced by an infusion of Huguenots – and adopted a nomadic life in many ways similar to that of the natives whom they conquered and exploited.[55] Other Afrikaners, as they called themselves, were able to save money and emancipate

[55] For the Boers' lifestyle during these years, see C. W. de Kiewit, *A History of South Africa, Social and Economic* (Oxford: Oxford University Press, 1941), pp. 19ff.

themselves from Company rule, becoming freeholders in the Cape itself. In 1814 the entire area, which at that time had some 22,000 white inhabitants in addition to an unknown number of others, passed from Dutch to British rule. The steady influx of white immigrants, British rather than Dutch, continued while the population was also augmented by the import of Asian labor. As happened in other British colonies, the need for revenue caused representative institutions to emerge from 1853 on; nineteen years later the Cape was granted full responsible government. Originally it was based on a color-blind, though property-based, franchise – the intention being that the more prosperous blacks would support the white minority against the rest.

Meanwhile, however, the introduction of British law, including above all the abolition of slavery, had caused conflicts with the resident Dutch. During the 1820s the latter started emigrating north and east, a movement which became institutionalized during the 1830s; coming to be known as the Great Trek, it ultimately involved a possible 15,000 people. Clashing with the native population – primarily the Zulu, Ndbele, and Xhosa tribes, at that time expanding in the opposite direction and setting up strong chiefdoms – the Boers defeated them in a series of wars that took place between about 1850 and 1870. The upshot was the establishment of two small republics, the Orange Free State and Transvaal, with constitutions ironically modeled upon that of the United States. In both of them the right to participate in politics was reserved for whites only. The remaining 80 percent or so of the population were excluded from the polity and, the lands on which they used to graze their cattle having been taken way from them, survived by squatting where they could and working for the Boers. The first British attempt to take over was defeated at Majuba Hill in 1881. But no sooner had this been accomplished than vast deposits of gold were discovered around Johannesburg. This led directly to an influx of immigrants from all over the world, the Jameson Raid, and so to the Boer War of 1899–1902.

Though 200,000 British troops were finally able to overcome the Boers, as early as 1907 self-rule was restored to them. In 1910 the Union of South Africa, made up of four former provinces (Orange, Transvaal, the Cape, and Natal) and populated by about 1,250,000 whites as well as perhaps four times as many others, came into being. Its first prime minister was Louis Botha, who, less than a decade earlier, had been commander-in-chief of the Boer army. From then on, but particularly after the country emancipated itself from its Dominion status in 1948, South African politics have been dominated by the relationship between the white minority (itself divided into English- and Boer-speaking groups) and the immense black majority.[56] The latter was constantly augmented by newcomers seeking employment in the continent's largest economy. The more it grew, the harsher the measures considered necessary to keep it in its place, i.e., as a cheap labor force with no political and hardly any personal rights. Though priding itself on being part of the West, South Africa during the 1950s and 1960s developed into a police state of the worst kind with laws against everything from free residence and mixed sporting teams to interracial marriage[57] – one which, though primarily intended to discriminate against the black population, was almost equally repressive on whites.

To summarize, the American Revolution which emancipated the original thirteen colonies permitted a modern state to emerge: one which, over the next two centuries, grew progressively more powerful and more centralized as one move after another enabled the federal government to take on additional functions and increase its authority at the expense of both the individual states and, some would say, the American people. Elsewhere developments took a different course. Experience had taught the British the futility of denying the inhabitants of their white colonies the rights which they themselves possessed and of which, indeed, they were proud; by and large they were ready to grant those inhabitants representative government almost as soon as it was demanded. In return, the Dominion status acquired by the colonies in question ensured that their foreign policies remained in British hands and that their resources and military manpower – even those of South Africa, however recent the defeat of the Boers – would remain available to the mother country during the critical era of total war. Though certainly not without their troubles – Canada in particular never outgrew the hostility between English and French and may still disintegrate into two or more states – all these countries were immensely successful in establishing stable governments, flourishing economies, and strong civil societies with well-developed institutions. The one exception was South Africa where prosperity, and indeed the state itself, belonged to the white minority only. The presence of a massive, economically backward, native population divided into numerous antagonistic tribes makes it doubtful whether the state can survive at all; but that is a question which, properly speaking, belongs to the last chapter of this book.

[56] See N. M. Stultz, *Afrikaner Politics in South Africa, 1934–1948* (Berkeley: University of California Press, 1974).

[57] See B. R. Bunting, *The Rise of the South African Reich* (Harmondsworth, UK: Penguin Books, 1969).

The Latin American experiment

Whereas much of the Anglo-Saxon expansion during the period 1600–1850 took place against the background of almost empty continents, the same was not true of the Spanish colonization of Central and South America. Estimates of the size of the native population on the eve of the Spanish arrival vary greatly; however, there is no doubt that, even after warfare, disease, malnutrition, and overwork caused a disastrous decline during the subsequent century, Amerindians still outnumbered Spaniards by a factor of between five and thirty to one.[58] Nor were the latter concerned with driving the former off, as was frequently the case in North America and Australia where the natives, accustomed to leading nomadic lives, were seen as useless by their conquerors. On the contrary, once the initial massacres were over, the importance of the natives to the economy was quickly realized. As a result they were penned in – sometime, literally so – and distributed *en bloc*, whether to private owners or to the church. As the conqueror of Mexico, Hernando Cortés alone received an estate or *encomienda* with 23,000 Amerindian serfs who owed him tribute and over whom he acted as landlord, governor, supreme justice, and chief of police all rolled into one. Other *encomenderos* benefited in proportion, estates with 2,000 tribute-payers or more living on them being by no means uncommon. Imitating their opposite numbers in Castile and Aragon, they set up private armies to enforce their power.[59]

Between 1542 and 1549, fears of feudalization, as well as horrifying reports concerning the atrocities being inflicted on the Amerindians, caused Emperor Charles V to change his mind. Working through the Conseio de las Indias (Council of the Indies) as the highest organ responsible for the colonies, he tried to abolish the *encomiendas*. A massive revolt ensued and Charles had to retreat; in the event the only change introduced was to limit inheritance, so that *encomiendas* that fell vacant reverted to the crown and all did so after the fifth generation. To compensate even for this limited change, the system of *repartimiento* or forced labor was introduced. Building on foundations previously laid by the Aztec and Inca empires, it obliged the Amerindians to work either for private individuals or else for the government in building roads, portage, and the like; for example, in Peru every able-bodied native had to spend

[58] For figures on the population in general, see A. Rosenblat, *La población indigena de America dese 1492 hasta la actualidad* (Buenos Aires: Editorial Nova, 1954), as well as W. Borah, *The Aboriginal Population of Central Mexico on the Eve of the Spanish Conquest* (Berkeley: University of California Press, 1963). Data on the ratio of whites to Amerindians in Mexico can be found in W. Borah, *New Spain's Century of Depression* (Berkeley: University of California Press, 1951), p. 18.

[59] For the early history of the *encomienda*, see B. Simpson, *The Encomienda in New Spain: The Beginning of Spanish Mexico* (Berkeley: University of California Press, 1966).

six months every seven years in the infamous silver mines.[60] Other natives remained bound to the *haciendas* by means of debt peonage, living and dying on the farms where they received their wages in kind. Particularly in the more remote regions where government power did not penetrate, this meant that they were completely at the mercy of the owners who both exploited them economically and exercised "political" rule over them. One way or another Amerindian labor provided the foundation both for any economic progress in the colonies and for the wealth that soon began to flow from them to Spain. Without them neither Peru nor, later, Mexico could have turned into the treasure-houses that they did.

Politically speaking, the government of Latin America was an extension of the one at home.[61] Discovered by Europeans at a time when the separation between ruler and state was only beginning to crystallize, the lands in question were seen as the property of the king who ran them with the aid of the above-mentioned *conseio*. The highest presence on the spot was that of the royal governors. Originally there were two, located in Mexico and Lima; much later two more were added at New Grenada (1717) and Buenos Aires (1778). Then came the captains-general. At first there were officers who served under the governors as commanders of the – rather scanty – military forces at their disposal; but later more were appointed and given their own districts to run, whether they were subdivisions of the viceroyalties or smaller ones that reported home directly. The third echelon of government consisted of the *corregidores* who fell into two kinds, those with responsibility for overseeing Spanish towns and *corregidores de indios* in charge of Amerindian *pueblos*. Each of the twelve governors and captains-general who eventually emerged was assisted by an *audiencia* of the juridical-executive council, while lower-level complaints were tried by itinerant justices or *oidores*.

As in contemporary Europe, the bureaucratic pyramid that eventually emerged was venal and shot through with corruption, as officials, having bought their posts, tried to compensate themselves and make a profit if possible. As in Europe, too, it tended to become more so as time went on. Its venality even constituted a check on the authority of the crown which it was supposed to serve – all the more so because, owing to distance and the difficulty of communication, many officials could do as they pleased. At a time when towns back home were being brought under control, an element of self-government was provided to those in the New World in the form of the *cabildos* or municipal councils. Each Spanish town had

---

[60] For a firsthand account of the system, see J. Juan and A. de Ulloa, *Discourse and Political Reflections on the Kingdoms of Peru* (Tulsa: University of Oklahoma Press, 1978), pp. 77ff.

[61] See E. G. Bourne, *Spain in America, 1450–1580* (New York: Barnes and Noble, 1962), pp. 227ff., for a brief account of the principal institutions.

one, made up of twelve *regidores* who were elected by the well-to-do citizens or *vecinos* and approved by the governor or captain-general; some even had the right to appoint their own successors. Under these circumstances the *cabildos* quickly turned into closed, self-perpetuating oligarchies which, as was often the case in early modern Europe also, ran the towns primarily in their own interests. During subsequent centuries the *cabildos* often declined as royal officials tightened their grip. But they never disappeared, and indeed whenever the crown wanted to introduce reforms its first step was to turn to the *cabildos* without whose cooperation nothing could be done.

These institutions, as well as the minor officials – scribes, constables, supervisors of markets, etc. – were not particularly original when compared to those of the homeland. The factor that modified, even transformed, them was the existence in Latin America of deep racial divisions. White females, whether free or slave, entered the colonies almost from the beginning. Here they formed a small minority, initially perhaps no more than 10 percent; thus the Spanish conquest of America was at the same time a conquest of native women who, in the words of one German mercenary serving the Spaniards in the Rio de la Plata area, were considered "very handsome and great lovers, affectionate and with ardent bodies."[62] By making the possession of the *encomiendas* dependent on the production of an heir, initially at any rate the crown encouraged those *encomenderos* who could not obtain spouses from Spain to marry local women; other cases (especially among the clergy) involved concubinage, outright sexual slavery, or casual liaisons. Whatever their duration and legal status, inevitably these unions resulted in mixed offspring. The situation was further complicated by the presence of black slaves. The first ones were brought in as early as 1502 from Spain itself. Later several millions were imported from Africa to replace the dwindling Amerindian labor force. Since, among them too, men formed the great majority, they had to turn to such Amerindian or *mestizo* females as came their way. The end result was the appearance of a fantastic number of different combinations which the Spaniards, always scholastically inclined, did their best to classify and catalogue.[63]

Though the gradations were often absurd, the prejudices behind them were very real. The European Middle Ages had not, by and large, been racially minded, preferring to classify people according to their religious faith. Later, attitudes changed. The succession of Charles V by Philip II

[62] U. Schmidel, *Derrotero y viaje España y las Indias*, E. Warnicke, ed. (Asuncion, Paraguay: Ediciones NAPA, 1983), p. 113.
[63] For two such catalogues, see M. Moerner, *Race Mixture in the History of Latin America* (Boston: Little, Brown, 1967), pp. 57–8.

marked the time when the early policy, which tolerated and even encouraged racial mixtures, came to an end. From then until the introduction of reform during the very last years of the colonial era, the home government deliberately sought to keep the *republica de españoles* separate from the *republica de indios*. Though interracial marriages were never prohibited, the two groups were governed by separate regulations. The most important one concerning the Amerindians was that they, and they alone, were subject to tribute. In addition they were prohibited from bearing arms or purchasing liquor; on the other hand, being considered "far from reason," they did not have to answer to the Inquisition. Between 1563 and 1680, when they were included in the great compilation that was published in that year,[64] a great many laws were issued whose purpose was to make members of the various racial groups take up separate residential quarters. They were also to register in separate churches, schools, guilds, and so on – a system not too different from the late unlamented one of apartheid and known to contemporaries as the *regimen de castas*.

In the case of individuals it was often all but impossible to determine who belonged to what group. No registers were kept, and people who looked white could usually pass as such; however, society as a whole had no doubt that dark was synonymous with inferior and mixed descent with illegitimacy. Throughout Latin America, the top of the sociopolitical heap was formed by recent arrivals from Spain and Portugal, known as *gapuchines* (spurred ones) and *chapetones*; they looked down on everybody else and monopolized all the most important offices, secular as well as ecclesiastical. Then came the native-born whites or *creoles* whose well-to-do members occupied seats on the *cabildos* and who also proved lower-level officials. Lower still were the poor, landless whites; but they too looked down on the various *mestizos* and *pardos*, let alone the blacks and Amerindians. Among the latter, pride of place was taken by the *caciques* or village chiefs who often collaborated with the Europeans and were sometimes promoted to *hidalgos*. With this exception the bulk of the population – white, mixed, Amerindian, and black – were almost entirely excluded from office, including ecclesiastical office as well as the universities and seminaries that led to them. Still, the supreme contempt that they felt for each other prevented them from uniting against their betters. Sticking to the remnants of its native language and religion, much of the Amerindian population in particular led a shadow-like existence in their own former lands. From time to time they made their presence felt by breaking into revolt, the largest of which was the one led by Inca Tupac

---

[64] *Recopilación de Leyes de los Reinos de las Indias* (Madrid: Paredes, 1668), book vi, title iii, articles 21–3.

Amaru – the assumed name of a *mestizo*, Jose Gabriel Condor-Canqui – in 1780–1.

It was only during the last third of the eighteenth century, under the reign of the Bourbon King Carlos III, that attempts were made to reform the system in the interest of strengthening royal control, reducing corruption, and giving the bulk of the population a somewhat greater stake in the government. The two top echelons of the administration, i.e., the viceroyalties and captaincies-general, were decentralized and their holders given greater power over defense in particular – including the raising of the first standing forces which, toward 1800, numbered approximately 20,000 men all told. Under them a new tier of government was introduced in the form of the *intendants*, salaried officials modeled upon those of France with responsibility for financial matters and public works. In an attempt to breathe new life into the *cabildos*, the old office of *corregidor* was abolished; henceforward the Spanish towns came under nonvenal *subdelegados* whose powers were less extensive. Another set of *subdelegados* was put in charge of Amerindian affairs with the aim of protecting them against the worst abuses committed by the landowners. In the event, and except for its success in ending the *repartimiento*, by and large the attempt to help the non-white population proved a failure as other forms of exploitation persisted, including tribute and the system whereby the *subdelegados* and other officials forced the population to buy from them specified quantities of specified products at prices which they themselves determined.

Visiting Mexico in 1803, the German explorer Alexander von Humboldt estimated that only one-third of the inhabitants lived even as well as the lower people in Spain, already at that time the most backward country in Western Europe;[65] in Peru, farther away from Madrid and harder to reform, the situation was even worse. However, for the upper classes the period following the end of the Seven Years War was one of considerable economic expansion.[66] In Europe demand for tropical products such as hides, cacao, coffee, tobacco, and sugar was soaring. The output of the latter alone is said to have grown tenfold between 1756 and 1800, whereas in the decades after 1788 total trade between Spain and its colonies grew fourfold. The profits provided the capital for a renewed interest in mining. After a long period of stagnation, technical improvements began to be introduced, often at the hands of German or German-trained experts who were recruited, paid, and sent to the colonies by the

---

[65] A. von Humboldt, *Political Essay on the Kingdom of New Spain* (Norman: University of Oklahoma, 1988), vol. I, p. 198.

[66] See V. Vives, ed., *Historia social y economica de España y America* (Barcelona: Teide, 1957–), vol. V.

crown. Combined with a population increase that made the necessary labor available, they soon led to a renewed flow of silver from Mexico in particular.

In theory these and other economic advances would have made the *creoles* grateful to the government which, by reforming the administration, had assisted them or at any rate made them possible. In practice, the opposite happened. At the top, the establishment of a modern civil service merely emphasized the extent to which the *americanos*, as they now started calling themselves, were excluded from it in spite of their property and other qualifications. At the bottom, the shift from venality to salaries caused many of the minor officials to lose their perks. An expanding economy found itself constricted by the old imperial system by which trade among the various colonies was prohibited and all transoceanic commerce had to be carried out exclusively with Spain by way of the famous *casa de la contratación* in Seville. Though some of the more onerous restrictions began to be removed during the 1770s, the situation resembled that which had existed in North America on the eve of the Revolution, with the difference that poor, backward Spain was far less capable of meeting its colonies' demand for manufactured goods than was Britain, the undisputed industrial giant of the age.

Beginning in the 1780s liberal ideas, imported first from France and then from North America, were able to pass censorship and began circulating. However, at best they touched only the wealthier part of the white population – the *gente distinguida*, consisting of government officials, army officers, merchants, professionals, and landowners who, though refusing any sort of self-rule to their dependent populations, wanted it for themselves. When the struggles for independence, prompted by Napoleon's conquest of the Iberian peninsula, broke out during the second decade of the nineteenth century, they were almost exclusively a question of whites fighting other whites as to who could participate in the government. A case in point is provided by one of the earliest "patriotic societies" which was formed in Buenos Aires in 1801. Membership was restricted to "men of honorable birth and good ways": in a racially based society, this translated into a ban on foreigners, blacks, mulattos, *zambos* (the offspring of blacks and mulattos), *mestizos*, and numerous other persons of mixed descent. Though the prohibition on the *mestizos* was subsequently dropped, the others remained in force, showing that there were limits to how low the society was prepared to stoop even in an enterprise so noble as wresting power from Spain.[67] Only in Mexico did the Amerindian and mixed-blood masses join the initial revolt, terrifying

[67] For this episode, see Rosenblat, *La población indígena*, vol. II, p. 155.

their betters and leading to a temporary rally to Spain. Here and else-where, the upshot was to replace a remote set of masters by another which was closer at hand, and one which turned out to be even more ruthless than those sent out by Madrid or Lisbon.

As Bolivar himself saw clearly enough,[68] against a background of slave ownership on the one hand and widespread poverty, apathy, and *de facto* serfdom on the other, the construction of abstract states would have proved very difficult – indeed the future which he forecast was one of "petty tyrants." It was made even more so because the politically con-scious populations were very small and, in sharp contrast to the situation in the United States where the original colonies were strung out along the seaboard and in easy contact with each other, scattered all over the rims of a vast continent. For example, Brazil in 1823 had fewer than 4 million inhabitants. At first sight this compared favorably with the United States in 1776; but, whereas the latter was a nation of flourishing farmers and urban residents, in Brazil the great majority were either black slaves or else a formless, near-destitute, racially diverse mass that included a remarkably high percentage of vagabonds. Other examples are Uruguay, which when it started its struggle for independence against Argentina had just 60,000 inhabitants, as well as Argentina itself which even as late as 1852 had 1,200,000 all told – including another class of men without fixed addresses, the *gauchos*. It is true that, between 1811 and 1821, all the newly independent countries adopted constitutions. They eman-cipated their colored populations, abolished tribute, and made all non-ecclesiastical civilians equal before the law (the military and the church were another matter, enjoying as they did *fueros* or privileges that put them beyond the reach of ordinary courts). However, centuries of dis-crimination, poverty, and isolation cannot be removed by fiat. In Brazil even slavery persisted until 1888.

Whatever the precise circumstances in which they lived, over 95 per-cent of the population continued to be in a position from which they could neither influence the government nor, which is even more sig-nificant, be controlled by it.[69] Among the tiny minority to whom this did not apply, to separate private interests from public affairs was almost impossible. Politics became, as they have often remained, a game of musical chairs between very small coteries; for example, in Chile the wife of one president (Manuel Bulnes, 1841–51) was the daughter of a presi-dent, the sister of a president, and the mother of a president. Taking into

---

[68] S. Bolivar, address to the Congress of Angostura, printed in *Selected Writings of Bolivar*, H. A. Bierck, ed. (New York: Colonial Press, 1951), vol. I, pp. 175–6.
[69] Figure from S. J. Stanley and B. H. Stein, *The Colonial Heritage of Latin America* (New York: Oxford University Press, 1988), pp. 32ff.

consideration local variations, generally one faction consisted of land-owners who supported centralized, authoritarian government with the aim of denying the rest of the population personal freedom (to say nothing of the right to participate in politics) and exploiting it more effectively. Their liberal opponents were typically urbanites, merchants, and professionals, but including a sprinkling of nonwhites who had somehow made good – often by way of the professions or the army which they joined and in which, thanks to exceptional ability, they rose. Their principal demands were drastic reductions in the influence of the church, including the confiscation of its immense landed property and the elimination of ecclesiastical courts; a federal, more democratic form of government; and the realization of personal freedom for their social inferiors from whom they hoped to receive support.[70] But even in those places where they could implement their platforms, democracy, hemmed in by a requirement for literacy and a high property qualification, never meant the enfranchisement of more than between 2 and 4 percent of the population, while the number of those entitled to hold public office was limited to a few thousand.

Against those handicaps, the only country that somehow succeeded in maintaining a political tradition unbroken by violence was Chile.[71] Here as elsewhere the bulk of the population was rural, illiterate, and dirt-poor, Between 1830, the year in which the opposing factions fought their last battle, and 1870, government tended to be in the hands of the conservative landowners. However, thanks to the fact that there were few Amerindians and that those who did exist were largely concentrated in the far south, at any rate a tradition of slavery, serfdom, and proprietary government were absent. When the transition to liberal rule came it was achieved by constitutional means; except for the privileged position of the armed forces and the fact that the franchise always remained rather narrow (when it ceased to be narrow it quickly led to the election of Salvador Allende as president in 1970), the resulting system of government was in many ways like that of the United States. This was not so in the remaining countries, where the wars of liberation merely marked the beginning of the struggles between the two groups. Often they were extremely violent with kidnapping, assassination, and sometimes the

[70] For a discussion of the two parties and their differences, see D. Bushnell and N. Macaulay, *The Emergence of Latin America in the Nineteenth Century* (New York: Oxford University Press, 1988), pp. 32ff.

[71] For the origins of Chilean politics, see F. J. Moreno, *Legitimacy and Stability in Latin America: A Study of Chilean Political Culture* (New York: State University of New York Press, 1969), ch. 4; and S. Collier, "From Independence to the War of the Pacific," in L. Tethell, ed., *Chile Since Independence* (London: Cambridge University Press, 1993), pp. 1–32.

extermination of entire families used as common weapons. Very frequently they created room for the emergence of *caudillos* or strongmen, a phenomenon once considered unique to Latin America but one which, following the establishment of many new states from 1945 on, has spread into other parts of the world as well.

Among the *caudillos* some stood at the head of one faction or another and mobilized their supporters from among their personal friends.[72] Many were army officers who sought to impose order even as they helped themselves to power at the head of *juntas* made up of their fellow officers. All had to be *muy hombres*, real he-men, but the few who came from obscure rural backgrounds were even more so; starting as bandit leaders of the oppressed local populations, they sometimes obtained local prominence if, fighting hard all the way, they did not get themselves killed first. Whatever the origins of the leading characters, during the century after independence virtually all of the newly created states underwent an endless series of civil wars: so in Argentina (until 1862), Bolivia (which, with no fewer than sixty revolutions, broke all records), Brazil, Colombia (some thirty civil wars), Ecuador, Mexico, Paraguay, Peru, Uruguay, and Venezuela (which had some fifty revolutions all told). From then to the present day perhaps the best thing that can be said of these and other Latin American states is that they did not wage too many wars against each other – though some of those they did wage, like the four-cornered struggle between Paraguay, Argentina, Brazil, and Uruguay in 1865–70, counted their victims in the hundreds of thousands and left the first-named country almost empty of male inhabitants. However, what they lacked in external conflict, they easily made up in terms of internal anarchy, coups, and countercoups.

To the extent that the endless civil wars permitted any economic development at all, the first half of the nineteenth century created a new situation. As Western Europe and North America entered the age of the industrial revolution the former Spanish and Portuguese colonies were unable to follow. Riddled with smuggling and corruption, the old imperial system had begun to break down even before independence was achieved;[73] but now it was abolished at the hands of both parties which, for once, found something on which they could more or less agree. Influenced by European ideas, the liberals favored free trade within the continent. Influenced by their interests, the conservatives were loud in demanding the right to exchange the crops and minerals that they pro-

---

[72] For a brief typology of the *caudillos*, see G. I. Blankenstein, *Constitutions and Caudillos* (Berkeley: University of California Press, 1951), pp. 34–7; and, at much greater length, J. Lynch, *Caudillos in Spanish America, 1800–1850* (Oxford: Clarendon, 1992).

[73] J. H. Parry, *The Spanish Seaborne Empire* (New York: Knopf, 1966), pp. 307ff.

duced for goods imported from overseas. As political instability prevented the accumulation of capital, industry was unable to develop. The
stream of factory-made European products easily overwhelmed the local
workshops, many of which were still home-based, nor was that stream
discouraged by government which often received the lion's share of its
revenue from tariffs. In particular, shipbuilding (which had been practiced in Mexico from the very beginning) and the manufacturing of
metals and of all but the most elementary textiles almost ceased. Luxury
goods came from France, those intended for mass consumption from
Britain and, increasingly, the United States. As had happened in much of
Eastern Europe during the sixteenth century and in Russia and India
during the nineteenth, the outcome was deindustrialization.[74]

To the extent that they were not limited to mere subsistence – still the
lot of a considerable part of the population – the new states' contribution
to the world economy was made almost exclusively in the form of food-
stuffs and raw materials. Though the towns did not disappear, their
economic role declined compared to the last decades of colonial rule.
They remained in existence mainly as administrative centers or, if their
geographical position permitted, *entrepôts* through which foreign products entered the country and spread inland. The towns' plight enabled
the various conservative factions – parties is too grand a word – to
maintain their power in opposition to the liberals and at the expense of the
remainder of the population. Particularly in Mexico and Brazil, the shift
of landed wealth out of the hands of Amerindian communities and into
those of private individuals went on throughout the nineteenth century,
whereas in Argentina, as in the United States, ownership of "empty"
spaces (meaning spaces inhabited by the native population) was settled
by means of the gun. In all three countries, and in others as well, the
resulting estates could often be measured in square miles rather than
acres. Except for luxury articles for the use of the master and his family,
they were almost entirely self-sufficient; regardless of what the law might
say, many landowners retained their own police forces, prisons, and even
instruments of torture as means for keeping their Amerindian and *mestizo*
dependents in check. Nor did conditions change very much during the
second half of the nineteenth century when an influx of foreign capital,
first British and then American, started. On the contrary, the foreigners
often conspired with the conservatives in order to preserve political
tranquility and a dirt-cheap, semi-servile labor force in what were known
as banana republics.

[74] On the emergence of the neocolonial economy, see C. Furtado, *The Economic Development of Latin America* (New York: Cambridge University Press, 1970); and Stanley and
Stein, *Colonial Heritage of Latin America*, ch. 5.

Entering the last quarter of the nineteenth century, many of the Latin American states were states mainly in name. If only because the various *caudillos* sought to reinforce their position by means of elections, almost all had gone through periods, albeit usually ones that were very brief, of constitutional government; Ecuador, for example, by 1895 had been blessed with no fewer than eleven constitutions. All had some kind of government bureaucracies, albeit ones that were very undeveloped and, owing to the extremely low salaries which were received by the employees, wide open to corruption. Each one also had its national currency, though all tended to be highly inflationary and none was ever able to develop into a recognized international means of exchange. Amply provided with national flags, anthems, postage stamps, and similar paraphernalia, they claimed to be sovereign in their external relationships; but even that claim was made somewhat doubtful by episodes that led to the creation of Panama out of Colombia's rib in 1903. They maintained a diplomatic apparatus, often one whose external splendor stood in inverse proportion to economic conditions at home. Several of them also sent representatives to the various international conferences that took place from 1864 on.

Another feature of the last quarter of the nineteenth century was the beginning of large-scale immigration into what had hitherto been a remarkably underpopulated continent. Previously, several Latin American governments had tried to attract immigrants; but the persistence of civil wars and the greater attractiveness of other regions, primarily the United States, made this impossible. Now, the largest numbers of immigrants came from Italy, Spain, and Portugal (most of the latter went to Brazil); but there were also numerous other groups including Irish, Germans, Chinese, and Japanese. Depending on the makeup of their original populations and on the number whom they absorbed, some countries became virtually white, as Argentina and Uruguay did. Others, such as Mexico and Brazil, turned into truly multiracial societies, whereas others still (particularly in the northeastern part of the continent) found that the entry of additional groups caused the distinctions between whites and Amerindians to become blurred and the *regimen de castas* to break down. Moreover, though immigration benefited agriculture – in Argentina alone the number of square miles under the plow increased from 3,730 in 1865 to 95,000 in 1915 – most of the newcomers came to live in cities. There they took on urban occupations in trade, industry, and services, thus forming the nucleus of a true proletariat. In the larger countries at any rate, the rise of mass societies finally put an end to the rule of the unstable, family-based coteries. Instead it gave rise to something like modern political parties, whether conservative or liberal, centralist or federalist, socialist, or even communist in outlook.

In the most important countries these factors, along with a degree of industrialization that began in the 1920s, brought the old tradition of *caudillismo* to an end. However romantic they may have been, Emilio Zapata and Pancho Villa – both of them rising from extremely humble rural backgrounds – had no successors. Their role in staging coups was soon filled by the various national armies. Not that those armies had been politically inactive during the previous century, but at that time they had often amounted to undisciplined rabbles hardly different from those raised, privately, by the various *caudillos*. While that situation has persisted in some of the smaller countries – notably those of Central America and the Caribbean – the armies which, starting with the 1930 coup in Argentina, began to play a dominant role in the life of some of the major ones were a different matter. Between 1890 and 1910 several of them were kicked into shape by foreign experts, whether German (who left their mark in the form of the goose-step and a predilection for Wagnerian music), French, or American. As of the last years before World War I all came to be based on conscription, though in practice it applied only to the lower classes whereas the rest either bought substitutes or, later, fled into the universities. Commanded by lifelong professionals, bureaucratically managed, and disciplined, after 1930 or so they often developed fascist and even nazi sympathies. Looking around, they saw civilian institutions as weak and corrupt, and themselves as the true embodiments of the state, the only organizations capable of rising above the narrow interests of faction and class.[75]

Disciplined or not, the long tradition of civil wars and coups meant that a key characteristic of the modern state – a clear separation between the forces responsible for waging external war and those charged with maintaining internal order – did not emerge. Busy as they were with the latter, the armies in question never became very good at the former. There was a time, toward the end of the nineteenth century, when the Chilean armed forces in particular seemed about to develop into a modern military organization; but in the face of opponents such as Peru and Bolivia there was little incentive for keeping them so even if the economic situation (governed by the collapse of guano prices after the outbreak of World War I when a method for capturing nitrogen from the air was discovered) had permitted it. Compared to other continents, military expenditure in Latin America had never been particularly high, usually amounting to no more than 3 or 4 percent of GNP. On a per capita basis it had even been

[75] For the development of Latin American armed forces during this period, see J. J. Johnson, *The Military and Society in Latin America* (New York: Praeger, 1976), chs. 3 and 4.

conspicuously low, e.g., $58 in Argentina, $40 in Brazil, $61 in Chile, and $11 in Mexico (figures for 1990–2).[76] However, the money that they do get they tend to spend less on modern arms than on instruments of internal control, including also extensive perks for the personnel in question. Outsiders have often been bemused by Latin American generals with their splendid uniforms and bemedaled chests – in a continent that, since the Chaco War of the 1930s, has been virtually free of interstate armed conflict, one wonders where they could have been earned. To their own people the armies in question took on a much more serious, not to say menacing aspect: true juggernauts whose power *vis-à-vis* their civilian society is mitigated primarily by the tendency of many of them toward corruption.

The years since 1940 have, in fact, witnessed any number of military coups which were naturally followed by military regimes. To adduce but a few examples, Argentina was under military government from 1943 to 1946 (when a colonel, Juan Peron, became president) and again in 1955–8, 1970–3, and 1976–83. Bolivia was under military rule in 1936–9 and 1943–6, whereas the period from 1964 to 1982 saw a whole series of military regimes. Brazil suffered a military coup in 1945 and another one in 1954; then came a period of military government that lasted from 1963 until 1978. Chile was under military rule from 1973 to 1990, Colombia from 1953 to 1957, Costa Rica in 1947 (after which the army was formally abolished) – and this list does not even exhaust the first three letters of the alphabet. In them and elsewhere both the periods of military rule and the intervals between them have often been marked by outbreaks of violence, some of which cost the lives of tens of thousands. Much of the time the military saw itself as the only institution capable of creating order out of the chaos left by corrupt, self-seeking politicians. Usually their intervention was meant to oppose a drift toward socialism or even communism – notoriously so in Argentina, Bolivia, Brazil, and Chile where, against the background of the Cold War, they received American backing in the form of advisers, funds, weapons, training, and sometimes much more. However, there were also cases when the army took power in the name of a left-wing social and economic program, as in Peru between 1968 and 1975.[77]

In minor republics such as Guatemala, Honduras, Panama, and Colombia, the military takeovers were often merely the instrument for advancing the interests of a few senior – sometimes even not so senior –

---

[76] Data from *Britannica Book of the Year, 1993* (Chicago: Encyclopaedia Britannica, 1993), pp. 552, 571, 583, 670.
[77] For a typology of Latin American military coups, see E. Liuwen, *Arms and Politics in Latin America* (New York: Praeger, 1967), pp. 132ff.

officers and their families. In the major ones the slogan under which the new rulers operated was usually modernization. Taking Brazil as our example, they sought to achieve economic stability, create the conditions for growth (as an alternative to revolution from below), and improve the infrastructure – including also educational and medical facilities for which purpose they often made use of their own, uniformed personnel. Above all else, they sought to end the traditional "coffee economy" by encouraging industrialization. Taking a strongly interventionist approach, they poured money into energy, transportation, and state-owned plants for import substitution, protecting them by tariff walls. They also tried to attract foreign capital by providing benefits such as tax breaks and the free withdrawal of hard currency; and they did their best to discipline the labor force by emasculating trade unions, prohibiting strikes, imposing wage controls, and the like.[78]

Often these measures worked for a while, bringing down inflation and creating the illusion of prosperity and progress – in Brazil, for example, economic growth between 1964 and 1968 was among the highest in the world. However, sooner or later a recession would occur owing to a drop in the value of exports, the tendency of the new state-sponsored industries to become entangled in their own bureaucracies, or both. Against a background of declining real wages, the ruling clique found themselves confronted by left-wing labor organizations. Suppressing the latter's open activities merely drove them underground, leading to acts of terrorism and sabotage. When the opposition was joined by the sons and daughters of the middle classes, often university students who were disturbed by the persecution and torture as well as the lack of political freedom, the game was up. As their own military supporters split between hardliners and those who favored greater freedom, the generals would give way, hold elections, and return to the barracks. Often, however, they did not go without dictating terms to their successors. This included an amnesty for the torturers, hardly any of whom were ever put on trial, as well as their own continuing right to act as the self-appointed watchdogs of the constitution, ready to step in again if they deemed it appropriate. Sometimes the military has formed a state within a state: so, for example, in Chile where they have their own delegates in parliament as well as dedicated sources of revenue (deriving from the export of copper) that are outside government control.

As the 1980s changed into the 1990s, the threat of communism receded – indeed Chile's military proudly proclaimed that it was in their country, and thanks to them, that the red tide first began to turn. Almost

[78] See T. E. Skidmore, *The Politics of Military Rule in Brazil* (New York: Oxford University Press, 1988), for an analysis of the period in question.

all countries returned to civilian government, while the enfranchisement of the poor and the illiterate, as well as women, created vastly larger electorates. These changes made some observers feel that armies were going the way of the *caudillos* and that the period of coups, revolutions, and military rule in the continent was finally coming to an end.[79] Even assuming this to be true, many Latin American states were confronted with a new problem. During the first century or so after independence it had been the rural areas, remote and often isolated owing to poor communications, that escaped the control of the state – which incidentally explains why, from Zapata down, they served as the starting point for so many *caudillos*. As of the last quarter of the twentieth century some governments still have difficulty controlling the countryside – one need only think of the civil wars in El Salvador and Nicaragua, the Sendoso Luminoso in Peru, and the Zapatista uprising in southern Mexico. However, another and often more serious problem has risen in the form of their inability to run the cities including, often, their own capitals.

The root of the problem is to be found in population growth. Since the end of World War II it has often been running at 2.5 to 3 percent a year; pushing millions of people out of the countryside and into the towns. Between the 1960s, when it was still possible to speak of the "urban–rural imbalance" as the root cause of all problems,[80] and 1990, many countries have seen the percentage of their people who live on the land and live by agriculture drop by some 60 percent. The winners, if that is the word, were the larger cities which witnessed phenomenal growth. The Federal District of Buenos Aires had 3,400,0000 inhabitants in 1950 and over 9,000,000 in 1992 (out of a total population of 33,000,000). For Caracas the figures are 700,000 and 2,000,000; for Lima 950,000 and 6,000,000; for Rio de Janeiro 3,000,000 and 5,000,000; for Santiago 1,280,000 and 5,300,000; and for Mexico City 2,800,000 and a whopping 16,000,000.[81] The centers of these and other cities – Latin America now has twenty-one urban concentrations with over a million people each, up from six in 1950 – often present the visitor with stunning displays of ultramodern architecture and all that is most advanced in contemporary Western civilization, including some of the world's heaviest concentrations of smog. However, they are surrounded by areas which, in developed countries, would not be recognized as cities at all: without paved streets, running water, sewers, illumination, or public buildings, merely

---

[79] For some optimistic views on the future of Latin America, see L. Diamond, et al., eds., *Democracy in Developing Countries: Latin America*, vol. IV (Boulder: Rienner, 1989); and O. Gonzalez Casanova, *Latin America Today* (Tokyo: United Nations University, 1993).

[80] J. M. Schmitt and D. D. Burks, *Evolution or Chaos: Dynamics of Latin American Government and Politics* (New York: Praeger, 1963), pp. 95ff.

[81] Figures from *Encyclopaedia Britannica* (London: Encyclopaedia Britannica, 1956); and the *Britannica Book of the Year, 1993*.

endless shanties grouped in slums variously known as *favelas*, *callamoas*, *barrios*, *chiampas*, or – in Argentina – *villas miseria*.

The populations of these slums are, of course, poorer than poor. Often their extreme want excludes them from the state-run education system; in spite of massive investments in education during the last few decades, the absolute number of illiterates in most Latin American countries is constant or growing.[82] The physical distance between *barrios* and the modern parts of the cities in question is often measured in hundreds of yards. The political distance is measured in centuries because, as far as the formers' inhabitants are concerned, president, cabinet, parliament, and even the bureaucracy might as well be on Mars. Here and there a clinic or a club for the elderly may be in operation, its dedicated personnel doing what they can to alleviate some of the worst misery. That apart, the only representatives of the state whom the slum residents are at all likely to encounter are the police. Often the latter are reinforced by military or paramilitary organizations as things become particularly bad and the inhabitants of more affluent neighboring areas demand action.

In brief, just as Latin American states seem to be approaching some kind of political stability at the top, most of them also appear to have failed in their attempt to integrate the poorer quarters of their cities as European ones did during the nineteenth century.[83] On the contrary, given the still continuing pressure of population the situation in many places may be worse than it was twenty or thirty years ago, with "stark poverty and the income distribution problem . . . measuring the failure of the post-war development process."[84] Like the underclasses of eighteenth-century Europe, the residents of the *barrios* are too poor and inarticulate to pose a political threat in the ordinary sense of that term. If they live outside the law, this lawlessness is directed primarily against each other; hence it is rarely even registered by the police who, in any case, are perceived as the enemy. In most cases the absence of leadership and organization means that the occasional riot which does take place is not translated into an uprising, let alone revolution; usually it fizzles out with a few dead but without the need for large-scale repression. On the other hand, the slums represent a place of refuge from the state, as well as an inexhaustible reservoir from which individuals and organizations operating outside the law can draw their followers.

Relying on the gun – in most Latin American countries weapons are

---

[82] Calculated from B. Klein and M. Wasserman, *A History of Latin America* (Boston: Houghton Mifflin, 1988), appendix, tables 1 and 3.

[83] See M. Edel and R. E. Hullman, eds., *Cities in Crisis: The Urban Challenge in the Americas* (New York: University of New York Press, 1989).

[84] Quote from the concluding section of E. Cardoso and A. Fishlow, "Latin American Economic Development, 1950–1980," *Journal of Latin American Studies*, 24, 1992, supplement, pp. 197–219.

easily available – these organizations and these individuals often create enclaves inside which their power is absolute or nearly so. Nor is it merely a question of the slums remaining outside the state's control; using a combination of threats and the economic benefits that drugs in particular can yield, strongmen emerge from the underworld to influence local and even national politics. Often they are able to corrupt the police, the armed forces, the bureaucracy, and the legislatures; nor are all heads of state necessarily out of their reach. Perhaps it is here that the state's greatest failure may be found. From Mexico down to the smaller republics, in many cases it is hard to say whom the members of its organs are really working for, which *vice versa* is one cardinal reason why the drug problem cannot be brought under control. All this is fed by, and comes on top of, the vast socioeconomic inequalities which, though perhaps no longer as firmly rooted in race as they used to be, still cause much of the population to live in what it pleases their governments to call "absolute poverty."[85] Enfranchised or not, they feel themselves excluded from any meaningful form of political participation; and indeed often the state's most important presence takes the form of brutalities inflicted by the police or the military as they raid the slum-dwellers' miserable quarters while searching for drugs, rebels, or – since the latter not seldom finance their operations by trading in the former – both.

In marked contrast to the situation in the United States and the British Dominions, the construction of states in Latin America has succeeded only up to a point. With few exceptions, most have been able neither to put all of their people under the rule of law, nor establish firm civilian control over the military and the police,[86] nor discover a durable balance between order and freedom; externally the invasions suffered by Granada in 1983, Panama in 1989, and Haiti in 1993 (to say nothing of the role played by the CIA in Chile as recently as 1973) are but the latest in a long series of reminders that the sovereignty of the smaller ones at any rate is conditional and depends on the goodwill of Big Brother. The history of many has amply confirmed the judgment of their founder, Simon Bolivar:

I agree with you [Gran Columbian foreign minister Estanislao Vergara] that the American continent is attracting attention by its scandalous behavior . . . order, security, life and everything else are constantly moving farther and farther away from our continent, which is fated to destroy itself.[87]

---

[85] See figures in Economic Commission for Latin America and the Caribbean, *Yearbook for Latin America* (New York: United Nations, 1984). As of the early 1990s, 3 percent *more* of Latin America's population were living in poverty than ten years earlier: A. F. Lowenthal, "Latin America: Ready for Partnership?," *Foreign Affairs*, 72, Winter 1992–3, p. 85.

[86] See most recently G. B. Demarest, "The Overlap of Military and Police Representatives in Latin America," *Low Intensity Conflict and Law Enforcement*, 4, 2, Autumn 1995, pp. 237–53.

Frustration in Asia and Africa

Historically speaking, the last societies to adopt the state as their dominant political entity were those of Asia and Africa. This is not to say that, before the advent first of European colonialism and then of the movement toward independence, all of these societies comprised mere disorderly masses and did not have government. On the contrary, Asia in particular contained some of the most ancient, most hierarchical, and most powerful empires of all time, whereas both Asia and Africa displayed a bewildering variety of political systems ranging all the way from the loosest tribes without rulers to strongly governed, relatively stable chiefdoms, emirates, and sultanates as the case might be. Yet it cannot be emphasized too often that government, even strong government, does not in itself a state make. From the Bushmen of the Kalahari to the forbidden city in Beijing, not one African or Asian society seems to have developed the concept of the abstract state as containing both rulers and ruled but identical with neither. The story of how they came to adopt that state, and with what results, forms the backbone of the present section.

The way European power spread from centers such as Lisbon, Amsterdam, London, and Paris is well known. The first to make their impact were the Portuguese. From about 1450 on they had been feeling their way south along the African coast; following the voyage of Vasco da Gama in 1494, during the sixteenth century they set up a chain of fortified trading posts that ranged all the way from Angola to Mozambique and from there on to Hormuz, Goa, Ceylon, Malacca, and Macao.[88] Portuguese power did not prove lasting, however, and during the first half of the seventeenth century much of the system they had built was taken over by the Dutch.[89] Forestalled in the rich, spice-growing regions of the Indonesian archipelago, as well as Ceylon, French and British entrepreneurs were active mainly in West Africa and India. In the former they traded in gold, ivory, and slaves – the last-named commodity often in return for guns that were used by the local rulers to obtain more slaves. In the latter it was a question of trading European products, as well as silver, for oriental ones such as coffee, tea, silk, and porcelain.

A factor which all these enterprises had in common is that they were overwhelmingly commercial by nature. As both the establishment of the first *encomiendas* and the arrival of the first settlers at Yorktown, Virginia, shows, in the Americas the aim had always been to dominate and to settle: not so in the Asian and African lands. Either because they were con-

---

[87] *Selected Writings of Bolivar*, vol. II, p. 724.
[88] C. R. Boxer, *Four Centuries of Portuguese Expansion* (Johannesburg: Witwatersrand University Press, 1961), ch. 1.
[89] C. R. Boxer, *The Dutch Seaborne Empire* (London: Hutchinson, 1965), pp. 22ff.

sidered unhealthy, because they were already densely populated, or because they belonged to relatively powerful rulers, the number of Europeans that they attracted was very small. There were neither towns nor extensive states; instead there would be a fortified post that either contained a settlement or, as time passed and the latter expanded, dominated it. The Spanish and Portuguese colonies in South and Central America had always been ruled by representatives of the crown, whereas the British ones in North America soon emancipated themselves from their concessionaires. This was not the case with the "factories" planted on the coasts of Africa and Asia, which for centuries were run by the various colonial companies who appointed their own officials as governors. It is true that those companies often received the support of rulers – Portuguese expansion in particular had started as a royal business enterprise and long remained no more than that. However, strictly speaking they were neither identical with the home government nor necessarily subservient to it – as is witnessed by the fact that the Charter of the Dutch East India Company described the Company as "sovereign." .

As mentioned above, between 1600 and 1715 the East and West India companies of Holland, Britain, and France often engaged each other in hostilities while their respective governments remained at peace, and *vice versa*. Even after this ceased to be the case, the companies continued to maintain their own bureaucracies and their own armies. Both were paid for out of the companies' own coffers, though their personnel were often interchangeable with that of the state, as officials, commanders, officers, and even entire troop units were transferred from one to another by lending or sale. Long after European states had begun building impersonal bureaucracies, long even after the French Revolution had abolished the remnants of feudalism and introduced the *levée en masse*, the tradition whereby the European overseas possessions were run by private enterprise persisted. The process of transition is best followed by the example of British India, far and away the largest and most important of the lot. The East India Company was started in 1599 as a purely private venture. In 1770 it became subject to parliamentary scrutiny and its senior man on the spot, Robert Clive, was impeached for corruption. In 1773 the Regulatory Act established the supremacy of Parliament over the Company and the first royal governor, Warren Hastings, was appointed. In 1813 the Company lost its monopoly over trade. In 1834 it was turned into a managing agency for the British government; following the Great Mutiny of 1857, India became a crown colony. In 1873 the Company, having lost its function, was dissolved, and in 1876 Queen Victoria was proclaimed empress of India.

While the shift from commercial ownership to rule by government was a prolonged process, territorial expansion took even longer. From the moment when Vasco da Gama blasted the Indian junks that tried to follow him out of the water, European technical superiority made itself felt primarily at sea[90] – thus explaining why the Dutch could dominate Indonesia (although it was only during the middle of the eighteenth century that they imposed direct rule on the interior) in the same way as the French and the British dominated the Caribbean. Where there were no islands, though, expansion into the hinterland was usually very slow. For example, the first British outpost on the Indian subcontinent dates to 1611, when the factory at Masulipatam was founded. By 1700 there were four – Fort St. George, Bombay, Calcutta, and Madras – but each came with only as much land as fell "within ye randome shott of a piece of ordnance."[91] Another six decades were to pass before French and Dutch competition was overcome and a series of wars was launched which broke the power of the Mogul empire and brought the entire country under control. Similarly, Spanish and Portuguese attempts to gain a foothold on the North African coast started late in the fourteenth century and a permanent one, Ceuta, was created as early as 1415. In 1471 another enclave, Tangiers, came under European domination; however, Charles V's attempt to hold on to Bizerta failed. It was only in the 1830s that the French effort to take over North Africa, nominally part of the Ottoman empire but in practice shared out by a large number of competing emirates, got under way. India apart, serious territorial expansion on the Asian mainland started even later.

By 1914 European technical superiority, now consisting not only of sailing ships and guns, but of steamships (which made it possible to penetrate inland by navigating rivers), railways, telegraphs, and quinine,[92] had led to the partition of the entire world between a very small number of competing states. The way was led by Britain which at peak succeeded in painting one-quarter of the globe pink. Then came France, then Russia, which beginning in the early nineteenth century occupied huge tracts of Asian territory at the expense of Turkey and Persia and thus brought large numbers of Muslims under the tsar's rule. Among the remaining colonial powers, the Portuguese and the Dutch stayed more or less where they were, neither adding nor losing much after 1820. Having already let go of its Latin American empire, Spain lost most of its

---

[90] See C. M. Cipolla, *Guns, Sails, and Empires: Technological Innovation in the Early Phases of European Expansion, 1400–1700* (New York: Pantheon, 1965).

[91] Agreement between the East India Company and the Marathas, quoted in M. Edwards, *Asia in the European Age, 1498–1955* (New York: Praeger, 1961), p. 34.

[92] For the role played by those technologies, see D. R. Headrick, *The Tools of Empire: Technology and European Imperialism in the Nineteenth Century* (New York: Oxford University Press, 1981).

remaining possessions to the United States in the Spanish–American War of 1898, retaining little more than the Spanish Sahara. Germany and Italy as latecomers to the game acquired a few mostly worthless pieces in Africa and the Pacific, whereas Belgium for lack of agreement among the rest was able to lay its hands on a huge and economically very valuable piece of central Africa. The driving power behind the imperialism of those days may be gauged from the fact that even the strongest non-European political entities, i.e., the Ottoman and Chinese empires as well as Iran, lost extensive territories and indeed came within a hair of being dismembered. Apart from them, only three countries escaped – Japan and Ethiopia (the latter until 1935–6) largely by their own efforts, Thailand because the British and French who occupied Burma and Indochina respectively preferred to keep it independent as a buffer zone.

Though the system set up by the colonial powers to administrate their newly won possessions varied, it is possible to classify them into two distinct types with the majority, as usual, falling in between. On the one extreme was the method adopted by the Belgians in the Congo, known as direct rule.[93] Originally the Congo was simply a royal estate, the king having both paid for its exploration out of his own pocket and fought for recognition by the remaining powers.[94] In 1908, after reports coming out of Africa described the domains as "a veritable hell on earth,"[95] an international scandal ensued and they were brought under state control. At the peak of empire Belgium had some 10,000 civil servants in Africa as well as a somewhat lager number of businessmen and ecclesiastics; the former two types of personnel were to some extent interchangeable as some bureaucrats, retiring while still comparatively young, joined private industry. Whatever the differences between them, the three pillars cooperated in breaking any opposition they encountered by the most brutal methods imaginable including, in the early days, chopping off arms. Having done so, they exploited the native population without giving them any political rights at all. Belgian businessmen recruited the Congolese to work in their plantations and mines. Belgian officials used force to keep them there (as well as ensuring that they perform all kinds of corvées, such as building roads), and Belgian clergy assuaged the conscience of everybody concerned while promising the natives a better existence in the next world if they obeyed their masters in the present one.

At the other extreme from the Belgian system was the British one in

[93] On the Belgian model, see C. Young, *Politics in the Congo* (Princeton: Princeton University Press, 1965).

[94] On the establishment of Belgian rule in Congo, see T. Pakenham, *The Scramble for Africa, 1876–1912* (New York: Random House, 1991), chs. 1, 14, 32, 37.

[95] See "The Congo Report," in P. Singleton-Gates and M. Girodisas, eds., *The Black Diaries of Roger Casement* (New York: Grove Press, 1959), p. 118.

Africa, often known as indirect rule. Initiated by Lord Lugard during his governorship of Nigeria in 1912–18, it received its classic statement in his work, *The Dual Mandate in British Tropical Africa* (1922). It placed much greater reliance on native chiefs – if necessary creating them where, as among tribes without rulers of East and South Africa, they had not existed previously. Whether old or newly created, the chiefs had the most important functions of government such as the right to wage war, make peace, and pronounce capital justice taken away from them.[96] The British also tried to suppress native customs, such as the ordeal, that they found "repugnant." For the rest they were content to leave the chiefs to administer their own peoples according to their own traditions, even to the extent of formally appointing them servants of the crown, paying them salaries, and inventing various symbols to emphasize the respect due to them. The system was cheap to run, the number of white administrators usually being only one per 70,000–100,000 natives; as Winston Churchill, who for a time served as colonial secretary, might have said, never did so few keep down so many with the aid of so little. Another striking advantage was that, to find out what the native customs really were, the British during the 1920s and 1930s launched a number of inquiries which in turn resulted in some of the finest anthropological studies of all time.

Regardless of the way they chose to administer their possessions, all the colonial governments ultimately brought about a weakening of native institutions. Some of this came about deliberately as chiefs were decapitated – sometimes, literally so – and tribes found themselves coming under European supervision in all matters of any importance; but in large part it was the result of economic pressures. Seeking to profit from their colonies, or at least to defray the expense of governing them, every one of the new administrations imposed taxes. In societies where money had previously been little known those taxes could only be paid in cash, thus forcing populations used to subsistence farming and barter to gear themselves to the demands of a monetary system by way of trade or work for wages. As Europeans, dispossessing the natives of their land, established mining operations and set up commercial estates for growing such crops as tea, coffee, rubber, or hemp, they created a demand for labor. Some of that labor remained rural but much of it drifted into the urban commercial and administrative centers newly established by the white man. Torn away from their villages, countless Asians and Africans came to live in the closest thing to destitute, near formless masses. Except for the discipline

---

[96] For a typical example of the way it was done, see the Niger Company's blank treaty, printed in L. L. Snyder, ed., *The Imperialism Reader* (Princeton: van Nostrand, 1962), pp. 61–2.

exercised in the workplace – for those who had employment – the members of these masses, like the inhabitants of the Latin American slums, encountered the government only during the occasional raids that the police launched into their miserable dwellings. Otherwise the two sides were content to leave each other alone, living in separate quarters, enlisting in separate institutions (if any), and, converts to Christianity apart, praying to separate gods as well.

Besides tearing society up by the roots, most of the colonial administrations – a notorious exception being the Belgian one, which made it all but impossible for natives to gain any kind of education beyond the elementary – also created new elites. Often the first step on the road to Westernization was provided by the missionaries who taught the three Rs as well as elementary Western social and cultural concepts. Then there were young villagers, often the relatives of chiefs, who were given some legal and administrative training so that they could help their elders dispense the kind of justice that the colonial rulers considered acceptable. Particularly in the British colonies, natives who had received a European education often went back to their homes as teachers. Others were taken into the lower ranks of the civil service. In the case of India, the first isolated cases of this kind occurred as early as the middle of the nineteenth century, and by 1909 the Viceroy's Council was even made to welcome its first Indian member. In North Africa and the former Ottoman possessions, this development began in the interwar period, whereas elsewhere it had to wait for the period after 1945. Finally, natives could aspire to travel overseas and get a European education – in the whole world there was no more exalted status than that of the "England returned." Usually this privilege was reserved for the sons of the very rich, whether chiefs who had succeeded in keeping part of their power or merchants who made use of the newly provided opportunities. However, there were always a few others who somehow made their way to a European metropolis and worked or begged their way through. One good example was Ho Chi Minh who, living in Paris between 1917 and 1923, was in turn employed as a gardener, sweeper, waiter, photo retoucher, and oven stoker. Another was Jomo Kenyatta who came to London in order to remonstrate against the British occupation of his country and stayed to study anthropology.

As the various states extended direct rule over their companies' overseas possessions, imperialism acquired a new ideology. From 1500 to 1800 it had been primarily a question of bringing the word of God on the one hand and of making a profit on the other; but neither of these were motives which the modern, publicly owned, secular state could admit. Accordingly, the period between 1840 and 1890 or so saw the emergence of the so-called civilizing missions.[97] Enlightenment ideas concerning the equality of man, let alone the example which "the noble savage" might set to a corrupt civilization at home, were thrown overboard. Their place was taken by social Darwinist notions of "dear" versus "cheap" races; as Senator Albert Beveridge (1862–1927) of the United States put it, "God has made us adept in government that we may administer [it] among savage and servile people"[98] (referring to the inhabitants of the newly captured Philippines). Spanning the turn of the century, highlighted by Rudyard's Kipling's invention of "the white man's burden," this line of thought persisted through World War I. In the end it led straight to the mandate system, first proposed by Ian Smuts in 1918,[99] and formally adopted by the League of Nations. Former Ottoman and German possessions in the Middle East, Africa, China, and the Pacific, whose inhabitants were considered unready for independence, were entrusted to the presumably benevolent guardianship of Britain, France, Belgium, South Africa, Japan, Australia, and New Zealand. Their task was to foster them until they were ready to stand on their own feet; an annual report on progress made had to be submitted to the permanent Mandates Commission. Needless to say, in many cases the way these and other colonies were governed did not change much during the interwar period. Still, theoretically, at any rate, the rationale behind this government did change – which in turn reflected doubts which many people in the "mother" countries began to feel concerning the justice of the colonial system as a whole.

In the long run the substitution of rule by the state for private ownership on the one hand, and the emergence of an articulate, Western-educated, native elite on the other, put the colonial administrations in an intolerable position. Regardless of the form of their government – monarchical or republican, authoritarian or democratic – at home the various states were seen as incorporating rulers and ruled; but in the colonies they found themselves ruling over people who were most emphatically *not* their members, thus contradicting the very principle on which they were based. Of all the imperial governments, only that of Russia tried to tackle the problem head on. Lenin and his associates were atheistic Communists. Coming to power, they insisted that the differences of religion and even race that separated the various regions of the former tsarist empire were less important than their unity, which supposedly was

[97] See above all L. Pyenson, *Civilizing Mission, Exact Science and French Expansion, 1870–1940* (Baltimore: Johns Hopkins University Press, 1993).
[98] Quotes from C. W. Dilke, *Greater Britain: A Record of Travel in English-Speaking Countries* (London: Macmillan, 1868), vol. II, p. 405; and M. J. Bonn, "Imperialism," in *Encyclopedia of the Social Sciences* (New York: Macmillan, 1932), vol. IV, p. 610.
[99] J. Smuts, *The League of Nations: A Practical Proposal* (New York: The Nation, 1918).

322 The spread of the state: 1696 to 1975

based on the international solidarity of the proletariat.[100] In theory each of the non-Russian countries composing the empire – including some that had been part of it for centuries, such as Belarus and Ukraine – was granted self-determination and the right to secede; in practice, they were forged into a single state. The upshot was the USSR, federal in name but highly centralized in fact. However nasty the life it offered to the vast majority of its inhabitants, at any rate it did not distinguish between citizens and those who merely came under its rule. On the contrary, provincial peoples, so long as they did not find themselves accused of treason – as happened, for example, to the Tatars during World War II – often had it better. Far removed from the centers of power, they were less likely to be terrorized than those who came directly under Stalin's eye.[101]

Elsewhere the situation was entirely different. Often separated from their colonies by thousands of miles of ocean and accustomed to taking a racist attitude when contemplating their inhabitants, the home governments never seriously attempted to merge them into single states – an idea which in any case would have been preposterous given the tremendous cultural distance that separated, say, a Dutchman from a Javanese or an Englishman from a Nigerian tribesman. From the time they were established to the moment they went free, most of the colonies had neither common institutions nor common citizenship with the mother country – at best such citizenship remained a privilege granted to a few colonial residents as a reward for outstanding achievement in the fields of economics or culture. Furthermore, wherever white settlers arrived, they tended to lead separate lives of their own. Interracial marriage was frowned upon if not forbidden outright, while the offspring of mixed couples were usually rejected by both communities and treated as the lowest of the low. To the natives the government and its institutions appeared as backing a privileged minority, intent on exploiting them, their resources, and their land. Whether a policy of integration, such as the one belatedly advocated (though never seriously implemented) by the French after 1945, could have developed into a genuine partnership between the homeland and its colonies and changed the course of history by preserving the various empires will forever remain unknown. However, the disintegration of the Soviet Union from 1989 on suggests that the answer to this question is negative.

[100] For the debates on this question, see V. I. Lenin, *The Right of Nations to Self-Determination* (New York: International Publishers, 1951), pp. 122ff.; and W. Connor, *The National Question in Marxist–Leninist Theory and Strategy* (Princeton: Princeton University Press, 1984), pp. 40ff.

[101] See on this entire question R. Pipes, *The Formation of the Soviet Union: Communism and Nationalism, 1917–1923* (Cambridge, MA: Harvard University Press, 1964), pp. 41–9, 242–93.

Particularly in Asia, the first nationalist stirrings made themselves felt even before World War I. Thus, in the Philippines the Nacionalista Party won an overwhelming victory in the elections of 1907, setting the country firmly on the road to eventual independence; in India the first National Congress was held in 1885, and some Indians began to receive voting rights (for provincial assemblies) from 1910 on. In contrast to earlier attempts by chiefs to resist subjugation and by tribes to prevent expropriation and exploitation, the early nationalist movements were mostly urban-based and spearheaded by well-educated, extremely articulate leaders: so in Egypt, occupied by the British in 1882; so also in the French colonies in North Africa. They were thus the fruit of attempts at modernization rather than of the traditional ways reasserting themselves, though in many cases a deliberate appeal was made to native cultural values by way of finding symbols around which the less educated masses could rally. While the urban elite began to flex its muscles, the countryside, which very often was left more or less to its own devices so long as order prevailed and taxes were paid, stagnated. Here politically organized opposition – as distinct from a religiously motivated one – as well as individual acts of revenge directed against the white settlers and their white collaborators only got under way at a much later date.

The early nationalist movements took the form of debating societies, newspapers, and agitation, all of them closely monitored by the police and not infrequently obstructed by the arrest and exile – sometimes, worse – of leaders. In 1904–5, they were given a tremendous boost by the Japanese victory over Russia which reverberated throughout the colonial world like a pistol shot in the dark. Having been "opened to the West," from 1853 on, Japan rapidly turned itself into a modern state. By the mid-1870s it possessed a parliamentary-type government, independent courts, a functioning bureaucracy, and armed forces based on universal conscription, as well as an education system that very soon found its mission in life by propagating a virulent form of nationalism and emperor-worship. Its triumph served as clear proof that the white man was not invincible and that he could be overcome at the place where it mattered most, i.e., the battlefield. These events were soon followed by those of World War I. Not only did many thousands of Indian, North African Arab, and African black troops serve in the armies of France and Britain, but tens of thousands of Chinese and Vietnamese laborers were transported to Europe where they were put to work behind the front. Returning to their own countries after the war many of these people were not content simply to resume their places as servitors of their colonial masters. In time they were to form a reservoir on which the nationalist movements could and did draw.

When self-appointed representatives of various colonial peoples sought to bring their claims in front of the Versailles Conference – which, after all, claimed to be based on the right to self-determination – they were destined to be disappointed. Dominating the conference as they did, France and Britain resolutely refused to let it discuss the fate of their own empires. Though somewhat more sympathetic, the United States was reluctant to take up cudgels against its allies on behalf of what were later to become known as Third World peoples; this left the USSR which, however, was in the midst of civil war and in any case was not represented at Versailles. Unable to make themselves heard, the people in question – one of them was Mahatma Gandhi – returned home, where they were very soon found at the head of the various nationalist movements. Some were right-, others left-wing in their orientation; as time went on and the Communists consolidated themselves in the USSR, many of the latter received Soviet aid in the form of advisers, training, and arms. In many colonial countries the interwar years were marked by agitation, demonstrations, boycotts, and riots as in India, Burma, and Indonesia. Here and there armed uprisings took place: in Ireland in 1920–2, Palestine (occupied by the British in 1917–18 and later transformed into a mandate) in 1919–22 and 1936–9, Egypt in 1919, Morocco in 1921–6, and Syria in 1926.

Before 1939, the one clear-cut case when a colonial country succeeded in getting rid of its masters was Ireland – though in the eyes of some the achievement remained incomplete as Ulster chose to stay under British rule. In addition several countries were granted at least nominal independence while remaining under the "protection" of foreign troops; this was the case in Egypt (the treaties of 1922 and 1936), Jordan (1927), Iraq (1932, but reoccupied by the British in 1941 following Rashid Ali's rebellion), and the Philippines (which became a commonwealth in 1935 but was occupied by Japan before it could develop further). India, too, was launched on the way to independence; the Government of India Act (1936) gave the vote to 35 million people and so enabled the nationalist Congress Party to gain electoral victories in eight out of eleven provinces. Elsewhere the armed uprisings that took place were suppressed, though sometimes only at the hands of massive forces – the Franco-Spanish army that finally defeated Abd El Krim numbered no fewer than a quarter of a million troops[102] – and at the cost of equally massive bloodshed. As it turned out, the triumph of Mussolini's legions, using tanks as well as poison gas dropped from aircraft in order to asphyxiate bare-footed, spear-carrying Ethiopian warriors, was the last of its kind. From this point

---

[102] See J. Gottmann, "Bugeaud, Gallieni, Lyautey: The Development of French Colonial Warfare," in Earle, *Makers of Modern Strategy*, pp. 249ff.

on the tide turned. Beginning in 1941 the armed forces of developed countries, however powerful and however ruthless, started suffering one defeat after another at the hands of popular uprisings in the countries that they occupied; but this is a subject to which we shall return in chapter 6.

However, the factor that really set the course of history against imperialism and in favor of the establishment of many new states all over Africa and Asia was World War II.[103] In Africa the war led to the permanent loss of the Italian empire (both the part located on the Mediterranean shore and the one in East Africa) and the temporary occupation by the Allies of the whole of French North Africa. In Asia, the Philippines, Hong Kong, Indochina, Malaysia, Singapore, Burma, Borneo, Indonesia, and New Guinea had all been overrun by the summer of 1942. The Japanese conquerors were, of course, themselves Asiatic and claimed to be operating in the name of a "Greater East-Asia Co-Prosperity Sphere." That their claim carried at least some credibility is proved by the fact that, wherever their troops appeared or even threatened to appear, they found some leaders as well as part of the population prepared to cooperate with them. This applied even to China, where for all the atrocities that they committed they also set up an alternative government to the one led by Chiang Kai-shek. Whether that cooperation would have lasted if the Axis had won the war and Japanese rule had become established is, of course, a different question. Be that as it may, the defeat of the old imperial powers, which sometimes culminated in abject and well-publicized surrender, dealt a tremendous blow to their prestige from which they never recovered.

If this were not enough, all the European imperial powers, both those which had "lost" and those which had "won," ended the conflict in a state of perfect bankruptcy. Some, notably Britain, were deeply in debt to their own colonies; others found their very survival conditional on handouts from the largest power, the United States. The latter in turn was not at all certain whether, on both moral and political grounds, it should support the continued existence of its former allies' empires.[104] Requiring allies in their Cold War against the Soviet Union, the Americans later reversed themselves and helped pay for, if they did not actually wage, numerous neocolonial campaigns. Yet it remains true that, looking back, the attempt to prop up imperialism appears almost preposterous, a manifestation of political and racial attitudes more like those of the nineteenth century than of the second half of the twentieth. As late as

---

[103] See R. F. Holland, *European Decolonization 1918–1981: An Introductory Survey* (New York: St. Martin's 1985), ch. 2.
[104] See W. R. Louis, *Imperialism at Bay, 1941–1945: The United States and the Decolonization of the British Empire* (Oxford: Clarendon Press, 1977), pp. 356ff.

1950 the Portuguese seriously tried to justify their rule in Angola by describing "the raw native" as an "adult with a child's mentality," while the Belgians in the Congo claimed (no doubt rightly) that "the majority of the population does not have an idea of what effective government is all about."[105] These and similar pretensions stood in stark contrast to the situation in Indonesia, for example, where the Dutch as the traditional "imperial" power did not have the capability to retake their possessions by their own efforts but had to rely on troops put at their disposal by Britain and Australia. Similarly, in Indochina the French attempt to restore their rule (1946–53) could never have lasted as long as it did had it not enjoyed massive American financial and military backing; when such backing was absent, as happened, for example, at Suez in 1956, the attempt collapsed almost at once.

Though often accompanied by bloodshed on an enormous scale – as in Algeria and, above all, Indochina – from 1945 on the march of Asian and African peoples toward forming their own states was inexorable. The first great steps were taken in 1945–8 when the Philippines, India, Pakistan, Burma, Ceylon, Lebanon, Syria, and Israel – the latter carved out of Palestine by means of a United Nations Resolution – rid themselves of their American and European masters. Indonesia, where the encouragement given by the Japanese to Sukarno and his nationalists precluded the return of the Dutch,[106] followed in 1949–50. From this point on new states became too numerous to list. At the Bandung Conference in 1955, the leaders of twenty-nine countries (all, with the partial exception of China, recently emancipated from colonial rule), representing over one-half of the world's population attended; over the next twenty years Africa alone contributed almost fifty new names to the growing list of sovereign states.

When the Portuguese territories of Angola and Mozambique went free in 1975, the process of decolonization was substantially complete, though there still remained the questions of Southern Rhodesia, Djibouti, Namibia, and Eritrea (the last named colonized not by a European country but, following 1945, Ethiopia). The late 1970s and 1980s saw those questions being resolved, invariably by the establishment of new states which, by way of asserting their equality with their older counterparts, at once applied for UN membership. The move toward self-determination continued as a number of small islands and island groups

[105] A. J. Alfrao Cardoso, *Angola Your Neighbor* (Johannesburg: Portuguese Embassy, 1955), p. 72; Foreign Ministry of Belgium, *Belgian Congo* (New York: Embassy of Belgium, 1954), p. 42.
[106] See H. J. Benda, *The Crescent and the Rising Sun: Indonesian Islam and the Japanese Occupation, 1942–1945* (The Hague: van Hoeve, 1958).

in the Indian and Pacific Oceans gained their independence. Additional states were created when the old Soviet Union broke up. Others such as Palestine and Chechnya, seem to be in the making; if successful, their example will no doubt serve as an inspiration for others still.

With hardly any exception, Asian and African states – whether born virtually *ex nihilo* or emerging as rejuvenated versions of older polities – entered life under the slogan of modernization, by which they meant radical improvements in health, education, and living standards which in many cases were hardly above subsistence level. Though dependent on many factors, such modernization presupposed nothing so much as political stability and a functioning bureaucracy; but such stability and such a bureaucracy could be established only in a minority of new states. The most successful ones by far are located in East and Southeast Asia. Some have a long tradition of political unity and/or ethnic homogeneity, others at any rate highly literate elites which in turn facilitated the transition and in some cases led to remarkable economic growth.[107] One might indeed argue that, toward the end of the twentieth century, the most successful states are located not in Europe – where this type of political organization originated – but in Japan, South Korea, Taiwan, and of course Singapore. All four have built impersonal and well-disciplined (although, from the individual's point of view, relatively authoritarian) bureaucracies and police forces. In none is the regime of a traditional type, and in 1995 an ex-Korean prime minister in particular was taught the consequences of confusing the state's property with his own. With some luck China, Thailand, Malaysia, Indonesia, Vietnam, and even Burma (should it get rid of its military rulers) may one day follow in their footsteps, though most of these countries are ethnically far more diverse and, in the case of China, may yet turn out to be too large and complex to be effectively ruled from a single center for very long.[108]   Elsewhere in Asia and Africa the situation is, by and large, much less favorable. One reason for this is extreme ethnic diversity. The old European states had centuries in which to build a national identity, a national language (though as late as the sixteenth century a resident of London, traveling to Kent, was considered by the local inhabitants to be speaking French), a national culture, and a national system of communications. No such unity existed elsewhere; from the Philippines to Ethiopia and from Iraq

---

[107] On the cultural traditions behind this phenomenon, see L. W. Pye, *Asian Power and Politics: The Cultural Dimensions of Authority* (Cambridge, MA: Belknap, 1985), particularly pp. 21–9.

[108] For an optimistic view of China's future, see B. B. Conable, Jr., and D. M. Lampton, "China: The Coming Power," *Foreign Affairs*, 72, 5, Winter 1992–3, pp. 137–49; for a pessimistic one, see G. Segal, "China's Changing Shape," *Foreign Affairs*, 73, 3, May–June 1994, pp. 43–58.

to Sudan, attempts to create it from above were often perceived as efforts by one group to establish itself at the expense of the rest. For example, in India the dominant language – itself divided into several mutually unintelligible dialects – is spoken by only 40 percent of the population. In addition there are thirty-three other languages spoken by at least a million people each (English, as the country's would-be official language, is spoken by only 5 percent). Pakistan's population consists of 55 percent Punjabis, 20 percent Sindhis, 10 percent Pathans, 10 percent Mujahirs, and 5 percent Baluchis; Urdu, which the government hopes to turn into the official language, is spoken by only a small minority. In Nigeria the three largest groups – Hausa, Yoruba, and Ibo – between them represent only 60 percent of the population, with the remainder divided among no fewer than 250 ethnic groups;[109] on the other side of the continent Ethiopia is said to contain 76 ethnic groups who speak 286 languages.[110] But the extreme in fragmentation is probably represented by Papua where a population of 2.5 million speaks over 700 different languages. Of African states, it has been claimed that most of them "share little but their own variety."[111]

This diversity was not created by the colonial governments. On the contrary, in some ways it was simply a result of the fact that, in the Third World, the state had failed to develop. Still, to the extent that they often joined together territories and peoples that had nothing in common – sometimes, by simply using a ruler to draw a line across a blank map[112] – the imperial powers contributed to it. This was the case in much of Africa during the last decades of the nineteenth century, and in the Middle East following the disintegration of the Ottoman empire when borders were created in flagrant disregard of ethnicity and religion as well as long-established social and economic patterns such as migration. Once they had established themselves, various European administrations deliberately played off one ethnic group against another as the British did in Cyprus (Turk against Greek), Palestine (Jew against Arab), India (Muslim against Hindu), and Nigeria (Hausa against everybody else). Even when this was not the case they tended to create new contrasts as between villages and the newly developing towns, Christians and others, Western-educated classes and those who stuck to their traditional ways. Sometimes different degrees of economic development

---

[109] For a discussion of African ethnic problems in particular, see B. Neuberger, *National Self-Determination in Postcolonial Africa* (Boulder: Rienner, 1986), pp. 14–15, 25ff., 34–6, 55–6.
[110] *Economist World Atlas and Almanac* (London: The Economist, 1989), p. 293.
[111] K. Manogue, *Nationalism* (London: Batsford, 1967), p. 13.
[112] P. J. Yearwood, "In a Casual Way with a Blue Pencil: British Policy and the Partition of Kamerun, 1918–1919," *Canadian Review of African Studies*, 27, 2, 1993, pp. 214–18.

among the colonies themselves led to the influx of strangers on a large scale. South Africa, for example, though already awash in cheap labor, attracted and still attracts more from the neighboring countries of Angola and Mozambique;[113] the same is true in some of the (relatively) more successful West African states. And this does not even take into account various white and Indian – in much of Southeast Asia, Chinese – minorities that were sometimes substantial and, even where numerically tiny, tended to dominate economic life. At the time independence was achieved, how the newly established states were to overcome these circumstances and function properly remained a mystery.

In fact, in many countries the mystery was soon solved. After the enthusiasm that had characterized the early years had subsided, it turned out that many if not most of the population remained attached to their own institutions: meaning – since the most important chiefs remaining from colonial times were systematically pushed aside – extensive networks of kin.[114] Alternatively, alienated from their homeland and flocking to the rapidly growing cities, they were left with hardly any institutions at all. Either way the state, however grandiloquent its pretensions and however colorful the symbols with which it bedecked itself, remained almost irrelevant to their lives. Against a background of widespread illiteracy, often the very concept of an abstract entity was all but incomprehensible – the more so since ideas of political authority remained crisscrossed by traditional notions concerning the power of religious and magic leaders who were closer to everyday life than the state's bureaucrats.

The bureaucracies themselves, such as they were, were shot through with corruption.[115] Some of their employees were Western-educated and, as a result, so alienated from the rest of the people as to make communication difficult if not impossible. Others regarded their posts primarily as a means of discharging their obligations toward their own relatives – an attitude that, far from being condemned, was often shared and even actively abetted by society at large or, at any rate, by those segments of it which benefited. The ensuing political vacuum resulted in chronic instability. Often it was aggravated by the search for short cuts toward development in the form of megalomaniac engineering projects (dams, power plants, airports, and the like), socialist- or communist-style

---

[113] See B. B. Brown, "Facing the 'Black Peril': The Politics of Population Control in South Africa," *Journal of South African Studies*, 13, 2, 1987, pp. 256–73, for the government's attempts to deal with the problem during the apartheid era.

[114] See N. Chazan, et al., *Politics and Society in Contemporary Africa* (Boulder: Rienner, 1992), pp. 77–82, 94–7.

[115] See J. M. Mbaku, "Bureaucratic Corruption and Policy Reform in Africa," *Journal of Social, Political, and Economic Studies*, 19, 2, Summer 1994, pp. 149–75.

economic regimes, or both. These in turn sometimes squeezed the population to such an extent that it dropped out of the market economy altogether, returning to subsistence farming as in parts of Africa. Elsewhere it resorted to illegal activities such as the drug-smuggling which is endemic in much of Southeast Asia and the former Soviet republics; and even, in the waters of both West Africa and Southeast Asia, to piracy.

One way or another, the state's attempt to involve all or even most of its population in some form of orderly political life often ended in failure. Consequently, during the last few decades there has hardly been any newly independent country in Asia or Africa that did not undergo some kind of coup, revolution, or violent internecine conflict between opposing ethnic and religious groups. Many countries have witnessed a whole series of such conflicts which pitted tribe against tribe, people against people, and often the military, as the best organized group and the one most familiar with modern technology, against the less organized civilians.[116] In Congo Brazzaville, as in Belize, Granada, and the Comorian Islands, governments were so weak that they were overthrown by a handful of NCOs or mercenaries, only to be restored, with equal ease, by small contingents of foreign troops called in for the purpose. Others fell into the hands of posturing madmen such as Idi Amin in Uganda and "Emperor" Bokassa in the Central African Republic. These and similar figures in other countries would have been comic if they had not set up regimes of terror and engaged in killing tens, sometimes hundreds, of thousands of their compatriots. On the other hand, in countries where strong government *was* established, the results were sometimes even worse – both Mao Tse-tung and Pol Pot counted their victims in the millions.

All over the two continents, and saving the above-mentioned success stories in East and Southeast Asia, almost the only two exceptions to the sad parade of one-party regimes, authoritarian regimes, military regimes, and tinpot dictators of every size, color, and description are India and Israel. Of the two, the former's achievement in maintaining an almost unbroken democratic tradition (except for the period of "totalitarian" rule in 1975–7) is especially impressive in view of its huge size, ethnic diversity, religious divisions, and extremely low per capita income. Yet even at present India, taking the opposite route from the United States during the first half of the nineteenth century, is slowly turning from a single state into a gathering of semi-autonomous provinces. It has witnessed and is still witnessing ethnic and religious disturbances in such places as Bengal, the Punjab, and Kashmir; some of these are so massive that, had they taken place in a country with fewer than 900,000,000

---

[116] The classic account remains E. N. Luttwak, *Coup d'Etat: A Practical Handbook* (Harmondsworth, UK: Penguin Books, 1969).

inhabitants, they would have merited the name of civil war.[117]

Israel, too, has maintained a democratic tradition in politics. Partly because most of its original population was of European stock and highly educated, partly because it has received and is receiving amounts of foreign aid that are unequaled in the whole of history, it has gone further in its quest for modernization than virtually any other developing country except Singapore. However, and even disregarding the residents of the West Bank and Gaza Strip who together make up almost 2 million people, it contains an Arab minority composing some 20 percent of the country's population of 5 million. The question of that minority's ultimate political allegiance, especially in view of the coming establishment of a Palestinian entity of some sort, has by no means been settled. As a result, the long-term outlook for the Holy Land as well may not be the kind of peace and economic integration with its neighbors that some Israeli leaders in particular see coming,[118] but a whole series of increasingly violent ethnic and religious conflicts.

As the twentieth century approached its end, the majority of new states in both Asia and Africa presented a sorry sight. At best they had achieved some kind of stability under a strongman, as in Syria, Jordan, and Libya, though such stability was probably temporary and only barely able to hide the intense religious, economic, and sometimes ethnic conflicts that seethed underneath. Others saw themselves torn by wars, sometimes extremely bloody ones as in Afghanistan, Sri Lanka, Somalia, Sudan, Rwanda, and Liberia to mention but a few. From Algeria through Egypt, Turkey, Iraq, and Iran all the way to Pakistan, Sri Lanka, Indonesia, and the Philippines, many had groups of guerrillas and terrorists operating in their national territories – even to the point where entire provinces had escaped control by the central government and were being held down, if at all, only by the massive presence of armed forces. In other places still the state remained an empty title; never having got its feet on the ground, it simply ceased to function as in much of Central and Western Africa in particular.[119] In view of these problems some even began to question whether the model of "one nation, one state" was suitable at all and whether the various societies would not be better served by some political structures different from those which, after all had, been imposed on them from outside.[120] Beyond vague phrases, however, the form of those

[117] See S. Kaviraj, "The Crisis of the Nation State in India," *Political Studies*, 42, 1994, pp. 115–29.   [118] S. Peres, *The New Middle East* (New York: Holt, 1993).

[119] For the plight of these states, see R. Kaplan, "The Coming Anarchy," *Atlantic Monthly*, February 1994, pp. 44–76.

[120] See R. Jackson, *Quasi-States* (London: Cambridge University Press, 1990); and B. Davidson, *The Black Man's Burden: Africa and the Curse of the Nation State* (London: James Currey, 1992), for the ethnic problems in question.

structures remains to be determined. Meanwhile many of the societies in question have been going their own way, circumventing the state, ignoring it, or turning it into a hollow shell.

What everybody has . . .

During the fifty or so years since 1945 the total number of states on this planet has more than tripled, leading to congestion and causing a second line of flagpoles to be added to the first in front of UN headquarters in New York. Among the newcomers a few are represented by states which, though they did exist before 1945, were initially excluded from UN membership owing to their defeat in World War II, including Germany, Italy, Japan, and a handful of others. However, the great majority comprise countries which, until recently, were not states by our definition of that term even in the (relatively few) cases when they did not lose their independence to others.

As the preceding pages have shown, the spread of the state from Western Europe, where it originated, to other continents had been far from uniform. While the earliest transplants of political institutions took place in Eastern Europe and Latin America, at least until the beginning of the twentieth century the most successful ones have been those initiated by the British in North America and Australasia. As the case of South Africa shows, they owe their success not to some outstanding political genius but to the fact that the continents in question were practically uninhabited, which in turn usually resulted from the systematic extermination of many natives and the expulsion of the rest. More recently some states have become very successful in East Asia where they built on foundations provided by ethnic homogeneity, ancient cultures, highly literate elites, and sometimes – as in Japan – extremely strongly governed polities.[121] In most other places, though, the story is at best one of mixed success. Neither in the states that came into being after the collapse of the Soviet Union, nor in Latin America, nor in large parts of Asia and Africa, do the rulers have much cause for congratulating themselves. The problems experienced by the so-called developed world – Western Europe, North America, Japan, Australasia – are, in many cases, bad enough. Those of the developing one, including also most of the former Soviet of republics in both Asia and Europe, are almost uniformly worse.

The doubtful value which often attaches to the term "state" is also indicated by other factors. Formally all are equal; in practice the differences among them are enormous and many, indeed, never have been

---

[121] On the authoritarian tradition in Japanese politics, see above all K. van Wolferen, *The Enigma of Japanese Power* (New York: Vintage Books, 1990).

greater. One extreme is represented by the United States with a surface area of 3,680,000 square miles, a population of 270,000,000 (the third largest), a GNP of $8.5 trillion, and global interests as well as armed forces that enable it to bring force to bear at any point on the globe. On the other end of the scale are some states with areas measured in a few hundred (or even a few dozen) square miles, populations numbering in the hundreds of thousands or less, and GNPs that are so small as to keep most citizens close to the subsistence level.[122] Having lost economic ground during the 1980s, many states whose representatives occupy seats in the General Assembly now have GNPs which cannot compare to the budgets of large cities or even universities in the developed world, let alone with the turnovers of large multinational corporations. No wonder the latter are often approached cap in hand by rulers of Third World countries (and not merely those of Third World countries either) eager for investment.

Since neither their police organizations nor their armed forces have achieved the degree of autonomy and cohesion necessary for functioning effectively, many are incapable of maintaining internal order, much less of defending themselves in foreign war. Nor is it at all rare for the forces and organizations in question to present a greater threat to their own governments than to anybody else: so, e.g., in much of Latin America; but so too in parts of East Asia where, to cite but one example, Thai leaders are engaged in an earnest debate as to whether the constitution, which explicitly permits the military to mount a coup, should also guarantee the population's right to resist one if it takes place. Some states are so poor that they do not even have the wherewithal to send representatives to the majority of other states which, in turn, do not bother to be represented in them. Their education systems have barely developed since 1950;[123] their transportation systems are in chaos, their borders practically uncontrolled, their currencies (if any, since some have chosen or been forced to adopt those of their more powerful neighbors) little more than colorful pieces of paper. And indeed their very existence may be noted by the rest of the world mainly through the exquisite postage stamps that some of them issue.

To present some of these states as if they were sovereign players in the international arena is a travesty of reality. Whether because of foreign penetration or because of their excessive dependence on a single category

---

[122] Between 1970 and 1990 the gap in per capita income between rich and poor countries increased from 14.5:1 to 24:1, according to data in World Bank, *World Tables 1991* (Baltimore: World Bank, 1991), table 1.

[123] The statistics of failure are presented in M. Meranghiz and L. A. Mennerik, "World-Wide Education Expansion from 1950 to 1980: The Failure of the Expansion of Schooling in Developing Countries," *Journal of Developing Areas*, 22, 3, pp. 338–58.

of exports, often their economies are at the mercy of others much more powerful than themselves. In addition to that, in some cases the rulers who inhabit the – often splendid – presidential palaces are not their own masters. Either they work for drug lords or, as used to be and still may be the case in several Central American and Caribbean countries, the intelligence services of foreign countries. In a few cases, notably Haiti under the Duvaliers (*père et fils*), Nicaragua under the Somoza family, Panama under Noriega, and the Ivory Coast under Houphouet-Boigny, even the distinction between the private and the public has remained fuzzy; nor was the situation very different in the Philippines during the Marcos regime or in Zaire while it was ruled by Mobutu. Acting as private individuals, the presidents of these countries, their wives, their mistresses, and their offspring were simultaneously the largest businessmen by far. In this capacity they raised private armies in addition to the official ones; freely plundered the resources of the state; and not seldom engaged in an astonishing variety of legal and illegal transactions that ranged from racketeering and drug-trafficking all the way to operating prostitution rings.

At best many of these countries continue to vegetate, maintaining some kind of stability and a more or less tolerable standard of living without inflicting any particular damage either on their own populations or on others. At worst they suffer from authoritarian government and/or chronic instability and civil war, ethnic strife, religious fanaticism, guerrilla terrorism, and narcoterrorism, which in turn reflect their governments' inability to control the remote and backward countryside, the sprawling townships, the private armies of druglords and populist leaders, or all of these. Some of these conflicts, such as the Nigerian civil war of 1967–9 and the Cambodian one of 1970–95, led to the deaths of millions. Others, such as the one in Sudan, have now lasted for decades on end and have reduced entire geographical districts to a shambles. As they are too weak to play the traditional game of the balance of power, the sovereignty of some of them is conditional on their neighbors' good will. Those neighbors recruit mercenaries to interfere in their internal affairs, help organize coups and countercoups, buy or intimidate presidents, and even replace their governments as they see fit.

As the twentieth century is coming to an end, the state, once a rare political construct confined to the western extension of a rather small continent, has spread its rule all over the world. Beginning with the French Revolution, which marked its transformation from a means into an end, to have a state of one's own became something of which people used to take extraordinary pride and for which they were often prepared to make every sacrifice including, where necessary, rivers of blood. From

Palestine to Chechnya, that is still true in some places; but in many of those the chances of the people in question ever establishing their own fully sovereign states are small. Conversely, and as I shall argue later in this volume, where sovereign states already exist and are long established, they are often regarded with sullen indifference, even hostility, which may be one reason why, far from attempting to guard their sovereignty, they are in the process of voluntarily relinquishing it to other entities supposedly more capable of serving the economic needs of their citizens. In many places, the moment of the state's greatest triumph may yet prove to be the beginning of its decline. What everybody has may turn out to be worth very little.

As we saw, the man who really "invented" the state was Thomas Hobbes. From his time up to the present, one of its most important functions – as of all previous forms of political organization – had been to wage war against others of its kind. Had it not been for the need to wage war, then almost certainly the centralization of power in the hands of the great monarchs would have been much harder to bring about. Had it not been for the need to wage war, then the development of bureaucracy, taxation, even welfare services such as education, health, etc. would probably have been much slower. As the record shows, in one way or another all of them were originally bound up with the desire to make people more willing to fight on behalf of their respective states.

To focus on the field of economics alone, the Bank of England as the first institution of its kind originated in the wars which Britain fought against Louis XIV.[1] Early in the nineteenth century the first modern income taxes were likewise the product of war, as were both legal tender and its most important specimen, the greenback. Later, to cite but three examples, neither some of the early attempts to provide social security, nor the abandonment of the gold standard in 1914, nor the Bolshevik Revolution (representing the attempt to institute total state control over an economy) would have come about in the form that they did, and at the time that they did, had it not been for the need of the state to mobilize its resources and wage war against its neighbors.

No less important than the massive contribution that war made to the state's structure and organization was its function as an emotionally unifying factor. Famous as they were, the writings of Rousseau, Herder, Fichte, Hegel, and the like were read by only a relative handful. It was only when the French state, after the Revolution, instituted the *levée en masse* – in which respect it was later followed by other states – that the Great Transformation took place and nationalism, fostered by every

---

[1] See M. Godfrey, "A Short Account of the Bank of England" (1695), printed in M. Collins, *Central Banking in History* (Aldershot: Elgar, 1993), vol. I, pp. 3–10.

means at the authorities' disposal, was turned into the dominant ideology of the nineteenth century. This is not necessarily to share the views of those who believe that the sovereign state, which admits no judge above itself, is the root cause of war; rather, I believe that the real reason why war exists is because men have always liked war, and women, warriors.[2] It does, however, mean that states can develop a strong appeal to the emotions only so long as they prepare for, and wage, war. If, for any reason, they should cease to do so, then there will be no point in people remaining loyal to them any more than, for example, to General Motors or IBM, which is tantamount to saying that much of their *raison d'être* will have been lost.

The first section of this chapter argues that the ability of states to go to war against each other has been diminishing since 1945. The second section explains how, faced with this loss, they adopted socialist ideas, turned inward, and constructed the modern welfare state, only to find, from about 1975 on, that such a system was no longer either economically affordable or, as some claimed, socially desirable. The third examines the way technology, which between 1500 and 1945 was such a great help in constructing the state, has turned around and is often causing states to lose power in favor of various kinds of organizations which are either not territorially based, or lacking in sovereignty, or both. The fourth section builds on the previous ones and argues that, in places as far apart as South Africa and the United States, many states are becoming less willing and able to guarantee the life and property of their citizens, with the result that this task is being increasingly delegated to other organizations. Finally, once all these building blocks are in place, the time will have come for looking into the future.

The waning of major war

The waning of major interstate war, which during the closing years of the century is still under way, was brought about primarily by the introduction of nuclear weapons. From the beginning of history, political organizations going to war against each other could hope to preserve themselves by defeating the enemy and gaining a victory; but now, assuming only that the vanquished side will retain a handful of weapons ready for use, the link between victory and self-preservation has been cut.[3] On the contrary, at least the possibility has to be taken into account

---

[2] See van Creveld, *Transformation of War*, ch. 6; and J. Keegan, *A History of Warfare* (London: Hodder Stoughton, 1993), part 2. For a recent survey of the vast bibliography on the subject, see J. M. G. van der Dennen, *The Origin of War: The Evolution of a Male-Conditional Reproductive Strategy* (Groningen: Origin Press, 1995), 2 vols.

that the greater the triumph gained over an opponent who was in possession of nuclear weapons, the greater also the danger to the survival of the victor. A belligerent faced with the imminent prospect of losing everything – as, for example, happened first to France and Russia and then to Germany and Japan during World War II – was all the more likely to react by pressing the nuclear button, or, indeed, by falling on it as his chain of command collapsed and he lost control.

Appearing as they did at the end, and as a result, of the largest armed conflict ever waged, nuclear weapons took a long time before their stultifying effects on future war were realized. During the immediate post-1945 years, only one important author seems to have understood that "the absolute weapons" could never be used;[4] whether in or out of uniform, the great majority preferred to look for ways in which the weapon could and, if necessary, *would* be used.[5] As always happens when people try to forecast the form of future conflict, inertia and the "lessons" of World War II played a part. So long as the number of available nuclear weapons remained limited, their power small compared to what was to come later, and their effects ill understood, it was possible to believe that they would make little difference and that war would go on more or less as before. To those who lived during or shortly after the war the outstanding characteristic of twentieth-century "total" warfare had been the state's ability to use the administrative organs at its disposal for mobilizing massive resources and creating equally massive armed forces.[6] Hence it was not unnatural to assume that such resources, minus of course those destroyed by the occasional atomic bomb dropped on them, would continue to be mobilized and thrown into combat against each other.[7]

At first, possession of nuclear weapons was confined to one country only, the United States, which used them in order to end the war against Japan. However, the "atomic" secret could not be kept for very long and in September 1949 the USSR carried out its first test.[8] As more and more weapons were produced and stored, there were now *two* states capable of

---

[3] See above all T. S. Schelling, *Arms and Influence* (New Haven, CT: Yale University Press, 1966), ch. 1.

[4] B. Brodie, et al., *The Absolute Weapons* (New York: Columbia University Press, 1946), ch. 1; Brodie, "The Atom Bomb as Policy Maker," *Foreign Affairs*, 27, 1, October 1948, pp. 1–16.

[5] The best history of nuclear "strategy" remains L. Freedman, *The Evolution of Nuclear Strategy* (New York: St. Martin's Press, 1981).

[6] See e.g. J. F. C. Fuller, *The Conduct of War* (London: Eyre and Spottiswode, 1961), pp. 321ff.

[7] P. M. S. Blackett, *The Military and Political Consequences of Atomic Energy* (London: Turnstile Press, 1948), ch. 10.

[8] For the Soviet road to the bomb, see most recently D. Holloway, *Stalin and the Bomb* (New Haven, CT: Yale University Press, 1994).

inflicting "unacceptable damage" on each other, as the phrase went. The introduction of hydrogen bombs in 1952–3 opened up the vision of unlimited destructive power (in practice, the most powerful one built was 3,000 times as large as the one that had demolished Hiroshima) and made the prospect of nuclear war even more awful. At the end of World War II there had been just two bombs in existence; but now the age of nuclear plenty arrived with more than enough devices available to "service" any conceivable target.[9] For the first time, humanity found itself in a situation where it could destroy itself if it wanted to. The decade and a half after 1945 saw the publication of widely read novels such as Aldous Huxley's *Ape and Essence* (1948), Neville Shute's *On the Beach* (1957), and Walter Miller's *A Canticle to Leibowitz* (1959). All three described the collapse of civilization following a nuclear exchange. All three had as their central message the need to prevent such an exchange at all cost.

Even as the possible effects of nuclear weapons were becoming clear, the two leading powers were busily developing better ones. The original device had been too large and cumbersome to be carried in any but specially modified versions of the heaviest bombers of the time; however, during the 1950s smaller and lighter versions were built that could be delivered by light bomber, fighter bomber, artillery shell, and even a light recoilless weapon operated by three men from a jeep. The acme of progress, if that is indeed the word, was represented in the form of ballistic missiles. Based on the ones developed by the Germans during World War II, by 1960 their range had been increased to the point where they were capable of delivering a hydrogen bomb from practically any point on earth to any other. The 1960s and 1970s saw missiles becoming much more accurate so that not only "area targets" – meaning entire cities – but pinpoint targets such as military bases could be aimed at and, with some luck, hit. Miracles of computerization led to the advent of multiple reentry vehicles (MRVs) and multiple independent reentry vehicles (MIRVs); this made it possible to put as many as ten warheads on top of a single missile. Also, both ballistic missiles and the smaller cruise missiles could now be based on the ground – either in fixed silos or on top of mobile railway cars – in the air, and at sea where hundreds upon hundreds of them were either put into submarines or mounted on the decks of World War II-vintage battleships which were especially refurbished for the purpose.

To focus on the United States alone, the number of available weapons rose from perhaps less than a hundred in 1950 to some 3,000 in 1960, 10,000 in 1970, and 30,000 in the early 1980s when, for lack of targets,

---

[9] See A. Enthoven, *How Much Is Enough?: Shaping the Defense Budget, 1961–1969* (New York: Harper and Row, 1971), for the kind of calculation involved.

growth came to a halt. The size of the weapons probably ranged from under 1 kiloton (that is, 1,000 tons of TNT, the most powerful conventional explosive) to as much as 15 megatons (15 *million* tons of TNT); although, as time went on and the introduction of new computers and other navigation aids permitted more accurate delivery vehicles to be built, there was a tendency for the yields of "strategic" warheads to decline to as little as 50–150 kilotons. With some variations, notably a preference for larger warheads and a greater reliance on land-based missiles as opposed to air- and sea-based ones, these arrangements were duplicated on the other side of the Iron Curtain. At its peak between 1980 and 1985 the Soviet arsenal probably counted some 20,000 warheads and their delivery vehicles. As in the American case, they were linked together by vast and intricate command-and-control networks consisting of bomb-proof command posts (some of them airborne), radar, satellites, communications, and the inevitable computers.[10] Their purpose was to serve warning against attack and make sure that the retaliatory forces would still be capable of doing their job even after "riding out" a nuclear attack.

By basing them on the ground, at sea, and in the air, as well as greatly increasing numbers, the nuclear forces themselves could be protected against attack, at any rate to the extent that enough of them would survive to deliver the so-called second strike. However, the same was not true of industrial, urban, and demographic targets. During World War II a defense that relied on radar and combined fighter with anti-aircraft artillery had sometimes brought down as many as a quarter of the bombers attacking a target: so, for example, in the case of the American raid against the German city of Schweinfurt in the autumn of 1943. Should the attack be made with nuclear weapons, though, even a defense capable of intercepting 90 percent of the attacking aircraft would be of no avail, since a single bomber getting through was capable of destroying the target just as surely as Hiroshima and Nagasaki were destroyed.

With the advent of ballistic missiles flying at hypersonic speeds, as well as cruise missiles flying so low that they could not be traced by ground-based radar, the problem of defending against attack became even more intractable. From the anti-ballistic missile area of the late 1960s all the way to the "Star Wars" program announced by President Reagan in 1983, tens of billions of dollars were spent and many solutions proposed; in the end, however, none of them appeared sufficiently promising to be developed and none were deployed on any scale. From a technical point of view, a missile that could be launched at another with a reasonable

[10] For the arrangements in question, see P. Bracken, *The Command and Control of Nuclear Forces* (New Haven, CT: Yale University Press, 1983).

chance of hitting it in mid-flight (though the meaning of "reasonable" remained in doubt) appeared feasible. However, how to deal with a missile carrying as many as ten warheads, let alone an attack consisting of numerous missiles and aimed at swamping the defense, was a different question altogether.

In the absence of a defense capable of effectively protecting demographic, economic, and industrial targets, nuclear weapons presented policy-makers with a dilemma. Obviously one of their most important functions – some would say, their only rightful function – was to deter war from breaking out. Previous military theorists, with Clausewitz at their head, had seldom even bothered to mention deterrence; now, however, it became a central part of strategy as formulated in defense departments and studied in think tanks and universities. On the other hand, if the weapons were to be capable of exercising a deterrent effect, the weapons had to be capable of being used. What is more, they had to be used in a "credible" manner that would not automatically lead to all-out war and thus to the user's own annihilation.

In the West, which owing to the numerical inferiority of its conventional forces believed it might be constrained to make "first use" of its nuclear arsenal, the search for an answer to this problem started during the mid-1950s and went on for the next thirty years. Numerous theories were developed; though none of them was ever put to the test, in retrospect they may be divided into three types. The first, proposed by Henry Kissinger among others,[11] suggested that an explicit agreement might be concluded concerning the kind of targets that might be subjected to nuclear bombardment as well as the maximum size of the weapons that might be used to destroy them. The second, variously known as "flexible response" and "selective options," also depended on agreement, albeit a tacit one. It rested on the hope that, in exchange for NATO not using every nuclear weapon in its arsenal against every kind of target, the USSR would exercise similar restraint and permit the war to remain limited in terms of geography, targets, or both – though this hope existed in spite of repeated Soviet statements to the contrary.[12]

The third, and most hair-raising, "solution" to the problem was proposed during the mid-1980s and was known as decapitation. Its adherents recognized that the chances of reaching an agreement, tacit or

---

[11] H. A. Kissinger, *Nuclear Weapons and Foreign Policy: The Need for Choice* (New York: Harper and Row, 1957), pp. 174–83.

[12] On these doctrines, which for the sake of brevity have been bundled together, see e.g. R. van Cleave and R. W. Barnett, "Strategic Adaptability," *Orbis*, 18, 3, Autumn 1974, pp. 655–76; and L. Etheridge-Davis, *Limited Nuclear Options: Deterrence and the New American Doctrine* (Adelphi Paper No. 121, Winter 1975–6; London: International Institute for Strategic Studies, 1976).

explicit, on the limitation of nuclear use in a war between the superpowers were anything but good; they therefore suggested that the new missiles and cruise missiles then coming into service should be used to "decapitate" the Soviet Union. By this they meant a series of superaccurate strikes that would eliminate the leadership and destroy its system of command, control, and communication, thus hopefully preventing it from launching an effective response.[13]

As the two last-mentioned strategies, dating to the 1970s and 1980s, suggest, by this time the apocalyptic fears so characteristic of the 1950s had to some extent evaporated. Such novels as John Hackett's *The Third World War* (1979) and Tom Clancy's *Red Storm Rising* (1984) enjoyed immense popularity – to say nothing of the latter's *A Debt of Honor* (1994), in which a team of American commandos is sent to demolish Japan's nuclear establishment *in order* that a war may be fought against that country. In the years before 1914, the popularity of military fiction was one indication of the approaching slaughter.[14] In Reagan's United States, presumably many people would have welcomed an opportunity to test the wonderful weapons put at their disposal by advancing technology. They might, indeed, have brought about a clash if it had not been for the restraining effect of nuclear weapons which, unfortunately, threatened to bring the fun to an end before it had even properly started; not by accident, both *The Third World War* and *Red Storm Rising* come to an end the moment such weapons are introduced. Whatever the precise relationship between fact and fiction, in practice the planners' attempts to devise "war-fighting" strategies for using the smaller bombs and superaccurate delivery vehicles came to naught. Deterrence, "the sturdy child of terror" as Winston Churchill had once called it, prevailed.

After the Cuban Missile Crisis, which for a few days in October 1962 seemed to have brought the world to the verge of nuclear doom, the superpowers became notably more cautious. There followed such agreements as the Test Ban Treaty (1963), the Nuclear Non-Proliferation Treaty (NPT, 1969), the two Strategic Arms Limitation Treaties of 1972 and 1977, and the cuts in the number of medium-range missiles and warheads that were achieved in the late 1980s by President Reagan and General Secretary Gorbachev. Each was brought about under different circumstances, but all reflected the two sides' willingness to put a cap on the arms race, as well as the growing conviction that, should a nuclear war break out, there would be neither winners nor losers. To date, the capstone of these agreements is formed by the one which was signed by

[13] C. S. Gray, "War Fighting for Deterrence," *Journal of Strategic Studies*, 7, March 1984, pp. 5–28.
[14] See I. V. Clark, *Voices Prophesizing War* (Harmondsworth, UK: Penguin, 1963), ch. 5.

Presidents George Bush and Boris Yeltsin and which provided for doing away with the more accurate delivery vehicles (the MIRVs). This was tantamount to an admission that "war-fighting" was dead, and that the only function of nuclear weapons was to deter.

By the time the Cold War ended, the number of nuclear states, which originally had stood at just one, had reached at least eight. From Argentina and Brazil through Canada, West and East Europe, all the way to Taiwan, Korea (both North and South), Japan, Australia, and probably New Zealand, several dozen others were prepared to construct bombs quickly, or were at any rate capable of doing so if they wanted to.[15] One, South Africa, preened itself on having built nuclear weapons and then dismantled them, although, understandably, both the meaning of "dismantling" and the fate of the dismantled parts remained somewhat obscure. Meanwhile, technological progress has brought nuclear weapons within the reach of anybody capable of producing modern conventional arms, as is proved by the fact that states like China, Israel, India, and Pakistan all developed the former years, even decades, before they began building the latter.

The entry of new members into the nuclear club was not, of course, favorably received by those who were already there. Seeking to preserve their monopoly, repeatedly they expressed their fears of the dire consequences that would follow. Their objective was to prove that they themselves were stable and responsible and wanted nothing but peace; however, for ideological, political, cultural, or technical reasons this was not the case elsewhere.[16] Some international safeguard, such as the Nuclear Non-Proliferation Treaty of 1969 and the London Regime of 1977, were set up, the intention being to prevent sensitive technology from falling into the hands of undesirable – which in practice meant those of Third World countries. However, the spread of nuclear technology proved difficult to stop. If, at present, the number of states with nuclear weapons in their arsenals remains limited to eight, on the whole this is due less to a lack of means than to a lack of will on the part of would-be proliferators.

Looking back, the fears of nuclear proliferation proved to be greatly exaggerated. Worldwide, the number of devices produced reaches into the high tens of thousands; fifty years after they were first introduced,

[15] See most recently T. Rauf, "Disarmament and Non-Proliferation Treaties," in G. A. Wood and L. S. Leland, Jr., eds., *State and Sovereignty: Is the State in Retreat?* (Dunedin: University of Otago Press, 1997), pp. 142–88.

[16] See e.g. *Public Opinion Quarterly*, 14, Spring 1950, p. 182 (the Soviet bomb); R. Ducci, "The World Order in the Sixties," *Foreign Affairs*, 43, 3, April 1964, pp. 379–90 (the Chinese bomb); and A. Myrdal, "The High Price of Nuclear Arms Monopoly," *Foreign Policy*, 18, Spring 1975, pp. 30–43 (the Indian bomb).

however, the only ones actually used in anger remain those dropped on Hiroshima and Nagasaki. First the superpowers, which were sufficiently terrified by the Cuban Missile Crisis to set up so-called hot lines; then their close allies in NATO and the Warsaw Pact, which signed various agreements designed to prevent the outbreak of accidental nuclear war; then the USSR and China, which settled their border dispute in 1991; then China and India, which have not seen a shot fired across their borders since the 1961 war between them; then India and Pakistan; and finally Israel and its neighbors – each in turn found that ownership of such weapons did not translate into as much military power as they had thought.

Instead, the nuclear arsenal tended to act as an inhibiting factor on military operations. As time went on, fear of escalation no longer allowed these countries to fight each other directly, seriously, or on any scale. As time was to show, the process took hold even where one or more of the nuclear states in question was headed by absolute dictators, as both the USSR and China were at various times; even when the balance of nuclear forces was completely lopsided, as when the United States possessed a ten-to-one advantage in delivery vehicles over the USSR during the Cuban Missile Crisis; even when the two sides hated each other "for longer than any other two peoples on earth" (Prime Minister Zulfikar Ali Bhutto of Pakistan), as in the case of India and Pakistan; and even when officials denied the existence of the bomb, as in both South Asia and the Middle East. In fact, a strong case could be made that, wherever nuclear weapons appeared or where their presence was even strongly suspected, major interstate warfare on any scale is in the process of slowly abolishing itself. What is more, any state of any importance is now by definition capable of producing nuclear weapons. Hence, such warfare can be waged only either between or against third- and fourth-rate countries.[17]

Since, in the years since 1945, first- and second-rate military powers have found it increasingly difficult to fight each other, it is no wonder that, taking a global view, both the size of the armed forces and the quantity of weapons at their disposal has declined quite sharply. In 1939 France, Germany, Italy, the USSR, and Japan each possessed ready-to-mobilize forces numbering several million men. The all-time peak came in 1944–5, when the six main belligerents (Italy having dropped out in 1943) between them probably maintained some 40 to 45 million men under arms. Since then the world's population has tripled, and international

---

[17] For a more detailed discussion of the decline of interstate war since 1945, see M. van Creveld, *Nuclear Proliferation and the Future of Conflict* (New York: Free Press, 1993), ch. 1; and E. Luard, *The Blunted Sword: The Erosion of Military Power in Modern World Politics* (London: Tauris, 1988).

relations have been anything but peaceful; nevertheless, the size of regular forces has declined to a mere fraction of the war years and is still declining.[18]

To adduce a more specific example, in 1941 the German invasion of the USSR, as the largest single military operation of all time, made use of 144 divisions out of approximately 209 that the Wehrmacht possessed; later, during the Soviet–German war, the forces deployed on both sides, but particularly by the Soviets, were even larger. By contrast, since 1945 there has probably not been even one case when any state used over twenty full-size divisions on any single campaign, and the numbers are still going nowhere but down. In 1991 a coalition that included three out of five members in the Security Council brought some 500,000 troops to bear against Iraq, which was only about one-third as many as Germany, counting field forces only, used to invade France as long ago as 1914. As of the late 1990s, the only states that still maintained forces exceeding 1.5 million (for the United States alone, the 1945 figure stood at 12 million) were India and China – and, of them, the last-named had just announced that half a million men would be sent home. In any case, most of those forces consisted of low-quality infantry, some of which, armed with World War I rifles, was suitable – if for anything – more for maintaining internal security than for waging serious external war.

While the decline in the number of regular troops – both regulars and, even more so, reservists – has been sharp indeed, the fall in the number of major weapons and weapons systems has been even more precipitous. In 1939, the air forces of each one of the leading powers counted their planes in the thousands; during each of the years 1942–5, the United States alone produced 75,000 military aircraft on the average. Fifty years later, the air forces of virtually all the most important countries were shrinking fast. The largest one, the United States Air Force, bought exactly 127 aircraft in 1995, including helicopters and transports;[19] elsewhere the numbers (if any) were down to the low dozens. At sea, the story has been broadly similar. Of the former Soviet navy, on which fortunes were spent and which as late as the 1980s appeared to pose a global threat, little remains but rusting surface vessels and old, undermaintained submarines that allegedly risk leaking nuclear material into the sea. The US navy is in a much better shape, but has seen the number of aircraft carriers – the most important weapons system around which everything else revolves –

---

[18] The International Institute of Military Studies, *The Military Balance, 1994–1995* (London: IISS, 1995), gives a country-by-country overview of the armed forces currently in existence.

[19] World War II figures are from R. Overy, *The Air War 1939–1945* (London: Europa, 1980), pp. 308–9; 1995 ones are from D. M. Snider, "The Coming Defense Train Wreck," *Washington Quarterly*, 19, 1, Winter 1996, p. 92.

go down from almost 100 in 1945 to as few as 12 in 1995. The United States apart, the one country which still maintains even one full-deck carrier is France; that apart, the carriers (all of them decidedly second-rate) owned by all other states combined can be counted on the fingers of one hand. Indeed, it is true to say that, with a single major exception, most states no longer maintain ocean-going navies at all.

In part, this decline in the size of armed forces reflects the escalating cost of modern weapons and weapons systems.[20] A World War II fighter bomber could be had for approximately $50,000. Some of its modern successors, such as the F-15I, come at $100,000,000 a piece when their maintenance-packages (without which they would not be operational) are included – which, when inflation is taken into account, represents a thousandfold increase. Even this does not mark the limit on what some airborne weapons systems, such as the "stealth" bomber, AWACS, and J-STAR – all of them produced, owned, and operated exclusively by the world's sole remaining superpower – can cost. And it has been claimed that the reluctance of the US Air Force to use its most recent acquisition, the B-2 bomber which carries a $2 billion price tag, against Iraq stems in part from the fact that there are simply no targets worthy of the risk.[21]

Even so, one should not make too much of the price factor. Modern economies are extraordinarily productive, and could certainly devote much greater resources to the acquisition of military hardware than they do at present. Thus, the cost of modern weapons systems may appear exorbitant only because the state's basic security, safeguarded as it is by nuclear weapons and their ever-ready delivery vehicles, no longer appears sufficiently at risk to justify them. In fact, this is probably the correct interpretation – as is suggested by the tendency, which has now been evident for decades, to cut the size of any production program and stretch the length of any acquisition process *ad calendas grecas*. For example, to develop the Manhattan Project – including the construction of some of the largest industrial plant ever – and build the first atomic bombs took less than three years; but the designers of present-day conventional weapons systems want us to believe that a new fighter bomber cannot be deployed in fewer than fifteen. The development histories of countless modern weapons systems prove that, in most cases, only a fraction of the numbers initially required are produced, and then only after delays lasting for years and years. The reason is that, in most cases, the threat – which would have made rapid mass production necessary and incidentally led to a dramatic drop in per unit costs – no longer exists.

[20] The best analysis of cost trends remains F. Spinney, *Defense Facts of Life* (Boulder: Westview, 1986).
[21] BBC World Service, television broadcast, 25 February 1998.

At the same time, yet another explanation for the decline in the quantity of weapons produced and deployed is the very great improvement in quality; this, it is argued, makes yesterday's large numbers superfluous.[22] There is, in fact, some truth in this argument. Particularly since guided missiles have replaced ballistic weapons in the form of the older artillery and rockets, the number of rounds necessary to destroy any particular target had dropped very sharply; as the 1991 Gulf War showed, in many cases a one-shot–one-kill capability has been achieved. On the other hand, it should be remembered that for every modern weapon – nuclear ones only excepted – a counterweapon may be, and in most cases has been, designed. However simple or sophisticated two opposing military systems, provided that they are technologically approximately equal, the struggle between them is likely to be prolonged and to result in heavy attrition.[23] Expecting more accurate weapons to increase attrition – as, in fact, was the case both in the 1973 Arab–Israeli War and the 1982 Falklands War, each in turn the most modern conflict in history until then – logically late twentieth-century states ought to have produced and fielded more weapons, not fewer. The fact that this has not happened almost certainly shows that they are no longer either willing or able to prepare for wars on a scale larger than, say, Vietnam and Afghanistan; and even those two came close to bankrupting the two largest powers, the United States and the USSR respectively.

To look at it in still another way, during World War II four of seven (five of eight, if China is included) major belligerents had their capitals occupied. Two more (London and Moscow) were heavily bombed, and only one (Washington, DC) escaped either misfortune. Since then, however, *no* first- or second-rate power has seen large-scale military operations waged on its territory; the reasons for this being too obvious to require an explanation. In fact, the majority of countries which did go to war – or against which others went to war – were quite small and relatively unimportant. For example, Israel against the Arab states; India against Pakistan; Iran against Iraq; the United States first against Vietnam and then against Iraq; and, for a few days in 1995, Peru against Ecuador. When the countries in question were not unimportant, as in the case of India and China during their prenuclear days, military operations were

---

[22] For some calculations pertaining to this subject, see N. Brown, *The Future of Air Power* (New York: Holmes and Meier, 1986), p. 88; J. A. Warden, III, "Air Theory for the Twenty-First Century," in K. P. Magyar, ed., *Challenge and Response: Anticipating US Military Security Concerns* (Maxwell AFB, AL: Air University Press, 1994), pp. 313 and 328; and D. T. Kuehl, "Airpower vs. Electricity: Electric Power as a Target for Strategic Air Operations," *Journal of Strategic Studies*, 18, 1, March 1995, pp. 250–60.
[23] See M. van Creveld, *Technology and War: From 2000 BC to the Present* (New York: Free Press, 1988), chs. 9 and 11.

almost always confined to the margins and never came near the capitals in question.

The significance of this change was that strategy, which from Napoleon to World War II often used to measure its advances and retreats in hundreds of miles, now operates on a much smaller scale. For example, no post-1945 army has so much as tried to repeat the 600-mile German advance from the River Bug to Moscow, let alone the 1,300-mile Soviet march from Stalingrad to Berlin. Since then, the distances covered by armies were much shorter. In no case did they exceed 300 miles (Korea in 1950); usually, though, they did not penetrate deeper than 150 or so. In 1973 Syria and Egypt faced an unacknowledged nuclear threat on the part of Israel. Hence, as some of their leaders subsequently admitted, they limited themselves to advancing ten and five miles respectively into occupied territory – to such lows had the formerly mighty art of "strategy" sunk.[24] In other places where nuclear powers confront each other, as between India and Pakistan, what hostilities still take place (across the remote and practically worthless glacier of Siachen) do not involve any territorial advances at all.[25]

As nuclear weapons restricted the scope of war, it is perhaps no wonder that conventional military theory stagnated. The thinkers who, during the interwar years, taught the world's armed forces how to wage wars with weapons and weapons systems based on the internal combustion engine – Giulio Douhet, John Frederick Fuller, Basil Liddell Hart, Heinz Guderian – did not really have successors worthy of them. It is often believed that, throughout the Cold War, the one thought that occupied the brains of the general staff in Moscow was how to conduct a 1940-style *Blitzkrieg*, only much bigger, faster, and more powerful; conversely, 90 percent of all NATO planning concerned the question how to stop such a *Blitzkrieg* in its tracks and then, perhaps, go over to the counteroffensive as the British had done at Alamein in 1942.[26] Through all this, the basic analytical terms used to understand large-scale military operations – such as advance, retreat, breakthrough, penetration, encirclement, front, line of communications, internal and external lines, direct and indirect approach – remained very much as they had been, with the result that Liddell Hart's *Strategy*, published for the first time in 1929, tended to be reprinted each

---

[24] For the effect of nuclear weapons on the Arab–Israeli conflict, see S. Aronson, *The Politics and Strategy of Nuclear Weapons in the Middle East* (Albany: State University of New York Press, 1992).

[25] For the ongoing Siachen conflict, see A. S. Wirsing, "The Siachen Glacier Dispute," parts 1, 2 and 3, *Strategic Studies*, 10, 1, Autumn 1987, pp. 49–66; 11, 3, Spring 1988, pp. 75–94; and 12, 1, Autumn 1988, pp. 38–54.

[26] See for example A. A. Sidorenko, *The Offensive* (Moscow, 1970; United States Air Force translation, Washington, DC: Government Printing Office, n.d.).

time a conventional war broke out.[27] Arguably, the only new concept that appeared on the scene since 1935 or so has been that of vertical envelopment.[28] Involving the use of aircraft and, later, helicopters in order to land troops to the enemy's rear, seize key points, and cut communications, vertical envelopment was used on a number of occasions during World War II. However, not since the Suez campaign of 1956 has any army tried to implement it on any scale; its use in counterinsurgency apart, the most innovative idea of all (which itself is over half a century old) has remained purely on paper.

Initiated by the development of nuclear weapons and accompanied by a drastic decline in the size of military establishments, the decline of major interstate war was also reflected in international law and mores. For centuries if not millennia, the most important reason why politically organized societies, including (after 1648) states, went to war against each other had been to carry out conquests and acquire territory. It was by sword and fire that Louis XIV conquered Alsace, Frederick II Silesia, and Napoleon (however temporarily) most of Europe; this was also the case in 1815 when Prussia emerged from the Napoleonic Wars in possession of the Rhineland, a territory that had never previously belonged to it, and when the United States occupied huge tracts of Mexican territory in 1846–8. As late as 1866 it was by war and the peace agreement concluded in its wake that Prussia annexed some of the north German states and Italy obtained Venice from Austria. Over the next half-century the acquisition of territory in Asia and Africa, where society had not yet been organized in states, continued and even accelerated. Not so in Europe itself. There, the spread of nationalism – meaning the growing identification of people with the state whose citizens they were – was probably already beginning to make conquest more difficult both to bring about and to legitimize.

In retrospect, the turning point in the process that eventually made the annexation by one state of territory belonging to others into a legal and practical impossibility probably came in 1870–1. Having won their war against France, the Germans like countless conquerors before them demanded payment in the form of real estate. That real estate was duly signed away by the newly established, but legitimate, republican government of Adolphe Thiers; however, it very soon became clear that, in sharp contrast to similar events in the past, the French people simply

---

[27] B. H. Liddell Hart, *The Decisive Wars of History* (London: Faber and Faber, 1929), reprinted as *Strategy: The Indirect Approach* in 1946 and 1954 and as *Strategy* in 1967 and 1991.

[28] See above all N. Browne, *Strategic Mobility* (London: Praeger, 1963); and R. Simpkin, *Race to the Swift* (London: Pergamon Press, 1985).

refused to let go. On the contrary, the very fact that they had been conquered by force caused Alsace and Lorraine to be designated "sacred"; during the second half of the twentieth century, that was to become the fate of *every* bit of occupied territory, no matter how insignificant. The land being sacred, they waited for *la revanche* which it was now the patriotic duty of every Frenchmen and Frenchwoman to prepare as best they could. As Bismarck himself had expressly foreseen,[29] the change in attitudes turned the annexation of the two provinces – carried out at the insistence of Moltke and the general staff – into the worst political error he ever made. From now on, every other state that nursed a grudge against Germany could invariably count on French support.

The idea that complete sovereignty, including the unrestricted right to wage war, was too dangerous to entertain in the age of modern technology suffered another blow as a result of World War I and the 10 million casualties (in dead alone) that it wrought.[30] Ever since the first half of the seventeenth century, numerous suggestions had been made to limit the right of states to make war against their neighbors. The idea was to establish some kind of international organization that would stand above individual states, arbitrate in disputes that broke out among them, and bring force to bear against disturbers of the peace. Sully apart, those who floated schemes of this kind included Abbé Cruce, William Penn, Jean-Jacques Rousseau, Immanuel Kant, John Stuart Mill, and the Swiss jurist Johann Bluntschli – in short, many of the leading intellectuals of the period between about 1650 and 1900.[31] Finally, in 1919, the vision was partly realized and the League of Nations established. Its Covenant, and especially Article 10, represented a new departure in international law. For the first time ever, the territorial integrity and political independence – in other words, the right to be free of conquest – of states were recognized as a fundamental international norm.

The next step was taken in 1928 and took the form of the Kellogg–Briand Pact. In this pact, originally designed by the foreign ministers of

[29] O. von Bismarck, *Reflections and Reminiscences* (London: Smith, 1898), vol. II, pp. 252ff.
[30] For what follows, see F. Przetacznik, "The Illegality of the Concept of Just War Under Contemporary International Law," *Revue de Droit International, des Sciences Diplomatiques et Politiques*, 70, 4, October–December 1993, pp. 245–94.
[31] For these and other attempts at international organization, see A. Saita, "Un riformatore pacifista contemporaneo de Richelieu: E. Cruce," *Rivista Storica Italiana*, 64, 1951, pp. 183–92; W. Penn, *An Essay Towards the Present and Future Peace of Europe* (Hildesheim: Olms, 1983 [1699]); Abbé de Saint Pierre, *A Scheme for Lasting Peace in Europe* (London: Peace Book, 1939 [1739]); O. Schreker, "Leibnitz: ses idées sur l'organisation des relations internationales," *Proceedings of the British Academy*, 23, 1937, pp. 218–19; E. Kant, *Plan for a Universal and Everlasting Peace* (New York: Garland, 1973 [1796]); J. Lorimer, *The Institutes of the Law of Nations* (Edinburgh: Blackwood, 1883–4), ch. 14; and J. G. Bluntschli, *Gesammelte kleine Schriften* (Nordlingen: Beck'sche Buchhandlung, 1879–81), vol. II, pp. 293–5.

the United States and France, the signatories formally undertook "to renounce war as an instrument of national policy." During the years that followed this obligation was joined by sixty-one additional states; since there was no time limit, technically speaking the pact remains in force to the present day.[32]

In the event, these and other "international kisses," as they have been called by their self-styled "realist" critics, failed to prevent the unleashing of World War II as the greatest war of conquest of all time. This, however, does not mean that, as indicators of the public mood, they were completely without significance. Once World War II was over, those persons considered most responsible for launching it were brought to justice in Nuremberg and Tokyo. The courts which were set up by the Allies used the Kellogg–Briand Pact as the legal basis for charging them with a new crime, such as had not been heard of since Hugo Grotius,[33] namely, planning and waging "aggressive" war.[34] The arguments of the defendants' lawyers, namely that this was a *post facto* indictment for a crime which had not been recognized as such at the time when it was allegedly committed, remained unheeded. The most important Nazi and Japanese war criminals were convicted – for this as well as other crimes – and, the majority of them duly executed. Moreover, thirteen months had not yet passed since the end of hostilities when the prohibition on aggressive war and the use of force in order to annex territory belonging to other sovereign entities were written into Article 2(4) of the United Nations Charter. As additional states joined the UN, in time the latter was to develop into the most subscribed-to document in human history.

Article 39 of the Charter left the decision as to what constituted aggression in the hands of the Security Council which, especially in view of the disagreements between its members, found the task remarkably difficult.[35] Nevertheless, it could be argued that the attempt to prevent states from enjoying the fruits of aggression in the form of territorial aggrandizement has been remarkably successful. The last time international war led to the annexation of territory on any scale was in 1945 when the USSR took over lands belonging to Poland (which itself annexed German lands), Germany, Czechoslovakia, and Japan; since then, though, international borders have become all but frozen. Remarkable as it seems, neither the Korean War, nor the three India–Pakistani wars, nor the India–Chinese war, nor any of the Arab–Israeli wars, ended with

[32] For these developments, see Przetacznik, "Illegality of the Concept of Just War."
[33] H. Grotius, *De Jure Belli ac Pacis* (Amsterdam: Jansunium, 1632), 2, 23, 13; 1, 3, 1.
[34] See G. Best, *War and Law Since 1945* (Oxford: Clarendon Press, 1991), pp. 181–2.
[35] For two attempts to grapple with this question, see Y. Melzer, *Just War* (Leiden: Sijthoff, 1975), pp. 83ff., and I. D. de Lupis, *The Law of War* (Cambridge: Cambridge University Press, 1987), pp. 58ff.

important pieces of territory being ceded by one side to another; indeed the great majority did not lead to any territorial changes at all. At most, a country was partitioned and a new international border created. This, for example, was what took place in Yugoslavia between 1991 and 1995. This, too, was what happened in Palestine in 1948–9 when Israel, having been established by means of a United Nations Resolution, occupied somewhat more territory than had been allocated to it by the Partition Plan. At that time King Abdullah of Jordan, who may have been acting in concert with Israel, used the opportunity to take over some 2,000 square miles known as the West Bank. However, in the whole world the only two countries to recognize the annexation were Britain and Pakistan; and in any case it has since been formally annulled.

Elsewhere the idea that force should not be used for altering frontiers, which was reaffirmed once again by UN Resolution 2734 of 1970, prevailed.[36] Before 1945, the attainment of military victory usually led to the surrender of the vanquished, a peace treaty, and the cession of territory; now, however, almost without exception, the most that an occupant could obtain was an armistice. Particularly in the Middle East, the state of no war, no peace that ensued proved itself capable of lasting for decades on end; as a result, many of the maps in current use have two lines marked on them, namely a green one showing the international border (which was in effect only during the first nineteen years after 1948) and a purple one indicating the cease-fire line that was established in 1967. Indeed, so strong has the prevalent bias toward the *status quo ante* become that it prevailed even in those cases when the defeated plainly did not have the ability to eject the victor. This is what happened when India occupied several thousand square miles of Pakistani territory in 1971, and also after China invaded Vietnam in 1979.

Moreover, the decline of major war has led to a change in the terminology by which it was surrounded. All but gone are a whole series of terms, such as "subjugation" and "the right of conquest," which even as late as 1950 or so formed a normal part of legal discourse in a work on international law written by such a highly civilized authority as His Britannic Majesty's Government's official adviser.[37] Of the two, the former has acquired an archaic, not to say outlandish, ring. The latter is regarded almost as a contradiction in terms; given that might, as exercised by one sovereign state against another, by definition can no longer create right. Gone, too, are the "war ministries" of the various states, every last one of which has had its name changed into Ministry of Defense, Ministry

---

[36] The relevant paragraphs are printed in S. D. Bailey, *Prohibitions and Restraints on War* (London: Oxford University Press, 1972), appendix 1, p. 162.
[37] H. Lauterpacht, *International Law: A Treatise* (London: Longmans, 1947).

of Security, or something of that kind. Needless to say, the change in nomenclature did not always mean a different kind of activity. As they had done for centuries past, "defense" officials of many countries continued to plan and prepare for wars at least some of which were aggressive. What it did was to emphasize the growing force of international law to delegitimize war, or, at any rate, of war as waged by one state against others.

The Iraqi invasion of Kuwait, which took place in 1990–1, marked yet another step toward the delegitimization of interstate war. Against the background of changing international norms, perhaps not since the time of Korea had there been a similar clear-cut attempt to occupy a sovereign state and wipe it off the map. The question of oil apart, no wonder Saddam Hussein faced the opprobrium of the whole world; as it turned out, he was unable to get his annexation recognized even by the handful of countries that supported him, such as Cuba, Jordan, Yemen, and Sudan.

On the other side of the dispute, the states that formed the coalition against Iraq did not respond by declaring war on their own accord. Following a precedent set in the matter of Korea in 1950, they asked the Security Council (in which, of course, their own influence was paramount) for a mandate to end the aggression or, in plain words, to throw the Iraqis out. As was noted at the time,[38] the procedure selected by President Bush raised the question of whether states still had the right to use force in order to pursue their interests, or whether they had to ask for permission in the manner of medieval princes appealing to the pope. Nor, as events were to show, was the precedent thus set without significance. Much of 1995 was spent wrangling over the question of whether NATO, as a mere alliance of sovereign states, was entitled to send troops to Bosnia without requiring a mandate from the United Nations. Early in 1998, as it was trying to punish Saddam Hussein for allegedly "stonewalling" the arms inspections to which Iraq had been subject for the last seven years, the United States found that going to war without permission from the Security Council would incur a heavy political price.

In law as well as in fact, as the twentieth century was approaching its end, interstate war appeared to be on the retreat. The right to wage it, far from being part and parcel of sovereignty, had been taken away except insofar as it was done in strict self-defense; even when states *did* wage war in strict self-defense (and precisely for that reason), they were no longer

---

[38] See G. Picco, "The UN and the Use of Force," *Foreign Affairs*, 73, 5, September–October 1994, pp. 14–18; and, in general, A. Roberts, "The United Nations: A System for Collective International Security?," in G. A. S. C. Wilson, ed., *British Security 2010* (Camberley Staff College: Strategic and Combat Studies Institute, 1996), pp. 65–8.

allowed to benefit by bringing about territorial change. Thus has such war lost its chief attraction. At the same time, as far as important states were concerned, the stakes were raised many times over by the introduction of nuclear weapons; no wonder that its incidence, among those states at least, was diminishing.

As to the interstate wars that still took place, with hardly any exception neither the size of the forces involved, nor the magnitude of the military operations that they witnessed, nor the threat that they posed to the belligerent's existence even approached pre-1945 dimensions. From the Middle East to the Straits of Taiwan, the world remains a dangerous place and new forms of armed conflict appear to be taking the place of the old.[39] Nevertheless, compared to the situation as it existed even as late as 1939 the change has been momentous.

The retreat of welfare

As the introduction of nuclear weapons and changing ideas on international law led to the loss of the state's ability to expand at its neighbors' expense, it turned its still considerable energies inward. Making use of tools such as statistics, taxes, the police, prison, compulsory education, and welfare, the state had been extending its power over civil society for centuries, imposing its own law, eradicating or at least greatly weakening lesser institutions in which people used to spend their lives, and building itself up until it towered over civil society. From about 1840 on socialist ideas, translated into practice, had worked in the same direction and helped bring about change; then the end of World War II, far from bringing about a period of relaxation, caused it to redouble its efforts.

On the declamatory level, the move toward the welfare state started during the war itself. Both Churchill and Roosevelt were well aware that the efforts made by workers on behalf of their state would have to be compensated; when they signed the "Atlantic Charter" of early 1942, they officially declared "freedom from want" to be one of the Allies' principal objectives. To bring it about, contemporaries pointed to the enormous increase in production which had been brought about by mobilization and the harnessing of all resources to the military effort. It was suggested that, if only a small fraction of those resources could be retained in the hands of the state and used for public purposes, it should be possible to solve or at least alleviate some of the most pressing social problems, such as poverty, unemployment (both of them very conspicu-

---

[39] See M. Kaldor, *New Wars for Old* (London: Pergamon, 1998, pp. 13–30); and the section on "The threat to internal order" in this chapter, pp. 394–408.

ous during the years of the Great Depression), inadequate health care, and insufficient access to secondary and tertiary education as a way toward a better life. Pointing the way ahead and serving as a model for many others all over Western Europe, Canada, and Australasia was the British Beveridge Report which was published in 1944 and paved the way toward far-reaching social and economic reforms. However, nobody expressed the prevailing sentiment better than an Australian statesman, John Curtin, who was prime minister throughout World War II; in his view, "predominantly government should be the agency whereby the masses should be lifted up."[40]

Broadly speaking, two series of steps were necessary to carry out this program. On the one hand, it was a question of concentrating much greater resources in the hands of the state – if not to the extent that this had been done during the war itself, then at any rate in comparison with the years before 1939. On the other, it was a question of devising new mechanisms for distributing those resources to those groups and those people who appeared to need them most. Both sides of the problem had this in common that, if they were to be tackled and solved, the number of those working for the state would have to be greatly increased with all that this entailed for career opportunities, promotions, and sheer power over society as a whole. From the beginning, in other words, the proposed reforms commanded a constituency in the form of the state bureaucracy and all its manifold organs – one which, over the next three decades, would prove capable of pressing its demands for greater state intervention in virtually all fields of life almost independently of the electorate's wishes.[41]

The first firm steps toward tightening the state's grip on the economy had, in fact, already been taken during the interwar period. Not only had levels of taxation never gone back to pre-1914 levels – a problem that affected even the country that was most reluctant to embark on the new course, i.e., the United States – but in one state after another there was a tendency toward the nationalization of industry. Among the most affected were newly established industries or those that were involved in the shaping of public opinion: for example, in Britain, the BBC (British Broadcasting Corporation) and General Electricity Board were both founded in the 1920s, and they soon developed into some of the largest organizations of their kind anywhere. In 1931 Ramsay MacDonald,

---

[40] Quoted in P. Wilenski, *Public Power and Public Administration* (Sydney: Hale and Ironmonger, 1986), p. 20.

[41] For a brief economic analysis of the factors behind the expansion of the state during the post-1945 period, see A. Peacock, *The Economic Analysis of Government and Related Themes* (Oxford: Robertson, 1979), pp. 105–17.

having assumed power as the first Labour prime minister, took London Transport out of private hands. In 1939 BOAC (British Overseas Air Corporation) was created by means of the merger of several privately owned firms, and soon achieved, as indeed it was intended to, a near-monopoly in the field. Across the Channel, France followed these British developments in 1936–9 when Leon Blum's Front populaire government nationalized very significant parts of the railway, armaments, and banking industries.

By way of further justifying the increased intervention of the state in the economy, several lines of thought were being developed. On the one hand, there was socialist and communist doctrine, going back to the *Communist Manifesto* and the *Critique of the Gotha Program* and most fully implemented in the Soviet Union. Throughout the interwar period, there existed a sprinkling of mostly middle-class, left-wing intellectuals in many European countries who looked at developments originating in Moscow as their shining example; feeling ashamed at what they called "poverty amidst plenty" (the British writer John Stacey), they argued that nation-alization would result in greater responsibility, fairer prices, increased efficiency, more rapid growth, the disappearance or at any rate flattening of the trade cycle, and an end to the class warfare which had bedeviled capitalist countries since at least the time of the industrial revolution.[42] In a curious way, many of the beliefs of these well-meaning people on the left were paralleled by the measures being implemented at that very time by the right-wing "totalitarian" regimes of Mussolini and Hitler, although, to be sure, in *their* case the extension of state control over both production and other fields (such as family life, in encouraging population growth) had at least as much to do with preparing for war than with any desire to "lift up the masses."

Left- and right-wing ideologies apart, for professional economists a further push toward increased state intervention was provided by a fa-mous book, John Maynard Keynes' *The General Theory of Employment, Interest and Money* (1936).[43] Written against the background of the Great Depression, it argued that *aggregate* supply and *aggregate* demand did not automatically balance each other, as had been argued by Adam Smith and so many of his successors. Instead, it was possible for demand to get locked in a situation where it constrained supply. As people failed to spend, the result would be a reduction of demand; and so on in a

---

[42] See, for Britain, E. J. Hobsbawm, *The Age of Empire* (Harmondsworth, UK: Penguin Books, 1989), pp. 239ff.

[43] For the way Keynes' influence made itself felt, see P. Weir and T. Skocpol, "State Structures and the Possibilities for Keynesian Responses to the Great Depression in Sweden, Britain, and the United States," in P. B. Evans, et al., eds., *Bringing the State back in* (Cambridge: Cambridge University Press, 1985), pp. 107–68.

downward spiral that was quite capable of lasting for years on end, making economies function at a fraction of their potential output, and even wrecking entire societies. Going against the traditional wisdom with its emphasis on balanced budgets and "sound" money, Keynes urged that the state should resolve such a situation by artificially stimulating demand. Whether this would be done by loosening credit, reducing taxes, or "deficit funding" – an elegant name for putting the printing press into operation – did not matter much; if necessary, all three methods were to be employed separately or in combination. The main thing was to get cash into people's hands. This would stimulate production, generate tax revenue for the state, and so on in a spiral whose direction, it was hoped, would be ever upward.

Whatever their precise origin, after 1945 the confluence of all these different modes of thought caused state intervention in the economy to explode. Among the first to take the road to the future was France. In 1946, it nationalized energy, including electricity, gas, and coal; the largest thirty-two insurance companies; the four largest deposit banks; Air France; as well as the aircraft manufacturer Berliet. Also caught in the dragnet were several firms accused of having cooperated with the German occupation regime, the most renowned of which was the car-maker Renault. In 1947–8 Labour, having established itself in power in Britain, followed. Coal, gas, steel, public transportation (railways, canals, and some road-hauling services) were all nationalized, leading to the creation of a whole series of huge corporations, all of which had names starting with the word "British." To one extent or another these measures were paralleled in other countries such as Italy, the Netherlands, Scandinavia, and even Canada, all of which significantly expanded public-sector ownership during the fifteen years after 1945. Among the important Western countries, only in West Germany did the current run in the other direction, the reason being that, already during the days of the Third Reich, nationalization had proceeded so far that it was a question not of expanding state holdings but of dismantling them. As late as the 1960s, and in spite of massive moves toward privatization (e.g., the sale of Volkswagen, which took place in 1959), the central government in Bonn continued to own very considerable parts of the economy, including 40 percent of the coal and iron sector, 62 percent of electrical-power generation, 72 percent of the aluminum industry, and 62 percent of the banking industry exclusive of the central bank.[44]

Most of the nationalizations which took place in the 1930s and 1940s had been carried out by left-wing governments for ideological reasons,

---

[44] Figures from H. van der Wee, *Prosperity and Upheaval* (New York: Viking, 1986), p. 307.

and in the face of opposition from the right. However, in country after country it became clear that the movement was in fact part of a long-term historical trend that conservative cabinets found themselves powerless to resist. Sometimes the need to provide employment acted as the decisive factor; in other cases it was a question of enabling bankrupt companies to continue providing essential services in fields as far apart as transportation and defense. For example, already in 1952–3 the new British Conservative government under Winston Churchill sought to restore steel back to private ownership; it failed, and not just because Labour threatened to renationalize in case it returned to power, but also because of interests which had grown up inside the government apparatus itself and which were already becoming vested. By 1967 British Rail and British Coal had become the world's largest employers outside the United States.[45] In Italy it was the ruling Christian Democratic Party, not some socialist government, which created ENI (Ente Nazionale Idrocarburanti) and EFIM (Ente Partecipazione et Finanziamento Industria Manifatturia), both of them holding companies in their respective fields of energy and manufacturing industry; later the same party also assumed responsibility for turning electricity generation into a government monopoly. Again it was the Conservative government of Edward Heath, not a Labour cabinet, which rescued the firm of Rolls-Royce in 1971. As it happened, this was the same year when the Republican administration of Richard Nixon, for very similar reasons (namely, the threatening bankruptcy of the firms in question) took over rail passenger service in most of the United States and created Amtrak.

Though in most countries the pace of nationalization showed signs of slackening after 1975, a few witnessed the greatest expansion of the public sector during the late 1970s and even the early 1980s. In Austria the socialist government of Bruno Kreisky, which was in office continuously from 1970 to 1987, carried out massive state takeovers of enterprises in such fields as steel, chemicals, and mining. In France, which for twenty-three years after 1958 was controlled by the Gaullists, the victory of François Mitterand in the 1981 elections led to dramatic increases in state control over everything from mining and steel through pharmaceuticals, chemicals, glass, and electric equipment to banking.[46] One of the last instances took place in Canada which in this respect

---

[45] G. L. Reid and K. Allen, *Nationalized Industries* (Harmondsworth, UK: Penguin Books, 1970), pp. 14–15.

[46] For French nationalizations during these years, see A. H. Hanson, ed., *Public Enterprise: A Study of Its Organization and Management in Various Countries* (Brussels: International Institute of Administrative Sciences, 1955), pp. 201–24; and J. P. van Ouderhoven, "Privatization in Europe," in K. K. Finley, *Public Sector Privatization: Alternative Approaches to Service Delivery* (New York: Quorum Books, 1989), pp. 168ff.

resembled Europe more than it did the United States. Here, electoral considerations and the need to prevent unemployment led to the nationalization of the – bankrupt – fishing industry in 1984.

Nor, during the decades in question, was the trend toward greater public ownership over industry limited to developed countries. On the contrary, many countries in the developing world proceeded even faster; considering that they regarded it as a major vehicle for modernization as well as a solution for every social problem. Thus the Mexican government between 1940 and 1980 founded 111 industrial enterprises, became a majority shareholder in 59, and a partner in 124 – 35 of which it was "forced" to save from bankruptcy.[47] In Chile by 1970 the state was sole or majority owner of forty-four of the largest companies including electricity generation, energy, and air transport; and this was *before* the socialist government of Salvador Allende took over 500 more during the three years when it was in office. In Argentina the expansion of the public sector was largely the product of the Peronist years between 1947 and 1955, showing once again how socialist and quasi-fascist ideas could meet. In Brazil it was carried out by the various military governments which ruled the country between 1963 and 1978, and which poured vast sums into industries considered vital to the national welfare such as chemicals, energy, cement, and arms.

However, even these developments were eclipsed by those which took place in Africa and Asia where, between 1960 and 1975 or so, the great majority of newly independent states adopted some kind of socialist development program that was heavily influenced either by the Soviet model or by the Chinese one. The outcome was a very large number of one-party political systems run on dictatorial or semi-dictatorial lines. Claiming to have liberated their peoples from imperialist "exploitation" and to be mustering the slender available resources for the public good, they nationalized – in other words, took over without compensation – virtually every form of economic enterprise, whether domestically or foreign-owned; beginning with the extraction of natural resources through energy production to the running of public transportation and even hotels. For example, in 1974 over three-quarters of Egypt's industrial production originated in state-owned plants.[48] Nor were minor enterprises, particularly in agriculture, exempt. From Vietnam to Tanzania, often even peasants engaged in little more than subsistence farming

[47] For additional data on the expansion of the state economy in Mexico, see O. Humberto Vera Ferrer, "The Political Economy of Privatization in Mexico," in W. Glade, ed., *Privatization of Public Enterprise in Latin America* (San Francisco: ICS Press, 1991), pp. 35–58.
[48] US Embassy, Cairo, *Egyptian Economic Trends*, occasional publication, March 1989, p. 8.

were deprived of their land – to the extent that it belonged to them in the first place – and concentrated in rural communes under tight state control.

While many developing states also tried to distribute at least some benefits in the form of free education and rudimentary medical care – e.g., China's "barefoot doctors" – the real triumph of the modern welfare state took place in Western Europe, Canada, and New Zealand. By the late 1960s these states had extended free education until it covered all high school students and many college and university students as well. They were providing some form of free (or, at any rate, heavily subsidized) medical service that covered every phase in the individual's life from ante-natal to geriatric care; they had instituted huge public housing and vocational training schemes, as well as insuring their citizens against unemployment, accident, sickness, and old age at levels which in most cases should permit those affected to hold their heads above water and which were sometimes remarkably generous. Some countries had also introduced paid maternity (and paternity) leave, child allowances, free legal aid to those who could not afford it, meals and nursing services for the disabled and the old, and countless other programs.

In the United States, as the world's richest society and the one most committed to free-enterprise capitalism, federal welfare schemes had made little progress since the days of the New Deal. However, in the late 1950s and early 1960s, it too was shocked into action by a number of inquiries which revealed how the less fortunate Americans lived amidst all the plenty by which they were surrounded.[49] Once the budget-minded Eisenhower had finally left office, reforms designed to correct this situation were started under the Kennedy administration. They were greatly accelerated by Lyndon Johnson who coined the term Great Society to describe them; in spite of the Republicans' conservative leanings, Democratic control of both Houses of Congress ensured they would be carried over into the Nixon and Ford eras as well. Taken together, they composed the greatest expansion of welfare in American history. Among the best-known programs were Medicare and Medicaid; foodstamps; SSI (Supplemental Security Income, a scheme for guaranteeing income to the elderly, the blind, and the disabled); WIN (Work Incentive Program, meant to provide adults with the opportunity for vocational training); and a very large number of programs designed to help individual groups from single parents to members of minorities.

[49] See in particular J. K. Galbraith, *The Affluent Society* (Boston: Houghton Mifflin, 1959), as well as M. Harrington, *The Other America: Poverty in the United States* (New York: Collier, 1962).

In both Europe and the United States – to say nothing of developing countries – the expansion of state-directed welfare led to an equally great growth of the bureaucracy. By the second half of the twentieth century, the number of ministries, which during the state's formative years in the seventeenth and eighteenth centuries had seldom exceeded four, had risen to something nearer twenty in many of the most advanced countries. The ministers of justice, of foreign affairs, of war, and of the treasury were joined by ministers for interior affairs, police, agriculture, transportation, communications, education, health, labor, welfare, trade and industry, aviation, energy, planning, housing, science and technology, and tourism. Some countries thought it indispensable to have a special minister for the infrastructure. Others considered that they could not get by without a portfolio for sport and leisure, while others still expanded their cabinets by including a minister who was responsible for ecological affairs and another to look after women. The number of government employees also grew by leaps and bounds: e.g., from 11 to 23 percent of the West European workforce between 1950 and 1980, and from 9.7 to 15.2 percent of the civilian workforce in the United States during the same period. In 1982 the Western countries with the largest number of government employees in the workforce were Sweden and Norway with 32 percent each. They were followed by the United Kingdom (22 percent), whereas France and the United States with 17 percent came near the bottom of the list.[50]

To support all these bureaucrats, the share of government spending as part of GNP grew to proportions which, except in periods of total war, were without precedent in history. To focus on a few countries only, between 1950 and 1973 it rose from 27.6 to 38.8 percent in France; 30.4 to 42.0 percent in (West) Germany; 26.8 to 45.0 percent in Britain; and 34.2 to 41.5 percent in the Netherlands.[51] Nor surprisingly, much of this increase was accounted for by the rise of various social services. Between 1940 and 1975 their share of GNP doubled in Germany (which, thanks to the Nazis, entered the period while in possession of a more developed system than any other Western country), trebled in the UK, quadrupled in the Netherlands, and quintupled in Denmark where the growth was

[50] Figures from G. K. Fry, *The Growth of Government* (London: Cass, 1979), p. 32; R. Higgs, *Crisis and Leviathan: Critical Episodes in the Growth of American Government* (New York: Oxford University Press, 1987), pp. 22–3; R. A. Freeman, *The Growth of American Government: A Morphology of the Welfare State* (Stanford, CA: Hoover Institution Press, 1975), p. 35.

[51] Figures from A. Milward, *The European Rescue of the Nation State* (London: Routledge, 1992), p. 35. For parallel figures on additional countries, see P. Flora and A. J. Heidenheimer, eds., *The Development of Welfare States in Europe and America* (New Brunswick, NJ: Transaction Books, 1981), p. 319.

from 4.8 to a whopping 24 percent.[52] On the other side of the Atlantic the corresponding US figures rose from 23 to 35.8 percent of GNP (total government spending at both the federal and state levels). The share of welfare payments grew from 8.9 to 20 percent of the federal budget, which meant that, from the second half of the 1970s on, "social" spending had easily become the largest part of government spending even in the one state whose commitment to "rugged individualism" was the strongest on earth.

As Northcote Parkinson had predicted in 1958, had the prevailing trends been allowed to continue then by the year 2195 every man, woman, and child in Britain would have been working for the government. That this did not happen was due above all to two factors, one external and the other internal. The external factor was represented by the 1973 Arab–Israeli War and the fourfold increase in the price of energy that came in its wake.[53] These events sent the majority of Western economies into a recession that lasted through most of the 1970s; from then until 1981 or so, each time the ministers of the Organization of Petroleum Exporting Countries (OPEC) held a meeting the world would hold its breath while waiting for the bad news which invariably followed. Nor were the economies of Western Europe and North America assisted by the intensification of East Asian, particularly Japanese, competition which took place during these years and which threatened to wipe out – in some cases, did wipe out – entire industries from textiles through automobiles and photographic equipment to consumer electronics. One way or another, in most West European countries, unemployment soared to levels double and triple those which had been considered normal during most of the 1950s and 1960s.[54] The system of payments which had been designed to enable the unemployed to keep their heads above water, and which often gave them generous benefits such as retraining and relocation, was swamped.

The other factor that drove the welfare state to the breaking point was its own success.[55] Whatever their precise form, the various programs had been designed to assist weak population groups such as the elderly, the sick, and, later, single mothers; however, it soon turned out that the

[52] N. Gilbert, *Capitalism and the Welfare State* (New Haven, CT: Yale University Press, 1981), table 7.2.
[53] For a short account of the impact of the "crisis" on the international economy, see W. M. Scammell, *The International Economy Since 1945* (London: Macmillan, 1983), pp. 193ff.
[54] For figures on Europe, see Milward, *The European Rescue of the Nation State*, p. 30; for the United States, *Monthly Labor Review*, 103, 2, February 1980, p. 75.
[55] J. Logue, "The Welfare State: Victim of Its Success," in S. R. Graubard, ed., *The State* (New York: Norton, 1979), pp. 69–88; M. Dogan, "The Social Security Crisis in the Richest Countries: Basic Analogies," *International Social Science Journal*, 37, 1, 1985, pp. 47–61.

greater the benefits offered, the larger the number of those entitled. For example, in Germany the number of people aged over sixty-five rose from 9.2 percent of the population in 1950 to 11.1 percent in 1961, 13.2 percent in 1970, and 15.5 percent in 1980.[56] Since the elderly get sick more often, but also because of the revolution in medical technology that took place during those very years, the cost of heath care rose dramatically;[57] this helps explain the near doubling of "social" expenditure (considered as part of either GNP or the state budget) that took place during the same period.[58]

To adduce another example, the number of children in the United States rose by 41 percent between 1952 and 1972, but the number of those eligible for benefits under the Aid for Dependent Children Program (AFDC) increased by a stunning 456 percent. The reason is that, given the rise in both illegitimacy and divorce (which by 1980 had increased from 26 to 50 percent of all marriages), a majority of children could now expect to spend at least some of their first eighteen years in a single parent household; similar developments took place in most other developed countries.[59] By way of a final case in point, Denmark with its remarkably generous system of sickness benefits (90 percent of the average industrial wage) discovered that the average number of sick days claimed by each worker per year doubled between 1967 and 1977.[60] Nothing could be better proof of the welfare state's amazing ability to aggravate the very social problems which it was destined to cure. In fact, the same had been true ever since the first programs had been instituted around the turn of the century.

Old habits are hard to discard. Trapped in the thinking of the previous two and a half decades, initially most of the governments confronted by these problems refused to look them in the face. Though slowing down, both the expansion of the welfare state and the wave of nationalizations that accompanied it continued through the first half of the 1970s, sometimes even into the second. Thus, in West Germany, the great improvement in provisions for the elderly came *after* Helmut Schmidt took over as chancellor in 1974. In Britain it was EEC membership which led to

[56] R. Tylewski and M. Opp de Hipt, *Die Bundesrepublik Deutschland in Zahlen 1945/49–1980* (Munich: Beck, 1987), p. 38; for Britain there are parallel figures in A. F. Stiletto, *Britain in Figures: A Handbook of Social Statistics* (Harmondsworth, UK: Penguin Books, 1971), p. 31.
[57] For some figures on this development, see C. W. Higgins, "American Health Care and the Economics of Change," in Finley, *Public Sector Privatization*, pp. 99ff.
[58] Tylewski and Opp de Hipt, *Die Bundesrepublik in Zahlen*, pp. 183–4.
[59] US data from Freeman, *The Growth of American Government*, p. 11; figures for selected other countries in L. Bryson, *Welfare and the State: Who Benefits?* (London: Macmillan, 1992), p. 193.
[60] J. Logue, "Will Success Spoil the Welfare State?," *Dissent*, Winter 1985, p. 97.

the introduction of maternity benefits in 1975, whereas the same year saw the European welfare state reach its apogee as unemployment benefits were increased and their average duration extended from twenty to forty-four weeks.[61] Similarly in the United States, Title XX of the Social Security Act consolidated a vast array of benefits in such a way that, between 1975 and 1977, the number of recipients rose from 2.4 million to 3.5 million, leading to a situation where almost half of the population were receiving payments of some sort.[62] Average social expenditure in the Organization for Economic Co-operation and Development (OECD) countries rose, reaching almost 25 percent of GNP.[63] The result, in every case, were government deficits and inflation. For example, the US federal government was *never* in the black from 1969 until 1998 (even now, the "balanced budget" allegedly achieved by the Clinton administration conceals an enormous gap in social security). In the late 1970s, Italy, Belgium, Britain, Japan, and West Germany were all running deficits in excess of 5 percent of GNP.[64] So did that world-renowned bastion of sound money, Switzerland – with the result that inflation ran between 3.6 percent in 1979 and 6.5 percent in 1981.[65]

By this time, though, a reaction was already setting in. Squeezed by a combination of rising taxes and inflation, and fearing a future which promised nothing but greater burdens, in one country after another the electorate signified its disgust with the welfare state and those who promoted it. For example, Canada from 1975 on started cutting the Unemployment Insurance Program with an eye to reducing expenditure. In 1977 the federal government in Ottawa put a cap on the amount of funding it provided for the provinces' social welfare programs;[66] from then on, the story has been one of more or less constant cuts.[67] In Britain the construction of public housing came to a halt in 1977, i.e., while the country was still under Labour government. A year later a program aimed at pushing people out of the state pension plan and into private funds was started, with the result that, by 1983, 45 percent of those concerned had

---

[61] Flora and Heidenheimer, *The Development of Welfare States*, p. 1,67.

[62] Gilbert, *Capitalism and the Welfare State*, pp. 52–4; J. L. Clayton, *On The Brink: Defense, Deficits and Welfare Spending* (New York: National Strategy Information Center, 1984), p. 101.

[63] The 1980 figure is from N. Ginsburg, *Divisions of Welfare* (London: Sage, 1992), p. 199.

[64] D. Cameron, "On the Limits of the Public Economy," *Annals*, January 1982, p. 46.

[65] Figures on inflation in Switzerland and other countries are from Scammell, *The International Economy Since 1945*, p. 216.

[66] S. B. Seward, *The Future of Social Welfare Systems in Canada and the UK* (Halifax, Nova Scotia: Institute for Research on Public Policy, 1987), p. 63.

[67] See W. Thorsell, "Canada Counts the Cost," in *The World in 1996* (London: The Economist, 1996), p. 67.

made the switch. For the United States, the decisive turning point at the grass-roots level was probably represented by the 1980 California citizens' tax revolt, which led to the adoption of Proposition 13 and demonstrated that people had had their fill of the ever-growing welfare state. In fact, the late 1970s and early 1980s saw the rise to power in both Britain and West Germany of conservative governments whose avowed purpose was to carry out a right-wing revolution, while in the United States President Reagan in his inaugural speech promised "to check and reverse the growth of government which shows signs of having grown beyond the consent of the governed."[68]

Since then, and with few exceptions such as Norway whose economy is kept afloat on a lake of oil, all over the world the news for the welfare state has been almost uniformly bad. The methods used to cut back on benefits and services have been numerous and varied. One such was to put an arbitrary ceiling on expenditure, thus cutting the quality of services and forcing people to look elsewhere. Then there was the introduction of means tests to limit the number of recipients; the substitution of tax credits for direct transfer payments, a method which often benefited middle-class families at the expense of lower-income ones; the broadening of the tax base so that welfare payments now counted as income; cuts in housing, education, and health programs; various changes in eligibility rules (such as raising retirement ages, and for Medicaid in the United States); requiring fees to be paid for services which used to be provided free of charge; and, in places where they existed, canceling or reducing subsidies for everything from cultural services (tertiary education, museums, libraries, the theater, the plastic arts, music) to housing, public transportation, and bread.

By the second half of the 1980s, there probably was no country left anywhere in the developed world that had not adopted at least some of these changes. However, even where the cuts had been kept to a minimum, the real quality of service was often eroded. The methods used were continuing inflation; lengthening waiting lists, as in the case of "nonessential" surgical procedures that might take months or years before they were carried out; and bureaucratic intimidation whose effect – whether deliberate or not – was to make sure that at least some of those entitled to benefits would not show up to claim them. For example, one study dating to the mid-1980s pointed out that an American widow with several children, one of whom was retarded, was entitled to participate in seven different welfare programs at both the state and the federal levels.

[68] The text of this speech can be found at http://www.cc.columbia.edu/acis/bartelby/inaugural/pres61.html, paragraph No. 13.

To obtain the benefits she would have to go to four different offices, complete five different forms, and answer 300 different questions. No fewer than 1,400 pieces of information were needed to determine the level of her income alone – and this before she ever saw a penny disbursed.[69]

As the various welfare systems shrank, the gaps between the incomes of rich and poor began to widen. The extent to which thirty or forty years of social legislation in the most advanced countries had succeeded in achieving its aim, i.e., promoting a more equal distribution of wealth, has often been debated; while data are often hard to obtain, if any conclusion emerges, it seems to be that it may have made a modest contribution in this direction.[70] However, beginning in the early 1980s there were unmistakable signs that whatever progress in this direction had taken place was being undone, or else soon would be. Thus, in Canada as one of the richest and most comprehensive welfare states, poverty rates which had fallen continuously from the mid-1960s on began to rise again, with the result that in 1985 one-fifth of all children were living in poverty.[71] In Britain the number of poor – defined as those with less than half the average EEC income – rose from 5 million in 1979 to 12 million in 1993, while the share of gross domestic product that the lowest 10 percent commanded dropped from 4 to 2.1 percent.[72] In the United States the share in national income of the poorest fifth of the population dropped by some 5 percent between 1977 and 1990, whereas the richest fifth became 9 percent wealthier.[73] In both the United States and Europe some of the hardest hit consisted of unskilled laborers who saw state-provided benefits – such as unemployment insurance – being cut even as their real wages fell;[74] first the United States, and then parts of Europe, witnessed the rise of the so-called working poor. Most of them were employees in service industries who did not enjoy benefits of

---

[69] E. E. Berkowitz and K. McQuaid, *Creating the Welfare State: The Political Economy of Twentieth-Century Reform* (Lawrence: University of Kansas Press, 1992), pp. 207–8.
[70] See Flora and Heidenheimer, *The Development of Welfare States*, pp. 202–4; M. Schnitzer, *Income Distribution: A Comparative Study of the United States, Sweden, West Germany, East Germany, and the UK* (New York: Praeger, 1972); A. B. Atkinson, *Poverty and Social Security* (New York: Harvester Wheatsheaf, 1989), pp. 48ff.; and J. A. Pechman, *The Rich, the Poor, and the Taxes They Pay* (Boulder: Westview Press, 1986), pp. 19–30.
[71] Seward, *The Future of Welfare Systems*, pp. 214, 218.
[72] *The Economist*, 11 September 1993.
[73] Congressional Budget Office, US House of Representatives, Ways and Means Committee, "The Changing Distribution of Federal Taxes, 1977–1990," February 1987, and "Tax Progressivity and Income Distribution," 26 March 1990.
[74] See E. B. Kapstein, "Workers and the World Economy," *Foreign Affairs*, 73, 3, May/June 1996, pp. 16–37.

any kind and, though holding jobs and often working long hours, were
unable to make a decent living.[75]

To justify and explain the changes that were taking place, economic
doctrine too was changing. Though Keynes himself died in 1946, his
ghost – in the form of generations of economists who worked out the
implications of the last of his equations – went marching on. He enjoyed
what was perhaps his greatest triumph in 1969 when, much to the
consternation of a few die-hard fellow party members, incoming Republican President Nixon announced that "I am a Keynesian." That triumph, however, was short-lived. The energy crisis brought about a
combination of inflation and stagnation which was previously considered
to be impossible and which was quickly given a new name, "stagflation."
From the mid-1970s on, it forced economists to take a fresh look at the
established Keynesian orthodoxy.

In some respects the new developments in the field of economic theory
merely constituted a return to older prophets, notably Gustav Hayek and
his so-called Austrian school who throughout the 1950s had criticized
Keynesian doctrines in the name of sound money.[76] Later the mantle of
leadership was assumed by Professor Milton Friedman of the University
of Chicago. Having been awarded the Nobel prize for economics in
1976, more than anybody else he initiated the emergence of so-called
monetary or supply-side economic theory. The notion that government
should deliberately incur budget deficits to iron out the business cycle
went out of favor as bad for entrepreneurship and productivity and good
only for inflation. Friedman's ideas were carried a step further by another
Nobel prize winner, Professor Robert Lucas, III, and his "rational-ex-
pectations" school. Previous economists had regarded states and their
populations as partners in a common enterprise; not so Lucas who, in a
way that was highly characteristic of the time, viewed them as opposed
players. Using the framework provided by game theory, he argued that
the former could not do *anything* to make their economies grow.[77]
Though few countries went that far, the upshot was the revival of
something closer to "classic" economic doctrine, including a strong

[75] For the United States, see R. B. Freeman and L. F. Katz, eds., *Differences and Changes in
Wage Structures* (Chicago: University of Chicago Press, 1995); for similar developments
taking hold in Germany as the largest EU country, see *Der Spiegel*, 39, 1997, pp. 96ff.

[76] An accessible collection of Hayek's ideas is C. Nishiyama and K. L. Leube, eds., *The
Essence of Hayek* (Stanford, CA: Hoover Institution Press, 1984).

[77] See P. J. Miller, ed., *The Rational Expectations Revolution* (Cambridge, MA: MIT Press,
1994), for a convenient summary. I wish to thank Prof. H. Barkai of the Economics
Department, Hebrew University, for providing me with a clue to this latest economic
hocus-pocus.

emphasis on balanced budgets, private enterprise, free competition, and the survival of the fittest.

By the mid-1980s, even the idea that the state should necessarily be responsible for looking after the currency – which for at least 400 years had been one of the pillars of sovereignty – found itself under attack.[78] Much as had been the case in England under the last Stuart kings, it was argued that governments were too powerful to be trusted with the management of money, as was evident from the inbuilt tendency toward inflation that had resulted as well as the highly irresponsible manner in which it was sometimes handled. Again, to date no state has gone so far as to put the management of the currency back into private hands; in other respects, however, the monetarists have long been triumphant. Economically speaking, much of the world found itself heading back to nineteenth-century capitalism – not by accident or apologetically, but as part of a well-thought-out, deliberate design. From Canada to New Zealand, the goal was to lower inflation and create the conditions for steady, unspectacular economic growth. This was to be achieved even at the cost of doing away with central planning, allowing the business cycle to run its course, and incurring insecurity for both employers and employees. In many places it also recreated what Marx in *Das Kapital* called the industrial reserve army – a more or less permanent core of unemployed people who could be, and were, used to keep the wages of the remainder within bounds.

As part of the new program, the industries which governments had spent so much money nationalizing during the years 1945–75 were being reprivatized. As it happened, many of the industries which European governments in particular took over were already in decline: so, for example, in the case of coal, whose place was being taken by oil; steel, which was increasingly being manufactured in Japan; and shipbuilding (ditto). The same was also true of railroads, which were being overtaken by motor transport. In other cases nationalization affected firms which had suffered years of neglect during World War II, with the result that their equipment had become run-down and they were badly short of capital. In time, many of the nationalized industries were further weakened by being run on political principles – as when they were made to provide unprofitable services, or employ too many workers, or keep their tariffs at artificially low levels, rather than along sound business lines

[78] E.g. R. L. Greenfield and L. B. Yaeger, "A *Laissez Faire* Approach to Monetary Stability," *Journal of Money, Credit and Banking*, 15, 1983, pp. 302–15; L. H. White, "The Relevance of Free Banking Today," printed in Collins, *Central Banking in History*, vol. I, pp. 434–49; R. Vaubal, "The Government's Money Monopoly: Externalization of Natural Monopoly," *Kyklos*, 37, 1984, pp. 27–58; and, above all, F. A. Hayek, *Denationalization of Money* (London: Hobart Special Paper, 70, 1978).

– to say nothing of the fact that senior posts in state-owned corporations were often treated not as jobs requiring expertise but as perks for politicians and bureaucrats in and out of office.

Be the precise reasons as they may, the hopes of those who had advocated nationalization, i.e., that it would permit profits to benefit the community as a whole instead of shareholders only, were seldom realized. From the late 1960s on, many of them began to hang like albatrosses round their owners' necks, employing vast numbers of superfluous workers and very often generated equally vast rivers of red ink. Thus, in Britain, all nationalized industries except gas were losing money, closing plants, and dismissing employees in a never-ending cycle which during the second half of the 1970s was reducing entire regions to poverty and despair.[79] In Italy, the state-owned industrial holding companies – IMI, ENI, EFIM, and IRI (the latter having grown into the largest employer in the country) – were all bankrupt by the mid-1970s. By the mid-1980s, the 20 percent or so of Austrian industry that was in government hands had turned into monuments of inefficiency and red tape. The list, which went on and on, was by no means limited to developed countries: witness, for example, the vast problems experienced by the Arab countries as well as numerous Latin American ones.

Whether in order to escape these losses, or simply as a means for raising money to cover their deficits, many governments were beginning to reprivatize the companies which during the previous decades they had spent so much money and effort acquiring; at the same time, they began contracting out services which they had previously provided in-house. The lead in both fields was taken by Britain, which during the years 1964–78 had been governed mainly by Labour but which in 1979 put the Conservatives back into office. Prime Minister Margaret Thatcher and her government were among the most strident representatives of the new economic conservatism. Acting with conscious, deliberate intent, they began offering to the public the shares of one state-owned company after another, including British Petroleum, British Aerospace, Cable and Wireless, Britoil (the company responsible for extracting North Sea oil), Associated British Ports, British Airways, British Steel, and National Freight, the government-owned road haulage corporation which had been in existence since the 1950s.

After Margaret Thatcher formed her second government in 1982, the pace of privatization accelerated. Additional slices of the above-listed companies were put on the market, together with British Gas, British Telecom, British Sugar, British Rail Hotels, Royal Ordnance, and parts

[79] See R. Pryke, *The Nationalized Industries: Policies and Performance Since 1968* (Oxford: Robertson, 1986), particularly pp. 237–66.

of British Leyland including the prestige car manufacturer Jaguar.[80] By 1988 nearly 40 percent of the industries which, in 1979, had been government-owned had been transferred back to private hands, while the proportion of GNP in the hands of the government had fallen from 10.5 to 6.5 percent. Some 650,000 people ceased to be state employees, and 90 percent of them also became shareholders either in the companies for which they worked or in others. Meanwhile, the percentage of all adults who owned shares tripled, a development which was itself regarded as creating a constituency in favor of continuing reform and which, in fact, had been deliberately planned for from the beginning. Plans were also announced for the complete or partial privatization of services such as water supply, sewage treatment, Crown Supplies (the central purchasing agency for all government departments, including the armed services), and prisons. In the field of health alone a whole series of ancillary services, including hospital cleaning, catering, and laundry were privatized between 1981 and 1988, as were the performance of abortions and the task of looking after the mentally ill. The result was a 33.5 percent drop in the number of ancillary jobs in the National Health Service. From the patients' point of view, it also spelt a considerable reduction in the quality of service provided and a rise in their cost.[81]

The road taken by Margaret Thatcher was often described as "the British cure," though "the British enema" might perhaps be more appropriate. During the 1980s, it provided a beacon for numerous other governments which followed along the same road. For example, in Italy between 1983 and 1989, the state holding companies sold off assets to the tune of $5 billion in order to cover their losses, including also such national symbols as the Alfa Romeo car maker, the Italtel communications group, and juicy chunks of the banking system with the Banco di Roma at their head. Though France's Socialist president Mitterand was destined to remain in office until 1995, here too the turning point was brought about by the elections of 1986; led by minister of finance Edouard Balladur, the government started selling off some state-owned companies in such fields as industry, insurance, banking, and finance. In 1987 alone the sum realized from these sales amounted to $11.5 billion. The number of people employed by the government fell by 800,000, while the number of shareholders – in other words, those who had bought up the newly privatized firms – increased by 5,000,000.

In West Germany, too, privatization gathered steam during the 1980s.

---

[80] For a full list of companies sold wholly or in part, as well as the sums realized, see S. Chodak, *The New State: Etatization of Western Societies* (Boulder: Rienner, 1989), p. 147.

[81] For the details, see R. Fraser, ed., *Privatization: The UK Experience and International Trends* (London: Longman, 1989).

Led by the Christian Democrat Helmut Kohl, the government – whose share was already smaller than in most other countries – sold off over fifty companies, including aluminum, chemicals, energy, vehicles, and banking. In Canada, the last important wave of state takeovers was accomplished in 1984. It was followed almost immediately by the massive sale of government-owned industries, including rail transportation, aircraft manufacturing, fish processing, ammunition, finance, mining (including uranium), nuclear energy, trucking, air transport, and power generation. And this continued in one economically developed country after another, from the United States – where Conrail was sold in 1982 – to the Netherlands and Belgium through Turkey, all the way to New Zealand and Australia.

Though taking a different form, the trend extended even to those very strongly governed states, South Korea and Taiwan. In both countries, Chaebol and Guanxiqiye (large industrial firms) were started by private individuals and always remained privately owned. During the so-called developmental period which lasted from the early 1950s to the early 1980s they were often so closely controlled by the state as to form virtually a part of it. Strongly *dirigiste* governments dictated what sectors should be developed. Having done so, they set out to provide the necessary prerequisites. These included custom barriers, a docile labor force, kept in check by law, the virtual absence of a social security network, and a suitable dose of Confucian propaganda,[82] and, as more resources became available, an improving infrastructure on the form of roads, telecommunications, electricity generating plant, ports, and airports. In return, the firms themselves provided governments, parties, and officials with massive subsidies, often amounting to bribes.

Around 1985, though, the pattern began changing. In part, this was because many of the most important industries in question had themselves become multinational, thus forcing them to pay more attention to the demands of foreign governments and international organizations. In part it reflected the gradual evolution toward democracy; as a new, prosperous middle class made its appearance, the old authoritarian forms of government came to be questioned. The cozy relationship between government and industry was now regarded as corrupt, leading to some spectacular trials of South Korean politicians in particular.[83] Then, in the middle of 1997, most East Asian countries were struck by a severe economic crisis. Their industries, having become accustomed to

---

[82] C. Jones, "The Pacific Challenge: Confucian Welfare States," in Jones, ed., *New Perspectives on the Welfare State in Europe* (London: Routledge, 1993), pp. 198–220.

[83] See K. J. Fields, *Enterprise and the State in Korea and Taiwan* (Ithaca, NY: Cornell University Press, 1995), particularly pp. 238ff.

the hothouse conditions provided by custom barriers and the "protection" of leading politicians, began to suffer from overcapacity. Prices of their real estate (which had often served as collateral for bank loans in aid of expansion) collapsed, their exports declined, and their currencies had to be devalued. At the time of writing it seems as if most of them will weather the crisis, albeit at the price of slowed-down growth and IMF-imposed reforms which will further weaken the relationship between government and industries.[84] Some, like Indonesia, may not.

Even as the majority of countries were privatizing as fast as they could, the movement was given a tremendous, and for the most part unexpected, boost by the collapse of the communist bloc. Coming to power in 1917, the Bolsheviks' proclaimed goal was to do away with all forms of private enterprise, and in fact most major resources and firms were taken over by the state within a few years. The onset of the New Economic Policy, or NEP, in 1923 delayed the completion of the process; by 1932, however, Stalin had eliminated all remaining "capitalists," not seldom by "liquidating" them, as happened to millions of peasants. The resources which collectivization made available were used to build up industry, with the result that, from the start of the first Five Year Plan in 1928, heavy industry in particular began to expand by leaps and bounds. By 1939, it had become the second largest in the world after the United States.[85]

After World War II left Germany in ruins, the Soviet lead over the remaining European countries increased, peaking between about 1965 and 1975.[86] Though they operated on a much smaller scale, the Soviet Union's proteges in Eastern Europe took a similar course during the twenty or so years after 1945 and, thanks in part to their abysmally low starting points, also enjoyed exceptional rates of industrial growth.[87] In particular, during the late 1970s and early 1980s, East Germany, a country of fewer than 20 million people, developed into the showcase of the East. It was being touted as the world's ninth-largest industrial power (after the United States, USSR, Japan, West Germany, France, Britain, Italy, and Canada), with a standard of living to rival Britain's.[88]

While the facade may have impressed some people – not, presumably, those who had actually visited East Germany and seen the empty shops –

---

[84] See D. Hale, "Test of the Tigers," *World Link*, September–October 1997, pp. 17–33.

[85] For figures, see Hillman, "Comparative Strength of the Great Powers," p. 146.

[86] For statistics on production, see R. Munting, *The Economic Development of the USSR* (London: St. Martin's, 1982), p. 133.

[87] See M. C. Kaser, ed., *The Economic History of Eastern Europe* (Oxford: Clarendon Press, 1986), vol. III, pp. 9ff., 19, 52, 95, 152, for data on the collectivization of agriculture in the countries in question as well as the resulting economic growth.

[88] I. Jeffries, "The DDR in Historical and International Perspective," in Jeffries and M. Melzer, eds., *The East German Economy* (London: Methuen, 1987), pp. 1–11.

by that time the rates of growth achieved by all communist countries were already beginning to fall. The highly centralized bureaucracies responsible for laying down plans and allocating resources had proven very successful in providing huge amount of standard products such as raw materials, power, steel, and chemicals.[89] Partly because of deliberate neglect, however, and partly because their methods proved ill adapted to meeting the infinitely varied demands of consumers, in agriculture and light industry they had been much less so. The first to fail was agriculture, forcing the Soviets to purchase American and Canadian wheat from 1963 on. Then came their failure and that of their satellites to adapt to the tougher conditions which prevailed on the international market from 1973 on, including specifically the rising price of oil; and finally they proved unable to effectively harness emerging technologies such as microelectronics and computers.[90] While many Soviet products had always had something crude about them, now they began looking as if they came out of some bygone Stakhanovite age – which was often actually the case. Productivity stalled and the gap between per capita income in East and West, which had seemed to close, began rising again.[91]

The first important communist country to start rolling back state control over the economy was, surprisingly, China. Once it had established itself in 1949, the Chinese Communist state had in some ways followed in the wake of its European comrades in arms, nationalizing the land and resorting to collectivization so as to squeeze the countryside and free resources for rapid industrialization. More than most, it allowed ideological considerations to throw its economy into chaos, first during the Great Leap Forward in 1957–61 and then during the even more destructive Cultural Revolution. So long as Mao lived, the Chinese economy, as well as Chinese society, wove a violent zigzag course between strict centralized planning and tumultuous populism; but his death in 1976, followed by the removal from the scene of his would-be successors in the form of the "Gang of Four," finally opened the way to reform.

In 1978 the Party's new secretary-general, Deng Xiao-ping, formally announced the "Four Modernizations" in the fields of science, agriculture, industry, and the armed forces. From then on there was no looking back. One field after another was thrown open to private enterprise; by

[89] For 1960 figures on Soviet production of these commodities, see G. A. Hosking, *History of the Soviet Union* (London: Collins, 1985), appendix C ("Selected Indices of Industrial and Agricultural Production"), pp. 483ff.
[90] See R. W. Judy and V. L. Clough, *The Information Age and Soviet Society* (Indianapolis: Bobbs Merrill, 1989), ch. 1.
[91] See R. E. Ericson, "The Soviet Economic Predicament," in H. S. Rowen and C. Wolf, Jr., eds., *The Future of the Soviet Empire* (New York: St. Martin's 1987), pp. 95–120; and W. Moskoff, *Hard Times: The Soviet Union 1985–1991* (Armonk, NY: Sharpe, 1993).

the late 1980s collective agriculture had all but disappeared and a stock exchange, the first to be permitted in China since 1949, was operating in Shanghai – as clear a sign as any that the processes which were overtaking other countries were operating here, too.

During the 1980s and 1990s, the willingness of the Chinese state to relax its hold over the economy led to phenomenal rates of growth. Often it was assisted by foreign (mainly Japanese and Taiwanese) capital pouring in in search of cheaper labor, as well as less stringent environmental requirements than the ones that existed in their own countries. While heavy industry tended to remain in the hands of the state and turned into monuments of backwardness and inefficiency, light industry and services were revolutionized as hundreds of thousands of new companies sprang out of the ground.[92] The changes were much more evident in the south than in the north, and along the coast than in the interior; urban areas tended to benefit more than rural ones, leading to peasant unrest as well as a vast migration from the latter into the former. For all the problems that growth created – including inflation and corruption on a massive scale – for the first time in its history China was acquiring something like a mass consumer class. Provided it could sustain the rate of growth achieved, the leadership could look forward to the day when their country would turn into the world's largest economic unit (by some measures it is already the third largest) even though there was still no prospect of ever matching the per capita product and living standards of the developed countries. As the end of the millennium approached, the major question confronting China did not so much appear its ability to pursue its drive toward economic growth, as whether that growth, and the social stresses that it generated, could be reconciled with the continuing dictatorship of the Communist Party.[93]

China's success in loosening state control over the economy without (so far) undergoing a major political upheaval was not emulated by most other communist countries. As already noted, Soviet recovery from the ordeal of World War II had been relatively quick. From the mid-1970s, however, growth slowed down, and by the time Brezhnev died in 1982 the Soviet leadership was aware that economically and technologically it was falling behind the West. Still his immediate successors, Yuri Andropov and Konstantin Chernenko, were reluctant to introduce far-reaching reforms. Given his KGB background, the former in particular

---

[92] By 1989 their number was put at almost a quarter of a million: J. P. Sterba, "Long March," *Wall Street Journal*, 16 June 1989, p. A4.

[93] For an in-depth discussion of the problem, see O. Schell, *Mandate of Heaven: The Legacy of Tiananmen Square and the Next Generation of China's Leaders* (New York: Simon and Schuster, 1994), particularly part V.

preferred to speak about the need to tighten discipline. By way of symbolizing his intentions, he launched a campaign against drunkenness.

When, after 1985, Mikhail Gorbachev *did* initiate fundamental changes, the road he took was the opposite from the Chinese one. Instead of relaxing the state's hold on the economy, Gorbachev introduced openness or *glasnost*. Instead of providing people with an incentive to work by opening the road to private enterprise, he permitted them to talk freely about politics. Talk freely they did, the main subject of conversation being the system's repeated and persistent failures. From the autumn of 1980 the Soviet Union had been involved in a bloody war in Afghanistan. When that adventure ended in defeat, in 1988, the Soviet leadership was left without an armed force which could have imposed unity on the country. Economic and, even more so, nationalist pressures manifested themselves; first the Baltic countries, then parts of Central Asia, broke away. In 1991 communism as a political regime collapsed with surprising suddenness. With it went perhaps the largest, most centralized, and militarily most powerful state that the world had ever seen, and, as far as can be judged at present, will see.

While the collapse was probably inevitable, in Gorbachev's defense it must be said that under his supervision it proceeded with remarkably little bloodshed. The same was not true after he left the scene. Out of the ruins there emerged no fewer than fifteen new republics; some of which lost no time in going after each other's throats and exterminating or driving out the members of ethnic minorities. Once the USSR started disintegrating the loss of Soviet control over, as well as the collapse of communism in, the countries of Eastern Europe was a foregone conclusion. As in the USSR, and mainly because communism seemed to have remarkably few people left willing to defend it, the process was for the most part a peaceful one – in Czechoslovakia it even earned the name "the velvet revolution." The major exception was Yugoslavia which went up in flames as its various constituent nationalities renounced the central government and embarked on a bloody civil war. Whatever the precise route taken, once the excitement subsided, all the countries in question discovered that forty-five years of state ownership and control had left their economies badly outdated and unable to compete in world markets. Partly to liberate their own citizens' energies, partly to attract foreign investment, all hastened to embark on a course of democratization, liberalization, and privatization. Since then, though the pace of reform has slackened in some places, in most it is still going on.[94]

Not only in West and East, but on every continent scarcely a country

---

[94] See R. Frydman, et al., *The Privatization Process in Central Europe* (New York: Oxford University Press, 1993).

could be found that was not privatizing as fast as it could.[95] Often this was done at the price of considerable social disruption: subsidies were cut, the prices of basic commodities went up, fees began to be required for services such as housing and medical care which had previously been provided free of charge or almost so, the size of the bureaucracy was cut, and state-owned firms disgorged streams of superfluous employees into labor markets that were ill equipped to absorb them. So powerful was the trend that it even reached countries whose very *raison d'être* since independence had been bound up with left-wing ideology such as Vietnam, India, Syria, Israel, Egypt, Tunisia, Algeria, and many others throughout Africa and Asia.

When "restructuring" proved too difficult a task, many developing countries were forced to turn to the World Bank and the International Monetary Fund. By early 1998 the latter had programs in no fewer than seventy-five countries with a total of 1.4 billion people; the list began with Albania and ended with Zimbabwe.[96] Staffed by adherents of the new supply-side economics, the two institutions provided their proteges with immense and badly needed loans. In return, they demanded thorough-going reforms including, above all, an end to deficit spending, the dismantling of the state-owned or -controlled sector, and the liberalization of financial markets. In addition they were to set up stable currencies; relax their hold on natural resources; allow foreign capital to enter; and provide the latter with various privileges, beginning with the right to repatriate profits freely and ending with the establishment of special "free-trade," meaning tax-free, zones.

Toward the year 2000, economic policy in most countries, like the science of economics which provided it with both an explanation and a justification, had made a complete about-turn. The trend toward greater state intervention in the economy which had started in the 1840s and gathered steam after 1900 or so was dead or dying; its place was taken by a renewed emphasis on private enterprise and competition. Often such competition and such enterprise manifested themselves in their wildest and least civilized forms: for example, as when the scramble for property that used to be government-owned led to the rise of the "Russian mafia." Often, too, it has been accompanied by incredible gaps between different

---

[95] For selected regions, see R. A. Ahene and B. S. Katz, eds., *Privatization and Investment in Sub-Saharan Africa* (New York: Praeger, 1992), and I. Harik and D. J. Sullivan, eds., *Privatization and Liberalization in the Middle East* (Bloomington: Indiana University Press, 1992); for a brief global overview, see P. Young, "Privatization Around the World," in S. H. Hanke, ed., *Prospects for Privatization* (New York: AOS, 1987), pp. 190–206.

[96] J. Sachs, "Recipe for Disaster," *World Link*, January–February 1998, p. 17.

social classes, a rising tide of organized and unorganized crime, and considerable misery for the great majority of the population, including in particular those – such as old age pensioners and the like – who for one reason or another were unable to break their dependence on a now bankrupt state.

Naturally the details varied from one region to another. In East Asia, as already noted, the virtual absence of a social security network meant that most important parts of the process were probably formed by the liberalization of markets, the loosening of the ties between government and industry, and a general tightening of belts. In the United States, carried on a wave of prosperity but divided between a Democratic president and a Republican Congress, politicians preferred to defer hard decisions as social security was threatened with bankruptcy soon after the year 2000. In much of Europe the welfare state still lingered on, more because of inertia and the lack of an alternative that would appeal to voters than for any other reason. In Ukraine, as in large parts of Eastern Europe, Central Asia, and Africa, the collapse of one-party communist and socialist regimes have left in their wake ruined economies that barely function at all. Almost everywhere governments struggled to retain at least parts of the welfare state, including above all elementary and secondary education. That apart, the dream of using government to "lift up" the masses was clearly in ruins and indeed even avowedly "left-wing" parties took a centrist stance and declared themselves no longer socialist. The old forms of political-economic organization have been largely discredited, and the search for others to take their place is on.

Technology goes international

As previous sections have argued, the rise of the state is inseparable from that of modern technology. Print, roads, railroads, telecommunications, and typewriters – to say nothing of weapons and weapons systems – were among the most important means that enabled the state to impose its power over every square mile of territory and every individual in the population. Separately and in combination, they made possible the establishment and operations of the armed forces, the collection of revenue, the transmission of laws and decrees, and the gathering of information, all in amounts, at speeds, and over distances that had previously been undreamed of. As it happened, the *first* use to which the early mechanical computers were put in the 1890s was to tabulate and collate the results of the US census. To look at it in another way, it is no accident that modern technology originated in Western Europe and that it has reached its highest development primarily in those parts of the world where states are strong and stable.[97] Conversely, those areas which for one reason or another have failed to establish powerful states are also, broadly speaking, the ones which lag behind in the generation and application of technology of every kind.

From the beginning, though, much of modern – meaning, in this context, post-1800 – technology bore a Janus face. On the one hand, it enabled governments to cast the net of sovereignty farther, and more tightly, than ever before, and thus helped them to control everything within their national borders. On the other, it tended to transcend those borders, crossing them and turning them into obstacles to progress. This was because, unlike its pre-1800 predecessors, much of modern technology can only operate when, and to the extent that, it is grouped into systems. A plow, a hammer, a musket, even a steam engine or a ship can do its job even in the absence of others of its kind; if numerous plows are used side by side, or many ships joined into a fleet, each one can still perform its function independently of the rest. Not so an individual railway train, or telegraph apparatus, or a telephone, each of which on its own is entirely useless. The number of such technologies is increasing every day; with them, what matters is the *network* of tracks, or wires, or switchboards, that connects each unit with countless others of its kind. Even more critical is the central directing hand that, laying down schedules and sorting out routes and priorities, enables them to communicate with each other at will, in an orderly manner, and without mutual interference.

The nature of modern technological systems may be explained by the example of the very first of them, namely the optical telegraph.[98] Dating to the last years of the eighteenth century and known after its inventors, the French brothers Chappe, it consisted of stations – either built into existing structures, such as church towers, or specially constructed ones – each of which was topped by a set of one horizontal and two vertical beams forming the letter H. Linked to each other by hinges, the beams were equipped with pulleys and ropes that allowed them to be set in 196 different positions, enough to cover the letters of the alphabet, punctuation marks, a number of selected syllables, words, and even entire phrases. Messages could be sent both by day and (using lamps) by night, either in clear or, by substituting letters for each other, in code. The

[97] For the state's use of the new technologies to control its population, see M. K. Matsuda, "Doctor, Judge, Vagabond: Identity, Identification and Other Memories of the State," *History and Memory*, 6, 1, 1994, pp. 73–94; B. Delmas, "Revolution industrielle et mutation administrative: l'innovation de l'administration française aux XIXe siècle," *Histoire, Economie et Société*, 4, 2, 1985, pp. 205–32; and, in greater detail, J. R. Beniger, *The Control Revolution: Technological and Economic Origins of the Information Society* (Cambridge, MA: Harvard University Press, 1986).   [98] See p. 251 above.

operator in each station was equipped with a telescope. He would pick up the signals displayed by the station before his own, write them down, and have his fellow operator transmit them to the next one. Depending on the topography the average distance between stations was in the order of four to five miles. The normal speed of transmission was around 200 or 300 miles per day, although much depended on atmospheric conditions (in fine weather some intermediate stations might be shut down) as well as on the length of the messages themselves.

As will be readily apparent, the efficiency of the system depended on the distances to be traversed as well as on its own density – the number of stations per square mile of territory. Below a certain distance it would offer no advantages at all, particularly if the messages were long and thus took a large number of beam-movements to transmit. Conversely, the longer the lines and the greater the number of directions in which they ran, the greater also the efficiency that it offered. National borders, even those of a country as large as France, merely stood in the way of achieving this efficiency. Already Napoleon had lines constructed which linked Paris with German and Italian cities; in 1809 they proved their worth by warning him that the Austrians had declared war and invaded the territory of his Bavarian ally. To perform their job, all stations, wherever located, had to be constructed on exactly the same principles and follow exactly the same procedures in regard to the nature of the signals, codes, priorities, and the like. Those procedures could be laid down only by a central headquarters which was also charged with making sure that they were obeyed. In other words, this earliest of all modern technological networks already had the potential of turning international and over-riding, if only for its own limited purposes, the differences between one sovereign state and another.

What was true of the semaphore system applied *a fortiori* to the electric telegraphs and railways which started making their appearance from the 1840s on; often running in tandem, at first both telegraphs and railways were constructed on a local scale, such as, to cite but two examples, the famous telegraph line by which Samuel Morse connected Washington, DC, with Baltimore and the equally famous length of track which connected Liverpool with Manchester. Originally, too, they tended to be privately owned; regardless of who owned them, however, the advantages of linking them to each other were very soon apparent. By the 1850s, at the latest, rail and telegraph systems belonging to different countries were often being integrated with each other by way of state-appointed *ad hoc* commissions. They laid down standards, operating procedures, orders of priority, and the like; the denser the traffic, the more imperative it was that these problems be solved. Conversely, a railway system designed solely for meeting the needs of a single state, such as the broad-gauged one constructed by imperial Russia and later passed to the USSR, provided some protection against invasion (a factor that was to prove particularly important in 1914–18 and 1941–5); however, by making transshipment necessary, it also acted as a barrier to Russian trade with other countries. Later, the same applied to attempts to build autonomous electricity grids, highway systems, and telephone networks, to say nothing of teleprinters and fax machines and computers.

In theory each state was, and still is, free to exercise its sovereignty and build its own networks to its own standards, however idiosyncratic, while at the same time ignoring those of its neighbors and refusing to integrate with them. In practice, states could do so only at the price of incurring a tremendous technological and economic cost. The current plight of North Korea is a perfect case in point. There, a xenophobic communist government has imposed isolation on its citizens, forcing them to become self-sufficient in all important respects and thus preventing them from making use of whatever comparative advantages they may have; the price to be paid was inefficiency and the inability to maximize the benefits of precisely those technologies that have developed most rapidly since 1945 or so, i.e., communication (including data processing) and transportation. The precise cost of isolation varies with circumstances and also depends on the size of the country in question. However, even in the case of the largest ones, it is still substantial – not for nothing has the United States, as the country with the largest economy of all, been switching over to the metric system. To avoid this cost, states had to gain access to international networks, which in turn forced them to grant foreigners access to their own. Furthermore, they also found it necessary to join the international bodies whose task was to regulate the technologies in question on behalf of all.

Another effect of advancing technology was to put an increasing number of environments which had previously been inaccessible to mankind within its reach. Some of these environments, such as the air and the bottom of the sea, had long been known to exist and, in small part, were explored and exploited; others, such as the electromagnetic spectrum, were recently discovered and turned out to be of an entirely new nature. Their effective use, even whether they could be used at all, often depended not on the whims of this country or that but on international cooperation. For example, without rules, procedures, and organizations which are responsible for allocating air space and coordinating communications, navigation, security, emergency services, and a whole host of other matters, the international civil transport aviation industry could not exist. Much the same is true for operations in outer space, underwater space, and of course electromagnetic space. Whether because the spaces owned by each country are too small, or because of the danger of mutual interference, all require that they be regulated on a scale, and by organizations, that are capable of looking beyond the needs of individual states.

Finally, a third way in which modern technology compelled governments to work together grew out of the ecological problems that it created.[99] As Charles Dickens' Coketown and the black satanic mills remind us, already during the nineteenth century industrialization was capable of polluting entire districts, spoiling their drinking water and filling the air with black smoke. But these problems were as nothing compared to the ones which made their appearance after 1945, and, even more so, since the rise of modern mass consumer societies in the most advanced countries. To the wastes, many of them toxic, created by industry itself – smoke, ashes, slag, and effluents of every sort – were added the emissions of automobiles, the lead from discarded batteries, the glass and aluminum from throwaway food and drink containers, and of course vast amounts of plastic and styrofoam used for packaging all sorts of products and, having served their function, left to litter the country for ever and ever.

Some of the pollutants went into the air, others into the ground, others still into the water – the oceans included – where not even fish were safe from them. While some remained strictly local nuisances, others were capable of making their effect felt hundreds and even thousands of miles from their point of origin. For example, global warming – the name speaks for itself – and the destruction of the ozone layer are caused by the emissions of power plants, factories, and automobiles, and represent planetary problems. Smoke generated by US industry will cause acid rain to fall in Canada. Poisonous materials poured into the Rhine by chemical plants which are located in Switzerland and Alsace will reach down the river all the way down to its mouth near the Hoek of Holland; and oil slicks developed in Egyptian territorial waters, for example, are liable to end up on the shores of Israel. The list of problems, once one thinks about it, is endless. However, perhaps the most dramatic demonstration of the global effects that pollution can have was given by the explosion that took place in the nuclear reactor at Chernobyl in 1986. From its place of origin near the Ukrainian city of Kiev the resulting radioactivity spread over much of the northern hemisphere, including Belarus, Poland, the Baltic states, Scandinavia, and Canada.

---

[99] See J. Vogler, "The Politics of the Global Environment," in C. Bretherton and G. Ponton, eds., *Global Politics: An Introduction* (Oxford: Blackwell, 1996), pp. 194–219; and M. S. Soroos, *Beyond Sovereignty: The Challenge of Global Policy* (Columbia: University of South Carolina Press, 1986), chs. 8 and 9.

With technology simultaneously creating the need for, and (by facilitating transportation and communication) encouraging the establishment of, international bodies it is not surprising that the first such bodies, appeared around the middle of the nineteenth century. Previously there had often been bilateral and multilateral alliances, some of which were intended to be permanent. A good example is provided by the "Concert of Europe," a loose association of states whose purpose was to prevent any individual member from expanding at the expense of the rest while simultaneously cooperating in suppressing Jacobinism wherever it might raise its head.[100] However, the International Telegraph Union represented something else. Its foundation, which took place in 1865, marked the first time when states created an organization in which they themselves were members but which at the same time had a legal persona of its own as well as a permanent staff and a permanent headquarters at which it could be reached. Within its own limited field, the organization was authorized to make decisions that were binding on states. It is true that no mechanism for enforcing those decisions was provided either at the time or afterward. But then one reason for this is precisely that, as experience has shown, in view of the very considerable disadvantages that resulted from remaining aloof, this and similar organizations could function tolerably well even without such a mechanism.

During the first forty years of its existence the ITU helped increase the number of international telegrams from 5 million to 82 million a year;[101] but even this only provided a glimmer of the future as technology began to invade additional sectors of the electromagnetic spectrum. Partly overtaken by the introduction of radio, in 1932 the organization was transformed into the International Telecommunication Union. In 1947 it was made into a specialized UN agency, and in the next year its headquarters were moved from Bern to Geneva. As constituted at present, the organization is anchored in a number of conventions that have been signed by member states. Its most important organs are the Plenipotentiary Council, which meets every five years, as well as the annual Administrative Councils. In addition it has a permanent secretariat and a variety of technical organs that are concerned with the allocation of radio frequencies, offering technical advice to member states, and the like.

Serving as a model for others to come, the ITU was followed by the International Postal Union (1874)[102] and the International Bureau of

---

[100] See A. H. Kissinger, *A World Restored: Metternich, Castlereagh and the Problems of Peace 1812–1822* (London: Weidenfeld and Nicolson, 1957), chs. 11 and 13.

[101] F. S. L. Lyons, *Internationalism in Europe 1815–1914* (Leiden: Sijthoff, 1963), p. 41.

[102] For its history, see M. W. Zacher, *Governing Global Networks: International Regimes for Transportation and Communication* (London: Cambridge University Press, 1996), pp. 182ff.

Weights and Standards (1875). A landmark of sorts was reached in 1884 when geographical space was standardized by making Greenwich into the prime meridian; previously Krakow, Uraniborg, Copenhagen, Ter-Goes, Pisa, Augsburg, Tierra del Fuego (in the Cape Verde Islands), Rome, Ulm, Tübingen, Bologna, Rouen, St. Petersburg, Washington, DC, Philadelphia, Munich, Brussels, Rio de Janeiro, Amsterdam, Christiana, Lisbon, Pultowa, Cadiz, Madrid, Warsaw, Paris, and Stockholm had all competed for the honor.[103] Hard on the heels of the meridian came Greenwich Standard Time, long resisted even in Britain ("an aggression more insidious in its advances than the papal one," complained an anonymous author in 1848) but made necessary by the railroads and now transmitted instantaneously by means of the telegraph. One by one those who objected – France, Haiti, Brazil and, in the United States, the city of Detroit – capitulated. Late nineteenth-century commentators expected a lot from these organizations. As one of them put it, "the victories of Alexander and Napoleon are cast into the shade by the triumphal procession of the tiny postage stamp around the world."[104]

By 1984 the number of intergovernmental organizations, which had stood at 123 in 1951 and 280 in 1972, reached 395;[105] in Europe alone thirteen selected states sent 391 representatives to regional organizations in 1988, as against only 101 in 1950.[106] Such organizations covered almost every conceivable field of human activity, from the regulation of air transport – the International Air Transport Association, IATA, was probably the only organization which counted more member states than did the United Nations itself – through the conservation of wildlife and the exploitation of the seabed all the way to the establishment of measures and standards and the disposal of hazardous materials. From Interpol to the International Customs Union, most of them had established their own headquarters and were employing their own bureaucrats. Though the latter continued as citizens of their states of origin, they were at the same time the servants of the organizations themselves. Like other bureaucrats they tended to develop a common outlook and common interests which often differed significantly from those of the member states; and indeed for them to do otherwise would have resulted in a loss of credibility. While individual states did their best to manipulate the

[103] R. K. Schaeffer, "The Standardization of Time and Place," in E. Friedman, ed., *Ascent and Decline in the World System* (London: Sage, 1982), pp. 71, 79.

[104] W. T. Stead, *The United States of Europe on the Eve of the Parliament of Peace* (New York: Garland, 1971 [1899]), p. 141.

[105] D. Held, "Farewell Nation State," *Marxism Today*, December 1988, p. 15.

[106] Figures from D. J. Puchala, "Western Europe," in R. H. Jackson and A. James, eds., *States in a Changing World: A Contemporary Analysis* (Oxford: Clarendon, 1993), p. 87, table 4–4.

organizations in question, clearly there were limits to what could be done. As the accession to the World Trade Organization of such formerly isolationist states as China indicates, to stay away from "the cobweb of agreements"[107] was tantamount to condemning oneself to something like a preindustrial existence.

While not itself the product of technological needs – by origin it was simply a coalition of states established to fight Germany and Japan in World War II – the UN has tended to take over many of these organizations and put them under a single roof. Like other international organizations, it has developed its own legal persona, well-established identity, and bureaucratic mechanism. The latter is by no means identical with that of individual member states whose interests it serves; if there is any correspondence at all, it is only to a very limited extent – witness the constant bickering between it and the United States as the strongest single member. In many ways its position resembles that of the medieval papacy: *vox populi, vox dei* (the voice of the people is like the voice of God), as the saying goes. Like the papacy, it is swerving from one financial crisis to another and is forever negotiating with members (formerly princes) who refuse to pay their debts. Like the papacy, its practical impotence is offset in part by the considerable moral authority which it wields.

If only because the UN is capable of offering a forum for a state's opponents to voice its grievances, to oppose it usually means incurring substantial costs in terms of public opinion. Being subject to UN sanctions can also be expensive – as is shown by the fact that, within a year of the ones against South Africa being lifted, the country's foreign trade leaped by no less than 38 percent.[108] Furthermore, as of 1995 the total amount of funding that was being channeled through the UN or its affiliated organizations stood at $10.5 billion. Of that sum, approximately $3.5 billion was used to maintain about 100,000 disciplined, well-armed troops, wearing blue helmets and scattered in seventeen different flashpoints around the world. Compared to the resources even of a second-rate member state, none of the three figures is terribly impressive. On the other hand, they are figures that cannot be matched by many, possibly even the majority, of UN members.

The organization responsible for wielding these resources for the common good is the Security Council. Acting as a sort of global executive, since the end of the Cold War it has become increasingly willing to invoke Chapter VII of the UN Charter and use force to police such states as either upset the international order or engaged in "intolerable" acts

---

[107] Zacher, *Governing Global Networks*, p. 230.
[108] *World Link*, March–April 1994, p. 99.

against their own populations: cases in point being, besides Iraq, Somalia, Bosnia, and most recently Rwanda. To back up its activity the General Assembly, playing the role of a global legislative, has adopted a whole series of resolutions dealing with basic human rights. In many ways these resolutions represent a return to seventeenth-century ideas of natural law. Expressly designed to put limits on sovereignty, theoretically they are binding not only on such governments as subscribe to them but on others as well.

Unlike the old League of Nations, which from the beginning did not include the most important power of all and which during the 1930s witnessed the withdrawal of other important powers, the UN has never been deserted by any country. Only once did any state walk out, as far back as June 1950, when Stalin ordered his delegation to leave the Security Council. Its absence, far from damaging the organization or benefiting the USSR itself, was used by the United States in order to push through a resolution that put UN troops into Korea; no wonder that, since then, not a single country however weak or strong has cared to repeat the experiment and leave its seat in New York unoccupied. In fact, so important has the UN become as a debating forum – occasionally, as a forum where practical resolutions are adopted and enforced – that the diplomatic services of most countries include few, if any, posts which carry greater weight than an ambassadorship to its headquarters along First Avenue; conversely, the representatives of the UN (and other international organizations) are known as ambassadors and granted diplomatic status just like those of sovereign states. All this adds up to a simple fact. In the late twentieth century, for any state to ignore the UN would be analogous to a commercial firm liaising with each of its competitors but failing to keep an eye on the stock exchange where the fate of all is determined.[109]

If, on the one hand, modern technology has done much to encourage the founding of international organizations that do not have territory and are not states, on the other it has forced and still is forcing states to join together into blocks whose territory is larger than that of individual members. To date, the best-known and most successful of these blocks is the European Union, which provides a tangible expression of the fact that the economic relationships generated by modern technology are on too large a scale to be dealt with effectively by individual countries. Originally the European Common Market had only six members and constituted no more than a free trade zone for coal and steel. Later the agreements were

---

[109] On the UN as a success story, see Report of the Commission on Global Governance, *Our Global Neighborhood* (Oxford: Oxford University Press, 1995), pp. 227ff., 266ff., and 305ff.

extended to other products as well, and common tariffs *vis-à-vis* the rest of the world were established.[110] Driven by the need to achieve economies of scale – often in direct competition with that other superstate, the United States[111] – the EEC has expanded, until it has become the unit with the third-largest number of people (after China and India) and the largest GNP on earth.

As important to our purpose, from the start the EEC represented more than a mere temporary arrangement between sovereign states. Like the other type of international organization just discussed, it was intended to be permanent. Like them, it has its own legal persona and institutions. Over the years it has developed its own legislature (the European Parliament, located in Strasbourg), its own high court, and its own executive. All three, but the last named one in particular, still fall far short of what one would expect from a unified sovereign state. Yet since 1963, when Community law was declared to be directly binding on the member states,[112] all three have certainly made their influence felt in the daily lives of people in all the member countries. Often this is done in entirely unexpected ways: as when the European Court ruled that the government of Ireland could not prevent its citizens from traveling abroad to have an abortion, or when the European Commission fined the British steel industry to the tune of £100,000,000 (1994), or when the same commission decided that Dutch clogs did not meet European footwear standards and that their manufacture should cease. By allowing the citizens of member states to move, live, and work freely – in some cases, also to have equal access to the social services offered by fellow members – the union has gone a considerable way toward creating a common citizenship. In 1979 it was provided with a permanent source of revenue in the form of 1 percent of value-added tax receipts, which is paid to it by each of the member states. Since then the union has become the first non-state organization in modern history to issue a currency of its own, and in the year 2002 that currency is scheduled to replace that of the member states.

Whether the European Union can or will grow into a single, sovereign United States of Europe is moot.[113] Some of the smaller member states

---

[110] For the early history of the EEC, see A. S. Milward, *The Reconstruction of Western Europe, 1945–1951* (London: Methuen, 1984); and E. B. Haas, *The Uniting of Europe: Political, Social and Economic Forces, 1950–1957* (Stanford, CA: Stanford University Press, 1968).

[111] See J. J. Servan-Schreiber, *The American Challenge* (London: Hamilton, 1968 [1967]), particularly chs. 1 and 2.

[112] See P. M. R. Stirk, *A History of European Integration Since 1914* (London: Pinter, 1996), p. 169.

[113] See W. Wallace, "Rescue or Retreat?: The Nation State in Western Europe, 1945–1993," *Political Studies*, 42, 1994, pp. 52–76, for a summary of the debate.

strongly support such a development; as of 1996 discussions were under way concerning the possibility of them surrendering the *liberum veto* which, until now, they have enjoyed. Others, particularly those with an imperial past and extra-European interests to consider, are more skeptical. In this context one should by no means overlook the fact that, in some ways, Europe is already more integrated than that other great federal entity across the Atlantic. For example, whereas US state universities routinely charge students originating in other states higher fees than those required of their own residents, such discrimination is expressly prohibited by a regulation issued by the European Commission and confirmed by the European Parliament. Also, the European banking system is more integrated than the American one, with the result that a German bank may find it easier to operate, say, in Sweden than a New York bank in neighboring New Jersey. A nucleus for a European defense force has been set up by Germany and France, and in some respects is already stronger than the armed forces of Britain, for example, on their own. In the future it will probably be joined by additional members.

On the other hand, development toward a single European superstate is hampered by the existence of other international organizations, whether smaller ones, such as the Nordic Council, or larger ones such as the North Atlantic Treaty Organization. Having established no fewer than 112 Nordic institutions, and counting 450 "Nordocrats" (1985), the Nordic Council forms an organization inside an organization. In practice it has put few obstacles in front of European integration; but in principle its continued existence (and that of similar groupings among other countries) within the context of a closer European Union is no more acceptable than, say, a formal alliance between Virginia, North and South Carolina, and Georgia would be in the United States. NATO for its part includes three non-European members, i.e., the United States, Canada, and Turkey. At the same time it excludes three European countries which *are* Union members, i.e., Austria, Sweden, and Finland. As the French in particular have repeatedly stated, the existence of NATO in its present form is clearly incompatible with continued movement toward European integration in what has traditionally been the most important field of all: namely, that of providing a common defense against outside aggression. Generalizing from this case, one might perhaps conclude that the obstacles which individual states such as Britain put in front of European unity are significant enough. However, in the long run even greater opposition is likely to come not from states but from other international organizations whose membership and purposes do not overlap.

Whatever the future of the European Community, its economic success has encouraged states in other parts of the world to create similar organizations. To date, none of them has progressed nearly as far as their model in creating common institutions and imposing a common law. On the other hand, multilateral arrangements aimed at reducing obstacles to trade, eliminating tariffs, achieving integration (as, for example, between the US and Canadian electricity grids and telephone networks), setting up a common economic front *vis-à-vis* the rest of the world, and dealing with ecological problems now number in the dozens and may be found in every continent. To list some of the most important ones only, 1959 saw the establishment of EFTA (European Free Trade Association) all of whose members later joined the European Union. In 1960 this was followed by LAFTA (the Latin American Free Trade Association, which incorporates Mexico and all Latin American countries except Guyana) as well as CACM (the Central American Common Market). UDEAC (Union douanière et économique de l'Afrique centrale, with Cameroon, the Central African Republic, Congo, and Gabon as its members) was founded in 1966, ASEAN (Association of South East Asian Nations, made up of Indonesia, Malaysia, the Philippines, Thailand, and Singapore) in the next year. An Andean Common Market (ACM), with Bolivia, Chile, Colombia, Ecuador, Peru and Venezuela as its members, has existed since 1969 and was later followed by MERCOSUR which includes Brazil, Bolivia, Paraguay, Uruguay, Argentina, and Chile. In 1975, the Economic Community of West African States (ECOWACS) was founded by Benin, Gambia, Ghana, Guinea, Guinea-Bissau, Ivory Coast, Liberia, Mali, Mauritania, Niger, Nigeria, Senegal, Sierra Leone, Togo, and Upper Volta. In 1994 the ratification of the North American Free Trade Agreement (NAFTA) by the United States, Canada, and Mexico showed that not even the largest and most productive economy in history can exist in isolation. Admittedly there are some exceptions, particularly in the Middle East where, since Nasser's death, state sovereignty has gained the upper hand over pan-Arabism.[114] Elsewhere, however, the list of agreements which already exist or are being negotiated is all but endless.

The declared purpose of all these agreements has not been to abolish political borders. Instead, those borders having been fixed in place (theoretically for all time to come), the goal is to reduce their economic importance, make it easier to move across them, and promote trade between the signatory states. Mindful of the experience of total mobilization in 1914–18, during the interwar years most of the great powers in particular had attempted to build trade empires in order to be as self-

---

[114] See M. Barnett, "Sovereignty, Nationalism and Regional Order in the Arab States System," in T. J. Biersteker and C. Weber, eds., *State Sovereignty as a Social Construct* (Cambridge: Cambridge University Press, 1996), pp. 148–89.

sufficient as possible; that, after all, was the declared aim of German, Italian, and Japanese imperialism. However, from 1945 on the most successful states have been those which, like Germany, Japan, South Korea, and Singapore, integrated into the world market. The larger the fraction of GNP that a state exported and imported – in other words, the better it used modern technology in order to maximize its comparative advantage – the greater by and large its economic success.[115] During the 1980s, even economic statistics, which are normally conservative, began to recognize the change by separating gross domestic product from gross national product. Other things being equal, the gap between the two provided a good index for the economic performance of any particular country; simultaneously, the very same figures tend to emphasize the fact that to calculate economic success in terms of individual countries is becoming less and less meaningful. For example, over 40 percent of all "Japanese" goods are now being produced outside Japan, in places as far apart as the United States, Europe, and Indonesia; and the figure keeps rising all the time.

Given this emphasis on international trade – as reflected in the doubling, between 1965 and 1990, of the percentage of world product which was exported[116] – it is perhaps not surprising that trading organizations which were represented in different states were often better positioned to use the opportunities provided than were states themselves. Unlike the latter, multinational corporations did not have citizens to protect, welfare payments to make, frontiers to cover, or sovereign territory to worry about. Free of these responsibilities and limitations, they were able to seize economic opportunities wherever they presented themselves, as soon as they presented themselves, and – a very important consideration – for only as long as they presented themselves. They could do so either on their own, by setting up branch offices, or else by forging alliances with their counterparts in other states. The methods used included common research and development; a division of labor in manufacturing so that parts provided by one firm would go into the products of another; shared access to distribution and service networks; the mutual acquisition of each other's stock; and, of course, outright mergers of the kind that took place in May 1998 when German-based Daimler Benz married American-based Chrysler.[117] Moreover, in most cases it was the multinationals, rather than states, which were the first to develop and deploy

---

[115] For some figures on the relationship between trade and economic growth for selected countries, see C. Mulhearn, "Change and Development in the International Economy," in Bretherton and Ponton, *Global Politics*, pp. 160–5.

[116] World Bank, *World Development* (Baltimore: World Bank, 1992), p. 235.

[117] See Scammell, *The International Economy Since 1945*, ch. 10.

the most modern technologies in fields ranging from aircraft through computers to telecommunications.[118] Both for this reason and because they were in a better position to make use of them, it was in their hands that such technologies really took off.

As has often been pointed out, multinational corporations need the state to provide stability and defense; also, the threat to sovereignty that they present is limited by the fact that those of their parts which operate within the jurisdiction of any given state had to obey that state's laws just as surely as national firms. Concerning the first point, I shall argue that, as some states at any rate become less capable of providing defense, parts of that task may themselves be taken over by the multinationals.[119] Concerning the second, the internationalization of business and the opening to foreigners of one stock exchange after another mean that a greater percentage of the assets belonging to the citizens of each state was likely to be located beyond its borders; and that vital economic decisions which affected such things as investment and employment inside each state were likely to be made by people over whom it had no control.

As the United States found out when it tried to protect its industry against imported Japanese automobiles, in many cases the measures contemplated to counter the trend were useless because the "enemy" was already within the gates, even assuming that the term fits at all, given that the vast majority of people employed on US soil by firms such as Honda, Mitsubishi, and BMW are themselves American, and sell their products to American customers. States that tried to resist the trend and went too far in their attempts to reimpose control risked finding themselves bypassed by prospective investors and abandoned by existing ones.[120] In a world where the role of interstate war was declining, the position of political leaders became increasingly dependent on their ability to deliver material prosperity. The latter itself was now being defined less in terms of welfare services, as during the years 1945–75, than in terms of attracting investment, providing jobs and creating growth. Special meeting places, such as the World Economic Forum in Davos, have even been set up where politicians are able to approach the multinationals cap in hands and launch their requests.

Another development implicit in the shift toward international trade was that governments, in the words of former British secretary of the treasury Denis Healey, found their ability to control their own currencies

---

[118] See J. H. Dunning, *Multinationals, Technology and Competitiveness* (London: Unwin Hyman, 1988), particularly ch. 6.

[119] See the section on "The threat to internal order" in this chapter, pp. 394–408.

[120] For an example of these developments as they affected two specific countries, see V. Dela Sala, "Capital Blight? The Regulation of Financial Institutions in Italy and Canada," *Governance*, 7, 3, July 1994, pp. 244–64.

"savagely crippled."[121] If a nation was to participate in international trade, its currency had to be convertible, as free as possible from unilateral administrative controls and capable of being exported anywhere without permission and at an instant's notice. But freedom from administrative controls put it at the mercy of the international market, particularly in a period when new computer technology enabled foreign currency transactions to be carried out instantaneously, twenty-four hours per day, and on a scale ($4 *trillion* a day in 1996) that not even the largest and richest states could match.

Gone were the days when, as during the period 1914–45, many important governments tried to create closed monetary systems and, at any rate insofar as their own citizens were concerned, lay down the value of their currencies by fiat. Gone, too, were the Bretton Woods Agreements which lasted from 1944 to 1971 and which pegged the various currencies to a US dollar which was itself pegged to gold.[122] Since 1971, when President Nixon in what he modestly described as "the greatest monetary reform in history" took the dollar off gold, all currencies have effectively been floating against each other. But whereas, before 1944, they were pegged to gold, now even that prop is gone and all that there is to support them is, often enough, the statistics which are compiled by economists.

To be sure, governments did not lose all influence over currencies. They could still manipulate the money supply, either balancing their budgets or failing to do so; too, they retained control over some key interest rates such as the discount rate (the rate at which the Central Bank lent money to the rest) and that which they paid on their own bonds. Furthermore, it has been pointed out that those involved in currency speculation might just as well be, and often are, not foreigners but the state's own citizens.[123] But that is precisely the point. Under the new liberal economics, the difference between the two is being eradicated in many ways. Citizens and foreigners act with equal ease, ignoring their respective governments while moving money in and out of any given country by pressing a button. Consequently the value of many currencies, including some of the most important, became subject to wild fluctuations which were often beyond the power of central banks, or even combinations of central banks, to regulate. From the point of view of

---

[121] Quoted in *The Economist*, 7 October 1995, p. 15. Lord Healey has explained his views at greater length in a lecture entitled "The New World Disorder," delivered to the Royal Geographical Society on 14 March 1995.

[122] For a short discussion of the system and its demise, see J. Agnew and S. Cobridge, *Mastering Space: Hegemony, Territory and International Political Economy* (London: Routledge, 1995), pp. 171ff.

[123] See e.g. D. Brash, "New Zealand and International Markets: Have We Lost Control of Our Own Destiny?," in Wood and Leland, *State and Sovereignty*, p. 58.

nonstate actors these fluctuations put a premium on hedging, which may be done by holding some of one's own assets in foreign currencies, or by borrowing in them.[124] And so the merry-go-round, also known as "casino capitalism,"[125] continued. It was subject to control, if at all, only by the IMF, itself a non-state actor.

Finally, the unprecedented development of electronic information services seems to mark another step in the retreat of the state.[126] Traditionally no state has ever been able to exercise complete control over the thoughts of all its citizens; to the credit of the more liberally minded among them, it must be added that they never even tried. The invention of print greatly increased the amount of information and reduced the cost at which it could be disseminated, but the ability to move that information across international frontiers remained limited by the need to physically transport paper (or set up printing presses), as well as language barriers. The latter in particular were important. Their existence meant that, small diplomatic and commercial elites only excepted, information tended to be distributed very much on a country-by-country basis.

In the event, the first of these problems was solved by the introduction of public radio broadcasting during the 1920s – leading to a situation where, in German-occupied countries during World War II, listening to enemy radio stations became a capital offense. The introduction of television, which relies on pictures instead of words, to a large extent eliminated the second. During the 1980s, cable and satellite television, as well as videotape, became widely available. Soon it began providing near-instantaneous coverage of events on a global scale; a decade later the advent of the Internet, which enabled individuals to communicate with each other instantaneously, at all places, at all times, and regardless of distance, time of day, or any other factor, presented an even greater revolution. As with the economy, individual states found themselves forced to relax their control over information in favor of people and organizations which were not sovereign, did not have territory, and were not states. It is certainly true that some media moguls, such as Ted Turner and Rupert Murdoch, have more influence over international affairs than do the majority of heads of state and their foreign ministers; but even the most powerful governments now tend to make policy very much with the so-called CNN factor in mind.[127]

---

[124] See K. Mehta, "Risky Business," *World Link*, January–February 1998, pp. 84–8.

[125] S. Strange, *Casino Capitalism*, New York, Blackwell, 1986.

[126] See W. Wriston, *The Twilight of Sovereignty: How the Information Revolution Is Transforming Our World* (New York: Scribner, 1992).

[127] See W. Wriston, "The Twilight of Sovereignty," *Fletcher Forum of World Affairs*, 17, 2, Summer 1993, pp. 117–30; J. F. Hodge, Jr., "Media Pervasiveness," *Foreign Affairs*, 73, 4, July–August 1994, pp. 136–45.

Though the role of the various information services in bringing down the former Eastern bloc cannot be measured, it was certainly very large.[128] In East Germany alone, 15 million out of 18 million people regularly watched West Germany television. Basing themselves on statements made by travelers, Western radio stations such as RFE, the VOA, the BBC, and DW claimed to have almost 100 million listeners in 1989; whether or not that figure was accurate, their role in helping move the USSR toward *glasnost* and *perestroika* was subsequently acknowledged by Mikhail Gorbachev.[129] Conversely, states such as China, Burma, Iran, and Saudi Arabia which attempt to put blinkers on their citizens' eyes and prevent them from accessing international information services will find that the price which they have to pay for their self-enforced isolation is considerable. In the long run, their struggle will almost certainly be hopeless.

Thus, and George Orwell in *1984* notwithstanding, as of the last years of the twentieth century it seems that modern technology has not ushered in an age of hermetically sealed empires, Engsoc, and thought control. To be sure, the obstacles to "globalization" remain formidable. They include not just the kind of nationalism and xenophobia found in many parts of the developing world in particular; but also the type of regional organization which, so far from opening countries up to world trade, tends to build blocks of them that are relatively closed to it. Regardless of whether it is globalism or regionalism which wins the struggle, the effect on individual states is similar.[130] The more important any state, the more likely it is to participate in a very large number of international organizations, be they global, regional, or merely technical. By so doing it gives up parts of its sovereignty in return for a say in its neighbors' affairs; meanwhile, its control over both its economies and its citizens' thoughts has undoubtedly declined.

Under such circumstances, the best that states can do is to swim with the trend. They must see to it that their citizens study foreign languages as well as the new international languages of data processing; join international organizations so as to make sure that their interests are not neglected; develop their communication and transportation networks,

---

[128] On the communist bloc's attempt to control information, and its failure to do so, see L. R. Sossman, "Information Control as an International Issue," *Proceedings of the Academy of Political Science*, 34, 4, 1982, pp. 176–88; and W. R. Roberts and H. Engels, "The Global Information Revolution and the Communist World," *Washington Quarterly*, 9, 2, 1986, pp. 141–55.

[129] See W. R. Roberts, "The Information Revolution I: A Breakdown in the East?," *The World Today*, 45, 6, 1989, pp. 95–6.

[130] See M. Svetlicic, "Challenges of Globalization and Regionalization in the World Economy," *Global Society*, 10, 2, May 1996, pp. 207–23.

which in most cases means integrating them with those of their neighbors; and exploit the new trading opportunities by lowering tariffs, providing stable and convertible currencies, opening financial markets, and providing "transparency" by allowing the free circulation of information about themselves, their economies, and their societies. Should they do so, they are likely to prosper; whereas those which, whether for religious or ideological or other reasons, refuse to do so have fallen behind and, to all appearances, are doomed to continue to do so. The days when a single state, however large and powerful, could hope to pull itself up by its own bootstraps, set up its own self-contained empire, and use its power to make a bid for its neighbors' territory or even world domination seem to be over.

The threat to internal order

As chapter 5 of this study showed, many Third World governments have always experienced great difficulty in taking violence out of the hands of people and organizations and monopolizing it in their own. From Colombia through Liberia to Afghanistan to the Philippines, they are often wracked by civil war, ethnic strife, religious struggles, guerrilla warfare, terrorism, narcoterrorism, or, as likely as not, some combination of all of these. With them the state has either continued to vegetate, sometimes for centuries on end, as in much of Latin America during its "hundred years of solitude"; or else it started falling apart almost before it was formed, as happened in parts of Asia and above all, Africa. Meanwhile, technological and economic developments are to some extent causing governments in the developed world to lose, or surrender, their ability to wage interstate war, provide welfare, dominate their economies, and control their citizens' thought. Therefore the question might well be asked: will they be able to retain their monopoly on the maintenance of law and order?

Perhaps the best way to approach the problem is this. From the middle of the seventeenth century until 1914, the armed forces of "civilized" governments – primarily those of Europe, but later joined by North American and Japanese ones as well – proved themselves more than a match for whatever opposition could be put up against them by other political entities and their societies. Over time, this advantage tended to grow: at Omdurman in 1896, a handful of Maxim Guns enabled those forces to wipe out entire columns of dervishes as if by magic. Their victories permitted them to expand until they controlled almost the entire world, and only three or four non-white countries escaped the domination which was often imposed on them by very small parties of foreigners from across the sea.

During the years 1918–39, the difficulties of holding on to the various colonial empires increased appreciably. In many places the imperialists were compelled to forge alliances with local elites, which were coopted into the lower echelons of government; more and more often, they hid behind a variety of treaties that conceded the appearance of power while preserving the reality. While the direction of change was thus quite clear, its extent should not be exaggerated. At the time when World War II broke out not a single Asian or African country had yet succeeded in ridding itself of its real masters, i.e., troops that were either white or organized by whites and run by them.

Over the last half-century, the change that has taken place is momentous. From France to the United States, there has scarcely been one "advanced" government in Europe and North America whose armed forces have not suffered defeat at the hands of underequipped, ill-trained, ill-organized, often even ill-clad, underfed, and illiterate freedom fighters or guerrillas or terrorists; briefly, by men – and, often, women – who were short on everything except high courage and the determination to endure and persist in the face of police operations, counterinsurgency operations, peacekeeping operations, and whatever other types of operations that were dreamt up by their masters.

In the event, perhaps the first to find out that the nature of war had begun to change were the Germans. Although as imperialists they were latecomers, before 1914 they had waged colonial warfare with the best. Both in Tanzania and in Namibia massive uprisings took place around the turn of the century, and in both countries they were suppressed with the utmost brutality. Either the natives, mounting frontal attacks in the belief that by being sprinkled with water they had been rendered bullet-proof, were mown down with the fire of modern weapons; or else, attempting to wage guerrilla warfare, they were fenced out and driven off into the desert where entire tribes were left to die of thirst. In the two countries together, the total number of victims probably reached several hundreds of thousands.

The early years of World War II once again provided German administrators and German soldiers with huge, comparatively underdeveloped territories in which to display their prowess. It was an opportunity which many of them, accustomed to years of racial propaganda and acting under Hitler's own explicit orders,[131] eagerly seized. Beginning already in 1941, and growing steadily worse thereafter, the German occupation of Yugoslavia and the Soviet Union in particular was so ruthless as to resemble, in many cases, genocide, with thousands upon thousands of

---

[131] See Hitler's own remarks on the subject as recorded in F. Halder, *Kriegstabeguch* (Stuttgart: Kohlhammer, 1962), vol. II, pp. 335–7, entry for 30 March 1941.

villages burnt and their inhabitants killed, whether as part of "anti-bandit" operations or for no reason at all. Yet the ferocity of the methods used by the Germans and their allies did not lead to peace and quiet; on the contrary, the greater the atrocities committed the fiercer, by and large, the resistance encountered. Though some countries were slower off the mark then others, subsequently that resistance spread to virtually every other country that was occupied by the Germans until, by the second half of 1944, much of Europe was ablaze.

Whether the operations of freedom fighters everywhere could have led to Europe's liberation from under the Nazi heel even in the absence of the various Allied armed forces will never be known. Suppose Germany to have "won" the war by concluding a peace treaty in the West and knocking out the Soviet Union, if only in the sense that large-scale operations against it would no longer be needed (as Hitler himself expected to happen).[132] In that case the Wehrmacht, reduced by demobilization to, say, 1.5 million men (twice as many as served in the active forces in 1939), would have been faced with the task of indefinitely keeping down *Lebensraum*, a "living space," consisting of several million square kilometers and populated by several hundred million people. Even in the relatively brief time of three to four years that the occupation in most countries lasted, the various resistance movements were able to inflict substantial damage in both casualties and materiel and to tie down hundreds of thousands of troops; in Yugoslavia alone an entire army group with almost thirty Axis divisions had to be maintained on a permanent footing, although admittedly only part of those were German.[133] Judging by the fact that, by the end of the war, guerrillas in such places as Yugoslavia, Greece, and northern Italy had succeeded in making the German position untenable, there is good reason to think that it could not have been done.

Faced with armed resistance on the part of the occupied populations, the Germans soon discovered that it was precisely the most modern components of their armed forces which were the most useless. Hitherto their tanks and artillery and fighters and bombers had experienced little difficulty in tearing the rest of the world's most advanced armies – including those of the three world powers with combined forces considerably larger than their own – to pieces;[134] but, confronted with small

[132] H. R. Trevor-Roper, *Hitler's Table Talk* (London: Weidenfeld and Nicolson, 1953), entries for 8 and 29 August 1942, pp. 621, 672–3.

[133] See M. F. Cancian, "The Wehrmacht in Yugoslavia: Lessons of the Past?," *Parameters*, 21, 3, Autumn 1993, p. 78, for the precise order of battle.

[134] See, most recently, K.-H. Frieser, *Blitzkrieg Legende: Der Westfeldzug 1940* (Munich: Oldenburg, 1995), which shows how, in 1940, the Germans were inferior to the Allies even in the number and quality of tanks.

groups of guerrillas who did not constitute armies, did not wear uniforms, did not fight in the open, and tended to melt away either into the countryside or into the surrounding population, they found themselves almost entirely at a loss. Like other conquerors after them the Germans learnt that, for counterinsurgency purposes, almost the only forces that mattered were those that were lightly armed: namely, police, infantry, mountain forces, special forces, signals, and, above all, intelligence of every kind. All had to operate on foot or else travel in light vehicles, preferably those that also possessed a crosscountry capability. Outside the towns they could be reinforced by reconnaissance aircraft, and, on such comparatively rare occasions as the opposition allowed itself to be caught in any strength, by a handful of artillery barrels and tanks. Still, there was no room in these operations for the Wehrmacht's pride and joy, i.e., its armored and mechanized divisions, and indeed, since the scale on which operations were conducted was usually very small, for hardly any divisions at all.

The discovery made by the Germans – and, to a lesser but still significant extent, their Japanese counterparts – during World War II has since been shared by virtually every other major armed force on earth. Among the first to encounter guerrilla warfare during the immediate post-war years were the French and the British. In point of ruthlessness their operations were very far from matching those of the Germans; still, particularly in the case of the French in Indochina and Algeria, they were ruthless enough. In both countries, the French attempt, supported by every modern weapon which they were capable of bringing to bear, to regain control of their colonies led to the deaths of hundreds of thousands and the destruction by fire and sword of entire villages, even districts. While the British did not go as far as this – the largest number of native victims in any of their colonial campaigns, i.e., the one which they waged in Kenya, seems to have stood at 10,000[135] – they too made routine use of capital punishment, torture, and the uprooting of entire villages whose inhabitants were moved into concentration camps.[136] Like the Germans, too, the British and the French armed forces discovered that it was precisely the most powerful weapons and weapons systems which were the most useless, being either too expensive, too fast, too indiscriminate, too big, too inaccurate, or all of these. As to the most powerful weapons of all, i.e., nuclear ones, against an enemy who was so dispersed and so elusive that he could barely be found, they were simply irrelevant.

---

[135] For the background to the conflict, see J. Kenyatta, *Suffering Without Bitterness: The Founding of the Kenya Nation* (Nairobi: East African Publishing House, 1968).

[136] For a brief history of the British attempts to hold on to their empire, see L. James, *Imperial Rearguard* (London: Brassey's, 1988).

Whether simultaneously or later on, the experience of the French and the British during the years 1945–60 has been shared by virtually every other modern armed force that tried its hand at the counterinsurgency game. The Dutch, Belgians, Spanish, and Portuguese were all forced to evacuate their colonies, as already related. Seeking to take the place of the supposedly demoralized French in Vietnam,[137] the Americans sent first advisers, then special forces, and then, from 1965 on, huge conventional forces into that small, backward, and remote country. Eventually the total number of those who served exceeded 2.5 million, while the largest number of troops present at any one time was 550,000. They were backed up by all the most powerful military technology available, including heavy bombers, fighter bombers, aircraft carriers, helicopters (the number of helicopters lost alone reached 1,500), tanks, artillery, and the most advanced communications system in history until then. The number of Vietcong, North Vietnamese, and civilian dead probably stood at between 1 and 2 million – to which, by standard calculations, three or four times as many wounded should be added – but to no avail. After eight years of fighting and 55,000 casualties in dead alone, it was the Americans who gave up and, with the last remaining personnel hanging on to the skis of their helicopters, evacuated Saigon.

From Afghanistan (where the Soviet army was broken after eight years of fighting) through Cambodia (where the Vietnamese were forced to retreat) and Sri Lanka (which the Indian army failed to reduce to order) to Namibia (granted its independence by South Africa after a long and bitter struggle) to Eritrea (which won its independence against everything that the Ethiopians, supported by the USSR, could do) to Somalia (evacuated by most UN forces after their failure to deal with the local warlords), the story is always the same. Each time modern (more or less), heavily armed, regular, state-owned forces tried their hand at the so-called counterinsurgency game, and each time they were defeated.

Perhaps one of the most interesting cases was the one of Israel in Lebanon. The Israeli–Lebanese border, which during the first twenty years after 1948 used to be the most peaceful of all, first became a source of trouble in 1968 when guerrillas belonging to the Palestinian Liberation Organization (PLO) started making their attacks. Four massive Israeli operations (1978, 1982, 1994, and 1996), as well as countless minor ones, failed to deal with the problem; though the guerrillas changed their names from PLO to Amal to Hizbullah, neither the ambushes directed against Israeli troops operating inside Lebanese territory nor the firing of rockets across the border into Galilee could be brought to an end.

---

[137] R. H. Spector, *Advice and Support: The Early Years of the US Army in Vietnam, 1941–1960* (New York: Free Press, 1985).

Particularly in April 1996, the Israeli Air Force and artillery – since the disintegration of the Soviet Union perhaps the second or third most powerful anywhere – rained down thousands of shells and missiles on a very small area in southern Lebanon. Guided by the most sophisticated electronic gear ever used in war, the response to the guerrillas' attacks was near-instantaneous and so accurate that virtually every round hit its target; the ability of Israeli helicopters to send missiles flying through preselected windows of high-rise buildings, even some that were surrounded by others in the middle of Beirut, was particularly impressive. Not for the first time, much of the area affected was turned into smoldering ruins. But when the smoke cleared, it was found that the number of Hizbullah guerrillas killed only amounted to 30 (out of a total butcher's bill of about 200 dead). The organization's ability to go on fighting was virtually unimpaired, and what damage it had suffered was quickly repaired.

The above examples could easily be reinforced by many others. They show that, from 1945 on, the vast majority of the larger guerrilla and terrorist campaigns in particular were waged in Third World countries; in other words, places where people were either trying to form states of their own or, on the contrary, where existing states had failed to assert their own monopoly over violence. Still it would not be true to say that the developed countries have remained immune to terrorism or that, in them, the problem does not exist. From Germany through France and Italy to Spain and Britain all the way to Japan – where Tokyo in 1995 witnessed two deadly poison-gas attacks – many of them have witnessed at least some terrorist acts take place on their national territories. Not seldom the attacks were deadly as dozens and even hundreds were killed or wounded; e.g., the number of those killed by, or in operations against, the IRA stood at 3,000 in early 1996, that is *before* the organization showed what it could do by wounding 200 in a single explosion (in Manchester) during May of that year. In these and other countries, the list of people and targets attacked includes prime ministers, prominent politicians, railway stations, railway tracks, buses, hospitals, shopping centers, office blocks, hotels, beer gardens, airports, aircraft in mid-flight, ships, and of course foreign embassies and diplomatic personnel.

Some of the attacks in question represented spillovers from struggles that were taking place in other countries, such as when Kurds fought Turks on German and Swiss territory; or else when Palestinian guerrillas and Israeli secret agents chased each other in places as far from each other as northern Norway and Latin America. In others the terrorists, though probably not without their foreign connections, are native-born or at least native-bred. Good examples are the late unmourned German and Italian Red Army Factions, which maintained ties with each other; the Irish

Republican Army, with its links to the United States and Libya; ETA (representing the Basques) in Spain and France; and the various Muslim organizations which have been operating in France and which, in early 1996, made the latter's capital look like an armed fortress. Often they are rooted in the ethnic and religious minorities which, whether legally or not, have entered the countries in question – in France, Germany, and Britain together, there are now approximately 10 million persons whose faith is Islam.

If only because they have to make a living, often terrorist organizations engage in ancillary criminal activities such as drug smuggling, arms trading, and, from the early 1990s on, dealing in radioactive materials such as uranium and plutonium. Repeatedly they have proved that they are capable of commanding fierce loyalties; in the Middle East and Turkey, even people willing to commit suicide (and go to heaven as their reward) have not been too difficult to find. The attacks by foreign-bred terrorists on the World Trade Center in New York, in 1992, and by native ones on the federal building in Oklahoma City in 1995, showed that not even the two largest oceans on earth can protect a country against terrorists' activities. The result was that, at the Atlanta Olympic Games in 1996, security officers outnumbered athletes two to one.[138]

How, in the face of these attacks, have the armed forces at the disposal of the state fared? That the most powerful weapons available to them, including specifically the heavy ones which account for the bulk of their budgets, are entirely useless against these and similar movements scarcely requires pointing out. What is needed are police forces, both in and out of uniform.[139] And in fact, since the onset of modern terrorism during the late 1960s and early 1970s, there is scarcely any advanced country which has not attempted to strengthen the "forces of order." Among the most common measures are the expansion of intelligence organizations and their coordination with each other; the establishment of special anti-terrorist squads trained in hostage-rescue operations and the like; the development and acquisition of a vast array of improved radio communications, "foolproof" identity cards, closed-circuit television cameras, metal detectors, X-ray machines, night vision devices, listening devices, automatic bomb-disposal devices, and, most recently, machines for detecting radioactive, chemical, and biological materials,[140] all backed up by computers in which data from these and other sources is stored, collated, processed, and sent to wherever it is needed, instan-

---

[138] CNN, *World Report*, 17 July 1996.
[139] See G. Daeniker, *The Guardian Soldier: On the Nature and Use of Future Armed Conflict* (New York: United Nations Institute for Disarmament Research, 1995).
[140] CNN, *World Report*, 16 March 1998.

taneously and often across borders as states try to coordinate their responses to the threat. The technology necessary for implanting electronic chips in human bodies, which would enable each of us to be instantly identified and our movements constantly tracked, is available and in use for the purpose of raising farm animals. Should the security forces in certain countries have their way, then it is only a question of time before the technology is applied to humans, first perhaps among criminals and children and old people (if they suffer from loss of memory) and then among wider population groups.[141]

As various groups concerned with the preservation of privacy are telling us, these developments are certainly disturbing. Perhaps even more disturbing, in face of the potential dangers – including, besides the ordinary bomb or guerrilla attack, chemical terrorism, biological terrorism, and nuclear terrorism – is the apparent inability of the various police forces to maintain the monopoly over violence in the hands of the state. Even in developed countries, the most that the majority of them can boast of is to have kept terrorism within "acceptable" boundaries. However, as people get used to watching terrorist actions unfold on television the definition of what constitutes "acceptable" seems to be stretched year by year. To some extent the change has been recognized by formal international law. In 1977 the Fourth Geneva Convention was signed, affording some protection to combatants who are not recognizable from a distance and do not wear uniforms while participating in military operations.[142]

Meanwhile, from Washington's White House to London's Downing Street, the change that has taken place is obvious even to the casual tourist. Entire city blocks in which presidents and prime ministers live and work, and which until not so long ago were open to pedestrian and vehicular traffic, are being sealed off and turned into fortresses; if only because nobody is willing to assume the responsibility, it is unlikely that, once closed, they will ever open again. Their protection is entrusted to uniformed – and, especially, nonuniformed – personnel with every imaginable technological device ready to hand. From Sweden to Israel, leaders who used to walk the streets freely and without an escort have long ceased doing so. They are now seen by the public, if at all, only when they are whisked from one place to another in their curtained, heavily armored cars; to mislead potential terrorists, there are not seldom several identical

---

[141] For a chilling account of technological possibilities in the field of surveillance, and their growing use in one country which traditionally has been among the freest on earth, see S. Davies, *Big Brother: Britain's Web of Surveillance and the New Technological Order* (London: Pan Books, 1996).

[142] See L. Doswald-Beck, "The Value of the 1977 Geneva Protocols for the Protection of Civilians," in M. A. Meyer, ed., *Armed Conflict and the New Law* (London: British Institute of International and Comparative Law, 1989), pp. 160ff.

cars in a convoy or even several convoys moving in different directions. The places in which they are expected to make scheduled appearances are routinely sealed off and searched, sometimes for days or weeks before the event, as are the surrounding areas. It is the kind of security such as a Cesare Borgia, constantly assassinating others and constantly fearing assassination himself, might have been proud of, and which, a generation or two ago, was only considered necessary to protect some of the world's worst dictators such as Hitler and Stalin.

In some ways, the rise of international terrorism merely represents the mirror image of everything we have been discussing so far. The weapons deployed by regular armed forces are often enormously expensive and require extensive logistic infrastructures as well as large crews – not so many of the devices which are used by the security forces in their attempts to combat terrorism, which are relatively cheap and therefore readily available to their opponents as well. Computers can be, and not seldom have been, broken into by hackers and crackers. Identification documents issued by the government, even high-tech ones, can usually be forged. Personal arms, listening devices, infrared night-vision devices, and simi-lar equipment used by the police are easily available off the shelf; and indeed the manufacturers are usually happy enough to sell them to whomever they can. If the police use sophisticated frequency-hopping radio apparatus to coordinate their work, then criminals and terrorists (as well as the journalists who chase them both) can do the same; they listen in to the network in order to evade their pursuers or, not uncommonly, send them on wild-goose chases. Similarly the transportation networks that make international communication and trade possible can be, and sometimes are, used by terrorists to run circles around states, their borders, and their sovereign territory.

But perhaps the most important factor involved in the rise of modern terrorism is the sheer multiplicity of states. At present there are almost 200 sovereign political entities, and additional ones are springing up almost daily. Among them, some are interested in stirring up trouble for their neighbors. Others seek to promote a variety of ideological and religious causes, while others still are ruled by people who are greedy for money and not too scrupulous about the ways of getting it. Thus it is virtually certain that, at any one time, at least several can be found which are ready to assist terrorists, if not against everybody, then at least against some.[143] Such assistance may take the form of bases, training, funding, documents, communications (by way of the diplomatic mail network),

[143] See e.g. P. Williams and S. Black, "Transnational Threats: Drug Trafficking and Weapons Proliferation," *Contemporary Security Policy*, 15, 1, April 1994, pp. 127–51.

transportation, arms, refuge, or all of these. A number of cases are even known when their embassies abroad have themselves turned into terrorist bases. They harbored personnel, smuggled arms, provided logistical support, and engaged in kidnapping operations.

If only because security is one of the most manpower-intensive fields of human endeavor – for example, in the early 1990s as many as *40* percent of the employees of American airlines in Europe consisted of security personnel – providing it can be extremely expensive. To secure a military base or turn a block of government buildings into a fortress is one thing; to offer the same kind of protection to an entire country is another. Even supposing it could be made affordable and effective, it would render ordinary life next to impossible by leading to an intolerable slowing down of the most ordinary activities. For these and other reasons – including, not least, the likelihood of being criticized in case of failure – many states are reluctant to engage their own forces in the task. At best they will train anti-terrorist units and keep them in reserve in case they are called upon to deal with high-profile emergencies such as bombings, kidnappings, and the like, whereas the financial and organizational burden represented by day-to-day security is something which, as experience shows, they are quite ready to shift to private industry and individuals.

Whether because the government has ordered them to – as in the case of civil aviation in many countries – or because they simply do not trust the state to provide them with reasonable security, individuals and private industry have, in fact, been looking after themselves to a growing extent and on a constantly increasing scale. Depending on the nature of the perceived threat, the citizens of many countries have become accustomed to having their belongings checked, and/or their persons searched, each time they enter a department store, movie house, football stadium, rock concert, or similar places where crowds gather and where a terrorist act is therefore both more probable and, should it in fact take place, likely to result in heavy casualties. From South Africa to Italy, some states now require that every bank be protected by metal detectors and double doors that will open only if and when the visitor's innocence (i.e., the fact that he or she does not carry arms) is verified. Individuals, neighborhoods, and corporations have tried to protect themselves against terrorism and crime by hiring private guards, erecting security fences, installing alarm systems and closed-circuit television, demanding proof of identity when entering buildings and installations (whether legally or not, the responsible personnel often insist on retaining the documents in question until the visitor leaves), requiring badges to be worn, and much more.

While not all countries are affected to the same extent, so far those measures seem to have done little to eliminate the problem. What they have done is to turn private security into a growth industry *par excellence* worldwide.[144] Thus, in Germany, the years from 1984 to 1996 saw the number of private security firms more than double (from 620 to 1,400) while employment in them increased by no less than 300 percent.[145] In Britain, not normally considered a particularly violent country, the number of employees in the field rose from 10,000 in 1950 to 250,000 in 1976;[146] as growth has continued since then, the point where there are more private guards then the state has uniformed active troops (whose number stood at 237,000 in 1995) must have been passed some years ago. Similarly in the United States, already by 1972 the private security industry had almost twice as many employees, and 1.5 times the budget, of all local, state, and federal police forces combined.[147] By 1995 the industry's turnover stood at $52 billion a year and was expected to reach twice that figure by the end of the century.[148] If present trends persist, then the day is in sight when American citizens pay more for private security than for their country's armed forces; the ratio between the two, which as of 1972 stood at 1:7, has since declined to 1:5 and is still going down. The number of those who are employed in the field, estimated at 1,600,000, already exceeds that of troops on active service. As of the early 1990s the American aviation industry alone was spending about a billion dollars annually to secure airports, install security devices, and screen passengers and their baggage; new devices, such as those needed to check on the transportation of radioactive materials, are being added almost daily. Some companies preferred to operate in-house, others hired outsiders, the reason being that, since the salaries paid by contractors are usually worse and there are fewer fringe benefits, doing so represents a way of cutting costs even at the expense of high personnel turnover and, often enough, bad security.[149]

Like so many others, the security industry is heavily centralized at the top. Some of the leading firms in the field are presently in command of private armies numbering in the thousands and more. In the developing

---

[144] See, for Germany, B. Jean d'Heur, "Von der Gefahrenabwehr als staatlicher Angelegenheit zum Einsatz privater Sicherheitskräfte – einige Rechtpolitische und Verfassungsrechtliche Anmerkungen," *Archiv des offentlichen Rechts*, 119, 1, March 1994, pp. 107–36; for France, F. Coqeteau, "L'état face au commerce de la securité," *L'Année Sociologique*, 40, 1990, pp. 97–124; and, for Italy, A. M. Ogliati-Vittorio, "La defesa armata privata in Italia," *Sociologia del Diritto*, 15, 3, 1988, pp. 47–71.

[145] *Der Spiegel*, No. 46, 1996, p. 37.

[146] N. South, *Policing for Profit: The Private Security Sector* (London: Sage, 1989).

[147] J. S. Kakalik and S. Wildhorn, *The Private Police: Security and Danger* (New York: Crane Russak, 1977), p. 18, table 2.1.

[148] Figures from B. Jenkins, "Thoroughly Modern Sabotage," *World Link*, March–April 1995, p. 16.

[149] For the working of the modern aviation security industry, see D. Phipps, *The Management of Aviation Security* (London: Pitman, 1991).

world, notably New Guinea, Sierra Leone, and Liberia, mercenaries have already been used to stage coups and countercoups. While mercenaries do not yet threaten the political stability of developed countries, the range of services they offer is astonishing. They include research and development, both of weapons and of scenarios; recruiting, training, and testing personnel of every sort, from simple guards to the kind who specialize in fortifying entire compounds and conducting sophisticated investigations; selling, renting, or leasing equipment that ranges from ten-cent plastic badges and crowd-control equipment all the way to million-dollar explosive detectors; vetting personnel, detecting fraud, conducting polygraph tests, and wiretapping; planning, building, and operating security systems of every kind; probing those defenses, also by means of specially designated "red" teams; not to mention so-called cowboy types of activity such as collecting debts, evicting trespassers, helping corporations deal with strikers, and obtaining evidence on everything from corruption to marital infidelity.

Security firms count among their clients not just private individuals, neighborhoods, and corporations but, in some cases, the government itself. The latter may turn to them either in quest of expertise which it does not have; as a method for cutting costs; or by way of circumventing its own personnel who, in some cases, are themselves the target of the investigation. In some developed countries, it is private security officers, working under contract with the state, who man border controls and check passports. In others, private guards have been granted powers of detaining suspects and escorting them to their designated prisons – to say nothing of the fact that the latter are themselves being privatized as fast as possible. While the United States alone has no fewer than 150 firms that specialize in making delinquent fathers pay up, even in a country as civilized as New Zealand a serious debate has taken place whether personnel working for private security should be allowed to participate in police roadblocks so as to catch debtors.[150] It is as if policy makers in many places are determined to bring the "police century" (1830–1945) to an end. Against the background of evidence that public faith in the police is declining,[151] the task of fighting criminals may revert back to the "thiefcatchers" in whose hands, in most countries, it had been until the time of the French Revolution and beyond.

From the men in the boardroom to the guards at the gate, the personnel employed by the private security industry are often ex-military, intelligence, and police in search of greener pastures. Sometimes prior service

[150] *Herald*, 27 June 1997, p. 1.
[151] See R. Robert, "Policing in a Postmodern World," *Modern Law Review*, 55, 6, November 1992, pp. 761–81.

in one of those bodies is a condition for being taken on by the industry in question. In other cases it is the policemen themselves who moonlight during their free time; they offer their services to everybody from the owners of sports teams to shopkeepers.[152] Their training, which is equivalent to that given to the members of the state's own security apparatus, is thus put at the disposal of purely private objectives. Provided the money is good – and some terrorist organizations, relying on protection money, drug trafficking, or the smuggling of nuclear materials, are said to own assets measured in the hundreds of millions of dollars[153] – it is not impossible that some of these people themselves will turn into terrorists at some stage in their careers. Either they will do so in their own countries or abroad; the latter is perhaps the more likely, and in fact the reemergence of mercenaries – soldiers of fortune, as they prefer to call themselves – in the service of both governments and their opponents is one of the outstanding developments of the last quarter of the twentieth century.[154] To put it in a different way, terrorists, members of the security industry, and the state's security establishment appear to be growing interchangeable in theory and, in at least some cases, in practice as well.

Clearly the impact of these developments differs sharply from one place to another, and some places remain much safer than others. Still, globally speaking, it is scant wonder that the struggle against terrorism does not appear to be making much headway. Should present trends continue, then the outcome is in sight, and indeed already now it is the subject of much science fiction[155] as well as the kind of games played on a personal computer. The provision of security – which since at least Thomas Hobbes has been recognized as *the* most important function of the corporation known as the state – will again be shared out among other entities.[156] Some will be territorial but not sovereign, i.e., communities larger than states; others, perhaps more numerous, neither sovereign nor territorial. Some will operate in the name of political, ideological, religious, or ethnic objectives, others with an eye purely to private gain.

[152] See J. Vardalis, "Privatization of Public Police," *Security Journal*, 3, 4, 1992, pp. 210–14.

[153] E.g., in the mid-1980s Abu Nidal's organization was supposed to have $400,000,000 stashed away in Swiss banks: P. Seale, *Abu Nidal: A Gun for Hire* (New York: Random House, 1992), p. 204.

[154] See the short discussion in Wilson, *British Security 2010*, pp. 59–60; also, in a paranoid but curiously parallel way, the accounts of the various private armies allegedly run by the British crown in places as far apart as Africa, Latin America, and Papua New Guinea in *Executive Intelligence Review*, 24, 34, August 1997.

[155] E.g., N. Stephenson, *Snow Crash* (New York: Bantam, 1992).

[156] See R. W. Mansbach, Y. H. Ferguson, and D. E. Lampert, *The Web of World Politics: Nonstate Actors in the Global System* (Englewood Cliffs, NJ: Prentice Hall, 1976), p. 297.

Whatever their goals, all will need money to survive. They will get it by contracting with states to do their dirty business for them, or by selling their services to other organizations, or by blackmailing the population;[157] for example, during the PLO's uprising against Israel all three methods were used, whether by different factions or simultaneously by the same ones. Conversely, and as is already the case in some places, it is likely that states will adopt the principle of "user pays." They will start charging fees for at least some kinds of security, such as providing assistance in case of a burglary, which used to be provided – to the extent that they were provided – free.

Thus the likelihood grows that the state will lose its monopoly over those forms of organized violence which still remain viable in the nuclear age, becoming one actor among many. Spreading from the bottom up, the conduct of that violence may revert to what it was as late as the first half of the seventeenth century: namely a capitalist enterprise little different from, and intimately linked with, so many others. Where princes and other military entrepreneurs used to contract with each other in order to make a profit – an Amsterdam capitalist, Louis de Geer, once provided the Swedish government with a complete navy, sailors, and commanders up to the vice-admiral included – in the future various public, semi-public, and private corporations will do the same. With some of them, security will form their main line of business, whereas with others it will be ancillary. Some will be legal, others criminal; although as time goes on and the various organizations and people interact with each other – if only in order to learn how to provide security better – the differences between them are likely to diminish.

In many so-called developing countries the situation just described already exists and has, indeed, never ceased to exist. Whether acting on their own – mounting private guards, even setting up entire armies – or by forming agreements with local insurgents, people and corporations are trying to safeguard their property and their operations, a situation often known as neocolonialism.[158] It is true that most citizens of most advanced countries are still able to sleep safely in their beds, albeit that more of those beds are coming to be protected by weapons and surrounded by walls. Thus, in Britain alone there are probably some 2 million illegal

---

[157] On these methods, see, in general, R. Naylor, "The Insurgent Economy: Black Market Operations of Guerrilla Organizations," *Crime, Law and Social Change*, 20, 1, July 1993, pp. 13–51; and, for a case study, K. Maguire, "Fraud, Extortion and Racketeering: The Black Economy in Northern Ireland," *Crime, Law and Social Change*, 20, 4, November 1993, pp. 273–92.

[158] See C. Clapham, *Africa and the International System: The Politics of State Survival* (Cambridge: Cambridge University Press, 1996), particularly part 3.

firearms.[159] As of 1997 the United States was dotted by 30,000 gated communities, a number which is expected to double in a few years; not surprisingly, there is some evidence concerning their residents' growing disinterest in, and disengagement from, public affairs.[160] Both for them and for their less fortunate countrymen, future life will likely become less secure, or at any rate more obsessed with security, than the one which was provided by the most powerful states of the past.

On the positive side, those same states are much less likely to engage each other in major hostilities – let alone in warfare on a global scale – than was the case until 1945. The devil's bargain that was struck in the seventeenth century, and in which the state offered its citizens much improved day-to-day security in return for their willingness to sacrifice themselves on its behalf if called upon, may be coming to an end. Nor, considering that the number of those who died during the six years of World War II stood at approximately 30,000 people *per day*, is its demise necessarily to be lamented.

The withdrawal of faith

Whereas, in 1830, Hegel praised bureaucracy as the "objective class" which put the public good above its own, and whereas, early in the present century, Otto Hintze sang "the lofty virtues" of civil servants and Max Weber saw the state administration as the embodiment of "goal-oriented rationality,"[161] today there is probably not an individual left in the world who believes that such are its attributes. In fact, the opposite is the case. In study after study produced from the 1960s on, state bureaucracies have been presented as endlessly demanding (the bureaucratic solution to any problem is more bureaucracy), self-serving, prone to lie in order to cover the blunders that they commit, arbitrary, capricious, impersonal, petty, inefficient, resistant to change, and heartless;[162] arguing against the extension of public health services, President Bush once described his own administration as having "the compassion of the KGB." "Red tape" has come to stand for anything that is evil, and one of the worst names that any person can be called is "bureaucrat."

---

[159] CNN, *World Report*, 30 September 1997.
[160] For the United States, see J. I. Bayne and D. M. Freeman, "The Effect of Residence Enclaves on Civic Concern," *Social Science Journal*, 32, 4, 1995, pp. 409–21.
[161] *Hegel's Philosophy of Right*, articles 202, 205, 294; O. Hintze, *Der Beamtestand* (Leipzig: Thieme, 1913), p. 17; M. Weber, *Economy and Society* (London: Allen and Unwin, 1923), pp. 249ff.
[162] Among the earliest critics were E. Strauss, *The Ruling Servants* (London: Allen and Unwin, 1961); P. Blau, *Formal Organizations* (London: Routledge, 1963); M. Crozier, *The Bureaucratic Phenomenon* (London: Tavistock, 1964); and others.

Perhaps even more striking is the fate that has overtaken the word "public" itself. In classical Greece, where the distinction between the private and the public was first invented, it was the public domain which enjoyed priority,[163] to the point that from private, *idios*, comes our modern "idiot." As the late twentieth century witnessed the demise of socialism, the situation has reversed itself. In most cases "public," meaning state-owned or -provided, has become synonymous with "second-rate." Whether correctly or not, the best that can be said about a school is that it is private (though such schools are called "public" in Britain) and expensive; the worst, that it is public and cheap. Depending on the country in question, much the same applies to medical services, housing (a field where "public" is usually synonymous with "run-down"), leisure facilities (ditto), transportation (other things being equal, it is only those who cannot afford a car who make use of public transportation), and other fields too numerous to mention. At a time publicly owned firms can survive only by claiming that they are as efficient as private ones,[164] the bias against anything public even seems to spread to basics such as drinking water. That which, as is still the case in many countries, is state-provided and comes out of the tap is considered undrinkable, not seldom with good reason, whereas that which is produced by privately owned bottling plants is supposedly fine.

Though "reducing paperwork" and "cutting the bureaucracy" have become successful electioneering slogans in many places, to date there are few if any countries in which the promise has been kept. In two decades of privatization, countless government-owned corporations around the world have been either sold off or shut down, often at the expense of their workers who found themselves joining the ranks of the unemployed or who have had to resign themselves to alternative employment which promised fewer fringe benefits. In addition, since 1980 scarcely a welfare system anywhere in the developed world has not cut the benefits that it offers and threatened to cut them again; the only difference between conservatives, and socialists such as Blair and Jospin, is that the latter promise to do so with less pain. In France during the last month of 1995 the outcome was widespread strikes and rioting. In the United States social security was threatened with bankruptcy[165] and, among many proposed solutions, there was even talk of privatizing it, which means that the government, while still forcing each of us to convert part of our earnings into compulsory savings, will no longer guarantee that the

[163] P. Rahe, "The Primacy of Politics in Classical Greece," *American Historical Review*, 89, 1984, pp. 265–93.
[164] E.g., France's nuclear industry: A. Rosenbaum, "The Grand Alliance," *World Link*, May–June 1996, p. 89.   [165] See *Business Week*, 5 April 1993, pp. 68–9, for the details.

money will in fact be there (even to the limited extent that this is done at present) when the time for payment comes.

To heap insult on injury, even in countries whose calls for rugged individualism, self-reliance, and privatization have been the most strident, the number of bureaucrats has not diminished: in the United States under Ronald Reagan, for example, it still managed to increase by 1 percent.[166] Nor has the share of GNP which they command declined. For example, in Britain it stood at 45.5 percent in 1993 versus 44 in 1978. For the European Economic Community as a whole the corresponding figures were 52 and 50 percent;[167] in 1996, following a decade of fiscal retrenchment, the French government was once again taking away a record 45.7 percent of GDP in taxes.[168] In the United States, too, the tax burden has remained more or less steady in spite of all the cuts in welfare that have taken place from the time that Republicans took power in 1981.

Thus the evidence is that, whether overtly and brazenly, or covertly and on the sly, the majority of modern states are demanding more and more while offering less and less. At best they compensate by developing the infrastructure and providing the conditions for vigorous economic growth, as is currently happening in the United States (albeit at the cost of a constant deficit in the external balance of payments, to the tune of approximately $120 billion a year), and as was the case until recently in several East and Southeast Asian countries. At worst they drive entire sectors of the workforce into tax evasion and even barter, as in Italy (between 1980 and 1990, the share of taxes in the Italian GDP increased from 30 to 42 percent).[169]

Possibly by way of compensating for their growing impotence, many states have also developed a disturbing habit of meddling in the most minute details of people's lives. In the Republic of Ireland, you cannot obtain information on contraception; in the Netherlands one has to ask government permission before painting one's front door in the color of one's choice. Some governments will tell you that you cannot place a bet outside the state-run lottery system (which insists on raking the profits to itself). Others decree that as a smoker you are a pariah, others that under certain circumstances you *must* turn informer on your family and neighbors (a method formerly reserved for the worst totalitarian regimes),[170] others that you are only allowed to listen to so many foreign songs on the

[166] *Statistical Census of the United States 1992* (Washington, DC: US Government Printing Office, 1992), p. 989.   [167] *The Economist*, 4 September 1993, p. 29.
[168] D. Geddes, "The Return of Orthodoxy," *World Link*, May–June 1996, p. 84.
[169] *Ibid.*, p. 129.
[170] R. W. Thurston, "The Soviet Family During the Great Terror, 1935–1941," *Soviet Studies*, 43, 3, 1991, pp. 553–74.

radio (ditto), others still that you do not even control your own body to the extent of using drugs or having an abortion.

To enforce these and other praiseworthy goals, and often driven by ecological requirements or else by the demands of minority groups, new laws and regulations fall like hail on a pane of glass. For example, by the late 1980s, the number of pages in the American *Federal Register*, the official journal publishing federal laws and regulations, was approaching the 100,000 mark, and they even controlled the shape of tubs in hotel rooms and the height of the jambs that could be put on their doors, nor did the agencies involved seem at all inclined to reduce their output after President Bush put a moratorium on new regulations in 1992.[171] These and countless other forms of intrusion can only lead to alienation and anger that is sometimes literally explosive. In a poll taken after the 1995 Oklahoma City bombing, 39 percent of US citizens asked said they saw the federal government as a threat to their rights and liberties.[172] Another poll showed that only 31 percent trusted the government "most or all of the time."[173] In turn, that government is sufficiently disturbed by the threat to set up special teams for dealing with the possible acts of chemical and biological terrorism in US cities – none too soon, since the first alleged attempt to launch such an attack was discovered by the FBI in February 1998.

More evidence for the state's waning ability to attract people's loyalties comes from the field of sport. As noted earlier, the modern notion that games and competition should be organized on national lines is a product of nineteenth-century nationalism on the one hand and the railways on the other. The nationalization of sport intensified after 1918, particularly in the totalitarian states which used it to prepare their peoples for war and which, in this respect as in so many others, merely went further than the rest.[174] It probably peaked between 1950 and 1980 or so when, in the USSR under Stalin, to attribute success in sport to any but patriotic motives was to risk punishment[175] and when Communist Chinese competitors, once admitted, invariably ascribed *their* success to Mao's thought. Since then things have changed as money has begun to play a

[171] S. R. Furlong, "The 1992 Regulatory Moratorium: Did It Make a Difference?" *Public Administration Review*, 55, 3, May–June 1995, pp. 254–62.
[172] CNN, *World Report*, 22 April 1995.
[173] *Herald Tribune International*, 11 February 1998, p. 7.
[174] H. Weiss, "Ideologie der Freizeit im Dritten Reich: die NS-Gemeinschaft Kraft durch Freude,'" *Archiv für Sozialgeschichte*, 33, 1993, pp. 289–303; for similar developments in at least one democratic country, see S. G. Jones, "State Intervention in Sport and Leisure in Britain Between the Wars," *Journal of Contemporary History*, 22, 1, 1987, pp. 163–82.
[175] See the example quoted in W. W. Kulski, "Can Russia Withdraw from Civilization?" *Foreign Affairs*, 28, 4, October 1950, p. 639.

larger role and nationality a lesser one. From the Olympic Games down, the most important competitions have become commercialized. While many events are still organized on national lines, in others both competitors and teams are sponsored (if not owned outright) by corporations which use them for advertising purposes and deduct them from their taxes.

The trend is most evident in expensive sports such as motor-racing and deep-water yachting where costs can easily reach into the millions of dollars. From them it spread to other sports where corporate logos have replaced national colors on the players' backs, often making them look like some particularly garish version of an overloaded Christmas tree. For example, the European Soccer Federation now allows the various competing "national" teams unlimited license in recruiting foreign (and not just European either) players into their ranks. In tennis, denationalization has reached the point where top-ranking players are often reluctant to represent their countries in the Davis Cup, which unlike the various "open" tournaments is still run on national lines, the reason being that it neither pays nor counts as part of the so-called grand slam – to say nothing of the fact that, having made their fortune, many of them prefer to live in tax havens rather than in their own countries.

Finally, the most obvious sign of people's feelings toward the state has been their declining willingness to fight on its behalf, with the result that in one country after another conscription has been brought to an end. The first important country to undergo the change was Japan, on which it was imposed from outside and where public opinion has since become strongly pacifist. Since then the list of states which have chosen to return to the eighteenth century and put their trust in all-volunteer, professional forces includes Britain (1960), the United States (1973), and Belgium (1994). France, the country which in 1793 became the first in modern history to introduce the *levée en masse* and in which it had long been regarded as symbolic of national unity, joined the trend in early 1996. A few months later even Russia's Boris Yeltsin was telling voters that, if reelected, he would end conscription.[176]

Once governments had abolished the draft they found, often to their chagrin, that it could not be restored. In the United States during the Carter administration an attempt to register young men as a preliminary toward possible conscription in a future national emergency met with resistance and had to be abandoned, while proposals aimed at establishing some other form of national service never even got off the ground.[177] Not only was American strategy during the 1991 Gulf War

[176] CNN, *World Report*, 18 May 1996.
[177] For one such attempt, see C. C. Moskos, *A Call to Civic Service* (New York: Free Press, 1988).

dictated almost entirely by the need to keep down casualties,[178] but a year
later the fact that Bill Clinton had evaded the draft during the Vietnam
War did not prevent him from beating a World War II veteran in his quest
for the presidency. Similar trends affect almost every other advanced
country, including even Israel which before 1982 was perhaps the most
belligerent society on earth.[179] Since then there has been a remarkable
decline in the willingness of its young people to serve the state by enlisting
in the standing army, let alone by risking their lives for it.[180]

Against these symptoms of declining faith it will be objected that, from
the Middle East to Chechnya, many of the organizations which have done
most to undermine the state are themselves trying to establish independent states.[181] It is in fact true that doing so is often one of their goals,
though by no means the only one; but even more remarkable is the fact
that many of them start contemplating how to lose their sovereignty even
before it has been attained. Thus, Quebec separatists hope to retain the
benefits of economic union with the rest of Canada, including a common
currency. No sooner had the former Soviet Union fallen apart than the
CIS, or Commonwealth of Independent States, was established with the
goal – only partly achieved – of saving those common institutions considered critical to the welfare of all.[182] As a result, ethnic Russians living
in the Baltic republics were allowed to participate in the Russian elections
of May–June 1996. Meanwhile at least one republic (Belarus) had still
not made up its mind whether it wanted to be independent or not.

Elsewhere in Europe five other newly established states, i.e., the Czech
Republic, Slovakia, and the three Baltic republics, are all actively seeking
to join the European Union. In the Middle East, the PLO, well aware that
an independent Palestinian state in the West Bank and Gaza Strip would
not be economically viable, has long been thinking about some form of
integration with Jordan, Israel, and possibly other countries; assuming
the region is heading toward peace and not war, in some ways such a
union is likely to come about whether the parties like it or not.[183] A final

[178] See M. R. Gordon and E. Trainor, *The Generals' War: The Inside Story of the Conflict in the Gulf* (Boston: Little, Brown, 1995), pp. 379–80.

[179] See M. van Creveld, "Conscription Warfare: The Israeli Experience," in R. G. Förster, ed., *Die Wehrpflicht: Entstehung, Erscheinungsformen und politische-militärische Wirkung* (Munich: Oldenburg Verlag, 1994), pp. 227–34.

[180] Interview with Lieutenant-Colonel Dr. R. Dovrat, chief of behavioral science, Israel Defense Forces, *Yedi'ot Acharonot* (Hebrew), 19 April 1996, pp. 10–16; interview with Minister of Defense Y. Mordechai, *Yedi'ot Acharonot* (Hebrew), 7 August 1996, p. 12.

[181] See F. Parkinson, "Ethnicity and Independent Statehood," pp. 322–45, and R. H. Jackson, "Continuity and Change in the State System," p. 348, both in Jackson and James, *States in a Changing World*.

[182] For the attempt to use the CIS for salvaging whatever can be salvaged from the former Soviet economy, see R. E. Ericson, "Economics," in T. J. Colton and R. Legvold, eds., *After the Soviet Union: From Empire to Nations* (New York: Norton, 1992), pp. 49–83.

[183] See S. Peres, *The New Middle East* (London: Weidenfeld and Nicolson, 1996).

case in point is represented by the former Yugoslav republics. No sooner did Croatia and Bosnia-Herzegovina become independent states – the latter even before it did – than they set up a federation. Like its fellow latecomers in Central and Eastern Europe, Slovenia is even now in the process of joining the European Union. As the foreign minister of one of those states told this author during a meeting at Davos, had his country not hoped to join the European Union, what would have been the point of breaking up Yugoslavia in the first place?

While states continue to carry out some important functions, two centuries after the French Revolution first enlisted modern mass nationalism, many of them seem to have run out of people who believe in them, let alone are willing to act as cannon fodder on their behalf. Sometimes this appears to have been the result of an unsuccessful war, as in the United States (following Vietnam and "the confidence gap"[184]) and the USSR (where a similar role was played by the failure in Afghanistan). Elsewhere it happened imperceptibly as growing integration with other states caused the sovereignty of each one to be whittled down, as in much of Europe.[185]

Whatever the precise processes, almost everywhere they have been accompanied by a declining willingness of states to take responsibility for their economies; provide social benefits; educate the young; and even perform the elementary function of protecting their citizens against terrorism and crime, a task which at best is being shared with other organizations and at worst simply let go. At the close of the second millennium, and in a growing number of places from Western and Eastern Europe all the way to the developing world,[186] the state is not so much served and admired as endured and tolerated. The days when, as used to be the case during the era of total war in particular, it could set itself up as a god on earth are clearly over.

[184] See S. M. Lipset, *The Confidence Gap* (Baltimore: Johns Hopkins University Press, 1987).

[185] See M. Dogan, "The Decline of Nationalisms Within Western Europe," *Comparative Politics*, 26, 3, 1994, pp. 281–305; also E. Pond, "The Escape from History," *World Link*, January–February 1998, pp. 64–70.

[186] For Western Europe, see above all W. Wallace, "Rescue or Retreat: The Nation State in Western Europe, 1945–1993," *Political Studies*, 42, 1994, pp. 52–76; for Eastern Europe, see U. Plasser-Fritz, "Politische Systemunterstützung und Institutionvertrauen in den OZE Staaten," *Österreichische Zeitschrift für Politikwissenschaften*, 23, 4, 1994, pp. 365–79; and for a detailed case study of one developing country, A. N. Longha, "Citizenship, Identity and Questions of Supreme Loyalty: The Case of Kuwait," *Forum for Development Studies*, 2, 1995, pp. 197–217.

Conclusions: beyond the state

As presented in this study, government and state are emphatically not the same. The former is a person or group which makes peace, wages war, enacts laws, exercises justice, raises revenue, determines the currency, and looks after internal security on behalf of society as a whole, all the while attempting to provide a focus for people's loyalty and, perhaps, a modicum of welfare as well. The latter is merely one of the forms which, historically speaking, the organization of government has assumed, and which, accordingly, need not be considered eternal and self-evident any more than were previous ones.

The first place to see this particular form of government was Western Europe, where it started developing around 1300 and where the decisive changes took place between the death of Charles V in 1558 and the Treaty of Westphalia ninety years later. Speaking very roughly, and skipping over the many differences that separated various countries, the process worked as follows. Having fought and defeated universalism on the one hand and particularism on the other, a small number of "absolute" monarchs consolidated territorial domains and concentrated political power in their own hands. Simultaneously, in order to wield both the civilian and military aspects of that power, they set out to construct an impersonal bureaucracy as well as the tax and information infrastructure necessary for its support. Once the bureaucracy was in place, its own nature – the fact that the rules of which it consisted could not be arbitrarily violated without risking a breakdown – soon caused it to start taking power out of the ruler's hands and into its own, thus spawning the state proper.

Closely associated as it was with the breakdown of the medieval world and the consequent civil and religious wars, the state was originally conceived principally as an instrument for imposing law and order on groups and people. About a century and a half after its birth, however, it met with, and proceeded to appropriate, the thunder of nationalism, thus providing itself with ethical contents. Constructed by and for war – often, as critics from Machiavelli on have noted,[1] by using criminal methods both against its competitors and against its own subjects – by this time it had grown much stronger than any other political organizations both in Europe and on the remaining continents. The result was that it spread to the rest of the world until, during the second half of the twentieth century, in one form or another its triumph had become all but complete.

To repeat the definition provided earlier, compared to previous forms of government the most important characteristics of the state are as follows. First, being sovereign, it refuses to share any of the above functions with others but concentrates all of them in its own hands. Secondly, being territorial, it exercises such powers over all the people who live within its borders and over them only. Thirdly and most importantly, it is an abstract organization. Unlike any of its predecessors at any other time and place, it is not identical with either rulers nor ruled; it is neither a man nor a community, but an invisible being known as a corporation. As a corporation it has an independent persona. The latter is recognized by law and capable of behaving *as if* it were a person in making contracts, owning property, defending itself, and the like.

As of the last years of the twentieth century, it is becoming apparent that the third characteristic of the state – the fact that it has a persona – is starting to make the other two redundant. In the main, the threat to the state does not come either from individuals or from groups of the kind which exercised the functions of government in various communities at various times and places before 1648. Instead it comes from other corporations: in other words, from such "artificial men" as share its own nature but differ from it both in respect to their control over territory and in regard to the exercise of sovereignty.

A few of the corporations in question are of a territorial nature, but the majority are not. Some are regional and larger than states, others smaller and merely local.[2] Some are intergovernmental, others nongovernmental. Some are primarily political by nature, others dedicated to different ends such as making money, protecting the environment, spreading some religious message, or propagating some special cause which may range from reducing pollution to animal rights. As one recent pundit put it,[3] though, all have in common that they are more attuned to modern technology, communication and transportation in particular, than the

---

[1] Most recently by C. Tilly, "War Making and State Making as Organized Crime," in Evans, et al., *Bringing the State back in*, pp. 169–91.

[2] For the shape that some such organizations might take, see K. Ohmae, "The Rise of the Region State," *Foreign Affairs*, 72, 2, Spring 1993, pp. 78–87; and, at the other end of the spectrum, G. Gottlieb, "Nations Without States," *Foreign Affairs*, 73, 3, May–June 1994, pp. 100–12.

[3] J. Mathews, "Power Shift," *Foreign Affairs*, 76, 1, January–February 1997, pp. 50–66.

state. As a result, some of them are able to grow much richer than most states; or take over some of the latter's functions; or evade its control by establishing colonies and moving their resources outside its borders; or influence the opinions of its citizens more than governments can; or (as in the case of numerous guerrilla and terrorist organizations) successfully resist it weapon in hand; or, not seldom, some combination of all these things.

In many instances the retreat of the state is voluntary. Such is the case, for example, when it sets out to evade its responsibilities by cutting back on welfare, social security, education, and the like; so also when it seeks to improve opportunities for trade by opening its borders, integrating its infrastructure with that of its neighbors, joining international organizations of various kinds, and submitting to such regulations as those organizations may lay down. In others it is involuntary: the product of vast economic, technological, and cultural forces which, although they affect different regions in different ways, are beyond the control even of the most powerful states, and which states can resist, if at all, only at the cost of being left behind as history bulldozes its way forward. Often, too, the process takes place by default. It is not so much a question of the state deciding to integrate or retreat as the slow erosion of the quality of the benefits which it can and does provide.

The obverse side of this coin is the feeling, which is prevalent among the citizens of many developed countries, that when the time for delivery comes the state just does not keep its promises, that it pays, if at all, in false coin. And that, in order to secure any kind of future for themselves and their children, citizens are left with no choice but to look after themselves in ways that are independent of, and may even stand in opposition to, the will of the state.

As the modern state abandons the commanding heights which it reached between 1945 and 1975, some of its most characteristic institutions are likely to decline. Among them are, naturally enough, state-owned economic enterprises (which from China to Britain are being either circumvented or sold); social security systems (whose share of GDP is declining just about everywhere);[4] the justice system (in some countries private justice, also known as "rent a judge," is already taking over as being both faster and cheaper than that which is provided by the state); the prison system (from Australia through Britain to the United States, all developed countries are desperately looking for a cheaper

---

[4] One of the few exceptions is Norway which, floating on a lake of oil, keeps them intact – but only at the cost of deindustrialization.

alternative to imprisonment and experimenting with private prisons);[5] the armed forces (many of which, having shrunk dramatically since the end of the Cold War, are even now seeking to take on new missions in everything from search and rescue to waging war on drugs); the police (who are being supplemented, and in some cases pushed aside, by private security forces); public schools (which, as well-to-do parents either send their children to private schools or revert to home schooling, are being turned into pens for the offspring of the underprivileged); publicly owned media (which, on top of the subsidies that they require, are often synonymous with boredom); and the statistical apparatus (which, to the extent that it still operates in terms of individual states, is becoming increasingly irrelevant). In one way or another, these and other services are being cut back all over the world.

As other organizations step into the shoes of the retreating state, they will no doubt seek to fill its role in many of these respects. Unlike the present members of the international community, all of which are sovereign, most of them will probably be unable to exercise exclusive control over a given territory; instead they will be forced to share that control with other organizations. Instead of being at least formally equal, as states are, some of them will no doubt be superior and others inferior. In other words, we are talking about a world whose legal structure will be more in harmony with political realities that already exist and which, in many ways and places, have never ceased to exist.

The organizations which, in the future, will carry out the functions of government will be more fragmented, more integrated with each other than those with which we have become familiar during the last 300 years or so. Unlike states, which in theory at any rate are each other's equals, they will also tend to form hierarchical relationships with each other. Sometimes sovereignty will be divided, as is currently happening in Northern Ireland and as may eventually happen in the Holy Land. A hierarchical structure in which some political entities are more equal than others also means that those entities will operate at one or more removes from their populations. This carries the danger that they will be less representative and less democratic than most modern states, much in the way that, already today, senior Eurocrats and the UN secretary-general are appointed or elected by governments rather than being voted for by the people of the European Union and the world respectively.

As used to be the case before 1648, all these organizations will interact with each other and bargain with each other. Occasionally, no doubt, they

---

[5] For the privatization of America's justice and prison systems in particular, see R. Fitzgerald, *When Government Goes Private: Successful Alternatives to Public Services* (New York: Universe Books, 1988), ch. 3.

will also make use either of their own forces or, which appears more and more likely, those of contractors in order to direct violence against each other. While such a situation will be nothing new to the inhabitants of much of the Third World – which is characterized by nothing so much as the fact that the state never succeeded in establishing an effective monopoly over violence – in many developed countries the effect on day-to-day security will almost certainly be adverse. People and organizations who used to rest peacefully in the bosom of the state will have to do, indeed already are doing, more to defend themselves, for example, by purchasing all kinds of specialized equipment; fortifying the premises in which they live and operate; mounting their own guards, whether in or out of uniform; and possibly even setting up their own armed forces under suitable commanders (retired officers and NCOs, no doubt).

Compared to what we have witnessed in 1914–45, most of the violence in question will almost certainly be local, sporadic, and on a rather small scale. There can be no question that the future has many conflicts such as Bosnia and Sri Lanka and Rwanda in store; not only will terrorists and guerrillas continue to make their presence felt in many countries, but the possibility of their resorting to chemical, biological, and even nuclear weapons cannot be ruled out.[6] Contrary to the fears of many and the hopes of a few, however, World War III – meaning a large-scale clash between superpowers each of which dominates the better part of a continent or hemisphere – will almost certainly not take place. But then, if it *does* take place and nuclear weapons *are* used in any numbers, then the result will be a return not just to pre-Westphalian days but to the stone age.

For people and organizations who are limited to individual states and dependent on them for their defense, livelihood, education, and other services, such a situation represents bad news. For groups as diverse as government employees and the recipients of social security (particularly those who hope to receive benefits in the future), the writing is on the wall. Either they start looking elsewhere for their economic status and, in some cases, even their physical protection; or else there is probably no future for them. As was also the case during previous periods when empires fell apart and feudal structures emerged, often looking elsewhere will mean losing their freedom by becoming the clients of the strong and the rich, whether in the form of individuals or, which is perhaps more likely for the majority, of corporations of various sorts. The reemergence of a politically deprived, disfranchised underclass similar to that which,

---

[6] Speaking on *Panorama* on 14 September 1997, General Lebed claimed that, out of 100 suitcase-sized nuclear bombs manufactured for the Soviet Union's special forces, two-thirds could no longer be accounted for.

even in the most "advanced" countries, continued to exist until the French Revolution and beyond appears likely. Some would say that, from California to Italy, it already exists in the form of so-called illegal aliens, guest workers, and so-called economic citizenship[7] – meaning people who, while subject to taxation and enjoying at least limited access to the justice system and social services provided by the host country, are without any political rights.

Conversely, organizations and people whose wealth and status are independent of the state, internationally oriented, and prepared to take advantage of opportunities that are opening up in every field from global communication and trade to providing private education stand to gain; and, as several analysts have argued,[8] are already gaining at the expense of all the rest. With the state weakening, many of them will undoubtedly find it both easier and more necessary to translate whatever advantages they have into direct political power. Instead of merely lobbying and bribing, as is the case today, they will rule – at least by carrying some of the functions of government, in regard to some people, and to some extent.

For each person, whether the coming changes will be good or bad depends on one's sex, family relationship, economic position, social status, occupation, organizational affiliation, and so on. Above all, it is a question of our willingness to discard old certainties and come to terms with the brave new world awaiting us. In some places change will be accomplished peacefully. The result will be unprecedented prosperity as national borders become less significant, technology advances, economic opportunities open up, and transportation and communications enable different cultures to fructify each other. Regional and local organizations will acquire a new lease on life; as is already happening in Spain (Catalonia), Britain (Scotland and Wales), Belgium (Flanders and the Walloon regions), and Australia (many of whose constituent states now have their own representatives abroad) *inter alia*. Finally, those who wish to escape at least some of the state's more meddlesome tendencies will be able to do so by moving elsewhere or simply linking up via the internet.

In other places, the retreat of the state will have less fortunate consequences. At best, the reemergence of the "market" at the expense of administrative controls and welfare will mean diminished security and, often enough greater turmoil. At worst, the tables may be turned and people may find themselves living under, or governed by, organizations that are less accountable and more authoritarian. Depending on circum-

---

[7] See S. Sassen, *Losing Control?: Sovereignty in the Age of Globalization* (New York: Columbia University Press, 1996), ch. 2.

[8] E.g., A. Toffler and H. Toffler, *The Third Wave* (New York: Morrow, 1980); and Reich, *The Work of Nations*, particularly part 3.

stances, such organizations may or may not be able to keep the peace, both among themselves and with whatever remains of the old states; in which case public authority may collapse, violence break out, the blood of both combatants and noncombatants flow, and at least a temporary reversion to more primitive ways of life ensue. There may even be a few regions and countries which will continue to vegetate much as they have always done, neither keeping up with the accelerating pace of change nor, it is to be hoped, falling into greater confusion than usual.[9]

On balance, the dangers and the opportunities are probably about equal. Neither is the retreat of the state to be regretted, nor will tomorrow's world be either much better or much worse than the one which is even now fading into the shadows. Asked about the shape of things to come, Mao Tse-tung once answered in a characteristic verse:

> The sun will keep rising
> trees will keep growing
> and women
> will keep having children.

[9] For the three possible outcomes – which they call "the postmodern state," "the premodern state," and "the modern state" – see H. H. Holm and G. Sorenson, "International Relations Theory in a World of Variation," in Holm and Sorenson, eds., *Whose World Order? Uneven Globalization and the End of the Cold War* (Boulder: Westview Press, 1995), pp. 202ff.

Index

Abdullah of Jordan, 352
aborigines, Australian, 6
Académie politique, 211
Accadian empire, 40, 42
Action française, 204
administrative revolution, 129–30
Admiralty Courts, 283
Adrian of Utrecht, as pope, 66; as
  humanist, 114
Adulteration of Food Act, British, 218
aediles, 26
aerarium, 33, 45
Afghanistan, 331; war in, 347, 414
Africanus, S. C., 33, 53; accused of
  peculation, 54
Afrikaners, 295–6
Agamemnon, King, 15
agentes rerum, 49
Agincourt, Battle of, 93
Aid for Dependent Children Program
  (AFDC), US, 363
Air France, 357
airpower, rise of, 254
Alagno, L. de, 98
Alba, duke of, 101
Albania, 376
Albert of Brandenburg-Ansbach, 69
Albert I of Habsburg, 76
Albiginsians, 64
Albrecht V of Bavaria, 102
alcabala, 116
Alexander the Great of Macedonia, 44, 47,
  224, 225, 383
Alexander VI, pope, 74
Alexander I of Russia, 120, 208, 270, 271
Alexander II of Russia, abolishes serfdom,
  273, 274, 275
Alfa Romeo, 370
Alfonso V of Aragon, 98
Algeria, 36, 331; retreats from socialism,
  376; war in, 397

Ali, R., 324
Allende, S., 305, 359
Allgemeines Landesrecht, 273
Amadeus VIII of Savoy, 80
Amal, 398
American Revolution, 196
Amin, I., 330
Amtrak, 358
anarchism, 185, 205, 207, 275
ancien régime, 129
Andean Common Market (ACM), 388
Andrea, V., 210
Andropov, Y. V., 374
Angkole, 15
Anglicanism, 68
Angola, 315, 326, 329
Annapolis Officer Academy, 211
Anne of Bohemia, 121
Anne of Brittany, 122
Anne of England, 134
Anne of Russia, 270
Antiochus III, 33; killed while robbing
  temple, 46, 54
Antiochus IV, 39
Anuak, 2
apartheid, 301
Aquinas, T., 51, 171
Arab–Israeli Wars, 347, 352, 362
Aragon, 89; united with Castile, 97–9, 100,
  298
architecture parlante, 199
archontes, 28
Argentina, 202, 261, 304, 306; settlement
  of, 307, 308, 310, 312, 343, 359, 388
Ariosto, 81
Aristotle, 22; criticizes Plato, 25, 137, 172;
  as model for Bodin, 176, 179, 186
Armenia, 36
Arndt, M., 200
Articles of Confederation, US, 284, 285
artillery, development of, 156, 158–9, 250

assignats, French, 230, 233
Association of South East Asian Nations
   (ASEAN), 388
Assyrian empire, 40
Atahualpa, 46
atéliers nationaux, 220
Athens, 25, 29, 32, 36, 54, 56, 108
Atlantic Charter, 354
Attic–Delic League, 32
auctoritas, 28
Augsburg, Confession of, 68
Augsburg, Peace of, 69, 85, 87
augusti, 38
Augustine, St., 170, 180
Augustus, C. O., 38, 44, 56, 168, 172, 225
aurea libertas, 277
Aurelius, M., 38; Capitoline statue of, 124
Austerlitz, Battle of, 120
Australia, 261, 281; unification of, 294–5,
   298, 321, 326, 343, 371
Austria, 36, 78, 84, 102, 129, 134, 142,
   144; taxation in, 154–5, 169, 186, 190,
   199; creates paper money, 230; adopts
   gold standard, 233, 251, 280, 290, 294,
   349, 371, 387
Austrian school, 367
Aztec empire, 36, 42, 43, 48, 298

Babylonian empire, 40
Bacon, F., 260
bailiffs, 92
Bakunin, M. A., 207
Bakwain, 9
Balladur, E., 370
Baltheassar, F. U., invents Swiss
   nationalism, 192
Banco di Roma, 370
band societies, 2, 5
Bandung Conference, 326
Bank Act, US, 286
Bank of England: establishment of, 228–9,
   230, 231; absorbed by state, 238, 336
Banque de France, 229; reestablished by
   Napoleon, 231
Barere, B., 245
Baruch, B., 239
Basel, Peace of, 81
Basque Liberation Movement (ETA), 400
Bassianus, V. A., 38
Bastille Day, 199
Bavaria, 69, 102, 136, 149; education in,
   212–13
Bayerische Motoren Werke (BMW), 390
Beccaria, C., 168
Becket, T., 62

Beer, F. von, 167
Belarus, 270, 322, 381, 413
Belgium, 221; adopts gold standard, 233;
   colonial empire of, 318, 321, 364, 371,
   412
Belize, 330
Bellamy, E., 210
Benedict XI, pope, 63
Benin, 388
Bentham, J., 140, 141, 168
Beria, L., 223
Berliet, 357
Bernhardi, T. von, 289
Berti, 5
Beveridge, A., 321
Beveridge Report, 355
Beza, T., 68
Bhutto, Z. A., 344
Bible, 3, 5, 6, 7, 13, 21, 40, 69, 170, 177
Big Government, 291
'big-men' societies, 22, 52
billets d'état, 229
Bismarck, O. von, 213, 217; introduces
   social security, 220; and annexation of
   Alsace Lorraine, 350
Black Death, 104
Blair, A., 409
Blanc, L., 220
Blanche of Savoy, 70
Blenheim, Battle of, 250
Blum, L., 356
Bluntschli, J., 350
Boccini, A., 223
Bodin, J., 70, 88, 145; and origins of
   modern state, 176–9, 181, 186, 187; and
   private property, 206
Boer War, 296
Bokassa, 330
Bolingbroke, H., 134
Bolivar, S., 304, 314
Bolivia, 306, 310, 388
Bolsheviks, 239, 275, 372
Boniface VIII, pope, 61; and quarrel with
   Philip IV, 62–3, 76
bonnes villes, 111
Books of Precedence, 265
Borgia, C., 74, 402
Borgia, R., *see* Alexander VI
Bosnia, 353, 385, 414
Bosworth Field, Battle of, 91, 107
Botha, L., 296
boule, 27
Bourbon family, 83
Bouvines, Battle of, 76
Braun, H., 211

Brazil, 304, 306, 308; under military government, 310–11, 343, 359, 388
Bret, C. de, 178
Bretton Woods Agreements, 391
Brezhnev, L. I., 374
Britain, 36; first census in, 147; abandons tax-farming, 152, 153, 155, 200, 204; rise of police in, 208, 213, 216, 217, 218; adopts social security, 221; establishes Bank of England, 228–9; creates legal tender, 230; taxation during World War I, 235, 236; mobilization for World War II, 241, 243, 251, 252, 253, 254, 256, 261, 263, 270, 273, 274; gains Canada, 284, 285, 290; and Canada, 292–3, 307, 316; expansion in Asia and Africa, 317, 321, 324, 326, 336, 352, 361, 363, 364, 365; retreats from welfare state, 369–70, 372, 386; and European Union, 387, 407, 409, 410, 412; see also England, Scotland
British Aerospace, 369
British Airways, 369
British Broadcasting Corporation (BBC), 355, 393
British Columbia, 293
British Gas, 369
British North America Act, 293
British Overseas Air Corporation (BOAC), 356
British Petroleum, 369
British Rail, 358
British Steel, 369
British Telecom, 369
Bubble Act, 228
Bucer, M., 68
Buganda, 15
Bulgaria, 36
Bulnes, M., 304
Bunyoro, 15
Bureau of Internal Revenue, US, 232
bureaucracy, in empires, 42, 50; under feudalism, 51; and early modern state, 128–30; expansion of, 136–7, 140–3; Prussian, 153, 191; and French Revolution, 198, 210; growth in World War I, 235; in Soviet Union, 239; in Russia, 269, 271; Polish, 278; American, 291; in Latin America, 308; in Asia and Africa, 327, 329, 355; and welfare state, 361; loss of faith in, 408–9
Burke, E., 140; and creation of legal tender, 230
Burkhardt, J., 74
Burma, 324, 325, 326, 327, 393

Burr, A., 286
Burundi, 14
Bush, G. S., 190, 343, 353; compares administration with KGB, 408
Bushmen, 2, 8
Byzantium, 17, 38, 44, 45, 47, 51, 59

Cabet, H., 220
cabildos, 300, 301, 302
Cable News Network (CNN), 392
caciques, 302
Caesar, G. J., 33, 38
caisse d'escompte, 230
California, 289; tax revolt in, 365
Caligula, C., 258
Calvin, J., 184
Cameroon, 388
Campus Martius, 30
Canada, 260, 284, 289; political history of, 291–4, 295, 297, 343, 355; creates welfare state, 357, 359, 360; retreats from welfare state, 364, 366, 368, 371, 372, 381, 383; and NAFTA, 388
Canaletto, J. A., 109
Canqui, J. G. C., 302
Cape Colony, 296
Capet, House of, 62
carabinieri, 166
Cardwell Reforms, 160
Carlist Wars, 248
Carlos III of Spain, 302
Carnot, L., 246
Carolingian empire, 12, 59–60, 210
Carter, J. E., 412
Carthage, 22, 56
casa de la contratación, 303
Casimir of the Palatinate, 95, 130
Castile, 89; united with Aragon, 97–9, 100, 114, 298
Cateau-Cambresis, Treaty of, 95
Cathars, 64
Catherine de Medici, 70, 95, 121
Catherine II of Russia, 270, 271; and Poland, 280
Catholic kings, 98
caudillos, 306, 308, 309, 311
censores, 54
Central African Republic, 330, 388
Central American Common Market (CACM), 388
central banks, expanding role of, 233–4
Ceylon, see Sri Lanka
Chaco War, 310
Charlemagne, 38; as universal emperor, 40, 60, 82

Charles the Bold of Burgundy, 78, 94
Charles V, Emperor, 41, 44, 66, 69; sacks Rome, 74, 81, 82, 87, 94, 99, 101; and *germanias*, 114, 116, 119, 122, 126, 130, 135, 159; testaments of, 172, 173, 176, 296, 301; North African campaigns, 317
Charles I of England, 70, 92, 107, 120, 124; revenue of, 149, 228
Charles II of England, 92, 282
Charles IV of France, 93
Charles V of France, 147, 415
Charles VI of France, 77, 178
Charles VII of France, 148
Charles VIII of France, 121, 122
Charles IX of France, 71
Charles XII of France, 94
Charles XII of Sweden, 120, 270
Charlotte of Savoy, 121
Charlottenburg Palace, 123
Chechnya, war in, 334, 413
Cheka, 208
Chernenko, C. U., 374
Chernobyl accident, 381
Cherokee, 8
Chiang Kai-shek, 325
Chile, 304, 305, 310; military government in, 311, 359, 388
China, 21; unification of, 22, 36, 38; and Confucianism, 39; bureaucracy in, 42–4, 45, 55, 56; and paper money, 226, 290, 321, 326, 343, 344, 345, 347; invades Vietnam, 352, 360; rolls back communism, 373, 393
Christianity: as religion of resignation, 39; as imperial religion during Middle Ages, 60–1; can no longer serve as basis of government, 176–7
Christina of Sweden, 131
Chrysler, 389
Churchill, W. S., 239, 319; and nuclear balance of terror, 342, 354, 358
Cicero, M. T., 29; defines *res publica*, 56, 176
cities, definition of, 20–1
city-states: concept of liberty in, 34, 53, 54, 170; education in, 210
civil society, in Hegel's work, 195; under totalitarian rule, 204, 258; absent in Russia., 268, 270–1; dominated by state, 354
Civil War, American, 231, 232; railways in, 250, 288–9, 293
Civil War, English, 73, 92, 107
Clancy, T., 342
Clausewitz, C. von, 245, 247

Clement IV, pope, 61
Clement V, pope, moves papacy to Avignon, 63
Clement VII, pope, 74, 82
Clinton, W. J., 1, 190, 364, 413
Clive, R., 316
Code Napoleon, 169
coercitio, 26
Colbert, C. S., 134
Colbert, J. B., 71; conducts *recherché de la noblesse*, 96, 145; estimates France's revenue, 149, 211
Cold War, 286; and Big Government, 291, 310, 325, 348, 384, 418
Colombia, 306, 308, 310, 384
Colonna family, 59, 74
Colorado, 209
Commonwealth of Independent States (CIS), 413
communeros, 99, 114
compagnies d'ordonnance, 148
concentration camps, 224
'Concert of Europe," 382
Conciliarists, 64
Condé, House of, 95
Condé, Louis de, 96, 103
Confucianism, as official religion, 39, 170
Congo, *see* Zaire
Congress Party, Indian, 323
Connecticut, 282, 285
Conrad I, Emperor, 61
Conrad IV, Emperor, 76
Conrail, 371
conscription, adopted by great powers, 252
conseil d'état, 140
Conseio de las Indias, 298
Constantine, Donation of, 65
Constantinople, fall of, 156
Constantinus, F. V., 84
Constitution, US, 284–5
Constitutional Act, Canadian, 292
consules (Italy), 104
consuls, 26
Continental Congress, 284
Copernicus, N., 121
Corinth, 32, 56, 206
Cormoran Islands, 330
corregidores, 113; *de indios*, 299
Cortés, H., 84, 298
corvee (forced labor), 49; in the Belgian Congo, 318
Costa Rica, 310
Council of Constance, 64
Council of Trent, 70

Counter-Reformation, 64; in Bavaria, 102; ends beatification of rulers, 123, 124; interrupts construction of diplomatic service, 134
County and Borough Police Act, UK, 208
cour des aides, 147
Court of Requests, 91
Crassus, M. L., 33
Crecy, Battle of, 93; use of gunpowder in, 156
Crevecoeur, H., 165
Crimean War, 261, 273
Croatia, 414
Crolie, H., 289
Cromwell, O., 73, 107; and administrative revolution, 130, 153
Cruce, Abbé, 350
cruzada, 69
Cuba, 291, 353
Cuban Missile Crisis, 342, 344
Cultural Revolution, Chinese, 373
currency, in chiefdoms, 17
cursus honorum, 26
cursus publicus, 53
Curtin, J., 355
custom, in tribes without rulers, 4
cynicism, 39
Cyprus, 328
Cyrus II, 172
Czartoryski family, 279
Czech Republic, 413
Czechoslovakia, 351, 375

Dabrowski, H., 280
Dahomey, 15
Daimler Benz, 389
Dante Alighieri, 76
Darius III, 44, 186
David, L., 199
Decembrist Revolt, 271
Declaration of Rights, 151
Declaration of the Rights of Man, 207
Deng Xiao-ping, 373
Denmark, 110, 144, 149, 220; adopts gold standard, 233; welfare state in, 361, 363
Department of Health and Human Services, US, 222
Deutsche Arbeitsfront, 240
Deutsche Welle (DW), 393
Deutschland über Alles, 200
Dickens, C., 381
dictator, Roman, 26, 33
Diderot, D., 11
Dinka, 2, 8
Diocletianus, G. A. V., 38, 225

Directory, the (France), 230
Disraeli, B., 293
Dluski, T., 280
Domesday Book, 88, 145
Dominions, British, 291–2
dominium, 53
Douhet, G., 254, 255, 256, 348
Drake, F., 160
Dreros, 24
Duma, 266
Dürer, A., 157
Duvalier family, 334
dvoriane, 265, 271, 273
Dyck, A. van, 124

East Germany, 372, 384, 389, 399
East India Company, 141, 161; history of, 316
echevins, 104
Economic Community of West African States (ECOWACS), 388
Ecuador, 306, 347, 384
Edict of Restitution, 85, 86
education: taken over by the state, 210–17; privatization of, 418
Edward I of England, 89, 106, 147
Edward II of England, 66, 90
Edward III of England, 90
Edward IV of England, 91
Eglantine, F. de, 199
Egypt, 36, 42, 171; nationalism in, 323, 324, 348, 359; retreats from socialism, 376
Eisenhower, D. D., 291, 360
El Salvador, 312
eleutheria, 34
Elgabalus, *see* Bassianus, V. A.
Elizabeth I of England, 41, 91, 160, 227
Elizabeth of Russia, 270
encomiendas, 298, 300
Encyclopédie, the, 204
Engels, F., 220
England, 67, 72, 73, 76, 88, 89, 97, 100, 106, 117; administrative revolution in, 129–30, 131, 133, 142; taxation in, 150, 175, 185, 207, 225, 226–7, 271; *see also* Britain
Enlightenment, the, 87, 180, 194; attitude to war, 243
ephors, 26
epicureanism, 39
Erasmus, D., 121, 154; as political theorist, 172–4, 176, 183
Eritrea, 326, 398
Escorial, 123

Eskimo, 2
Esther, 40
Etats généreaux, 148
Ethiopia, 318, 326, 328
Etruscans, 22
Eugenius IV, pope, 64
eunuchs, as officials, 45, 50
European Commission, 386, 387
European Court, 386
European Free Trade Area (EFTA), 388
European Parliament, 386, 387
European Union, 385–8, 410, 413, 414
Evans-Pritchard, E. E., 2

Fabius, Q. M. Cunctator, 33
Factory Acts, UK, 218
Fajardo, S., 137
Falklands War, 347
fealty, 52
Federal Bureau of Investigation, US, 209, 411
Federal Emergency Relief Agency, US, 222
Federal Reserve System, US, created, 234
Federalist Party, US, 286
Felix V, pope, 64
Ferdinand I, Emperor, 83, 111
Ferdinand II, Emperor, 85, 120
Ferdinand I of Aragon, 98, 226
Ferdinand II of Aragon, 66, 91; marries Isabella of Castile, 98, 113
Ferry, J., 215
Feu, J., 82
feudalism, 50; and failed empires, 51–2, 54, 57, 58, 61
feuding, in tribes without rulers, 6, 11
Fichte, J. G., 194–5, 196, 336
Fifth Amendment, US Constitution, 232
Finland, 221, 387
fiscus, 45
Filmer, R., 184–5
Five Year Plan, USSR, 372
Flamininus, C. T., 31
'flexible response," 341
Flodden, Battle of, 119
Florence, 80, 108, 148, 175, 206
Florida, 284; taken from Spain, 289
forced currency, 230, 233; during 1930s, 237
Ford, G., 360
Ford, 336
foreign ministries, rise of, 133–4
Fornovo, Battle of, 115
Fouché, J., 167, 169
Fourier, F. M. C., 218

"Four Modernizations," Chinese, 373
Four Year Plan, German, 240
France, 36, 71, 72, 86, 97, 100, 104, 107; towns in, 111, 117, 123, 124, 130; venal offices in, 131, 133; diplomatic service of, 134, 135; venality abolished in, 139–40, 142, 143–4; first census held in, 147, 148; taxation in, 150, 151, 153, 155, 157, 164, 169, 176, 178, 184, 185, 186, 196, 204, 207, 213; nationalizes education, 214–15, 217, 218, 220, 226, 227; attempts at paper money, 229, 231; adopts gold standard, 233, 243, 251, 253, 255, 260, 261, 263, 270, 273, 274, 307, 316; expansion in Africa and Asia, 317, 321, 324, 338, 344, 345, 351; and welfare state, 358, 361, 370, 379, 387, 395, 399, 400, 409, 412
Francis I, Emperor, 120, 188, 190
Francis I of France, 41, 66, 69; captured by Charles V, 82, 83, 84, 94, 119, 122, 126, 148, 159, 163
Frankfurt am Main, 110
Frederick III, Emperor, 80, 120
Frederick I of Prussia, 102
Frederick II of Prussia, 120, 133; and bureaucracy, 136, 138, 139, 142; and taxation, 153, 163, 190; and education, 212; creates paper money, 230, 246, 250, 269; partitions Poland, 279, 349
Frederick William I of Prussia: prohibits the sale of offices, 132; and education, 212
Frederick William II of Prussia, 138
Frederick William III of Prussia, 138, 213
Frederick William, the Great Elector of Prussia, 102, 131, 150, 279
French and Indian War, 284
Friedland, Battle of, 270
Friedman, M., 367
Fronde, 96, 135
Front populaire, 356
fueros, 304
Fugger family, 83
Fuller, J. C. H., 254, 255, 348
Füssli, H., and Swiss nationalism, 192
fyrd, 19

gabelle, 111, 147
Gabon, 388
Galileo, G., 73; as model for Hobbes, 179
Gallipoli campaign, World War I, 295
Gama, V. da, 315, 317
Gambia, 388
Gandhi, M., 324

"Gang of Four," 373
Garfield, J. A., 262
Gattinara, M., 81
Geer, L. de, 407
General Electricity Board, UK, 355
General Medical Council, British, 218
General Motors, 337
generalités, 133
Generalkommissaren, Prussian, 135
Geneva, 112; and Rousseau, 192
Geneva Convention, 401
Genghis Khan, 258
Genoa, 108, 148, 226
George III of England, 134, 155
Georgia, 282; ends proprietary
　government, 288, 387
Germany, 196, 205; education in, 213,
　216–17, 218; social security in, 220–1;
　under National Socialism, 222–3; adopts
　gold standard, 233, 237; mobilizes for
　World War II, 241, 255, 260, 274, 280,
　291; colonial empire of, 318, 338, 344,
　345, 350, 351; *see also* East Germany,
　West Germany
gerousia, 27
Gerson, J., 171
Gestapo, 223
Gettysburg, Battle of, 288
Ghana, 388
Gibbons, E., 188
Gibbons v. Ogden, 286
Giles of Rome, 61
giro banks, 230
glebi adscripti, 52
Glorious Revolution, 180; and defense of
　private property, 207
Gneisenau, A. von, 247
Goebbels, J., 204
Goering, H., 240
gold standard: in Britain, 229; universal
　adoption of, 233; in World War I, 234;
　abandoned, 236
Golden Bull, 78, 100
Gonsalvo de Cordoba, 159
Gonzaga, F., 80
Gonzaga family, 79
Gorbachev, M. S., 375, 393
Goths, 12, 21
Gourmay, V. de, 137
Government of India Act, UK, 324
Gracchus brothers, 38
Granada, 314, 330
Grant, U., 232
Granvelle, N. P., 70, 116
Grassaille, C. de, 82

Great Britain, *see* Britain
Great Depression, 236, 355, 356
Great Leap Forward, China, 373
Great Northern War, 132, 279
Great Schism, 63–4
Great Society, US, 360
Great Transformation, 336
Great Trek, 296
Greater East-Asia Co-Prosperity Sphere,
　325
Greece, 36, 255; resists German
　occupation, 396
greenback, creation of, 232, 336
Greenwich Standard Time, 383
Gregoire, H., 197
Gregory VII, pope, 61
Gregory XI, pope, 63
Gresham, T., 227
Grotius, H., 161, 190, 351
Groves, L., 257
Guatemala, 310
Guderian, H., 348
Guicciardini, F., 75, 126
Guinea, 388
Guinea-Bissau, 388
Guise, House of, 95, 103
Guizot, F., 196, 214
Gulf War, *see* Persian Gulf War
gunpowder, invention of, 156
Gustavus Adolphus, 86, 131, 159
Gustavus Vasa, 69

Habsburg family, 76, 81, 83; launch Thirty
　Years War, 84; and Switzerland, 115,
　173
Hackett, J., 342
Hadrianus, M. A., 38
Hahn, O., 257
Haiti, 314, 334
Hambach Festival, 200
Hamburg, 110
Hamilton, A., 286
Han dynasty, 55
Hannibal, 32
Hansa, the, 105; decline of, 109–10
Hardenberg, K. A. von, 139, 154
Harrington, J., 260
Hastings, W., 316
Hawaii, 12; comes under US protection,
　289
Hayek, G., 367
Healey, D., 390
Hearst, W. R., 289
Heath, E., 358
Hebner, J., 144

Hegel, G., 142; deifies the state, 195–7, 203, 336
Heidelberg, Alliance of, 105
Helvetic Society, 192
Henry IV, Emperor, 61
Henry I of Castile, 97
Henry III of Castile, 97
Henry IV of Castile, 97
Henry I of England, 88
Henry II of England, 62, 88
Henry III of England, 89, 97, 106
Henry IV of England, 91
Henry V of England, 91, 93
Henry VI of England, 91
Henry VII of England, 91
Henry VIII of England, 66, 69, 71; and religion, 72, 73, 82, 83, 84, 91, 122; and administrative revolution, 130, 142; revenue of, 148, 163, 227
Henry II of France, 95, 101, 122
Henry III of France, 71, 72, 130, 145, 176
Henry IV of France, 70, 84, 96, 112, 119, 121, 123, 128, 131, 178, 227
Hepburn v. Griswold, 232
Herder, J. G. von, 193–4, 259, 336
Herodotus, 246
Herzl, T., 203
Hesse, 102
Himmler, H., 223
Hintze, O., 408
Hiroshima, bombing of, 258, 340
Hitler, A.: and nationalization, 240, 259; and welfare state, 356, 395, 402
Hizbullah, 398, 399
Ho Chi Minh, 320
Hobbes, T., 73; invents the state, 178–9; and absolutism, 180–1; and human equality, 186, 188, 189; compared with Hegel, 195; and private property, 206, 242, 260, 336, 406
Hofgericht, 79
Holy Roman Empire, 75, 78; in folklore, 80–1, 83; at Peace of Westphalia, 86, 100, 103, 150, 157, 164, 263
Home Office, UK, takes over police, 208
Homer, 24, 118
Honda, 390
Hopkins, H., 222
Houphouet-Boigny, F., 334
household ordinances, 130–1
Huguenots, 71, 72, 95, 112; in South Africa, 295
humanism, 65, 70, 71
Humboldt, A. von, 302
Hume, D., 182

Hundred Years War, 66, 90, 93; and French towns, 111; use of artillery in, 156
Hungary, 78, 80, 249
Hussein, S., 353
Hussites, 64–5
Hutu, 14
Huxley, A., 339
huyscarls, 16

Iceland, 146
Iliad, 24, 118
'imperial presidency,'' 291
Imperial Statute, British, 292
imperium, 23
Inca empire, 37; imperial religion in, 38; taxation in, 43, 47, 48, 59, 210, 298
income tax, 152–3, 232, 336
India: comes under British rule, 316; starts move to independence, 320, 323, 324; heterogeneity of, 328, 330, 343; and Pakistan, 344, 347, 348; retreats from socialism, 376
Indians, North American, 2, 5, 7
Indonesia, 263, 324, 325, 327, 331, 372, 388
indulgentia, 40
industrial revolution: and nationalism, 200–1; and war, 249; Russia left behind by, 272–3, 356
Infantado, duke of, 99
inflation, in Rome, 225; and early attempts to establish paper money, 225–6; in World War I, 234–5; in World War II, 237
Innocent III, pope, 61, 62
Innocent VIII, pope, 74
Innocent IX, pope, 86
Inquisition, 66, 100; in Latin America, 301
intendants, 96, 113, 132, 135; abolished, 139, 145–6; in Latin America, 302
Internal Revenue Act, US, 232
International Air Transport Association (IATA), 383
International Bureau of Weights and Standards, 383
International Business Machines (IBM), 337
International Customs Union, 383
International Monetary Fund (IMF), 372, 376, 392
International Postal Union (IPU), 382
International Telegraph Union (ITU), 382
Internet, the, 392
Interpol, 383

Iran, 226, 331, 347, 393
Iraq, 324, 328, 331, 347, 385
Ireland, 59, 190, 221; gains independence, 324, 386, 410
Irish Republican Army (IRA), 399
Iroquois League, 11
Isabella of Castile, 97; marries Ferdinand II of Aragon, 98, 113, 227
Isabella of England, 90
Islam, as official religion, 39
Isonzo, Battles of, 254
Israel (biblical), 13, 21, 326
Israel, 326, 330, 330, 331, 343, 344, 352; retreats from socialism, 376, 381; in Lebanon, 398–9, 407
Italy, 36, 215; under Fascism, 222–3; adopts gold standard, 233, 236, 237; mobilization for World War II, 241, 260, 291, 308; colonial empire of, 318, 322, 344, 349; creates welfare state, 357, 364, 369, 372, 396, 399, 403
Ivan III, 264
Ivan IV the Terrible, 41, 278
Ivory Coast, 324, 388

Jackson, A., 231, 287
Jackson, F. T., 289
Jacobeans, 197, 200
Jagellonian dynasty, 277
Jahn, L., 200
James, Duke of York, 282
James of Viterbo, 61
James I of England, 120, 121; revenue of, 149
James III of Scotland, 78
James IV of Scotland, 119
Jameson Raid, 296
Janissaries, 42
Japan, 41, 51, 61, 215; mobilization for World War II, 241, 252, 261, 263; war against Russia, 275, 289; colonial empire of, 318; defeats Russia, 323, 327, 332, 338, 343, 344, 351, 364, 384, 399, 412
Jena, Battle of, 190
Jivaro, 8
Joan of Arc, 93
John of England 62, 88, 120
John of Gaunt, 66
John of Paris, 62
John XXII, pope, 64
John II of Aragon, 98
John I of Castile, 97
Johnson, L. B., 291, 360
Jordan, 324, 352, 353
Joseph II, Emperor, 167, 188

Judea (biblical), 13
Julius II, pope, 74
July Monarchy, 169
juros, 227
justice: in chiefdoms, 17; in city-states, 28–9; in empires, 39; and church, 66–7
justices of the peace, 132, 218, 219

kakoi, 14
Kammergericht, 79
Kansas, 221
Kant, I., 194, 350
Kellogg–Briand Pact, 350, 351
Kennedy, J. F., 360
Kenya, 397
Kenyatta, J., 320
Keynes, J. M., 356
KGB, 208, 374, 408
khaliff, religious position of, 38
King, G., 146
king's two bodies, 177–8
Kipling, R., and 'White Man's Burden,'' 321
Kissinger, H. A., 340
Knights Templar, 63
Kohl, H., 371
Königgrätz, Battle of, 214
Korean War, 290, 348, 352
Kosciuszko, T., 280
Kosice, Pact of, 276
kosmos, 24
Kreisky, B., 358
Kriegsakademie, 247
Krim, A. El, 324
Kropotkin, P., 207
Krupp, firm of, 250
kshatriya, 21
Kublai Khan, 226
Kulturkampf, 217
Kuwait, 290; invaded by Iraq, 353

laissez faire, 217; abandoned by US, 222
Lancaster, House of, 91
Landeshoheit, 86
Landschulregiment, 212
Latin American Free Trade Association (LAFTA), 388
Laud, W., 70
Lavoisier, A., 146
Law, J., 229
law: in tribes without rulers, 4; in Greece and Rome, 25, 29; in empires, 39; common, 91, 103; in Bodin's work, 176; in Hobbes' work, 179, 189; of nature, 182; and early nationalism, 193;

imposed on lower classes, 207–8; concerning welfare, 219; in Russia, 269, 271; in Prussia, 273; international, 352
League of Nations: foreshadowed by Sully, 84; adopts mandate system, 321, 350
League of the Public Weal, 94
Lebanon, 326, 331
legal tender, creation of, 230, 232, 336
Legnano, Battle of, 105
Leibnitz, G. W., 191
Leipzig, Battle of, 248, 270
Lenin, V. I., 237, 275; and nationality question, 321
Leo X, pope, 74
Leonardo da Vinci, 157
Lerma, duke of, 70
lèse majesté, 171; replaced by treason, 205
levée en masse, 206, 245
Lewis the Bavarian, 77, 78; as Empire incarnate, 171
L'Hôpital, M., 69
Liberia, 331, 388, 405
libertas, 33
liberum veto, Polish, 277, 279
Libya, 36, 400
lictores, 30
Liddell Hart, B., 253–4, 255, 256, 348
Lipsius, J., 70, 127, 145
liturgies, 33–4
Livingstone, D., 9
Lloyd George, D., 221, 235, 239
Locke, J., 54, 180–2; and separation of powers, 183, 185, 186, 188, 189, 196, 204; and private property, 206; and US Constitution, 285
Lodi, Peace of, 72
Lodovico II Il Moro, 80, 126
logistai, 54
Lollards, 64
Lords Appellant, 90
Louis IX of France, 92, 120, 122, 123, 131
Louis X of France, 93
Louis XI of France, 66, 74, 93, 94, 98, 111, 121, 128, 178
Louis XII of France, 71, 94, 121, 148, 178
Louis XIII of France, 86, 96, 121, 124, 131, 149
Louis XIV of France, 71; ends noble uprisings, 96–7; suppresses municipal elections, 113, 120, 121, 122, 127, 131; builds diplomatic service, 134, 143, 145, 149, 150, 153, 169, 181; and French state, 183, 184, 186, 187, 188; and French education, 211, 229, 242, 250, 336, 349

Louis XV of France, 123, 138, 142, 242
Louis XVI of France, 146, 188
Louis of Poland, 276
Louis-Philippe, 214
Louise of Prussia, 139
Louisiana, 144
Louvois, F. M., 71, 145
Loyseau, C., 128
Lucas, R., 367
Ludendorff, E., 255
lugal, 21
Lugard, F., 319
Luigi III of Mantua, 80
Luna, A. de, 97
Luneville, Peace of, 212
Luther, M., 68, 69; visits Rome, 75; starts Reformation, 175, 184
Lützen, Battle of, 120
Lydia, invention of money in, 224

McCullogh v. Maryland, 286
MacDonald, R., 356
Macedonia, defeated by Rome, 31
Machiavelli, N., 71, 73; and papacy, 75, 109, 114, 126; writes *The Prince*, 174–6, 180, 183, 415
Maecenas, G., 56
Magdeburg, sack of, 86
magistrates, 23, 25–6, 28–30, 34, 53
Magna Carta, 89
Mahan, A. T., 289, 290
majordomo, 13
Majuba Hill, Battle of, 296
Malaysia, 263, 325, 388
Mali, 388
Malplaquet, Battle of, 242
Mandarins, 42–3
mandate system, 321
Manhattan Project, 257, 346
Mantua, 80
Mao Tse-tung, 12, 330, 373, 411, 421
maps, 55, 143
Marco Polo, 226
Mare, N. de, 165
maréchaussée, 166
Margaret of Parma, 116
Maria Theresa, empress, 131, 188
Marie of Burgundy, 116
Marie Antoinette, 188
Marie Louise, 188
Marsellaise, 199
Marshall, J., 285; and expansion of US federal government, 286
Marsilius of Padua, 76–7
Martin V, pope, 64

Martinet, J., 160
Marx, K., 8, 119, 207, 220, 368
Maryland, 282
Masai, 2, 8
Massachusetts, 221, 282, 285
Matilda of England, 88
Maurice of Nassau, 159
Maurice of Saxony, 101
Mauritania, 388
Maxentius, M. A., 37
Maximilian I, Emperor, 78, 79, 80, 100, 120
Maximilian of Mexico, 289
Mazarin, J., 71, 96; suppresses municipal independence in France, 113, 149
Mazzini, G., 196, 197, 248
Mead, M., 290
Medicaid, 360, 365
Medicare, 360
Medici, Cosimo de, 124
Medici family, 79, 122; and Machiavelli, 175
Medina Sidonia, duke of, 99
Meiji Restoration, 215
Meitner, L., 257
Melanchthon, 68
Mendez de Haro, L., 70
Menelaus, 24
mercenaries, 31, 34; in middle ages, 158, 249, 330, 334
Meru, 9
messenger systems, 19, 51, 53
Methodism, 184
Mexico, 289, 298, 302; revolt against Spain, 303–4, 306, 307, 308, 310, 314, 349; and NAFTA, 388
Michelangelo, B., 157
Michigan, 209
Micronesia, 2
Milan, 80, 108, 206
military-industrial complex, 291
militia perpetua, see standing armies
Mill, J., 350
Miller, A., 339
Ming dynasty, 42, 48, 55
Ministry of Food, British, 241
Ministry of Health, British, establishment of, 218
Ministry of Munitions, British, 239
Ministry of Public Education, Polish, 280
Ministry of State Domains, Russian, 271
Mirabeau, V. R., 139
Mirrors for Princes, 176, 184
Mississippi Company, 229
Mitsubishi, 390

Mitterand, F., 358, 370
Mobutu, S. S., 334
Mogul empire, 37, 56
Mohammed, 38
Moltke, H. von, 214, 252, 350
money, 51, 55; origins of, 224–5; early attempts at creating paper money, 226–7; and Bank of England, 228–9, 259; in Poland, 276; during total war, 238, 259
Mongols, 157
Monroe Declaration, 289
Montesquieu, C. de, 132; and modern state, 180–3, 186, 189, 204; and private property, 206; on war, 243, 272; and US Constitution, 285
Montmorency, House of, 95
More, T., 70; and religious toleration, 71, 145
Morgarten, Battle of, 158
Morocco, 36, 324
Morse, M., 379
Mortimer, 90
Möser, J., 193
Mozambique, 315, 329
mugwe, 9
Mühlberg, Battle of, 101, 120
multinationals, 333, 389–90
Murdoch, R., 392
Mushin-Pushkin, I., 267
Mussolini, B., 204, 236; and nationalization, 240; and welfare state, 356
Mycene, 12

Namibia, 326, 395
Nantes, Edict of, 72, 112
Naomi, 3
Napoleon Bonaparte, 120, 138; builds modern French bureaucracy, 139–40; increases taxation, 151; and police, 167, 188, 190; defeats Prussia, 194, 199, 207; and education, 214, 223, 230; military methods of, 246–8; and military technology, 250, 286, 303, 348, 379, 383
Napoleon III, 199, 260
Nasser, G. A., 388
Natal, 296
Natchez, 14
national debt, US, 150
National Health Service, British, 370
nationalism, rise of, 193–6; adopted by French Revolution, 197–9; in nineteenth century, 200–3; American, 289

Navarre, 89
Navigation Acts, 283
Ndbele tribe, 296
Necker, J., 146
Nelson, H., 162
neocolonialism, 407
Nero, C. D., 44, 186, 225
Netherlands, the, 71; religious conflict in, 72, 82, 104, 115; revolt against Spain, 116–17; adopts French administrative system, 140, 144, 152, 161, 220, 226, 243, 263; create welfare state, 357, 361, 371, 410
New Deal, US, 222, 291, 360
New Economic Policy (NEP), USSR, 372
New Guinea, 2, 325, 405
New Hampshire, 282
New Jersey, 282, 387
New Orleans, Battle of, 286
New South Wales, 294
New Zealand, 220, 281, 295, 321, 343, 360; retreats from welfare state, 368, 371, 405
Newfoundland, 293
Nicaragua, 312, 334
Nicholas of Cusa, 81
Nicholas I of Russia, 34; expands police, 208, 271, 274
Niger, 388
Nigeria, British rule in, 319, 328, 388
Nihil Novi, Act of (Poland), 277
Nijmegen, Conference of, 78, 144
Nixon, R. M., 291, 358, 367; takes dollar off gold, 391
NKVD, 208
Nogaret, G. de, 63
Nordic Council, 387
North, F., 141
North American Free Trade Agreement (NAFTA), 388
North Atlantic Treaty Organization (NATO), 341, 344, 348, 353, 387
North Carolina, 387
North Korea, 343
Norway, 123, 255; welfare state in, 361, 365, 399
Nuclear Non-Proliferation Treaty, 342, 343
nuclear weapons, impact on war, 338–44
Nuer, 2
Nymphenburg, 123

Odysseus, 15
Odyssey, 24, 118
officer schools, founding of, 211

Oglethorpe family, 283
OGPU, 208
oidores, 299
oikumene, 40
Olaf, St., 16
Olivares, G. de Guzman, 70; and paper money, 227
Olmedo, Battle of, 97
Olympic Games, modern, 202; as terrorist target, 400; privatization of, 414
Ontario, 293
Orange Free State, 297
ordeals, 6
Oregon, 221
Organization for Economic Co-operation and Development (OECD), 364
Organization of Petroleum Exporting Countries (OPEC), 362
Orléans, duc de, 229
Orsini family, 59
Orthodox Church, Russian, controlled by Peter I, 267–8
Orwell, G., 242, 393
Osse, M. von, 165
ostracism, 25
Otto I, Emperor, 78
Otto IV, Emperor, 76
Ottoman empire, 41, 210, 328
OVRA, 213
Owen, R., 218
Oxenstierna, B. V., 131

Pacheo, D. L., 99
Page, W., 130
Paine, T., 186
Pakistan, 326, 328, 331, 343; and India, 344, 348, 352
Palais Royal, 123
Palestinian Liberation Organization (PLO), 398, 407, 413
Panama, creation of, 308, 310, 314, 334
Papal State, establishment of, 73–4, 131, 148
Paraguay, 306, 388
Parkinson, N., 362
Paulette, 131
Pavia, Battle of, 82, 94, 119
pays d'élection, 135; abolished, 139, 149
pays d'état, abolished, 139, 149
Peace Act, 132
Peasants' Revolt, 68, 110
Peel, R., 208
Peloponnesian War, 33, 54
Penn, W., 350
Pennsylvania, 282

Pepys, S., 243
Perenot, N., *see* Granvelle, N. P.
Pericles, 30; accused of peculation, 54
Peron, A., 310
Persian empire, 39, 40, 44, 51, 224
Persian Gulf War, 290, 347, 412
Peru, 299, 302, 306; under military
    government, 310, 312, 347, 384
Pestalozzi, J. H., 193
pet banks, 231
Peter of Portugal, 98
Peter I the Great of Russia, 260; and serfs,
    265; reforms of, 266–8, 269, 270, 272,
    279
Peter III of Russia, 120, 269; abolishes
    obligatory service for nobles, 270
Pharaoh, 40, 162; as son of Ra, 171
Philip II Augustus of France, 62, 76, 92,
    128
Philip III of France, 92
Philip IV, the Fair of France, 62, 76
Philip V of France, 93
Philip VI of France, 93
Philip II of Spain, 44, 69, 70, 84, 95;
    defeats Spanish nobility, 99–100, 114;
    and the Netherlands, 116, 120, 121,
    130, 135; threatened by own
    bureaucracy, 137, 142, 173, 184, 301
Philip III of Spain, 70, 120
Philip IV of Spain, 70, 120
Philip V of Spain, 188
Philippines, 82; comes under US rule, 321,
    326, 331, 334, 388
Phoenicians, 22
Picolomini, A., 81
Piedmont, 260
Pithou, P., 70
Pitt, W., the elder, 134
Pitt, W., the younger, 152
Pizarro, F., 46
Plato, 25; on military professionalism, 31,
    192, 210
Plutarch, 31
poison gas, 253
Poitiers, Battle of, 93, 119
Pol Pot, 330
Poland, 59, 78, 110, 134, 255, 264, 270;
    from fourteenth to eighteenth centuries,
    276–8; turned into Russian protectorate,
    279; in nineteenth century, 280–1, 351,
    381
polemarchs, 26
police: original meaning of, 117, 165; rise
    of, 166–7; nineteenth-century expansion
    of, 208–10; in totalitarian countries,
223, 258; in Latin America, 313–14;
    recent reinforcement of, 400–1; switch
    to private security, 403–6, 418
polis, 22; political system of, 23, 24, 33, 54
political science, 70; takes place of religion,
    184
politiques, 71
polygamy, in chiefdoms, 12–13
Polynesia, 12, 16, 18
pomes'ti, 264, 265
Pompadour, J. A. Poisson de, 138
Pompey, G. M, 33
Pompone, S. A, 134
pontifex maximus, 27, 38
Pope, A., 144, 189
Portugal, 67, 98, 243, 263, 308
potlatching, 18
Potocki family, 278, 279
praetors, 26, 28
Pragmatic Sanction, 65
Predikanten, 72
Prerogative Courts, 91
prévots, 92, 166
prikazy, 267
printing press, 56; and modern
    bureaucracy, 136, 377, 392
prison, rise of, 168–9, 258; privatization of,
    417–18
private property, defense of, 207
procuratores, 135
'Progressives," American, 289
Prokopovich, F., 267, 268
Protectorate, the (England), 73, 107, 131
provocatio, 29
Prussia, founded, 69, 73, 102, 103;
    dealings with the Hansa, 109–10, 124,
    129, 131; and venal offices, 132–3, 134,
    135, 136, 138; ruled by bureaucracy,
    138–9, 149; taxation in, 153–4, 155,
    164, 190; defeated by Napoleon, 194,
    207; education in, 212, 213–14; military
    system of, 247, 251; and railways, 252,
    260, 270
Ptolemy IV Philopater, 48
Pueblo, 8
Pulitzer, J., 289
Punic War, Second, 26, 32, 33
Puritans, 70, 73; emigration to New
    England, 282

quaestores, 26, 49
Quebec, 293; separatism in, 413
Quebec Act, 292
Queensland, 294
quippu, 46

Radio Free Europe (RDF), 393
Radziwil family, 278, 279
railways, 208; introduction of, 250–3, 260;
    in Russia, 274, 377–9
Raleigh, W., 160
Rathenau, W., 239, 240
Raw Materials Department, Germany, 239
Reagan, R., 340, 342, 365, 410
recherché de la noblesse, 96
reconquista, 99
Reform Bill, UK, 141
Reformation: role in weakening the
    church, 67; divides Europe, 72, 84; in
    France, 95, 112, 118, 134, 176
Regeringsform, 131
Regulating Act, UK, 141
regidores, 104; in Latin America, 300
regimen de castas, 301, 308
Reichsgericht, 79
Reichsregiment, 81
religion: in tribes without rulers, 8–10; in
    chiefdoms, 15; in city-states, 27; in
    empires, 38; as foundation of political
    power, 171–2; discarded by Machiavelli,
    174–5; replaced by sovereignty, 176;
    Hobbes and, 180; and modern state,
    184
Renault, 357
repartimiento, 298, 302
republica de españoles, 301
republica de indios, 301
Republican Party, US, 286
res publica, 37; defined by Cicero, 56, 176
Res Publica Christiana, 87
Restoration, the, 73, 248
Resumption Act, US, 232
reth, 9
"Return to the People," 275
"Revenge of the People," 275
Revolution, French, 73, 129, 139–40, 144,
    148, 185; welcomed by Hegel, 195;
    adopts nationalism, 197; adopts levée en
    masse, 206, 245, 336, 405, 414
Revolution, Russian, 237, 281, 336
Revolutions of 1848, 167, 220, 248–9
rex in regno suo imperator est, 76
Rhineland League, 105
Rhode Island, 282
Richard, Duke of York, 91
Richard I Lionheart of England, 88, 135
Richard II of England, 66, 90
Richard III of England, 91, 121
Richelieu, A. de, 71, 96; and
    administrative revolution, 130; and venal
    offices, 132, 135, 178

Robertet, F., 130
Robespierre, M. F., 198
Rocroi, Battle of, 242
Rohan, House of, 95
Rolls-Royce, 358
Roman Republic, 248
Rome, 22; republic, 23; people's
    assemblies in, 25, 26, 29; army of, 30–1;
    turns into empire, 37, 38; bureaucracy
    in, 42–3, 48, 53, 54, 55; papal rule over,
    74–5, 82; Machiavelli on, 75; as center
    of papal state, 108–9, 135, 206
Roon, A. von, 214
Roosevelt, F. D., 222; devalues dollar,
    236, 354
Roosevelt, T., 289
Root, E., 289
Rothschild, L. W., 235
Rouget de Lille, C. J., 199
Rousseau, J. J., 11; initiates the Great
    Transformation, 191–2; and education,
    211, 218, 259, 272, 336, 350
Rubens, P., 124
Rudolf I, Emperor, 76
Russia, 134, 154; police in, 208; creates
    paper money, 230; adopts gold standard,
    233; invaded by Napoleon, 247, 251,
    260, 261; in seventeenth and eighteenth
    centuries, 264–70; emergence of civil
    society in, 271; in nineteenth century,
    272–6, 278, 286, 307; defeated by
    Japan, 323, 338, 412
Ruth, 3
Rwanda, 13, 331, 385

St. Blois, Edict of, 148
St. German-en-Laye, 148
Saint-Simon, Duke of, 122
Saint-Simon, H. de, 219
Samuel, 10
San Michele, M., 157
Sargon, 22
Saudi Arabia, 12, 393
Saxe, M. de, 244
Saxony, 102, 195
Scharenhorst, G. von, 247
Schiller, J. von, 194
Schmalkaldic League, 101
Schmidt, H., 363
Schöffen, 104
Schönbrunn Palace, 123
Scotland, 67, 190
scutagium, 158
Secret Service, US, 209
secretaries of state, 130

Security Council, UN, 345, 351, 353, 384, 385; *see also* United Nations
Sedan, Battle of, 260
Sedantag, 200
Sejm, 276–7
Senate, Roman, 27–8, 31, 33, 38, 225
Sendoso Luminoso, 312
Senegal, 388
seneschal, 92
separation of powers, 25, 39; proposed by Locke, 180–1; Montesquieu and, 182–3; adopted by United States, 285
Seven Years War, 161, 163, 242, 245, 302
Severus, S., 48
Sforza family, 79, 124
Shaka, 19
Sherman, W. T., 251, 288
Shilluk, 9
Shute, N., 339
Sierra Leone, 388, 405
Sigismund, Emperor, 76
Silhon, J. de, 130
Singapore, 325, 327, 331, 388, 389
Sinope, Battle of, 272
Sixtus IV, 74
Slavophiles, 275
Slovakia, 413
Slovenia, 414
Smith, A., 55; on transportation, 287
Smuts, I., 321
Snell, W., 143
Sobieski, J., 279
Sobornoe ulozhenie, 264
'social question," the, 207
social security, rise of, 220–1; in Canada, 293–4; retreat of, 364–6, 371
social war, 38, 108
société d'états, abolished, 140, 186
Socrates, 29
sodalities, 3–4; as basis for warfare, 7, 11
Soli, 48
Solomon, King, 12
Solon, 25
Somalia, 331, 385; war in, 398
Somoza family, 334
Sorbonne, 69
South Africa, 281, 292; history of, 295–7, 321, 336, 384, 398, 403
South Australia, 294
South Carolina, 152, 387
South Korea, 327, 343, 371, 389
sovereignty: in the ancient world, 34; defined by Bodin, 176–7; in Hegel's work, 195; and World War I, 350;

retreat of, limited by United Nations, 385, 418
Soviet Union, 222, 235; forced currency in, 237; bureaucracy in, 239–40, 269, 291; and nationality question, 322, 324; disintegration of, 327, 338, 341, 344, 347, 351,model welfare state, 356; economic failure of, 372–3, 374–5, 385, 396, 411, 413, 414
Spain, 36, 59, 67, 69, 72, 74; under Charles V, 82, 83, 95, 97; united by Catholic kings, 98, 100, 103, 107; towns in, 111, 113–14, 134, 135; adopts French administrative system, 140, 157, 161, 175, 184, 188, 202, 217; tries to create paper money, 227, 230, 243, 251, 263, 289; and South American empire, 299–304, 308; loses colonies, 317–18, 400
Spanish–American War, 290, 318
Spanish Succession, War of, 83, 150, 161, 188, 243
Sparta, 26, 27, 31, 54, 108
Spartacus, 33
Speenhamland system, 218
sport, nationalization of, 201–2
Sri Lanka, 315, 326, 331
Stacey, J., 356
Stalin, J. V., 75, 237, 322, 372, 385, 402, 411
standing armies, 160
Stanhope, J., 134
Stanislaw II Poniatowski of Poland, 279
Star Chamber, England, 91
'Star Wars" program, US, 340
state, the: defined, 1; origins of term, 126–7, 128; territorial character of, 133–4; product of bureaucracy, 137; gathers statistics, 145–7; monopolizes war, 155–65; and crime, 169–70; crystallization of, 178–9; theoretical construction completed, 183; as basic human unit, 185; from means into end, 189; adopts nationalism, 190–1; fascist, 204; takes over education, 210–17; and social security, 216–22; totalitarian, 222–3; and money, 224, 238; develops military technology, 249–50; adopts conscription, 252; builds nuclear weapons, 257; and science, 260; culminates in total war, 262; Russian, 272; Anglo-Saxon, 297; in Latin America, 314; in Asia and Africa, 328, 331–2, 333–5; faces nuclear weapons, 338–48; ceases to expand, 349; builds

up welfare, 354–61; undermined by modern technology, 379–81; multiplicity of, 402; retreat of, 414, 418–19
statistics, origins of, 145–7
Statutes of Praemunire, England, 65
Stein, H. K., 139, 154
Stephen of England, 88
Sterne, L., 185
stoicism, 39
Stolypin, P. A., 275
Strategic Arms Limitation Treaties (SALT), 342
strategoi, 26
strategy, decline of, 348
strel'tsy, eliminated by Peter I, 267
Sudan, 5, 328, 331; civil war in, 353
Sueur, H. le, 124
Sukarno, 327
Suleiman the Magnificent, 41, 84
Sully, M. de Bethune, 72, 84, 86, 113, 187, 350
Sûreté, 167
Swabian League, 105
Sweden, 69, 73, 86, 110, 134, 144, 146, 175, 220, 227, 264; defeated by Peter I, 270; welfare state in, 270, 387
Switzerland, 36, 59, 81; becomes independent, 86, 110; towns in, 115, 190; adopts gold standard, 233, 399
sycophancy, 29
synoikismos, 22
Syracuse, 36, 56, 206
Syria, 36, 324, 326, 331, 348; retreats from socialism, 376
Syrian War, 54
szlachta, 276

table holidays, 268
Tacitus, C., 12, 15
taille, 111; instituted to pay for standing army, 148
Taiwan, 327, 334, 371
Talleyrand, C. M. de, 198
T'ang dynasty, 42
Tanzania, 359, 395
taxation: in chiefdoms, 17; in city states, 32–3; in empires, 42, 43–4, 46, 49; under feudalism, 50, 51, 53, 56; and medieval church, 64; in Holy Roman Empire, 79; in early modern Europe, 150–1, 190; in nineteenth-century America, 232–3; during World War I, 234–5; during World War II, 237; in Petrine Russia, 266–7; in Poland, 277, 278; in welfare state, 363, 365

technology, military: development of, 249–51; in World War II, 256–7
telecommunications: monopolized by state, 240, 261, 378; undermine sovereignty, 379–80, 390
telegraph, 208; introduction of, 251, 378–9
Telemachus, 24
terrorism, modern, 399–401
Test Ban Treaty, 342
Teutonic Order, 69
Texas, 289
Thailand, 318, 327, 388
Thatcher, M., 369, 370
Themistocles, 32
themosthetai, 28
Theodore II of Russia, 265
thetes, 13
Thiers, A., 349
Third Department, Russian, 208, 274
Thirty Years War, outbreak of, 85–6, 96; effect on German unity, 102, 110, 132, 144, 153, 159, 169, 227, 243
Tiberius, J. C., 44
Tiglat Pileser III, 43, 47, 162
Tilly, J. T. von, 103
timaion, 55
Togo, 388
tort, 4
trace italienne, 157
Trajanus, M. U., 36, 162
Transvaal, 296
Trastamara, House of, 97
treason, 205
Treitschke, H. von, 289
trésoir d'épargne, established, 148
Trevelyan, C., 141
Trojan War, 15
Trotsky, L., 249
Troyes, Treaty of, 93
Truman, H. S., 291
tumultus, 28
Tunisia, 36; retreats from socialism, 376
Turenne, H. de, 244
Turgot, A. G., 230
Turkey, 331, 371, 387, 400
Turner, T., 392
Tutankamun, 46
tyranny, 34

Uganda, 330
Ukraine, 322, 377
unam sanctam ecclesiam, 61, 63, 76
Union douanière et économique de Afrique centrale (UDEAC), 388

United Kingdom, *see* Britain
United Nations, 326, 332, 351, 352; rules over war and peace, 353; embraces other international organizations, 383, 384–5, 418; *see also* Security Council
United States, 147, 150; adopts separation of powers, 183, 185, 207; rise of police in, 209; universities in, 216, 217, 220; and social security, 221–2, 231; creates Federal Reserve System, 234; government during World War I, 234–5, 236, 241, 252, 256, 261, 274; first constitution of, 284; artificial creation, 285, 287; civil war in, 288; 'chip-on-the-shoulder nation'', 290; expansion of government, 291; and Canada, 293, 294, 304, 305, 307, 318; imperial mission of, 321, 324; and decolonization, 325, 330, 332, 336; uses nuclear weapons, 338, 341–2; armed forces of, 345–6, 347, 349, 351, 353, 355, 358, 359; builds welfare state, 360–1; welfare state dismantled, 362–3, 364, 365–6; and privatization, 371, 372, 377; and United Nations, 384–5, 386; and NAFTA, 388, 390, 395, 400, 404; private police in, 405; develops gated communities, 408, 409, 410, 411, 412, 414
Urban IV, pope, 63
Urena, count of, 99
Uruguay, 306, 308, 388
US Bank, 231, 286
USSR, *see* Soviet Union
Utraquist Church, 65
Utrecht, Treaty of, 116

Valla, L., 65
Vasari, G., 124
Vattel, E., 164
Vauban, S. le Prêtre de, 143, 246
Vega, G. de la, 47
Velazquez, D., 124
"velvet revolution," 375
venal offices, 131–2
Venezuela, 306, 384
Venice, 80, 108, 109
Vergara, E., 314
Versailles, 123
Versailles Conference, 324
Vespasian, T. F., 42
Vicksburg, Battle of, 288
Victoria of Great Britain, 316
Vidocq, F., 167
Vienna, Congress of, 270

Vietnam, 290, 327; war in, 347; invaded by China, 352, 359; retreats from socialism, 376, 397–8, 413
Vikings, 282
Villa, P., 309
Villalar, Battle of, 114
Virgil, P., 84
Virginia, 144, 282, 315, 387
Virginia Plan, 285
virtù, 175
Visconti, G., 80
Visconti family, 79
Voice of America (VOA), 393
Volkswagen, 241, 357
Voltaire, F. M. A., 145, 186, 188, 204
votchiny, 264, 265

Waldensians, 64
Wallenstein, A. von, 103
Walpole, R., on taxation, 152
wanax, 21
war: in tribes without rulers, 7–8; in chiefdoms, 17–18, 19; as waged by empires, 41–2; in Middle Ages, 155–6; prisoners of, 161; monuments to, 162; in eighteenth and nineteenth centuries, 164; monopolized by state, 170, 188; French Revolutionary and Napoleonic, 191; as supreme test of the state, 196; increasing size of, 242–3; and industrial revolution, 249–50; modern theories of, 253–5; and nuclear weapons, 338–44; since 1945, 397–400
War Industries Board, US, 239
War of 1812, 286, 288
War of Devolution, 187
Wars of Liberation, German, 199, 213
Wars of the Roses, 91
Warsaw Pact, 344
Warwick, earl of, 91, 103
Washington, G., 279, 286
Waterloo, Battle of, 250
"Way of the People," 275
Webb, B., 215
Weber, M., 258, 408
Wesley, J., 184
West Germany, 357, 361, 363, 364, 365; and privatization, 370–1
West India Company, 161, 316
West Point, 211
West Virginia, 209
Weston v. Charleston, 286
Westphalia, Peace of, 86, 102, 160, 191, 415
White Mountain, Battle of, 85

Wild, J., 166
"Will of the People," 275
William of Ockham, 76–7
William Rufus, 88
William the Conqueror, 88
William the Silent of Orange, 72, 116
William I, German Emperor, 214
William II, German Emperor, 142
William IV of Bavaria, 101–2
William III of England, 134, 154, 187
Wilson, W., 262
Winstanley, G., 144, 210
Wolsey, T., 70
World Bank, 376
World Economic Forum, 390
World Trade Organization, 384
World War I, 215, 234, 237; and property
  rights, 238, 252; logistics in, 253, 256,
  259, 261, 275, 290, 309, 321; and Third
  World nationalism, 323, 345
World War II, 235; taxation in, 237;
  mobilization for, 241, 242; as total war,
  255–8, 259, 290, 291, 293, 309, 312,
  322, 324, 332; use of nuclear weapons

in, 338, 339, 340, 346, 348, 349, 351;
and origins of welfare state, 354, 368,
372, 374, 384, 392; as turning point in
warfare, 395, 408, 413
Worms, Diet of, 81
Württemberg, 102

Xenophon, 172
Xerxes, 40, 48, 246
Xhosa tribe, 296

Yeltsin, B., 343, 412
Yemen, 353
York, House of, 91
Yugoslavia, 255, 352, 396, 414

Zaire, Belgian rule in, 318, 326, 334, 388
Zapatista movement, 312
Zeydlitz, K. von, 211
Zheng He, 45
Zimbabwe, 376
Zionism, 203
Zulu, 15, 19, 296
Zwingli, H., 68